Report on Conditions of Work and Promotion of Livelihoods in the Unorganised Sector

NATIONAL COMMISSION FOR ENTERPRISES
IN THE UNORGANISED SECTOR,
GOVERNMENT OF INDIA

Chairman

Arjun K. Sengupta

ACADEMIC FOUNDATION
NEW DELHI

www.academicfoundation.com

First published in 2008
by

ACADEMIC FOUNDATION
4772-73 / 23 Bharat Ram Road, (23 Ansari Road),
Darya Ganj, New Delhi - 110 002 (India).
Phones : 23245001 / 02 / 03 / 04.
Fax : +91-11-23245005.
E-mail : academic@vsnl.com
www. academicfoundation.com

Cataloging in Publication Data--DK
Courtesy: D.K. Agencies (P) Ltd. <docinfo@dkagencies.com>

India. National Commission for Enterprises in the Unorganised Sector.
Report on conditions of work and promotion of livelihoods in the unorganised sector.
p. cm. Chairman: Arjun K. Sengupta.
Includes bibliographical references (p.)
ISBN 13: 9788171886784
ISBN 10: 8171886787

1. Informal sector (Economics)--Government policy--India. 2. Employees--India--Economic conditions. 3. Agricultural laborers--India--Economic conditions. 4. Minimum wage—Law and legislation--India. 5. Employee rights--India. 6. Labor laws and legislation--India. I. Title.

DDC 330.954 22

Printed and bound in India.

10 9 8 7 6 5 4 3 2 1

सत्यमेव जयते

Dr. ARJUN K. SENGUPTA
Chairman

NATIONAL COMMISSION FOR ENTERPRISES IN THE UNORGANISED SECTOR GOVERNMENT OF INDIA

19th Floor, Jawahar Vyapar Bhawan
1, Tolstoy Marg, Janpath
New Delhi-110001 INDIA
Telefax : +91-11-2370 1111, 2370 1112

D.O.No.A-25021/21/2006-NCEUS

Dated: 6.8.2007

Dear Prime Minister,

The National Commission for Enterprises in the Unorganised Sector has prepared a detailed and comprehensive Report on **"Conditions of Work and Promotion of Livelihoods in the Unorganised Sector"**, analyzing the conditions of work and issues in livelihood promotion along with a set of recommendations for the unorganised sector. This Report deals with these issues in the non-agriculture sector, focusing separately on wage workers, self-employed workers and women workers. It also profiles agricultural workers with special emphasis on marginal and small farmers as well as labourers. The Report further focuses on the regulatory and promotional issues arising out of our detailed analysis.

This detailed work forms the basis of the Commission's earlier Report on "Comprehensive Legislation for Minimum Conditions of Work and Social Security for Unorganised Workers" incorporating two Bills, one for the Unorganised Non-Agricultural and another for Agricultural Unorganised Workers, which was submitted to you on July 7, 2007.

The final chapter of this Report contains a package of measures for farm and non-farm sectors in the form of an Action Programme for addressing the main issues in an integrated manner. The Commission believes that an immediate implementation of the proposed Action Programme would make a visible and significant impact on improving the productivity and employment in the unorganised sector.

Yours sincerely,

Arjun Sengupta

Dr. K P Kannan
Member

Dr. R S Srivastava
Member

V K Malhotra
Member Secretary

Dr.T S Papola
Member(Part-time)

B N Yugandhar
Member(Part-time)

Dr. Manmohan Singh,
Prime Minister of India,
PMO, South Block,
New Delhi-110011.

Preface

The constitution of this National Commission for Enterprises in the Unorganised Sector in September 20, 2004, was one of the first steps taken by the UPA Government, in pursuance of its Common Minimum Programme that committed itself "to ensure the welfare and well-being of all workers, particularly those in the unorganised sector who constitute 93 percent of our workforce". Although the Indian economy experienced a reasonably high growth rate till then, this was not seen as inclusive enough by the majority of the population. The policies pursued by the new Government made "inclusive growth" as its central plank.

It is in this background that the Commission has examined the conditions of work as well as livelihood issues of the unorganised workers, who form the overwhelming proportion of the Indian workforce. The picture that it has presented is based on the latest available set of data from the Sixty-first Round of the National Sample Survey in 2004-05. This has been supplemented with data from other sources such as the Special Survey of Farmers carried out by the NSS in 2003.

One of the major highlights of this Report is the existence and quantification of unorganised or informal workers, defined as those who do not have employment security, work security and social security. These workers are engaged not only in the unorganised sector but in the organised sector as well. This universe of informal workers now constitutes 92 percent of the total workforce. We have also highlighted, based on an empirical measurement, the high congruence between this segment of the workforce and 77 percent of the population with a per capita daily consumption of up to Rs. 20 (in 2004-05) whom we have called "Poor and Vulnerable". The number of persons belonging to this group increased from 811 million in 1999-00 to 836 million in 2004-05.

On the employment front, the low rate of growth during 1993-94 and 1999-00 gave way to a higher growth rate of employment during 1999-00 to 2004-05. But the additional employment created during this period was entirely informal, whether in the unorganised or organised sector.

The Commission has carried out a detailed analysis of the various dimensions of the challenge confronting the informal or unorganised workers. They work as so called self employed or wage workers, sometimes located in their homes but mostly outside. Some are lucky to have some kind of regular work but majority of wage workers are employed on a casual basis. Most get wages that are too low to enable them to come out of their poverty, not to speak of overcoming their vulnerability. Discrimination is the norm when it comes to women, children, bonded or migrant workers. Such positions of disadvantage are often reinforced by one's social identity, rural location and, above all, low or no education.

The situation calls for immediate steps to ensure minimum conditions of work for the unorganised workers as well as measures for livelihood promotion. The Commission has, therefore, proposed two comprehensive Bills for unorganised agricultural and non-agricultural workers to ensure minimum conditions of work as well as a minimum level of social security. It has, further, proposed a number of measures to improve the livelihood of unorganised sector workers.

The Commission is aware that there have been concerted efforts by the Government during the last three years to address some of the constraints and problems faced by the poor households in general and workers in the unorganised sector in particular. The enactment of a National Rural Employment Guarantee for rural households is, in our view, a historic move. The launching of the National Rural Health Mission is another important milestone. The schemes and projects under the Bharat Nirman address some of the critical constraints in infrastructure faced by rural India and, by implication, the poorer segments of the population whose livelihood opportunities are, by and large, in the unorganised sectors of the economy. The latest decision to strengthen the Sarva Shiksha Abhiyan to address the problems in school education and to increase the allocation to the educational sector is a much needed foundational initiative.

Formidable social and administrative challenges do exist in ensuring the effective implementation of these initiatives. There is also the scope for adopting a new agenda strengthening existing initiatives as well as taking new initiatives which will give a sharper focus on the poor and vulnerable who constitute the majority of the informal or unorganised workers.

On the basis of its detailed assessment, the Commission has recommended a 13 Point Action Programme that will, in our view, not only provide a minimum standard for conditions of work and social security but also provide a modicum of livelihood opportunities to the 92 percent of the unorganised workers in this country. We believe that these measures are within the administrative and fiscal capacity of the Government, and if implemented within a short period of time, will have a significant impact on the lives of the working poor.

The journey is long and hard. But we are confident that the inherent dynamism of India's democracy will be able to negotiate it successfully, building on the ongoing reform process and the high rate of economic growth.

Arjun Sengupta
Chairman
National Commission for Enterprises in the Unorganised Sector

New Delhi
August 6, 2007

Acknowledgements

The Commission wishes to acknowledge the contributions made by a large number of persons in the finalisation of this report. The Commission benefited by the discussions in the Advisory Board as well as the suggestions made by several members of the Board. A background paper for this report was prepared by a research team of the Institute for Studies in Industrial Development led by Dr. T. S. Papola. Four other background papers were prepared by Dr. Kamala Sankaran, Dr. Naveen Chandra, Dr. Atul Sood and Dr. Praveen Jha. Dr. Kamala Sankaran also assisted the Commission in the preparation of the Draft Bills. Editorial support was provided by Dr. N. K. Nair.

Officials of the Government of India, especially the Ministry of Micro, Small and Medium Industries, Labour and Employment, and the Departments of Labour in the States provided useful feedback to the Commission, and in a number of cases, arranged for visits and meetings by the Commission. The representatives of trade unions, other organisations of the workers in the unorganised sector, academics, experts and social activists participated in discussions with the Commission in New Delhi and in the States visited by the Commission. The Commission also benefited from discussions on the Bill in a number of fora and regional consultative meetings arranged by the organizations of unorganised workers, the Institute of Human Development, New Delhi, Institute of Social and Economic Change, Bangalore, the Institute of Development Studies, Jaipur, Department of Economics, Jadavpur University, Kolkata.

We have also interacted closely with experts in the International Labour Office, both in Geneva and New Delhi, on a range of issues relevant to the subject of this report.

The Commission takes this opportunity to thank the above individuals and organizations that have contributed towards the preparation of the Report and the Bill.

It is our pleasant duty to place on record our deep appreciation of the valuable services rendered by the staff of the Commission. Shri Mahesh Kumar, Director, shouldered the main responsibility for coordinating all the activities related to the preparation of this Report. Professor Jeemol Unni, Consultant, provided valuable support in the analysis and writing of this report. Valuable advice on the design, processing and analysis of NSS unit level data was provided by Dr. G. Raveendran. Excellent research assistance was provided by Ms. Swati Sachdev, Shri Ajaya Kumar Naik, Ms. T. Shobha and Ms Richa Singh. Shri S.V. Ramanamurthy, Director provided advice and assistance on statistical issues. Shri D. P. Singh, Under Secretary, provided critical inputs on the legal regulatory framework. Ms. Manisha Shridhar, Joint Secretary, Shri Suresh Kumar, Under Secretary, and Shri H.S. Chhabra, Section Officer and the whole team of supporting staff provided excellent services in the functioning of the Commission in general and the preparation of this Report in particular.

Contents

List of Tables

List of Figures

List of Boxes

List of Appendix Tables

List of Annexures

1 Introduction

India's Informal Economy

1.1 This Report is focused on the informal or the unorganised economy which accounts for an overwhelming proportion of the poor and vulnerable population in an otherwise shining India. It concentrates on a detailed analysis of the conditions of work and lives of the unorganised workers consisting of about 92 per cent of the total workforce of about 457 million (as of 2004-05). For most of them, conditions of work are utterly deplorable and livelihood options extremely few. Such a sordid picture coexists uneasily with a shining India that has successfully confronted the challenge of globalisation powered by increasing economic competition both within the country and across the world.

1.2 The shining India's achievements are no doubt remarkable especially from a macroeconomic perspective. It is not only marked by the high performance in aggregate economic growth but also in many other parameters. India's real national income grew by 125 per cent during the economic reform period of 1992/93 - 2005/06 compared to 97 per cent during the previous period of the same duration. Consequently the per capita income increased by 77 per cent during 1992/93 - 2005/06. There has been a heightened sense of buoyancy in the economy during the last three years with the growth rate exceeding 9 per cent per annum. The savings rate of the economy has risen from a long time average of 22-24 per cent to 30 per cent in recent years with a corresponding increase in investment rate currently exceeding 30 per cent. Growth in exports has averaged to around 20 per cent per annum matched by a similar rate of growth in imports. The steady flow of remittances and earnings from invisible exports as well as increasing flow of foreign investments has swelled the foreign exchange reserves to more than 200 billion US Dollars. The foreign exchange rate has remained remarkably stable, even though the Rupee has been strengthening against the US Dollar in the last few months. The external debt burden of the country is not only within manageable limits but also one of the lowest in the developing countries.

1.3 Such a buoyancy in the economy did lead to a sense of euphoria by the turn of the last century. However, a majority of the people, who did not have even Rs. 20 a day for consumption, were not touched by this euphoria. At the end of 2004-05, about 836 million or 77 per cent of the population were living below Rs.20 per day and constituted most of India's informal economy. About 79 per cent of the informal or unorganised workers belonged to this group without any legal protection of their jobs or working conditions or social security, living in abject poverty and excluded from all the glory of a shining India. Recognizing this paradox, the Common Minimum Programme (CMP) of the United Progressive Alliance promised to initiate measures for the welfare of the common people by addressing, inter alia, the concerns of the workers in the unorganised sector. The CMP expressed this resolve in a number of places when it stated:

"The UPA government is firmly committed to ensure the welfare and well-being of all workers, particularly those in the unorganised sector who constitute 93 per cent of our workforce. Social security, health insurance

and other schemes for such workers like weavers, handloom workers, fishermen and fisherwomen, toddy tappers, leather workers, plantation labour, beedi workers, etc. will be expanded."

"Enhance the welfare and wellbeing of farmers, farm labour and workers, particularly those in the unorganised sector and assure a secure future for their families in every respect."

"The UPA administration will ensure the fullest implementation of minimum wage laws for farm labour. Comprehensive protective legislation will be enacted for all agricultural workers."

Constitution of a National Commission for the Unorganised Sector

1.4 In order to fulfil the above commitment, the Government of India, among other measures, constituted a National Commission for Enterprises in the Unorganised Sector (NCEUS) vide Ministry of Small Scale Industries Resolution No. 5(2)/2004-ICC dated 20th September, 2004, to act as an advisory body and watchdog for the informal sector. The detailed terms of reference of the Commission and its past and present composition are given in Annexures 3 and 4 of this Report.

1.5 The Commission submitted its first Report on Social Security for Unorganised Workers on 16th May 2006 recommending the creation of an entitlement of a national minimum social security for all the eligible unorganised workers. These proposals are again reiterated in the recommendations of this Report. The Commission strongly believes that the creation of an entitlement for a national minimum social security will be a historic decision towards ensuring a bare minimum of protection to the vast multitude of unorganised workers in the country.

1.6 As a prelude to this detailed analytical as well as recommendatory Report, the Commission submitted to the Prime Minister, on 7 July 2007, a concise Report with two draft Bills - one for the unorganised workers in agriculture and another one for those outside agriculture-recommending legislation for a set of minimum conditions of work as well as a national minimum social security. The main arguments for these recommendations were drawn from this detailed Report.

1.7 This Report focuses on the conditions of work of the informal or unorganised workers, both in the unorganised and organised sectors. The Commission recognises that wage workers (i.e. employed by others), whose conditions of work are of concern, constituted only 36 per cent of the workers in the unorganised sector in 2004-05. For the remaining 64 per cent who are self-employed (see Appendix A1.1) promotion of livelihood opportunities is the prime route for improving their conditions of work. This is also true, if not directly, for the wage earners. As such, the Report has covered these two dimensions of the problem and by implication the entire terms of reference. In that sense, this is an overarching Report that not only analyses the issues but also recommends a framework within which these twin issues can be addressed. Detailed Reports on such specific issues listed in the terms of reference are under preparation. These include access to credit, marketing and related issues, development of skills and, a strategy for employment promotion.

Conceptualising the Unorganised Economy: Sector Vs Workers

1.8 The use of the term 'organised' and 'unorganised' as used in India is internationally known as 'formal' and 'informal'. In the Indian context the enterprise concept (i.e. to define the unorganised sector) and the employment concept (i.e. to define unorganised employment) lack in conceptual clarity and uniformity across the sub-sectors of the economy. For example, the Central Statistical Organisation uses the term organised enterprise as small units with ten or more workers with power or 20 or more workers without power for the manufacturing sector. However, the absence of similar statistical data till now prevented this definition being extended to the service sector. Employment in the unorganised sector has hitherto been derived as a residual of the total workers minus workers in the organised sector as Reported by the Directorate General of Employment and Training (DGET). The DGET figures, however, fail to capture the informal/unorganised employment in the formal/organised sector - a phenomenon, which is becoming increasingly significant in the Indian economy.

1.9 These definitional and statistical issues have been examined and deliberated in detail by the Commission

"The unorganised sector consists of all unincorporated private enterprises owned by individuals or households engaged in the sale and production of goods and services operated on a proprietary or partnership basis and with less than ten total workers".

and the findings and recommendations are being brought out in a separate Report since they have implications for future design of surveys and compilation of data. Since the 55th Round Employment Survey of the National Sample Survey Organisation (NSSO), it is possible to apply a uniform definition of both the sector concept and the employment concept to distinguish the organised/ formal from the unorganised/informal. Using the following two key definitions the Commission separated the unorganised sector from that of the organised sector as well as unorganised employment from that of organised employment (NCEUS forthcoming). The organised/ unorganised terms are used interchangeably with formal/ informal and as such they are consistent with the international definition as recommended by the ILO.

1.10 First, we define the unorganised sector in the following way:

> *"The unorganised sector consists of all unincorporated private enterprises owned by individuals or households engaged in the sale and production of goods and services operated on a proprietary or partnership basis and with less than ten total workers".*

1.11 The Commission considers all agricultural activities undertaken on agricultural holdings, either individually or in partnership, as being in the unorganised sector. According to this definition, it excludes only the plantation sector and other types of organised agriculture (e.g. corporate or co-operative farming) and covers a very large part of agriculture.

1.12 The definition of the unorganised enterprise constituting the unorganised sector given here is a generic one in the sense that it has no legal personality of its own (other than the person who owns it); it is small in employment size and, more often than not, associated with low capital intensity and labour productivity. The diverse nature of these enterprises is often a response to the demand for a variety of low-price goods and services produced in different modes of self-employment, unpaid family labour and wage work (often concealed as self-employment under different forms of putting-out systems).

1.13 Second, we define unorganised or informal employment as follows:

> *"Unorganised workers consist of those working in the unorganised enterprises or households, excluding regular workers with social security benefits, and the workers in the formal sector without any employment/ social security benefits provided by the employers".*

1.14 The employees with informal jobs generally do not enjoy employment security (no protection against arbitrary dismissal) work security (no protection against accidents and illness at the work place) and social security (maternity and health care benefits, pension, etc.) and therefore any one or more of these characteristics can be used for identifying informal employment.

1.15 In this Report, those who form the universe of unorganised workers are without adequate legislative or other support for employment and/or conditions of work. In general, we can expect a correspondence between unorganised workers without social security and workers without protection for conditions of work and promotion of livelihood benefits, particularly in the unorganised sector.

Size and Relationships

1.16 The Commission has prepared direct estimates of employment in the unorganised sector based on its definition given earlier. As per these estimates, on January, 2005, the total employment (principal plus subsidiary) in the Indian economy was 458 million, of which the unorganised sector accounted for 395 million (Table 1.1). This direct estimation shows that the unorganised sector constituted 86 per cent of total workers in 2004-05 (Appendix A1.1) [1].

1.17 Of the 395 million unorganised sector workers, agriculture accounted for 253 million and the rest 142 million are employed in the non-agriculture sector

"Unorganised workers consist of those working in the unorganised enterprises or households, excluding regular workers with social security benefits, and the workers in the formal sector without any employment/ social security benefits provided by the employers".

1 The percentage of workers in the unorganised sector by states is presented in Appendix A1.3

2 The percentage of unorganised workers by states is presented in Appendix A1.3.

Table 1.1: Relationship between Sector and Type of Employment (UPSS), All Workers 1999-2000 & 2004-05

Sector/Worker	Total Employment (Million)		
	Informal/Unorganised Worker	Formal/Organised Worker	Total
		1999 - 2000	
Informal/Unorganised sector	341.3 (99.6)	1.4 (0.4)	342.6 (100.0)
Formal/Organised sector	20.5(37.8)	33.7 (62.2)	54.1 (100.0)
Total	361.7 (91.2)	35.0 (8.8)	396.8 (100.0)
		2004 - 2005	
Informal/Unorganised Sector	393.5 (99.6)	1.4 (0.4)	394.9 (100.0)
Formal/Organised Sector	29.1 (46.6)	33.4 (53.4)	62.6 (100.0)
Total	422.6 (92.4)	34.9 (7.6)	457.5 (100.0)

Note : Figures in brackets are percentages.
Source : NSS 61st Round 2004 - 2005 and NSS 55th Round, 1999-2000, Employment-Unemployment Survey. Computed.

(Appendix A1.1). The proportion of non-agricultural worker in the unorganised sector rose from 32 per cent to 36 per cent between 1999-2000 and 2004-05. The agriculture sector consists of almost entirely unorganised workers who are mainly the self-employed (65 per cent) and the casual workers (35 per cent). Even in the non-agriculture sector nearly 72 per cent of the workers are in the unorganised sector, an increase of 4 percentage points from 68 per cent in 1999-2000. These workers are mainly the self-employed (63 per cent). The rest of the workers in the non-agriculture unorganised sector are more or less equally distributed between the regular (17 per cent) and casual categories (20 per cent).

1.18 Only about 0.4 per cent of the unorganised sector workers were receiving social security benefits like Provident Fund, and this proportion had not changed since 1999-2000 (Table 1.1). Thus, the informal workers in the unorganised sector number 393.5 million (i.e. 394.9 million less 1.4 million). The Commission has further estimated the total number of unorganised/ informal workers at 423 million, 256 million in the agriculture sector and 167 million in the non-agriculture sector (Appendix 1.2)[2].

1.19 We can now see the inter-relationship between the organised/unorganised sector and organised/ unorganised employment . This is shown in Table 1.1. Since data from the 61st Round of the NSS are now available we are in a position to compare our estimates of the 55th Round (1999-00) with those for 2004-05. The total employment in the economy has increased from 397 million to 457 million between the two NSS rounds. The change in the organised or formal employment has been nil or marginally negative (i.e. 35 million in both the years). Therefore, the increase in total employment has been of an informal kind i.e. 61 million (from 362 to 423 million) or 17 per cent. However, if we view the increase from a sectoral point, employment increased by 8.5 million or 16 per cent (from 54.1 million to 62.6 million) in the organised sector. *What this means in simple terms is that the entire increase in the employment in the organised sector over this period has been informal in nature i.e. without any job or social security. This constitutes what can be termed as informalisation of the formal sector, where any employment increase consists of regular workers without social security benefits and casual or contract workers again without the benefits that should accrue to formal workers.*

1.20 Thus, the categories of workers who comprise unorganised workers/informal employment are the following:

[3] This is based on the recommendation discussed in the Seventeenth International Conference of Labour Statisticians (ICLS) held in 2003 endorsing a set of guidelines to complement the resolution concerning statistics of employment in the informal sector adopted by the 15th ICLS. A conceptual framework to identify the inter-face between workers in the informal sector and in the informal employment is in ILO 2002a.

1.21 *Wage Workers in the Unorganised Sector:* Wage workers are persons employed for remuneration as unorganised workers, directly by employers or through agencies or contractors. Wage workers include casual and temporary workers, migrant workers, or those employed by households including domestic workers. Wage workers also include regular workers in the unorganised sector. Different groups of wage workers face different types/ grades of vulnerabilities, which we examine at length in this Report.

1.22 *Self-employed in the Unorganised Sector:* These are persons who operate farm or non-farm enterprises or engage in a profession or trade, either on own account, individually or with partners, or as home-based workers. Own account workers include unpaid family workers also.

1.23 *Unprotected Wage Workers in the Organised Sector:* Unprotected workers in the organised sector are mainly in the categories of regular, casual and contract workers who remain unprotected because of non-compliance of the provisions of the existing laws. This is a growing segment in the organised sector.

1.24 *Regular Unorganised Workers,* referred to in 1.22 and 1.24 above, are those working for others and getting in return salary or wages on a regular basis.

Homeworkers as a Distinct Category

1.25 From a statistical point of view, homeworkers are usually classified under the category of the self-employed. We have separated this category since a significant share of women workers belong to this segment. They warrant separate treatment from a policy point of view. It should be noted that there are two types of home-based workers; (i) independent employers or own account workers (purely self-employed), and (ii) dependent sub-contract workers. The term homeworker is used to designate the second category of dependent workers only. The ILO Home Work Convention No. 177, adopted in 1996, refers exclusively to homeworkers, a category not included in the International Classification of Status in Employment, ICSE-93. It defined a homeworker as a person who carried out work for remuneration in premises of his/her choice, other than the work place of the employer, resulting in a product or service as specified by the employer, irrespective of who provided the equipment, material or inputs used. This is a sub-category of a broader category of home-based workers. The homeworkers fall in an intermediate position between the self-employed and the wage workers, or the employee. Consequently they may also Report themselves as either wage workers or as self-employed workers in a survey.

1.26 For the first time in 1999-2000, the NSS Employment and Unemployment Survey canvassed some special questions to enable the direct estimation of the number and proportion of homeworkers. These were a set of questions on the place of work and nature of contracts. The homeworkers as a whole were estimated at nearly 8.2 million workers of whom about 4.8 million were women. The homeworkers constitute about 7.4 per cent of the unorganised non-agricultural workers (Appendix A1.4). Available studies show that in the manufacturing sector in India product outsourcing from large firms to small firms has been on the increase. We anticipate that further subcontracting from the smaller firms to homeworkers could have increased the size of the homeworkers. Unfortunately the NSS 61st Round, unlike the 55th round, does not allow us to estimate the size of the homeworkers because the survey did not include specific questions on the nature of contract.

Poverty, Vulnerability and Informal Work Status: the High Congruence

1.27 When 92 per cent of the country's workforce is employed in the informal or unorganised economy (i.e. those who work in the unorganised sector plus the informal workers in the organised sector), it is but natural that there is a high congruence between the poor and the vulnerable segments of the society (who may be called the common people). But, there is an empirical challenge to demarcate, the segments that constitute the group of the poor and the vulnerable and then to link them up with the informal economy. The Commission has therefore attempted, as a first approximation, to measure this category by dividing the total population of the country into six groups based on their consumption

While the percentage of population below the poverty line has come down, albeit at a slower rate during the nineties and until recently compared to in the eighties, the movement is within the group of broadly poor (41 per cent) or the poor and vulnerable (77 per cent) of the population.

Table 1.2: Population in Different Expenditure Class

S.No.	Expenditure class	1993-94	In Million 1999-00	2004-05
1.	Extremely Poor (up to 075PL)	103	87	70
2.	Poor (0.75Pl to PL)	172	174	167
3.	Marginally Poor (PL to 1.25PL)	168	200	207
4.	Vulnerable (1.25PL to 2PL)	290	349	392
5.	Middle Income (2PL to 4 PL)	139	167	210
6.	High Income (>4PL)	24	26	44
7.	Extremely Poor and Poor (1 + 2)	274	262	237
8.	Marginal and Vulnerable (3 + 4)	458	549	599
9.	**Poor and Vulnerable (7 + 8)**	732	811	836
10.	**Middle and High Income (5 + 6)**	162	193	253
11.	Total	894	1004	1090
	Expenditure class		**Percentage share and average consumer expenditure per capita per day in Rs. (pcpd)**	
1.	Extremely Poor (up to 075PL)	11.5	8.7	6.4 (9)
2.	Poor (0.75Pl to PL)	19.2	17.3	15.4 (12)
3.	Marginally Poor (PL to 1.25PL)	18.8	19.9	19.0 (15)
4.	Vulnerable (1.25PL to 2PL)	32.4	34.8	36.0 (20)
5.	Middle Income (2PL to 4 PL)	15.5	16.7	19.3 (37)
6.	High Income (>4PL)	2.7	2.6	4.0 (93)
7.	Extremely Poor and Poor (1 + 2)	30.7	26.1	21.8 (11)
8.	Marginal and Vulnerable (3 + 4)	51.2	54.7	55.0 (18)
9.	**Poor and Vulnerable (7 + 8)**	81.8	80.7	76.7 (16)
10.	**Middle and High Income (5 + 6)**	18.2	19.3	23.3 (46)
11.	Total	100.00	100.00	100.00 (23)

Note:
1. Figures in bracket denote average consumer expenditure per capita per day in Rs.
2. PL refers to Poverty Line.

Source: Computed from unit level data of NSS 61st Round 2004 - 2005, NSS 55th Round 1999-2000 and NSS 50th Round 1993-94, Employment-Unemployment Survey.

expenditure. The first four are clubbed together to get the segment of the common people. The first group of "Extremely Poor" are those who have a monthly per capita consumer expenditure of up to three-fourths of the official poverty line (i.e. an average of Rs.8.9 per capita per day (pcpd) in 2004-05); the second group "Poor" are those between the Extremely Poor and up to the official poverty line (average expenditure of Rs. 11.6 pcpd); the third is called "Marginally Poor" with per capita consumer expenditure of only 1.25 times the poverty line (i.e. Rs.14.6 pcpd); and the fourth called "Vulnerable" have per capita consumer expenditure of only two times the poverty line (i.e. Rs.20.3 pcpd). In 2004-05, the Extremely Poor constituted 6.4 per cent, the Poor 15.4 per cent, the Marginally Poor 19.0 per cent. These three constituted 41 per cent of the population. If the vulnerable are added to this group the total accounts for 77 per cent of the population (Table 1.2). We would categorise this 77 per cent, totalling 836 million people, with an income roughly below $2 in PPP terms, as the poor and vulnerable segment of the Indian population.

1.28 *While the percentage of population below the poverty line has come down, albeit at a slower rate during the nineties and until recently compared to in the eighties, the movement is within the group of broadly poor (41 per cent) or the poor and vulnerable (77 per cent) of the population.*

1.29 In Table 1.2 we present the various poorer classes along side, what we call, Middle Income and High Income for the three time periods since the early nineties. What is significant to note is the reduction in extreme poverty from close to 12 per cent to 6 per cent between 1993 and 2005. Similarly the share of the poor has also come down from 19 to 15 per cent. Equally significantly we find that the share of the marginal group has hardly changed while the share of the vulnerable increased from 32 to 36 per cent. The overall gain has been quite limited from a staggering 82 per cent to just 77 per cent. Given the increase in population, even this gain has not meant a decrease in the total burden because the total population of the poor and vulnerable increased from 733 million to 836 million. Much of the reduction in poor is in the groups of extremely poor and the poor but they remained within the overall category of the marginal and vulnerable.

1.30 The other side of the picture is the increase in the high income group from 18 to 23 per cent that now totals 254 million compared to 163 million in the early nineties. More significantly, there has been a very noticeable growth in the consumption of the next category whom we call the "Middle Income" with a per capita consumption two to four times the poverty line and a last category say, the "High Income" class with a per capita consumption above four times the poverty line. The compound rate of growth of consumption of these two groups have been high; 4.3 per cent and 6.2 per cent a year respectively compared with less than one per cent increase a year in the consumption of groups identified as the "Extremely Poor", "Poor" and "Marginal". If we include the fourth group of "Vulnerable", then the growth rate increases to 2.8 per cent a year. We have also analysed the details of the monthly consumption expenditure of the different poverty groups. The overwhelming fraction of consumption of the first four groups, the poor and vulnerable, consists of cereals, pulses and other food items and some essential non-food items. The share of consumption expenditure of the Middle and High Income Groups consists, understandably, much less of cereals and essential non-food items, but overwhelmingly so of the other non-essential non-food and food items as well as durable goods.

Table 1.3: Percentage Distribution of Expenditure Classes by Social Identity, Informal Work Status and Education, 2004-2005

Sl. No.	Economic Status	Social Categories (percentage share in own total)				Percentage of Un-organised Workers	Education[1]	
		STs/SCs	All OBCs except Muslims	AllMuslim except STs/SCs	Others* (without STs/SCs, OBCs & Muslim)		Illiterates	Primary and below Primary
1	Extremely Poor	10.9	5.1	8.2	2.1	5.8	8.1	5.0
2	Poor	21.5	15.1	19.2	6.4	15	19.0	14.2
3	Marginally Poor	22.4	20.4	22.3	11.1	19.6	22.2	19.4
4	Vulnerable	33	39.2	34.8	35.2	38.4	36.9	40.0
5	Middle Income	11.1	17.8	13.3	34.2	18.7	12.8	18.9
6	High Income	1	2.4	2.2	11	2.7	1.0	2.5
7	Extremely Poor and Poor (1+2)	32.4	20.3	27.4	8.5	20.8	27.1	19.2
8	Marginal and Vulnerable (3+4)	55.4	59.6	57.1	46.3	57.9	59.1	59.4
9	**Poor and Vulnerable (7 + 8)**	**87.8**	**79.9**	**84.5**	**54.8**	**78.7**	**86.2**	**78.6**
10	**Middle and High Income (5+6)**	**12.2**	**20.1**	**15.5**	**45.2**	**21.3**	**13.8**	**21.4**
	All	100.0	100.0	100.0	100.0	100.0	100.0	100.0
	All (million)	**302**	**391**	**138**	**258**	**423**	**270**	**164**

Note: 1. Refers to persons aged 15 and above.
Source: NSS 61st Round 2004 - 2005, Employment-Unemployment Survey. Computed.

1.31 As will be seen in Table 1.3, what is quite significant is that 79 per cent of the informal or unorganised workers, 88 per cent of the Scheduled Castes and Scheduled Tribes, 80 per cent of the OBC population and 84 per cent of the Muslims belong to the poor and vulnerable group. They have remained poor at a bare subsistence level without any job or social security, working in the most miserable, unhygienic and unliveable conditions, throughout this period of high economic growth since the early nineties. There have been some *inter se* changes within this total group, such that the proportion of the Extremely Poor and the Poor has come down, while the number of marginally poor and the Vulnerable groups have increased. But the percentage of population suffering from poverty and vulnerability has remained substantial. The illiterates have a very high probability of being poor or vulnerable, almost nine out of ten, and they are predominantly unorganised workers. Even with education up to only primary level 83 per cent are in the poor and vulnerable group. Education can be a liberating capability but access to it is made difficult, if not impossible, by such inherited characteristics as lower social status, rural origin, informal work status and gender or a combination of these. These issues (of the relationship between social origin, educational status and work status) have been analysed by us in greater detail in subsequent chapters.

1.32 The relationship between poverty and vulnerability and the type of employment that the unorganised workers engage in, is brought out in Table 1.4. Among these workers, the 21 per cent belonging to Middle and High Income groups are mostly self-employed or regular workers. The category of self-employed here are the ones with sufficient capital and skills, such as urban traders and independent skilled workers or professionals. Regular employees could be those whose services are critical to the running of small informal enterprises or establishments such as accountants or master craftsmen or such similar critical skilled workers. The high congruence between informal work status and poverty/vulnerability becomes almost complete in the case of casual workers, 90 per cent of them belong to the group of poor and vulnerable. In this sense, the analysis contained in this Report on the conditions of informal workers is also a commentary on the conditions of life of those whom we have chosen to characterise as poor and vulnerable who constitute the common people of the country.

Table 1.4: Percentage Distribution of Unorganised Workers across Expenditure Classes

Status	Total	Self-employed	Regular wage workers	Casual workers
Poor and vulnerable	78.7	74.7	66.7	90.0
Higher income group	21.3	25.3	33.3	10.0
Total	100.0	100.0	100.0	100.0

Source: Same as in Table 1.3.

1.33 The socio-economic and educational correlates of the poor and vulnerable population quantified here are no doubt based on the official poverty line (which we also use in the rest of this Report) but to illustrate the true dimensions of the problem we have constructed the well-being categories used in the preceding analysis. We must however mention here that the Commission is aware of the vigorous debate, both at the level of the government (especially the state governments) and among the social science academic community about whether the official poverty line realistically captures the prevailing levels of deprivation. Apart from the fact that this level is based on a consumption basket of nearly two generations ago (1973-74) and the unsatisfactory nature of its indexation, it conveys only one dimension of poverty in terms of income or its surrogate, consumption expenditure. A revisit of the official poverty line as a first step towards the recognition of the multidimensional nature of poverty is perhaps overdue.

1.34 It is quite evident that the Indian growth story has been characterized by a rapid growth of middle class and the rich, expanding their consumption of non-food, non-essential and durable items and thereby providing a huge market of 253 million people that includes imports of these items from the global market. There is no doubt that this "Shining India" has expanded in the past and is still expanding at a very high rate. But this picture is spoiled by a virtually stagnant consumption expenditure and miserable working and living conditions of the 77 per cent of our population who are poor and vulnerable. This group includes the overwhelming population of the *dalits* and *adivasis,* OBCs and Muslims. This is the other world which can be characterised as the India of the Common People, constituting more than three-fourths of the population and consisting of all those whom the growth process has, by and large, bypassed.

Rationale for a Social Floor

1.35 It is this reality of the high congruence between the informal economy and the poor and vulnerable that has led the Commission to examine the twin issues of conditions of work and promotion of livelihood. By no means are the recommendations in this regard adequate to address the magnitude of the problem. *The first step, in our view, is to create a social floor and nobody is allowed to fall below that level as a matter of social priority and a bottom line of our developmental programmes.*

1.36 While many schemes and projects exist, there are very few which are in the nature of entitlements. The recent and significant exception is that of the National Rural Employment Guarantee. In the present Report we document the status of conditions of work and earnings in the unorganised sector and those of the informal workers in the organised sector wherever relevant with a view to identifying the kind of measures that would help in improving their lot. We have focussed on the following five issues out of the six and have translated them into two Draft Bills - one for workers in agriculture and the other for those in non-agriculture - for consideration of the Government.

I. Issues relating to the working conditions and welfare of workers. These include two distinct components: physical conditions of work and the duration and the timing of work. The physical conditions at the work place would include space, ventilation, illumination, temperature, humidity, hygiene and so on, that affect the health and safety of workers. Issues related to duration and timing of work include the length of the work day, the spread over, hours of rest, overtime work, and hours of work per week, night work, and paid holidays during the week and so on.

II. Issues relating to the remuneration at work, wage levels, wage forms, pay period, advances and so on.

III. Issues relating to social security benefits for the workers. (As mentioned earlier, this was dealt with in the first Report of the Commission submitted to the Government on 16 May 2006.)

IV. Issues relating to the industrial/labour relations. These include issues related to the trade unions such as recognition and registration and mechanisms available to workers in the unorganised sector for redressal of grievances and disputes.

V. Issues relating to the conditions of work of disadvantaged workers, such as forced labour, bonded and child labour and disadvantaged groups arising from discrimination based on gender, caste, religion or any such characteristic of the workers.

VI. And finally and most importantly, issues relating to expanding employment and employability, through enterprise development, technology, marketing and credit enhancement and through skill development and training.

1.37 While providing a social floor related to the first five issues are the main subject matter of the two draft Bills we have proposed, the issues related to expanding employment and employability are the subject matters of an agenda for livelihood promotion.

An Agenda for Livelihood Promotion

1.38 The Commission recognises that livelihood promotion is the only route through which we can deal with the issues of conditions of work and related aspects of poverty and vulnerability of those who are called the self-employed. Given the empirical reality that the self-employed largely consist of own account workers with or without assistance from family labour, the notion of 'livelihood promotion' takes a broader meaning than what may be called 'enterprise promotion'. Own account workers are workers as well as micro entrepreneurs because both these characteristics merge into one. Their conditions of work are similar to the wage workers (e.g. a street vendor or a rickshaw puller pulling his own vehicle) and often strive to make a meagre income by 'self exploitation' through lengthening the working day. However, they also need to employ the skills of an entrepreneur in sourcing inputs and selling their products. Moreover, for the wage workers, too, especially those working in the unorganised sector, the conditions of work can not be divorced from the conditions of the small enterprises (usually run by the self-employed) in which they are employed. Hence, the promotion of livelihoods and the growth of enterprises have relevance for them as well.

1.39 Livelihood issues are related to one's capabilities, access to assets and entitlements as well as opportunities for income generation. The fact that the self-employed form the majority of workers in the Indian economy has not, so we feel, sufficiently dawned on the popular consciousness. In agriculture, the self-employed are the farmers who constitute 64 per cent of the total agricultural workers. Within the category of farmers, 86 per cent are marginal or small farmers (i.e. operating up to 2 hectares of land) accounting for 45 per cent of the area cultivated. Outside agriculture, the self-employed constitute around 63 per cent in the unorganised sector (Appendix A1.1). This includes the own account workers, assisted by the family workers (also referred to as unpaid) and those who employ one to nine workers.

1.40 The challenge is to ensure minimum livelihood security to the poor self-employed and wage employed workers and to improve their livelihoods on a sustained basis. Further, what, out of this range of security needs of the unorganised sector workers, can be provided by legislation and what can be developed through promotional policies or programmes? The Commission has taken the position that the conditions of work including a minimum of social security should be an entitlement backed by national legislation. For promoting livelihood there should be a public programme and an institutional mechanism to monitor, review and further develop from time to time with a dedicated National Fund to which the Common Minimum Programme of the UPA government is committed. In order to expand employment and improve the livelihood of those dependent on the unorganised sector, the Commission has formulated an action programme consisting of a number of immediate measures.

The Need for Ensuring Minimum Conditions of Work

1.41 The recognition of the need to ensure socially acceptable conditions of work is based on the basic principles of moral philosophy and human dignity and rights, which have also been adopted as international covenants by bodies such as the International Labour Organisation and others concerned with human rights and development. In practice they have been followed at varying pace in different countries dictated by, among other things, social norms and the resultant national ethos governing development and human dignity.

1.42 In India the basic principles governing state policy as enshrined in the Constitution, directly or implicitly, ask for ensuring these conditions for all workers. They have also been put in practice by passing several legislations prescribing the principles and procedures to be followed by the enterprises in to the employment of workers. Some of them apply to all workers but most cover only the workers in larger enterprises, namely, those employing more than a certain number of workers. The principle that the standards should be applied to all workers is accepted but their application by law has been confined to only the larger enterprises, or what has come to be known as the "organised sector", presumably because of non-affordability of the compliance cost by small or unorganised sector enterprises and difficulties in implementation. In view of the fact that the conditions of work prevailing in the unorganised sector are found to violate some of the basic tenets of human dignity, these assumptions need to be seriously examined for their validity and for explaining ways of ensuring the minimum standards at workplace for all the workers.

1.43 The Commission has examined in this Report these issues in detail including a brief overview of the international practices. Apart from the normative argument for ensuring minimum conditions of work for all workers, the Commission is also of the view that there are also strong economic arguments for providing these conditions. Some of these arguments are briefly discussed below.

Issue of Minimum Wages

1.44 One of the important issues, which have been focused upon in the context of conditions of work, is the issue of minimum wages. Although a large number of countries around the world, including developed market economies have minimum wages (see Chapter 10), there are still strong advocates of the position that wages in the labour market should not be regulated, especially in the context of the unorganised/informal sector. Advocates of non-regulation would argue that the labour market itself would set a 'floor' to wages, either because of supply and demand, or because of efficiency considerations. Moreover, they would argue that setting a wage would result in lowering employment and hence growth.

1.45 These questions demand a detailed analysis of the level at which minimum wages are set, their implementation in the economy and the relationship between minimum wages and other variables. Detailed examination of the large number of studies suggests that there is no clear-cut evidence that minimum wages deter employment.

1.46 The link between minimum wages and growth is also generally construed to be positive in a majority of studies on the topic. Minimum wages are known to have a positive impact on wages through their impact on productivity and by reducing transaction and training costs to employers, which could result from a high turnover. If there is an economy-wide implementation of minimum wages, their macro economic impact through expansion in aggregate demand on economic growth may be quite significant. Further, from a development perspective, wages, as income, go to enhance human development and thus contribute to enhancing productivity and lower unit costs.

1.47 An important set of questions pertains to the impact of minimum wages on the earnings of workers (and hence on poverty). The impact of minimum wages on poverty of the labourers would be positive as long as the increase in daily earnings can offset any potential decline in employment. Some studies have argued that even if the impact of minimum wages on poverty is positive, there could be distributional impacts, since employment effect could be negative for marginal workers. Here again, international studies indicate a positive impact of minimum wages on poverty, even among groups, which have been suggested to be vulnerable. A detailed study of the impact of minimum wages on poverty in developing countries in Asia and Latin America also suggests that there is a negative relationship between minimum wages and poverty (Lustig and McLeod 1997).

1.48 Thus, without going into the question of the level of minimum wages and other specific issues at this stage, the Commission is of the clear view that minimum wages will have a positive impact both on employment and on growth of the Indian economy and will also be conducive to reducing poverty. It has, thus, advocated the introduction of a National Minimum Wage (see Chapter 13) related to the requirements of subsistence and minimal health, education and housing requirements. Individual States and trades could set up higher minimum wages carefully considering their viability. But for the country as a whole the national minimum wage will be the basic standard that would apply to all workers, organised or unorganised. The Commission is aware that there may be a gap in the implementation of that national minimum wage, but fixing it legally will be the first step towards its effective implementation and also a signal to the investors to design their production plan taking that into account, setting up for the dynamic forces increasing productivity to accommodate an increasing level of wages.

Regulation of Working Conditions

1.49 Another significant set of issues in the labour market relates to the working condition of workers, including issues such as length of the working day, payment of overtime, holidays, safety conditions etc. In recent decades, the East Asian experience is characterised as one in which firms were able to increase production by lengthening the working day. This is often used as an argument in the Indian case to buttress demands for relaxing regulations on the length of the working day, wherever such regulation exists.

1.50 There is a limited but useful amount of literature available on the impact of the length of the working day on worker productivity. This literature establishes that elongation of the working day beyond an 'optimum' number of hours reduces the per-hour productivity of the worker (i.e. it is subject to diminishing marginal productivity).

1.51 The other aspect of the length of the working day is linked to wages i.e. in the case of daily time rate wages, elongation of the working day would lead to lower hourly wages. However, this is subject to the arguments considered earlier in the context of minimum wages. In fact, a standard application of economic theory demands that workers be paid a higher wage rate for work beyond standard hours because of the steeply increasing disutility of such work (for the workers). This is usually provided through the application of overtime wage rates the world over.

1.52 The inescapable conclusion is that the arguments for the regulation of working conditions ensue not only from the protection of workers and their rights as well as concerns with basic dignity of work, but also from the logic of enhancing productivity and growth, even though such logic may not be immediately obvious to individual employers.

Discrimination and Conditions of Disadvantaged Labour

1.53 Conditions of workers in the Indian labour market are defined by the conditions of their social existence, particularly for women. In this Report, we have highlighted the plight of women unorganised workers to focus public attention on the continuing and widespread discrimination across sectors and occupations. While labour market discrimination is often manifested in job typing and lower remuneration, discrimination outside the labour market takes the form of lower work participation rate. The situation becomes further debilitating when gender disadvantage is superimposed on other disadvantages such as low social status, low education and rural location.

1.54 The other prominent forms of disadvantaged labour are such groups as migrant, bonded and child labour. Such groups of workers are mostly, if not only, in the unorganised sector and belong to low status communities, who suffer from social exclusion of one kind or another. These conditions include low levels of human resource development, low social acceptability in high status and high value jobs, and (in the case of women) low mobility and low valuation of the work performed. These conditions combine with discrimination in the labour market to result in labour market segmentation, low wages and poor working conditions to workers belonging to these groups.

1.55 These outcomes are then justified on the basis of differentials in productivity, whereas these supposed differentials are themselves results of the specific ways in which the labour market functions. Similar justification is also given for the continuation of child labour (to which another argument regarding the relative dexterity of child workers is also added) who also mostly belong to the poor and the socially discriminated groups.

1.56 The Commission has examined these arguments thoroughly and rejects them completely. We are of the view that the existence of social discrimination and social segmentation, along with the existence of unacceptable forms of work such as child labour and forced labour militates against growth and development, and that it is the duty of the State to ensure that the grounds for such treatment are demolished.

Need for Levelling Up the Informal Sector

1.57 In the Commission's view, the dualistic nature of the Indian economy has significantly moved away from the textbook division of agriculture and non-agriculture (often referred to as traditional and modern) sectors and has been replaced by the informal and formal dichotomy, cutting across the sectors. The challenge is to transform the informal sector and reduce the gap between the formal and informal. That calls for a conscious strategy of 'levelling up' the informal sector rather than 'levelling down' the formal sector. This has been the historical experience of the now developed countries that enjoy high levels of income and human development. Public policies and instruments are therefore required to be shaped and tuned for such a process of 'levelling up'. The costs of dithering or delay could be socially and politically unacceptable in an electoral democracy of unequal voters.

Role of the State and Other Institutions

1.58 In this era of globalisation driven by the ideology of economic liberalisation, it is quite evident that the role of the state has changed ever since the decline of the Keynesian paradigm of macro economic management and its corollary of state-led development in poor developing countries. But the state's basic responsibility towards provision of certain minimum conditions of work, including minimum wages and social security, cannot be brushed aside. And it has not been brushed aside even in the advanced capitalist countries who swear by the ideology of economic liberalisation and its concomitant, free market economy. In fact, these countries as a group continue to lead the rest of the world in providing what may be called decent conditions of work, minimum wages and social security. The role of the employer is also clearly recognized. However, besides the state and employers, there is a third form of institutional mechanism, the civil society that also plays a role in delivering protection and promotion. This appears in the form of the trade unions, social networks and voluntary organizations and associations advocating protection and promotion of the labouring poor in the society. The institutional mechanisms to deliver these instruments are found in the institutions of private (employer), public (government), and civil society.

1.59 The Commission has earlier listed (see 1.37) five sets of issues important to guarantee decent conditions of work for the unorganised workers. The extent to which each type of institution can be responsible for securing these strategic conditions can be judged by a number of criteria. In those cases, where the unorganised worker has a clearly identifiable employer and the employer has the capacity to pay, the employer has the primary responsibility of ensuring basic conditions of work. In such cases, the role of the government is of regulation and enforcement. But in cases where the employer cannot be identified or does not have the capacity to pay in creating appropriate conditions of work, the responsibility of the state in creating appropriate conditions of work will be paramount. Given the weak state of voice and representation of the unorganised workers, the state and the civil society organisations mentioned earlier have an important role in contributing to an industrial and labour relations environment in which the minimum conditions of work of the unorganised workers can be secured. Similarly, for the promotion of livelihoods of the unorganised sector workers, the state has the most critical role, particularly in the provision of public goods and policies. Others can play an important part, both independently, and in conjunction with the State. But in all these subjects, the primary duty bearer, in our view, is the state which alone is constitutionally mandated to enforce society-wide regulations and create conditions for the development of the economy.

Procedure Followed in the Preparation of the Report

1.60 The Commission began with consultations with its Advisory Board. Subsequently, two draft Bills were prepared and placed in the public domain. Copies of the draft Bills were sent to several of the stakeholders including state governments, trade unions and other organisations working for, and with, the unorganised workers.

1.61 Comments and suggestions on the draft Bills were received from a number of ministries, state governments, trade unions, and workers' organizations. The Commission also requested the state governments for specific information on a number of issues, relating to the existing laws and their implementation. Visits were organised to a number of states in early 2007, during which consultations were held with the departments of labour, trade unions, industry associations, and other stakeholders. Views of the stakeholders were particularly sought on the advisability of having a single draft Bill for all unorganised workers or separate Bills for agricultural and non-agricultural workers. The comments and responses received formed the basis for the preparation of this Report and the revised draft Bills.

1.62 The Commission also asked a few experts to prepare background papers to guide its work. The main analytical work in the preparation of the Report and the draft Bills was carried out internally with the assistance of the technical staff of the Commission. Most of the findings presented here refer to the latest available period i.e. 2004-05 based on the 61st Round of the National Sample Survey. Working on the unit level data made available by the National Sample Survey Organisation, a number of empirical findings have been generated for the first time. In particular mention may be made of the effort to bring out the gender, social identity and educational dimensions of various issues.

1.63 Once a draft version of the Report was completed it was placed in the public domain through the website of the Commission for comments and feedback from all interested stakeholders. Subsequently regional consultations in Jaipur (2nd May 2007), Ranchi (11th May 2007), Bangalore (22nd May 2007) and Kolkata (2nd June 2007) were organised to discuss the draft Report with the representatives of unorganised workers, small industry, government officials, scholars and social activists.

1.64 The draft Bills and the Report were reviewed by the Advisory Board in its meeting held on 28th May 2007 before finalisation.

Framework of the Report

1.65 This Report is organised as follows. Chapters 2 to 4 deal with the workers outside agriculture and within that, wage workers and the self-employed separately. Chapters 5 and 6 focus on women workers and other disadvantaged workers such as migrants, child labourers and bonded labourers. The intention here is to draw the attention of all concerned on the specific problems faced by these groups of workers. Chapters 7-9 deal with agricultural workers. While Chapter 7 gives a socio-economic profile of the agricultural workers, Chapter 8 deals with the conditions of agricultural wage workers and Chapter 9 concentrates on the conditions of work of farmers especially the small and marginal ones. Chapter 10 discusses the international experiences with regulations for minimum conditions of work. Subsequent Chapters in the Report deal with the existing framework of regulation of conditions of work and promotional policies. It also delineates the recommendations of this Commission. Specifically, Chapter 11 discusses the provisions relating to minimum conditions of work mainly for wage workers in India. Chapter 12 discusses the promotional issues and a framework for the unorganised sector in India.

1.66 Chapter 13 contains the Commission's recommendations as well as the main provisions of the two draft Bills proposed by it. Given the plight of the large majority of the informal workers in the country, the Commission has drawn up an immediate agenda for action in the form of an Action Programme for implementation by the Central Government based on the analysis and recommendations in the Report as well as discussions with various stakeholders. This is given in Chapter 14.

2 Unorganised Non-agricultural Workers: Socio-economic Profile

Introduction

2.1 By international standards, especially of the East and South East Asia, India's 40-42 per cent labour force participation rate is not high. But, as we have seen in Chapter 1, the absolute number of workers is a staggering 457 million by the latest count in 2004-05. Of this more than 92 per cent are what we call the unorganised or informal workers i.e. those who work in the unorganised sector as well as those in the organised sector, but without any job or social security. In this report, we first deal with the unorganised non-agricultural workers who constitute around 167 million in 2004-05. These workers, along with those working in agriculture, are really the unprotected although the official classification used is 'unorganised'. While textbook theory on economic development predicts the transfer of labour from agriculture to the rest of the economy as it transforms in to modern, experience of the developing countries has, by now, established the presence of a large pool of informal workers outside agriculture. The transition to formal or organised worker status seems to be significantly long and no one has a clear answer as to how long this process is likely to continue. The exciting debate in the popular press in India on the benefits of the high speed of the economy's aggregate growth has hardly shown any concern when it comes to the plight of the vast pool of informal or unorganised workers in all the sectors of the economy. It is therefore imperative to bring to light, as much as possible, the conditions of this section of workers if the country is serious about its declared objective of inclusive growth and, by implication, overall and balanced development.

2.2 This chapter gives an overview of the socio-economic profile of the unorganised or informal workers other than those engaged in agriculture. Workers in agriculture (discussed in Chapters 7-9) constitute a category in itself and are, mostly unorganised or informal. We have examined access to land (i.e. land possessed), which is an important asset even for those in non-agricultural activities because of the safety net it provides in a labour market that is not only discriminatory but also irregular in employment with low wages or income earning opportunities. We also examine the educational levels, social background (i.e. caste/community), labour market outcomes in terms of employment status and finally the incidence of poverty.

2.3 The predominant share of unorganised workers belongs to those working in the unorganised sector. They can be classified as wage workers and the self-employed. Wage workers can be either 'regular workers' or 'casual workers'. Self-employed can be 'homeworkers' or 'other' self-employed.

2.4 Limited access to human and physical capital among the unorganised workers acts as a major constraint on access to jobs or growth of self-employed activities. We have given special attention to analyse the levels of education in rural and urban areas and land ownership of the non-agricultural workers in rural areas. At one level, vulnerability is observed in terms of access to organised sector jobs. At another there are differences within the unorganised sector in conditions of work among casual wage workers, regular workers and self-employed workers and more generally between organised and unorganised workers.

2.5 There is keen public interest in and a public debate on affirmative action. Scheduled Castes and Scheduled Tribes have been guaranteed affirmative action through Constitutional protection. For Other Backward Classes, both central and state governments have adopted different norms and kinds of affirmative action. A recent report (GOI 2006), on the socio-economic conditions of Muslims has brought out the relative backwardness of this community in a number of states as well as on an all India level. In this report, we have noted that social status, along with education and gender, has also contributed to the vulnerability of unorganised workers.

2.6 These socio-economic characteristics are discussed in this chapter as they together determine the entry into the various segments of the labour market in terms of their status, industry in which they work and the occupations they undertake. Finally, the socio-economic status as well as the labour market niche that the workers find themselves determines their relative deprivation in terms of incidence of poverty. We finally discuss the poverty profile of the workers across segments of the labour force and socio-religious groups.

Physical and Human Capital

Land Distribution

2.7 The land distribution data (see Table 2.1) reveals that 7.5 per cent and 15.4 per cent of the agricultural and non-agricultural workers are totally landless. Landless and sub-marginal farmers (having up to 0.4 hectare or one acre) together comprise as high as three fourths of the non-agricultural workers. Not surprisingly, the highest percentage of landless and land-poor is among the wage workers in agriculture. The high incidence of landlessness or near landlessness among the agricultural wage workers and non-agricultural workers is perhaps the principal reason for they pursuing wage work or being in non-farm sector in rural India. About 17 per cent of the self-employed (cultivators) in agriculture are also land-poor.

Table 2.1: Percentage Distribution of Rural Workers by Land Size Classes and Sector of Occupation 2004 - 2005

Employment Status	Landless & Sub-Marginal	Marginal	Small	Medium-Large	Total
			Agriculture Unorganised		
Wage Worker in Agriculture	77.4 (19.3)	14.9	5.8	1.9	100.0
Self -employed in Agriculture	17.3 (1.1)	27.9	24.8	29.9	100.0
Agricultural Workers	38.4 (7.5)	23.4	18.1	20.1	100.0
			Non-agriculture		
US: Casual Workers	79.7 (16.0)	13.6	4.4	2.3	100.0
US: Regular Workers	74.1 (17.5)	12.7	7.1	6.1	100.0
US: Self-employed Workers	76.0 (13.8)	13.2	6.1	4.7	100.0
Unorganised Sector	76.7 (14.8)	13.2	5.8	4.3	100.0
Organised Sector	69.4 (17.3)	14.6	8.0	8.1	100.0
Non-agricultural Workers	75.0 (15.4)	13.6	6.3	5.2	100.0

Note:
1. Land Possessed in hectares: Landless (< 0.01), Sub-Marginal (0.01 - 0.40), Marginal (0.41 - 1.00), Small (1.01 - 2.00), Medium-Large (> 2.00).
2. Figures in parenthesis indicate share of landless workers.

Source: NSS 61st Round 2004 - 2005, Employment-Unemployment Survey. Computed.

Majority of the wage and self-employed workers in rural non-agricultural unorganised sector are landless and sub-marginal land-holders with very small land holdings of less than 0.4 hectares.

Fig. 2.1: Percentage Distribution of Rural Unorganised Non-agricultural Workers by Land Size Class and Socio-Religious Groups 2004 - 2005

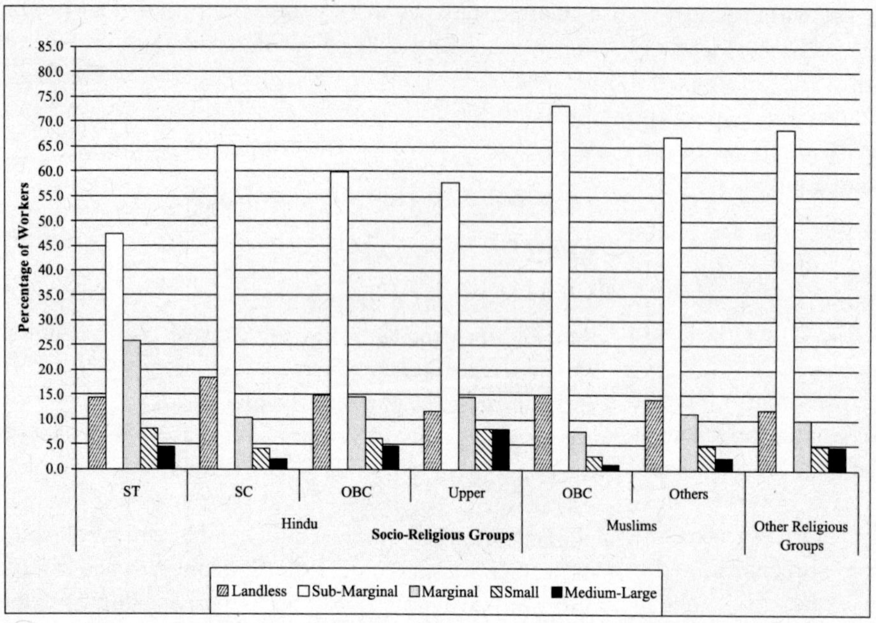

Source: NSS 61st Round 2004 - 2005, Employment-Unemployment Survey. Computed.

Although these small plots/homesteads may provide some food security to these workers, they are also likely to seek wage work for their subsistence.

2.8 Among the agricultural workers, a small share of agricultural labourers (15 per cent) had marginal holdings, while 28 per cent of the self-employed had marginal holdings. The large landholders with more than 2 hectares of land constituted about 30 per cent of the self-employed in agriculture.

2.9 The land distribution in non-agricultural rural India sheds light on their economic profile. Workers in the organised sector are a little more likely to be landless than those in the unorganised sector. This probably indicates that their human capital endowments may be better than their physical assets (which will be examined in the next section), which facilitates their entry in to the coveted organised sector jobs.

2.10 Majority of the unorganised sector workers had sub-marginal holdings as noted earlier. Landlessness is the highest among Hindu SCs and Muslim OBCs and Others and the least among Hindu upper castes. There was not much difference across socio-religious groups in the landholding status of non-agricultural unorganised sector workers, except that Hindu SCs and Muslim OBCs tended to have a slightly larger proportion of sub-marginal holdings while Scheduled Tribes had a larger share of the marginal holdings (Fig. 2.1 and Appendix Table A2.1).

2.11 Thus, the rural non-agricultural wage workers and self-employed workers have no viable means of earning a livelihood through farming, which perhaps results in their resorting to non-farm work. These workers probably also have low educational attainment levels and hence are concentrated in manufacturing and petty trading activities and production related occupations in the unorganised sector (as we shall see below) as they lack the skills for moving in to formal sector work or more productive occupations.

Educational Profile

2.12 Education is a significant attribute and an asset to an individual. In the present era, education is necessary to obtain gainful, productive and remunerative employment. The average years of schooling have been computed for the workers in the organised and unorganised non-agricultural sectors and in the unorganised agricultural sector by imputing average years to each level of reported education (see note to Appendix A2.2). In addition, mean years of schooling were computed for the unorganised workers in the organised sector (specifically for regular workers) as well.

2.13 The average number of years of schooling of all non-agricultural workers was 6.5 years (Appendix A2.2 and Fig. 2.2). There is a marked difference in the mean years of schooling between workers in the organised sector (9 years) and unorganised sector (5.6 years)[1]. Obviously, education is an important asset that helps entry into

[1] The mean years of schooling, of organised sector workers was above the unorganised workers for both men and women in rural and urban areas across the states (Appendix A2.3). The mean years of schooling among men was higher in Kerala, Maharashtra, Himachal Pradesh, Gujarat and Chhattisgarh in rural areas and Jharkhand, Uttaranchal, Kerala, Gujarat and Maharashtra in urban areas. The pattern for women is slightly different in Kerala, Punjab, HP, Maharashtra and Uttaranchal in rural areas and Uttaranchal, Punjab, Haryana, Kerala and Maharashtra in urban areas, having higher mean years of schooling.

Fig. 2.2: Mean Years of Schooling of Non-agricultural Workers by Sector and Sex 2004 - 2005

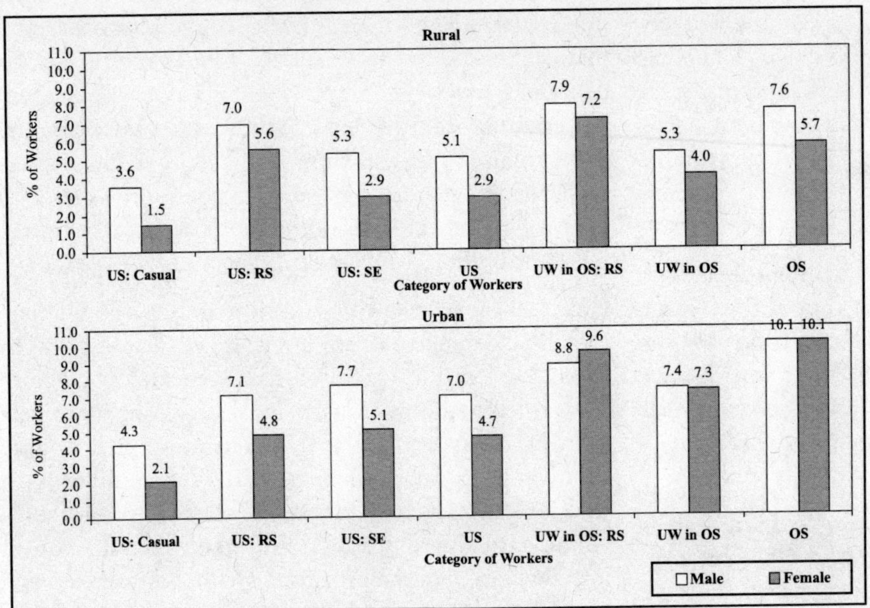

Note: Unorganised Sector (US); Unorganised Worker (UW); Organised Sector (OS); Regular Workers (RW); Self employed (SE); Unorganised Worker in Organised Sector (UW in OS).
Source: ibid.

coveted organised sector jobs. Unorganised workers in the organised sector had 6.2 years of schooling while regular unorganised workers had 8.5 years, equivalent to the organised sector workers. Entry into the organised sector even as an unprotected (unorganised) worker required higher mean years of schooling. The fact that regular workers with similar mean years of schooling actually obtain jobs without social security protection is yet another indicator of the informalisation process in the organised sector.

2.14 The difference in years of schooling between unorganised agricultural and non-agricultural workers in rural areas is 1.8 years. The agricultural workers have, on average, only 2.8 years compared to rural non-agricultural workers having 4.6 years (Table 2.2). The difference of rural agricultural workers from all non-agricultural workers is 2.4 years. The difference is less dramatic than the case between the organised sector and unorganised sector workers.

Table 2.2: Mean Years of Schooling of Rural Unorganised Agricultural Workers 2004 - 2005

Employment Status	Male	Female	Total
Agricultural Labourer	2.4	1.0	1.8
Self-employed in Agriculture (Cultivators)	4.5	1.9	3.4
Agricultural Workers	3.7	1.6	2.8

Source: Same as in Table 2.1.

2.15 The gender difference in mean years of schooling is striking for all workers (2 years), more so within the unorganised sector (2.4 years). The difference between mean years of schooling of men in the organised and unorganised non-agricultural sectors is about 3 years. The same difference between women in the two sectors is 4.4 years (Appendix A2.2). Women with higher education are able to compete with men for jobs in the organised sector and the difference in years of schooling is only about 1 year overall. Remarkably, there is no gender difference in mean years of schooling in the urban organised sector. Low access to education and lower levels of education keep the women mainly in the unorganised non-agricultural or agricultural sectors. To put differently, a woman's class and social origin determines the level of education and correspondingly her status in the labour market, if she participates in it.

2.16 Men and women workers in the organised sector in urban areas have same mean years of schooling. In fact the women regular unorganised workers in the organised sector have even higher mean years of schooling, 9.6 compared to 8.8 for men (Fig. 2.2). This probably reflects the gender bias in women's entry into the organised sector so that even with higher levels of schooling they are in regular jobs as unorganised workers.

2.17 While there is a difference of more than 2 years of schooling between men and women in the agricultural sector, it is markedly higher among the cultivators, 2.6 years, compared to the agricultural labourers (1.4 years) (Table 2.2).

A woman's class and social origin determines the level of education and correspondingly her status in the labour market, if she participates in it.

2.18 Mean years of schooling of the casual wage workers is the lowest among the non-agricultural workers in the unorganised sector, 3.5 years, though it is still, on average, one year higher than of the agricultural workers in rural areas. While the difference in years of schooling among the casual workers is not very striking across rural and urban areas (Fig. 2.2), it is markedly different across gender. Women casual workers have only 1.8 years of education, on average, while men have 3.9 years (Appendix A2.2)

2.19 Self-employed men workers in urban areas have mean years of schooling higher than that of the regular workers in the unorganised sector, at least two years less than those in the organised sector. There is a distinct difference between the mean years of schooling between rural and urban self-employed workers, both men and women.

2.20 The profile of workers by levels of education depicts the above differences more distinctly. In rural areas the percentage of men and women with low education (i.e. up to primary level) is higher than those with education above middle level in the unorganised sector, especially so for women (Fig. 2.3). A higher share of rural women has low education irrespective of whether they are in the organised or unorganised sector. Further, unorganised workers in the organised sector (especially the unorganised regular workers in the organised sector, Appendix A2.4) mimic the education levels of the organised sector workers (Fig. 2.3)[2].

2.21 Share of workers with low education is high among men and women casual workers in rural and urban unorganised sectors and among women self-employed workers (Fig. 2.3). Among the men in the unorganised sector in urban areas, self-employed workers are the most educated group, more than a 60 per cent of them have education above middle level. As we shall see later, this is reflected in the higher returns to informal enterprises in urban areas compared to in rural ones. Though there may not be a direct correlation between human capital and returns, proximate variables such as ownership of physical capital may all compound to result in higher returns to the educated persons Self-employment is a 'catch all' category and can be broadly divided into those with physical capital and human capital and those without. The lower levels of self-employed are the working poor, often closer to casual workers, in such occupations as street vending, rickshaw pulling, beedi rolling, etc.

2.22 Lower level of education among the workers creates vulnerability at two levels. It first denies access to "good jobs" in the organised sector. Second, it confines the workers to mostly casual manual jobs. Women workers in rural areas are the worst victims of this double disadvantage. In rural areas illiteracy coupled with extremely low levels of education means remaining stuck in the agricultural sector. The recent phenomenon of informalisation of the organised sector, however, leaves a lot of better educated workers in the organised sector with unprotected jobs.

Fig. 2.3: Percentage of Workers' Educational Attainment Levels in Non-agricultural Sector by Sector and Sex 2004-05

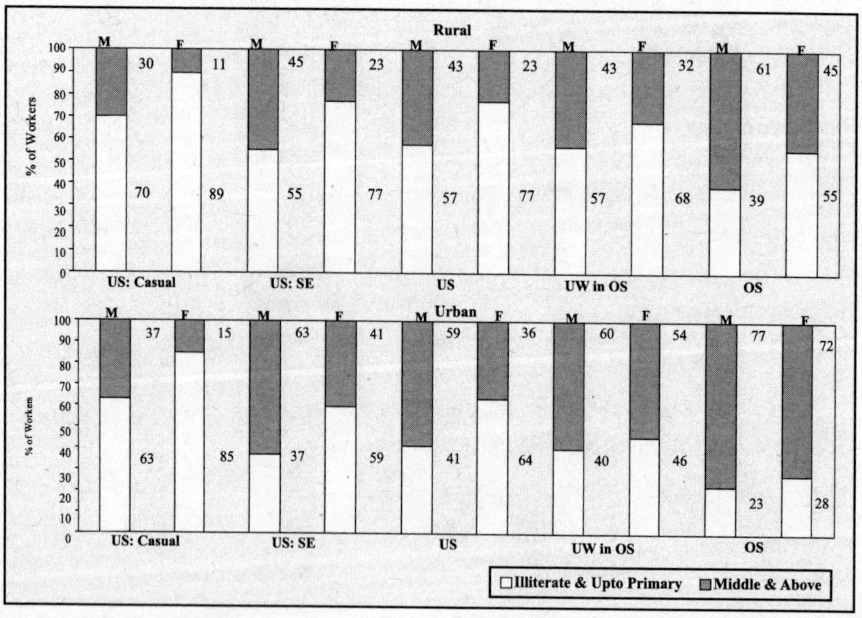

Note : M=Male; F=Female
Source: ibid.

[2] The spatial variations in educational attainments of workers in the unorganised non-agriculture reflect (Appendix A2.5 and A2.6) the same pattern in rural and urban areas. The share of those with up to primary education is the least in the states with the highest mean years of schooling. The share of unorganised non-agricultural workers with education up to primary level is high in Rajasthan, eastern and central states in the case of rural areas and Jammu and Kashmir and Andhra Pradesh in the case of urban men and women.

2.23 A third vulnerability stems from the socio-religious group to which the workers belong. Certain castes and tribes have been identified as socially backward over the centuries and have been notified as Scheduled Castes and Scheduled Tribes. For centuries they were at the bottom of the social structure in India. There are provisions in the Constitution that allow for reservation of jobs and admissions to higher education for these socially under-privileged groups. A number of other castes have also been identified as backward classes on economic and social considerations, such as the artisan groups. Most of these scheduled communities and backward classes belong to the Hindus. Further, some religious communities such as the Muslims are also economically backward leading to vulnerability in the labour market. Here we consider the socio-economic profile of the unorganised sector workers by socio-religious groups and discuss the dimensions of their vulnerability.

2.24 All workers outside agriculture had, on average, 6.5 years of schooling. Among the social groups, the STs had the lowest average years of schooling, 3.8 years, followed by Muslim OBCs, Hindu SCs and Muslim Others with only slightly higher achievements. The upper caste Hindu workers had the highest average years of schooling at 9.5 years. Among all the groups the

Fig. 2.4: Mean Years of Schooling in Non-agriculture by Sector, Sex among Socio-Religious Groups 2004 - 2005

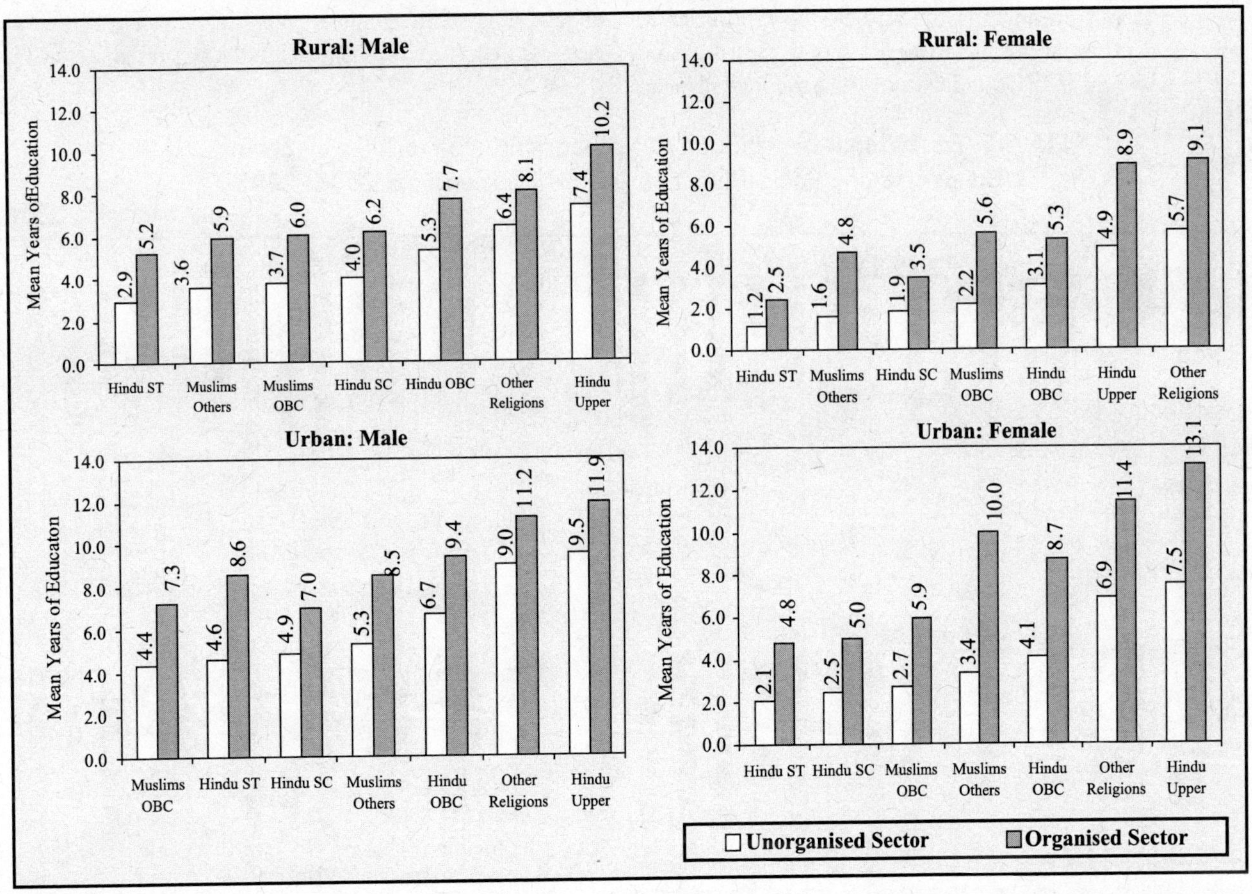

Source: ibid.

Mean years of schooling among the socio-religious groups rose for Hindu ST, SC, OBC upper castes, with the Muslims being closer to the Hindu SC. Absolute number of mean years of schooling was higher for all socio-religious groups among the organised sector workers compared to those in the unorganised sector, men compared to women and in urban compared to rural areas.

unorganised sector workers had lower years of schooling than the organised sector workers. Mean years of schooling among the unorganised non-agricultural workers rose steadily from Hindu STs to SCs, OBCs and upper castes from 2.9 years to 8.3 years (Fig. 2.4). The Muslim workers had mean years of schooling closer to the Hindu SCs with Muslim OBC having average years of schooling slightly lower and Muslim Others marginally above the Hindu SCs (Appendix A2.7 - A2.9).

2.25 Difference in years of schooling across the casual and self-employed workers was also marked. The self-employed workers clearly had higher mean years of schooling compared to the casual workers, though lower than of the regular workers among men and women in rural and urban areas (Appendix A2.7 - A2.9). Casual women labour among the ST and SC communities in rural and urban areas and women among the rural and urban Muslims (OBCs and Others) had the lowest mean years of schooling of about one year. The broad pattern in years of schooling remained the same among the socio-religious groups, rising from STs to upper castes, the Muslims being closer to the SCs, with only the absolute number of years being higher for all groups among the organised sector workers compared to those in the unorganised sector, men compared to women and urban compared to rural areas.

2.26 The unorganised worker in the organised sector, on the whole, had mean years of schooling close to those in the unorganised sector and followed the pattern across socio-religious groups as identified earlier. Among the regular unorganised workers STs and Muslims had, on average, higher levels of education than their counterparts in the organised sector, but still found themselves in unprotected jobs. Among the upper caste Hindus, mean years of schooling of the regular unorganised workers was one year less than their counterparts in the organised sector. The

Fig. 2.5: Educational Distribution of Non-agriculture Workers by Sector and Gender among Socio-Religious Groups (Percentage) 2004 -2005

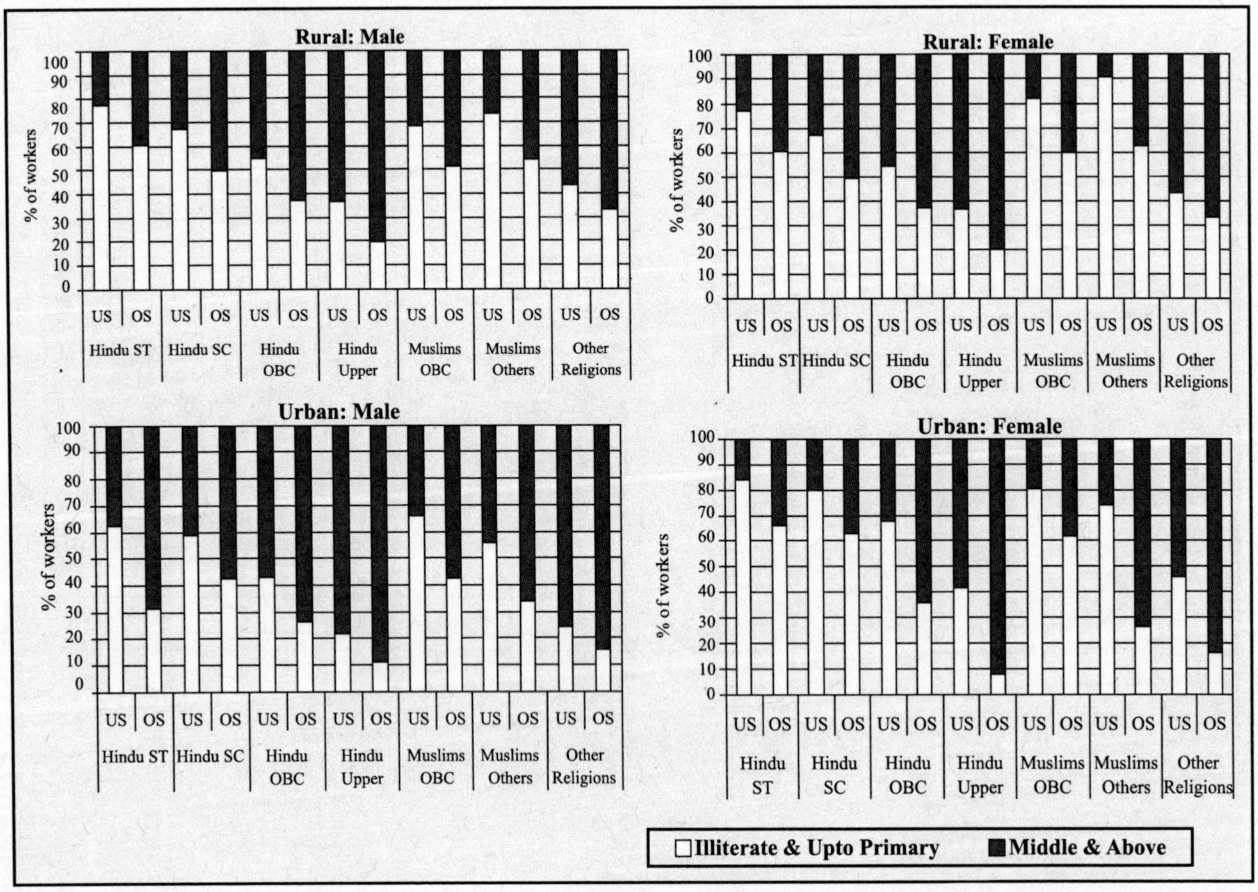

Source: ibid.

STs, OBCs and Muslim men in rural areas faced a similar situation of higher mean years among the regular workers in unprotected jobs (Appendix A2.7 to Appendix A2.9).

2.27 A distinct pattern across socio-religious groups is clearly noted in the proportion of workers with education up to primary level and those with education above the middle level. Low educational attainment was most prominent among men and women ST and Muslim OBC unorganised non-agricultural workers. Upper caste Hindus had much higher educational attainments than all other social groups (Fig. 2.5).

2.28 Percentage of workers with higher levels of education is distinctly higher in the organised sector in the case of all social groups, followed by regular workers in the unorganised sector. The only exception is the upper caste self-employed men in urban areas who are better educated than the regular workers in the unorganised sector. These upper caste men probably have the advantage of access to both human and physical capital, partly because of their superior social status, which allows them to engage in more remunerative self-employed activities.

Labour Market Entry

2.29 The level of educational attainment of workers would influence their labour market entry in terms of status, sector, industry and nature of work or occupation undertaken by them. The level of education was seen to have an effect on entry into the organised sector of the economy. In rural areas access to land also enabled them to enter into the agricultural sector as self-employed workers, often as cultivators.

Activity Status

2.30 Overall, while 29 per cent of men workers were able to access organised sector jobs, only about 27 per cent of the women were able to do so. While men and women from the upper castes and other religious groups were most likely to get organised sector jobs, Muslims, both OBC and others, both men and women, were least likely to do so (Table 2.3). While the high levels of education among the upper castes explained this difference, in the

Table 2.3: Proportion of Non-agriculture Workers by Employment Status, Sector and Gender among Socio-Religious Groups (Percentage) 2004-2005: All India

Employment Status	Hindu				Muslims		Other Religious Groups	All Socio-Religious Groups
	ST	SC	OBC	Upper	OBC	Others		
	Total: Male							
Unorganised Sector: Casual	30.4	25.0	15.5	6.0	15.7	15.1	15.3	15.1
Unorganised Sector: Regular Workers (RW)	8.7	11.4	13.1	13.2	12.3	13.7	12.7	12.7
Unorganised Sector: Self Employed	25.3	34.9	45.0	43.2	60.5	52.9	38.6	43.4
Unorganised Sector (Total)	**64.4**	**71.4**	**73.7**	**62.4**	**88.5**	**81.7**	**66.7**	**71.2**
Unorganised Worker in OS: RW	**5.3**	**5.9**	**6.6**	**8.3**	**3.3**	**4.5**	**7.3**	**6.6**
Unorganised Worker in OS	**20.8**	**15.1**	**12.7**	**11.9**	**7.1**	**9.9**	**12.9**	**12.6**
Organised Sector (OS) (Total)	**35.6**	**28.6**	**26.3**	**37.6**	**11.5**	**18.3**	**33.3**	**28.8**
All Workers	**100.0**	**100.0**	**100.0**	**100.0**	**100.0**	**100.0**	**100.0**	**100.0**
	Total: Female							
Unorganised Sector: Casual	25.3	15.3	9.8	5.6	8.5	8.5	7.9	10.4
Unorganised Sector: Regular Workers (RW)	6.6	14.6	11.0	13.2	7.3	7.3	16.5	11.7
Unorganised Sector: Self Employed	36.9	45.2	55.0	44.4	71.6	71.6	36.2	51.0
Unorganised Sector (Total)	**68.7**	**75.1**	**75.8**	**63.2**	**87.4**	**87.4**	**60.5**	**73.1**
Unorganised Worker in OS: RW	**5.6**	**7.3**	**8.1**	**10.7**	**4.0**	**4.0**	**10.2**	**7.9**
Unorganised Worker in OS	**23.8**	**16.6**	**15.2**	**14.4**	**7.1**	**7.1**	**16.5**	**14.7**
Organised Sector (OS) (Total)	**31.3**	**24.9**	**24.2**	**36.8**	**12.6**	**12.6**	**39.5**	**26.9**
All Workers	**100.0**	**100.0**	**100.0**	**100.0**	**100.0**	**100.0**	**100.0**	**100.0**

Source: Same as in Table 2.1.

Fig. 2.6: Distribution of Non-agricultural Workers by Employment Status, Sector & Sex among Socio-Religious Groups (Percentage) 2004 - 2005

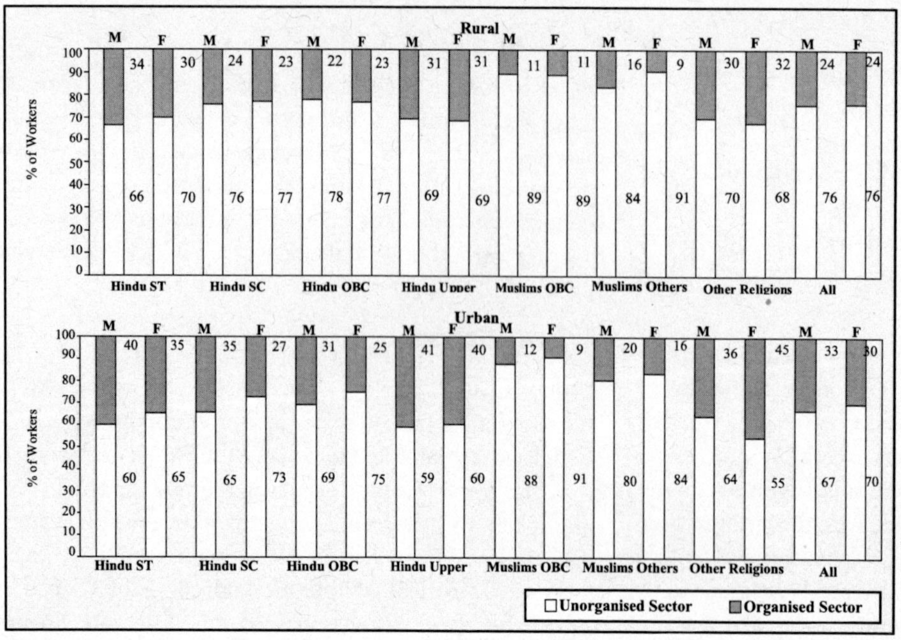

Source: ibid.

case of SCs and STs affirmative action in their favour led to better access to organised sector jobs (even if they were at the lower levels) compared to Muslims.

2.31 At the other extreme, the highest proportion of casual workers in the non-agricultural unorganised sector is in the case of ST men and women (30 and 25 per cent respectively), followed by the SCs (Table 2.3). The upper caste Hindus are least likely to be casual workers and most likely to be self-employed workers even in the unorganised sector. The proportion of casual workers among the Muslims is close to that of the OBC for women, which is lower than the SCs/STs but higher than the upper caste workers (Fig. 2.6 and Appendix A2.10). Among both men and women Muslims are predominantly employed as self-employed workers in the unorganised sector. Women have an overwhelming presence as self-employed workers in the unorganised sector (more than 70 per cent Appendix A2.10).

2.32 Differences across the socio-religious groups are more marked in the urban areas, with the proportion among Muslim workers employed in unorganised sector being significantly higher than in the case of any other socio-religious group (Fig. 2.6). The upper caste Hindu men and women are more likely to be in the organised sector. Even in the unorganised sector they are less likely to be casual workers and more likely to be regular workers and self-employed workers. Among the ST men in rural areas and women in rural and urban areas are most likely to be casual workers. In rural and urban areas alike Muslim men and women are most likely to be self-employed workers in the unorganised sector.

2.33 In urban areas, most Muslim OBC women workers in the unorganised sector are self-employed (about 73 per cent), followed by women from Muslim Others and other backward classes, SCs and upper caste Hindus. Men in these communities are almost equally likely to be self-employed, though Muslim men have much higher proportion in self-employment, especially among the OBC. Lower levels of education and lack of access to land among the Muslims are likely to be proximate causes.

Industrial Profile

2.34 About 71.6 per cent of all non-agricultural workers are in the unorganised sector[3]. Among the industrial categories, more than 95 per cent of the workers in trade and employment by private households are in the unorganised sector. More than three-fourth of the workers in other services, hotels and restaurants, transport storage, etc and construction are in the unorganised sector.

2.35 Outside agriculture, manufacturing is one of the most important segments in both the organised as well as unorganised sectors of the economy. Women workers in the unorganised sector, are predominantly concentrated in manufacturing, about 48 per cent (Fig. 2.7). In the unorganised sector nearly 33 per cent of the men are concentrated in trade, followed by manufacturing, 23 per cent. In the organised sector, women are largely engaged in other services (41 per cent), while men are diversified into other industry groups. Among the unorganised workers in the organised sector, both men and women are concentrated in the manufacturing sector. The construction industry is also a major employer of the regular workers unorganised workers.

2.36 We shall profile these workers by industry groups in the next chapter and see where the various

Fig. 2.7: Distribution of Non-agricultural Workers across Industrial Categories by Sex (Percentage) 2004 - 2005

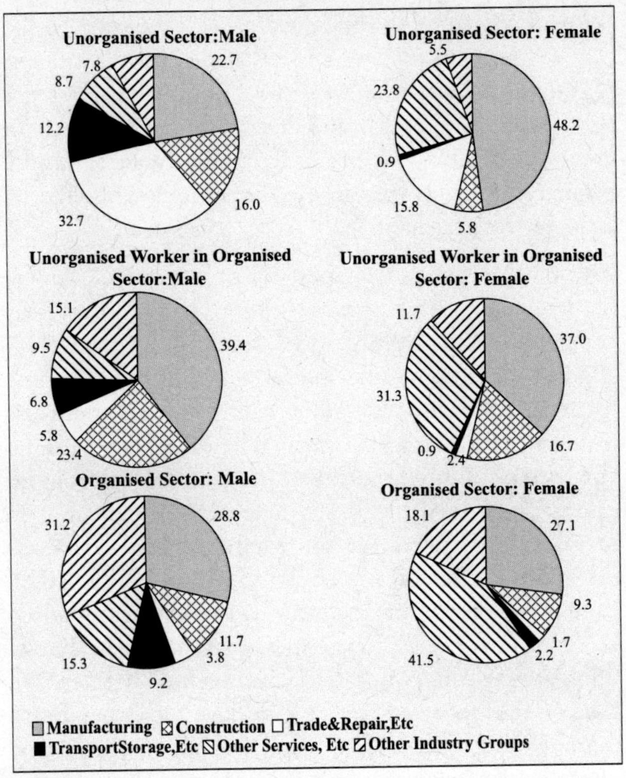

Source: ibid.

segments of the wage workers are concentrated. The effort will be to study the working conditions and assess the constraints faced by them in order to visualize promotional policies for the self-employed.

Occupational Profile

2.37 Certain Occupational Groups were almost entirely concentrated in the unorganised sector, e.g. sales workers (Appendix A2.12)[4].

2.38 Women are concentrated in production related occupations in the unorganised manufacturing sector whereas men are predominantly in sales activities in the unorganised sector (Table 2.4).

2.39 Occupational profile of the casual workers in the unorganised sector (non-agricultural) is predominantly in production and related work (Appendix A2.13). Variations are visible between men and women. Concentration of men in production and related work is greater than in the case of women. Women casual workers have a slightly more diversified occupational profile, being 76 per cent in production related activities and 22 per cent in service sectors.

2.40 Similarly, non-agricultural self-employed workers in the unorganised sector are concentrated in production related activities. The gender profile is just the opposite of that of the casual workers. While in casual work men are concentrated in production work, among self-employed workers it is the women who are more concentrated in production work (Appendix A2.13). A little more than one-third of the self-employed men

Table 2.4: Distribution of Non-agricultural Workers across Occupational Groups by Status and Gender (Percentage) 2004 - 2005

Occupational Category	Unorganised			Organised		
	Male	Female	Total	Male	Female	Total
Professional, Technical, etc	4.5	6.5	4.9	16.2	33.9	19.6
Administrative, Managerial	9.4	7.3	9.0	6.3	2.8	5.6
Clerical, etc	1.9	1.0	1.7	19.1	13.9	18.1
Sales	26.6	15.3	24.2	3.6	1.3	3.1
Service	6.9	19.6	9.6	9.4	11.8	9.8
Farmers & Related	0.2	0.1	0.2	0.6	0.4	0.6
Production, Transport & Related	50.5	50.2	50.4	44.8	36.0	43.1
All Occupational Categories	100.0	100.0	100.0	100.0	100.0	100.0

Source: Same as in Table 2.1.

[3] The state level pattern is presented in Appendix A2.11.
[4] The state level pattern is presented in Appendix A2.12.

workers are engaged in sales and production related activities. The occupational profile of the non-agricultural self-employed workers in rural and urban areas is not very different, though the concentration of women in production related work is slightly higher in the rural areas.

Incidence of Poverty

2.41 The access to human and physical assets determines the access to jobs and self-employed activities as we have seen earlier in the chapter. The resultant status of workers is reflected in the incidence of poverty within the segments of the labour market. Therefore we finally discuss here the incidence of poverty among the various segments of the workforce.

2.42 The percentage of persons below the poverty line (head count ratio) during 1999-2000 as estimated by the Planning Commission based on NSSO 55th Round Consumer Expenditure Survey was about 26.1 per cent for the country as a whole, 27.1 per cent for the rural population and 23.6 per cent for the urban population. This estimate was based on a mixed recall period. In 2004-05, NSSO 61st Round, using a similar recall period the Planning Commission obtained much lower poverty ratios of 21.8 per cent for the country in 2004-2005, 21.8 per cent in rural and 21.7 per cent in urban areas. However, using a uniform recall period of 30 days, the poverty estimates generated by the Planning Commission for 2004-05 was 27.5 per cent for the country, 28.3 per cent in rural and 25.7 per cent in urban areas.

2.43 Our estimates of the poverty ratio, based on the mixed recall period and using the Employment and Unemployment Survey schedule was also 21.8 per cent in the aggregate, with urban poverty slightly higher, 21.9 per cent compared to rural poverty, 21.7 per cent. In the case of those in the work force, the poverty ratio was slightly lower than that of general population, 19.3 per cent, 18.7 per cent in rural areas and 21.0 per cent in urban areas. This was primarily due to the fact that the general population also included households without even a single working member.

2.44 Workers in the unorganized sector had a much higher incidence of poverty (20.5 per cent) than their counterparts in the organised sector (11.3 per cent), almost double[5]. This is an indicator of inadequate income levels and the extent of vulnerability of workers in the unorganised sector (Table 2.5). The difference between the workers' poverty ratios in the organised and unorganised agriculture was much lower than that in the non-agricultural sector where poverty ratio was distinctly higher (again almost the double). Further, though workers' poverty ratio in the urban organised sector is marginally lower than in rural areas that of unorganised urban workers (25.5 per cent) is greater than that of the unorganised rural workers (19.3 per cent). Among the unorganised non-agricultural workers poverty ratios are 24.1 per cent and 17.2 per cent in urban and rural areas respectively. The poorer conditions of work of the unorganised sector workers, who constitute about 70 per cent of the urban workforce, perhaps worsened

Table 2.5: Poverty Ratios of Workers by Industry and Sector, 2004-2005

Industry	Sector	Unorg. Sector	Org. Sector	Unorg. Worker in Org Sector	Unorg. Worker	Org. Worker	All Workers
Agriculture	Total	20.5	16.5	18.9	20.5	13.8	20.4
	Rural	17.2	11.2	17.0	17.2	3.5	15.7
Non-agriculture	Urban	24.1	10.4	20.4	23.7	4.3	19.6
	Total	20.6	10.7	18.7	20.4	4.1	17.8
All	Rural	19.3	12.0	17.0	19.2	5.4	18.7
	Urban	25.5	10.7	20.7	25.1	4.5	21.0
	Total	20.5	11.3	18.7	20.4	4.9	19.3

Source: Same as in Table 2.1

[5] Across the states, the poverty levels in the unorganised non-agriculture are the highest in the eastern and central states (where the mean years of schooling are low), the only exception being the rural areas in Chhattisgarh and Uttaranchal and urban areas in Maharashtra (Appendix A2.14). Only in Bihar, Orissa, Jharkhand, West Bengal, Tamil Nadu, Gujarat and Punjab are the unorganised agricultural workers' poverty ratios higher than those of non-agricultural workers.

the lot of all urban workers resulting in higher poverty ratio.

2.45 The poverty ratios of unorganised sector workers and unorganised workers are similar (20.5 per cent) across all sectors and in the rural and urban areas. Within the organised sector a large proportion of workers are without regular contracts and social security benefits, as we shall see in the next chapter. These unorganised workers had poverty ratio not significantly lower than the workers in the unorganised sector, 18.7 per cent. The formal workers in the organised sector are hardly poor (less than 5 per cent). It is, thus, not difficult to find why the formal jobs with social security benefits in the organised sector are the coveted jobs in the country and are highly sought after.

2.46 A striking difference exists between the poverty ratios of the casual, regular and of the self-employed workers in the non-agricultural sector. The casual workers in urban areas are the worst off with more than 35 per cent of them being below the poverty line irrespective of whether they were in the organised or unorganised sectors (Table 2.6). In rural areas also the casual workers are the worst off, but with lower poverty ratios, about 22 per cent in both the organised and unorganised sectors[6]. About 21 per cent of the self-employed in the unorganised sector in urban areas and 16 per cent in rural areas are below the poverty line. The regular workers in the organised sector are the least likely to be in poverty.

Table 2.6: Poverty Ratios among Non-agricultural Workers by Category of Workers 2004-2005

Category of Workers	Rural		Urban	
	Organised	Unor-ganised	Organised	Unor-ganised
Casual Worker	21.9	23.1	35.0	41.5
All Workers	11.2	17.2	10.4	24.1
Self Employed	11.2	15.9	11.4	21.4
Regular Workers	5.2	11.5	6.8	20.2

Source: Same as in Table 2.1

2.47 All workers belonging to socially backward and minority communities within the unorganised sector and unorganised non-agricultural workers are more vulnerable in terms of poverty (Table 2.7 and Appendix A2.16). We had observed that human capital and access to better jobs among the Hindus improved from STs, SCs to OBCs and upper castes, with the Muslims somewhere between the SCs and OBCs. A similar pattern is observed in the poverty ratios also with STs being the worst off and upper caste Hindus having the best status, in both the rural and urban areas. The poverty ratio of the Muslim OBC workers is closer to the Hindu SCs, about 40 per cent in urban areas. In rural areas, the Muslim Others has a slightly lower poverty ratio of 21.5 per cent compared to the Hindu SCs. This at least partly indicates that labour market characteristics, which are determined by the structural factors do impact on the well-being of the workers.

Table 2.7: Poverty Ratios among Unorganised Sector Workers by Social Groups2004-2005

Social Group	Rural	Social Group	Urban
Hindu ST	35.7	Hindu ST	48.6
Hindu SC	26.2	Muslims OBC	39.7
Muslims OBC	21.5	Hindu SC	38.9
Muslims Others	21.5	Muslims Other	33.6
All Unorganised Workers	19.3	Hindu OBC	27.5
Hindu OBC	15.8	All Unorganised Workers	25.5
Other Religions	15.4	Other Religions	14.0
Hindu: Upper	8.4	Hindu: Upper	10.2

Source: Same as in Table 2.1.

Conclusion

2.48 Our analysis of the national level data clearly brings out, once again, that a substantial proportion of wage workers in agriculture and all workers in non-agriculture are either landless or land-poor. This has implications for seeking any kind of work in the non-agricultural labour market as well as in securing a living wage. To this must be added the absence of any meaningful educational endowment that is so crucial in determining the quality of employment and the ability to secure reasonable wages. The segments of the workforce that are better endowed have access to better and possibly more remunerative jobs.

[6] Similar pattern of high level of poverty among casual workers is noted in all the states (Appendix A2.15).

2.49 The average years of education received by the workers in the unorganised sector (6.6 years) is about 3.5 years less than that received by workers in the organised sector (10.1 years). Women received fewer years of schooling than men in all segments of the workforce. Further, the difference among organised and unorganised women workers was even greater, about 4.4 years. Casual workers have lower years of education and higher illiteracy. They are at the bottom of the educational ladder. The first two levels of vulnerability created by low levels of education and poor access to assets (e.g. land) are that it denies access to "good jobs" in the organised sector and that it confines one to casual manual labour. Thus, while educated workers may or may not get more employment, they definitely get better quality jobs.

2.50 The third dimension of vulnerability is introduced by the socio-religious groups to which the workers belong. While the ST and SC populations are protected, to some extent by affirmative action, Muslims are overwhelmingly concentrated in unorganised sector and in self-employed activities to meet their livelihood needs. Hindus other than SCs/STs and OBCs fare the best. With better educational and land possessed status, they are able to access better jobs as well as have more productive self-employed activities particularly in urban areas. Indeed, there could be a certain range of variation across the states but the overall picture has conveyed a mutually reinforcing mechanism in terms of assets, education and social status.

2.51 The labour market status and characteristics have its final impact on the well-being or its opposite, poverty. The poverty ratios are the highest among the casual workers in the unorganised sector both in rural and urban areas. However, it appears that social status has an overbearing influence on poverty compared to the work status. What we have seen is that SCs and STs have a higher incidence of poverty than casual workers both in rural and urban areas. For all other social groups poverty ratios are lower than that of casual workers. Casual work status and SC/ST status emerge as a deadly combination in its association with incidence of poverty. The vulnerabilities of a casual labour market and the social handicaps of being at the bottom of an oppressive social order are indeed too powerful to demand any further explanation.

3 Wage Workers in Non-agricultural Sector

Introduction

3.1 Based on the evidence presented and discussed in the last chapter, the Commission is of the view that the socio-economic profile of the unorganised workers in general and workers in the unorganised sector in particular presents a picture that is in sharp contrast to the otherwise improving image of the Indian economy. The strong association between the low social status and the unorganised or informal nature of workers also brings out the social dimension of economic deprivation. In this chapter, we focus our attention on the conditions of wage workers in the non-agricultural sector. As of 2004-05 there are about 52.9 million wage workers in the unorganised non-agricultural sector and 76.7 million unorganised or informal workers that include the informal wage workers in the organised sector. Taken as a whole, the conditions of informal wage workers are nothing but deplorable. The failure to ensure a modicum of human dignity at work to this vast multitude of working poor should have received far more political and policy attention than what has been the case hitherto. The continuing discourse on minimum wages is 60 years old if one takes the Minimum Wages Act of 1948 as the formal starting point. There is a plethora of minimum wages across the states and occupations. Compliance to minimum wages has been more an exception than the rule. Although much debate has taken place on the need for a national minimum wage that should act as a floor level, there is as yet no statutory backing to the various recommendations. Based on a notional national minimum wage, as recommended by the NCRL (also known as Hanumantha Rao Commission) of 1991, this Commission has found to its dismay that about half of the men workers and about 87 per cent of the women workers in urban areas and 40 per cent of the men workers and 81 per cent of the women workers in rural areas get wages that are below this notional national minimum. Thus, we hardly require to emphasise the need to improve the conditions of women workers.

3.2 Where do the wage workers work? Popular impression is that it is a highly heterogeneous group. If we ignore the social heterogeneity, what we find is concentration in a small number of activity groups. More than 90 per cent of men workers are either engaged in some kind of manufacturing, construction, trading or transport activities. Similarly more than 90 per cent of women workers are engaged in either some kind of manufacturing, construction activities or just domestic services. Based on this broad picture and further such disaggregation as are necessary, this Chapter focuses on the conditions of work in their different manifestations. We first look at the physical conditions of work followed by occupational and health hazards and basic amenities like drinking water and sanitation. Then we examine the employment contracts or their absence and wages

Box 3.1: Limitation of data

More often, the Labour Bureau surveys on the working and living conditions in the unorganised sector have been designed to collect data on factories that are already covered under the Factories Act and, in fact, are part of the organised sector. The surveys do not cover the self-employed workers, they do not include small enterprises that are run mainly on family labour and occasionally hire workers (own-account enterprises). According to the National Sample Surveys on employment and unemployment, the self-employed account for about 53 per cent of the workforce in India and the own account enterprises account for about 90 per cent of all enterprises in certain industries. Thus, a limitation of the Labour Bureau surveys would be that they exclude the self-employed and all hired workers employed in own-account enterprises. The Labour Bureau surveys also suffer from at least one more major methodological flaw, i.e., the questionnaire on conditions of work is canvassed with the owner of the enterprise. Thus wherever the owners of the enterprises were aware of the acceptable norms for conditions of work, the responses were always in full conformity with the norms. For example, on the question on provision of bonus to workers (annual bonus or festival bonus), the data from the Labour Bureau surveys showed that about 80 per cent of the enterprises in the unorganised sector provided their workers with a bonus and that too at a minimum rate of 8.33 per cent of the basic wage, which happens to be the regulatory requirement under the Payment of Bonus Act. Therefore either the surveys cover the organised sector where workers are receiving their bonus, or the data are simply biased as the respondent is the owner of the enterprise. Another striking feature of the Labour Bureau surveys is the negligible share of casual workers in the unorganised sector. All these render use of the data difficult. Some of the reports of the Labour Bureau have at times attempted to present results of the surveys by size of enterprise, the smallest class being of 1-10 workers and the largest being of 50- 100 workers. Despite the limitations of the surveys discussed above, data on the 1-10 workers category give some indications of the conditions of work in the unorganised sector. Wherever, such data are available, we have used them to highlight specific conditions of work. Given these limitations of the Labour Bureau surveys the working conditions on the ground are likely to be much worse.

and their relationship with minimum wages. We have assessed the extent to which casual workers actually obtain daily wages above or below the notional national minimum. The analysis in this Chapter also includes examination of the conditions of regular workers in the unorganised sector, which constitutes a small share of the total.

3.3 At the outset, the Commission would like to point out that the vastness of the unorganised sector and its unregulated nature has led to a situation where data on the conditions of work in the unorganised sector are scanty. This was realised by the first National Commission on Labour (also known as Gajendragadkar Commission) in its report submitted in 1969. It recommended the conduct of detailed studies about the conditions of work in the unorganised sector (NCRL 1969). Following this recommendation, the Labour Bureau under the Ministry of Labour, Government of India began surveys and collecting data on the conditions of work in selected industries. Labour Bureau has been regularly publishing these reports on the "Working and Living Conditions" since 1977, initially restricting the location of the studies to certain urban centres and later extending the coverage to the whole country. In all, the Labour Bureau has conducted over 40 industry specific studies and a dozen location specific studies on the subject. There are, however, not many attempts by researchers to analyse the data from the Labour Bureau surveys probably because of the poor quality of data that stem from several problems with the methodology adopted (Box 3.1).

3.4 In our view, the data on important aspects of conditions of work in the unorganised sector should be obtained through surveys of workers, which could be supplemented with a survey of enterprises by independent investigators to obtain data on physical conditions of work such as space, illumination, ventilation, humidity and hygiene. There is a large body of literature that deals with working conditions in industries and industrial clusters based on surveys done by independent researchers. Very few researchers have, however, attempted to compare the situation on the ground with a set of minimum standards or norms. For example, of the several studies on wage levels and earnings in the unorganised sector, only a handful have made an attempt to compare the wages and earnings with the prevailing statutory minimum wages. This limitation apart, the research studies provide a wealth of details on the conditions of work in the unorganised sector. The discussion in this Chapter is largely based on findings of such research.

Profile of Wage Workers

3.5 Casual workers tend to be the least protected and have the lowest levels of earnings. As we noted in Chapter 1 the casual workers constituted about one fifth of the workers in the unorganised non-agricultural sector. In 2004-05 about 53 per cent of the casual workers were in the construction sector, followed by 19 per cent in the manufacturing sector. Within the manufacturing sector textile industry was the largest employer of casual workers, both men and women (Fig. 3.1). This was followed by other non-metallic mineral products and food products. The former includes brick-kilns and pottery work. For men casual workers other manufacturing industries form a large source of employment as well which could include motor vehicles, auto components, machinery etc.

3.6 Regular workers constituted about 17 per cent of the non-agriculture workers in the unorganised sector. Regular men in the unorganised sector were well distributed between manufacturing, trade and transport, storage etc. The women regular workers were concentrated in other services, such as education and health, and manufacturing (13 per cent each). An overwhelming 54 per cent of the regular women workers in the unorganised sector were hired by private households mainly in domestic services (Fig. 3.2).

3.7 The process of informalisation we referred to in Chapter 1 is reflected in the composition of regular unorganised workers in the organised sector. Majority of such male workers are in the manufacturing sector and the women are in the services sector, again in education, health etc.

Fig. 3.1: Percentage Distribution of Unorganised Sector Casual Non-agricultural Workers across Industry Groups 2004 - 2005

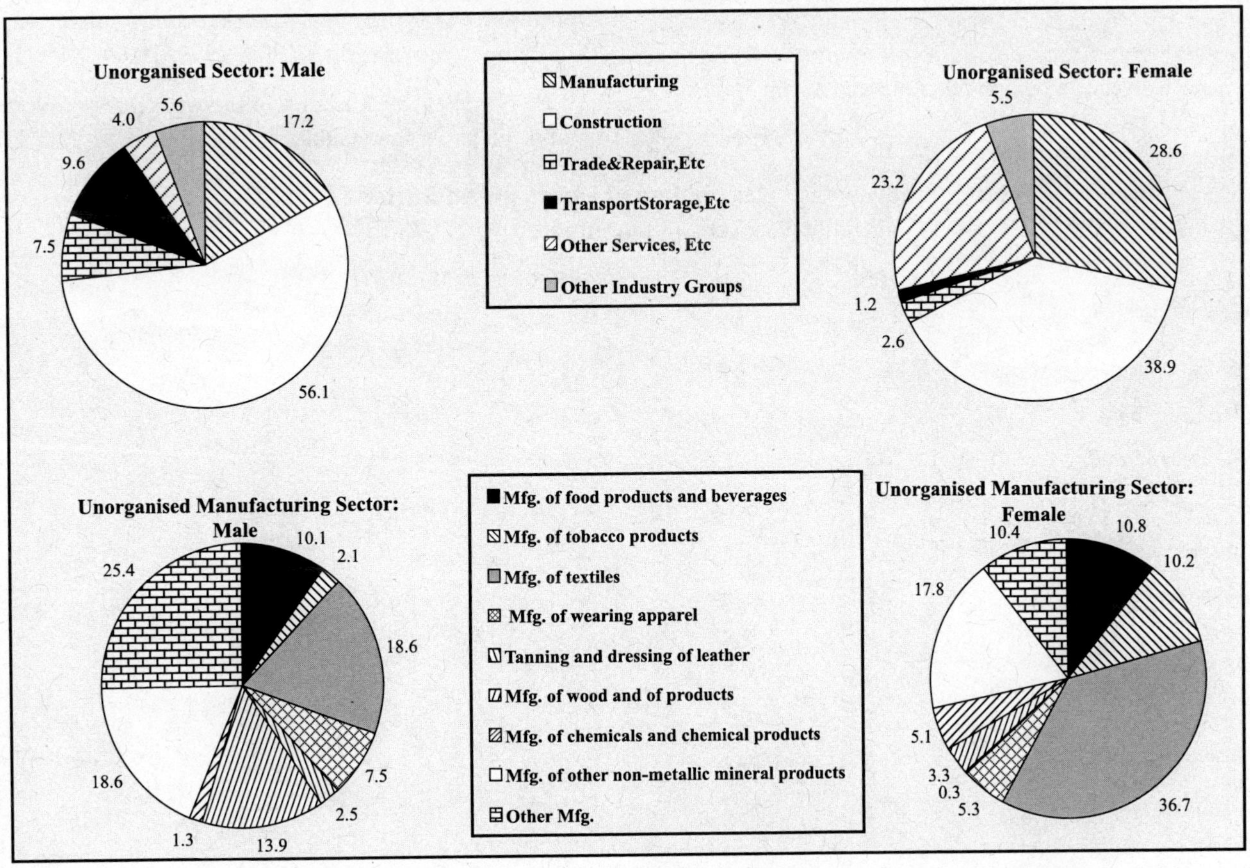

Source : NSS 61st Round 2004-2005, Employment-Unemployment Survey. Computed.

Fig. 3.2: Percentage of Regular Non-agricultural workers across Industry Groups 2004 - 2005

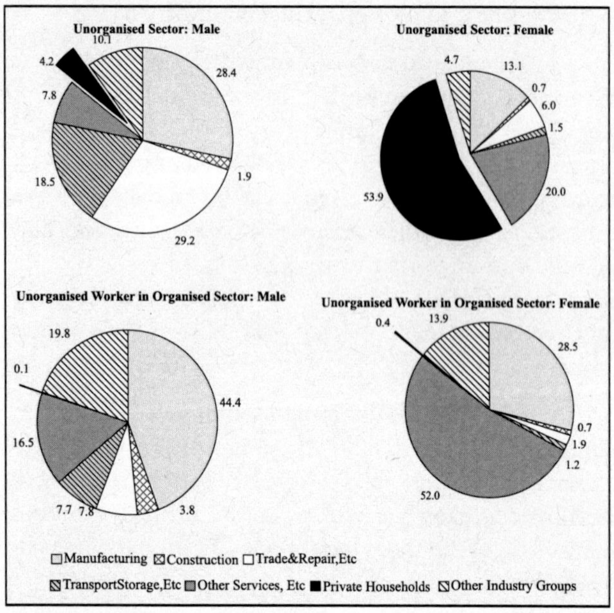

Note: The slice depicts workers employed by private households.
Source: ibid.

3.8 In the unorganised manufacturing sector the regular women workers are concentrated in the manufacture of tobacco and textile products, while men are more diversified in the other manufacturing industries (Table 3.1)

Physical Conditions at Work Place

3.9 Important components of the physical conditions of work are space, volume (space and height of work place), ventilation, illumination, temperature, humidity, hygiene and cleanliness (Box 3.2). Also important is the provision of protective equipments against loss of life and limbs (amputations). Numerous studies have pointed out the poor working conditions in the unorganised sector in India. In survey after survey and industry after industry, researchers have noted that physical conditions of workers are inhuman. For example, studies in the leather tanning industry have found that workers without footwear worked for long hours with their bare feet soaked in chemicals, animal wastes and decomposing offal (Usha 1984; Banerjee and Nihila 1999: Nihila 2002). In the fish processing units in the export zones, a study found that the "floors are permanently wet and slippery, with open puddles of 'black ink' seeping from fish innards" (Dewan 2001). Similarly, studies on the conditions of workers in the manufacture of locks, beedi rolling, diamond cutting, textiles including handlooms and powerlooms, artistic metalware and so on have all pointed to the pathetic conditions under which workers engage in production for long hours (Sekar and Mohammad 2001; Labour Bureau 2000; 1998; 1996; 1992b; 1992a).

3.10 Some of the attributes of the working conditions may not be easily measurable, and data on them may be

Table 3.1: Percentage Distribution of Unorganised Sector Casual and Regular Workers in Manufacturing 2004-05

Industry Group	Casual	Regular	Casual	Regular	Casual	Regular
	Male		Female		All	
Food products and beverages	10.1	11.4	10.8	8.7	10.3	11.1
Tobacco products	2.1	0.5	10.2	18.9	3.9	2.3
Textile products	18.6	14.5	36.7	20.4	22.7	15.0
Wearing apparel	7.5	11.5	5.3	10.9	7.0	11.4
Tanning and dressing of leather	2.5	3.3	0.3	3.9	2.0	3.4
Wood and of products	13.9	4.2	3.3	1.8	11.5	4.0
Chemicals and chemical products	1.3	3.0	5.1	7.2	2.1	3.4
Other non-metallic mineral products	18.6	2.3	17.8	1.4	18.4	2.2
Other Manufacturing	25.4	49.3	10.4	26.8	22.0	47.1
All Manufacturing	100.0	100.0	100.0	100.0	100.0	100.0

Source: NSS 61st Round 2004 -2005, Employment-Unemployment Survey. Computed.

Box 3.2: Physical Conditions of Work

Space

Factories Act specified a minimum floor space of 36 square feet per worker and a minimum volume space of 500 cubic feet per worker.

Average workspace was 30 square feet and volume space was 272 cubic feet per worker in Mumbai leather accessories manufacturing. The share of workers with workspace below the norms set by the Factories Act was 78 per cent. Similarly, the share of workers who worked with volume space below the norm was 92 per cent (Pais 2002).

Lighting

Labour Bureau surveys in the textiles found that only 17 per cent of the workers surveyed had proper lighting (Labour Bureau 1998).

In the beedi industry, where a large part of the work is done in home-based settings, only 40 per cent of the workers undertook beedi rolling activity under sufficient illumination (Labour Bureau 1996).

Health

Labour Bureau surveys in the unorganised sector found that in all industries surveyed, the minimum requirement of a first aid kit was not provided for in 50 per cent or more of the enterprises. In fact, in industries such as carpet weaving, beedi rolling, marine fishing, and metalware, the proportion of enterprises without a first aid kit was 90 per cent (Various Labour Bureau Studies).

qualitative and subjective (such as 'good, very good, bad and poor'). On such attributes, the norms are also likely to use terms such as "sufficient", "adequate" and "decent". There are, however, other aspects that are measurable, e.g. space, volume (space and height of work place), ventilation, illumination, temperature, humidity and dust level can be measured using easily available measuring instruments. The norms for such aspects are also easy to set and in fact, agencies such as the Occupation Safety and Health Administration of the United States of America (OSHA) have standards set for each of these variables. In India, in the organised sector, the Factories Act (1948) also provides standards for some of these variables through the rules for the implementation of the Act.

3.11 On the unorganised sector, however, there are very few studies that have made attempts to measure attributes of the physical working conditions such as space, volume (space and height of work place), ventilation, illumination, temperature and humidity. Studies have noted that large numbers of workers were cramped in a tiny room, or that the roof the work shed was very low making the work place hot, humid and stifling (Pais 2002; Breman 1996). Studies also found that the workspace was same as the living space for the worker and her family and the result was the highly inadequate working space as was the living quarters (Pais 2002; Desai and Raj 2001; Breman 1996; Engelshoven 1999). The Factories Act does not clarify whether the space norms are inclusive of machinery or not (Pais 2002).

Ventilation, Temperature and Humidity

3.12 Proper ventilation is very important in certain industries such as chemicals, metallurgy, leather tanning, pottery, brick-kilns, meat and fish processing, manufacture of matches and fireworks. Labour Bureau surveys and field studies by individual researchers have noted the poor ventilation (Labour Bureau 1996; 1981, Sekar 2003; Ghosh 2004; Vidyasagar and Kumarbabu 2001; Jeyarajan 2002). Some studies have also identified health hazards (for example respiratory diseases) that can be directly related to inadequate ventilation at work place and long exposure to dust and fumes (Roy 2000). Studies have repeatedly shown that work in the match manufacturing and fireworks industry in Sivakasi was under inappropriate ventilation (exposed to fumes, chemicals). One consequence of inadequate ventilation has been the shift of work to late evenings and nights during hot summers (Pais 2003). Again, night work, apart from being in contrast to the natural cycle, involves other requirements with regard to working place such as adequate illumination, provision for breaks, rest and so on.

3.13 According to design consultants and housing regulations, the minimum window area should be at least 5 per cent of the floor area of the room with a minimum of 5 sq ft[1]. Windows should also provide access to direct sunlight. A study in the leather accessories manufacture in Mumbai shows that about half the workforce has been denied access to this minimum ventilation. An important raw material used in the leather accessories, synthetic rubber based adhesive is highly inflammable. Adequate ventilation is also essential to provide for fire safety. The surface area of the window has been less than norm mentioned above in the case of 50.4 per cent of the enterprises affecting about 50.9 per cent workers covered in the study (Pais 2002). It was found that "workers in the leather accessories manufacture worked under inadequate ventilation and illumination." Natural ventilation from windows was inadequate and was not supplemented by the use of the exhaust, table or ceiling fans. Most of the enterprises had ceiling fans, however, over half the workforce had to share a fan with 5 workers. During the summer months, the temperature at the work place reached 50 degrees Celsius under the low asbestos roof. Thus workers were compelled to take a break from work during mid-day to escape from the extreme heat. To compensate for this break of about 2 hours, they worked through the evening into the night and at times till 1 am the next morning (Pais 2003).

3.14 In the diamond cutting industry in Surat, a study found "small rooms without air conditioning or ventilation, stuffed with machinery" (Engelshoven 1999). Another study in the same industry found 8-10 workers sitting cross-legged on the floor of a small room with no ventilation or fresh air, but well-lit with neon tubes (Breman 1996). The work place was hot and humid and a number of researchers who visited these work places have reported that the workers were seen "without wearing anything on their upper part" and with a towel hanging around their neck to "dry hand and face of sweat that runs profusely" (Desai and Raj 2001; Breman 1996; Engelshoven 1999).

3.15 The glass bangle industry in Firozabad in UP operates on primitive and obsolete technology (Ghosh and Sharma 2003). The environment within the workshops is severely polluted with toxic chemical fumes, high temperatures and coal dust.

Illumination

3.16 Proper illumination is necessary to protect not only the workers' eyes but also from injuries such as from moving parts of machines and sharp cutting tools. Adequate illumination of the work place is required in general but specifically for three reasons. One, the work after sunset means appropriate lighting for night work is necessary. Two, as certain production involves intricate operations that are performed manually by the workers using hand tools. For example, all cutting operations are done with the use of a sharp knife or weaving of carpets with intricate designs. In such instances, proper illumination is necessary for both the safety of the worker and for maintaining quality in the production process. Three, as the main raw inputs can be of different colours, textures and surfaces appropriate lighting is essential for matching the colour and textures as in carpets weaving. Appropriate lighting is necessary in the manufacture of leather footwear or accessories, in operations involving cutting leather and assembling the leather accessories so that the grain is maintained. In the unorganised sector, where a large part of the work is done on piece rates and the workers end up paying penalty for mistakes, errors and bad quality of work due to inadequate illumination is a double punishment. A large part of the carpet weaving in the unorganised sector is home-based or based in small workshops. While the lighting in such work place seems adequate in general, it is insufficient for the carpet weaving operations or for work such as zari embroidery. Workers have to strain themselves with tiny knots, involving different types of threads and colours. In the long run, this has affected the eyesight of a large number of workers involved in carpet weaving (Raj and Srivastava 2000, John and Ghosh 2002). Similarly surveys of working conditions in the Aligarh lock making industry found that there was inadequate lighting at the work place (Sekar & Mohammad 2001).

3.17 In the diamond cutting industry, since the owners cannot take risks with the quality of output, the raw material being very expensive, generally it is found that illumination is at least adequate in the workshops (Breman 1996). In this industry, it has been found that employers provided adequate lighting while compromising on other working conditions such as space, temperature and humidity. Workers were found crammed in tiny, hot and humid workshops that were otherwise well lit (Breman 1996).

[1] Housing standard according to HUD's Manufactured Housing Standards and Oregon's one and two family dwelling code in the United States.

Occupational Hazards, Health Conditions and Safety Measures

Dangerous Work, Loss of Life and Limbs

3.18 The Second National Commission on Labour highlighted that the working conditions in certain unorganised sector industries such as underground mines, ship breaking, fire works and match industry were dangerous and full of hazards. It noted that workers in underground mines were at the risk of loosing limbs or lives due to fire, flooding and collapse of roof, emission of (toxic) gases and the failure of ventilation systems in the underground mines (SNCL 2002).

3.19 Loss of limbs and amputations due to accidents occur most often when workers operate unguarded or inadequately safeguarded machines such as mechanical power presses, power press brakes, powered and non-powered conveyors, printing presses, roll-forming and roll-bending machines, saws including band saws, portable and table saws, shears, grinders and slitters, drilling machines, grinding machines and milling machines (OSHA). The hazard of loss of limbs and amputation can be identified and avoided through guarding, safe work practices, employee training, administrative controls and operating in a safe manner. The best way to prevent amputations caused by stationery or portable machinery is through machine safeguarding. Guards provide physical barriers to hazardous areas. They should be secure and strong, and workers should not be able to bypass, remove, or tamper with them. Guards should not obstruct the operator's view or prevent employees from working. Devices (such as sensors) help prevent contact with points of operation and may replace or supplement guards. Devices can interrupt the normal cycle of the machine when the operator's hands are at the point of operation. In the fish and meat processing units the Second National Commission on Labour has suggested that employers should provide workers with protective equipment such as aprons, gloves and gumboots (SNCL 2002).

3.20 Loss of limbs or amputations is widespread and involves a variety of activities and equipment. According to the Occupation Safety and Health Administration of the United States of America (OSHA) every year, thousands of workers lose fingers, hands, feet, and other body parts "mostly through compression, crushing, or by getting them caught between or struck by objects." A large number of such injuries involve fingertips.

3.21 In India, the Second National Commission on Labour has noted that the rate of accidents in the Indian mining industry was very high when compared with similar situations in other countries. There is a high rate of fatalities in the ship breaking industry in India (SNCL 2002). About 20 per cent of the deaths had been caused by falling objects, while 25 per cent of the deaths were due to fire. In the match making industry in Sivakasi, deaths were reported due to fire. Deaths were also reported in the homes of home-based workers in the industry. A study in the slaughter and meat processing industry in Delhi found that workers including child workers sustained a very high level of injuries (SNCL 2002). The study of brick-kiln workers in Tamil Nadu found hazardous working conditions, cases of loss of limbs, particularly foot being cut by spades (Dharmalingam 1995).

3.22 In the SSI units in Greater Mumbai (Dewan 2005), the major occupational hazard was fire. With the open and loose wire connections, crammed conditions with both workers and storage of materials, this should not be surprising. Over nine-tenths of the units reported having a fire extinguisher majority of which were not working. Masks, hand gloves and shoes that should be ideally compulsory in such manufacturing units were not provided to workers. Of the 446 workers interviewed only 7 were provided masks, 5 with shoes, and 11 with hand gloves. Of these, 3 women had masks and 8 were provided aprons. Nearly 95 per cent of the units reported having a first-aid kit, but they were of poor quality. Almost none has tincture, antiseptic cream or bandages. Most just had a few analgesic tablets.

3.23 There was no official compensation for work related injuries. Obtaining it was purely based on the quality of relationship between the owner and worker and that too confined only for the permanent employees. Even among the permanent workers only one-tenth had their medical bills reimbursed, and less than 4 per cent were given some cash, mainly in the computer division (Dewan 2005). No temporary workers received any

Every year, thousands of workers lose fingers, hands, feet, and other body parts "mostly through compression, crushing, or by getting them caught between or struck by objects." A lag e number of such injuries involve fingertips (OSHA).

medical benefits and even in the case of work related injuries taking leave implied loss of pay and often loss of job as well. The logic being that the owner could not stop production to wait for the injured worker. Surprisingly, only 52 per cent of the women and 48 per cent of the men, mainly employed for more than five years, subscribed to the Employees State Insurance Scheme (ESIS).

Occupational Diseases

3.24 The Second National Commission on Labour has pointed to the high incidence of lung diseases such as tuberculosis and pneumoconiosis among underground mine workers. There is a danger of workers in the glass bangle industry suffering from respiratory disorders and tuberculosis due to the toxic fumes and smoke within the factories and the high level of coal dust. Dyes and chemicals used in textiles and carpet weaving are health hazards to the workers and a serious environmental problem (SNCL 2002). A study of migrant workers in silica mines in Allahabad found significantly large number of workers suffering from tuberculosis and silicosis (Roy 2000). In the fish processing units in the exports zones, a study found that "lifting and carrying of 200 kg or even 400 kg rubs packed with fish and ice" on wet and slippery floors "often lead to falls, injuries, strained muscles, hernia and slip discs" (Dewan 2001). The study also documented health problems such as permanent damage to the uterus of women workers, coughs, shivering bouts etc. due to continued exposure to freezing temperatures.

3.25 The Hand Block Printing textiles cluster in Jaipur is at least 500 years old and hand print naturally dyed textiles. Block printing was a family tradition among the Chhipa community located in Sanganer. There are many health hazards in this trade. The work requires a lot of stamina since the worker has to stand and walk for about eight hours a day. Almost half the workers in the sample said that they could not work for more than ten days in a month due to lack of stamina. The dyes created problems for the workers since they had to hit the block with their palms which caused hardened/dead/numb skin. Skin related problems created by allergy to dyes while hitting the block were reported by 75 per cent of the workers (IDS 2006). Improper ventilation in the worksites was also reported by the workers. Health hazards and job insecurity become inter-related problems in this sector and affect the earnings of the workers.

3.26 Workers in the brick-kiln industry suffer from respiratory problems arising from living and working 24 hours of the day in the fumes emanating from the furnace. Workers had persistent cough and complained of body ache and exhaustion. Rudimentary facilities like drinking water and absence of health care contributed to their vulnerability to disease. The women and children were equally exposed to the harsh life in the 'bhattas' (Varma and Kumar 2006).

Drinking Water, Washing Facility, Rest Rooms, Crèche and Canteen at Work Place

3.27 The Building and Other Construction Workers (Regulation of Employment and Conditions of Service) Act, 1996 provided for the principal employer, contractor or sub-contractor of construction workers to provide for facilities in the workplace such as safe drinking water, urinals and toilets separately for male and female workers, first-aid, and crèche for children of the workers on sites where the number of women workers is greater than 20. The Contract Labour and Inter-state Migrant Workers Act which is also applicable to the construction workers required the provision of living accommodation of specified standard. The Tamil Nadu Manual Workers (Regulation of Employment and Conditions of Work) Act, amended in 1994, has similar provisions for working condition and special provision for women.

3.28 Most studies that have enquired into the working conditions in the unorganised sector tend to report that the employers provided workers with drinking water. Labour Bureau surveys showed that in beedi making, textiles, powerlooms, agarbati, stone quarry, fireworks, saw mills, oil mills and dal mills, toys and doll industry and readymade garments, over 90 per cent of the workers had access to drinking water (Labour Bureau 1992c). The potability of the drinking water is, however, not tested and reported. While most enterprises in the unorganised sector have some arrangement for the provision of drinking water for the workers, studies have found that workers themselves make own arrangements in those cases where the employers do not provide this facility.

3.29 No study has found facilities such as crèche, canteen and shelter for rest or recreation of workers in the unorganised sector. Exceptions are in beedi making and cashew nut processing in Kerala. Studies carried out in these two industries all over India found that only in Kerala, the workers were provided with facilities such as crèche and canteen. Resting place was provided to some workers in stone quarrying and in construction industry. The quality of these facilities was, however, of such low standard that it could be safely held that no such facilities were provided to workers in these industries as well (Labour Bureau 1979; Vaid 1997; Suryanarayanan 2004).

3.30 The construction industry involves a large number of women workers, a number of them young mothers with infant children. Surveys in the construction industry have found that crèche facilities are not available on worksites (Labour Bureau 1979; Vaid 1997; Suryanarayanan 2004). An all India study and many state level studies have noted the lack of welfare measures such as crèches for children, rest-rooms for workers, separate toilets for women and potable drinking water. If housing was provided it was generally unfit for human living. Further, it was observed that there were no complaints from the workers or the labour administrators (Suryanarayanan 2004). One of the consequences of not having adequate crèche facility was that the children were often engaged in helping the workers and over time were inducted into the workforce. In fact the workers begin their working life very young and continue till old age without any provision for old age benefits.

3.31 The fish processing industry in the coastal areas of Maharashtra and Gujarat obtain their workers mainly from Kerala. Almost all of them are younger and unmarried women who are in great demand because of their skill in cleaning and separating the variety of fish species caught from the sea. The working conditions are very poor and the women also live in hostel like accommodation. These women are vulnerable to sexual harassment and, being away from their own community, have no way to protect themselves. Workers' organizations are slow to reach them. Of late, concerned social action groups have come together to articulate the problems of these workers and demand remedial measures from respective governments.

Housing and Sanitation

3.32 A large number of unorganised sector activities, especially in the urban areas, are in clusters, often formed in a particular area due to historical reasons. With the expansion of activities and the number of enterprises in the clusters grow even while there is not enough space. Examples are lock making industry in Aligarh, diamond cutting in Surat, brassware in Moradabad, leather saddlery in Kanpur, leather tanning in Chromepet in Chennai, glass bangle industry in Firozabad, leather accessories manufacture in Kolkata, Kanpur and Mumbai, zari embroidery in the slums of Mumbai, Varanasi and so on. A large number of workers in these enterprises also live in the surroundings of the cluster if not within the workshop itself. Thus, the unorganised sector clusters face extremely limited facilities for sanitation. Open sewer drainage systems, overflowing drains, flooding during monsoon etc lead to unhygienic living and working conditions for workers. In these slums not many housing units or workshops have attached toilet facilities within the premises. In the leather accessories manufacture in Dharavi only about one per cent of the enterprises (and workers) had access to toilet facilities within the premises. All others had to use public toilets or open spaces within the slum.

3.33 Another set of unorganised sector activities are carried out on the site. Examples are building constructions, roads, highways and bridge constructions, stone quarrying, coal mining and so on. In these settings, workers are provided with "temporary residential sheds which lack minimum facilities" (SNCL 2002). The Labour Bureau surveys in several industries in the unorganised sector over the years have found that about 3.5 per cent workers in beedi making and between 2 and 3 per cent of the workers in the powerlooms sector were provided with housing facility (Labour Bureau 1992b). It is common for migrant single workers in the unorganised sector to also sleep at the place of work (Sekar 2003; Pais 2003; Breman 1996; Engelshoven 1999). Work tools, implements, unfinished products are pushed to a side to make space for the workers to sleep in the workshops (Pais 2003). A study of the working conditions in slaughter-houses found that the workers including child workers slept within the slaughter house with all the dirt and stench from decaying carcass and offal (Sekar 2003).

3.34 The only industries where relatively larger number of workers are provided housing is in economic activities that are not undertaken in homes or industrial sites, but on worksite, often away from workers' normal place of residence. Examples are construction, brick-kilns, stone quarrying and other mining activities. The quality of such housing leaves much to be desired. Few

An All India study and many state level studies have noted the lack of welfare measures such as crèches for children, rest-rooms for workers, separate toilets for women and potable drinking water.

studies have found that unorganised sector workers had urinal and toilet facilities at work. Studies have repeatedly shown that even in industries employing large number of women workers there was no separate toilet and wash facilities for them.

Hours of Work, Duration of Work Day and Weekly Holidays

3.35 Various labour and industry regulations in India (Factories Act 1948; Minimum Wages Act 1948; Shops and Establishments Act 1948) lay down rules that no adult worker shall be required to work for more than 9 hours a day and for more than 48 hours a week. The regulations also restrain the spread over of working period including rest interval not to exceed 10.5 hours in a day. On an average, the working hours in an establishment with 6 days a week would be 8 hours a day. Thus we consider a regulatory norm of 8 hours a day as normal working hours and any work done beyond 8 hours a day on a regular basis would be considered work beyond normal working hours.

3.36 The labour and industry regulations provide for occasional overtime work. The law stipulates that the wages received by the workers for work done beyond the normal working hours, i.e. during overtime, should be at twice the rate of the normal wage received. Regulations provide for one day off from work per week with wages and oblige employers to provide workers with paid off during National holidays and on the occasion of certain holidays.

3.37 Work by coolies, porters, workers in the fishing industry and rag pickers worked over very long spread over, lasting up to 52 hours as in the case of marine fishing industry. In other sectors where it was found that working hours were more regular. In fireworks, match making, brassware, glass bangle manufacture, diamond cutting, powerlooms and so on, workers started very early in the morning, e.g. 6 a.m. in the case of fireworks in Shivakasi, and the work-day ended very late in the evening. In Dharavi's leather accessories manufacture, it was common to start work at 8 a.m. and continued till 1 a.m. the next morning, with 2-3 half-hour breaks for lunch and dinner. The total spread over is between 15 and 17 hours a day. A study of handloom sector in Kanpur found that the work was organised in such a way that wages were based on a 12 - 15 hours work/ day while in the powerlooms sector in the same town it was a 8 hours/ day (Mishra and Srivastava 2002).

3.38 Long hours of work in the unorganised sector have been highlighted by numerous studies (Joshi and Joshi 1976; Anand 1991; Acharya and Jose 1991; Das 1994; Swaminathan 1998; Ghosh 2004; Pais 2003). Long hours of work also seem to be the trend in the new and emerging sectors such as the business process outsourcing (BPO). A recent study has shown that BPO workers did not get a weekly holiday (Babu 2004). In the software industry, about 23 per cent of the workers worked for more than 9 hours a day on an average (Abraham and Sharma 2005).

3.39 Casual leave, earned leave and sick leave for workers in the unorganised sector are not provided by the employers. It is a feature of the unorganised sector that work goes on for 7 days a week. In some instances the work is for 6 days a week with a one day break. In such cases, workers are given a day off from work without wages. Piece rated workers have reported not working on one day a week (for example beedi workers). However, this weekly off is often without wages. Construction workers have reported a day off from work per week without wages (Suryanarayanan 2004, Labour Bureau 1979, Labour Bureau 1995a).

3.40 The Maternity Benefits Act, (1961) provides for a minimum maternity leave of six weeks to a pregnant woman immediately following her delivery or miscarriage. The provision of paid maternity leave seems to be very rare in the unorganised sector, though the Labour Bureau surveys and some other researchers have found limited instances of women being given maternity leave without pay. The women workers were assured of a job when they returned from maternity leave.

3.41 Holidays with wages for festivals or a festival bonus seem to be in practise in different unorganised sector industries. For example, the Labour Bureau surveys in the unorganised sector have found that 74 per cent of the beedi workers had received festival holidays with some wages, 83 per cent of the workers in the garment industry had also received some compensation along with festival holidays. In other sectors such as metalware, powerlooms

Contrary to regulatory norm, long working hours seem to be a normal feature of unorganised sector in India and workers are engaged in work for 10 to 12 hours a day. In some industries, the daily wage is for a fixed work day of 10 hours.

and handlooms, toy and doll industry, saw mills, oil mills and dal mills more than half the hired workers were provided with paid festival holidays.

3.42 A study conducted in 33 industrial estates of Greater Mumbai in 2004 recorded the conditions of 446 workers in 109 small scale units (SSI) in the manufacturing sector (Dewan 2005). One third of the workers were in the plastics industry with an equal proportion of men and women. Metal and metal-based products had 45 per cent women workers. About 20 per cent of the workers were engaged in equal proportions in the chemical and electrical products industry. The sectors where women out numbered the men were in the others category including oil filtering and packing, jewellery and jewellery packing, gift-wrapping, health care, medical products, courier services and computer data entry. Only 18 per cent of all respondents worked for the legal 8-hour day, 73 per cent worked for a normal shift of 10 hours. The normal shift for the remaining 9 per cent was 12 hours. There did not seem to be much difference in the hours of work by gender. Thus, factory work did imply more than full hours of work per day once one obtained such work.

3.43 According to the Brick and Tiles Manufacturers Federation, (New Delhi) there are nearly 22000 brick-kilns in and around Delhi (in Ghaziabad, UP, Faridabad and Haryana) with a workforce of nearly 3 million (Gupta 2003). The workers are mainly agricultural labourers recruited by labour agents/ kiln owners' contractors during lean agricultural seasons. An advance is paid to the workers for the entire period and for the entire family, excluding the old and the disabled move to the kiln to work for the full season of about 6 months. Only the male workers are registered as workers in the muster roll of the employer and the rest of the family remains invisible to statistics, policy and social protection provisions. Working hours for all workers are about 12-14 hours, including for the women who are not on the muster rolls (Gupta 2003). The day starts at 6.00 a.m. for the women with her housework chores and a little later for the men who start the preparatory work. The workers have an hour of rest in the afternoon. The day ends at 6.00 p.m. for the men and women. While the men proceed to rest, women begin her household chores such as preparation of the evening meal. Her day ends only around 10.00 p.m. when she has served the meal and cleaned the utensils etc. The double burden of work for women is quite clear.

Employment Contracts

Employment Opportunities and Recruitment Methods

3.44 Employment is obtained in the unorganised sector mainly through three modes, the importance of these three modes vary from activity to activity and industry to industry. First, is by 'standing at the factory gate', second is through a family, caste and community based network and third is through labour contractors or 'Jamadars'. There is a total absence of any form of formal publicity for employment; no newspaper advertisements or posters in public places announcing job vacancies etc. Occasionally, employers stick notices such as "Wanted: Sample tailors", "Wanted skilled workers for shirt making" and "Wanted: Packers". Posters with "Wanted Sales Man" or "Wanted Typist" are not uncommon in the unorganised services sector. Workers without access to caste or community networks have to shift from one 'factory gate' to another till they get a job. The Labour Bureau surveys show that a large part of the unorganised employment in the industries such as textiles, garments, powerlooms, agarbati and toys and dolls, is obtained at the 'factory gate' (Labour Bureau 1998; 1995b; 1992c; 1992a; 1992b). Migrant labour are particularly disadvantaged if they have to get jobs at the factory gate. All these imply limited job choices and low levels of mobility for workers in the unorganised sector.

3.45 In the SSI units in Greater Mumbai (Dewan 2005) most workers were recruited through relatives and friends. Some workers reported that they had to go from unit to unit for several months before obtaining the current job. Some women reported specific forms of recruitments applicable only to them. They were brought in by contractors to finish urgent 'order-jobs', the terms of employment last for anywhere between 4 - 18 weeks. The employer apparently paid a one-time price of Rs.800 per girl to the contractor, and the workers insisted they did not have to pay any 'cut;' to the contractor. A few workers said they had registered at the Employment Exchange where they receive unemployment allowance

A study of the construction industry found that only the male workers are registered as workers in the muster roll of the employer and the rest of the family remains invisible to statistics, policy and social protection provisions (Gupta 2003).

of Rs.50 per day. But they stopped going to the Exchange since it costs them Rs.80 each day to reach there.

3.46 Contract labour refers to all those workers who are employed by or through labour contractors on the work of any enterprise. Contract labour can be distinguished from the direct labour in terms of employment relationships with the principal employer and the method of wage payment. Unlike direct employment, contract workers do not receive wages directly from the principal employer. The contractor is responsible for the conditions of work of the contract workers. Contract labour in India is regulated under the Contract Labour (Regulation and Abolition) Act 1970. The aim of the Act is to provide for the regulation of contract labour in certain economic activities and for abolition in other circumstances. Under this Act, contract labour has been prohibited in certain industries. The Act does not apply when a contractor employs less than 20 workers and this has lead to manipulations by employers and contractors (SNCL 2002).

3.47 Contract labour was found in large numbers in certain activities in the unorganised sector such as in stone quarrying, beedi rolling, rice shelling, brick-kiln and construction. Labour Bureau surveys in the unorganised sector brick -kilns found that all the workers were through some form of contracting (Labour Bureau 1982). In construction, an estimated 10.7 million construction workers, accounting for 83 per cent of all construction workers in India in that year, were employed through contractors and did not receive minimum employment protection and benefits whatsoever (Vaid 1997).

3.48 In the activities where contract labour is predominant, the contract system forces migrant workers to be available 'on call' through jamadar, mistry, mukaddam or other regional expression through a system of advances and loans (Suryanarayanan 2004, Srivastava 2005; Ghosh 2004). A major draw back of the contract labour system is that typically the working conditions are poor and neither the contractor nor the principal employer takes responsibility for the workers' welfare (NCRL 1991; Suryanarayanan 2004).

Work Contracts and Wage Forms

3.49 The nature of employment contract gives us an idea of the extent of security and regularity of the work involved apart from providing an idea of the other work related benefits that workers might have access to. The National Commission on Rural Labour observed that workmen employed through middlemen or contractors do not receive wages in full measure (NCRL 1991).

3.50 Studies on workers and employment in the formal and informal sectors have categorised workers in several ways, in terms, for example, of the nature of employment or work contracts, security of employment, and ownership of productive assets. Standing (1983) suggests a number of detailed criteria to categorise work contracts that include duration: casual, daily, piecework, fixed term, "permanent"; basis of payment: time rate (hourly, etc.), piece-rate, product share; frequency of payment: at regular intervals, upon completion of job, irregular, including timing of bonuses; medium of payment: cash, kind, meals etc. provision of a service, work, or favour; relative autonomy: timing and amount of work, and intensity of effort/productivity or not; freedom of employment relations: ability to change employers, ability to combine with other (work) activities; linkages with other contracts: credit, land, employment of family members. In India, the NSSO classifies workers as self-employed, regular employees and casual workers. The Labour Bureau categorises hired workers as permanent, temporary, casual and others. The share of each of these categories of workers differs vastly by industry. According to the Labour Bureau surveys, temporary workers dominated employment in rice shelling, match industry, marine fishing, woollen carpet manufacture, metalware industry, lime manufacturing units, powerlooms, fireworks, agarbatti manufacture and toy and doll industry accounting for over half the workforce in these industries (Labour Bureau 1992c). In fact, the surveys found that the share of temporary workers was 100 per cent in rice shelling, 99 per cent in match making and 97 per cent in marine fishing operations. In a study of workers in the low-income households in Mumbai, Acharya and Jose (1991) classify workers as permanent workers, contract workers, temporary workers and other workers. In a study of workers in the informal sector ceramic industry Das (2003) classifies workers as regular and irregular based on work related benefits. Despite the heterogeneity in the informal sector, workers can still

A part of workers' wages is paid as informal commissions to the middlemen (Srivastava 2005).

be classified into some basic categories (Carr and Chen 2001)[2]. Based on the location of work, workers in the unorganised sector can be classified as those based in industrial sheds, home-based workers, workers on work site (such as construction workers), workers without fixed location (such as street hawkers).

Contracts of Workers in the Unorganised Sector and Unorganised Workers

3.51 The NSSO Employment and Unemployment Survey of 2004-05 canvassed a few special questions on the nature of the contracts and benefits accruing to wage workers, which point to the conditions of work of casual and regular workers. Nearly all casual and almost all regular workers (above 90 per cent) in the unorganised sector did not have a written contract (Table 3.2). In contrast, about half of the wage workers (including casual) in the organised sector had written contracts. The category of unorganised regular workers in the organised sector was not very different from their counterparts in the unorganised sector with about three fourths of them not having written contracts.

3.52 Another important condition of work that is a clear necessity to guarantee decent work is the eligibility for paid leave. Less than 10 per cent of the wage workers in the unorganised sector were entitled to the facility of paid leave (Table 3.3). The regular workers in the unorganised sector were only a little more fortunate with about 20 per cent of them being eligible.

3.53 At the other extreme, about 60 per cent of the workers in the organised sector were eligible for paid leave (Table 3.3). However, it is interesting that this minimum condition of work was not available to all the workers even in the organised sector. The informalisation process has generated a large segment of workers within the organised sector without minimum conditions of work. We have termed them as unorganised workers. Only about 15 per cent of these unorganised workers in the organised sector were eligible for paid leave, the situation being a little better for regular workers with slightly more than a quarter of them being eligible for paid leave.

3.54 More than two-fifths of the workers in the SSI units in Greater Mumbai were employed for more than five years. However, only 7.2 per cent of them had a permanent status. There was apparently no gender discrimination on permanency since a large proportion of clerks and data entry operators were women. The rest, 92.8 per cent of the total workers, were temporary and

Table 3.2: Percentage Share of Non-agricultural Wage Workers without Contract by Sector and Gender 2004 - 2005

Employment Status	Rural	Urban	Total	Rural	Urban	Total	Rural	Urban	Total
		Male			Female			Total	
Unorganised Sector: Casual	99.1	98.9	99.0	98.8	98.5	98.7	99.0	98.8	99.0
Unorganised Sector: Regular Workers (RW)	93.0	92.1	92.4	90.1	93.0	92.3	92.5	92.3	92.4
Unorganised Sector: Wage Workers	97.2	94.8	96.0	96.0	94.8	95.3	97.0	94.8	95.9
Unorganised Worker in Organised Sector: RW	77.8	73.2	80.4	68.5	62.6	73.4	75.6	70.2	79.0
Unorganised Worker in Organised Sector: Wage Worker	88.1	86.0	87.0	81.6	81.4	81.6	86.5	85.1	85.8
Organised Sector: Wage Workers	60.8	47.6	52.7	64.6	47.9	55.4	61.6	47.6	53.2
Wage Workers: All	81.2	68.7	74.2	78.3	70.1	73.7	80.7	69.0	74.1

Source: Same as in Table 3.1.

2 Carr and Chen (2001) have classified workers in the informal sector as follows

a) Employer: Owners of informal enterprises, owner operators of informal enterprises

b) Self-Employed: Own-account workers, heads of family businesses, unpaid family workers

c) Wage Workers: Employees of informal enterprises, casual workers without a fixed employer, homeworkers (also called industrial outworkers), domestic workers, temporary and part-time workers, unregistered workers

Table 3.3: Percentage Share of Non-agricultural Wage Workers Eligible for Paid Leave by Sector and Gender 2004 - 2005

Employment Status	Rural	Urban	Total	Rural	Urban	Total	Rural	Urban	Total
		Male			Female			Total	
Unorganised Sector: Casual	0.9	0.9	0.9	1.3	3.2	2.1	1.0	1.2	1.1
Unorganised Sector: Regular Workers (RW)	17.2	18.3	17.9	21.8	0.1	20.5	17.9	18.7	18.4
Unorganised Sector: Wage Workers	5.9	11.5	8.7	7.9	14.6	11.8	6.2	12.1	9.2
Unorganised Worker in Organised Sector: RW	25.6	28.1	24.3	35.2	34.8	35.5	27.9	30.0	26.6
Unorganised Worker in Organised Sector: Wage Workers	11.7	16.7	14.2	16.9	24.8	20.3	13.0	18.3	15.6
Organised Sector: Wage Workers	47.7	66.2	59.0	39.3	63.8	52.8	45.9	65.8	57.8
Wage Workers: All	24.3	41.7	34.0	25.5	40.5	34.1	24.5	41.5	34.0

Source: Same as in Table 3.1.

this tallied with the employer's registers where 94.5 per cent of the workers were not recorded. Multi-tasking is the norm for both men and women. Gender stereo-typing seemed to be more or less broken down with women being engaged in all activities except carpentry. Women were engaged as machine operators, turners, technicians and mechanics. They also did drilling, rolling, printing, buffing punching and painting and were engaged in pipe-making, coil-finishing, weighing, cutting etc. (Dewan 2005). Men also performed all the women-specific jobs including packing.

Wages and Earnings of Workers in the Unorganised Sector

3.55 It was the wage-structure that was gendered though the same activity was performed by men and women. Literacy had no role to play in the wage determination except for those who are 'employees' (permanent). Dewan (2005) found that the wage structure could be divided in to three categories:

Category 1: At the bottom of the pyramid wages of women ranged from Rs.27 to 47 per day and for men from Rs.37 to 67 per day.

Category 2: In the middle of the pyramid, women who are engaged solely in packing get Rs.32 per day, while men get Rs.48. Male loaders are presumed to carry more weight and get Rs.60 while women get Rs.27- 30 per day. All the peons were men and received a monthly salary of Rs.1400 - 2000 depending on the length of service.

Category 3: At the upper level the wage rate is determined mainly by the length of service and is applicable only to those who have worked for more than 5 years in the unit.

3.56 The monthly income was affected by the fact that while wages were calculated on a daily basis it was paid only monthly. Only 6 days of the week were taken into account and the compulsory holiday in the week was unpaid. As we had noted earlier most of the workers worked for more than the legal 8 hours per day. The overtime wages added little to the monthly income because it was really an extension of the working day from 10 hours to 12 hours. The extra two hours were recorded in a register and when this added up to a full workday of 10 hours an extra day's wage was received. "The overtime therefore did not increase the wages but merely added to a normal work-day" (Dewan 2005).

3.57 In a study of the garment export industry in the National Capital Region in Delhi Singh and Sapre (2007) observed that written contracts were issued to very few skilled workers only. Three kinds of contracts were

The informalisation process has generated a large segment of workers within the organised sector without minimum conditions of work.

identified: skilled workers were mainly engaged as permanent workers and offered regular contracts; contract workers were engaged through contractors; piece rate workers were paid on the basis of work finished. The skilled workers category consisted mainly of men. In 2002, the Minimum Wages for skilled workers was Rs.3091 per month in the NCR. For semi-skilled workers it was Rs.2833 per month and for unskilled workers it was Rs.2497 per month. The study found that about two-fifths of the women and one fourth of the men got less than Rs.2000 per month. At the other extreme, about 13 per cent of the men got more than Rs.3500 or above minimum wages, while only 5 per cent of the women did so.

3.58 In an interesting case study of sales workers in shops in Ernakulam district in Kerala (Patrick 2001) found discrimination in wages paid to women sales workers. It was hypothesized that the employers deliberately underestimated the women's probable length of stay in the job. Even if recruited as permanent workers they were employed only till they were married. It was assumed that women were only temporary participants in the workforce and this justified the low wages paid to them. The women themselves often underestimated the possible length of stay in the employment further strengthening the justification. Low levels of unionization of the women workers also increased the chance of discrimination. The women received an average of Rs.448 per month, which was half of the Minimum Wage as prescribed by the Shops and Establishments Act, Rs.881 per month in 1991. The male-female wage gap was the lowest among the youngest workers and rose steadily for the older workers across the sectors. Women workers in the age-group 21-25 years earned almost 89 per cent of the male wage while women workers aged 41-45 years earned only 76 per cent of the male wage. However, experience was rewarded and women workers with more than eight years of experience had lower wage-gap with the male counterparts.

3.59 A survey of construction workers on sites in Tamil Nadu found that none of the workers received the minimum wages of Rs.40 prevailing in 1993 (Suryanarayanan 2004). Women were paid Rs. 20-25 and men received Rs. 30-35. No employment cards or wage slips were issued. Again in 1997 a survey of 77 construction sites across the country showed that contract labour in the construction industry were mainly landless rural migrants who entered the industry through Jamadars or Mistris. While most of the workers were hired for nearly 25 days for 9 -12 months, it took them nearly 10 - 15 years to become skilled workers. The wages of skilled workers was generally higher than the statutorily prescribed wage. However, gender discrimination was well entrenched and women workers were paid much less than the men for similar work. The all-India study observed that the benefits of most of the provisions of the laws relating to wages and provident fund did not reach the construction workers and contract labour.

3.60 The Committee constituted to study the conditions of work of unorganized labour in Tamil Nadu (GOTN 1998, quoted in Swaminathan 2005) observed active gender discrimination in wages practiced by many industries. In the 'appalam' manufacturing industry, "Equal wages for equal work is something utopian and hitherto unheard of by the workers in this occupation. A female worker doing identical work in this occupation is denied 50 per cent of the wages given to the male worker. A male worker earns around Rs.40 per day while a female worker is paid only Rs.20 per day". Similarly in the coir industry while a male worker earned Rs.40 per day the female is paid anywhere between Rs.25 and Rs.27. In the match and fireworks industry while the women and children were engaged as homeworkers in processes de-linked from the factory, the men worked in the factory. Obviously this has implication for wages and other benefits.

3.61 The brick-kiln industry is a low technology activity with a strict division of labour. The moulder who prepares the pit and moulds the bricks is paid per 1000 bricks. He uses the services of the women and children of the family to mould the mud and to carry the moulded bricks to dry in the sun. In Haryana the moulder was paid Rs.121 per 1000 bricks which included the payment for his family. The loader loads the bricks into the kiln which includes carrying the dried bricks to the kiln with the help of a cart and animals. The stacker arranges the bricks into the kiln and the 'rapaswala' covers it with earth in preparation for the firing. All these workers are paid per 1000 bricks and get Rs.50, 11 and 8 respectively. The 'nikasi' or un-loader removes the baked bricks from the kiln and stacks them according to the quality of the bricks. The women are engaged in this activity and also clean the kiln after the bricks are removed. The 'nikasi' is paid about Rs.28-31 per 1000 bricks. The firemen fire the kiln and watch over it all through the operation to see that the bricks are properly burnt. They are paid Rs.2200 per month (Gupta 2003).

3.62 Since the kotadoria work in Rajasthan is a family enterprise one cannot clearly distinguish the gender differential in wages. However, this is a predominantly female economic activity and the women themselves consider it a supplementary source of income (IDS 2006). The gender differential in income is seen clearly in the case of income of the weavers compared to the master weavers who are all men. While the income per weaver was reported as Rs.554 per month, that of the master weaver was reported as Rs.5359 per month. Other workers such as loom repairer, yarn trader etc. got monthly incomes in the range of Rs.600 - 800. The exploitative nature of the income is seen in the unequal relationship between the weaver and the master weaver. The method of exploitation includes delayed payments and this can be up to 6 months. The payment is partial and about 20 per cent is given when completing the first 'paan' (a part of the fabric), another 20 per cent after the second paan and when the third paan is completed they get the full payment for the first paan. Therefore at any point in time 60 per cent of the wages remain unpaid. This money is used by the master weaver as working capital to maintain the production chain. This is a large hidden cost borne by the weavers.

3.63 Overtime Wages: There is gender discrimination in the payment of overtime wages. The wages were already determined by the length of service and gender. Overtime 'single' wages were given to those who were employed for less than five years and one and a half times for those between 5 and 10 years, and 'double' the wages were paid to those employed for more than a decade. The basis of calculation of overtime rates is even more exploitative. Wage rate for a person working for 10 hours say Rs.37 is computed by dividing the daily wage by 10 to get Rs.3.7 for 'single', Rs.5.55 for one and a half and Rs.7.4 for a 'double'. Thus, overtime rate for those working for a 12 hours day becomes Rs.3.08, Rs.4.62 and Rs.6.16 for the respective categories (Dewan 2005). Even this was not available because the work was not available. Workers complained that the lack of work to cover up for the low wages is a major problem.

3.64 Leave Benefits: The unpaid compulsory holiday during the week was treated as a break in service. Besides some of the women reported that they were laid-off for one week every two months even though they had been working in the same unit for five years. A permanent male worker complained that he got no provident fund though he worked for more than 30 years in the same unit. Only 7 per cent said they got provident fund benefits (Dewan 2005).

3.65 Almost 70 per cent of the men and 76 per cent of the women workers said they got no paid leave ever. Dewan (2005) reported that three fourths of the workers did not get the three compulsory public holidays, Republic Day, Independence Day and Maharashtra Day. The gender discrimination noted here was that as high as 54 per cent of such workers were women. Again 56 per cent of the 30 per cent who did not get a day off for festival were women. In the SSI sector gender discrimination is noted in all aspects particularly in wages when there is hardly any difference in the tasks performed by them.

Statutory Minimum Wages

3.66 The Minimum Wages Act 1948 fixes the minimum wages payable to any person who is in an employment specified in the schedule. The Minimum Wages Act is applicable to "every person who is employed for hire or reward to do any work, skilled or unskilled, manual or clerical, in an employment specified in the schedule and in respect to which minimum rates of wages have been fixed. This includes an out-worker to whom any articles or materials are given out by another person to be made up, cleaned, washed, altered, finished, repaired or otherwise processed for sale." The authority that fixes minimum wages for a given employment through a government notification and enforces this Act is the state government. The minimum wage consists of two components. The first is the basic rate per day or per month and the second component is called the "special allowance". The basic rate for a given industry and for a given class of employees is fixed once in every few years and varies by location of work in rural and urban areas, city and towns. The special allowance, or cost of living allowance, is revised every six months and varies by the place of work. Once in every few years, the basic rate is itself revised upwards to reflect the current prices at the time of the revision.

3.67 Under the Minimum Wages Act, the procedures for fixing and revising of minimum wages are vague. The Act says that "when fixing minimum wages in respect of any scheduled employment for the first time or in revising minimum rates of wages so fixed, the appropriate government shall either (a) appoint as many committees or sub-committees as it considers necessary to hold enquiries and advise it in respect of such fixation or revision, as the case may be or (b) by notification in the official Gazette, publish its proposals for the information of persons likely to be affected thereby and specify a date on which the proposal will be taken into consideration." After considering the advice of the committee or committees appointed or response to the Gazette the government shall fix or revise the said minimum wage rates.

3.68 By the Apprentices Act 1961, the minimum wages for apprentice-helpers should amount to seventy five per cent of the minimum statutory wage of a skilled worker in the same category. Minimum wages are applicable to piece-rated as well as time-rated workers. For the piece-rated workers the minimum wage per piece should be calculated in such a way that "wages are not less than the minimum time-rate" (GOM 2001).

3.69 The Minimum Wages Act covers all workers in scheduled employments, in the formal and the informal sectors[3]. In 2002, in the central sphere minimum wages act covered only 47 scheduled employments. In the same year the highest number of employment schedules was 90 in Tamil Nadu while the lowest number of schedules was 15 in Manipur.

3.70 In the words of the Second National Commission for Labour the Act "is meant to ensure that market forces, and the laws of demand and supply are not allowed to determine the wages of workmen in industries where workers are poor, vulnerable, unorganised, and without bargaining power" (SNCL 2002). Minimum wages are to be paid by all employers "irrespective of the capacity of the employer to pay" (Anant and Sundaram 1998). In a 1982 judgment, the Supreme Court of India ruled that employing workers at wage rates below the statutory minimum wage levels was equivalent to forced labour, prohibited under Article 23 of the Constitution of India, even though economic compulsions might drive one to volunteer to work below the statutory minimum wage.[4]

3.71 The Minimum Wages Act also provides for regulation of hours of work, overtime wages, and benefits related to leave and holidays to workers. According to the hours of work regulation, a "normal working day" should not exceed 9 hours for an adult worker, including at least one break of 30 minutes. According to the overtime work regulation, any work beyond the "normal working day" should be considered as overtime work and the worker[5] is required to be compensated at twice the statutory minimum wage for the overtime work.

3.72 A major criticism of the implementation of the Minimum Wages Act is that it is applicable only to certain employments and does not include all workers. Thus, if a state government fails to include a particular employment within an industry in the employment schedule, the Minimum Wages Act does not cover all workers in that industry.

3.73 Many scholars have studied minimum wages legislation and its application to workers in the informal or unorganised sectors in India. Most studies show that, the Act has not been used to safeguard the interests of the poor and the informal sector workers. Anant and Sundaram (1998) showed that several states have a statutory minimum wage well below the poverty line. While fixing the minimum wages many state governments did not take into consideration the minimum requirement of a family of three consumption units, as prescribed under the Act (Bhagat 1997). Scholars have observed that that "infrequent revisions and inadequate cost of living adjustment" have been the marked features of statutory minimum wages and have led to a fall in real minimum wages over time (Bhagat 1997; Jhabvala 1998). Part of the reason for the ineffectiveness of minimum wags lies in the design and structure of the Minimum Wages Act, specifically in the absence of appropriate criteria for fixing the minimum wages, power to grant exemptions, inadequate sanctions and cumbersome penalties (Sankaran 1997). It has been shown for the city of Ahmedabad that only about 30 per cent of the workers in the unorganised sector are officially covered by the employment schedules of the Minimum Wages Act. Even within these industry groups the majority of the workers do not in fact obtain wages above the prescribed minimum wages (Unni 1998).

3.74 This has also led to a situation where there is a vast difference in the minimum wages set for different

A large proportion of unorganised workers remain outside the protection of the Minimum Wages Act in 2002.

3 For a detailed discussion on the development of policies related to minimum wages in India see Sankaran (1997), Anant and Sundaram (1998), Unni (1998). For a brief history of the minimum wages legislations in the developed countries in the last decade of the 19th century and early 20th century see Sankaran (1997).

4 People's Union for Democratic Rights vs. Union of India AIR 1982 SC 1473, cited in the report of the National Commission for Labour (SNCL 2002).

5 7 hours for adolescent workers and 4.5 hours for child workers.

employments within a state and across the states. In some of the smaller states such as Arunachal Pradesh, Haryana, Himachal Pradesh, Meghalaya, and Punjab, there is not much difference between minimum wages set for different employments, while in others such as Karnataka, Kerala, Tamil Nadu, Uttar Pradesh, there is a large difference between the minimum wages set. For example in Tamil Nadu, the highest and lowest minimum wage per day in 2003 was Rs.54 and Rs.110 respectively.

Minimum Wages and Piece Rates

3.75 Both piece-rated wages and time-rated wages exist in the unorganised sector in India. Piece rated and time-rated work is not specific to any particular industry, but in certain industries the prevalence of piece-rated work is relatively higher. If an industry had both time-rated as well as piece rated wage forms, male workers are more likely in time-rated jobs. Similarly, jobs that require higher levels of skills and education tend to be time-rated (Mishra and Srivastava 2002). Wage forms may or may not depend on the skill level of workers. In industries such as leather goods manufacture it was found that skilled workers worked on time-rated or piece-rated contracts, while unskilled workers were obliged to work on time-rated work contracts.

Comparison of Workers Earnings with Minimum Wages

3.76 Most studies on conditions of employment in the unorganised sector have examined wage levels and earnings of workers. There are, however, few studies that attempt to compare the wage earnings of workers with the statutory minimum wages. That there are a large number of studies with wage data and relatively smaller number of studies, which compare wages with statutory minimum wages is perhaps because they are not applicable to all types of employment, or because they are not revised frequently or simply because they are set so low that the comparison do not provide additional information other than suggesting that wage levels are low. One study in the small-scale unorganised sectors of Mumbai found that nearly 60 per cent of workers in the garments and pharmaceutical industry and about 90 per cent of the workers in the engineering industry received wages below the statutory minimum wages. The study also estimated that the wage earnings of about 20 per cent of the workers were about half the statutory minimum wage level (Gothoskar et. al. 1998). Bhagat (1997) reported that the daily wages in her area of study were below the minimum wages, while Chandra (1999) has observed that minimum wages were fixed below the prevailing wages.

3.77 In a study of construction workers in Tamil Nadu in 1993, it was found that none of the workers received the statutory minimum wage of Rs.40. As already noted earlier, while men were paid between Rs.30 and Rs. 35, women were paid between Rs.20 and Rs. 25 (Suryanarayanan 2004). Studies have also shown that minimum wages not paid to casual workers employed in the central public works projects (Suryanarayanan 2004), and to agricultural workers in Haryana (Rawal 2006). Pais (2003) found that if hours of work were taken into account, 87 per cent of the workers in leather accessories manufacture in Mumbai's unorganised sector did not receive minimum wages. In a survey of beedi workers across 11 major states in India, the Labour Bureau found a large variation in the piece rates received by workers. After examining the productivity of workers, the survey estimates that about 65.6 per cent of the beedi workers did not receive a minimum wage.

Notional Minimum Wage

3.78 In order to cover all workers, irrespective of type of employment, the Second National Commission on Labour has proposed a comprehensive legislation on a National Minimum Wage. The National Commission on Rural Labour (1991) had suggested a similar "basic minimum wage" in rural areas at Rs.19.6 (1991 prices) and Rs.25 for urban areas. It also stressed that minimum wages should be based on cost of living index and should therefore reflect any variation in the minimum wages from state to state or region to region.

3.79 The 28th Indian Labour Conference in 1985 recommended a national basic subsistence level of wage below which no wage may be fixed regardless of the nature of work, nature of employment and other considerations. In the absence of uniformity in minimum wages the Central Government adopted the concept of

The Commission uses two norms for Notional Minimum Wages in this Report: The National Minimum Wage of Rs. 66 and the alternative NCRL 'basic minimum wage' of Rs. 49 in rural and Rs. 67 in urban areas.

the national floor level minimum wage and fixed it at Rs. 35 per day in 1996, based on the recommendations of the National Commission on Rural Labour (1991). This national floor level minimum wage was then raised to Rs. 40 per day in 1998 and to Rs. 45 per day with effect from 1.12.1999 and Rs. 50 with effect from 1.09.2002 keeping in view the rising consumer price index.

3.80 The Central Advisory Board constituted under Section 8 of the Minimum Wages Act, 1948 set up a Working Group to go into the codification of the Minimum Wages and other issues (MOLE 2003). Based on the recommendations of the Central Advisory Board the National Minimum Wage has been last revised upwards to Rs. 66 per day with effect from 1-02-2004. All states have been requested to ensure fixation of wages in all the scheduled employments not below Rs. 66 per day (MOLE 2007).

3.81 The Commission records its objection to a National Minimum Wage, which does not adjust for differences in prices in rural and urban areas and across the states. However, in view of the fact that this is an accepted National Minimum Wage in the analysis below we use it as a norm to compare the wages received in various industrial sectors in rural and urban areas. In addition we use the "basic minimum wage" suggested by the National Commission on Rural Labour (1991), to arrive at a notional minimum wage of Rs.49 in rural and Rs.67 in urban areas at 2004-05 prices. The Consumer Price Index for Agricultural Labourers and the Consumer Price Index for Industrial Workers were used to inflate the wages for rural and urban areas respectively. Besides the National Minimum Wage of Rs.66, we also use the NCRL 'basic minimum wage' as an alternative Minimum Wage norm for rural and urban areas to compare the average daily wages per worker.

Minimum Wages among Casual Workers

3.82 The average daily wages of casual workers in urban areas was higher than that in rural areas for both men and women workers. A comparison of the average daily wage earnings from the NSSO with the National Minimum Wage norm and the alternative NCRL (1991) norm for rural and urban minimum wages, show discrepancies. When a uniform National Mimimun Wage norm of Rs. 66 is used the rural workers are distinctly worse off than the urban workers irrespective of the gender. In fact nearly all (96 per cent) the rural casual women workers get wages below Rs. 66. About 84 per cent of all casual workers in rural areas get wages below Rs. 66 compared to only 57 per cent of them in urban areas (Appendix A3.1 and Appendix A3.2). When the NCRL minimum wage is disaggregated for rural and urban areas the urban casual workers are worse off than the rural counterparts. About 49 and 88 per cent of the men and women in urban areas (Appendix A3.2) and nearly 41 and 81 per cent of men and women in rural areas (Appendix A3.1) respectively received wages less than the NCRL minimum wage norms.

3.83 The difference in percentage below the national minimum wage norm (Rs. 66) between men and women is more marked in non-agriculture than in agriculture, and in urban than in rural areas (Fig. 3.3 and Fig. 3.4). Among industry groups the percentage of men below the minimum wage norm is highest in trade, where as among women it is highest in manufacturing in rural and urban areas (Fig. 3.3 and Fig. 3.4).

3.84 We earlier highlighted the major manufacturing industries where there was a concentration of casual workers. In rural areas the lowest average daily wage was received by workers in the tobacco industry, (mainly women). About 92 per cent of them received wages below the National Minimum Wage norm (Appendix A3.3). Workers in the wood and wood product industries, (mainly men), had the highest average daily wage and less than 40 per cent of them were likely to have wages lower than the National Minimum Wage.

3.85 In the manufacturing sector, the average daily wages of casual men workers appeared close to the National Minimum wage of Rs. 66. However, nearly 60 per cent of them received wages below the norm and many of the industries groups had average wages below the norm (Appendix A3.4). More than 90 per cent of the women casual workers in all the industry groups on average had wages well below this norm.

3.86 At the state level, Madhya Pradesh and Orissa had the highest percentage of casual non-agricultural workers receiving wages below either of the minimum wage norms in both rural and urban areas (Fig. 3.5 and

The casual agricultural workers in rural areas were worse off compared to non-agricultural workers with nearly 87 per cent of the men and 97 per cent of the women receiving wages below the notional minimum.

Fig. 3.3: Percentage of Casual Workers with Wages below National Minimum Wage of Rs. 66 across Industry Groups by Gender 2004-2005: Rural

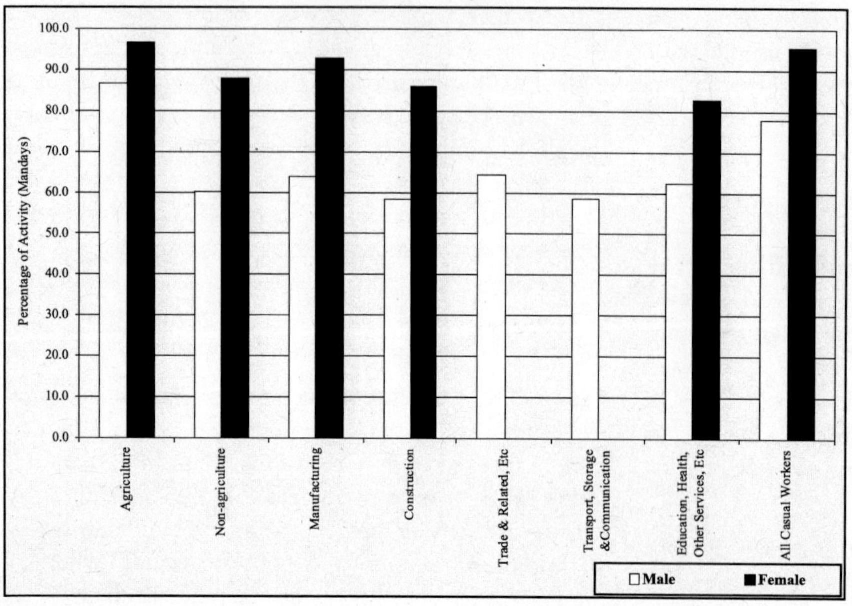

Source: ibid.

Fig. 3.6). Kerala and Punjab recorded the least percentage of casual non-agricultural workers receiving wages below the norms.

Minimum Wages among Regular Workers

3.87 As we have emphasized in the earlier chapters, the regular workers were working in both the organised and unorganised sectors. We also showed how the regular workers in the organised sector did not get the benefits that should accrue to them in this sector. These workers constituted the unorganised workers in the organised sector. We now look at whether the regular workers in the unorganised sector received wages above the norm and also whether the unorganised workers (regular) in the organised sector were obtaining the minimum wages.

3.88 Regular workers in the unorganised sector received daily earnings (Rs.72 in rural and Rs.84 in urban areas) higher than the casual workers in rural and urban areas, women received slightly more than half the male wage earnings (Appendix A3.1, Appendix A3.2, Appendix A3.5 and Appendix A3.6). The regular workers without social security benefits or unorganised workers in the organised sector received the highest average daily wage earnings (Rs.113) in urban areas, but not so in rural areas (Rs.72), women regular workers received between half and two thirds of the male earnings.

3.89 As in the case of casual workers the percentage of workers who received wages below the norm varies depending on the use of the National Minimum Wage or the NCRL wage, differentiated by rural and urban prices. About half of the regular workers in the unorganised sector received below the National minimum wage norm. In the urban areas the situation was the same if we consider the NCRL norm, but the proportion below the minimum wage declines to about one-third in rural areas. This further emphasises the fact,

Fig. 3.4: Percentage of Casual Workers with Wages below National Minimum Wage of Rs. 66 across Industry Groups by Gender 2004-2005: Urban

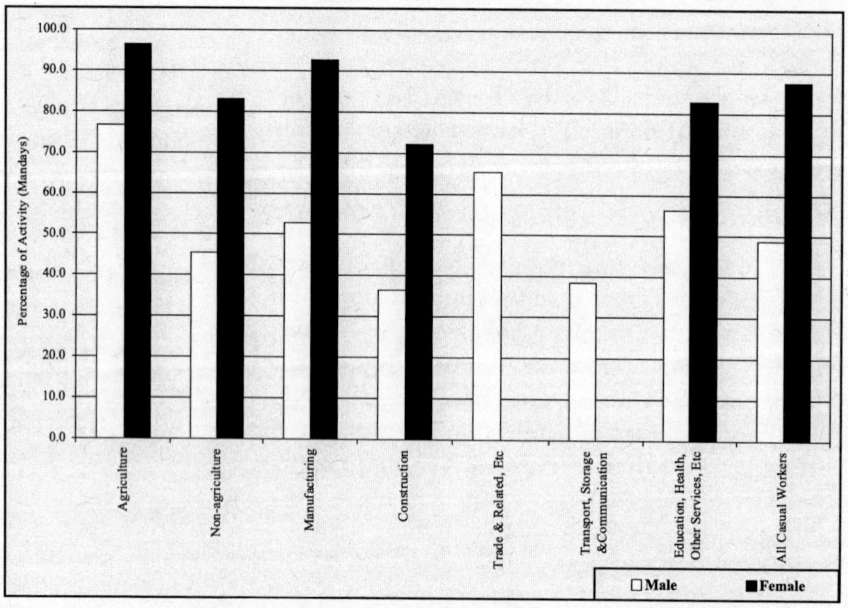

Source: ibid.

Fig. 3.5: Percentage of Rural Non-agricultural Casual Labour with Wages below Minimum Wage 2004 - 2005

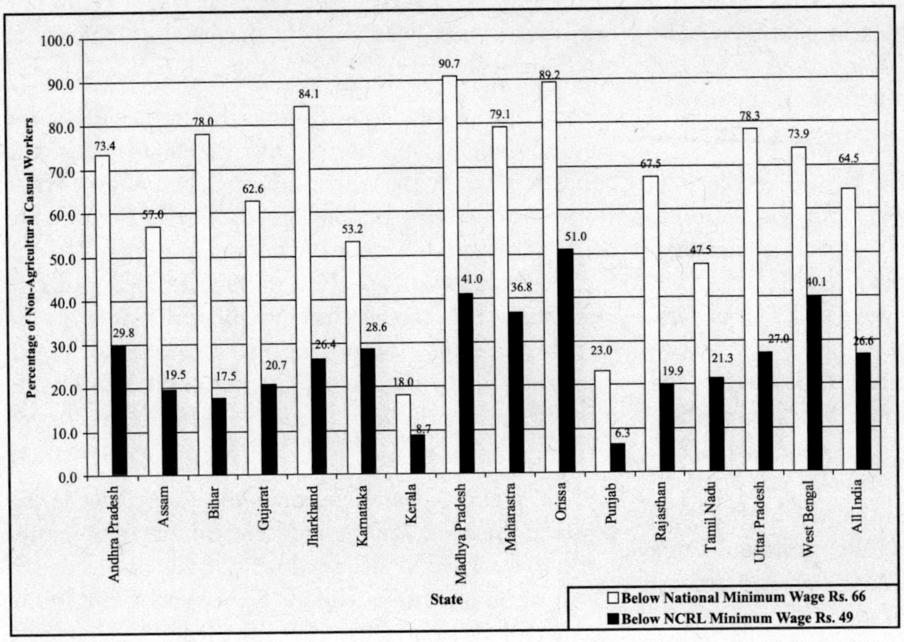

Source: ibid.

mainly in construction and manufacturing. Within the manufacturing sector textile industry is the largest employer of casual workers followed by other non-metallic mineral products and food products. Among the regular workers in the unorganised sector, while men are concentrated in construction, trade and transport and communication, women are overwhelmingly concentrated in other services, particularly in private households with employed persons. They also have a significant share in the construction and manufacturing sectors. Thus, the nature of occupations in which men and women tend to predominate are still varied and governed by gender role patterns.

that even the regular workers have poor working conditions, particularly in the unorganised sector or as unorganised workers.

3.90 The brief comparison of wages of individual workers with notional norm for minimum wages shows that the reach and effectiveness of the Minimum Wages Act is limited. The analysis also shows that vulnerable wage workers include the regular workers in the unorganised sector. Casual women workers were the worst off compared to men and to regular workers who were not particularly well off either.

Conclusion

3.91 The wage workers are concentrated in a few selected industrial categories and unlike the popular notion there is thus not much heterogeneity in terms of the nature of the industry in which they are employed. Among the casual workers, both men and women are employed

3.92 The physical conditions of work, occupational health, working hours and remunerations of wage workers in the unorganised sector were examined through case studies and found to be deplorable. The conditions

Fig. 3.6: Percentage of Urban Non-agricultural Casual Labour with Wages below Minimum Wage 2004 - 2005

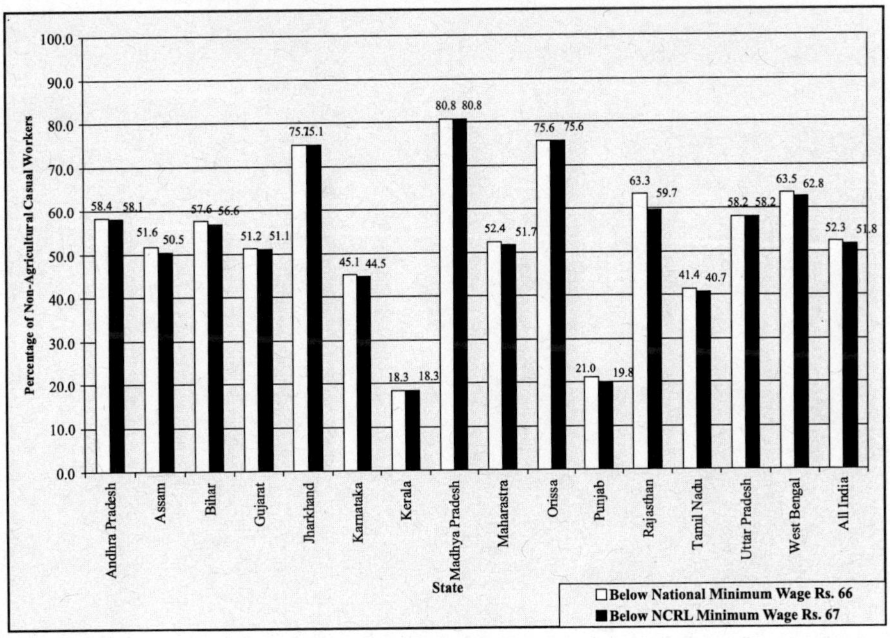

Source: ibid.

of work of the regular wage workers in the unorganised sector were only slightly better than that of the casual workers. Large majority of them have no written contracts and less than one-fifth was entitled to paid leave. The regular unorganised workers in the organised sector had better conditions, but a large proportion of them were also without written contracts. Only about a quarter of them were entitled to paid leave.

3.93 The Commission utilized both the National Minimum Wage (Rs. 66) and the "basic minimum wage" suggested by the National Commission on Rural Labour, to arrive at a notional minimum wage of Rs.49 in rural areas and Rs.67 in urban areas at 2004-05 prices using the Consumer Price India for Agricultural Labourers and the Consumer Price Index for Industrial Workers to inflate the wages in rural areas and urban areas respectively. The share of wage workers securing wages below the National Minimum Wage norm is significantly high across industries, clearly indicating that the minimum wage regulations are hardly being followed and applied in most industries. In fact, 85 per cent of all casual workers in rural areas and 57 per cent of them in urban areas get wages below the minimum wages. The difference in percentages of workers below the minimum wage norm in rural areas and urban areas is more marked for the non-agricultural workers, with urban workers being considerably worse-off. The casual agricultural workers in rural areas were worse off compared to non-agricultural workers. The share of the regular unorganised workers in the organised sector who received wages below the minimum wage was slightly better than the other categories of workers.

3.94 Given the overwhelming empirical evidence the Commission has no hesitation to conclude that, the conditions of work of the unorganised sector wage workers are nothing but deplorable. They are entitled to neither any paid leave nor the minimum wages. Besides, their concentration in a few industries is a probable indication of the non-availability of work opportunities elsewhere. Thus, in terms of not only one but several dimensions and criteria pertaining to conditions of work, the wage workers in the unorganised sector are a deprived lot.

3.95 Such a conclusion points to the need for laying down, at the least, a minimum standard for conditions of work, a national floor below which no trade or occupation based minimum wage should be set and a minimum package of social security. Given the federal character of the polity, these minimum standards should be applicable to the whole country backed by national legislation. Adding on to these minimum standards should then be left to individual states depending on their regional context and conditions.

4 Self-employed Workers in Non-agriculture

Introduction

4.1 We would like to highlight the fact that, from an employment point of view, Indian economy is dominated by what is called the 'self-employed'. There is some fuzziness in this concept since, as we shall see subsequently, it conceals more than it reveals. The latest figures (2004-05) suggest that this category accounts for the majority of the workforce (56.5 per cent), followed by casual workers (28.3 per cent) and regular workers (15.2 per cent). The share of the self-employed is much higher if we take the unorganised sector as a whole.[1] Of course, what is referred to as the self-employed in agriculture is nothing but various categories of farmers - marginal, small and big - so long as they derive their principal income from own cultivation and not wage labour. The self-employed in agriculture (which is mostly, if not always, synonymous with unorganised sector) has been estimated at about 166.2 million. In non-agriculture, which is the focus of this chapter, they are around 92.1 million as of 2004-05. Share of the self-employed is much higher among women than men in rural areas while in urban areas the share is more or less the same for men and women (Table 4.1).

4.2 The sub-categories within the self-employed are largely dictated by work status. Broadly there are three sub-categories. The largest is the 'own account workers' accounting for 46 per cent of the unorganised sector workers. They work on their own using their labour power and often stretches it to longer working hours to eke out a living leading to what Chayanov, a Russian economist, called 'self exploitation' when referring to the Russian peasantry of the nineteenth century. The second category is that of the 'unpaid family worker'. As the name suggests they do not get an independent remuneration though they contribute to the family income. They are also referred to as 'contributing family member'. The third refers to the 'employer' i.e. those who hire at least one wage worker but less than 10 total workers according to our definition of the unorganised sector. When a person is an own account worker or an employer with at least one hired worker, the economic unit also acquires the characteristic of an enterprise. What it essentially means is that the own account worker or the small employer, apart from using one's own labour, has also to deploy his organisational or entrepreneurial skills because he or she is forced to deal with the market while purchasing inputs and selling the output as well as organising production. Fig. 4.1 illustrates the linkages among workers, enterprises and the self-employed. The fuzziness, however, does not end here.

[1] There were wide state level variations. Self-employed formed about 85 per cent of the unorganised non-agricultural workforce in Bihar, close to 70 per cent in Orissa, Uttar Pradesh and West Bengal and less than 50 per cent in Kerala and Himachal Pradesh (Appendix A4.1).

Table 4.1: Percentage of the Self-employed Workers in Unorganised Non-agriculture 2004 - 2005

Employment Status	Rural			Urban			Total		
	Male	Female	Total	Male	Female	Total	Male	Female	Total
Own Account Worker	50.2	38.6	47.6	47.0	35.4	44.7	48.6	37.1	46.2
Employer	1.0	0.3	0.8	3.5	0.6	3.0	2.3	0.4	1.9
Unpaid Family Worker	9.1	37.7	15.4	11.1	26.1	14.0	10.1	32.3	14.7
Self Employed	60.3	76.5	63.9	61.6	62.0	61.7	61.0	69.8	62.8
All Workers	**100.0**	**100.0**	**100.0**	**100.0**	**100.0**	**100.0**	**100.0**	**100.0**	**100.0**

Source: NSS 61st Round 2004 - 2005, Employment-Unemployment Survey. Computed.

Fig. 4.1 Workers and Enterprises in the Unorganised Sector

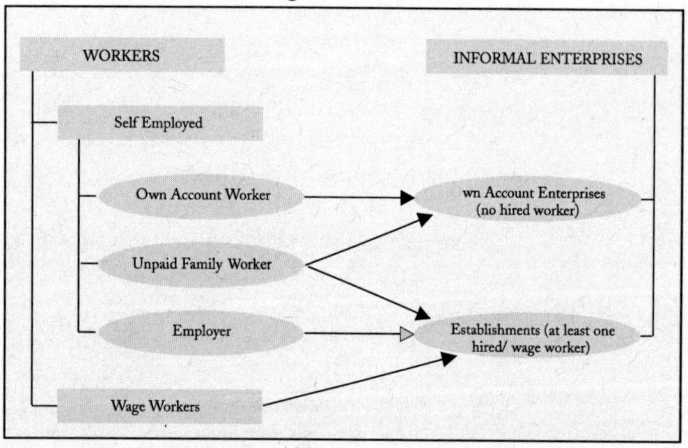

4.3 Another dimension of the fuzziness comes from the inclusion of homeworkers. All those who work out of their homes are also included in the self-employed. We have tried to separate them for special treatment since it is mostly the women workers who find themselves in this category. The use of the home as their place of work is dictated by several considerations including their responsibilities relating to care of the family members, community norms and related factors. They are, in essence, the disguised wage workers. Their employment is mostly under the system of 'putting-out'. The homeworkers are an even more difficult category when considering regulation or promotion of livelihood policies. This is because they are often invisible due to their location of work and have characteristics of both wage and self-employed workers. It therefore becomes difficult to decide at whose door the burden of compliance with basic norms of the conditions of work should be placed and to what extent promotional policies should include them. In such cases the role of the state in providing certain minimum conditions of work and address other promotional needs becomes greater. These issues are highlighted in this Chapter.

4.4 While the statistical classification has to be followed for purposes of highlighting the magnitude involved, the Commission realises that it is not best suited to a discussion of the conditions of work and livelihood promotion. As such, we confine ourselves only to a brief overview of the main economic characteristics of these tiny enterprises. Subsequently, we move on to deal with the conditions of work and livelihood issues of homeworkers and then to selected economic activities in which self-employment is predominant. These are food processing, handloom weaving, street vending and rickshaw pulling.

4.5 The Commission considers it important to also emphasize the fact that the category of self-employed, unlike that of casual workers, is not necessarily and uniformly poor. As we shall see later in this Chapter, there are those with some significant physical and/or human capital and also those with very little capital. Independent professionals such as doctors, architects, lawyers, accountants, small workshop owners, urban shop owners, etc. may be self-employed but with incomes that are several times higher than a street vendor, rickshaw puller or a handloom weaver. Our focus and concern here is on the latter groups, who lack the critical minimum by way of either physical or human capital or both. It would be useful to have an illustrative list, which is given in Table 4.2.

Table 4.2: Two Types of Self-employed by Income

Low income self-employed who are closer to or marginally above casual workers	High income self-employed who are closer to or higher than regular workers
1. Handloom weavers (mostly women).	1. Independent professionals (such as doctors, lawyers, artists and accountants).
2. Chikan workers (mostly women).	2. Shop owners in urban areas.
3. Street vendors.	3. Rice mill owners.
4. Food processors.	4. Workshop owners.
5. Rickshaw pullers.	5. Commission agents.
6. Rag pickers.	6. Brokers of real estate, housing, etc.
7. Beedi rollers (mostly homeworkers).	7. Owners of small hotels and restaurants.
8. Agarbatti makers (mostly women).	
9. Potters.	
10. Bamboo product makers.	

Two Types of Enterprises

4.6 The Commission notes that the constraints faced by informal enterprises are often co-related with their size in terms of employment and assets. In order to capture these differences in sizes we have examined the characteristics and constraints of own account enterprises (OAE) i.e., without hired workers, separately from the establishments with hired workers[2].

4.7 Majority, of the informal enterprises, 87 per cent, are OAEs (Table 4.3), more so in the rural areas, where they account for nearly 94 per cent. Among the rest, establishments with hired workers, about 11 per cent of total enterprises have 2-5 total workers and less than 2 per cent have 6-9 total workers (Table 4.3)[3].

4.8 The total workers in them are also concentrated in the OAEs, 73 per cent in all areas[4] and 87 per cent in rural areas. They include both owner operators and family labour. In fact 33 per cent of all workers work in single owner operated units. Of the rest 26 per cent of workers, about 19 per cent are in establishments with at least one hired worker and 2-5 total workers. About 7 per cent is in establishments with at least one hired worker and with 6-9 workers. The workers in these latter establishments include three kinds: employers, family labour and hired workers.

4.9 The concentration of workers in own account enterprises is a little lower in urban areas, 58 per cent. Nearly 30 per cent of the workers are in establishments with 2-5 workers and 11 per cent are in establishments with 6-9 workers. This reflects the concentration of larger units in the urban areas. In fact the contrast with rural areas is very sharp.

Table 4.3: Percentage of Enterprises and Total Workers by Enterprise Size 1999-2000

Enterprise Type	Enterprises			Worker		
	Rural	Urban	Total	Rural	Urban	Total
OAE: Owner Operator	61.8	51.9	57.5	40.1	27.2	33.8
All OAE	94.2	78.4	87.4	87.5	58.7	73.4
Establishments 2-5 workers	5.2	18.4	10.9	9.5	29.8	19.4
Establishments 6-9 workers	0.7	3.1	1.7	3.0	11.6	7.2
Establishments	5.8	21.6	12.6	12.5	41.3	26.6
Total	**100.0**	**100.0**	**100.0**	**100.0**	**100.0**	**100.0**

Note: OAEs are enterprises with no hired workers; Establishments are enterprises with hired workers.
Source: NSS 55th Round 1999-2000, Informal Sector Enterprises. Computed.

Own Account Enterprises constitute about 87 per cent of informal enterprises with 73 per cent of all workers engaged in them.

2 The data used in this analysis are from the Survey of Informal Enterprises collected by the NSS 55th Round, Schedule 2.0 in 1999-2000.
3 There is not much variation across the states in the size of informal enterprises. Kerala has the lowest share of OAE (Appendix A4.2).
4 The number of workers by size of the enterprises across the states varied from 57 per cent in OAE in Kerala to 91 per cent in Orissa (Appendix A4.3).

4.10 The implication of this distribution is that conditions of work in the majority of self-employed/ informal enterprises are dependent on the owner operator himself. Similarly, the predominance of small sized enterprises implies that the burden of assuring good conditions of work would mainly fall on small enterprises. Here size is a manifestation, especially in such activities as mentioned in the first column of Table 4.2, of the poor economic condition of the so called employer or entrepreneur. The challenge is to transform such tiny enterprises into viable units with greater volume of business to ensure the required minimum conditions of work. Alternatively, and perhaps more realistically, the challenge is to bring them together under a collective umbrella like associations/cooperatives/self-help groups of enterprises to promote business on the one hand and provide some minimum conditions of work on the other. Such instances are often found in certain trades or industries such as handloom weavers, food processors, etc.

Own Account Enterprises

4.11 Majority of the self-employed workers were in own account enterprises as owner operators or as family labour. Therefore in order to visualise any programme for the promotion of their livelihoods, we must understand the characteristics of these own account enterprises. The productive capacity of the enterprises can be used to judge the scale of the operation of the informal enterprises. It would also determine to what extent the small enterprises can provide good working conditions to its own family and hired workers and also indicate to what extent the state has to help bear part of this responsibility. The scale of operation and productive capacity of the OAEs and establishments reveal themselves in the value of assets and gross value addition of the enterprises.

4.12 The Commission is quite aware of the limitation of this approach. What the official surveys bring out are the results arising out of the methodologies usually applied to formal enterprises and related economic units with clear cut distinction between wages and profits on the one hand and labour inputs in terms of regulated mandays and working hours on the other. We well recognise the absence of such clear cut distinctions in the case of informal enterprises. The lengthened working days as well as increased number of working days in a year are common practices in order to generate income that is often just sufficient to meet the subsistence requirements of the family. Correspondingly, there is hardly any distinction between wages and profits since the objective is to maximise income net of purchased inputs. This is what is reflected in the figures of gross value added. However, given the current data base and system of data collection, there is hardly a substitute to get a rough idea of the economics of these tiny enterprises, essential for policy purposes. Available qualitative information on problems relating to livelihood issues may therefore, in our view, need to be taken as complementary to the quantitative analysis.

Value of Assets

4.13 The informal enterprises operate with both their own assets and by hiring fixed assets. The own account enterprises operate with relatively low average value of fixed assets, about Rs.39 thousand per enterprise. This

Fig. 4.2: Own Account Enterprises: Fixed Asset per Enterprise and Gross Value Added Per Worker (Rs.) 1999-2000

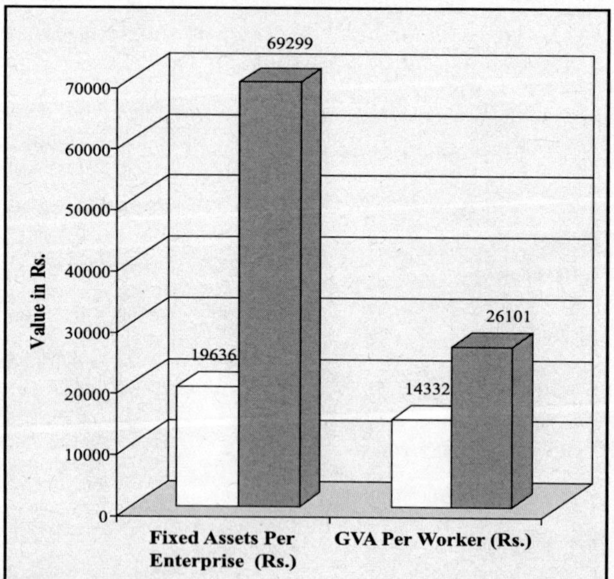

Source: NSS 55th Round 1999-2000, Informal Sector Enterprises. Computed.

Investment in terms of value of fixed assets is low in OAEs. Rural OAEs have even lower investment levels than urban OAEs.

indicates the small scale of operation and the consequent lower returns they are likely to get from such investment. The own account enterprises in the urban areas were marginally larger in terms of the size of investment with an average value of fixed assets of nearly Rs.70 thousand. Again the contrast with those in rural areas is striking with the average value of fixed assets being only Rs.20 thousand per enterprise (Fig. 4.2).

4.14 The OAEs mainly use their own fixed assets with 85 per cent and 60 per cent of them reporting not using any hired assets in rural and urban areas respectively. The urban enterprises have higher value of assets and when these enterprises do hire assets the value of hired assets is almost double the value of their own assets. The urban enterprises have a bigger scale of operation and also get a higher return on their investments, as we shall see below.

4.15 Besides the small average size of fixed assets, nearly 37 per cent of the OAEs were found to have assets of less than Rs.5 thousand (Fig. 4.3), 43 per cent of them rural and 27 per cent of them urban. Barely 8 per cent of all OAEs and about 17 per cent of the urban OAEs, had investment of more than rupees one lakh. Overall, a large percentage of enterprises were mainly engaged in some form of survival operations rather than carrying on with a business activity in the proper sense of the term. As mentioned earlier, these are strategies to meet household expenses on a continuing basis rather than to generate profits based on returns to investment and costing of one's own (as well as family's) labour.

Gross Value Addition

4.16 The low scale of operation of these enterprises can be judged from their low value additions. The average annual gross value added per worker[5] in OAEs is a minimal Rs.19 thousand per annum or Rs. 1583 per month. In urban areas the gross value addition is higher at Rs.26100 per annum or Rs.2175 per month, while it is only about Rs.14 thousand per annum in rural areas or Rs. 1167 per month (Fig. 4.2). At the prevailing price level in the year 2000, a rural family required Rs.327.56 per capita per month to cross the officially determined poverty line. In urban areas it was Rs. 454.11 per capita per month (Box 4.1).

Fig. 4.3: Distribution of Value of Fixed Assets Rs. per Enterprise in Own Account Enterprises, 1999-2000

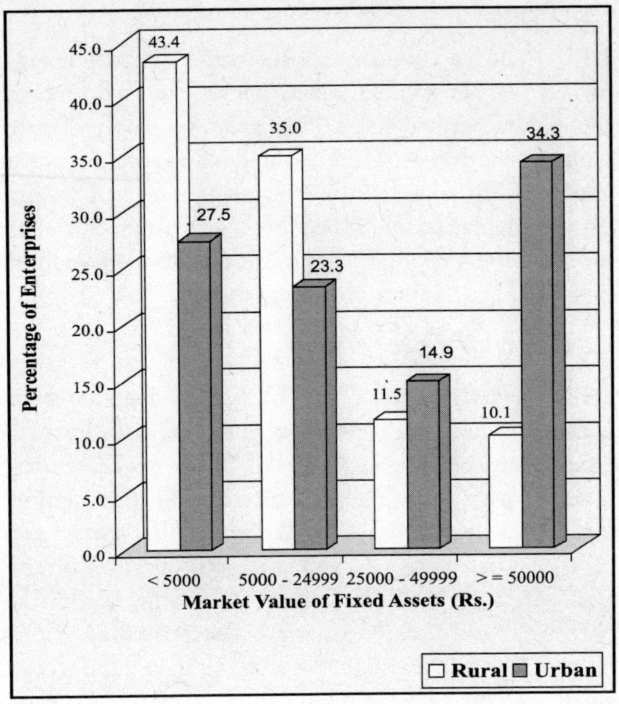

Source: ibid.

Box 4.1: Value Addition per Worker of OAEs less than Notional Minimum Incomes

Value added per worker in the OAEs can be considered as equivalent to income of the worker since he does not hire workers and the scale of operation is such that only minimal capital is used. We consider a notional daily minimum wage using the floor level wage as on 01.12.1999 of Rs. 45 (MOLE, 2007), multiplied by 159 working days in the year and 1.89 earnings units per family to arrive at annual notional floor level minimum annual income of Rs. 13523 in 1999-2000 (MOLE, 2003). This is the absolute notional minimum income required by a worker to sustain livelihoods. The percentage of OAE within the unorganised non-agriculture having gross value added per worker below this notional minimum income in rural areas is a staggering 57 per cent. The percentage of OAEs in urban areas with below the notional minimum income is almost one-third (30 per cent). Thus, a very large proportion of the own account enterprises do not have sustainable livelihoods, particularly in the rural areas.

Nearly 37 per cent of OAEs have average value of fixed assets less than Rs. 5000. Rural OAEs are more likely to be smaller than the urban oaes.

5 Two part-time workers considered as one worker

Gross value added per worker is on average Rs.19000 per annum in all OAEs, and only Rs.14000 in rural OAEs. Urban OAEs have higher value addition at Rs.26000 per annum.

4.17 Own account enterprises (with no hired workers) earned very low value added per worker. The larger enterprises, particularly in urban areas, were only slightly more productive. The family labour based enterprises are also likely to be self-exploiting their own and family labour. These enterprises therefore require some assistance from the state or other institutions for the promotion of their livelihoods through various means.

Location of Enterprises

4.18 Nearly 40 per cent of the OAEs operated from within the household premises, even more so in rural areas, 46 per cent (see Appendix A4.4). The manufacturing activities were most likely to be carried out from within the household premises, 76 per cent in rural and 63 per cent in urban areas. Besides a large proportion of the OAEs in trade, hotels in rural areas and other services in both rural and urban areas were also carried out from homes. This implied that the size of the enterprise was small and obviously the returns from them would also be low. More than 50 per cent of own account trade and hotels were carried out in urban areas from fixed and permanent structures or from "designated business places". Such units were likely to be more productive. About 14 per cent of the hotels were run from fixed but temporary structures, which could be "Dhabbas" or tea stalls as well.

Constraints Faced by Own Account Enterprises

Growth Status of Enterprises

4.19 The OAEs were asked about their perception of the status of their enterprises in terms of growth and the nature of major problems faced by them. Nearly 64 per cent of them responded that their units were stagnating, while only about 18 per cent said that the units were expanding and another 10 per cent felt that their units were contracting. In spite of the difference we noted earlier among rural and urban units in terms of value of assets and value additions there was not much difference in their perception about growth by location or by the industry group.

Registration of OAE

4.20 The characteristic of the informal enterprises is the lack of registration under the Factories Act and the lack of incorporation. In true nature, majority of the OAEs were not registered with any agency, particularly in rural areas. However, about 11 per cent of the enterprises in urban areas were registered with the local bodies and about 5 per cent under the Shops and Establishments Act (Table 4.4). This is perhaps necessary for enterprises with a certain size to be able to operate legally.

Table 4.4: Percentage of OAEs by Type of Registration Agency 1999-2000

Registration Agency	Rural	Urban	Total
No Registration	90.4	76.3	84.9
License Issued by Municipal Corporation/Panchayat/Local Body	5.6	11.5	7.9
Partnership Act	0.1	0.1	0.1
Shops and Establishments Act	0.6	5.6	2.6
Government Boards/ Commissioners	0.5	1.0	0.7
Road Transport/ Motor Vehicle Act	1.3	3.1	2.0
Others	1.5	2.2	1.8
Total	**100.0**	**100.0**	**100.0**

Source: Same as in Table 4.3.

Problem Faced by Enterprises

4.21 The major problem reported was the limited access to credit followed by marketing and infrastructural constraints. Competition from large units was also an important problem faced by these tiny enterprises (see Box 4.2). Given the fact that a large proportion of these units were not registered, their ability to access credit remained rather limited.

Self-employed in Establishments with Hired Workers

4.22 What is officially classified as Own Account Enterprises, owner operated sometimes with the help of unpaid family labour, dominate the group of self-employed enterprises. Establishments with hired workers

Nearly 40 per cent of OAEs operated from household premises, 12 per cent without a fixed structure and 7 per cent were mobile. Only 30 per cent of OAEs operate from fixed premises with permanent structure.

BOX 4.2: Problems Faced by Own Account Enterprises

Shortage of credit was the most serious problem faced by the OAEs. Lack of marketing and infrastructural facilities and competition from large units were the other major problems reported. However, nearly 30 per cent of the OAE operators felt they did not face any serious problem.

Shortage of credit was noted by the majority of OAEs as the most serious problem and this was true for urban and rural areas (nearly 38 per cent of OAEs). While OAEs in all industry groups felt credit was a major issue, it was most commonly noted by trade and hotels and restaurants in rural and urban areas.

Three other serious problems identified were lack of marketing and infrastructure facilities, local problems and competition from larger units. Lack of marketing and infrastructural facilities and other local problems were considered a greater problem in rural areas. Competition from larger units was noted as an issue in double the OAEs in urban compared to rural areas. Such competition was particularly felt by OAEs in manufacturing, construction and trade.

Source: Based on NSS unit level data, Informal Sector Enterprises, 1999-2000.

or the employer category consisted of only 13 per cent of the enterprises and 26 per cent of the workers in the informal enterprises (Table 4.3). There is however, a vast difference in the economic condition of these two types of enterprises in the sense that those with hired workers had some physical capital worth the name and correspondingly a much higher level of output per worker that was more than twice that in the own account enterprises or worker category.

Value of Assets

4.23 The average value of fixed assets in the establishments with hired workers is nearly Rs.3 lakhs, which is well above the average investment in OAEs of Rs.39000 (Table 4.5). Clearly the scale of operation of establishments with hired workers is quite different. In fact, the value of average fixed assets in the larger establishments with 6-9 workers is even higher at more than Rs.6 lakhs. Another striking difference between the OAEs and these establishments is the large average

Table 4.5: Fixed Assets per Enterprise (Rs.) in Establishments by Employment Size 1999-2000

Employment Size	Rural	Urban	Total
2-5 Workers	118272	286658	241663
6-9 Workers	216603	745336	632165
Establishments	129334	353209	295013

Source: As in Table 4.3.

Fig. 4.4: Percentage of Value of Fixed Assets per Enterprise (Rs.) in Establishments with Hired Workers, 1999-2000

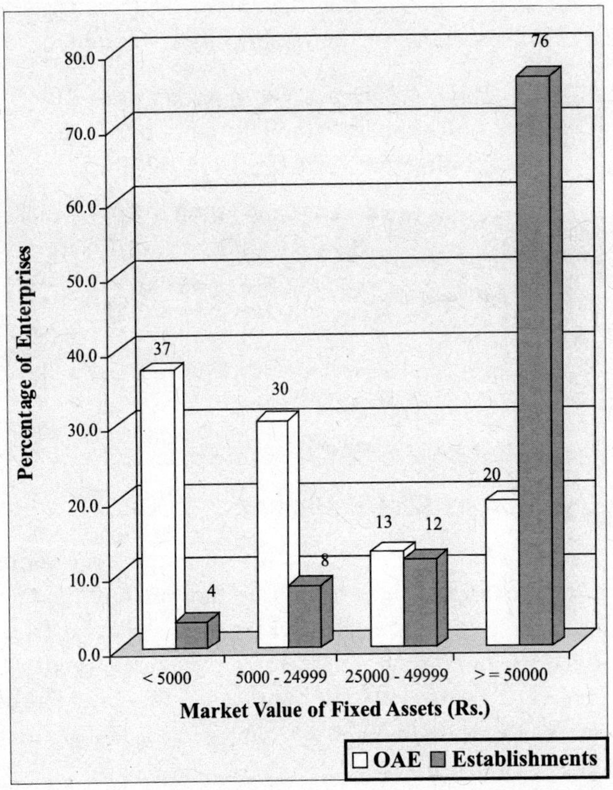

Source: ibid.

Nearly 64 per cent of OAEs reported they were stagnant and less than 20 per cent reported expansion.

value of fixed assets that is hired in. Obviously the returns to investment are higher in these larger units warranting the use of higher value of hired assets as well.

4.24 Differences in the scale of operation with the OAEs are also observed in the distribution of enterprises with fixed assets of less than Rs.5000 (Fig. 4.4). While nearly 37 per cent of the OAEs were in this category only less than 4 per cent were so in the establishment with hired workers. At the other extreme, nearly 43 per cent of the establishments had value of assets of more than Rs. One lakh compared to only 8 per cent of the OAEs.

Gross Value Addition

4.25 Gross value addition in the establishments with hired workers at Rs.39000 is nearly double that of the OAEs (Table 4.6 and Fig. 4.5). Establishments in the urban areas have distinctly higher value addition, just as we had observed for the OAEs. The differences in the value of fixed assets and value addition are indicative of the fact that the nature of products itself would be varying in the establishments compared to the OAEs and in urban compared to rural areas.

Table 4.6: Gross Value Added per Worker in Establishments by Employment Size (Rs.) 1999-2000

Employment Size	Rural	Urban	Total
2-5 Workers	27,414	38,707	35,906
6-9 Workers	22,803	54,253	47,584
All Establishments	26,303	43,061	39,068

Note: Two part time workers are treated as one full time worker.
Source: Same as in Table 4.3.

Location of Establishments

4.26 Larger size of the operation and the more formal nature of the business are indicative of the fact that three-fourth of these enterprises operated from fixed premises with a permanent structure. About 46 per cent of the OAEs operated from household premises, while only 14 per cent of the establishment did so (Table 4.7).

Fig. 4.5: Fixed Assets and Gross Value Added per Enterprises in OAE and Establishments (Rs.) 1999-2000

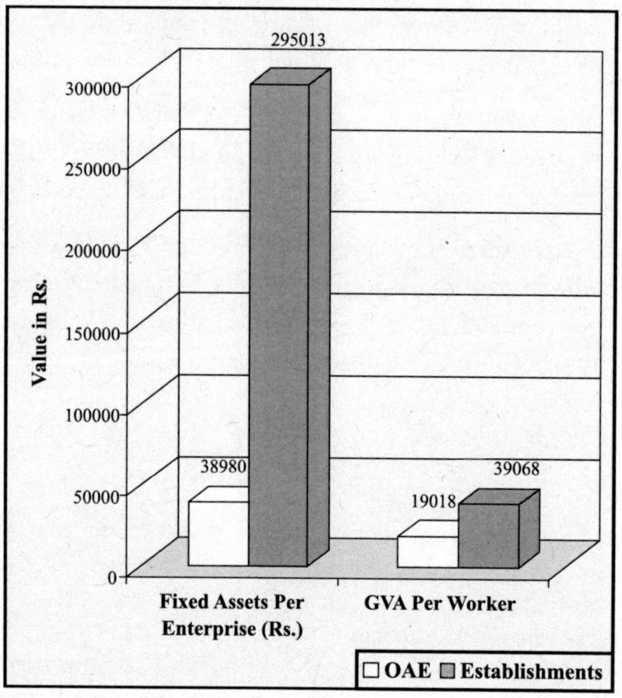

Source: ibid.

Table 4.7: Percentage Distribution of Establishments by Location of Enterprise 1999-2000

Location	Rural	Urban	Total
Within Household Premises	22.8	10.8	13.9
With Fixed Premises & Permanent Structure	58.2	83.0	76.5
With Fixed Premises & Temporary Structure	2.8	1.6	1.9
With Fixed Premises but Without Structure	2.5	0.7	1.2
Mobile Market	4.1	0.7	1.6
Without Fixed Premises	4.0	0.8	1.6
Construction Site	5.5	2.4	3.2
Total	100.0	100.0	100.0

Source: Same as in Table 4.3.

Establishments with hired workers had, on average, much higher investment per enterprise than the OAEs. Returns to investment were perhaps higher warranting higher value of hired fixed assets.

While 37 per cent of the OAEs had value of assets less than Rs. 5000, only 4 per cent of establishments with hired workers had such low investment. Nearly 73 per cent of the larger enterprises had value of assets more than Rs. One lakh, compared to only 8 per cent of OAEs.

Constraints Faced by Establishments

Growth Status of Establishments

4.27 The responses of the entrepreneurs regarding the growth status of their enterprises were, however, not very encouraging. Nearly 50 per cent of them reported that they were stagnating. This was only slightly smaller than the 64 per cent of the OAEs that reported that they were stagnating. About, 30 per cent said that they were expanding. This was larger than the 18 per cent of the OAEs that reported the same response. This reflects the heterogeneity even among the establishments with hired workers, besides their clear differentiation with the OAEs.

Registration Status

4.28 Unlike the OAEs almost 90 per cent of which were not registered under any agency, more than half of the establishments with hired workers were registered with some agency.[6] In urban areas, 30 per cent were registered with the local bodies and another 16 per cent were registered under the Shops and Establishments Act (Table 4.8). This difference may be because of the size of the establishments were greater and this required some legal registration for them to operate.

Table 4.8: Percentage of Self-employed Establishments by Type of Registration Agency 1999-2000

Registration Agency	Rural	Urban	Total
No Registration	57.8	43.1	46.9
License Issued by Municipal Corporation/Panchayat/Local Body	20.6	29.1	26.9
Partnership Act	0.4	0.5	0.5
Provident Fund Act	0.0	0.1	0.1
Shops and Establishments Act	2.2	16.3	12.7
Government Boards/ Commissioners	3.7	4.4	4.2
Road Transport/ Motor Vehicle Act	9.4	1.7	3.7
Hotels and Restaurants Act	0.2	0.3	0.3
Others	5.6	4.5	4.8
Total	**100.0**	**100.0**	**100.0**

Source: Same as in Table 4.3.

4.29 As in the case of the OAEs the problem of shortage of capital was faced by the establishments as well (Box 4.3). This may be compounded by the lack of registration which may impede their capacity to obtain credit from institutional sources.

Homeworkers as a Special Category

4.30 In our classification, the self-employed workers are classified into independent self-employed and homeworkers or dependent sub-contract workers operating from home. The homeworkers, also called industrial outworkers, are identified in the ILO Convention No. 177 as discussed in Chapter 1.

4.31 While the self-employed organise all facets of their production or service activity, the homeworker manufactures products based on the specifications of the parent enterprise or contractor, which also often supplies the raw material. Under the putting-out system, the homeworkers often have to purchase, repair, and maintain their own tools or machines, bear the costs of some inputs (e.g., garment workers often have to buy their own thread), transportation to and from the contractor or firm, and infrastructure (space, utilities, etc.). Manufacturing or retail companies typically "put-out" labour-intensive work that does not require heavy machinery. Homeworkers, like the self-employed, are not directly supervised, but like the wage workers they typically do not market final products, or negotiate prices.

4.32 Of the 69 million self-employed non-agricultural workers in the unorganised sector in 1999-2000 about 12 per cent are homeworkers[7]. The percentage of homeworkers is much higher among women. Out of nearly 16 million self-employed non-

Half of the large enterprises with hired workers were stagnant while 30 per cent were expanding.

6 There was variation in registration status across the states by size of the enterprise. Enterprises in Kerala and Gujarat were most likely to be registered (Appendix 4.5)

7 There was considerable variation across the states in percentage of homeworkers among the self-employed, ranging from 6 per cent in Gujarat to nearly 24 per cent in Tamil Nadu and 22 per cent in West Bengal (Appendix A4.6).

Box 4.3: Problems Faced by Establishments with Hired Workers

While the scale of operation of the establishments with hired workers was much greater than OAEs the reported problems faced by them were similar. Shortage of capital was the major problem faced by both the large and small informal enterprises. Competition from larger units was the second most prominent reported problem faced by the enterprises with hired workers, while this was only one of the problems faced by the OAEs. Where as lack of infrastructural facilities was noted by both small and large enterprise as a problem, the large establishment also noted power related problems as a major issue of concern. More than a quarter of establishments with hired workers also reported that they did not face any specific problem.

Source: Based on NSS unit level data, Informal Sector Enterprises, 1999-2000.

Table 4.9: Number (in Million) and Percentage of Self-Employed and Homeworkers in Non-agricultural Unorganised and Manufacturing Sectors 1999-2000

Status	Male	Female	Total
		All Workers	
Self Employed: Independent	49.5 (93.5)	11.2 (69.9)	60.7 (88.1)
Homeworkers	3.4 (6.5)	4. 8 (30.1)	8.2 (11.9)
All Self-employed	52.9 (100.0)	16.0 (100.0)	68.9 (100.0)
		Manufacturing Sector	
Self-employed: Independent	10.1 (79.9)	4.6 (50.8)	14.6 (67.7)
Homeworkers	2.5 (20.1)	4.4 (49.2)	7.0 (32.3)
All Self-employed	12.6 (100.0)	9.0 (100.0)	21.6 (100.0)

Note: Figures in brackets denote percentage.
Source: NSS 55th Round 1999-2000, Employment and Unemployment. Computed.

agricultural women about 30 per cent are homeworkers (Table 4.9).

4.33 Homeworking in the manufacturing sector is what can be clearly identified as a system of production often within a global or domestic value chain. Among the nearly 22 million manufacturing sector workers about 32 per cent are homeworkers, while among the 9 million women manufacturing workers, nearly 50 per cent are homeworkers (Table 4.9). The pie charts (Fig. 4.6) clearly show the predominance of homework among women in both rural and urban areas in the manufacturing sector. In urban areas more than half the women manufacturing workers are homeworkers.

Fig. 4.6: Categories of Self-employed Workers in Non-agricultural Unorganised Sector (million) 1999-2000

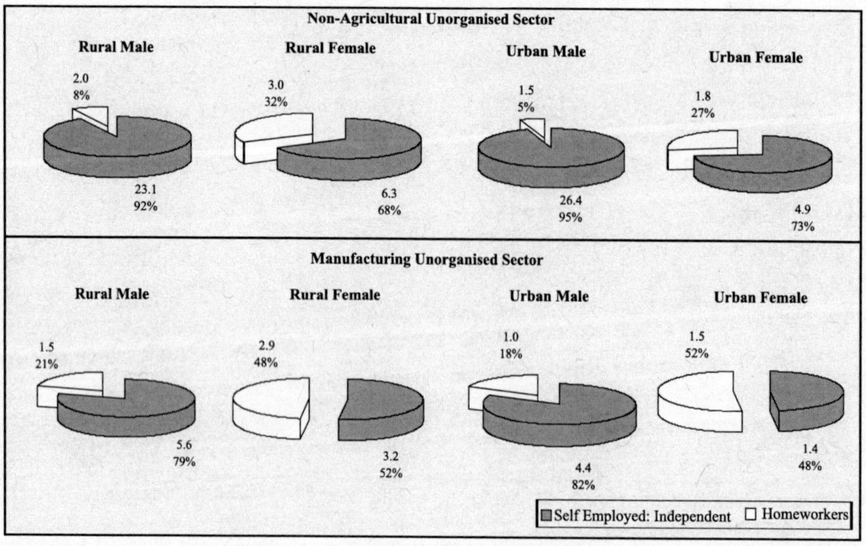

Source: NSS 55th Round 1999-2000, Employment and Unemployment. Computed.

Forms of Homeworking

4.34 Employment status of the self-employed workers and the homeworkers can be considered to be along a continuum of dependence, from being completely independent to being fully dependent on the contractor/middleman for design, raw material and equipment and being unable to negotiate the price of the product. Within this continuum of dependence, the literature on industrial subcontracting distinguishes between two types of 'business arrangements', one that contracts out production without providing raw materials and the other that provides raw materials etc. (Watanabe 1983). The first is called 'horizontal subcontracting'. This implies a subcontracting relationship exist, but with more independent production relationships, so that the status of the homeworker is closer to an independent self-employed worker. The second is called 'vertical subcontracting', which tends to create more of a dependent relationship and where except for lack of supervision the status is closer to a wage worker. The predominant mode of homeworking among the manufacturing sector self-employed workers is that of vertical sub-contracting or the most dependent relationship, accounting for about 70 per cent of the total (68 per cent for men and 71 per cent for women).

Conditions of Work of Self-employed Workers

4.35 Certain industry groups were identified as having a large proportion of unorganised workers (Chapter 2). Unorganised sector workers in self-employed non-agriculture are concentrated in manufacturing and trade (Fig. 4.7). The gender difference is striking. While women self-employed workers are concentrated overwhelmingly in manufacturing (60 per cent), men are predominantly in trade (42 per cent). The predominance of manufacturing activities among women is partly due to their engaging in homework in a putting -out system as we shall see later in this chapter. This also accounts for almost half of the women unpaid family workers in the manufacturing sector.

4.36 Own account workers constituted the largest segment of the self-employed. The manufacturing sectors where they were concentrated were food processing, tobacco products, textiles, wearing apparel and non-metallic mineral products (65 per cent) (Fig. 4.7). Large proportions of these workers, particularly women, were engaged as homeworkers in sub-contracting chains. This is clearly visible in the manufacture of tobacco products, which is largely done by homeworkers. The women own account workers, were concentrated in manufacture of tobacco products, mainly beedi-rolling, textile products and wearing apparel. Large parts of all these activities are likely to be in homework.

Fig. 4.7: Percentage of Unorganised Non-agricultural Workers across Industry Groups 2004-05

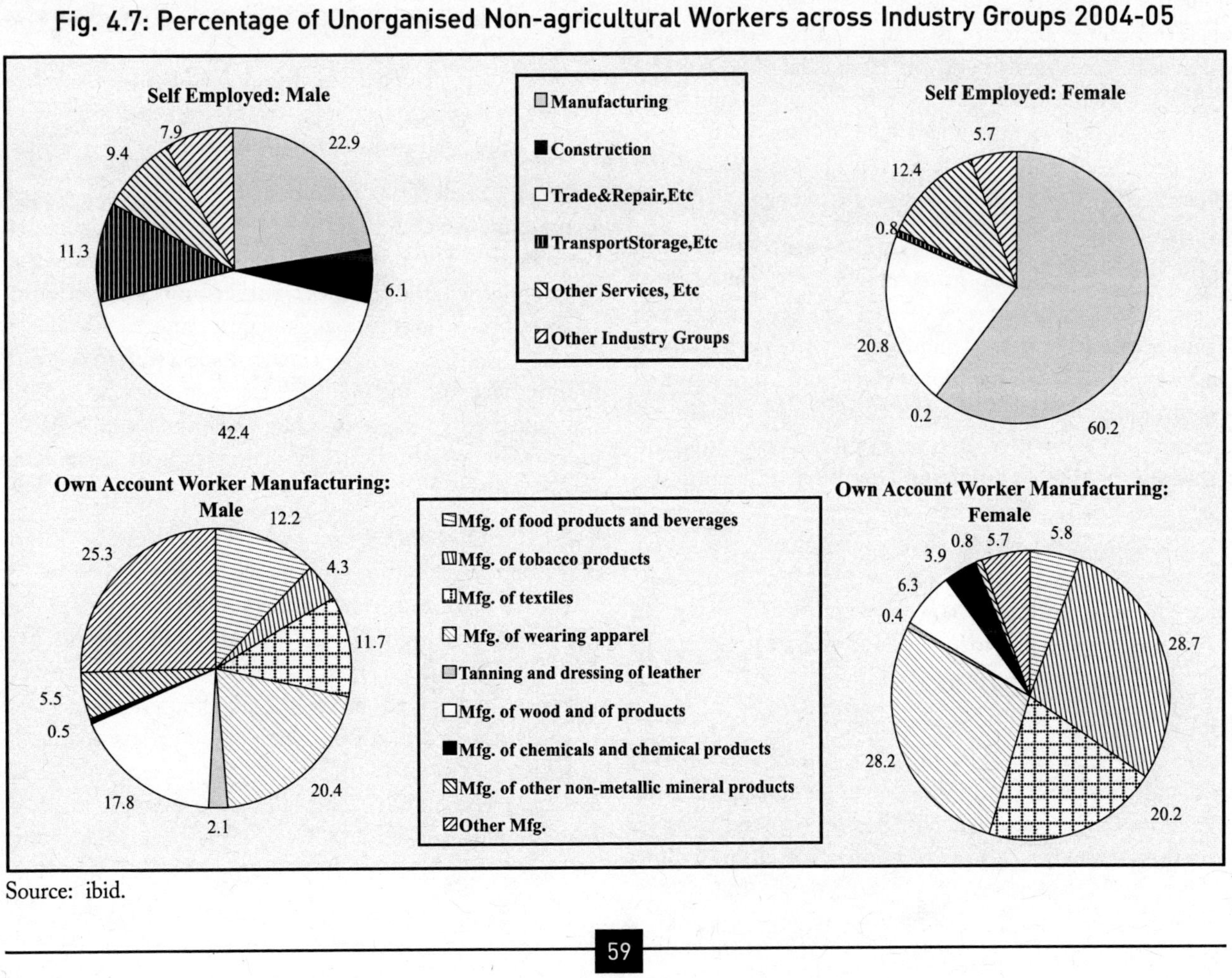

Source: ibid.

4.37 In this section we provide a brief profile of the self-employed workers in these industry groups based on the case studies to highlight their conditions of work and identify their needs. While most of these identified sectors have mainly independent self-employed workers, beedi-rolling within the tobacco industry and wearing apparel have a larger proportion of homeworkers and are profiled in the next section.

Textile Industry: Case of Handloom Sector

4.38 Handloom weaving of cloth, an occupation of ancient vintage, continued to be the main source of livelihood of a large number of families in the country - a little over 2.5 million by a census conducted in 1995-96. This occupation is the lowest in the hierarchy of technologies of textile manufacturing. Broadly, the factory system of production at the top has also been on the decline. The intermediate technology of power looms, organised in small factories and workshops, has been on the expansion taking advantage of both low cost of production as well as electromechanical technology. While the handloom sector is also differentiated by low productivity looms and somewhat better ones and the consequent differentiation in quality of production, the socio-economic correlate is that it is the occupation of an artisan community who are by and large poor. The existence of multistructural mode of production combined with the livelihood imperatives of large numbers of people has presented this industry as a classic case of the dilemmas involved in technological change.

4.39 Given the employment and livelihood dimensions, state intervention has been a major source of support to the sustenance of this industry and of the families involved in it. A number of items were reserved for production in the handloom sector and a development commissioner for handlooms coordinates the central government's initiatives in supporting and promoting this sector. A National Handloom Development Centre was also established. Some tax concessions were extended. At the state level, several state governments gave active support to the formation of weavers' cooperatives, marketing support systems such as para-statal marketing organisations and provided relief and welfare programmes for the handloom workers.

4.40 The initiation of economic reforms gave way to a new paradigmatic shift in policy. State support was gradually reduced, the number of items reserved for the handloom sector was also curtailed and special schemes for the production and procurement of cheaper cloth under Janata Cloth Scheme was dissolved in 1996. The tax concessions enjoyed by the handloom sector were also withdrawn. With the focus on maximising exports, cotton and yarn found their place in exports leading to a higher cost of inputs for the handloom sector. All these 'level playing fields' worked to bring down the already meagre standard of living of the workers and their families that perhaps added momentum to the decline of the industry.

4.41 The handloom industry can be found all over the country but its concentration is mainly along the eastern part of the country - from Tamil Nadu in the south to Assam in the north-east. The policy shift, first in 1985 and then in a stronger way in 1996, led to a crisis of survival of the handloom workers and their families. In Tamil Nadu and Andhra Pradesh it led to suicides, starvation leading to public provision of emergency food relief, unemployment and unrest. The dissolution of the Janata Cloth Scheme led to the stoppage of procurement of the produce from the primary cooperative production units by the apex cooperative societies. For example in Dubakka, a well-known and once prosperous handloom centre in Andhra Pradesh, the number of looms declined to 700 in April 2001 from an earlier high of 1500. While the fragmented and unorganised handloom workers here sought refuge in suicides, the better organised handloom workers in many parts of Tamil Nadu took to public protest by organising hunger marches to the capital city, Chennai, as well as in several localities.

4.42 The decline of the handloom industry has been an ongoing one and the advent of powerlooms accelerated the process. The problem for handloom workers is that there is no demand for these workers in the powerlooms sector since no traditional skills are required. While it would be desirable to have a technological shift to enhance productivity and income, the losers are not necessarily the gainers. This poses a huge dilemma and calls for policies for rehabilitation and provision of sustainable livelihood mechanisms.

4.43 As recent statistics on workers and families dependent on handloom weaving are hard to come by, the Government of India has conducted two Censuses of the Handloom Industry, in 1987-88 and in 1995-96. The 1995-96 Census recorded 34.7 lakh handloom weavers in the country and a total of 25.2 lakh households engaged in the industry. However, there was actually a decline in employment in the handloom sector since the 1987-88 Census recorded 43.7 lakh handloom weavers and 30.6 lakh weaver households. Of the 34.7 lakh handloom weavers in the country in 1995-96, 16.5 lakh were full-time weavers. Majority of them, about 9.9 lakh worked independently while 2.4 lakh weavers worked under cooperative societies and 2.9 lakh under master weavers. Over and above this there were 17.3 lakh persons engaged in preparatory works of which 5.4 lakh worked on a fulltime basis (NCAER 2007).

4.44 A comparison between the two Censuses however showed another more worrisome feature, a decline in the productivity per loom and per worker. This together with the decline in the number of weavers and looms resulted in an overall decline in the production of fabric in the handlooms sector over the period. The production per day per worker declined from 1.48 meters to 1.33 meters and the production per day per loom from 2.63 meters to 2.49 meters during the period. This decline in production per worker and per loom would have an impact on the earnings per day of the weavers and also on the overall earnings of the weaver households.

4.45 In order to capture some aspects of the current conditions in the industry , the Commission carried out studies of the handloom industry in Uttar Pradesh and Bihar. The fixed capital investment on looms in Uttar Pradesh ranged from Rs.42000 to just above Rs. One lakh (Table 4.10). Most of the weavers reported to have invested in the loom in the last five years. The average investment per unit per year was however quite minimal and was probably only in the maintenance of the loom. The average annual income received per weaver was a modest Rs.26000 -35000. The situation in Bihar was just a little worse than in UP. The fixed capital investment, investment per year and the average incomes in Bihar were also lower than the units in UP.

4.46 The weavers operated under different forms of organization in Andhra Pradesh. They worked under the co-operative system, or under a master weaver, or contracted through middlemen or were independent self-employed weavers. Within each system also they could either operate from home or in a work shed or the Karkhana system. The independent weavers were found to have the highest monthly income, Rs.7000/month, while the workers within the Karkhana system in both the co-operative and master weaver systems earned the least, about Rs.1200/month. Again majority of these workers, 63 per cent, were below the poverty line. Nearly 40-50 per cent of the weavers under the other systems were also below the poverty line with the exception of the independent weavers (Dev 2005).

4.47 ***Demand for Handlooms and Employment:*** The sample households in Uttar Pradesh reported a decline in demand for the handloom products. This resulted in the closing down of working looms by almost 40 per cent and it directly affected the employment generated as well. Weaving was a household activity and all members of the household including the children, as well as hired workers, were involved. The number of family workers declined from 220 to 207 in the last five years, while the hired workers declined from 457 to 211, less than half. Obviously, faced with the decline in demand, the households would try to retain as many activities as possible within the family units and reduce the number of hired workers.

4.48 ***Problems of Raw Material and Marketing:*** It was observed that the problems of raw material supply and marketing were closely linked. Over the last decade the weavers have become highly dependent on the traders and the co-operative societies for meeting their raw material demand and marketing their products. The traders were rich and influential people and contracted to large buyers from all over the country. Often even the co-operative societies had to obtain work orders from the various agencies and traders who procured the products and send them to various showrooms all over the country and also to the export markets. The weavers, whether working independently, within the co-operative structure or under master weavers, came under this marketing chain and were reduced to a sort of putting-out system. Selling in the local market is not a good

Table 4.10: Investment in Looms and Weavers' Earnings in Uttar Pradesh (Rs) 2006

	Azamgarh District	Bijnore District	Varanasi District
Fixed Capital Investment in Loom	106820	43533	42833
Investment per Unit per Year	1865	1239	2580
Average Income per Weaver	34754	26532	34030

Source: A.K. Singh et. al. 2006

Two Census of Handloom Industry (1987-88 and 1995-96) recorded a decline in employment in the handloom sector. Further there was decline in the productivity per loom and per worker, which had an impact on the earnings per day of the weavers.

option since the prices are very low. The result of this form of a closed structure of supply of raw material and marketing meant that the weavers were not able to bargain or get a good price for their efforts. They remain highly dependent on the trader or co-operative society for procuring orders.

4.49 ***Deferred Payment and Indebtedness:*** A further problem faced by the local weavers was that the payment for the product was not made on time. As we have noted earlier for other 'homeworkers', deferred payment is another reason for the reduction in incomes.

4.50 Two thirds of the respondents in the survey in Uttar Pradesh also reported that they had taken loans, mainly from the co-operative society and also from friends and relatives. Number of people taking loans from banks was negligible. There are no special provisions for weavers to access loans from the banks. The average loan taken was about Rs.23000.

4.51 ***Technology:*** Majority of the weavers still used the traditional pit-looms rather than the frame looms. Most of the weavers said that they used new designs and products. The quality of the colour dyes had also improved. However, only half of the respondents had adopted these changes. Some of them reported that the increase in cost due to these changes was about 10 per cent. The increased returns to these investments were not in proportion to the increase in costs and therefore many weavers did not adopt the new methods. More pervasive was the shift in the product from only sarees to more of dress materials. Also marked was a shift from using only natural fibres such as silk and cotton for weaving to the use of synthetic fibres.

4.52 Since much of the handloom industry is home-based, a major constraint noted was the poor and traditional quality of the premises in which the looms were set up. The thatched roof, if not repaired regularly, resulted in leaking. The water drops stained the cloth and rendered large losses. The orders for such stained products were often cancelled. The weavers then tried to sell the products on their own leading to even lower prices.

The Food Processing Industry

4.53 Within the manufacturing sector, the food processing industry is one where the self-employed workers are concentrated. About 5 per cent of the self-employed workforce in all industry groups was in this industry in 1999-2000. The prospects for this industry are considered bright in both the domestic and export markets. Importance of the food processing industry is also because it increases value addition and creates gainful employment for the masses. Studies show that the food processing industry has been opting for the new technology so that its employment elasticity has been reducing till the early nineties (e.g. Mamgain 1996). There has been a moderate increase in capital intensity in grain processing, bakery products, cocoa, chocolate, sugar confectionery and other food products, leading to increase in factor productivity of capital and labour.

4.54 A survey of food processing units in six Indian states conducted in 1997 (Suryanarayanan and Rao 2000), found that 56 per cent of the units were sole proprietorships, 22 per cent were partnerships, 17 per cent were private limited companies and only about 4 per cent were corporations or others. The predominant form of ownership is as enterprises in the informal sector. However, 90 per cent of the units reported that they obtained a license for the commencement of production either from the District Industries Centres or Directorate of Industries and Small Scale Industries offices. The food processing units surveyed were dairy products, fruits and vegetables processing, grain mills processing, bakery products and cocoa and sugar confectionary. Majority of them, 80 per cent, reported that they worked at more than half the installed capacity, and half of them reported capacity utilization of at least 75 per cent, the most common being the grain mills. The single largest problem reported by the units was accessing capital and credit. The next most common problem was marketing and competition followed by securing raw materials.

4.55 Detailed studies on the rice milling industry, a common sight throughout the country, are far and few. A recent study by Kaur, et. al. (2007) presents the formal-informal dichotomy of the enterprises in the rice-milling industry and provides some useful information on the organisation and economics of rice processing units in Punjab and West Bengal. The formal rice mills differ from the informal ones in the size of labour, licenses required and the nature of technology used.

4.56 There was an estimated 6,823 rice processing units in Punjab as on January 1, 2001, out of which 1,965 (29 per cent) were rice mills in the formal sector. The

Control of the trader on raw material and marketing of the handloom products, resulted in poor bargaining power of the weavers.

rest (71 per cent) were hullers and mini-shellers in the informal sector. In West Bengal, 90 per cent of the rice mills are hullers, 0.7 per cent is hullers cum shellers and only 8.8 per cent are modern rice mills. Though the number of modern rice mills has gone up, official statistics still records only 562 modern mills in 2001, while the informal rice husking mills is reported to be around 37,000 in 2002. Between 1990 and 2000 rice production is said to have increased in West Bengal by 19 per cent and modern rice mills by 36 per cent, while husking mills rose by 300 per cent.

Technology

4.57 There are four main systems of technology and ownership operating in rice processing in Punjab: private processing of basmati, cooperative sector mills, custom milling for government agencies and custom milling for individual consumers. Processing in the first three systems is in the modern mills, mainly in the formal sector and registered under the Factories Act. The fourth system of hullers and mini-shellers with small processing capacities and relatively simple technology are unregistered firms in the informal sector. The average processing capacity of rice mills in Punjab was one thousand kilos or more per hour, while the processing capacity of hullers was less than 100 kilos and of mini shellers between 100 kilos and 200 kilos per hour. Thus the units in the informal sector were quite small in capacity. The quality of rice processed in the informal sector is low and these units mainly engaged in custom milling of paddy retained by the farmers for home consumption.

4.58 In West Bengal the informal husking mills used older technology with greater wastage of paddy and lower value by-products, compared to the formal rice mills. This was partly due to poor entrepreneurship but mainly due to the limited infrastructure and institutional support, mostly the limited credit facilities.

Costs of Formality

4.59 In Punjab the capital required for the equipment of huller mills is around Rs.4000-5000. Land and buildings cost about Rs.20000-350000. The buildings are used for other purposes as well, since rice milling is a seasonal activity. The total cost of the mini-shellers is Rs.50000-100000 and they too engage in a range of agro-processing activities.

4.60 In West Bengal the estimated cost for setting up the mill was between Rs.70 lakhs and over Rs.1 crore. The cost of setting up a new husking mill was estimated at less than Rs.2 lakhs, with land and building cost of Rs. 90 thousand, equipment of Rs.60 thousand and deposit to Electricity Company of Rs.40 thousand. While the procedures for setting up a unit have been simplified and the transaction costs have been reduced, a major hurdle that still remained was getting an electricity connection.

Workers

4.61 In both states while the entrepreneurs of the mills in the formal sector are well educated the informal sector owners in the survey had mostly not completed high school. Of the over 143,000 workers in the industry in Punjab less than 4 per cent are in informal units. However, with varying terms and conditions, less than 1 per cent get social security benefits and about 5 per cent receive provident fund benefits, the majority are informal workers in the formal sector. They are mostly casual workers engaged through contractors and earn daily minimum wages working for 10-12 hours a day. In Punjab the hullers mainly work with family labour while the mini-shellers sometimes employ a hired worker, while mainly using one or two family workers. These units work for about half a day and for 3-4 months in the year.

Rates of Return

4.62 In Punjab the net return on the informal mills is quite low, ranging from Rs.5000 to Rs.25000 a year. Most of them undertake other activities in the same unit, which form the main source of their income.

4.63 In spite of all the problems faced by the informal units in West Bengal the rates of return on investment were estimated to be higher, at 20-30 per cent, than that of the formal mills, 10-20 per cent. One of the reasons could be that the formal units were often the part of a value chain with a number of intermediaries. Millers reported that the difference in the price received by the producers and paid by the final consumer (net of processing costs) was Rs.200-500 per quintal of rice, though this varied by quality and the like . This was mainly due to the high margins charged by the middlemen, high transport and storage costs. Many of these costs were not faced by the informal husking mills and thus their returns were likely to be higher. Therefore, there are some benefits to being informal and operating in a smaller, local market. We should also note that the higher returns are on rather low capital investment in the informal sector units compared to lower returns on fairly higher levels of capital investment.

Petty Trade in India: Street Vendors/ Hawkers

4.64 The street vendors interact with different segments of urban population and have a specific role in urban society and space. The primary role of street vendors is that they provide a source of livelihood and employment to especially the poor classes. They create their own employment - 'an uncertain form of entrepreneurship' (Jhabvala 2000). Thus, in a way, they help to reduce unemployment and poverty by providing remunerative employment.

4.65 In spite of the fact that the street vendors have a significant role in the daily lives of all individuals in the urban areas, they are considered a hindrance in the urban space by government officials as well as the urban vehicle owners, who believe that they clutter the urban space and prevent smooth flow of traffic. The essence of the problem lies with the legal system of the cities, which fails to provide any space to street vending as an activity and recognize its significance in retail trading and with the attitude and perceptions of the people.[8]

The Legal Framework-Municipal Laws and Urban Space

4.66 On the legal side, the street vendors fall under the purview of two authorities - the traffic police (who deal with the flow and regulation of traffic and safety of the citizens using the road) and the Municipal Corporation, (which regulates the use of pavements and trade). The laws pertaining to the street vendors are formulated by the municipal authorities that invoke their respective Municipal Acts, the Indian Penal Code/ Police Act and the urban planning department; as there is no special Act for the street vendors.

4.67 The municipal and police laws of various cities vary with regard to the legal status of the hawkers (Box 4.4). In most of the cities, hawking and street vending are at least considered a legal activity, except in Kolkata where the Municipal Act prevents any type of street vending and the punishment for the same is rigorous imprisonment for up to three months or a fine of Rs. 250 (Section 371 of Kolkata Municipal Act, 1997). The 'Statement of Objects and Reasons' of the same Act state it as a "non-bailable offence" (Bhowmik undated, http:/ /www.streetnet.org.za/ English/page10.htm).

4.68 Even in other cities, the legal provisions are far from one that encourage or ease the problem of street vendors. In Patna, Bangalore, Bhubaneshwar, Ahmedabad and Mumbai license/ permission has to be obtained for street vending from a specific authority, generally the Municipal Commissioner. It is indeed ironical that while at the global level free trade and removal of licenses are stressed upon, the poor people who are actually generating employment for themselves have to take permission to start the activity. Besides, in most cities a license fee has to be paid, the amount of which varied from Rs.150 per month in Bangalore to Rs.200 per month in Mumbai (Table 4.11). In addition, it is allowed only as a temporary activity in Patna or for a short period of only three years in Bhubaneshwar. The timings and zones or areas in which hawking can be undertaken are also specified in

Box 4.4: Legal Status of Vendors in Imphal

In a study of seven cities in India, it was found that only two of them, Bhubaneshwar and Imphal, had some provisions for street vending. The Manipur Town and Country Planning Act, 1975, clearly provides for space for street vendors (Bhowmik undated, http://www.streetnet.org.za/English/page10.htm) A three-year agitation by the street vendors of the city (mainly women) in 1992 culminated in the municipality giving legal status to hawkers and releasing funds for improvement of the market by building metalled roads, covered drains and raised plinths around the stalls of hawkers. Although it charges a fee from the hawkers, it is in lieu of the facilities that are provided.

In contrast in Patna, the police can arrest a street vendor without a warrant and convict or fine the person if found violating any law. In Kolkata hawking is a non-bailable offence. In Mumbai and Ahmedabad the municipality can inspect any goods being hawked and remove, evict, seize and destroy goods, if the provisions of the license are violated and the hawkers whose structure is destroyed or whose goods are confiscated have to incur the expenditure for the destruction/ removal of the structure.

[8] This section is mainly based on a study of seven cities conducted by National Alliance of Street Vendors (NASVI) (Bhowmik undated, http://www.streetnet.org.za/ English/page10.htm).

most cities like Bangalore. There is a cap on the number of licenses that would be issued. Besides the common problems, those specific to the city exist. In Patna, to obtain a license, elaborate details pertaining to the articles sold, place, time of sale and also the stall/ booth details from which it would be sold, need to be specified. Provision of these details is a hurdle for most hawkers who are generally illiterate. In most cities, the street vendors are imposed heavy fines and harsh punishment if found without license or working against the regulations.

4.69 The issue of urban space and planning is the second segment of government machinery under whose purview the vending activities fall. With the exception of Imphal[9], urban land use and town planning ignore the hawkers and neither distinctly identify public spaces for retail trade and hawkers nor allow for mixed land uses so that hawking can be continued in residential areas, which are the natural markets for them. While urban town planning allows specific car parking spaces, the hawkers are termed as encroachers upon public land. (Labour File 1998a; Lahiri 1998).

4.70 Restrictions, cumbersome procedures involved in procuring license and costs - economic and otherwise - involved, dissuade even those vendors who are willing to obtain a license. Further, the limit on the number of licenses is coupled with the hesitancy to accept hawkers and hawking as a legal means of earning a livelihood, with a specific place in urban space. This results in hawkers operating without licenses and in any suitable space as no space is earmarked for them. As a consequence, municipal officers, traffic policemen, and the local musclemen take advantage of the situation. To continue to operate, the hawkers have to resort to illegal gratification of the demands of these vested interest groups in the form of payment of bribes and haftas, besides the fines. Even this fails to ensure that they will not be evicted/ arrested or that their goods will not be confiscated as was revealed by the interactions with the hawkers, in the course of the NASVI study in some cities (see Box 4.5 for Constitutional Provisions).

Social Profile of Vendors

4.71 The number of street vendors varies from one city to another ranging from 1.5 to 2 lakhs in metropolis like Mumbai and Kolkata to 30000 in small cities like Bhubaneshwar. The share of women street vendors is the highest in Imphal, where it is primarily a women's domain. In other cities, the share of women street vendors varies in the range of 30 per cent; in Kolkata it is as low as 15 per cent, probably due to the harsh treatment meted out to vendors. In most cities surveyed by NASVI, the constant dealings with the police, municipal officers and musclemen tended to make the environment highly insecure for women - who had to bear not only the hackling and pay bribes but were also exposed to snide comments and inappropriate behaviour from these groups. In spite of hardships the need for a source of income drove them into the trade, though most women tended to support their husbands by helping them at their stalls or making things at home for them to sell.

4.72 The scheduled castes and other backward castes dominate the trade. Exceptions are only in eastern India, e.g. all classes in Bhubaneshwar and upper and middle castes in Kolkata are in the trade. Approximately 25-30 per cent of the street vendors in the cities are illiterates and another 20-24 per cent have only primary education. This indicates that they tend to take up the activity as last resort to obtain a living. However, in the metropolis of Kolkata, Mumbai and even in Ahmedabad the closure of various industries led to the retrenchment of the workers, who had no option but to take up the activity. In these three cities, they form a major portion of the street vendors.

Earnings, Livelihood and Problems of Vendors

4.73 The vendors' earnings are very low and vary from trade to trade and from location to location. The men's average daily income is around Rs.70 in most cities except Patna, where it is slightly lower. Women earn considerably less - Rs.40 per day (Table 4.11). The earnings are higher for hawkers who sell garment and

The lack of recognition of the role of street vendors culminates in a multitude of problems faced by them: obtaining license, insecurity of earnings, insecurity of place for hawking, gratifying officers and musclemen, constant eviction threat, fines and harassment by traffic policemen.

9 In Manipur Town Planning and Country Planning Act 1997, 4 - 6 shops and 10 hawkers per 1000 persons are allowed in the residential areas (Bhowmik, NASVI, http://www.streetnet.org.za/English/ 10.htm).

non-perishable goods and for food stalls. The earnings are also higher in commercial than in residential areas.

4.74 The monetary problem is compounded by the fact that they have scarce resources for their trade and need to obtain credit by borrowing. Most of the street vendors report having borrowed from moneylenders who charge exorbitant interest rates. In Bhubaneshwar the credit is obtained from the wholesalers in the form of advances to be paid back at the end of the day at rates up to 110 per cent (Bhowmik undated, http://www.streetnet.org.za/English/ page10.htm). Sometimes the interest rate exceeds to 100 - 125 per cent or even 10 per cent per day (Jhabvala 2000).

4.75 The courts in India as well as organisations of and for the street vendors assert that government cannot ignore the street vendors (see Box 4.6). As a result of the efforts of organisations of the self-employed, a National Alliance of Street Vendors of India (known as NASVI) was formed, in 1998, to articulate the problems and demand the rights of vendors. At the same time a call for 'do tokri ki Jagah' was taken up in Parliament when Ela Bhatt, founder of SEWA in Ahmedabad, moved a resolution in the Rajya Sabha on August 5, 1998 demanding the formulation of a National Policy on Hawkers and Vendors and sought to improve their rights based on the framework proposed at the Bellagio Declaration (Labour File 1998a, 1998b).

4.76 As a result of these efforts, a National Policy on Street Vendors was formulated by the Government of India in 2004 (www.mhupa.gov.in/policies/natpol.htm accessed on 16th May 2007). Realising that there is need for a revision of this policy, the Government of India

Box 4.5: A Case for Hawking/Vending: Constitutional Provisions

Hawking and Vending need to be legalized as a means of earning a livelihood and integrated into the urban frame/ space, transport planning, infrastructure planning and town planning as has been undertaken in cities like Chandigarh and Manipur (Lahiri 1998; Tiwari 2000a; Singh 2000; Singh 2004). The Constitution of India lend support to the above argument.

Provisions Enshrined in the Constitution of India:

- Article 14, Fundamental Right: Right to Equality states, " The State shall not deny to any person equality before the law or the equal protection of the laws within the territory of India.", subject to "reasonable restrictions on the exercise of the right conferred by the said sub-clause."
- Article 19 (1) (g) of the Indian Constitution states that all citizens have the Fundamental Right "to practise any profession, or to carry on any occupation, trade or business"
- Article 38 (2) states "The State shall, in particular, strive to minimise the inequalities in income, and endeavour to eliminate inequalities in status, facilities and opportunities, not only amongst individuals but also amongst groups of people residing in different areas or engaged in different vocations."
- Article 39 (a) states "The State shall, in particular, direct its policy towards securing that the citizens, men and women equally, have the right to an adequate means of livelihood"
- Article 41 states "The State shall, within the limits of its economic capacity and development, make effective provision for securing the right to work, to education and to public assistance in cases of unemployment, old age, sickness and disablement, and in other cases of undeserved want."

(**http://lawmin.nic.in/coi.htm;** Seminar 2000; Advani 1998; Labour File 1998a; Lahiri 1998)

Each of these indicates that hawkers like any other individual have the right to sell goods and earn their own livelihood.

At the Bellagio Conference, 1995 vendors from several countries (11 cities) met and formed an alliance to fight for the rights of street vendors. They called for formulation of national policies for street vendors for protection, promotion and supportive policies from governments and also efforts by vendors themselves (Labour File 1998b).

Box 4.6: A Case for Hawking/Vending: Court Proceedings

Plea from a vendor, Sodan Singh:

"What I would like to request all of you, the privileged lot is to give me a regular Tehbazari Right...., give me a place to sit and hawk....., or if nothing is possible please show me a way to earn my bread." (Menon, 1998).

- **Sodan Singh & Others vs New Delhi Municipal Corporation:** The judgement referred to the fact that as per the Constitution of India Article 19 (1) the street vendors had a right to practice their trade. However, as per Article 19 (6) the state had the right to subject this right to reasonable restrictions, but as street vendors cannot chose the place to sell on the streets, the duty to delineate the place of work for them falls on the state (Lahiri 1998). The Supreme Court ruled that "The right to carry on trade or business mentioned in Article 19(1) of the Constitution, on street pavement, if properly regulated cannot be denied on the ground that the street areas meant exclusively for passing or re-passing and no other use" (Sodham Singh versus NDMC 1989, quoted in IDS 2006).

- In spite of the court orders the condition of street vendors has not changed. The Sodan Singh & Others vs New Delhi Municipal Corporation in August 1988, paved the way for formation of Thareja Committee, which proposed provision of place of work to street vendors who gave proof of regular vending in the form of three challans or Tejhabari slips of paper. Most vendors being either illiterate or with little education had not saved these slips. Taking advantage, hawkers reported that officials sold the older challan slips at high price. Further appeal resulted in court directing the Committee to use even local and government records as proof. However, Sodan Singh even in 1998 reported that little had changed (Menon 1998).

- Similar other court cases directing the state to delineate a place for hawkers: K Sundarshan vs Commissioner, Corporation of Madras (AIR 1984 Mad 292); Francis Coralie Mullin (AIR 1981 SC 746) and Olga Tellis vs. Bombay Municipal Corporation (AIR 1986 BC 180); Gulamali Gulamnabi Shaikh vs Municipal Commissioner (1986 GLH 616) to mention a few (Advani 1998).

asked the NCEUS to examine it and suggest such revisions as are necessary. On the basis of its report, a new National Policy on Street Vendors was formulated in 2006 (www.nceus.gov.in). The salient features of this policy are given in Box 12.3 in Chapter 12.

Non-Mechanized Land Transport: Rickshaw Pullers

4.77 One of the most neglected and vulnerable segments of workers in the land transport sector are the Rickshaw pullers. The initial large wooden wheeled hand pulled rickshaw had been replaced by the cycle rickshaw in most cities of India today. The cycle rickshaws first came into existence in India in the early forties of the last century (Shyam 2000). The profile of rickshaw pullers interestingly does not vary markedly across the cities. They are primarily migrants, driven from their homes in rural areas by abject poverty and in other cases by unemployment or lack of suitable jobs. The rickshawalas are thus primarily migrants from the different states of Bihar, Uttar Pradesh, Madhya Pradesh, Orissa and Rajasthan (Menon 2000; Majumdar 2006). They are either landless or own small plots of land from 5 to 10 khattas, which is generally dry and of low yield. Even other-wise, these small land holdings can be tilled by one adult member of the family and others are rendered idle and need to migrate to city for additional source of income, as the produce from these lands is not adequate to even feed their own families for more than a few months (Mukherjee & Mukherjee 2000; Menon 2000; Shukla 2000a; Shukla 2000b; Majumdar 2006). In Allahabad, 20 per cent of the rickshawalas were cultivators and 1 per cent agricultural labour. About 50 per cent of them in the city belonged to non-agricultural labour households. Only 8 per cent of the rickshawalas had the main occupation of the household as that of rickshaw pulling (Majumdar 2006).

4.78 A survey of the Rickshawalas in Nasik revealed that 40 per cent of them were illiterate and 38 per cent had less than secondary education (Mitra undated). However, in some cases, the educated youth in dire

Table 4.11: Conditions of Work, Livelihood and Earnings of Street Vendors across few Indian Cities

VARIABLE	PATNA	BHUBAN-ESHWAR	BANGALORE	IMPHAL	AHMEDABAD	MUMBAI	KOLKATA
Number	80000	30000	30000	7000	100000	200000	150000
Reason for Hawking (per cent)	Only means of earning a livelihood	Lack of skills for other employment/ lack of other jobs		Poverty	Retrenchment (30per cent)	Retrenchment (30per cent)	Retrenchment (55per cent)
Per cent Women	33	18.50	25	93	40	30	15
Social Group (Highest per cent)	SC (31)	General (44)	SC		SC+OBC(80)	OBC (51)	Upper & Middle Castes (60)
Per cent Illiterate & Per cent Primary Educated	27; 40	29; 24	37; 38		26; 24	25; 22	27; 23
Hours of Work	10	10	10 - 12		10 - 12	10+	10(city) - 15(commuting)
Credit Source (Highest per cent)	Moneylenders (79)	Wholesalers[1] (48)	Moneylenders				
Average Daily Income: Male; Female (Rs.)	50; 33	60; 35	70; 40	40 (female)	70; 50	70; 40	70; 35
Illegal Payment to Appease Policemen (Rs.)	2 p.d.	No rampant extortion in the city	Rs. 3 - 6 p.d. Yes		Rs. 10 p.d.	2- 10 p.d. 5 - 20 p.d. [2]	Daily Payment
Illegal Payment to Appease Municipal Officers (Rs.)	Varies						
Illegal Payment to Appease Local Musclemen (Rs.)	2 per day[3]	Yes	-		Rs. 10 p.d.		
Legal Licenses and other Fees (Rs.)	Fine Rs. 10		150 p. m ; Fine Rs. 50 - 100	31(no license) 7(license) p.m.		2 p.d. (male); 1p.d. (female)[4]	
Problems of Women (Highest per cent)	Lack of Protection (96per cent)	Lack of toilet		Problem from police	Lesser problems	Harassment by police & municipal officers	Insecure environment
Municipal Law Relating to Hawking (Year)	1951	1950; 1968	1964;1966; 2000	1989; 1992	1950; 1960	1950; 1960	1980; 1997
Urban Land Use with Provision for Hawking	No	Yes	Yes	Yes	No	No	No
Presence of Union	No	No	No	No	Yes	Yes (14per cent)	Yes
Average Monthly Income Spent on Hawkers Goods by:							
Low Income (Rs.)	800		800		900	1000	800
Middle Income (Rs)	3000		2500		1500	2000	1700
High Income (Rs)	1500		1500		2000	3000	2000

Notes: [1] as advance and paid daily after sale; [2] as bribe in lieu of pavti or charge to keep pavement clean; [3] Rangdhari Tax; [4] as Pavti

Source: Bhowmik undated, NASVI, http://www.streetnet.org.za/English/ page10.htm.

conditions are forced to take up the task though they are over educated for the job. In other cities, local conditions, e.g. closure of factories in Kanpur have resulted in the retrenched workers taking it up in the absence of any other occupation (Shukla 2000a).

4.79 Rickshaw pulling does not demand any technical skills and, hence, the unskilled agricultural migrants find it an easy option. Rickshaw pulling does not require capital either as rickshaws are available for hire at fixed rates per day. Acquiring a rickshaw in a city requires that the person knows someone who can introduce him to the rickshaw owner. Interestingly, in cities like Delhi and Patna, the city municipal commissioner lays down that an individual can have license for only a single rickshaw. Only widows and physically challenged persons can have up to 5 licences. There has been segmentation in the trade wherein one can clearly identify the rickshaw owners and rickshaw pullers separately. One rickshaw owner in Delhi acknowledged having 500 rickshaws and said that there were many such owners, though illegal. Despite the upper limit set by MCD of a total of 99000 licences; it is widely acknowledged that there are more than 5 lakh rickshaws plying in the city (Menon 2000). Similar is the case in Kanpur, where though the licences have been only up to 25 thousand rickshaws, around 5 lakh rickshaws ply in the city, according to the officials (Shukla 2000a). The number of licences to be provided in any city is limited on the pretext that rickshaws cause congestion. Besides in cities like Delhi the licences are provided only twice a year (Tiwari 2000b) (Box 4.7).

Box 4.7: Recognition of the Rickshaw Puller

The richshaw pullers are not recognised within the transport system. They are cheap modes of transport to low-income people, are pollution free and provide employment to seasonal migrants. There are at least seven categories of motorised and non-motorised vehicles. A transport policy that recognises the rickshaw-pullers in the transport hierarchy is required. A left service lane for them to ply on and special stands to park are the minimal requirements of planning for rickshaw pullers (Tiwari 2000b).

4.80 Purchase of a rickshaw requires a large sum of money (Table 4.12). Besides the purchase cost, the actual cost of the licence and the additional cost of bribes etc also should be incurred. City studies of rickshaw pullers from Delhi, Kolkata, and Nasik reported the large amounts to be paid by the rickshaw pullers to police and municipal authorities (Mukherjee & Mukherjee 2000; Mitra undated). Exploitation by the authorities and policemen is facilitated by the fact that the rickshaw pullers are generally not aware of the varied laws and rules that exist. The Delhi Municipal Cycle Rickshaw

Table 4.12: Earnings and Livelihood of Rickshaw Pullers across the Cities (Rs.)

City	License Fee	Actual Money to be Paid	Hiring Charges	Earnings in a Day	Number of Rickshaw in City (with licences in brackets)
Kolkata			20	20 - 50	
Delhi	50	200 - 250	20	20 - 25	5 lakhs plus (73000)
Kanpur	150 p.a.(road tax) + 5.76 (driving license)	250 (road tax) + 25 - 50 (driving licences)	25 per day or 15 for 12 hours	80 - 150	50000 plus (23400)
Patna	14.50	50	15 - 20	40 - 125	90000 (35000)
Allahabad	160 (Rickshaw) + 20 (For Rickshaw Pulling Licences)			1900 per month (approx. 160 per day)	31812 (14099) 2004-2005
Nasik	27 p.a.	500 - 600 (for license) + per cent per day (tax to tax clerks)	25	68 per cent say < 50	15000 and decreasing

Source: Compiled from Mukherjee & Mukherjee 2000; Tiwari 2000b; Shukla 2000a; Shukla 2000b; Mitra undated; Majumdar 2006.

Policy (1982) lays down that it would issue a certificate for the applicant/puller, which will help him apply for a loan from the State Bank of India, or any other nationalised bank up to Rs 900 or even higher if the rickshaw costs are higher (Menon 2000). Banks are, however, reluctant to implement the scheme for one or the other reason. That the rickshaw pullers are unaware of such schemes is also widely acknowledged.

4.81 Besides the problems with the authorities - governmental and police - the rickshaw pullers have to deal with the rickshaw owners as well. The relationship with the rickshaw owners is one of patron - client kind (John 2000). Their earnings are meagre in larger cities like Kolkata and Delhi and best in cities/towns like Kanpur, where they are one of the most important modes of transport. However, in all cities without exception a large part of their earnings are used up for paying the rickshaws' hiring charges. Though the repair and maintenance and release of the rickshaw, if impounded, is mostly undertaken by the owners rather than the pullers (Menon 2000); even the hiring charges in some cases like in Kolkata, where earnings are really low are only enough for paying the dues and to sustain themselves (Mukherjee 2000). They can hardly save anything for sending to their family back home each month.

Living and Working Conditions

4.82 Most of the rickshaw pullers stay in jhuggies or unauthorized colonies, owner's workshops or even below staircases, on footpaths, under hanging balconies on the roadside, in their rickshaws or in the open space (Mukherjee & Mukherjee 2000; Tiwari 2000b; Shukla 2000b; Mitra undated; Majumdar 2006). Few, like in Kolkata, can afford to take up rooms, sharing with other co-workers. In Patna, the people like in dirty common rooms (Box 4.8). There are no rickshaw parking stands (Shukla 2000b) or shelters where they can rest and no facilities for them to have food and water.

4.83 The plight of rickshaw pullers is accentuated by the low technology used in the design of the rickshaw. The cycle rickshaw comprises the front bicycle frame, lower angle iron chass and wooden passenger seat. Ironically, the bicycle components are considered best when they are the heaviest (Shyam 2000). The traditional rickshaw weighs at least four times the normal bicycle, i.e. around 1 quintal (Shukla 2000b). The basic bolted-on unit is inflexible and misaligned making the task of rickshaw pulling inefficient and extra tedious. Besides, the lack of gear system makes the rickshaw puller act as one producing different torque as per loading and road conditions (Shyam 2000). This structure is highly unfavourable for the puller with evident consequences for his health and has remained unchanged, inspite of some recent efforts to introduce technical improvements.

4.84 The stressful life with no rest day (as they cannot afford it) coupled with unhygienic living conditions and limited food results in poor health of most workers. Diseases like backache, tuberculosis, asthma, hernia, weak eyesight, and underweight are common. They have no medical insurance or health care facilities, forcing them to consult quacks when ill.

Conditions of Work and Constraints of Homeworkers

4.85 A number of activities in the unorganised sector are carried out from home-based enterprises. The industries where home-based employment dominated or account for equal proportion of industrial shed based employment are handlooms, beedi, artistic metalware, agarbati and so on. In other industries such as garments, a large part of the production is outsourced to home-based workers. A relatively larger proportion of the vulnerable sections of the workforce such as unpaid family workers, child workers and women workers are likely to be involved in home-based work, most often as homeworkers. Homeworkers are less likely to be organised and unionised and hence have less bargaining

Box 4.8: Shelters for Rickshaw Pullers

In Patna, place of shelter was created for the rickshaw pullers separately in 1975, termed as "rain baseras". These are hired common rooms in dirty by lanes or open areas. Even most of these have been captured by teashops and/or are used for other unlawful activities (Shukla 2000b).

In this era of liberalization, when India talks of open market regime and removing government controls, the restriction for the number of licences provided for plying rickshaws in any city raises several questions (Tiwari 2000).

power vis-à-vis their employers. Some studies show that homeworkers receive relatively lower amount of wage and non-wage benefits as compared to workers based in industrial premises (Labour Bureau 1996).

4.86 On the positive side, homework offers some advantages to families. Primarily, it offers employment and hence an opportunity to enhance and diversify their income. It also saves workers travel time and offers the flexibility to do other tasks. Men usually pursue another economic activity (e.g., agriculture in rural areas or seasonal work). Women generally perform their domestic responsibilities, while also contributing to family income through homework. The work and the experience can eventually trigger the entrepreneurial capabilities of some workers and subcontractors. Some homework activities may lead to the start up of small units (Mehrotra and Biggeri 2007).

4.87 These advantages are severely masked by the disadvantages faced by the homeworkers. In India, in a situation marked by surplus labour, piece rates to homeworkers are known to be very low. Work conditions can be exploitative if there are few alternative opportunities in the area or if work is available only as bonded labour. The exploitation of the homeworker by local employers can be just a first step in the exploitation through the global value chain (McCormick and Schmitz 2002). Homeworkers have little or no access to markets and the final consumer. Lack of unionization can also be an important source of the vulnerability of homeworkers. Child labour is an important part of homework, often necessitated by the need to generate additional income for the household (Bhat 1994; Pais 2003).

4.88 There is evidence to show that efforts to regulate illegal labour practices such as child labour in hazardous industries have led simply to a shift of production from industrial sheds and workshops to home-based settings. In fact, it shifts the illegal labour practice from more organised industrial settings to unorganised settings of home-based production.

Value Chain and Share of Homeworkers

4.89 Many of the activities undertaken by homeworkers are conducted within a value chain, which is sometimes connected globally. The value chain contains a number of intermediaries between the homeworker/producer and the final consumer. An example of a global value chain is in the garment industry. At the upper extreme are the international retailers such as GAP or Wal-Mart. These retailers mainly operate through export houses or large exporters themselves. The export houses contract out the orders to contractors who in turn may sub-contract it to sub-contractors. The actual production may be done in large factories, small factories or by homeworkers. The production process may be broken up and some part of this work, sometimes the more intricate hand work such as embroidery work, is done by the homeworkers. Depending on the complexity in the value chains and the number of intermediaries in the chain the bargaining power of the homeworker is reduced. The distance between the final consumer and the homeworker also creates ambiguity with regard to who is responsible for providing higher wages and social security benefits (ILO 2002b).

4.90 The study by Mehrotra and Biggeri (2007) found that "between homeworker at one end of the spectrum, and the retailer at the other end, there are usually four or five intermediaries. The number of intermediaries and the bargaining strength of the homeworker have implications for the share of the final consumer price that accrues to the homeworker. There may also be sector-specific technology-related factors, which determine the homeworkers' earnings. It was found that for a commodity that costs Rs.100 to a consumer, homeworkers receive Rs.15 in zardoshi; Rs.17 in beedi, and Rs.2.3 in incense sticks/agarbatti. The latter is said to be so low because the cost of perfuming the incense stick is high. (Fig. 4.8). The retailer obtains high shares in zardoshi - as with most high-valued garments and clothing products. In beedi and incense sticks, manufacturers obtain high shares, primarily because brand-names are important in these industries".

Fig. 4.8 Margins in Homework

	Price paid by Consumer	Price received by Homeworker
Zardo hi	R . 100	Rs. 15.00
Beedi	R . 100	Rs. 17.00
Agarbatt	Rs. 100	Rs. 2.30

Source: Mehrotra and Biggeri 2007

Low income

4.91 The homeworkers earn very little, are paid on piece rate, at very low rates, and are often dependent on the middlemen for work and wages. Based on the 1999-

2000 NSS data, it was noted that enterprises involved in contract work at home (homework) received annual incomes much lower than the other enterprises. In fact the women homeworkers received incomes that were close to Rs.27 per day or way below any acceptable norm (Table 4.13).

Table 4.13: Annual Incomes (Rs) of Homeworkers and Non-Homework Enterprises in India 1999-00

Enterprise On contract Work	Homework		Non-Homework	
	Organised	Unorganised	Organised	Unorganised
Casual Worker	21.9	23.1	35.0	41.5
All Workers	11.2	17.2	10.4	24.1
Self Employed	11.2	15.9	11.4	21.4
Regular Workers	5.2	11.5	6.8	20.2

Source: Unni and Rani 2005a

Hours of work and Seasonality

4.92 Homeworkers often do not have adequate work throughout the year. There is seasonality in the work with wide variations in the hours of work available per day and also the wages received per day. In a survey of beedi, agarbatti and zardoshi work it was noted that the women homeworkers received as low as Rs.27 in the peak season and worked for nearly 7 hours (Table 4.14). In the lean season they work, on average, for less than 5 hours and received even lower wages of less than Rs.6.

Table 4.14: Seasonality of Work among Homeworkers: Earnings and Hours of Work

	Wages per Day (Rs)		Hours per Day	
	Male	Female	Male	Female
Peak Season	60.00	27.00	7.7	7.0
Lean Season	11.34	5.88	5.0	4.6

Note: Sectors covered were beedi,. Agarbatti rolling and zardoshi work.

Source: Homenet South Asia and ISST 2006.

Delayed or Deferred Payments

4.93 One of the common exploitative practices adopted by the middlemen is to deduct wages for 'rejection'. Many a times, the middlemen withhold partial payment to maintain a hold on the worker and to discourage him/her from leaving for competitors. The strategy of denying work to the most vocal leader amongst the workers is often adopted by the traders. Besides homeworkers also take care of the overhead costs which eats into their profits. Not being organized, many homeworkers lack bargaining power. In two (of the three) sectors, in over nine out of ten cases there are no delays in payment; but in one sector (zardoshi) there are delays in nearly 4 out of 10 cases. The homeworkers tend to remain with the same contractor, even in the absence of written agreements or benefit payments. The inertia in seeking alternatives is accounted for by the high opportunity costs of change (i.e., lack of alternative or excess supply of labour), debt bondage, delayed payments, and contractors preferring to keep workers isolated (Mehrotra and Biggeri 2007).

The Case of Homeworkers in Beedi-Rolling

4.94 Beedi rolling is one economic activity in the unorganised sector that is regulated under the Beedi and Cigar Workers (Conditions of Employment) Act, 1966. In many parts of the country in the early 1970s beedi-rolling was mainly undertaken in the factory. However, by the 1980s beedi-rolling shifted to the household sector mainly as home-based work. This was perhaps due to better implementation of the provisions of the Act. This shift also went hand in hand with a larger proportion of women engaged in this activity.

4.95 In many parts of Tamil Nadu, for example, beedi rolling is undertaken as a family enterprise. Women who work in beedi rolling also work as assistants to other activities like ring-making, leaf cutting, closing the beedi ends, etc. The assistants would not get any wages, but their productivity was added to the main worker. The ring maker got variable wages, if he collected the beedis from the factory for labelling he got Rs. 3 per 1000 beedis, but if he got it collected by someone else he got Rs.1.5-2.0 per 1000 beedis (Saravanan 2002).

Rejection, Supply and Quality of Raw Material

4.96 Since the 1970s a minimum wage was fixed for beedi rolling, but the workers rarely got this wage. Two methods were used to reduce wages, one, while supplying the leaves and tobacco to make 1000 beedis, sufficient amount was not provided. The workers purchased the extra amount from the market for which they paid themselves, or the contractor refused the beedis or refused to give further work. A second method was to demand 110 beedis instead of 100 and then reject 10 beedis, on the count that they were not of the specified size. After all these deductions the worker would be paid about two-thirds of the actual stipulated wage. All these were hidden costs borne by the beedi-rollers (Saravanan 2002).

4.97 One of the problems faced by beedi workers was that the quality and availability of raw material is uneven. This resulted in low incomes and also greater rejection of the output that affected their incomes. In a survey conducted in Karnataka, about 37 per cent of the workers felt that the quality of raw material was substandard, while 12 per cent felt that it was some times substandard. Further, the women workers reported that the registered companies supplied raw material required for only three to four days as against six to seven days in the past. In fact, in one of the villages it was reported that, on account of reduced supply of raw material, the per capita rolling had come down from 1,000 to 600 beedis per day. "In the villages where both registered and unregistered companies were operating, the workers filled in the gap in the raw material availability by contracting the work for the latter. In fact, the combination of registered companies and tax-free beedi companies provided material sufficient for the week in (some) places" (Rajasekhar and Sreedhar 2001; ILO 2003).

4.98 Rejection of beedis on the grounds of poor quality and providing less than the required amount of raw material were methods used to reduce the wage payments and keep the wages below the Minimum Wages. Some of the contractors in a study reported, "Sometimes we reject all the beedis of a worker intentionally and this is not due to any sense of revenge but just to make up our own expenses. And therefore we sell these beedis in the market at higher rates" (ILO 2003).

Indebtedness

4.99 With low level of income and uncertain employment in the beedi industry, the workers are unable to meet their basic necessities and other social and cultural responsibilities. The level of indebtedness among them is very high. According to a survey in Tamil Nadu (Saravanan 2002) of the 71 respondents, 30 per cent had loans of less than Rs.1000 while the remaining 70 per cent were indebted for more than Rs.10000. A few among the latter had borrowed even up to Rs.100000. Since most of the beedi workers did not have land or other properties for security they relied either on the contractors or non-institutional sources like moneylenders, relatives, friends and neighbours. Institutional credit facilities could not be availed of without security. Of the recorded 89 transactions only 11 per cent were with the institutional sources like banks and cooperative societies, 18 per cent with the moneylenders, 17 per cent with the beedi contractors and the remaining 54 per cent with relatives and friends.

Health Problems of Beedi Homeworkers

4.100 Most of the studies reported health problems of the homeworkers, mainly respiratory problems due to inhalation of the tobacco dust and body ache due to the peculiar posture that had to be maintained at all times of work. The common diseases that the beedi-workers suffered from were asthma, tuberculosis, spondilitis and back-strain (ILO 2003).

Conclusion

4.101 Self-employed is a catch-all category and hides a good proportion of workers who can only be described as disguised wage workers. This is because a majority of the self-employed are own account workers i.e. working as tiny enterprises often with the help of family labour or with one or two hired workers. Many others such as homeworkers are under the putting-out system whereby raw materials are supplied to them by agents or establishments who purchase the processed output. The category of self-employed in fact outweighs the share of wage workers in the Indian economy, both in agriculture and outside it.

4.102 When we analyse the problems of own account workers who are also called own account enterprises, it is quite important not to be misled by the concepts and categories as applied to business operations. Statistically the family members assisting such tiny enterprises are called the 'unpaid family workers'. This is more a statistical artefact and a situation of non-payment for one's work because the objective is to increase the family's

Hidden costs of homework:

- *Rejection of product on the ground of poor quality*
- *Deferred or delayed payment*
- *Use of own infrastructure and electricity - home as workplace*
- *Supply of poor quality and inadequate raw material*

income through such self-employed activities. What is of importance to note is the self-exploiting nature of these family enterprises where the members seek to make a living by lengthening their working day as well as working most of the days in a year.

4.103 Such economic units have a dual character; that of enterprises and workers. As tiny enterprises, they do need such support as greater access to credit, marketing and infrastructure. Many of them such as those in handloom weaving also need better technology. Weak or even the absence of organisational capital is a critical problem. The numerous tiny enterprises need some kind of associational umbrella so that they can demand better support systems, engage in creating common facilities, procurement of raw material and marketing of products.

4.104 Enterprises that hire workers, especially those hiring between 6 and 9 workers, are somewhat better placed than the smaller ones. The fixed capital of the former is eight times higher than the latter. Even then their fixed capital (estimated at Rs.3 lakhs in 2000) is considerably lower than the threshold for defining a micro enterprise (i.e. Rs.25 lakhs) under the Micro, Small and Medium Enterprise Act of 2005. Given the high proportion of such enterprises in the small scale sector, this alone points to the need for concerted attention to this segment.

4.105 The case studies discussed here represented the mixed bag of self-employed. But they all share certain common problems. Access to credit is a major one. Their conditions of living are so poor that several promotional measures are also called for to improve their living standards and consequently their human capital. Absence of good health and education acts as debilitating factors in their ability to secure a reasonable living. Therefore the promotional measures have to be designed and implemented both from the angle of enterprises as well as that of the worker.

5 Women Workers in Non-agriculture

Introduction

5.1 The Commission is of the view that the problems of the women workers in general and in the unorganised sector in particular deserve special emphasis and focus in view of their marginalised position within the class of workers. Even when women are not employed in the sense of contributing to the national output, a considerable share of their time is consumed by socially productive and reproductive labour. This is what is called the 'double burden of work' that distinguishes women from men. For women workers in the informal economy the double burden of combining the tasks of production and reproduction is even more arduous because they are already engaged in activities that require long hours to obtain a subsistence wage.

5.2 Having said that, the problem of women workers should not be reduced to this general and somewhat simplified formulation. The differentiation within women in general and women workers in particular is also a fact of life. This behavioural differentiation is influenced by their basic social and economic characteristics. This is evident in Table 5.1 and Table 5.2, which present the difference between men and women workers and the status of women from rural areas (as a proxy for economic background since the rural economy is dominated by agriculture) and rural women belonging to the bottom layer of the Indian society i.e. SCs and STs. It is quite clear that the position of women workers in rural India is considerably lower than that of women in general. But the bottom layer is constituted by women belonging to the lowest social status groups. A comparison of selected indicators given in Table 5.2 shows that urban women workers in general are better off than even rural men workers. But this advantage is somewhat dented when we look at the status of urban women belonging to SCs and STs. However, rural women workers in general seem to be more disadvantaged than even the urban SCs/STs women workers.

5.3 Therefore the Commission is of the view that while women workers constitute a marginalised category within the class of workers in general, there are layers of subordination determined by structural factors such as the initial conditions of social status and economic sector to which they belong. This is quite evident in the case of women workers in the unorganised sector.

Conceptualising Women's Work

5.4 We discuss the problems of women workers in the following order: (a) the larger issue of double burden of work, (b) women workers and their invisibility, and (c) conditions of work as well as discrimination. We begin by an examination of the double burden of work that more often than not determines their availability for and location of work. Then we go on to characterising the nature of women's work taking into consideration two of their distinct characteristics, the socio-cultural norms that restrict their workspaces and the double burden of production and reproduction activities. These

Table 5.1: Select Characteristics of Women Workers 2004-2005

Indicator	Male	Female	Rural Female	Rural Female SCs/STs
Total Workers (UPSS in million)	309.4	148.0	124.0	44.9
Labour Force Participation Rate	56.0	29.0	33.3	37.9
Work Force Participation Rate	54.7	28.3	32.7	37.5
Percentage of Regular Workers in Total Workforce	18.2	8.9	3.7	3.1
Percentage of Self-employed in Total Workforce	54.2	61.1	63.7	51.1
Percentage of Casual Labour in Total Workforce	27.5	30.0	32.6	45.8
Percentage of Unorganised Workers in Total Workforce	90.7	95.9	98.0	98.6
Percentage of Unorganised Sector Workers in Total Workforce	84.0	91.3	94.5	95.0
Percentage of Workers in Agriculture & Allied Activities	48.9	72.8	83.34	86.2
Percentage of Out of School Children in Relevant Age Group (5 - 14 years)	15.5	20.7	23.5	28.5
Mean Years of Schooling (all workers)	5.4	2.5	1.9	1.2
Mean Years of Schooling (Unorganised Non-agr. Workers)	6.1	3.7	2.9	2.0
Mean Years of Schooling (Rural Unorganised Agr. Workers)	3.7	NA	1.6	1.1
Percentage of All Workers Up to Primary Education (including Illiterates)	55.6	80.7	85.0	90.7
Percentage of Unorganised Non-agr. Workers Up to Primary Education (including I Illiterates)	49.2	70.8	77.1	84.7
Percentage of Unorganised Agricultural Workers Up to Primary Education (including Illiterates)	68.8	87.8	88.0	92.2
Percentage of Homeworkers in Self-employed (Unorganised Non-agriculture) [1]	6.5	30.1	32.0	-
Percentage of Workers with only Subsidiary Work	1.9	24.9	26.1	23.5
Wage Rate of Rural Agricultural Labourers (Rs.per manday)	47.9	NA	33.1	33.1
Wage Rate of Rural Non-agricultural Labourers (Rs.per manday)	67.5	NA	44.0	45.8
Percentage of Casual Labourers (Rural) not Getting Notional Minimum Wage of Rs. 66	78.0	NA	95.6	95.4
Percentage of Casual Labourers (Rural) not Getting NCRL Minimum Wage of Rs. 49	40.9	NA	80.9	80.7

Note:
1. Data pertain to 1999-2000.
2. UPSS: Usual Principal and Subsidiary Status.

Source: NSS 61st Round and 55th Round 2004 - 2005 and 1999-2000, Employment-Unemployment Survey. Computed.

Conceptualizing women's work
- *Invisibility: lack of "designated business place of work"*
- *Double burden of production and reproduction activities.*

Table 5.2: Rural-Urban Differences between Men and Women Workers 2004-2005

Indicator	Urban Men	Urban Women	Rural Men	Urban Women	Rural Women (SCs/STs)
Percentage of Regular Workers in Total Workforce	40.6	35.6	9.0	3.7	3.7
Percentage of Workers with Education Secondary & Above	44.4	29.8	18.4	14.3	6.3
Wages of Casual Workers (Rs. per manday)	74.3	43.6	54.6	44.0	34.7
Percentage of Workers with only Subsidiary Work	1.4	18.8	2.1	16.2	26.1

Source: NSS 61st Round 2004 - 2005, Employment-Unemployment Survey. Computed.

characteristics as well as limited opportunities ensure that their participation in the conventionally defined productive work is low. A woman, therefore, engages as a subsidiary worker, in part-time work and with considerable domestic duties, and yet is available for additional work. In the next section we discuss gender discrimination that women face in terms of the sexual division of labour and the low valuation of her skills. In the final section specific issues of conditions of work related to women in the three categories of workers, i.e. wage workers, self-employed and homeworkers, are brought out. The conditions of women workers are discussed taking into account these distinguishing characteristics of their work highlighted earlier. Women self-employed worker operated proprietary enterprises are compared to male operated proprietary enterprises in terms of the scale of operation and the nature and problems faced. Among the homeworkers we note a number of unaccounted for hidden costs that affect the earnings and reduce the wages actually paid. We also discuss the work undertaken by girl children as a special category since the roots of gender discrimination are sown at a young age.

Double Burden of Work

5.5 The reproductive role of women is less visible and less recognized by the society. She engages in multiple livelihood activities to fulfil her productive and reproductive role. The Central Statistical Organisation of the Government of India provided official visibility to this double burden of work through a pilot study of utilization of time by men and women in six states in 1998 (CSO 2000). The report classified the activities based on the 1993 System of National Accounts (SNA) into three categories: (i) those coming under economic activities that are included in the SNA; (ii) those that are not currently included in the SNA but are characterised as extended SNA, which include household maintenance and care for the children, old and the sick in the household; and (iii) non-SNA consisting of the social and cultural activities, leisure and personal care. Since productive and reproductive roles performed by women are equally necessary for the well-being and regeneration of the society, the study found that women spend a disproportionate amount of time in what is called extended SNA. On the other hand men spend a much greater time in SNA activities than women. As for non-SNA activities, the difference was not as striking as in the case of extended SNA. These are presented in Table 5.3. In short women spent 17 per cent more time in SNA plus extended SNA activities compared to men. The result of this high work intensity is seen on the lower levels of health and well-being of the women compared to men. Women's situation in the informal economy is graver since the conditions under which they labour in the SNA activities are already precarious. This intensification of work time, especially in the so called self-employment, has consequences for her and the development of her children.

5.6 Among women in the prime age group, 15- 59 years, 53 per cent in rural and 65 per cent in urban areas, were engaged in domestic duties by principal status in 2004-05 (Table 5.4). In contrast, only 0.4 per cent of the men were primarily engaged in domestic work. These women undertook a number of activities that helped their

Women spend nearly 35 hours a week on care of children, old and the sick at home and household maintenance compared to less than 4 hours spent by men.

Table 5.3: Weekly Average Time (hours) Spent on SNA, Extended SNA and Non SNA Activities by Gender and Place of Work (Combined for Six States)

Activities	Rural		Urban		Total	
	Male	Female	Male	Female	Male	Female
SNA	42.3	22.5	41.1	9.2	42.0	18.7
Extended-SNA	3.7	33.9	3.4	36.4	3.6	34.6
Non SNA	122.0	111.5	123.5	122.4	122.4	114.5
Total	168.0	168.0	168.0	168.0	168.0	168.0
Total Persons	22285	21130	10305	9549	32590	30679

Note: Time Use Survey was conducted in 18,591 households spread over 6 selected states namely, Haryana, Madhya Pradesh, Gujarat, Orissa, Tamil Nadu and Meghalaya.
Source: CSO 2000.

household to save incomes, if not to directly earn it. Fetching water and free collection of firewood, including preparation of cow-dung cakes, were the predominant activities in rural areas. In urban areas, these were fetching water, sewing and tailoring and tutoring children free of cost. Many of these activities are included in the count of extended SNA activities as discussed above. If all these were to be included as economic activities the participation rates of women would be considerably higher than what has been currently estimated. Since the work force participation rate of women belonging to SCs/STs is higher (Table 5.8), the participation in additional domestic duties is lower than that of all women. Among those engaged in additional activities a higher share reported preparation of cow dung cakes, fetching water and free collection of goods (Table 5.4). Women from the lower social strata were more likely to engage in economic activities and in addition in free collection of goods perhaps due to lower economic status of their households. However, one should also note that inclusion

Table 5.4: Additional Activities Undertaken by Women (Age 15 - 59 years) usually Engaged in Domestic Duties, Principal Status (Percentage) 2004-05

Additional Activities	Rural	Urban	Total [SC/ST]
Per cent Engaged In Domestic Duties	53.3	65.0	56.8 [49.1]
Kitchen Garden, Orchards, etc	16.1	3.3	12.1 [14.0]
Household Poultry, Dairy, etc	34.0	4.1	24.8 [28.2]
Cow Dung Preparation for Household Fuel	47.4	5.9	34.6 [42.7]
Tutoring for Free	7.5	13.8	9.5 [6.1]
Bring Water from Outside Household Premises	45.4	20.5	37.7 [53.4]
For Household Use/ Consumption			
Free Collection of Fish,Fruit, Veg, etc	16.4	1.2	11.7 [20.8]
Free Collection of Firewood, etc	40.4	6.0	29.7 [47.2]
Sewing, etc	30.2	27.3	29.3 [28.2]
Husking Paddy	14.6	3.2	11.1 [14.0]
Grinding Food Grains	15.5	7.5	13.0 [15.1]
Preparation of Gur	3.9	1.7	3.2 [3.5]
Preservation of Meat, Fish	5.3	3.0	4.6 [5.4]
Making Baskets, Mats	7.0	2.6	5.7 [6.5]

Note: Figures in parentheses are the corresponding shares of SC/ST women.
Source: NSS 61st Round 2004-2005, Employment-Unemployment Survey. Computed.

of these extended SNA per se is not going to give a higher income to the women. What it means is the absence of recognition of the kind of work, which although not in the realm of monetisation, is important to the sustenance of the family as well as the economy. Recognition of the women's contribution to extended SNA could, and should, lead to greater appreciation of public policies for the welfare of women.

5.7 What is brought out in Table 5.4 is the percentage of women engaged in additional work while reporting themselves as principally engaged in domestic duties. These types of work are essentially economic in nature and add to the income in one way or another. However, such additional burden of work is a common feature among the poorer women because of their limited purchasing power to buy these consumption goods.

Availability for Additional Work

5.8 In spite of the stress from the double burden of work, the economic condition forces many women to be available for additional work. More than one third of these women engaged in domestic duties for the major part of the year by principal status (Table 5.5) reported that they would engage in productive activities if such work was available within the confines of their homes. It is significant to note that a quarter of those willing to work at home were also willing to work full-time. This is a clear indication that the two dimensions of women's work participation, highlighted earlier, viz. social norms and the exigencies arising out of the double burden of work, restrict her mobility and hence the choice of the place of work.

5.9 The type of activities they are willing to engage in are mainly spinning, weaving and tailoring in rural and urban areas and animal husbandry in rural areas (Table 5.6). It is easy to see that they can undertake these activities at home. Nearly 60 per cent of the women reporting their availability for work at home said they had the necessary skill/experience to carry out the activities of their choice. This merely implies that they were opting to work at home on activities that they were capable of undertaking.

Non-conventional Place of Work

5.10 The fact that women workers have restricted mobility because of which their capacity to engage in economically productive work is restricted is clearly brought out by their place of work. The conventional idea of a workplace is the office, factory or an institution. In 2004-05 only half of the total non-agricultural workforce and as little as one-third of the women workers worked in conventionally designated workplaces. This implied that about 89 million men and only about 10 million women workers had a conventional place of work, either of their own or belonging to the employer. The enterprises in the unorganised sector are mainly unregistered units. Only 40 per cent of the total and 18 per cent of the women workers in the unorganised sector had a designated place of work. Their rural-urban distribution is shown in Table 5.7. About 23 per cent of all unorganised sector workers worked from their own homes. Among women this was as high as 54 per cent, taking rural and urban areas together, having risen by 5 percentage points from 1999-2000.

5.11 Lack of a clear-cut employer-employee relationship in the case of the self-employed and outworkers/ homeworkers and lack of a designated place of work for the majority, particularly of women, adds to the problem of invisibility of such enterprises. It also

Table 5.5: Percentage of Women (Age 15 - 59 years) in Domestic Duties Willing to Accept Work at Home, Full-time and Part-time, by Sector2004 - 2005

Nature of Work	Rural	Urban	Total
Per cent Engaged In Domestic Duties	**53.3**	**65.0**	**56.8**
Willing to Accept Work At Home	35.7	29.4	33.7
Regular: Full Time	23.0	28.5	24.5
Regular: Part Time	71.9	67.8	70.8
Occasional	5.1	3.6	4.7
Total	**100.0**	**100.0**	**100.0**

Source: Same as in Table 5.2.

Restrictions on Mobility of Women
Social norms and exigencies of double burden of work influence choice of the place of work of women.
Women engaged primarily in domestic duties are willing to work within their homes.

Table 5.6: Percentage of Women (Age 15 - 59 years) in Domestic Duties Willing to Accept Work at Home by Type of Work acceptable by Skill/ Experience to undertake, by Sector 2004 - 2005

Type of work	Rural	Urban	Total
Per cent Engaged In Domestic Duties	**53.3**	**65.0**	**56.8**
Willing to Accept Work At Home	**35.7**	**29.4**	**33.7**
Animal Husbandry	44.6	11.8	35.8
Food Processing	3.0	7.5	4.2
Spinning, Weaving, Tailoring	34.6	50.3	38.8
Manufacture. of Wood, Leather	1.8	1.7	1.7
Others	16.0	28.7	19.5
Total	100.0	100.0	100.0
Per cent Having Skill/ Experience for above Work	**56.1**	**58.0**	**56.6**

Source: Same as in Table 5.2.

makes it difficult for such units to approach the formal financial institutions such as banks for credit.

5.12 Workers engaged in enterprises on a casual basis tend to change employers frequently. It is relatively easy for the employer then not to recognize the workers and then to deny him any additional benefits. The problem is compounded if the workers are engaged in the enterprises based in the employers' home. In rural and urban areas together about 13.5 per cent of women and 3.5 per cent of men unorganised sector workers were so engaged (Table 5.7).

5.13 Unorganised workers, in both self-employed and wage employed categories , remain, by and large, legally unrecognised as workers, which implies that the existing laws related to minimum wages or social security are not applied to them. Besides the lack of legal recognition, lack of a designated "business place" also works to increase their vulnerability and exposes them to exploitation by the authorities. Further, the dispersed nature of workplace makes organisation of these workers and enterprises more difficult, further adding to their invisibility.

Table 5.7: Percentage of Unorganised Sector Non-agricultural Workers by Location of Work 2004 - 2005

Location of Workplace	Rural			Urban			Total		
	Male	Female	Total	Male	Female	Total	Male	Female	Total
No Fixed Workplace	13.1	3.9	11.1	6.2	1.6	5.3	9.6	2.8	8.2
Own Dwelling	18.6	61.2	28.1	12.9	45.9	19.3	15.7	54.1	23.7
Own Enterprise	20.6	9.2	18.1	29.6	9.6	25.7	25.2	9.4	21.9
Employer's Dwelling	3.4	7.3	4.2	3.7	20.7	7.0	3.5	13.5	5.6
Employer's Enterprise	15.8	6.0	13.6	24.8	11.7	22.3	20.4	8.7	17.9
Street Fixed Location	3.9	1.9	3.4	4.5	2.4	4.1	4.2	2.2	3.7
Street Without Fixed Location	5.6	2.6	4.9	7.1	3.2	6.3	6.3	2.9	5.6
Construction	15.5	5.8	13.3	8.3	3.4	7.3	11.8	4.7	10.3
Others	3.5	2.1	3.2	2.9	1.5	2.6	3.2	1.8	2.9
Total	100.0	100.0	100.0	100.0	100.0	100.0	100.0	100.0	100.0

Source: Same as in Table 5.2.

More than half of women workers in the unorganised non-agricultural sector work from their own homes. Another 10 per cent work in the employer's home or in their own enterprises. Rural women non-agricultural workers are even more likely to work at home than urban women.

Nature of Work Participation of Women

5.14 Women's work participation rates reflect the twin characteristics of their work highlighted above, double burden of productive and reproductive responsibilities and being confined to non-conventional spaces of work. These features together with the poor access to human and physical capital, highlighted in Chapter 2, leads to much lower participation of adult women in the workforce than men (Table 5.8). The disparity in work participation across rural and urban areas is also large. While nearly half the rural adult women participate in the workforce, only a little more than one-fifth of the urban women do so. This is partly explained by the self-employment on land or engagement in livestock related activities (e.g. taking care of cattle) in the rural areas. However, the work participation rates for women belonging to SCs/STs are significantly higher than women in general. Such a high work participation rate for rural women does not mean that their economic condition is better than their counterparts in the urban areas. In fact, the reality is to the contrary, given the low level of wages in rural areas, highly restricted work opportunities (mostly in agriculture and related activities) and the social constraints imposed especially on those who come from the bottom layer of the social hierarchy. A higher work participation rate in such a context is more likely the result of economic hardships than the availability of work opportunities. This is also corroborated by the low level of education of rural women workers as discussed in Chapter 2. As highlighted in Table 5.1, the low level of education is a serious handicap for not only women workers in general but rural women in particular. Here again the bottom layer is the rural women belonging to SC/ ST categories.

Table 5.8: Workforce Participation Rates by Gender by Usual Status (Percentage)

Year	Rural Male	Rural Female	Urban Male	Urban Female
		All Workers		
1993-94	55.3	32.8	52.1	15.5
1999-00	53.1	29.7	51.8	13.9
2004-05	54.6	32.7	54.9	16.6
		For SC/ST Workers		
1993-94	56.6	39.8	50.8	20.6
1999-00	54.0	36.3	49.9	18.9
2004-05	55.0	37.5	53.5	20.8

Source: NSSO 2006a

Subsidiary Status Work

5.15 Another prominent characteristic of women's work force participation is that even within the low participation of women, a large part is of subsidiary work status, nearly a quarter of the women workers (Table 5.9). Subsidiary status workers are non-workers or the unemployed persons engaged in an economic activity for part of the year. In rural areas, about 26 per cent of the women participating in the workforce did so only for part of the year, or were subsidiary workers, and in urban areas about 19 per cent of them work only in subsidiary capacity. Again the societal compulsions and double responsibilities would partly explain this phenomenon. The interesting feature is that it is mainly the self-employed women who engage in work in a subsidiary capacity (34 per cent) and, to some extent, women casual workers, who perhaps tend to have fewer employment opportunities. In the case of the casual workers it would be the compulsions and pressures of survival that make them work in their principal capacity. In marked contrast, a negligible proportion of men work as subsidiary workers.

5.16 Increase in employment in the recent period until 2005 indicates a disturbing feature, viz. growth of workers in the subsidiary status category. There is a sharp growth of regular workers in subsidiary status, particularly in urban areas, among both men and women (Table Unni and Raveendran 2007). This is a form of erosion in formal or full-time jobs and the increase in informal part-time jobs. Interestingly, there is also the growth of subsidiary self-employed non-agricultural activity in urban areas in the recent decade, particularly among women. This is, of course, an understandable phenomenon, viz. persons trying to make ends meet in the urban informal labour market.

Conditions of Women's Work

5.17 In the earlier chapters on wage and self-employed workers in the unorganised sector we have

Table 5.9: Share of All Workers (all ages) with Only Subsidiary Work by Sector and Gender (Percentage) 2004 - 2005

Employment Status	Rural			Urban			Total		
	Male	Female	Total	Male	Female	Total	Male	Female	Total
Casual Labour	1.0	12.0	5.0	1.6	15.4	4.8	1.1	12.3	5.0
Regular Workers	0.8	5.0	1.6	0.9	3.6	1.4	0.9	4.1	1.5
Self-employed	3.0	34.6	15.1	1.8	31.3	8.3	2.7	34.2	13.7
Total Workers	2.1	26.1	10.8	1.4	18.8	5.1	1.9	24.9	9.4

Source: Same as in Table 5.2.

discussed several issues of conditions of work including from the point of view of women workers. To the extent possible, the analysis highlighted the differences between men and women workers in the unorganised sector. In this section we therefore discuss only specific issues related to women alone for the various categories of wage workers, self-employed, homeworkers and the case of girl children.

Gender Discrimination

5.18 Discrimination on the lines of gender is not always overt. It appears in very subtle forms such as in the nature of work performed, the skills required to perform the work and the valuation of these skills and the technology used by men and women.

Sexual Division of Labour

5.19 In a study of the garment industry in Tiruppur (Vijayabaskar 2002) and Delhi (Singh and Sapra 2007) it was noted that there was a rise in the relative importance of daily wage and home-based work in the garment industry with large proportion being women workers. In Tiruppur the entry of migrant workers into the knitwear industry was noted in three phases and the last phase in the late 1980s and early 1990s saw a large influx of women wage workers. A growing feminization of the workforce was observed in the Tiruppur knitwear industry with women constituting 21 per cent of the work force in 1985, which increased to 34 per cent in 1998. The incidence of child labour was noted in the industry where about 90 per cent of the children were girls.

5.20 Women workers in Tiruppur were concentrated in the lowest paid category of workers receiving substantially lower wages than men. Women were concentrated in embroidery, cleaning, finishing, tagging and packaging. More recently, women are entering into stitching in large numbers. There is a clear sexual division of labour and with the introduction of machines this has further been augmented and facilitated. The fashion masters are the most skilled and this category is exclusively reserved for male workers. Machine attendants carry out the actual process of knitting, control, adjust and monitor the process with the assistance of helpers. Female workers are mostly helpers in these units and their chance of moving from helpers to attendants is nil, while the male workers are able to make this vertical movement. This very clear sexual division of labour has implications for the wages earned, permanency in the job and the possibilities for upward mobility in the industry. Obviously, the women receive lower wages and have limited job mobility in the hierarchy of the knitwear industry (Neetha 2002). The Commission's visit to the garment factories in Tiruppur confirmed these features of the industry.

5.21 The garment industry operates in India within subcontracting supply chains. These supply chains are sometimes small and at the local level, while some operate for export houses who supply to international retail brands. In Ahmedabad city, the smallest supply chain was observed where the local ready-made shop

Gender discrimination at the workplace is subtle and is reflected in the nature of work performed, valuation of the skills and the technology used by men and women.

acted as a sub-contractor to local retail shops. The owner bought cloth from the local mills and sub-contracted the ready-made garment stitching to home-based workers, mainly women in the city. Such local chains also operate as small factory units sub-contracting out the garment making, sometimes, to smaller home-based units. The largest operation was conducted by a medium sized unit which hired about 100 men and 50 women in its premises and made a branded jeans of denim cloth bought from the large textile mills. Various processes within the supply chain such as washing and finishing of the jeans were also contracted out to other units (Unni and Bali 2002).

5.22 There was a clear sexual division of labour in the garment making processes and also in the type and quality of garments contracted. Among workers stitching ready-made garments in the local supply chains, only 12 per cent of the women stitched pants, while 36 per cent of the men did so. The majority of the women stitched frocks and hosiery garments. Men were also engaged in the cutting of the garments, the most specialized activity, supervision, procuring orders and marketing. Women were engaged in minor activities like cutting the loose threads, stitching the buttons and other finishing and ornamentation work. This sexual division of labour that relegated the women to the lowest categories of work resulted in lower piece-rate wages and lower overall monthly incomes (Unni and Bali 2002).

5.23 In the occupations related to the textile industry, we see clearly that the jobs of supervisors and machine operators are male dominated, while the preparatory work of making of fibre and yarn, spinning and winding are dominated by women (Fig. 5.1). In the garment industry women tailors are not too few, but it is the kind of garments that they stitch that makes the difference in valuation. Sewing and embroidery works are clearly dominated by women. Our observation in Chapter 4 that the wearing apparel industry has a large proportion of own account workers and homeworkers may be recalled here.

5.24 A number of national and international studies have documented the sex-typing of jobs and occupations by women (e.g. Anker 1998). Occupational segregation represents a form of discrimination when large segments of the labour force are in essence restricted from entering many occupations. Anker (1998) argues that the Asia/Pacific region has a relatively low level of occupational segregation by sex, compared to other regions of the world. Women are often restrained by vertical segregation within an occupation. Vertical segregation occurs when men and women in the same occupation hold different jobs in terms of rank and pay. In other words, women have fewer opportunities for advancement or management within an occupation.

5.25 A documentation of occupational segregation therefore may reveal that women are concentrated in certain occupations within a broad group. But occupational segregation alone will not be able to show that women in similar occupations receive lower wages than men by typing them by jobs that are deemed inferior. The vertical segregation of the nature implied by Anker (1998) will not be evident. In the services sector, health and education (including the organised

Fig. 5.1: Occupational Distribution among Weavers, Spinners and Related Occupations and Tailors and Related Occupations: All Workers 2004-05

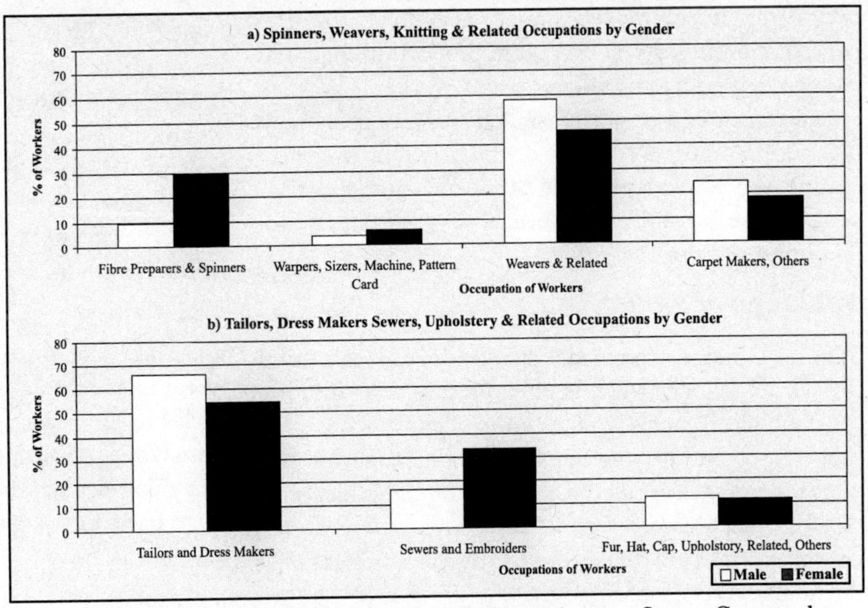

Source: NSS 61st Round 2004-2005, Employment-Unemployment Survey. Computed.

Fig. 5.2: Occupational Distribution among Physicians and Other Health Related Workers, All Workers, 2004-05

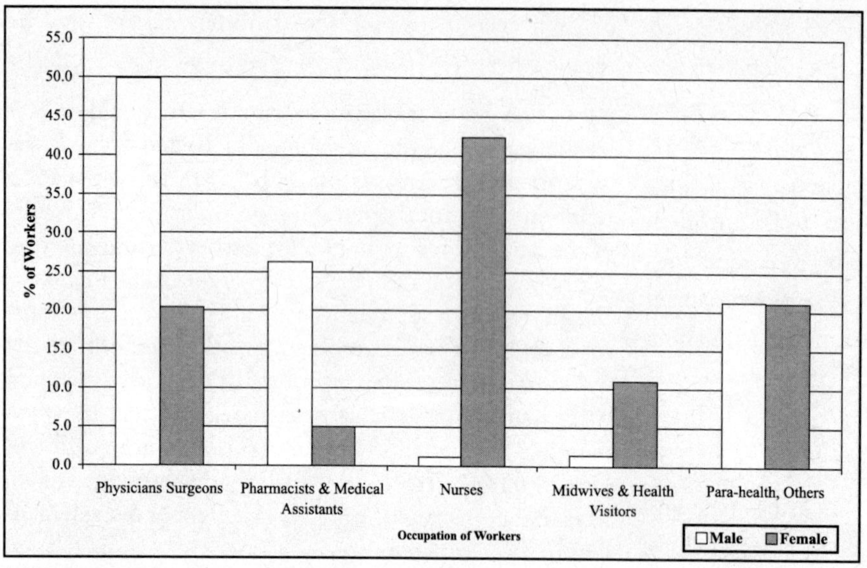

Source: ibid

5.27 Sexual division of labour was observed in the garment export industry where the hierarchy was such that men were the supervisors since men tailors "do not like to take orders from women". In the supervisory category usually women supervised only women. Men tended to be placed in all the 'critical' skilled jobs and were consequently paid higher wages. Hand embroidery done by women was the most skill and time intensive, but paid the lowest wages, i.e. women's skills were systematically undervalued. Studies have brought out that women also did the most monotonous jobs, such as checking, button stitching and thread cutting, the drudgery was greater and the wages were lower (e.g. Rao and Husain 1997). In the textile and wearing apparel industry all jobs done by hand and involving minimal or low level equipment is delegated to the women. The myth of "nimble fingers" is also used to relegate much of the work done by hand to women. So while women sew the buttons, do the hemming and hand stitching, they also do the embroidery work, zardosi and stitching of sequences to the dresses. This latter is a very skilled activity, but is valued very low because it is seen as women's work.

sector), have a large proportion of women regular workers. In the health sector, women are clearly concentrated as nurses, midwives and para-health workers, all likely to get lower wages than men who are concentrated as physicians or in particular jobs even within the category of para-health workers (Fig. 5.2). In the education sector the occupational segregation is very clear. Men are prominently in the higher education sector, and women in rural areas are mainly in pre-primary. A lot of them are likely to be aganwadi workers, ayahs etc. In urban areas women workers are prominently primary school teachers. In the construction industry a very large proportion men and women are concentrated as casual workers. Women are clearly categorized as unskilled workers in a broad 'others' category. Women do have some presence among the brick-layers and stone masons and tile-setters. The possibility of vertical segregation cannot be obtained from these data.

Valuation of Skills

5.26 What we have described above is a sexual division of labour, which is often used as a justification for dubbing women's work as low skilled. It is observed that in most industry groups there is a hierarchy of jobs where the women are placed at the bottom. This hierarchy of jobs is then used to value the jobs where women are concentrated as low skilled even if it involves exceptional talent and years of informal training.

5.28 Similar examples can be found in almost all industries. In the ceramic industry or in brick-kilns, preparation of the mud or clay is a skilled activity. If the consistency of this raw material is not correct, the pottery will disintegrate and the houses built of the brick would collapse. This work is done by women but is valued as one of the lowest as we described in Chapter 3 on wage workers. Women in this activity are paid the least, well below minimum wages.

5.29 In the agricultural sector, while the men undertake ploughing and harvesting, the women do the weeding. While ploughing is important, weeding involves back-breaking work. The gender discrimination is such that while minimum wages are fixed separately for ploughing and harvesting, there is most often no minimum wage fixed for weeding)

5.30 The sexual division of labour in the society is reflected in the division of labour in the workplace. This is then used to argue that the activities or segments where the women are concentrated are low skilled. The consequence of this sex-typing of jobs is two fold: even women with requisite skills find it difficult to get into the so called "male" jobs and the ones in which the women are concentrated are categorised as "low skilled" and receive lower wages.

Number of Women Workers in Non-agriculture

5.31 We have distinguished three types of workers in Chapter 1, namely, the wage workers, the self-employed and the homeworkers. Half of the 22 million women non-agricultural workers in the unorganised sector in 1999-2000 were independent self-employed workers. Nearly 29 per cent or 7 million were wage workers (Table 5.10). About 5 million or 21 per cent were homeworkers, more or less disguised wage workers. The major difference in the rural and urban workforce was the higher share of independent self-employed women workers and also a higher share of homeworkers in rural areas.

5.32 While we are not able to separate out the homeworkers from the self-employed, the total self-employed women constituted 21 million in 2004-05[1] (70 per cent of the workforce in the unorganised sector), having increased from 15 million in 1999-2000 (71 per cent). At least some part of this increase in self-employed would be increase in homeworkers. The proportion of women wage workers grew in the unorganised sector from 29 per cent to 30 per cent during the period, or 7 million to 9 million workers.

Casual and Regular Women Workers

5.33 Wage workers in the unorganised sector are distinguished into regular and casual workers. Among the women wage workers, less than half or 47 per cent were casual workers. The casual workers were mainly engaged in construction and manufacturing sectors, 39 per cent and 29 per cent respectively. A smaller proportion (20 per cent) was engaged as domestic workers in private households. These women were clearly undertaking manual work in these sectors (Appendix A5.1).

5.34 Regular workers formed about 53 per cent of the women wage workers. One striking feature of the regular women workers is that nearly 54 per cent were employed by private households in domestic services, a rather steep increase from 37 per cent in 1999-00. In the majority of cases the only reason why they are probably categorised as regular workers is that they receive a salary on a regular basis. Their working conditions, in terms of wage earnings, and benefits received were likely to be quite close to the casual workers. The conditions of work of domestic workers in regular work are highlighted in Box 5.1. Overwhelming majority of the domestic women workers, nearly 84 per cent in urban areas and 92 per cent in rural areas, were found to get wages below the

Table 5.10: Number and Percentage of Unorganised Non-agricultural Female Workers 1999-00 and 2004-05

Category of Employment	Number (Million)			Percentage		
	Rural	Urban	Total	Rural	Urban	Total
			1999 - 2000			
Wage Employment	2.6	4.0	6.6	21.7	37.3	29.1
Self-employment: Independent	6.3	4.9	11.2	52.9	45.9	49.6
Home Workers	3.0	1.8	4.8	25.4	16.8	21.3
Total	**11.9**	**10.6**	**22.5**	**100.0**	**100.0**	**100.0**
			2004 - 2005			
Wage Employment	3.7	5.2	8.9	23.5	38.0	30.2
Self-employment	12.1	8.5	20.6	76.5	62.0	69.8
Total	**15.8**	**13.7**	**29.5**	**100.0**	**100.0**	**100.0**

Source: Same as in Table 5.1.

1 In 2004-05 the 61st Round data do not allow us to distinguish homeworkers from the self-employed, hence for major part of the analysis in this chapter they are clubbed with the self-employed workers.

Box 5.1: Domestic Workers

Female and children domestic workers constitute a large portion of today's migrant worker population. Sadly, they also join the category of migrant workers, most being at the risk of exploitation and human rights abuse. Working in the unregulated domain of a private home, mostly without the protection of national labour legislation, allows for female domestic workers to be maltreated by their employers with impunity. Women are often subjected to long working hours and excessively arduous tasks. They may be strictly confined to their places of work. They are frequently the victims of sexual harassment and, in the very worst cases, rape and torture. Thus, women as well as children working as domestic servants are often forced to work in sub-human conditions with no job security, no benefits and no dignity. A study estimated that 78 per cent of the domestic helpers in 12 cities were females. The increasing demand for domestic workers in all big cities and towns of the country played a major role in the migration of women from rural or tribal areas. Most of them are from poor families and are illiterates. Due to the lack of education and skill they become easy victims of exploitation.

The biggest problem faced by the domestic workers across the country is their non-recognition as workers. The domestic workforce is excluded from labour laws that look after important employment-related issues such as conditions of work, wages, social security, provident funds, old age pensions, and maternity leave. Though the Indian government's Ministry of Labour has adopted legislative measures for social security and welfare of unorganised workers, these, if at all effected, are typically applicable to those employed in agriculture, construction, trade, transport, and communication; domestic workers are left out. They do not come under labour laws - they have no right to workers' compensation, weekly holidays and minimum wages. Even the Child Labour (Prohibition and Regulation) Act, 1986, does not include domestic workers. But attempts were made to introduce legislation to improve the lot of the domestic workers but the Domestic Workers Bill was stalled in 1990 and again in 1996.

There are estimated 4 million women domestic workers in India. Of them, 92 per cent are women, girls and children, 20 per cent are under 14 years of age and 25 per cent are between the ages of 15 to and 20. In Mumbai alone, there are an estimated six lakh domestic workers of whom 80,000 work full-time.

Good example of struggle for the rights of domestic workers is The Human Rights Law Network (HRLN), who argues for their status as regular workers and consolidation of the existing laws in their favour. Other organizations such as the Pune Shahar Molkarin Sanghatana (Pune City Domestic Workers Association), started in 1980, prepared a charter of rights, trained a group of women to become spokespersons, and initiated action. After repeated and lengthy protests by this organization in Pune and other parts of Maharashtra, on August 10, 2000, they managed to issue a Maharashtra Government Resolution to regulate the domestic workers. Although there has been no noticeable progress, the pay structure and the leave arrangement has now been formalized.

A survey done as recently as June 2005 by the Stree Jagruti Samiti of Bangalore illustrates how government-fixed minimum wages are inadequate even today. The study report that the minimum wages fixed by the government and paid by employers are not high enough to cover food, leave, housing, medical expenses and educational needs. It found that the average expenditure per month of a domestic worker's family, living in a slum, was Rs.5189 (Rs.173 per day) of which Rs.1959 (Rs.65 per day) was for food, Rs.1221 for school fees, Rs.817 for repayment of loans, Rs.555 for rent, Rs.293 for health care, Rs.279 for electricity, Rs.185 for transport, Rs.54 for water and Rs.62 for other miscellaneous expenditure. The minimum wage of Rs.1600 (Rs.53 per day) fixed by the government was insufficient even to cover the food needs of the average family, leave alone other needs.

Some areas for immediate policy intervention are: Granting status of worker and dignified working conditions, developing a suitable legislative mechanism and mobilisation to form unions.

Souirce: Barat (2004), Dhavse (2004), Ramirez-Mchado (2003), Sharma (2003)

National Minimum Wage of Rs.66 per day (Chapter 3). Nearly 13 per cent of the regular workers in the unorganised sector worked in the education sector. These workers could include primary school teachers, anganwadi workers and even ayahs and sweepers who received a regular salary. The SC/ST women wage workers have a somewhat narrower set of work opportunities compared to women wage workers in general. Working as domestic servants (private households), in manufacturing, construction and trade account for 91 per cent of such workers compared to 82 per cent for all women workers.

Women Self-employed Workers

5.35 As we have noted earlier, the self-employed workers are not a homogeneous group. They are divided into the employers i.e., those who hire workers on a more or less regular basis, own account workers, who do not hire workers regularly and unpaid family helpers. Majority of women were own account workers, 53 per cent (Appendix A5.2). However as we noted earlier a large proportion of them are actually homeworkers. Here again, workers belonging to SC/ST groups have a somewhat narrower range of opportunities. One of the stated advantages of self-employment for women is that they can undertake work at their pace and convenience. However, this results in the dis-advantage of limited opportunities and lower earnings.

Female Proprietary Enterprises

5.36 We observed above that nearly 53 per cent of the self-employed women were own account workers (Appendix A5.2). This implies that they were actually operating own account enterprises, though these were mainly concentrated in manufacturing and trade. The NSSO informal enterprises survey, 1999-2000 found that about 12 per cent of the proprietary enterprises were operated by women and these were mainly own account enterprises[2] (Table 5.11). Approximately 10 per cent of the workers in proprietary enterprises were engaged in the female proprietary enterprises.

5.37 We present below a comparison of the female proprietary enterprises with the male proprietary enterprises in order to understand the scale, returns and problems faced by women A typical female proprietary enterprise had a value of fixed assets of about Rs.30500, which was less than half the value of fixed assets of the male proprietary enterprises (Rs.71700). While this was true of both rural and urban enterprises, the female enterprises in the urban areas were much larger with value of assets nearly 6 times that of the rural enterprises (Fig. 5.3 & 5.4). Clearly the urban enterprises operated by women had a distinctly larger scale of operation. This pattern is similar to self-employed enterprises in general that we noted in Chapter 4.

5.38 The scale distinction of rural and urban female OAEs is noted in the fact that about 34 per cent of them have value of fixed assets of less than Rs.1000, in comparison to nearly 18 per cent of them in urban areas. At the upper end of the spectrum about 28 per cent of the urban female proprietary OAEs have value of assets greater than

Table 5.11: Percentage of Enterprises and Workers in Proprietary Enterprises, 1999-2000

Sector	Male Proprietary			Female Proprietary			Proprietary
	OAEs	Establish-ments	Total	OAEs	Establish-ments	Total	Total
			Enterprises				
Rural	81.5	5.4	86.9	12. 9	0.2	13.1	100.0
Urban	70.0	19.1	89.1	9.7	1.2	10.9	100.0
Total	76. 6	11.3	87.8	11.5	0.6	12.2	100.0
			Workers				
Rural	76.8	11.5	88.2	11.2	0.5	11.8	100.0
Urban	53.7	36.6	90.3	7.3	2.4	9.7	100.0
Total	65.8	23.5	89.2	9.4	1.4	10. 8	100.0

Note: OAE = Enterprises with no hired worker.
Establishments = Enterprises with one or more hired workers.
Source: NSS 55th Round 1999-2000, Informal Sector Enterprises. Computed.

Only about 12 per cent of own account proprietary enterprises were operated by women.

2 Proprietary enterprises and workers are defined using the NCEUS definition of unorganised sector.

Fig. 5.3: Fixed Asset per Reporting Enterprise among Proprietary Enterprises (Rs.) 1999-2000

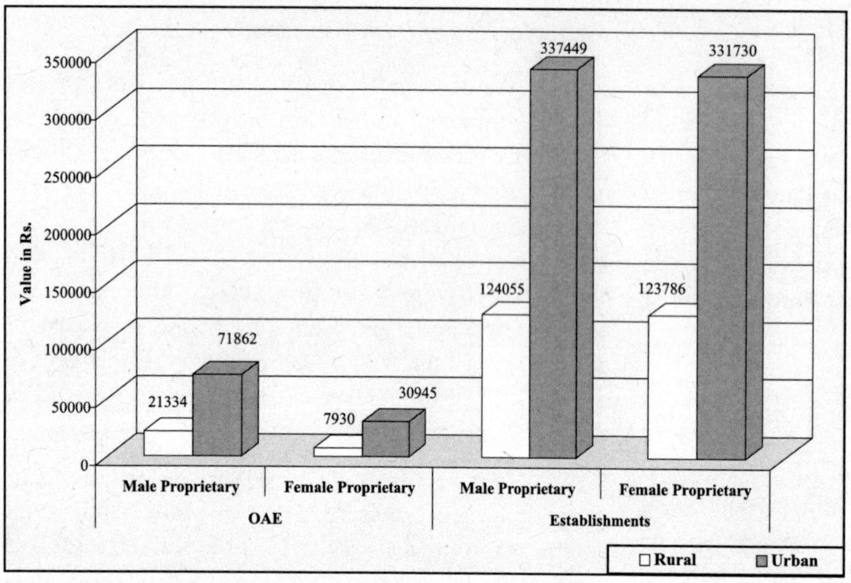

Note: OAE = Enterprises with no hired worker.
Establishments are with one or more hired workers.
Source: NSS 55th Round 1999-2000, Informal Sector Enterprises. Computed.

Rs.25000 compared to only 7 per cent of the rural female enterprises. The scale of operation of women operated units is distinctly very tiny particularly in rural areas.

5.39 The smaller scale of operation in terms of investment also results in smaller gross value addition of the female own account enterprises compared to those owned by the males (Box 5.2). The average annual gross value added per worker in the female OAEs is only Rs.9000 compared to Rs.20000 among the male OAEs. The differential between urban and rural female OAEs is also marked, with the urban units having double the value addition of the rural units (Fig. 5.5).

5.40 We noted in Chapter 4, that nearly 40 per cent of the OAEs were operating from household premises, less so in urban areas (28 per cent). A much larger share of the female OAEs, nearly three-fourth, operated from household premises. Female OAEs operating from home in the urban areas were only slightly lower, at about 68 per cent (Table 5.12). The lower scale of operation and the value addition of the female proprietary enterprises are partly explained by the phenomenon of home-based enterprises. As we shall see later in the section on homeworkers, a larger proportion of the female proprietary enterprises operating from household premises are working on sub-contract, less so in urban areas. These units are likely to be operated by homeworkers, which

Fig. 5.4: Percentage Distribution of Value of Fixed Assets (Rs. per Enterprise) in Own Account Enterprises Proprietary Enterprises 1999-2000

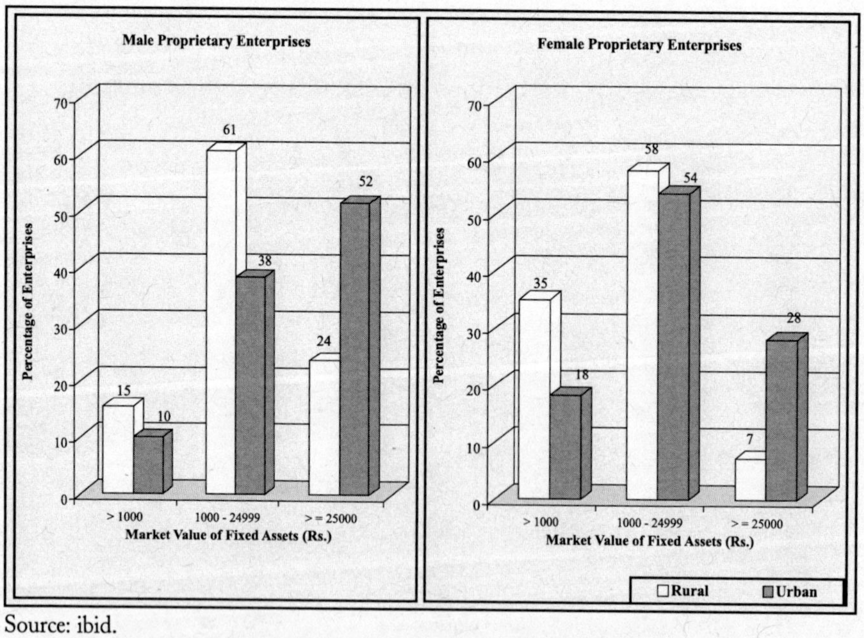

Source: ibid.

Scale of operation of women proprietary enterprises was much smaller than those operated by men. Nearly 30 per cent of women operated enterprises had value of fixed assets less than Rs. 1000 and average value addition per worker was Rs. 9000.

Fig. 5.5: Gross Value Added Per Worker among Proprietary Enterprises (Rs.), 1999-2000

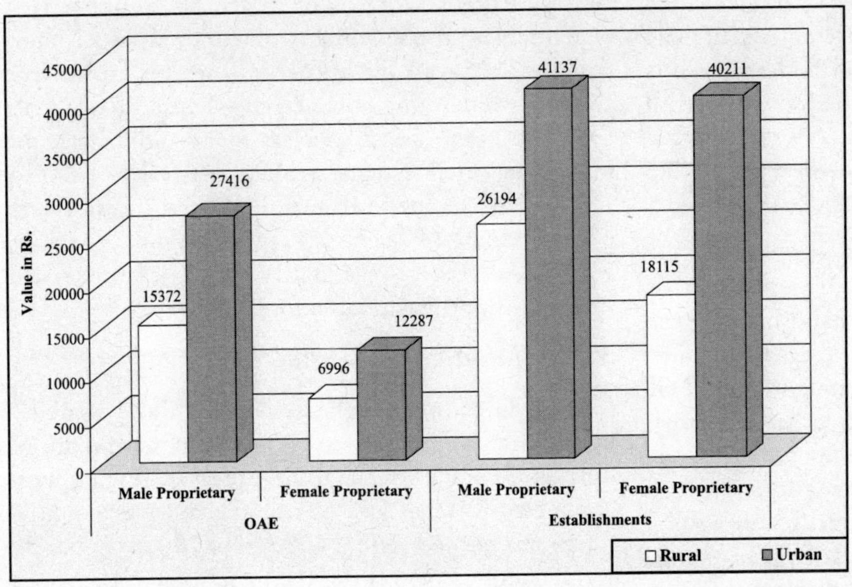

Source: ibid.

Table 5.12: Percentage of Enterprises Located At Home 1999-2000

Sector	Male Proprietary			Female Proprietary		
	OAEs	Establish-ments	Total	OAEs	Establish-ments	Total
Total	33.7	14.3	31.2	76.9	20.1	73.9
Rural	40.7	22.8	39.5	81.8	35.4	80.9
Urban	22.8	11.1	20.3	68.4	16.1	62.8

Note: Figures are percentage to the total in each category.
Source: Same as in Table 5.11.

partly explain the low value addition of female proprietary enterprises. The higher value addition among female proprietary units in urban areas may reflect the lower proportion in homework.

5.41 There was not much difference in the perception of the growth status of the male and female proprietary enterprises. Nearly 70 per cent of the female OAEs against 64 per cent of the male OAEs felt that they were stagnant and only 14 per cent (19 per cent of male OAEs) reported that the units were expanding. It is possible that in enterprises operating with low capital base and poor value addition, the difference between the male and female proprietors was not very significant and therefore the overall similar proportions reporting stagnancy reflect the overall poor prospects for these enterprises.

5.42 In spite of the poor value addition, low value of fixed assets and poor growth prospects of the female own account enterprises, 38 per cent of them reported that they faced no particular problem

Box 5.2: Below Notional Minimum Income of Female Proprietors

Value added per worker of OAE can be used as a proxy for incomes of OAEs due to the small scale of operation and the owner operated nature of the enterprise. We had estimated a notional floor level minimum annual income of Rs. 13523 for 1999-2000 (Box 4.1, Chapter 4). Overall, nearly 83 per cent of the female proprietary OAEs had incomes lower than the notional minimum compared to 41 per cent of the male proprietary OAEs.

In rural areas 89 per cent of the female proprietary OAEs had gross value addition per worker lower than an annual notional minimum income compared to 52 per cent of the male proprietary enterprises. In urban areas 72 per cent of the female proprietary OAEs having gross value addition per worker lower than an annual notional minimum income compared to 24 per cent male proprietary OAEs. In other words the small segment of female proprietors was more than twice likely to be poor compared to their male counterparts.

Nearly 36 per cent of female own account proprietors were homeworkers, operating on contract or sub-contract arrangements. Less than 4 per cent of the male proprietors were homeworkers.

(Appendix A5.3). This was higher than that reported by the male OAEs. Of the female units reporting problems the majority noted shortage of capital as the most serious problem. The major difference with male OAEs was that nearly 12 per cent of the female units reported other problems, not specified, compared to very few of the male units stating any unspecified problem. It is likely that the female enterprises face other problems that restrict their growth, which are not being clearly captured by the survey.

5.43 One problem more specific to women is that they are subject to various forms of harassment in the workplace. Verbal and physical violence against women has been an age-old method of subjugating women. This is used in the workplace to further strengthen the sexual division of labour and keep women at the bottom of the work hierarchy. Such harassment leads to stress and reduces the productivity of the workers. It can also be used to curb upward mobility or, as a consequence, inhibits growth of the women operated enterprises.

Conditions of Homeworkers

5.44 Nearly three-fourths of the female proprietors and OAEs, operated from home (Table 5.13). It is possible that much of the female proprietary units are actually homeworkers doing sub-contract work. About 36 per cent of the female OAEs were found to be undertaking sub-contract work at home, only a quarter of them were so in urban areas (Table 5.13). These units are, in all likelihood, homeworkers.

Hours of Work

5.45 A study of three industries reported that the women homeworkers worked for about 7 hours a day (Homenet South Asia and ISST, 2006). A major problem faced by the women homeworkers was the seasonality of work. The working hours varied depending on the seasonality of work so that a 7 hours day was only available in the peak season. In the lean seasons women got only about 4 hours of work per day. The home-based weavers and handmade paper makers reported that the peak season was for about 7 - 8 months in the year and 3- 4 months were lean periods. Some workers also reported months with no work at all. Such seasonality of work reduces the incomes that they are able to earn.

Value Addition in Homework

5.46 The homeworkers were subject to direct exploitation by the contractor for whom they produced. The contract under which these activities were conducted differed and one of the more exploitative forms was of piece-rate work. About 79 per cent of the women and 63 per cent of the men homeworkers were paid on a piece-rate basis (NSSO 2001a, Table 16).

5.47 The homeworkers are dependent on the sub-contractor for supply of work, raw material and sale of finished goods. They are also isolated from their fellow women workers in the same trade. This dependence on the contractor together with the isolation undermines their ability to bargain for higher piece-rates, timely payments or overtime pay. The annual gross value addition of the female homeworkers is, on average, Rs.5500 (Table 5.14), much lower than even the female OAEs, Rs.9000. The average value of fixed assets engaged by them is also very low at Rs.6000. The very low value addition per annum would be reflected in the very low annual earnings, much below the nominal norms we had indicated earlier.

Table 5.13: Percentage of Homework Proprietary Enterprise in Total OAEs and Establishments 1999-2000

Sector	Male Proprietary			Female Proprietary		
	OAEs	Establish-ments	Total	OAEs	Establish-ments	Total
Total	33.7	14.3	31.2	76.9	20.1	73.9
Rural	40.7	22.8	39.5	81.8	35.4	80.9
Urban	22.8	11.1	20.3	68.4	16.1	62.8

Source: Same as in Table 5.11.

Piece-rate Wages and Hidden Costs

5.48 The homeworkers are paid piece-rate wages for the work delivered. This wage has many hidden costs, including use of the house and electricity. Delayed payments and arbitrary cuts in wages on the pretext of poor quality also add to the hidden costs (Box 5.3).

Homeworkers faced problems of seasonality with peak and lean seasons where both hours of work and earnings varied substantially.

Table 5.14: Gross Value Added per Worker and Fixed Assets per Enterprise of Homework (Rs.) 1999-2000

Sector	Male Proprietary	Female Proprietary	Male Proprietary	Female Proprietary
	Gross Value Added Per Worker (Rs.)		Value of Fixed Assets Per Enterprise (Rs.)	
Rural	8826	5270	13917	3800
Urban	13409	6343	39131	13914
Total	10435	5544	22341	6229

Note: Homework constitutes of OAEs located at home and working solely/ mainly on contract.
Source: Same as in Table 5.11.

Changing as well as complicated designs due to fashions when no training is provided for adds to the costs since one has to learn the new work from family friends or neighbours utilizing valuable time of both the informal trainers and trainees. Some not so hidden costs are the cost of inputs such as thread for the garment workers and maintenance of equipment. All these are often not factored into the wages leading to extremely low net wages per day.

5.49 The piece rate wages vary considerably by products and also change with the season. In Indore stitching of saree falls for Rs. 20-22 for 1000 falls, where the cloth is given, but the cost of thread and electricity has to be borne by the worker. A shirt is stitched for Rs. 21 for a dozen and better quality ones for Rs. 8 for just one shirt. In the lean period this can come down to Rs. 8 per dozen. In Uttar Pradesh, home-based chikan workers on piece-rate can earn from Rs.20-25 per day to Rs.10-15 per day. In Ahmedabad, frocks were stitched for Rs.35 per day. Making of Agarbatti earns Rs. 48 - 80 per day in Madhya Pradesh, but only about Rs.28 per day in Ahmedabad. Overall, piece-rate wages tend to be below minimum wage norms (Homenet South Asia and ISST 2006).

Girl Child Workers

5.50 Within the class of women workers, there is the subset of girl child workers. Although the latter is only 2.6 per cent of the total women workers, the problem of out of school girl children is a larger one. The issues relating to child workers are discussed in the next chapter along with what we call other disadvantaged workers such as migrant workers and bonded labourers.

Conclusion

5.51 The Commission considered it important to highlight the special problems of women workers and hence this Chapter. While women workers in general constitute a marginalised category within the class of workers, the ground reality also forces us to recognise the different layers within this subordination. Rural women workers occupy a lower position compared to their urban counterparts. But the lower most layer is constituted by those belonging to the bottom strata of the society i.e. SCs and STs. This kind of stratification also brings out that women who are at the upper social stratum especially with higher educational capabilities are better off than the rural men workers in general. The inescapable conclusion is that while gender is a strong differentiating factor in the Indian labour market it is mediated by one's class and caste/ community position in the society.

5.52 What is generic to the condition of women workers as a whole is their double burden of work.

Box 5.3: "Hidden costs" borne by Homeworkers

In Imphal, home-based weavers earn Rs.90 per piece of mekhla (sarong) or cotton/woollen shawls over two days. The piece rate has however gone down since the last year to half, Rs.45/ per piece due to an increase in the number of weavers. About 22 per cent of the home-based weavers and 44 per cent of the handmade paper makers reported problems such as delayed payments which added to the "hidden costs". A women silk mekhla sarong homeworker in Imphal can earn Rs. 600-700 per piece over seven days. But the "hidden costs" are that the trader or contractor who contracts this work can return the sarong even after two to three years if it remains unsold (Homenet South Asia and ISST 2006).

Value addition per worker of women homeworkers was even lower than that of the women own account enterprises

Women's time use in economic activities that give them a return is limited but their participation in such economic activities that add to the economic output of the household (called extended SNA) far exceeds that of men. Therefore, taking these two together, women spend, on average, 17 per cent more time than men.

5.53 Women in general have, for reasons discussed here, lower work participation rates. But for rural women they are not only higher but also closer to men. These rates are higher for women belonging to SCs/STs than the other women. Higher work participation rates per se do not indicate a higher level of welfare. What it points out is the economic compulsion driving women to engage in whatever work that comes by in order to make a living. Only when higher work participation rates are accompanied by higher educational capabilities and/or asset and income (as in the case of a section of urban women), higher work participation rates become meaningful from a welfare and, especially, income point of view.

5.54 The lower work participation rates conceal in good measure the subsidiary status of the work of women. A quarter of the women workers report themselves as in subsidiary status compared to just two per cent of men. Although women work for more time (including activities that are not recognised as economic work as such), they reported as available for additional work. One third of them were available for work if that was based at home. Despite lower earnings, home-based work offers them the flexibility to calibrate income-earning activities with household responsibilities.

5.55 The conditions of work, as discussed in this chapter as well as in Chapter 3, especially of women wage worker, are quite dismal. Women workers are also subjected to various forms of discrimination including job-typing which gives them a lower wage compared to men. Among the women wage workers, a significant proportion (54 per cent) is reported as regular workers. As we have seen, this, in no way, indicates a higher labour status since more than half of them work as domestic servants (reported as workers in private households) where longer hours of work, very few holidays and lower wages are the prevalent norm.

5.56 The position of self-employed women is only marginally better than of the wage workers. Their capital base is low and consequently their value addition is also low. One third of them operate from their own homes.

5.57 The overall picture that emerges is one of greater disadvantage for women workers in general and those belonging to rural as well as SCs/STs in particular. Apart from such inherited disadvantages as lower social position, a number of other factors also contribute to such a picture. These are their limited asset position, access to resources, and low level of education and skill. Education, and consequently some ability to acquire formal skills, could be a moderating force but this aspect presents a dismal picture. About 71 per cent of the women workers in India are either illiterates or have education only up to the primary level compared to 49 per cent for men. For rural women this is as high as 88 per cent but the highest percentage with such low education are the women workers belonging to SCs/STs i.e. 92 per cent. The overall situation of women workers calls for interventions of a promotional nature from different entry points but with a strong emphasis on education.

6 Other Disadvantaged Workers: Migrants, Child and Bonded Labourers

Introduction

6.1 A running theme of this report as well as the Commission's earlier report is on social security to the unprotected unorganised workers. They are, by definition, disadvantaged workers. The degree of disadvantage, if one may say so, varies from segment to segment. The earlier chapter discussed the gender dimension of this disadvantage and its manifestations in terms of the conditions of work, access to capital and earnings. There is yet another segment of disadvantaged workers who perhaps constitute the bottom layer of the working class in the country. These are the migrant workers, particularly the seasonal migrants, child labourers and bonded labourers. These workers are highly vulnerable on account of their lack of physical assets and human capabilities coupled with their initial conditions of extreme poverty and low social status. This results in their low bargaining power in the labour market that further reinforces their already vulnerable state and traps them into a vicious circle of poverty and deprivation. Not only is it more difficult for them to find avenues for gainful work, but it is also harsh when some such work is found. The conditions of work are often miserable, hours of work long, wages meagre and security of work non-existent.

6.2 Migrant workers are mostly those who are driven from their homes in search of means of earning a livelihood. Lacking any skills and assets they tend to end up in the unorganised sector, both in rural and urban areas. Such labourers are often sourced by labour brokers. More often than not, they end up in rural areas as farm labourers and construction workers or rickshawalas or street vendors in urban areas. Women from poor rural households often end up as domestic servants in urban centres. The bonded labourers have a different kind of predicament, with no freedom to change their employment. Sometimes the disadvantages of migration and bondage intersect as in the case of migrant bonded labourers in construction sites, quarries and brick-kilns. The problem of child labourers is more complex and is intertwined with the twin issues of poverty and lack of access to quality school education. It is also not rare to find situations when a child worker is a migrant and bonded to the employer. As the susceptibility of these workers to exploitation is greater and the reasons for their plight in the work arena are specific to each and related to their societal position and context, this Chapter explores the working conditions of these disadvantaged migrant workers, child labourers and bonded labourers in separate sections.

Migrant Labour

6.3 Migration by individuals and/or households is undertaken for both economic and social reasons. These include migration by virtue of marriage, as has been the case of a large majority of the female migrants or due to economic reasons such as for seeking better employment opportunities. Migration can be within the country, i.e. internal migration which can be within the district, intra/ inter district or intra/inter state (rural to rural, rural to urban, urban to rural and urban to urban) or it can be international migration. Here we primarily deal with the working conditions of internal migrant wage workers and focus on semi-permanent or seasonal migrants in the informal sector, who are at the lowest end of the spectrum of migrant workers. They comprise the petty self-employed and the unskilled casual wage workers who are highly disadvantaged and vulnerable and are subject to extremely adverse working conditions and economic exploitation. The migrant workers are largely in the unorganised sector, which is why they face exploitation at the hands of employers and middlemen who help them get employment in destinations away from their places of origin.

6.4 In India there is large scale migration of unskilled wage labourers from not necessarily the resource poor areas but also the areas which have widespread poverty, low demand and wages for unskilled labour. They migrate to areas where there is greater demand for such labour. These comprise both rural to rural and rural to urban migration. Examples of the former are the migration of poor rural labourers from Bihar and eastern Uttar Pradesh to Punjab and Haryana and those from Maharashtra to Gujarat. Examples of rural to urban migration are the ones from Jharkhand to Delhi, Orissa to Gujarat (especially in urban industries in Surat), Bihar to Mumbai and Delhi and so on. Migration is critical for the livelihood of these poverty ridden, skill and asset deficient persons, especially in rural areas which include economically and socially backward groups such as the tribal and other deprived groups. They are further disadvantaged because of the absence of laws that specifically address their problems. There is one law pertaining to inter-state migration that is conspicuous by its rather poor implementation resulting in the persistent vulnerability of the migrant workers especially the unskilled and the poor.

Table 6.1: Percentage Distribution of Migrants by Place of Last Residence, Age, Sex & Reason for Migration 2001

Reason		Total	Rural	Urban
Work/Employment	Total	9.5	.4	19.7
	Male	28.1	16.9	38.0
	Female	1.7	1.2	3.2
Business	Total	0.9	0.4	1.8
	Male	2.6	1.5	3.5
	Female	0.2	0.2	0.3
Education	Total	1.1	0.6	2.0
	Male	2.5	2.1	3.0
	Female	0.4	0.2	1.1
Marriage	Total	49.6	62.5	23.6
	Male	2.3	4.0	0.8
	Female	69.6	77.9	44.2
Moved after Birth	Total	5.0	4.8	5.5
	Male	9.9	13.5	6.8
	Female	2.9	2.4	4.4
Moved with Household	Total	13.7	8.6	23.9
	Male	19.4	17.9	20.7
	Female	11.3	6.2	26.8
Others	Total	20.2	18.6	23.4
	Male	35.2	44.1	27.3
	Female	13.9	11.9	20.0

Source: Census of India 2001, Table D-5.

Definition and Size of Migrants

6.5 There is some conceptual difficulty in defining migration. This is mainly because people move away from their place of residence or origin for varying time intervals. At one end is the long term/ permanent migration and at the other is the short duration one of less than a year. Between these two extreme points, the varying time periods have to be reckoned within any meaningful understanding and measurement of migration. In addition to the time dimension, there is also the aspect of reason for migration. This has not drastically changed over the years. As shown in Table 6.1, employment continues to be the main reason for men while marriage is the main reason for women. In the case of men, employment as a reason for migration was seen to rise in the nineties. This could be reflective of the impact of structural changes on availability of employment opportunities, largely generated in urban centres and that too for the more skilled among the workers. With improved infrastructure and connectivity migration has been facilitated as information regarding opportunities is available in far off places. This has led to greater mobility of workers, a welcome fact, if it arises out of choice and not sheer economic compulsion. According to the 2001 Census, the total migrant population in the country was 314.5 million. Both the Census and the NSSO indicate that the rate of migration has increased.

6.6 Among those migrating for work and employment purposes, long term/permanent migration (above 10 years) has the highest share (Table 6.2). This has declined slightly since 1991 (from 56 per cent to 54 per cent) while the 1-9 years category has shown a rise to 28 per cent in 2001 from 21 per cent in 1991. Short duration migration over the years has shown a slight decline from 3.0 per cent in 1991 to 2.8 per cent in 2001.

6.7 However, the Census and the National Sample Survey underestimated the seasonal and short-term migration, while aspects of more permanent migration were captured well. Indeed, the NSSO for 1992-93 and 1999-00 suggest that there has been a decline in short duration migration through the nineties. As per the 1999-00 NSSO, 10.9 million workers migrated for 2 - 6 months of which 8.5 million were in rural areas. Among the rural migrants 3 million were females. Short duration out-migrants constituted 2.1 per cent of the rural employed persons and 1.3 per cent of the urban employed of which 3.1 per cent (rural) and 1.5 per cent (urban) were casual labourers. The 1999-00 NSSO results show

Table 6.2: Percentage Distribution of Migration by Duration of Stay 2001

Duration of Residence		Total Migrants			Migrants who Stated Work/ Employment as the Reason for Migration		
		Total	Male	Female	Total	Male	Female
Less than 1 year	Total	2.8	4.5	2.1	7	6.1	13.7
	Rural	2.9	6.2	2	15.3	13.8	21
	Urban	2.7	3	2.5	3.3	3.1	5.6
1-4 years	Total	15	17.8	13.9	23.5	23.1	26.7
	Rural	13.8	17.2	12.9	28.1	28.4	27
	Urban	17.6	18.3	17	21.5	21	26.4
5-9 years	Total	13.4	13	13.6	17.7	18	16
	Rural	12.7	11.3	13.1	16.6	17.2	14.1
	Urban	14.7	14.5	14.9	18.2	18.3	18
1-9 years	Total	28.4	30.8	27.4	41.3	41.1	42.7
	Rural	26.5	28.5	26	44.6	45.6	41.1
	Urban	32.3	32.7	31.9	39.7	39.3	44.4
10 years and above	Total	54.2	39.2	60.6	51.6	52.8	43.5
	Rural	57.5	32.7	64	40	40.6	37.8
	Urban	47.7	45	50.1	56.9	57.6	49.9

Source: Census of India 2001, Table D-3.

that there has been a shift in favour of the more regular and self-employed among migrants and a reduction in the casual workers among males in both rural and urban areas. However in the case of women the increase has been in all the categories and more in the case of casual labour in both rural and urban areas.

6.8 Temporary or short duration migrants need special attention because they face instability in employment and are extremely poor. They are engaged in agricultural sector, seasonal industries or in the urban sector as casual labourers or self-employed (Srivastava and Sasikumar 2005). By all accounts, the numbers of such migrants is much larger than that estimated in the official sources. The NCRL (1991) estimated the number of seasonal migrants at 10 million in rural areas alone. Such migrants work in agriculture, plantations, brick-kilns, quarries, construction sites and fish processing. Some estimates suggest that the total number of seasonal migrants in India could be in the range of 30 million (Srivastava 2005)

6.9 Migrant workers form a substantial proportion of both the organised and unorganised workforce in urban India. In the early 1990's a study (Acharya and Jose 1991) of low-income households in Mumbai city found that 80 per cent of the workers were migrants. During recent times it is observed that regional imbalances in development within the country along with rising unemployment have accelerated the pace of migration. The rural poor, especially from the low productivity eastern and central states, migrate to western and southern India where jobs are being created especially in urban centres. Rural-urban migration is found to be temporary or semi-permanent.

Social and Educational Profile of Migrant Wage Workers

6.10 Migrant casual workers belong to the poorest sections of the population characterised by meagre human capabilities and capital assets. It is the absence of resources or lack of access to resources in their native places that force them to migrate to other regions in order to eke out a living. Migrant labour is a compensating mechanism used by households to reduce their disadvantageous position. Poor migrant households are characterized by lower education levels, lower levels of income from agriculture, and an inferior geographical location (Haberfeld et.al. 1999). Migrant labourers primarily belong to socially deprived groups such as Scheduled Castes and Scheduled Tribes and other weaker sections including women and children. Among the ST and SC migrants short duration migration is higher, being 2 per cent and 1 per cent respectively, compared to an overall rate of 0.7 per cent in the case of all short duration migrants (NSSO 2001b). Migration in the working age group of 15-59 years is very high. This percentage is much higher for rural persons, 86 per cent, compared to the urban migrant persons, 78 per cent. Search for employment or better work opportunities is one of the prime reasons for migration, especially from rural areas where employment opportunities are very limited and entrenched in the agriculture sector which generates a seasonal demand for labour. Thus, during lean periods in agriculture the casual labourers migrate to urban and semi-urban areas in search of employment.

6.11 While migration is high among both the highly educated and the illiterates, among the seasonal temporary migrants the proportion of the least educated is very high (Srivastava and Sasikumar 2005). Based on the census estimates, illiteracy among migrants is found to be very high at 48 per cent. While the majority of migrant population in rural areas are illiterates the urban counterparts show a lower share of illiterates at 27 per cent. Lack of employment opportunities for the less educated (or less skilled) lead to migration as a strategy for survival.

Employment Profile of Migrant Wage Workers

6.12 A recent study (Srivastava and Sasikumar 2005) found that migrants are engaged in different kinds of employment in rural and urban areas. In rural areas self-employment is the main activity followed by casual work with 33.4 per cent male migrant workers and 44.2 per cent of female migrant workers in 1999-00. In urban areas, 55.6 per cent male migrant workers are primarily engaged in regular employment followed by 31.1 per cent in self-employment and 13.3 per cent in casual work. The respective figures for urban female migrant workers are 35.1 per cent, 39.7 per cent and 25.1 per cent. Casual unskilled migrant wage workers, thus, comprise a significant section of the migrant workers, particularly among rural female migrant workers.

6.13 Migrant workers at the upper end of the spectrum i.e., those in the organized sector or at the higher rung of employment, are much better off than those who migrate at the lower end of the spectrum. The latter comprise unskilled casual labourers or petty traders or small time self-employed like cart and rickshaw pullers who either migrate from rural to urban areas or urban to urban areas in search of better employment opportunities mainly as a survival strategy. The rural to rural shift mainly comprises agricultural labourers while the shift to urban areas is mainly into the unorganised sector as construction workers or as unskilled workers in industrial units.

6.14 More than half of the migrant workers are constituted by those in agriculture. The proportion was significantly higher for females (82 per cent) compared to males (32 per cent). In the non-agricultural sector migration in the category other than household industries is very high.

6.15 Labour force participation rate (LPR) is higher among migrants compared to non-migrants as this category, particularly the males, faces displacement from their native lands mainly in search of employment. The difference between migrants and non-migrants is particularly noticeable in rural areas especially for females. The young (less than 15 years of age) register a slightly higher LPR compared to the non-migrants in that age group.

6.16 Unemployment rate (those seeking/available for work) among migrants is much higher than the non-migrants, particularly in urban areas where the gap between migrants and non-migrants is higher. Unemployment among the young (15 - 30 years) is higher compared to those above 30 years of age. New environs and lack of knowledge/awareness about employment opportunities available along with alienation faced on account of being non-natives place the migrants at a more disadvantaged position than the non-migrants.

Conditions of Migrant Workers

6.17 Migrant workers, particularly at the lower end, including casual labourers and wage workers in industries and construction sites, face adverse work as well as living conditions. This group is highly disadvantaged because they are largely engaged in the unorganized sector with weakly implemented labour laws. Migration often involves longer working hours, poor living conditions, social isolation and inadequate access to basic amenities. It is the poor households that largely participate in migration to eke out a living. Thus, states where poverty levels are very high including Bihar, U.P and Orissa have a high rate of out-migration to relatively better off states such as Punjab, Haryana, Maharastra and Gujarat. These groups of migrants are characterized by meagre physical and human capital assets and belong to socially deprived groups such as the Scheduled Castes (SCs) and Scheduled Tribes (STs) and weaker groups such as the women.

6.18 The poor migrant workers are extremely vulnerable and often resort to employment through exploitative contractors and middlemen rather than taking up individual contracts directly with their employers. This greatly increases the dependency of the group on these middlemen and accentuates risks and uncertainty. In the rural agricultural sector employment is mainly through such middlemen who recruit at entry points such as railway stations and bus stands, while in the urban informal sector friends and relatives also act as the link between the employer and the migrant worker. To reduce costs and risks migrant workers also seek employment on their own and move in groups.

6.19 A number of cases cited in Srivastava and Sasikumar (2005) indicate that in the unorganised sector there is a high degree of organised migration such as in construction industry where workers are recruited through contractors who fix wages and also retain some parts of their earnings. Sometimes, as in case of domestic maids, agencies and voluntary organizations get involved as mediators for employment as the women mainly come from tribal areas. Further even those who enter the market independently have to face the dominance of contractors and sub-contractors.

6.20 Migrant wage workers often face economic exploitation when they are paid wages which are lower than what are received by local counterparts. Employers prefer migrant labourers to local workers because of the former being cheaper. Statutory minimum wage rate guidelines are rarely observed. Wages for women migrant workers are lower than the male migrant workers. For example, in the construction industry they are treated as

Migrant workers, particularly at the lower end, including casual labourers and wage workers in industries and construction sites, face adverse work as well as living conditions. This group is highly disadvantaged because they are largely engaged in the unorganized sector with weakly implemented labour laws.

assistants and given unskilled manual worker's wages. Further, payments are irregular and, sometimes, are not made in time. Piece rates are prevalent as it provides greater flexibility to the employers. Migrant workers also prefer this system as it assures some savings. However, often migration interlocks credit and labour such that the net returns to labour may have no relation to wages in the destination areas.

6.21 Migrants from backward regions are willing to accept any distress wages as long as they have access to employment. In the bargain they undercut the employment prospects of the local labour. Their excess supply also contributes to reducing the wage rate.

6.22 The wage payments in the public sector also vary from project to project (Srivastava and Sasikumar 2005). Private contractors hired by public sector often flout the labour laws and minimum wage legislation. Temporary migrants who migrate in times of higher seasonal demand for labour also face instability in employment and fluctuations in wages. Insecurity is further accentuated by the segmented labour markets, lack of regulation and dominance by labour contactors and vulnerability of the workers.

6.23 Work conditions of migrant workers are severely adverse with long working hours in hazardous environs. The migrant workers, in most cases, stay at the work site in temporary huts and shanties. Often the employer expects them to be available for work all 24-hours of the day. There is no fixity of hours. This is not only true of workers at construction sites or mines and brick-kilns but also in the case of domestic servants who stay at the employers' places and are expected to be available for work round the clock, irrespective of the nature of work. Women migrant workers are even more insecure because of the odd work hours. They face exploitation in terms of adverse working conditions, lower wages and insecure living conditions and, at times, sexual harassment.

6.24 Deplorable living conditions increase the health hazards of the migrant workers making them more susceptible to disease and infection because of the unhygienic living conditions. Occupational health problems are also high especially for those working at the construction sites, quarries and mines as lung related health issues become common among them. Employers do not take care of the safety measures which increase the rate of accidents. Temporary status of the workers limits their access to public health services and programmes. Women are not given maternity leave. That childcare facilities and crèches are also not available forces the women to bring children to workplace and to expose them to health hazards. Problems such as body-aches, sunstrokes and skin irritation are endemic among the workers, such as in the fish processing units where the conditions are damp, dingy and dirty. The extremely unsanitary working conditions cause infections. There are reports of eye irritation, respiratory disorders, arthritis, rheumatism, skin disorders and nausea. There are occupational hazards and accidents and the managements provide no compensation.

6.25 Lack of a permanent residence often adversely affects education prospects of the children of the migrant workers who in the process are deprived of even the basic elementary education. While the families of the migrant workers who stay back in the native places face financial/economic and social/emotional insecurities and the migrant is also left isolated and lonely in an alien environment.

Living Condition of Migrants

6.26 Migrant workers not only face adverse working conditions, their living conditions are also often deplorable. With little or no assets of their own, the migrant wage workers often live in temporary hutments located at the site of work, such as in case of construction industry. There is no facility of safe drinking water or hygienic sanitation. Often they live on pavements or in slums, stations and parks in the cities. In the case of temporary migration, the migrants are not able to make use of the public distribution system due to non-availability of ration cards.

6.27 Over the years there has been massive poverty-induced migration of illiterate and unskilled workers into mega cities such as Mumbai, Delhi, Kolkata, and Chennai. These workers are absorbed in poor urban informal sectors and eke out a living in miserable conditions in urban slums, which has also contributed to urban degradation. Since these metropolises have failed to provide migrants and residents minimum shelter and subsistence employment poverty, unemployment, extreme

Deplorable living conditions increase the health hazards of the migrant workers making them more susceptible to disease and infection because of the unhygienic living conditions.

housing shortages and frequent breakdowns of essential urban services (like water, electricity, sewerage and transport) are visible in these cities (Bhagat 2005). Further, since employment generation in the mega cities is limited, especially because of the capital intensive industrialisation, the incoming illiterate and unskilled migrants are absorbed in very poorly paid urban informal sectors which are characterized by low productivity, insecurity and exploitation. Such kind of migration helps avoid starvation, yet it does not improve the economic conditions of the migrants.

6.28 Migrant workers, thus, suffer for lack of regulated working hours and harsh working and living conditions but have also been facing social consequences in terms of the wrath of local elements. There are several instances of migrant labourers being made victims by terrorists such as in Kashmir, Punjab and more recently in Assam. Several studies have pointed out that the migrant workers should be assured right to safe and adequate accommodation, right to organize, right to safe travel, assured minimum wages and access to health and education services.

Conditions of Women Migrant Wage Workers

6.29 As already mentioned and health services. They gain access only to low paid work available above, women migrant workers face even greater insecurity and are more prone to exploitation than their male counterparts. Women casual workers are largely engaged in construction sites, fishing industry as in the case of coastal areas or more prominently as domestic maids. Their presence is also visible in brick-kilns, personal services such as entertainment, housekeeping, child-care in the unorganised sector. Millions of women migrants face hazards that reflect the lack of adequate rights, protection and opportunity to migrate safely and legally. Migrant women workers are a marginalized group and there is a gross neglect of their concerns. This can be attributed to their lower socio-economic status and the under-valuation of their work. Their situation is weakened by the gender stereotypes and biases, leading to discrimination, besides the additional fear of sexual assaults and exploitation. As per 1991 census there were almost 3 million migrant women who cited employment and business as the reasons for migration (Rustagi undated). The states that reported higher women migration for economic reasons are Tamil Nadu, A.P, Gujarat, Karnataka, Kerala and Maharastra. Interestingly, these are also the states with relatively higher levels of industrialisation, commercialisation of agriculture and a higher share of workers outside agriculture. It is plausible that changes in aspirations that accompany economic growth and diversification are also factors that propel more women to migrate for work. Women are more concentrated in the shorter duration and distance (more intra-state than inter-state) migration than their male counterparts.

6.30 Migrant women suffer from difficulties of gaining employment compared to migrant men. Even when they are hired, the terms and conditions are more adverse and wages paid lower than for men and local female wage workers. Very often the norms of the Minimum Wage Act 1948 are not followed. They are paid in piece rates and are hence preferred by employers as it helps them in cost cutting. There is no fixity of working hours. They are made to work for long hours with no commensurate increase in wages. The work environment is like a captive work place (Rustagi undated). Work conditions are extremely arduous. Often, as in the construction industry, women workers are illiterates and unskilled. They are unaware of the prevailing wage rates and accept work at lower wages. Most women remain manual, load carrying and unskilled workers. Wages are not paid in time and are more like a subsistence allowance.

6.31 Living conditions are deplorable with workers residing in make shift shanties and huts with no access to drinking water and other basic amenities. Often women workers move with the family and have the additional burden of domestic chores and child rearing. Inevitably,

A study of migrant workers in Mumbai city noted that 48 per cent of them lived in one room accommodations, 57 per cent had no toilet facilities, 36 per cent had no water facility, 44 per cent lived in kuchha or semi-pucca houses, 32 per cent used gunny bag, straw, tin sheets as raw material for their houses. Even a long term stay as migrants did not improve their deplorable conditions. Duration of stay in the city varied from 10 years (37 per cent), 10 - 19 years (29 per cent) and more than 20 years (34 per cent).

their health suffers. They also suffer from malnutrition. That maternity benefits are not provided further worsens their situation. Child-care facilities are also lacking subjecting their children to the hazards at the work place as they have to accompany their parents to the work site. They are thus also deprived of basic education. The conditions of migrant domestic servants, highlighted in Chapter 5 of this Report, bring out the many facets of deprivation, vulnerability and exploitation faced by women They constitute nearly 18 per cent of the children migrant workers.

Child Labour

6.32 There has been a secular decline in the incidence of child labour reported in India. Of the two main sources of information - Census and the National Sample Survey Organisation - we have relied mainly on the latter since this report is based on the data from this source. Both the sources show a decline in children principally engaged in work. As per the Census, the total number of child workers declined from 11 million in 1991 to 3.6 million in 2001. Similar decline is also evident in the NSSO results but the estimated total number was 13.3 million in 1993-94 and 8.6 million in 2004-05. They constituted about 6.2 per cent of children in the age group 5-14 years in 1993-94 and 3.4 per cent in 2004-05. The absolute number and proportion of working male children were more than those of girl children (Table 6.3).

6.33 The overall decline in child workers is attributable to increasing awareness, greater participation in education by children from poorer households, efforts by the state, international organisations such as the UNICEF, the ILO and national and international non-governmental organisations towards elimination of child labour, and the regulatory framework. All stakeholders

Table 6.3: Number and Percentage of Children (5 - 14 years) across Usual Status by Gender

Usual Status	2004 - 2005			1993-1994		
	Boys	Girls	Total	Boys	Girls	Total
			Numbers (million)			
Labour	4.7	3.9	8.6	7.3	6.0	13.3
Non-Workers	16.1	20.5	36.6	22.2	32.0	54.1
Out-of-School(Labour Pool)	20.8	24.4	45.2	29.4	38.0	67.4
Students	113.9	93.2	207.1	84.4	61.3	145.8
All (5 - 14)	134.7	117.6	252.3	113.9	99.3	213.2
			Percentage			
Labour	3.5	3.3	3.4	6.4	6.1	6.2
Non-Workers	12.0	17.4	14.5	19.5	32.2	25.4
Out-of-School(Labour Pool)	15.4	20.8	17.9	25.9	38.3	31.6
Students	84.6	79.2	82.1	74.1	61.7	68.4
All (5 - 14)	100.0	100.0	100.0	100.0	100.0	100.0

Note:
1. Labour includes the unemployed.
2. Labour pool includes child labourers and non-workers.
3. Non-workers are children who are neither in school nor at work.

Source: NSS 61st and 50th Rounds, 2004 - 2005 and 1993-1994, Employment-Unemployment Survey. Computed.

Out-of-school children comprise the workers and the non-workers. They together signify a measure of deprivation among children and can be considered as a potential labour pool, always being at the risk of entering the labour force. They constitute nearly 18 per cent of the children.

in the effort to eliminate child labour recognise the close relationship between provision of primary education and the elimination of child labour.

6.34 The Commission does not consider it appropriate to view child labour purely from a definitional point of view of who is a worker and who is not. This is because there is a significant proportion of children who are out of school and who are not reported as child labour, 14 per cent in 2004-05. Given the conditions in poor households it is quite possible that these children are engaged in some activity by way of helping their parents, either to take care of the younger siblings or old parents when the parents are away for work or in activities that are not perceived as income-earning by the reporting parents. Out-of-school children comprise the workers and the non-workers. In our view, they together signify a measure of deprivation among children and can be considered as a potential labour pool, always being at the risk of entering the labour force. They constitute nearly 18 per cent of the children; 15 per cent boys and 21 per cent girls. The increased participation of children in schools had led to a substantial decline in the children at risk since 1993-94 but in absolute numbers the potential child labour pool still remains very high at 45.2 million.

6.35 Interestingly, the states with higher incidence of child labour are not necessarily the ones with high incidence of out-of-school children although there are some states that find a place in both. States with child labour above the all-India average were Andhra Pradesh, Orissa, Rajasthan, Meghalaya, Karnataka, Chattisgarh, Uttar Pradesh, West Bengal and Maharashtra (Table 6.4). States with out-of-school children that are higher than the all India average were Bihar, Jharkhand, Uttar Pradesh, Rajasthan, Arunachal Pradesh, Madhya Pradesh, Orissa and Chattisgarh. The latter are basically the poor states with very low levels of human development, often referred to as BIMARU. Orissa and Arunachal Pradesh are outside the acronym of BIMARU but the position of Orissa is quite close to them in several respects.

6.36 The fact that 21 per cent of the children are deprived (i.e. child labour plus out-of-school children) should be reckoned as a major socio-economic problem and one that is bigger than the narrowly defined child labour. While child labour is a major problem only in 9 states, child deprivation is more widespread in the country except in the three states of Kerala (3 per cent), Tamil Nadu (5 per cent) and Himachal Pradesh (9 per cent) (Appendix A6.1).

6.37 The association between economic and social deprivation and child labour has been long established in India and other countries. Fig. 6.1 shows a clear negative association among the per capita household expenditure and the incidence of child labour and out-of-school children. The incidence of child labour and out-of-school children was also clearly associated with the socio-religious status of the household (Fig. 6.2). The ST and Muslim households had the highest incidence of child deprivation labour. Hindu SCs and OBCs followed closely. The incidence of child deprivation as well as child labour among Muslims is higher than among Hindu SCs. This is different from the earlier patterns of deprivation across socio-religious groups,

Table 6.4: States with High Incidence of Child Labour and Out-of-School Children (Labour Pool) (5 - 14 Years) (Percentage) 2004 - 2005

State	Male	Female	Total
		Child Labour	
Andhra Pradesh	6.1	7.1	6.6
Orissa	5.3	4.6	5.0
Rajasthan	3.8	5.9	4.8
Meghalaya	5.8	3.3	4.6
Karnataka	4.3	4.8	4.6
Chhattisgarh	3.6	5.5	4.5
Uttar Pradesh	4.7	3.4	4.1
West Bengal	4.3	3.2	3.7
Maharashtra	3.2	3.7	3.5
All India	**3.5**	**3.3**	**3.4**
		Out-of-School Children	
Bihar	29.9	40.1	34.4
Jharkhand	20.0	27.4	23.4
Uttar Pradesh	20.3	25.7	22.8
Rajasthan	15.6	29.2	22.2
Arunachal Pradesh	19.7	24.1	21.7
Madhya Pradesh	17.3	26.4	21.5
Orissa	17.3	23.7	20.4
Chhattisgarh	14.0	23.0	18.6
All India	**15.4**	**20.8**	**17.9**

Source: NSS 61st Round 2004 - 2005, Employment Unemployment Survey. Computed.

Fig. 6.1: Incidence of Out of School Children (Labour Pool) and Child Labour (5 - 14 Years) across Quintile Groups (Percentage) 2004-05

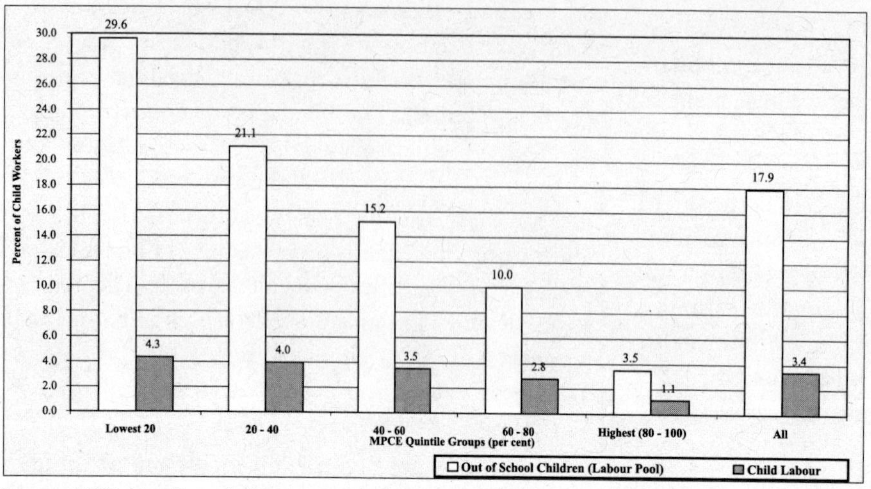

Source: NSS 61st Rounds 2004 - 2005, Employment-Unemployment Survey. Computed.

wherein Muslims in general were better off than the Hindu SCs and worse off than the Hindu OBCs. The artisan tradition among the Muslim community may partly explain the higher incidence of child labour besides the relative deprivation of the group.

6.38 It has been argued by scholars that poverty or lack of employment opportunities is not a sufficient condition for the existence of child labour (Chandrasekhar 1997). Child labour is also significantly and negatively associated with opportunities for education of children (Wiener 1991; Nangia 1981). The high incidence of child deprivation indicates that part of the problem may manifest as child labour and a larger part as lack of opportunity or access to attend the school. While 3.4 per cent of the children are child labourers, the proportion of out-of-school children is 18 per cent for the country as a whole. Across both the expenditure quintile groups and the socio-religious groups, higher the incidence of child labour, higher has been the incidence of out-of-school children other than child labour. Nearly 30 per cent of the children among the lowest 20 per cent of the households (in terms of expenditure) are out-of-school (Fig. 6.1). Similarly, nearly 28 per cent of Hindu ST children and 25 per cent of Muslim children were out-of-school (Fig. 6.2). The inherent problem, thus, lies not in dealing with child labour alone, but with the entire gamut of the out-of-school children, which is a manifestation of not merely poverty or economic deprivation but also the extent and nature of educational facilities and its easy access to the socially weaker sections.

Fig. 6.2: Incidence of Out-of-School Children (Labour Pool) and Child Labour (5 - 14 Years) across Socio-religious Groups 2004 - 2005

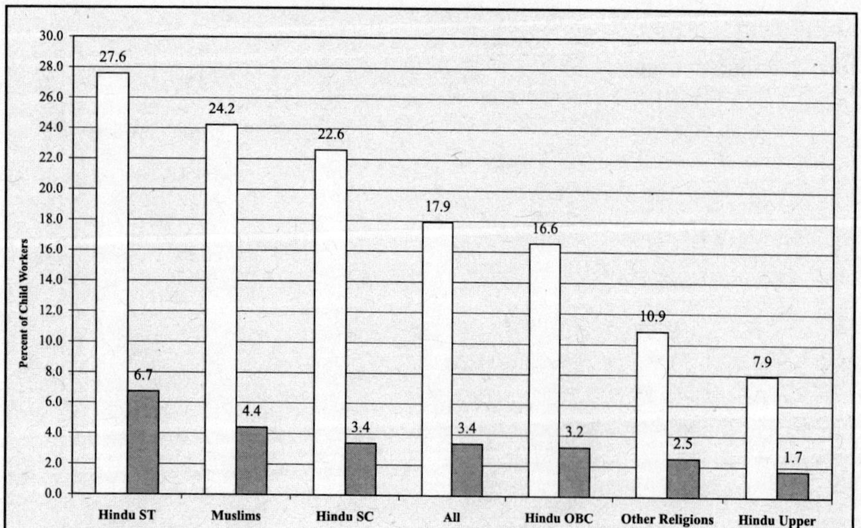

Source: ibid.

Conditions of Work

6.39 There were about 9 million child labourers in 2004-05, of which majority were in rural areas (Table 6.5). The percentage of child labour was also slightly higher in the rural areas, 3.7 per cent compared to 2.5 per cent in urban areas. About two-thirds of the children were engaged in family enterprises as helpers, while more than one-third were engaged as paid wage workers. However, in urban areas, nearly half the child labourers were wage workers.

6.40 Two thirds of the child workers were engaged in

Table 6.5: Child Labourers (5 - 14 years) by Sector 2004 - 2005

	Rural	Urban	Total
Child Labour (million)	7.0	1.5	8.6
Child Labour (as per cent of all children)	3.7	2.5	3.4
Per cent of Self- employed to Total Workers	66.5	51.0	63.9
Per cent of Wage- employed to Total Workers	33.5	49.0	36.1

Source: Same as in Table 6.4.

agriculture. It seems that majority of the working children were helping in the family farms in rural areas but the sector still accounted for 72 per cent of the casual wage child labourers and 9 per cent of the regular workers. Nearly one-fifth of the girls and 14 per cent of the boys worked in manufacturing industries and another 10 per cent of the boys were engaged in trade (Table 6.6).

Table 6.6: Percentage of Child Workers (5 - 14 years) across Industry Groups by gender 2004 - 2005

Industry Group	Boys	Girls	Total
Agriculture	62.8	71.1	66.6
Mining	0.1	0.4	0.2
Manufacturing	14.4	20.5	17.2
Electricity	0.0	0.0	0.0
Construction	3.0	0.8	2.0
Trade	10.6	1.6	6.4
Hotels	4.4	0.4	2.5
Transport	1.2	0.1	0.7
Real estate	1.2	0.0	0.6
Education	0.0	0.0	0.0
Health	0.0	0.1	0.0
Community	1.8	1.6	1.7
Household	0.5	3.4	1.8
Total	**100.0**	**100.0**	**100.0**

Source: Same as in Table 6.4.

6.41 India's child labour policy is two-fold: a ban on such labour in certain hazardous industries and its regulation in others. It is, however, found by independent researchers as well as Census of India that child workers continue to be employed in hazardous industries as well as in others. A large proportion of the children engaged in the manufacturing sector, the second highest industry group using child labour, are likely to be exposed to the risk of being in such hazardous occupations as wage labourers.

6.42 Industries employing child labour are highly fragmented with complex structures where much of the work is done through a system of sub-contracting to small, unorganised sector enterprises (home-based and otherwise), which are paid on piece rates. Part of the complexity of the industrial structure and the forms of subcontracting are a result of efforts to evade child labour regulations and other similar measures (Ghosh and Sharma 2003; Sekar and Mohammed 2001; Burra 1989). Independent researchers have found child workers in large numbers in home-based industries such as beedi making, match industry, carpet production, lock making, glass bangle making, hosiery and so on, all identified as hazardous industries under the Child Labour Act of 1986 (e.g. Ghosh and Sharma 2003: Laskar 2000; Goyal 2005). There is also blatant violation of the law as well as human rights in the small workshops where children continue to work in dangerous working conditions.

6.43 Studies by the V.V.Giri National Labour Institute looked at the conditions of work of child workers in different industries and reported that they worked for more than 8 hours a day. In fact, only those child workers who were also attending school worked for less than 8 hours a day. School going children attended school for 6 hours a day and then spent another 4-6 hours working (Ghosh 2004).

6.44 Child labour helps employers by depressing general wage levels in these industries. The general finding of recent studies on working conditions of children is that child workers worked as much as and as long as adult workers received no wages (as apprentice) or a fraction of the adult wage, which was itself very low. They faced inhuman and even dangerous working conditions. Scholars have observed that within the unorganised sector, child workers are the worst affected. Not only have they lost their childhood and opportunities for education, they face conditions at work that are at par with adult workers and, in some cases, even worse since they do not have the bargaining power to demand their rights. Any national policy that aims at improving the conditions of work in the unorganised sector should aim at elimination of all types of child labour in agriculture as well as in the unorganised non-agricultural sector enterprises. Since the banning of child labour through legislation (confined to the hazardous industries) has not proved to be very effective, further legislative effort should aim at regulating child labour and restricting their employment in all sectors, consistent with the needs of their development. In Chapter 13, the Commission has made specific recommendations in this regard, Further, efforts should be made to promote relevant, child-centred primary education of good quality, and expand employment and livelihood opportunities for adult workers.

Girl Child Workers

6.45 We estimated that there were nearly 8.6 million child workers less than 14 years of age in 2004-05 of whom 3.9 million were girls. Majority of these children were working in the agricultural sector. In the age group of 10- 14 years, however, about 5.4 per cent of boys and 4.9 per cent of girls in rural areas were working in their principal capacity. Among the urban children, about 4.4 per cent of the boys and 2.4 per cent of the girls were working in their principal capacity (Fig. 6.3). Majority of these children would be helping in the family farms or family enterprises. The girls are likely to be helping their mothers in the homework activities that they may be engaged in. Further, in the age groups 10- 14 years about 2.5 per cent of the girls in rural areas and nearly one per cent in urban areas were working at least part of the year (in subsidiary status).

6.46 While nearly 90 per cent of the boys and girls in this age group were in school in urban areas, in rural areas the gender discrimination is much deeper. Nearly 87 per cent of the boys in rural areas were in school where as only about 77 per cent of the girls were in school. Of the girls 10-14 years of age, nearly 11 per cent in rural areas and 5.5 per cent in urban areas were helping their mothers and were primarily engaged in domestic work. A negligible proportion of the boys were

Fig. 6.3: Percentage of Boys and Girls in Principal Work, Attending Education and Domestic Duties (Usual Principal Status) by Age Group, Sector and Gender 2004 - 2005

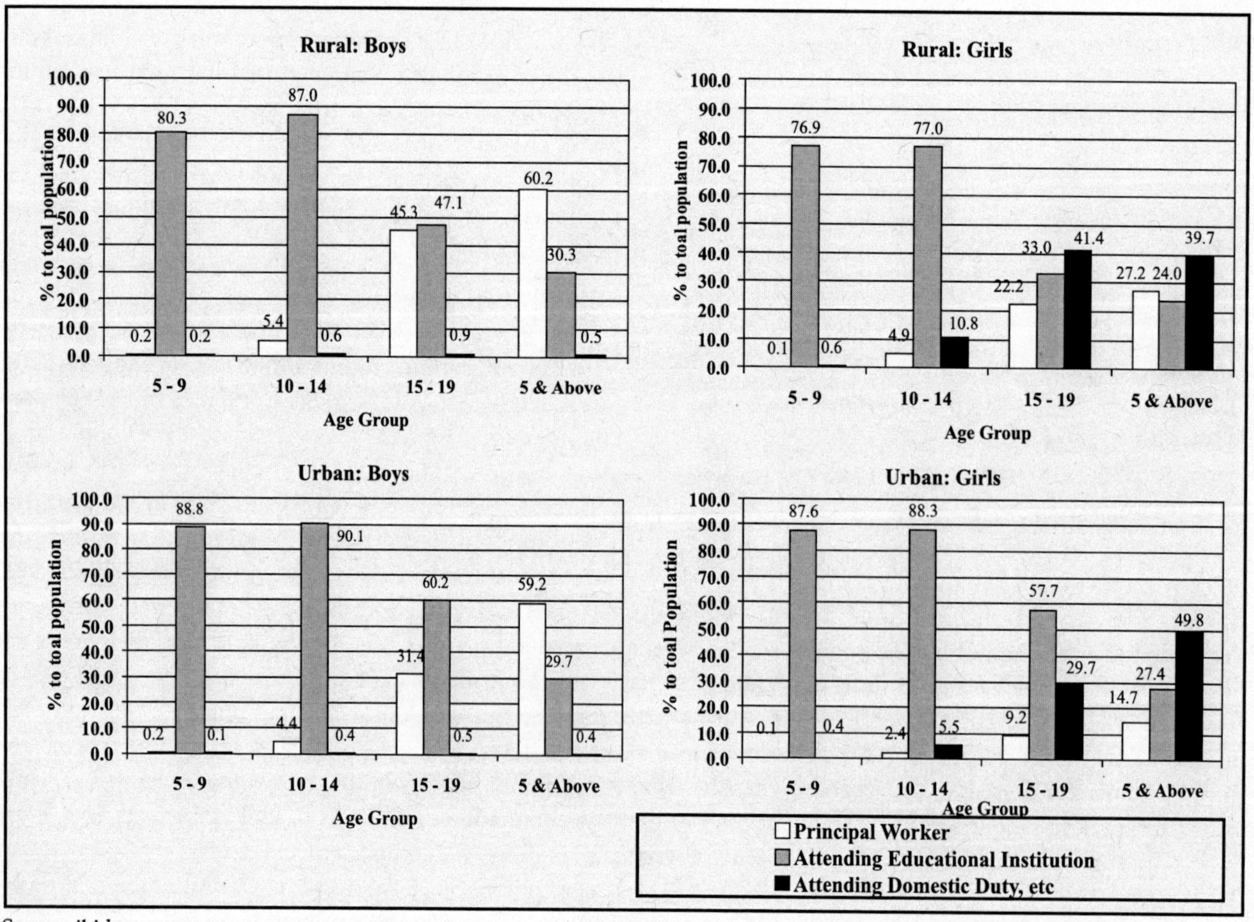

Source: ibid.

engaged in domestic work. Thus, while the girls were not officially engaged in work, they were working by the extended SNA concept and perhaps helped to relieve their mothers to participate in the workforce.

6.47 About half of the 11 per cent of girls, engaged in domestic duties in rural areas, collected water and firewood and prepared cow dung cakes for fuel. As we saw earlier, a large proportion of the adult women also engaged in these activities. Clearly the girls were helping out their mothers in these activities, which could be categorized as work. Collection of water and to some extent fending for other fuel sources are activities carried out by a large proportion of the 5.5 per cent girls in urban areas as well. Other tasks performed by girls in rural areas are husking paddy, grinding food grains and sewing. All these activities may keep the girl child out of the school as well.

6.48 The main issue about the girl child is that the characteristics of their work participation and engagement in domestic duties reflect those of the adult women. The two dimensions of women's work, viz. the social and cultural norms and double burden of work, appear to be operating on the girl child as well. Being kept out of school and helping the mother in work and domestic duties, would reduce her capacity to compete in the labour market in future. Her future is, thus, in jeopardy even from the age of 10, if not from earlier. This is particularly true of the girls in rural areas. It is possible that majority of these girls also belong to the poor households and are being used by their families to maintain their subsistence incomes.

Bonded Labour

6.49 Bonded labour is illegal in India since the enactment of the Bonded Labour System Abolition Act (1976). Despite the law there are instances of forced labour or servitude in most parts of the country. Forced labour, slave labour and servitude are characterized by compulsions, whether customary or otherwise. In India it has often been found that bonded labour stems from a creditor-debtor relationship between the employer and the employee, whereby the debtor enters into labour as a means to repay the debt and does not receive wages for the work rendered by him to the creditor, who reckons it as a return of the debt. Very often the bondage is not confined to the debtor alone but his family members are also co-opted as bonded labourers. The bondage continues to the next generation. It involves adverse contractual stipulations not justified by law or even by the prevailing state of the market. Bonded labour relationships are also usually reinforced by customs or by force. Thus, bonded labour relationships are not purely economic contracts, even though employees may enter into them 'voluntarily' because of economic compulsions. Bonded labour, thus, refers to a long-term relationship between the employee and the employer, cemented through a loan, by custom or by force, which denies the employee various freedoms including to choose his or her employer, to enter into a fresh contract with the same employer or to negotiate the terms and conditions of her/his contract (Srivastava 2005).

Incidence and Socio-economic Profile of Bonded Labour

6.50 The first systematic survey on bonded labour was undertaken by the Gandhi Peace Foundation and the V.V. Giri National Labour Institute in 1978 and estimated the number of bonded labour in India then to be 2.62 million. On the initiative of the Supreme Court, a study found that in 1995 there were still about a million bonded labourers in Tamil Nadu alone (Sugirtharaj and Sait 1995). Weaker sections of the society including the Scheduled Castes, Scheduled Tribes and the OBCs accounted for 76 per cent of all bonded labour. Bonded child labour formed about 10 per cent of the total. Number of cases of bonded labour actually reported by the Director General of Labour Welfare of the Ministry of Labour, Government of India has been so miniscule that it is hardly a problem in the country. The total number of bonded labour reported for 1997 was 6000 and it declined to 304 in 2005-06 (Table 6.7). Given the official apathy and absence of any concerted effort, it is extremely difficult to say how reliable these figures are. At the same time, the Ministry of Labour estimated that between 1996 and 2006, about 2.86 lakh bonded labourers were in different states and, of these, about 2.66 lakh were rehabilitated (Tables 6.7 and 6.8). The National Human Rights Commission (NHRC) has been active in the effort to identify and rehabilitate bonded labour.

6.51 A high proportion of the bonded labourers were from the Scheduled Castes (61.5 per cent) and the Scheduled Tribes (25.1 per cent). The proportion of backward and deprived groups is found to be very high among bonded labourers across various studies. A number of cases of bonded labour in agriculture, construction, mines and brick-kilns have been reported from the states of Punjab, Haryana, Delhi, Uttar Pradesh,

Table 6.7: Incidence of Bonded Labour Reported

Year	Incidence of Bonded Labour Reported (Number)	Year	Incidence of Bonded Labour Reported (Number)
1997-98	6000	2002-03	2198
1998-99	5960	2003-04	2465
1999-00	8195	2004-05	866
2000-01	5256	2005-06	304
2001-02	3929		

Source: GOI (2004-2005)

Madhya Pradesh, Andhra Pradesh, Tamil Nadu, Rajasthan and Karnataka and most of these labourers are from the Scheduled Tribes or Scheduled Castes and are migrants. SCs/STs constitute a major share among the bonded labourers because, being a socially relegated group with no physical and human assets, they are often trapped by the debt burden and taken as bonded labourers. They have no means to redeem their situation and are subject to exploitation by the higher castes. Among the employers, 89 per cent were agriculturalists. The Gandhi Peace Foundation survey categorised bondage into inter-generational bondage; child bondage; loyalty bondage; bondage through land allotment and widow bondage (Srivastava 2005). The vulnerable groups including SCs/STs, women and children, are more easily taken in as bonded labourers in several industries like woollen, carpet and silk weaving, gem cutting and polishing.

6.52 Bonded labourers are mostly found in agriculture as also in several activities in the unorganised sector. Among the sub-sectors, the incidence of bondage is probably the highest in quarries and open mines. These industries are characterized mainly by the predominance of manual processes, seasonality, remoteness and contract migrant labour. Brick-kilns are another industry, which reportedly continues to have a sizeable incidence of bonded labour. Among industries for which recent evidence has accumulated are power looms, handlooms, rice mills, sericulture and silk weaving, woollen carpets, fish processing, and construction. Bonded labour, including of children, has been identified in a number of other sectors such as the circus industry and domestic work. Incidence of bonded labour is also found to be relatively high among migrant labour, child labour and forest tribal populations (Gupta 2003).

6.53 In view of the overwhelming evidence revealed by a number of studies and surveys, it is highly unlikely that the magnitude of bonded labour is only a miniscule as reported by the Ministry of Labour. Increasingly also, as is evident from the discussion above, the bonded labourers are from the lowest segment of migrant labourers and child labourers.

Table 6.8: Number of Bonded Labour Identified, Released and Re-habilitated by the Centrally Sponsored Scheme during 2005-2006

States	Identified and Released upto 31-3-05	Rehabilitated upto 31-3-05	Central Assistance Provided in Rs Lakh upto 31-3-05
Andhra Pradesh	37,988	31,534	850
Bihar	13,651	12,974	389.28
Karnataka	63,437	57,185	1578.18
Madhya Pradesh	13,087	12,200	163.26
Orissa	50,029	46,901	903.34
Rajasthan	7,488	6,331	72.42
Tamil Nadu	65,573	65,573	1661.94
Maharashtra	1,398	1,325	9.55
Uttar Pradesh	28,236	28,236	577.07
Kerala	823	710	15.56
Haryana	551	49	0.93
Gujarat	64	64	1.01
Arunachal Pradesh	3526	2,992	568.48
Chhattisgarh	124	124	12.4
Punjab	69	69	6.9
Uttaranchal	5	5	0.5
Jharkhand	196	196	19.6
West Bengal	5	5	0.5
TOTAL	**2,86,245**	**2,66,283**	**6830.42**

Source: GOI (2004-2005)

Conditions of Bonded Labour

6.54 Bonded labourers work under extremely restricted work environment. They are at the mercy of the employer who exploits them economically and physically with no commensurate returns. Their economic freedom is curtailed entirely and they have no means to break-free and redeem their situation. Having no power to organise themselves, their miserable conditions are perpetuated and extended to their family members.

6.55 As mentioned earlier, bonded labourers largely belong to the deprived and weaker sections such as the Scheduled Caste community (such as in Punjab) and the Scheduled Tribes and women and children. They have no freedom to choose employment, to right of movement, to use village commons, etc; and endure long working hours. They are also physically abused at the slightest attempt to protest. Wage payment is tied up with the debt and is practically never received. Sometimes, coarse cereals are given to survive (Srivastava 1999). The system involves the repayment of the loan through labour but the wages are so meager that the labourer remains in perpetual bondage. Moreover, if freedom is desired, the employers charge a high rate of interest. The bonded labourers could also be sold to other employers and the debt obligation transferred.

6.56 Bonded labourers working in brick-kilns, mines, and in a number of other sectors, are often employed through middlemen. It is found that labour recruitment and deployment was based on a system of advances, controlled by contractors, who were paid commissions, deductible from the workers' wages. In a significant proportion of cases, the debts were carried over from one season to the next, with the contractors acting as informal guarantors of the loan. Wages were adjusted at the end of the season and the workers received a portion of their wages at the end of each week or fortnight. They can be transferred from one employer to another.

6.57 Working and living conditions in these brick kilns/construction sites/mines are very poor and there was a near total absence of any regulation, with none of the labour legislation being implemented. There are restrictions to movement and interaction with the non-bonded labourers.

6.58 There has been some change in the nature and incidence of bonded labour in India as a result of various factors, including the impact of social change and social movements, economic modernisation and state intervention. While these processes have impacted positively on the unfree status of labour in traditional agriculture and in some other sectors, the incidence of bonded labour still remains high in some segments of the unorganised industry. Emergence of bondage in newer forms is one of the reasons that make it more difficult to enforce the existing legislation.

Conclusion

6.59 The three segments of disadvantaged workers discussed here - migrant, child and bonded labourers - no doubt, belong to the bottom layer of India's working poor. Quite often they intersect each other, for example, a migrant bonded labourer or a migrant child labourer. Majority of the men migrate for economic reasons. Although migration as a percentage of the work force may not be high (about 8 - 10 per cent), the numbers involved are, indeed, quite large. More importantly, most of the migrants are poor and take recourse to it as a strategy for survival. High share of the less educated among these seasonal migrants and the fluidity of their place of living and jobs (nature and industry), culminate in their reliance on contractors and middlemen to obtain jobs, leading to greater exploitation and deplorable living conditions. The limited social networks of these migrants further increase their vulnerability in the labour market. There is a dire need to recognize the migrant workers and their multiple disadvantages to improve their working and living conditions. Registration and education of the migrant workers can probably go a long way in realizing a measure of such improvement.

6.60 Child labour continues to be a menace in the country but one that shows steady improvement. The problem is in fact confined to only a few states. However, a larger perspective of considering all out-

Bonded labourers have no freedom to change employment, to right of movement, to use village commons and endure long working hours. They are also physically abused at the slightest attempt to protest. Wage payment is tied up with the debt. The bonded labourers can be sold to other employers and the debt obligation transferred.

of-the-school children brings to the fore the ever continuing nature of what we call child deprivation. About 21 per cent of the children are out of the school as of 2005 and that numbers around 45 million. A narrow focus on child labour-centred schemes and projects, in our view, misses this larger dimension of a very basic problem with long-term adverse implications for human development and quality of living. A pro-poor strategy of growth and development that gives special emphasis on up-lifting the poorest sections of the population alone would constitute an effective response to one of the basic maladies afflicting the Indian society. That would, per force, shift attention to the conditions of work, earnings and basic livelihood requirements of the workers in the unorganised sector.

6.61 The problem of bonded labour is one that is conditioned by what one adopts as the definition. A verdict of the Supreme Court has stated that all those who do not get the statutory minimum wage should be presumed to be treated as bonded labour. A more generic definition could be the unfree nature of labour in terms of changing his or her employer. Such a definition would shift the focus to such bondages as the ones emanating from debt. No credible estimate of the magnitude of bonded labour is yet available. In any case, the Commission views the problem as a huge one in view of the overwhelming empirical evidence arising from a number of studies and surveys. Official statistics have tended to underplay the incidence of bonded labour. In fact, it is almost a non-existent problem if one takes the reported figures of bonded labour seriously.

6.62 Our examination of the conditions of work of these segments of disadvantaged workers confirms not only the sad plight of these workers, but also the multiple manifestations of deprivation even outside the work sphere. It reflects how the work and livelihood issues tend to get even more entangled, especially for these workers. The economic deprivation of these workers results in their further exploitation in the labour market, thereby resulting in a vicious circle. The plight of these segments of workers and their family members represents the acute side of a suffering India that only shines for a minority at the top.

7 Agricultural Workers: Socio-economic Profile

Introduction

7.1 In some countries 'unorganised workers' or 'informal workers' are identified as the urban self-employed and in some others the urban self-employed as well as the urban casual workers. This Commission has taken a broader view by extending the definition to the rural economy in general and agriculture in particular. This is mainly because, if informality is used to denote the unprotected nature of work, the rural workers are equally vulnerable. Moreover, rural economy is more dominated by self-employment than the urban one. As such, the Commission has examined the conditions of work and livelihood issues of agricultural workers in the same spirit as it did with regard to its earlier report on social security. By common practice, unless otherwise specified, agriculture refers to crop cultivation, forestry, fishing, hunting and livestock rearing. For the sake of brevity and common usage, self-employed in agriculture are referred to in this Report as farmers and wage workers as agricultural labourers. Together they are referred to as the agricultural workers.

7.2 The total number of agricultural workers in India has been estimated at 259 million as of 2004-05. They form 57 per cent of the workers in the total workforce. About 249 million of them are in rural areas and that works out to 73 per cent of the total rural workforce of 343 million. Their share in total rural unorganised sector employment is 96 per cent while in unorganised agricultural sector it is 98 per cent. Nearly two-thirds of the agricultural workers (64 per cent) are self-employed, or farmers as we call them, and the remaining, a little over one-third (36 per cent), wage workers. Almost all these wage workers (98 per cent) are casual labourers. The farmers are a differentiated group and size of land holding is a good proxy for this differentiation. As elsewhere in the Report, we focus on the more vulnerable segments of the self-employed workforce, viz., marginal and small farmers, although comparisons with medium and large farmers are also made whenever necessary.

7.3 This Chapter provides an overview of the agricultural workers and the specific problems and issues of farmers and agricultural labourers are discussed in the subsequent two chapters. Here we examine the composition of agricultural workers in terms of gender, age, socio-religious groups and education. The incidence of poverty has been subjected to a detailed examination by size of land operated as well as socio-religious groups. The differentiation is not confined to farmers alone; it is equally applicable to agricultural labourers as well, if we go by their social identities. As in the case of non-agricultural workers, those belonging to SC and ST categories emerge as the most vulnerable among the agricultural workers also.

Size and Nature of Agricultural Workforce in India

7.4 The share of the agricultural workforce has declined gradually during the two decades

Table 7.1: Structural Transformation in Indian States 2004-05: Share of Employment and Income in Agriculture

Less than 50 per cent	51-60 per cent	More than 60 per cent
Kerala (35, 14)	Haryana (50, 28)	Orissa (61, 28)
Tripura (37, 24)	J & K (51, 32)	Nagaland (61, 35)
Tamil Nadu (45, 14)	Sikkim (53, 21)	Karnataka (61, 19)
W Bengal (46, 22)	Maharashtra (54, 11)	Himachal Pradesh (62,21)
Punjab (48, 37)	Gujarat (56, 17)	Uttaranchal (64, 25)
	India (58, 27)	***More than 65 per cent***
	Uttar Pradesh (59, 32)	Assam (66, 29)
	Manipur (59, 26)	Madhya Pradesh (67, 28)
	AP (60, 29)	Mizoram (68, 17)
	Rajasthan (60, 27)	Bihar (71, 42)
	Jharkhand (60, 22)	Meghalaya (71, 22)
		Arunachal (73, 27)
		Chhattisgarh (75, 22)

Note: Figures in brackets are the shares of employment and income respectively in agriculture.
Source: Employment figures are from the 61st Round of the National Sample Survey and income figures are from the National Accounts Statistics published by the Central Statistical Organisation.

with diversification of the rural employment to non-agricultural activities. However, agricultural workers still constituted 56.6 per cent of the total workers in 2004-05, down from 68.6 per cent in 1983. In rural areas, agricultural workers constituted 72.6 per cent of the total workers in 2004-05, down from 81.6 per cent in 1983 (Table 7.1). The decline during this period of two decades is quite slow but, nevertheless, significant from a historical point of view when the rural economy was synonymous with agriculture. The situation is still one of overwhelming presence of agriculture but the signs of economic diversification are quite strong, albeit, slow.

7.5 The absence of faster diversification is partly due to the lack of new economic opportunities for women. While men migrate as well as take up new employment opportunities in rural areas, women find themselves at a disadvantage, as already discussed in Chapter 5. Therefore, the share of agricultural workers in the female workforce is very high, 72.8 per cent in 2004-05, while for males it is much lower at 48.9 per cent. There appears to be a faster rate of occupational mobility out of agriculture among men than among women. The latter remain more bound to rural areas and to agriculture due to socio-cultural and structural causes. The share of the agricultural workers to total workforce declined at a faster pace between 1994 and 2005 compared to between 1983 and 1994 particularly among males. The share of agricultural workers was particularly high in Karnataka, Maharashtra, Bihar, Uttar Pradesh, Madhya Pradesh and Orissa while Kerala and West Bengal have the lowest[1].

7.6 While agriculture no longer dominates the Indian economy in terms of national output, it still dominates in terms of employment. Such a lopsided structural transformation (where a declining share of income is not accompanied by an equivalent decline in employment) is the result of jobless growth in manufacturing and overall declining employment elasticity. However, the scenario is more nuanced showing sharp regional variations. As of 2004-05, there are at least five states, which have achieved a broad structural transformation in the sense that agriculture's share accounts for less than 50 per cent in both income and employment. At the other extreme, there are seven states with an overwhelming burden of employment in agriculture say, 66- 75 per cent. In the remaining fifteen states structural transformation is round the corner for at least one-third (Table 7.1).

7.7 The faster shift out of agriculture among male workers compared to female workers is expected to result in what is termed as feminization of the agricultural workforce. According the NSSO data, the share of female agricultural workers among total agricultural workers remained almost stable between 1983 and 1993-

[1] Appendix Table A7.1 gives the state-wise share of agricultural workers in the rural workforce. Across the states the pace of decline has been sharp in Kerala, Himachal Pradesh, Haryana, Rajasthan, Punjab and West Bengal. The gap between the percentage of male and female agricultural workers has been widening over the years across all the states, particularly where diversification into non-agriculture has been faster among men such as in Himachal Pradesh, Gujarat, Haryana, Jammu and Kashmir, Punjab and Rajasthan. While in the relatively poorer states and states where there has been slower diversification such as Orissa, Bihar, Madhya Pradesh, Andhra Pradesh and Karnataka the gap between male and female agricultural workers has been lower.

Fig. 7.1: Women's Share in the Agricultural Workforce (Percentage) 1983 - 2004-05

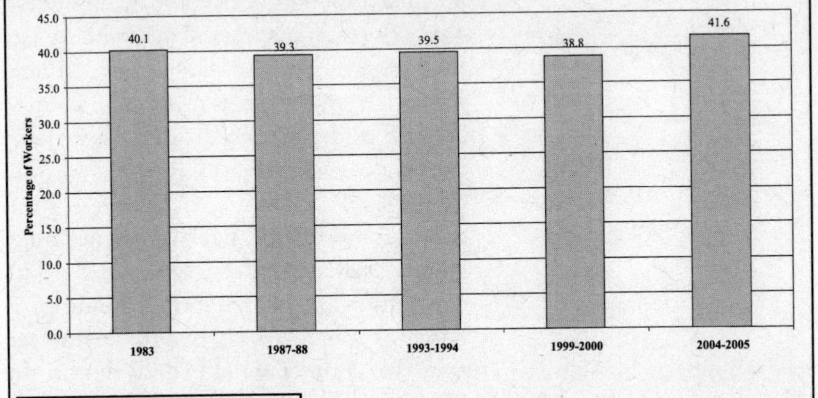

Source: Based on NSSO 1987; 1990; 1997; 2001a; 2006a

94, before declining to 38.8 per cent in 1999-00 (Fig. 7.1). However, in 2004-05 the share of women in the agricultural workforce increased to 41.6 per cent.

7.8 Farmers have a major share within the agricultural workforce though there has been a gradual decline in their percentage from 63.5 in 1983 to 57.8 in 1999-00. The obverse is true in the sense that the share of agricultural labourers rose over this period. Between 1999-00 and 2004-05, the percentage of cultivators increased to 64.2, the highest level achieved in 15 years (Table 7.2)[2]. Since the per capita availability of land has continued to decline in rural areas, and agricultural growth rates have been low over the period, the reversion to self-employment probably reflects insufficiency of alternative economic activities. Another explanation is that while the growth rate of NSDP in agriculture has been 1.7 per cent per annum between 1999-00 and 2004-05, normal monsoons were reported during all the years since 1999-2000 except in 2002. This is probably reflected in the increased number of farmers in agriculture during 1999/00 - 2004/05.

7.9 Among female agricultural workers, the share of those working as farmers has been slightly lower than for males in the earlier years. However, in 2004-05 the share of farmers among men and women was almost equalized 64.4 per cent among women and 64 among men agricultural workers.

Table 7.2: Numbers and Percentage Shares of Farmers in Total Agricultural Workers

	1983	1987-88	1993-1994	1999-2000	2004-2005
	Numbers (Million)				
Male	79.5	83.4	88.0	85.3	96.8
Female	52.0	54.7	55.2	51.9	69.4
Total	131.5	138.0	143.2	137.3	166.2
	Percentage to Total Agricultural Workers				
Male	64.2	65.6	61.1	58.6	64.0
Female	62.6	66.4	58.6	56.4	64.4
Total	63.5	65.9	60.1	57.8	64.2

Source: NSS 38th, 43rd, 50th, 55th and 61st Rounds, 1983, 1987-88, 1993-94, 1999-2000 and 2004-2005, Employment and Unemployment Survey. Computed.

7.10 In the past several decades, agricultural employment has increased primarily as a result of land augmenting technological changes, propelled by the enhanced irrigation. These changes made possible both an increase in sown area through higher cropping intensity as well as greater labour use per sown hectare. There has also been a fairly dramatic growth of employment in the non-crop agricultural sub-sectors such as dairy farming and livestock. Recent studies show that the impetus of such technological changes has virtually petered out in the past several years and agricultural growth has acquired a more labour saving character. The faster growth of the (unorganised) non-farm sector has also provided the scope for occupational diversification. At the same time, one must recognise the residual character of agricultural self-employment. If the non-farm sector does not provide adequate remunerative employment opportunities, there are always possibilities of agricultural involution, with the sector retaining a growing part of the workforce through fragmentation and sharing of work, in the absence of alternatives.

7.11 Over the last two decades the agricultural workforce grew at 1.1 per cent per annum while the total workforce grew at 2.0 per

[2] State-wise shares are given in Appendix Table A7.2. Across the states Assam, Jammu and Kashmir, Himachal Pradesh, Uttar Pradesh, Punjab, Haryana and Rajasthan have a very high share of farmers. Southern states of Andhra Pradesh, Kerala, Tamil Nadu and Karnataka along with Orissa, Maharashtra, Gujarat and West Bengal have a substantial share of agricultural labourers. During 1993-94 and 2004-05 all the states except Jammu and Kashmir, Himachal Pradesh, Karnataka, Madhya Pradesh, and West Bengal show an increase in the share of farmers.

Table 7.3: Growth Rate (Percentage) of Agricultural and Total Workers

			1983/94	1994/05	1983/05
Rural	Male	Agriculture	1.5	0.5	1.0
		Total	1.9	1.5	1.7
	Female	Agriculture	1.2	1.4	1.3
		Total	1.4	1.7	1.5
	Total	Agriculture	1.4	0.9	1.1
		Total	1.8	1.6	1.7
Total	Male	Agriculture	1.2	1.3	1.3
		Total	2.3	2.0	2.1
	Female	Agriculture	1.5	0.5	1.0
		Total	1.8	1.9	1.8
	Total	Agriculture	1.4	0.8	1.1
		Total	2.1	1.9	2.0

Note: Usual Principal and Subsidiary Status Workers.
Source: NSS 38th, 50th and 61st Rounds, 1983, 1993-94 and 2004-2005, Employment and Unemployment Survey. Computed.

cent per annum (Table 7.3). Male employment, both agricultural and total, grew at a faster rate than total employment. A comparison of employment growth rates between 1983/1993-94 and 1993-94/2004-05 shows that the growth rate of agricultural employment decelerated sharply in the last decade, from 1.4 to 0.8 per cent. Although the growth of total employment also declined from 2.1 per cent during 1983/1993-94 to 1.9 per cent during 1993-94/2004-05, this deceleration was clearly not so sharp. Finally, it is the growth rate of female employment in agriculture that has shown a much sharper decline. It is obvious from these results that the potential of the agricultural sector to absorb the incremental workforce has declined. Further, technological changes and changes in cultivation practices in agriculture also appear to be restricting the scope of women's employment in this sector.

Distribution of Landholdings

7.12 Since the cultivable land area is more or less fixed, and since most parts of the country follow the principle of partible inheritance, the land area available per household has been steadily declining, making it more difficult for households to subsist on agriculture. At the same time the land distribution remains unequal although both the pattern of land ownership and operation have been subject to change due to the state policy (on land reforms), and both temporary (such as leasing and mortgage) and permanent transactions (sale and purchase). The ownership holdings show high concentration ratios, which remained quite steady since the early sixties. The concentration of operational holdings is however much lower though fluctuating over the years. This is mainly due to the land leasing practice according to which the small and marginal holders are able to lease-in land from the medium and large holders.

7.13 The proportion of households with no land possessed increased from 13 per cent in 1993-94 to 14.5 per cent in 2004-05[3]. The share of households with marginal holdings also increased during the period from 59 per cent to 62 per cent. Shares of small, medium and large holdings declined slightly. This pattern of land

Table 7.4: Percentage of Agricultural Worker Households by Size of Land Possessed Rural 2004 - 2005

Land Possessed	Agricultural Labour Household	Farmer Household	All Rural Households
Landless	19.7	0.6	13.1
Sub-Marginal	62.3	14.6	44.8
Marginal	12.9	30.7	18.7
Small	4.1	26.5	12.2
Medium-Large	1.0	27.5	11.2
All	100.0	100.0	100.0

Note: Landless (< 0.01), Sub-Marginal (0.01 - 0.40), Marginal (0.41 - 1.00), Small (1.01 - 2.00), Medium-Large (> 2.00) Hectares.
Source: NSS 61st Round 2004 - 2005, Employment-Unemployment Survey.

The potential of the agricultural sector to absorb the incremental workforce has declined. Further, technological changes and changes in cultivation practices in agriculture also appear to be restricting the scope of women's employment in this sector.

[3] Appendix Table A7.3 gives the pattern of landholdings by states.

distribution contributed to a decline in the average size of holdings from 1.0 hectare in 1993-94 to 0.8 hectares in 2004-05 (NSSO 2006a).

7.14 Poor asset base and landlessness are the prime reasons why workers in rural areas work as agricultural labourers. The share of landlessness among the agricultural labourers was 19.7 per cent in 2004-05. More than 60 per cent of the agricultural labourers had sub-marginal holdings up to 0.4 hectares and that remained more or less constant over the period. Landlessness or small size of holdings forces the workers to engage as labourers to maintain their subsistence levels (Table 7.4). Among the farmer households nearly 15 per cent had sub-marginal holdings, while another 30 per cent had marginal holdings. Such small size of land holdings among farmer households made cultivation unviable. The members of these households are likely to be engaged in casual labour in agricultural and non-agricultural activities (NSSO 2006a).

7.15 Over the years the number and area under marginal and small farms (operational holdings) has been increasing (Table 7.5). By early nineties, nearly 63 per cent of the holdings and 16 per cent of the area was under less than 1 hectare holding size. Approximately 18 per cent of the holdings and area was under less than 2 hectares holding size. In 2002-03 around 22 per cent of the operated area was under marginal holdings and another 21 per cent was under smallholdings. The main message is that 86 per cent of the marginal and small farmers operate around 43 per cent of agricultural land while 14 per cent of the medium and large farmers operate around 37 per cent of the land. Given the high proportion of the small and marginal farmers who are also dependent on the large and medium farmers for inputs, we concentrate on the working conditions of this group. Further, large and medium farmers are principally employers and thus enjoy far better working conditions than the former group.

7.16 Large-scale commercial or capitalist farming/ cultivation is undertaken at a very limited level. Increased demographic pressure on land has led to continuous decline in farm size and landlessness. Even while there has been a fall in the share of agricultural income in the economy the decline in the dependence on the sector for employment, particularly in the rural areas, has not been as rapid. While the share of the sector in the national income has declined to less than one-fourth, the share in total employment, as noted before, is still around 57 per cent in 2004-05. Small size of holdings limits the benefits of scale of operations and also thwarts the capacity of the farmer to make investments and gain access to credit. Increased risks and low profitability in recent times has further increased the vulnerability of the small and marginal farmers.

Education Level

7.17 With the ongoing commercialisation of agriculture, crop diversification, introduction of new technologies and the imperative for better information processing, education has to be reckoned as a key input

Table 7.5: Distribution of Operational Holdings and Area by Size, All India

	Operated Area	1953-54	1961-62	1971-72	1981-82	1991-92 Kharif	2002-03 Rabi
			Operational Holdings as per cent to Total Rural Holdings				
Marginal	39.2	39.1	45.8	55.5	62.8	69.7	70.0
Small	20.9	22.6	22.4	19.5	17.8	16.3	15.9
Medium & Large	40.0	33.3	31.9	25.0	19.5	14.0	14.1
			Operational Holdings as per cent to Total Area				
Marginal	4.4	6.9	9.2	11.5	15.6	22.6	21.7
Small	10.0	12.3	14.8	16.6	18.7	20.9	20.3
Medium & Large	84.6	80.8	76.0	71.9	65.7	56.5	57.9

Note: Marginal (Less than 1.00), Small (1.01 - 2.00), Medium-Large (> 2.00) Hectares.
Source: NSSO Survey on Land Holding, Various Rounds.

About 86 per cent of the marginal and small farmers operate around 43 per cent of the agricultural land while 14 per cent of medium and large farmers operate around 37 per cent of the land

in any attempt at overall development and modernization of agriculture and improve the welfare of the people dependent on it. However, the historical legacy as well as the contemporary reality have contributed to a situation of low level of education of agricultural workers i.e., farmers and agricultural labourers. The position of women in this group is nothing less than pathetic. About 86 per cent of agricultural labourers and 72 per cent of farmers are either illiterate or have education only upto the primary level (Table 7.6), which is hardly adequate to assimilate, let alone apply, a fraction of the new information generated for better agricultural practices and management. In the case of female agricultural labourers this was as high as 93 per cent while for males it was 81 per cent even in 2004-05. Of the total agricultural labourers only 12 per cent were educated up to the primary school level, 10 per cent had middle and less than 4 per cent had education up to secondary school and above. Though agricultural labourers on the whole have low levels of education, the male-female gap is substantial. About 37 per cent of the male agricultural labourers have primary and middle level education while only 16 per cent of the female agricultural labourers have attained this level.

Table 7.6: Percentage of Educational Attainment of Rural Agricultural Workers, 2004-2005

Education Level	Male	Female	Total	Male	Female	Total
	Agricultural Labourers			Farmers		
Illiterate & Below Primary	65.9	85.5	74.1	45.7	74.0	57.5
Primary	15.7	7.5	12.3	16.2	10.8	14.0
Middle	13.3	5.3	10.0	18.9	9.5	15.0
Secondary	3.7	1.2	2.6	10.3	3.9	7.6
HS & Above	1.5	0.4	1.0	8.9	1.9	6.0
Total	**100.0**	**100.0**	**100.0**	**100.0**	**100.0**	**100.0**

Note: Agricultural Labourers are usual status (principal and subsidiary) casual workers in agriculture.
Source: Same as in Table 7.4.

7.18 The level of education among the small farmers is only marginally better. The women farmers have high levels of illiteracy or education only up to primary level. Among the small farmers, 62 per cent of men and 85 per cent of women belong to this group. Only about 20 per cent of the male small farmers and 6 per cent of the female small farmers had levels of education above secondary schooling.

Poverty among Agricultural Labourers

7.19 Agricultural labourers are the most marginalised group among the rural poor who constitute the bottom layer in the poverty ladder. Overall, poverty estimate for agricultural labourers at 28.4 per cent is much higher than the poverty ratio for agricultural workers as a whole, at 19.9 per cent (Fig. 7.2.).

7.20 The poverty ratios vary substantially across socio-religious groups. Nearly 40 per cent of the Hindu STs engaged as agricultural labourers are below the poverty line, followed by Muslim agricultural labourers at 31.5 per cent, and SC Hindus at 31 per cent. These three poorest groups are followed by agricultural labourers in Other Religions at 26.1 per cent that includes SCs belonging to the Sikh community and Dalit

Fig. 7.2: Poverty Ratio among Rural Agricultural Labourers by Socio-Religious Groups 2004 - 2005

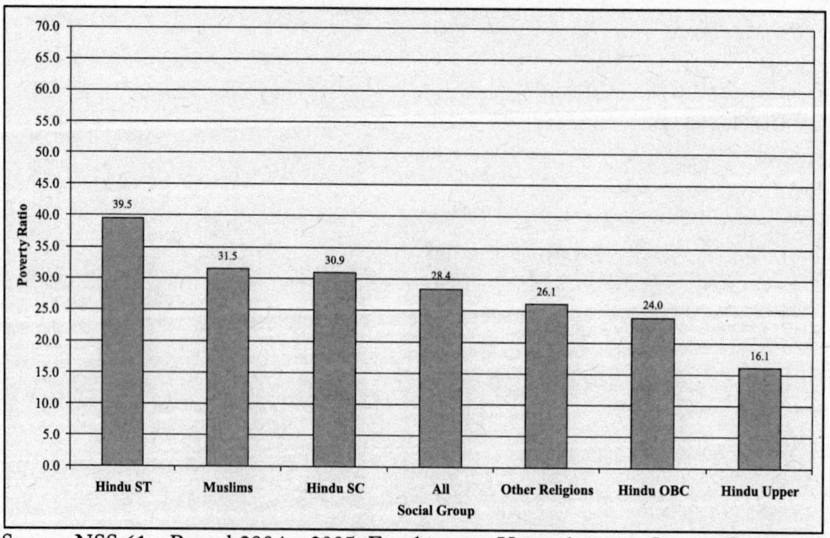

Source: NSS 61st Round 2004 - 2005, Employment-Unemployment Survey. Computed.

Christians and Adivasis and Hindu OBCs (24 per cent). The Hindu upper castes even among agricultural labourers are the least likely to be poor, 16 per cent.

7.21 Thus, the poverty level among agricultural labourers is very high. The occupation of agricultural labour was obviously not one of choice and the poorest among each social group undertook it only when one was forced into it. With little human and physical capital these groups were left with no option but to take up low paid wage labour in agriculture, which helped them to just about subsist. What this decomposition of agricultural labourers into socio-religious groups indicates is the existence of many structural constraints that are often mediated through one's social status/identity. Despite the fact that the agricultural labourers as a group form the bottom layer of the working class, the differentiation arising out of social identity is indeed striking. The historical weight of social exclusion coupled with the absence of any fall back mechanism of social security or protection is indeed a powerful initial condition debilitating this section of the working poor.

Poverty among Farmers

7.22 The small holding size among the majority of farmers makes the marginal and small farmers, especially in rain-fed agriculture, one of the most impoverished in the rural areas after agricultural labourers. The poverty ratio of all farmers is nearly 15 per cent, which is lower than for all the agricultural workers in the unorganised sector at 19.9 per cent. But the poverty ratio is very high among the landless farmers who are likely to be in animal husbandry, forestry etc., followed by the sub-marginal farmers. The poverty ratio declines with land size and the large land cultivators are the least likely to be poor (Fig. 7.3). The sub-marginal and marginal farmers are undoubtedly among the most economically impoverished and vulnerable sections.

7.23 The overall poverty ratios of farmers by socio-religious groups follow the pattern observed for all workers in Chapter 2. The ST farmers are the most vulnerable with one-third of them being in poverty. About one-fifth of the SC self-employed agricultural workers are in poverty and 16 per cent of the Muslims. The upper caste Hindus were the least likely to be in poverty (Table 7.7).

7.24 The STs landless farmers had an overwhelming poverty ratio of 68 per cent. These workers are likely to be forest dwellers who eke out a living probably by collecting non-timber forest products as tribal communities in many parts of the country have been traditionally doing. More than one-third of the tribal communities with sub-marginal, marginal and small holdings were poor, i.e, there is little variation across land size classes. The landless among the SCs and OBCs were also poorer than the landed agricultural self-employed. Muslim farmers with sub-marginal holdings were the poorest. It is evident that the small and marginal farmers are economically worse off. But here again, there is differential incidence of poverty mediated by one's social identity. Size of land does help reduce poverty but there are other factors that have to do with one's social position to translate the

Fig. 7.3: Poverty Ratio among Farmers by Land (Possessed) Size Classes, Rural 2004 - 2005

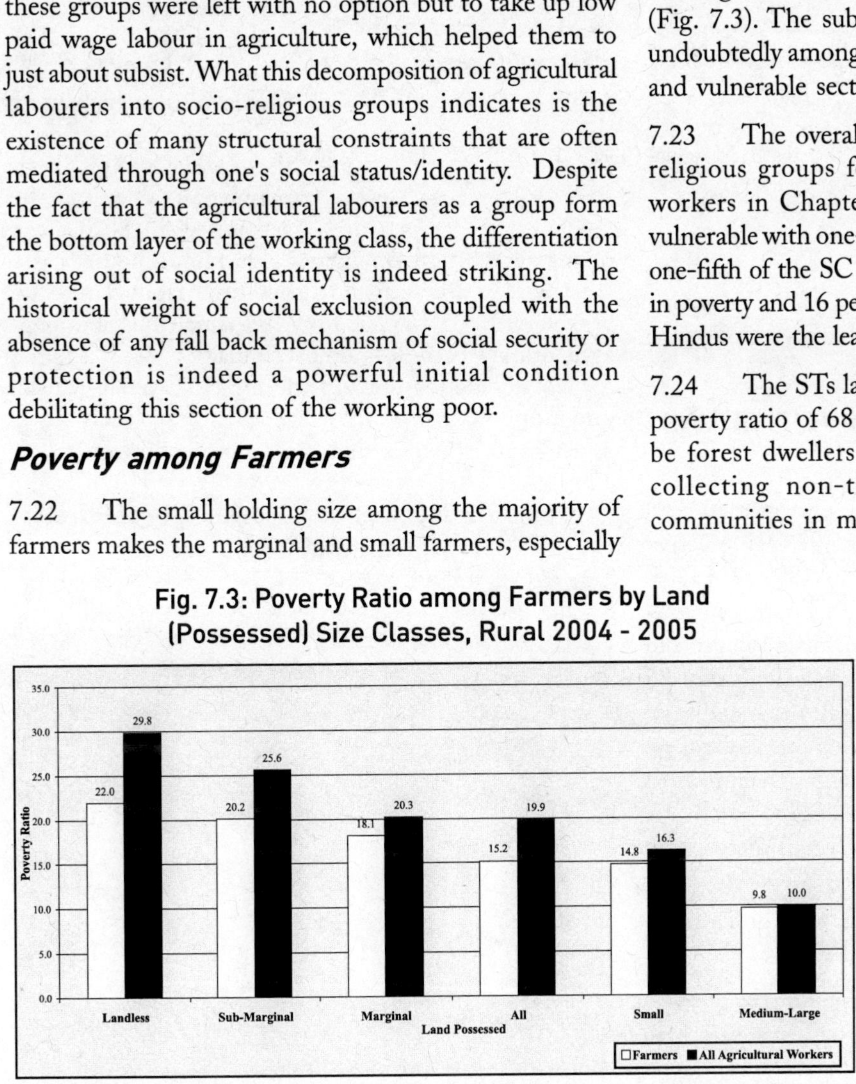

Note: Landless (< 0.01), Sub-Marginal (0.01 - 0.40), Marginal (0.41 - 1.00), Small (1.01 - 2.00), Medium-Large (> 2.00) Hectares;
Source : ibid

Despite the fact that agricultural labourers as a group form the bottom layer of the working class, the differentiation arising out of social identity is indeed striking. The historical weight of social exclusion coupled with the absence of any fall back mechanism of social security or protection is indeed a powerful initial condition debilitating this section of the working poor.

Table 7.7: Poverty Ratios among Farmers by Socio-Religious Groups and Land (Possessed) Size Classes, Rural 2004 - 2005

Land Size	Hindu STs	Hindu SCs	Hindu OBCs	Hindu Upper Castes	Muslims	Other Religions	All
Landless	68.4	29.1	18.1	1.6	4.7	26.6	22.0
Sub-Marginal	41.5	24.8	18.8	10.3	23.1	10.2	20.2
Marginal	34.4	21.5	17.5	6.4	19.5	17.6	18.1
Small	33.2	18.0	12.3	6.9	12.1	16.8	14.8
Medium-Large	29.7	14.5	6.8	6.1	7.1	6.4	9.8
All	33.3	20.8	13.0	6.9	16.4	12.6	15.2

Note: Landless (<0.01), Sub-Marginal (0.01 - 0.40), Marginal (0.41 - 1.00), Small (1.01 - 2.00), Medium-Large (> 2.00) Hectares
Source: Same as in Table 7.4.

asset position in to one of wellbeing. Social networking and education could be among them. Those belonging to SCs and STs are especially vulnerable even among the group of farmers.

Socio-economic Profile of Agricultural Labourers

7.25 The share of agricultural labourers in total rural workforce declined from 30 per cent in 1993-94 to 25 per cent in 2004-05 after rising slightly in 1999-00 (Table 7.8). The share of female agricultural labourers in total female workforce is higher than that of male labourers in male workforce, the former showing a decline from 35 per cent to 29 per cent during the period with a slight rise to 36.5 per cent in 1999-00. This implied that while there was a positive growth of 1.3 per cent per annum of agricultural labourers till 1999-00, it declined at nearly 1.5 per cent in the next five years. Overall there was a slight decline of agricultural labourers during the decade 1993/94 - 2004/05 (Table 7.9).

Table 7.8: Percentage of Agricultural Labourers in Total Workforce in Rural Areas

	1993-94	1999-2000	2004 - 2005
Male	27.3	28.3	23.2
Female	35.0	36.5	29.2
Total	30.0	31.2	25.4

Source: NSS 50th, 55th and 61st Rounds, 1993-94, 1999-2000 and 2004-2005, Employment and Unemployment Survey. Computed.

Social Composition

7.26 Agricultural labourers as a group consist largely of those belonging to Scheduled Castes and Scheduled Tribes (46.7 per cent in 2004-05) and OBC category (33.9 per cent) (Table 7.10), which partly reflects the proportion of these social groups in the population. They together accounted for 80 per cent of the agricultural labourers. The Hindu higher castes are the least likely to be agricultural labourers (8 per cent in 2004-05). While the male-female distribution of agricultural labourers is almost similar for SCs it is higher for females among the STs and OBCs. Overall, Muslim and upper caste women are even less likely to be agricultural labourers than their male counterparts.[4]

Table 7.9: Number and Growth Rate of Rural Agricultural Labourers

Year	Male	Female	Total
		Estimated Agricultural Labourers (millions)	
1993-94	51.2	36.6	87.9
1999-2000	55.7	38.0	93.7
2004 - 2005	50.8	36.2	87.0
		Growth Rate (per cent)	
1993-94/ 1999-2000	1.69	0.74	1.30
1999-2000/ 2004-2005	-1.82	-0.97	-1.47
1993-94/ 2004-2005	-0.08	-0.12	-0.10

Source: Same as in Table 7.8.

Gender and Age Composition

7.27 The age composition has only marginally changed over the years. The share of child agricultural

[4] Appendix A7.4 gives the state level social composition of agricultural labour households. There is considerable variation within the tribal belt of Madhya Pradesh, Orissa, Gujarat, Chhattisgarh and Jharkhand having a higher share of STs among the rural agricultural labour households. Conversely SCs are higher in those states where STs were low. The proportion of STs among the agricultural labour households has not shown significant changes between 1999 and 2005 while the share of SCs among the agricultural labour households showed a sharp increase in Haryana and Himachal Pradesh.

labourers came down from 3.2 per cent to 1.9 per cent during 1993/94 - 2004/05 (Table 7.11). The incidence of child female agricultural labourers (2.4 per cent) is higher than for child male labourers (1.5 per cent). The share of the older labourers (above 60 years) has remained more or less constant at about 5 per cent. The working age group (15 - 59 years) constituted about 93 per cent of the agricultural labourers in 2004-05. The trend is towards an ageing agricultural labour population. The age groups below 35 years in general show a decline in agricultural labourers whereas the age groups above 35 years show an increase among both men and women. This is partly due to the younger rural poor looking for somewhat better paying non-agricultural employment opportunities propelled by some increase in educational attainments, however meagre it is. Working as agricultural labourers is the last resort, given its low social status, low earnings and irregular employment often reinforced by social oppression in the event of assertion of rights or dignity.

Table 7.10: Percentage of Rural Agricultural Labourers by Socio-Religious Groups 2004-2005

Socio-Religious Group	Male	Female	Total
Hindu STs	13.0	16.4	14.4
Hindu SCs	32.0	31.4	31.7
Hindu: OBCs	32.0	36.6	33.9
Hindu: Upper Castes	8.4	7.5	8.0
Muslims	9.8	3.7	7.3
Other Religions	4.9	4.4	4.7
Total	**100.0**	**100.0**	**100.0**

Source: Same as in Table 7.8.

Table 7.11: Age Composition of Rural Agricultural Labourers (Percentage)

Age Group	1993-94	2004 - 05	1993-94	2004 - 05	1993-94	2004 - 05
	Male		Female		Total	
5 - 9	0.1	0.0	0.2	0.1	0.2	0.0
10 - 14	2.4	1.5	3.9	2.4	3.0	1.9
Child Labour< 15	2.6	1.5	4.1	2.4	3.2	1.9
15 - 19	11.4	11.0	10.2	9.3	10.9	10.3
20 - 34	39.5	37.8	42.4	39.3	40.7	38.4
35 - 49	30.0	33.4	29.1	34.0	29.6	33.6
50 - 59	10.7	10.9	10.1	10.4	10.4	10.7
Working Age Group 15 - 59	91.7	93.2	91.7	93.0	91.7	93.1
60 & Above	5.8	5.3	4.2	4.5	5.1	5.0
5 & Above	100.0	100.0	100.0	100.0	100.0	100.0

Source: NSS 50th and 61st Rounds 1993-94 and 2004-2005, Employment and Unemployment Survey. Computed.

Socio-economic Profile of Farmers

7.28 The definition of a farmer in the NSSO Situation Assessment Survey of Farmers 2003 differs from the other definitions in the sense that it included plantation and horticulture crops and animal husbandry as activities undertaken by a farmer while a cultivator was distinguished as the one who engaged in crop cultivation. An income criterion was not taken as a base to define a farmer household as done in Rural Labour Enquiry Reports to define rural labour households. The NSSO Situation Assessment Survey of Farmers 2003 states that 60 per cent of the rural households are farmers. Among these farmer households a large majority are marginal and small farmers (83 per cent). This Survey is the most comprehensive information available on the conditions of the farmers (Box 7.1).

7.29 Majority of farmer households belong to the OBC category (42 per cent), followed by the others (28 per cent). SCs and STs together constitute thirty-one per cent of the farmer households. It is evident that among the socially and economically backward groups such as SCs and OBCs majority of the holdings are of less than a hectare (Table 7.12). The SCs

Size of land does help reduce poverty but there are other factors that have to do with one's social position to translate the asset position in to one of wellbeing. Social networking and education could be among them. Those belonging to SCs and STs are especially vulnerable even among the group of farmers.

Box 7.1 Definition of Farmers

The NSSO Situation Assessment Survey of Farmers 2003, gives a more precise definition of a farmer as ".... a person who possessed some land and was engaged in agricultural activities on any part of that land during the last 365 days. Agricultural activity was taken to include cultivation of field and horticultural crops, growing of trees and plantations such as rubber, cashew, coconut, pepper, coffee, tea, etc; animal husbandry, poultry, fishery, piggery, bee-keeping, vermiculture, sericulture, etc. By cultivator it was meant a farmer who had been engaged in activities related to production of crops by tillage and ancillary jobs" (NSSO 2005, p 1). A Farmer household was defined as one that had at least one member as a farmer.

in particular have more than half of their holdings of less than half a hectare. Over nine-tenths of SC farmers are either sub-marginal/marginal or small land holders. Among the higher castes even while the share of less than one hectare is substantial, their proportion in the larger land size categories is the highest, particularly in the above four hectare category. The economically vulnerable group of small and marginal farmers thus mainly comprise the socially relegated groups such as SCs, STs and OBCs, while the higher castes enjoy a better asset ownership in terms of land. Having said that, the Commission would emphasize the dominance of marginal and small farmers of all socio-religious groups in Indian agriculture.

Table 7.12: Percentage Distribution for Social Groups of Farmer Households by Land Size (Hectares) Categories 2003

Social group	Sub-Marginal	Marginal	Small	Medium	Large	Total
STs	24.8	37.4	19.7	12.1	6.0	100.0
SCs	56.4	26.5	9.9	4.8	2.4	100.0
OBCs	35.2	32.3	16.9	9.5	6.0	100.0
Others	29.3	29.2	19.6	12.9	9.1	100.0
Total	**35.9**	**31.1**	**16.8**	**10.0**	**6.2**	**100.0**

Note: Sub-Marginal (< 0.4), Marginal (0.40 - 1.00), Small (1.01 - 2.00), Semi-Medium (2.00 - 4.00), Large (> 4.00) Hectares.

Source: NSS 59th Round 2002 -2003, Situation Assessment Survey of Farmers. Computed.

7.30 Cultivation remains the primary activity of the farmer households. About 96 per cent of the total land possessed by such households is devoted to this activity (Table 7.13). There is little variation across the different farm sizes. Only among the near landless, i.e. those with less than 0.01 hectare of land, dairying and other farming of animals is a major activity. Orchards and plantation remains low at 3 per cent. This does not increase with increase in farm size. In fact the proportion is the highest for less 0.5 hectare size. Overall there is minimal diversification of activities among the farmers. Largely they engage in cultivation and, to a limited extent, in plantation with the near landless mainly in dairying.

Table 7.13: Percentage of Farmed land Among Different Agricultural Activities 2003

Land Size (Hectares)	Cultivation and Allied Agriculture	Orchardsand Plantations	Dairy	Fishery	Other farming (Animals, bees, poultry, etc)
< 0.01	14.3	1.7	68.8	0.0	15.2
0.01-0.40	93.3	5.3	0.8	0.4	0.3
0.4-1.00	95.9	3.2	0.4	0.4	0.1
1.01-2.00	96.5	2.9	0.3	0.2	0.2
2.01 - 4.00	96.1	3.3	0.3	0.2	0.1
4.01 -10.00	96.7	2.7	0.3	0.1	0.2
> 10.10	97.5	2.0	0.2	0.1	0.2
All	**96.2**	**3.1**	**0.4**	**0.2**	**0.1**

Source: Same as in Table 7.12

Income and Consumption Level

7.31 Share of income through cultivation is the highest at 46 per cent while share of wage income is also very high at 39 per cent. The fact that marginal and sub-marginal holdings owning less than 1 hectare of land constitute nearly 45 per cent of the farmer households (Table 7.4) explains the high share of wage incomes in the total income of farmer households. Such households

Table 7.14: Percentage of Income by Source and Farm Size 2003

Land Size (Hectares)	Wages	Cultivation	Farming of Animals	Non Farm Business Receipts	Total
< 0.01	77.9	0.8	4.6	16.7	100.
0.01-0.40	59.6	18.1	5.8	16.5	100
0.4-1.00	39.8	43.3	6.2	10.7	100
1.01 - 2.00	25.5	63.3	4.1	7.1	100
2.01- 4.00	17.7	74.8	1.6	5.9	100
4.01 - 10.00	8.6	82.3	0.2	8.9	100
> 10.10	5.8	86.1	1.2	7.0	100
All	**38.7**	**45.8**	**4.3**	**11.2**	**100**

Source: NSSO 2005a

have to supplement their income through wage labour to maintain subsistence levels (Table 7.14).

7.32 Share of wages is very high for marginal farmers. Income from wages declined with increase in farm size while that from cultivation increased (Table 7.14). Small and marginal farmers have a more diversified portfolio than the medium and large farmers. This is probably because income from cultivation is not enough to support the household, and hence wage labour, animal rearing and other sources of income are sought.

7.33 Income from cultivation constitutes an important source of earnings for farmer households. At the all India level the average monthly income from cultivation alone in all sizes is Rs.969 (Table 7.15). Across all the farm sizes income of a marginal farmer from cultivation is a paltry Rs.435 while that of a large farmer is Rs.8321. The average monthly income of a marginal farmer household is one-twentieth of the income of the large farmer household. Since the share of small and marginal farmer in the total number of holdings is very high and their income is very low the average income for all size groups from cultivation is very low.[5]

7.34 Average monthly income of a farmer household from all sources is estimated as Rs.2115 per month while monthly per capita income is as low as Rs.385 at all India level. Average monthly income ranges from Rs. 1380 for land size less than 0.01 hectares to Rs.9667 for land size 10 hectares and above (Fig. 7.4). The highest monthly income from all sources considered is reported in Jammu and Kashmir (nearly Rs.5500) followed by Punjab (Rs.4960) and Kerala (Rs.4004). Lowest average income (Rs.1062) was reported in Orissa, followed by Madhya Pradesh (Rs.1430) and Rajasthan (Rs.1500).

7.35 Farmers have come to be identified as a highly marginalized section of the population. After the agricultural labourers, small and marginal farmers are identified as the most impoverished section. Recent trends in agricultural growth performance have indicated a

Table 7.15: Average Monthly Income from Cultivation by Size of Holding 2003

Holding Size (Hectares)	Income in Rs
Marginal	435
Small	1578
Semi-Medium	2685
Medium	4676
Large	8321
All Sizes	969

Note: Marginal (Less than 1.00), Small (1.01 - 2.00), Semi-Medium (2.00 - 4.00), Medium (4.00 - 10.00), Large (> 10.00) Hectares.
Source: NSSO 2005a

Along with liberalization the sector has been exposed to the price fluctuations in the global market, which has increased the risks of the farmers. Increased use of purchased inputs and mechanization has increased the cost of cultivation of the farmer. These along with low prices have reduced the viability of farm operations and stability of farm incomes.

[5] State wise average monthly income from cultivation is given in Appendix Table A7.5. Average income from cultivation is the highest in Punjab, followed by Jammu & Kashmir, Assam and Haryana. Lowest income from cultivation is in Rajasthan and Orissa. Among the marginal farmer households, those from Jammu & Kashmir, Assam, Kerala, Jharkhand, West Bengal, Bihar and Maharashtra have average income from cultivation per farmer household higher than the national level. Punjab and Haryana, which have a high average income from cultivation per farmer households, have much below the national level among the marginal farmers. Among the small farmers the states with high average income from cultivation per farmer household include Punjab and Haryana. Marginal and small farmer households in Rajasthan, Orissa, Madhya Pradesh, Andhra Pradesh and Tamil Nadu have very low average income from cultivation.

Fig. 7.4: Average Monthly Expenditure and Income by Farm Size for Rural Farmer Households: All-India 2003

Average Monthly Income by Farm Size

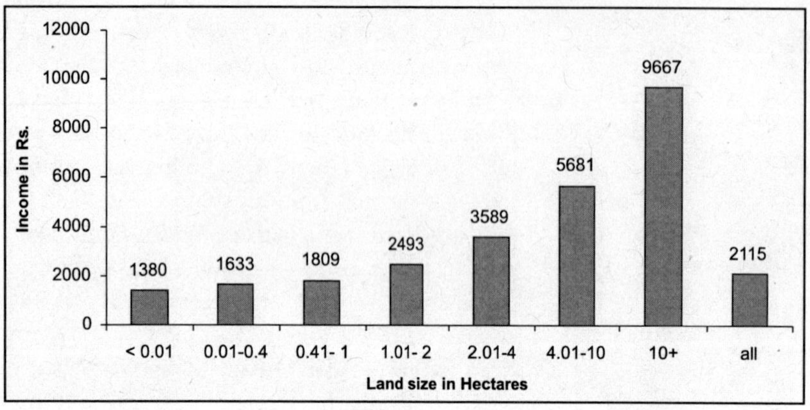

Average Monthly Consumption Expenditure by Farm Size

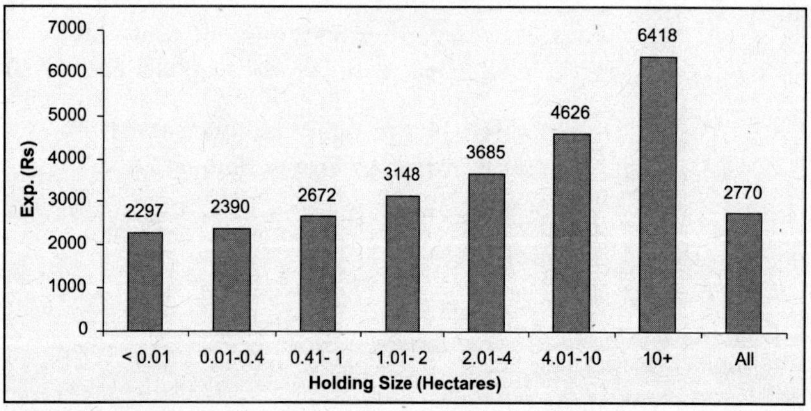

Source: NSSO 2005a

deceleration in output and stagnancy in employment. Along with liberalization the sector has been exposed to the price fluctuations in the global market, which has increased the risks of the farmers. Increased use of purchased inputs and mechanization has increased the cost of cultivation of the farmer. These along with low prices have reduced the viability of farm operations and stability of farm incomes. Thus, there has been an increase in indebtedness of the farmer households to meet the production expenditure and consumption needs. A large majority are marginal and small farmers and their condition is still worse off as they are not in a position to meet the increased risks in production that appear with increased dependence on free market and reduced support from the state. This is leading to increased distress among the farmers, driving them to extreme measures such as suicides, which have been on the increase, particularly in the states of Andhra Pradesh, Maharashtra, Kerala, Karnataka and Punjab. This will be clearer in Chapter 9 in which we examine the issue of farmer suicides in more details.

7.36 Pattern of average monthly consumption expenditure by farm size further confirms the economic status of the small and marginal farmers compared to the medium and large farmers. The average expenditure levels increase with size of land holding, being above Rs.6000 for large farmers (Fig. 7.4). That the average monthly expenditure of a farmer household at Rs.2770 is higher than the monthly income of Rs.2115 indicates that the expenditure levels are higher than the income, especially for the small and marginal farmers. The threshold of land size where monthly income of farmer household is higher than the monthly expenditure is 2 hectares. The income levels of farmers below this land-size group are not able to meet the consumption needs of the household. Thus, to meet their expenses the households resort to loans. This along with increased use of monetized inputs leading to high costs of cultivation has lead to increased indebtedness among farmer households. The large farmer's average monthly expenditure is well below the average monthly income.

Conclusion

7.37 Agricultural workers i.e., farmers and agricultural labourers, are largely in the unorganised sector and are an extremely impoverished and a vulnerable group. Within this group, agricultural labourers are worse off compared to the farmers/cultivators. Agricultural

Expenditure levels of farmer households are higher than income for small and marginal holdings upto the size of 2 hectares. These households are unable to meet their consumption needs and have to resort to borrowing.

labourers are characterised by extreme poverty levels. With no physical and human capital assets, they take up wage work in manual agricultural activities. The socially backwards like the Scheduled Castes and Scheduled Tribes agricultural workers are the most vulnerable within the group. Farmers are slightly better off than the agricultural labourers as they have some capital base in land on which they undertake agricultural activities. Farmers are also characterised by high poverty levels because of the predominance of marginal and small farmers among them. Marginal and small cultivators have very little resources and also have to supplement their incomes through wage labour. Their income levels are below their consumption expenditure levels. This leads to high indebtedness among them. Recent deceleration in agriculture through the nineties has made them even worse off. Further, marginal and small farmers belonging to Scheduled Castes and Scheduled Tribes are the worst in terms of poverty levels and economic status. The medium and large farmers are better off in terms of their economic position. Given this socio-economic profile of agricultural workers, the following two chapters are devoted the examination of the working conditions of the agricultural labourers and farmers in greater detail.

8 Agricultural Labourers

Introduction

8.1 As we saw in Chapter 7, agricultural labourers, estimated at 87 million in 2004-05, constituted 34 per cent of about 253 million agricultural workers i.e., farmers and agricultural labourers. The socio-economic profile drawn in the previous chapter highlights their extremely miserable economic condition. Agricultural labourers are characterised by poor physical and human capital and also the highest poverty levels. Socially backward groups like the Scheduled Castes and the Scheduled Tribes feature prominently in the group. Agricultural labourers take up manual activities in agriculture in return for wages. Almost all of them are casual labourers. With agriculture largely in the unorganised sector and with little regulation or social security cover, agricultural labourers remain vulnerable to poor working conditions and economic exploitation. In this chapter we review the working conditions of agricultural labourers.

Wage Levels

8.2 Agricultural labourers' wages can be paid either on hourly basis or, also in some cases, by a piece rate system. The former is linked to the hours worked by the labourer while the latter is related to the actual productive work done in physical units. The piece rate system provides greater flexibility to the employer as it varies with the amount of work done and also has greater scope for manipulation. In the agriculture sector wages in kind still co-exist with wages in cash. Wages in kind are the food grains given in return for the work instead of cash, often in coarse cereals. Overall, wage levels of agricultural labourers have been very low and their growth rates decelerated through the decade 1993/94-2004/05 (Table 8.1).

Table 8.1: Wages and Growth in Wages of Casual Agricultural Workers

Gender	Wage Rate (Rs./ Manday)		Growth Rates (Per cent / Year)	
Male	1993-94	37.9	1993-00	2.8
	1999-00	44.8	2000-05	1.4
	2004-05	48.1	1993-05	2.2
Female	1993-94	26.5	1993-00	3.0
	1999-00	31.6	2000-05	1.1
	2004-05	33.4	1993-05	2.1
Total	1993-94	33.7	1993-00	2.9
	1999-00	40.0	2000-05	1.3
	2004-05	42.6	1993-05	2.2

Note: Wage rates given here are per manday and in 2004-05 real prices.
Source: NSS 50th, 55th and 61st Rounds 1993-94, 1999-2000 and 2004 2005, Employment and Unemployment Survey. Computed

8.3 Average daily earnings of an agricultural worker are as low as Rs. 43 per manday in 2004-05. Wage rates of agricultural labourers, as observed by a number of studies (Unni 1997; Sarmah 2001; Srivastava and Singh 2005 and 2006), have shown a decelerated growth in the nineties compared to the eighties. While, at the same time, wages for manual work in non-agriculture have grown at a reasonable rate. This led to a widening of the gap between agricultural and non-agricultural wages. The ratio declined from 0.66 in 1993-94 to 0.62 in 1999-00, but rose slightly to 0.65 in 2004-05 (Table 8.2). Non-agricultural manual wages were, thus, 1.5 times higher than agricultural manual wages. Gender disparity within agriculture is also high though the ratio of female wages to male agricultural manual wages has remained unchanged at about 0.70 since 1993-94 indicating that male wages are 1.4 times the female wages.

Table 8.2: Disparities in Agricultural Wages

	Ratio of Female Wage Rate to Male Wage Rate	Ratio of Agricultural Wages to Non-agricultural wages
1993-94	0.70	0.66
1999-00	0.71	0.62
2004-05	0.69	0.65

Source : Same as in Table 8.1

8.4 The Rural Labour Enquiry Reports give earnings data, including earnings in cash and kind, for different types of agricultural and non-agricultural operations, such as, ploughing, sowing, transplanting, weeding, harvesting, cultivation, forestry, plantation, animal husbandry and fisheries. The all India details are summarized in Table 8.3 and state level details for 1999-2000 are given in Appendix Table A8.1. Across the social groups there are not much disparities though wages for STs are slightly lower than for the other groups. Wages in kind constitute 15 per cent of the total wage. This ratio is slightly higher for children and females compared to males and also for SCs compared to the other groups.

8.5 The Minimum Wages Act, 1948 is the only statutory legislation which ensures minimum wages to workers in agriculture. The respective state governments fix the minimum wage. In Chapter 3 we discussed two separate norms for minimum wages that we use to compare the existing wage rates in different industry groups. The first is the National Minimum Wage of Rs.66 irrespective of the rural-urban location. The second is the minimum wage of Rs. 49 for rural areas as proposed by the National Commission for Rural Labour (NCRL). However, the prevailing wage rates were often found to be much lower than either of these minimum wage norms (Fig. 8.1). In 2004-05 about 91 per cent of the agricultural

Table 8.3: Average Daily Earnings (Rs.) of Workers in Rural Labour Household in Agricultural Operations - All India at 1999-00 Prices

Category of Households	Men		Women		Children	
	1993-94	1999-2000	1993-94	1999-2000	1993-94	1999-2000
			All Classes			
Total	34.1	40.58	24.3	28.57	19.5	24.32
Cash	29.3	34.26	20.4	23.82	15.9	20.57
Kind	4.8	6.32	3.9	4.75	3.7	3.75
			Scheduled Castes			
Total	34.6	41.89	25.0	29.6	20.9	26.28
Cash	28.5	34.31	20.0	23.24	15.7	21.19
Kind	6.0	7.58	4.9	6.36	5.2	5.09
			Scheduled Tribes			
Total	29.4	33.19	23.7	26.44	17.3	22.41
Cash	25.2	28.56	19.7	22.58	14.0	19.63
Kind	4.3	4.63	4.0	3.86	3.3	2.78
			Other Backward Classes			
Total	-	40.93	-	28.42	-	22.72
Cash	-	34.43	-	24.19	-	19.05
Kind	-	6.5	-	4.23	-	3.67

Source: Rural Labour Enquiry 1999-2000.

Fig. 8.1 Percentage of Rural Agricultural Labourers with Wages below Minimum Wage, 2004 - 2005

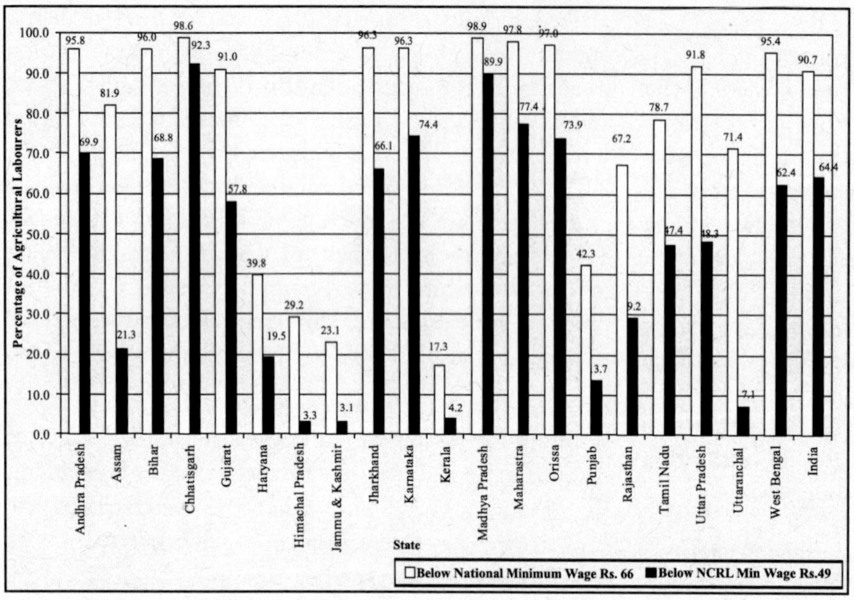

Source: NSS 61st Round 2004-2005, Employment-Unemployment Survey. Computed.

labour mandays received wage rates below the National Minimum Wage and about 64 per cent below the NCRL minimum wage norm in rural areas.

8.6 Lack of minimum standards in daily wage rates in most of the states is alarming. However, there are some bright spots in this otherwise depressing scenario. In Kerala, Jammu and Kashmir and Himachal Pradesh, 71 - 83 per cent of the agricultural labourers get minimum wages above the National Minimum Wage of Rs.66 per day whereas almost all such labourers get above the NCRL minimum wage norm of Rs. 49 per day. The situation in the agriculturally prosperous states of Punjab and Haryana and also in Uttaranchal (now Uttarakhand) is similar only if we go by the NCRL minimum wage norm although nearly 20 per cent of agricultural labourers in Haryana do not get even this lower wage. About 60 per cent of the agricultural labourers in Haryana and 58 per cent of them in Punjab get wages above the National Minimum Wage of Rs.66. These states report, in any case, a high average daily wage rate for agricultural labourers compared to other states. The fact that such industrially advanced and urbanised states as Maharashtra, West Bengal and Andhra Pradesh are in the same league as the predominantly agrarian states of Bihar, Madhya Pradesh, Chattisgarh, Jharkhand and Uttar Pradesh perhaps reflects the extreme rural-urban disparities and the consequent weak bargaining power of agricultural labourers in these states. Such a grim reality of widespread non-payment of what, in our view, a very modest minimum wage norm is in sharp contrast to the emerging reality of the Indian economy as a rapidly growing one.

Pattern of Employment

8.7 A number of studies indicate a decline in growth rate of agricultural and rural employment during 1993-00 compared to the preceding decade, by all measures of employment (Chadha and Sahu 2003; Planning Commission 2002; Bhattacharya and Sakthivel 2004). Our own estimate shows that the growth rate of employment in the agricultural sector stagnated at 0.2 per cent per annum during 1994-00 (Srivastava 2006). Within the agricultural sector crop cultivation, which accounts for the major share of employment by operation (77 per cent in 1999-00) also showed a very low growth rate at 0.5 per cent per annum during 1994-2000. Agricultural labourers are mainly engaged for manual work in cultivation such as sowing, reaping, harvesting and total employment in manual cultivation also showed a dismal rate of growth of 0.7 per cent per annum during the period (Srivastava 2006). A number of factors

In 2004-05 about 91 per cent of the agricultural labourers received wage rates below the National Minimum Wage and about 64 per cent below the NCRL minimum wage norm in rural areas. Lack of minimum standards in daily wage rates in most of the states is alarming. However, there are some bright spots in this otherwise depressing scenario. In Kerala, Jammu and Kashmir and Himachal Pradesh, 71 - 83 per cent of the agricultural labourers get minimum wages above the National Minimum Wage whereas almost all such labourers get above the NCRL minimum wage norm.

contributed to this slow down in employment in agriculture sector. Prime among these was a lower investment in irrigation, drought proofing and agricultural research because of which there was no intensification of farming in rain-fed and dry-land areas. This also led to slowing down of land augmenting technical changes. Further, institutional factors led to acceleration in the adoption of labour saving changes particularly due to rising wages during the eighties. There is a shift away from agriculture to more remunerative non-agricultural employment among the rural workers. There are, thus, both demand and supply constraints on employment generation in the agricultural sector.

8.8 Employment days for agricultural wage labourers is characterised by great degree of uncertainty because of seasonality of manual operations such as sowing, weeding, harvesting etc. in crop cultivation. There could be ups and downs in employment days depending on the agricultural performance during the year. Years when agriculture has been good and monsoon has been appropriate employment days would be higher and vice-versa. However, between 1993-94 and 2004-05 there was a secular decline in the number of days of wage employment available to agricultural labourers, from 224 to 209 (Table 8.4).

8.9 The male-female gap in wage employment days is also significant for agricultural labourers. The wage employment days available for female agricultural labourers were 196 in 1993-94, which declined to 184 in 2004-05. Wage rates, as observed earlier, were also much lower for females, male wage being 1.4 times higher than of the female agricultural labourers.

8.10 These average days of employment for wage labourers conceal a great deal of regional variations. During the Commission's visit to the agriculturally prosperous district of Anand in Gujarat, groups of women agricultural labourers complained about lack of adequate work. They reported around ten days of work on an average in a month. They also complained about the farmers' new practice of employing them for half-a-day paying a wage of Rs.15 or sometimes Rs.20. 'Kam Do' (Give us work) was the constant refrain of these workers during the meeting. Similarly, in another visit to West Bengal, groups of rural labourers from 24 Parghanas voiced similar concerns and many women, especially 'santhals' (tribal), reported a wage rate of Rs.25 per day.

8.11 There are no fixed hours of work as there are no laws to act as guidelines for the working conditions of agricultural workers. Wage labourers are subject to long working hours at meagre wages well below the minimum wage limit. Further, due to lack of opportunities, there is high level of unemployment and underemployment leaving the labourers with little bargaining power.

8.12 The agricultural labourers engage in other activities as well, perhaps in self-employment such as cultivation on small farms or animal husbandry. The average total employment days were 279 in 1993-94, which also declined to 262 in 2004-05. The women agricultural labourers had lower total days of work, which also declined in 2004-05.

8.13 The seasonality in agricultural operations is a major reason why the labourers have to migrate to other regions to look for work during lean periods. Out of the total days in a year an agricultural labourer is rendered unemployed (seeking/available for work but not working for want of work) for 51 days in 2004-05 (Table 8.5). The number of days of unemployment varied in different years, being lower in the earlier years. This reflects the varying demand for labour due to seasonality and the weather conditions of the year. Women agricultural

Table 8.4: Wage Employment Days for Rural Agricultural labourers: Casual, All

	1993-1994	1999-2000	2004-2005
Male	244	235	227
Female	196	199	184
Total	224	220	209

Source: Same as in Table 8.1

Table 8.5: Employment, Unemployment and Out of Labour Force Days of Rural Agricultural Labourers

	Year	Days Unemployed	Days not in Labour Force
Male	1993-94	33	24
	1999-00	44	26
	2004-05	53	23
Female	1993-94	26	101
	1999-00	31	95
	2004-05	47	94
Total	1993-94	30	56
	1999-00	39	54
	2004-05	51	53

Source: Same as in Table 8.1

labourers in rural areas tended to be out of the labour force for more days in a year, almost double of the men. As we saw in Chapter 5 on women workers, while being out of paid work, they engaged in a number of activities that helped save incomes such as free collection of fodder and fuel. also declined in 2004-05.

Unemployment and Underemployment

8.14 Unemployment rate, which is the number of persons unemployed per 100 persons in the labour force, is computed for usual status agricultural labourers by current daily (CDS) status (Table 8.6). The unemployment rate for agricultural labourers by the CDS is quite high in rural areas by any standard; 16 per cent for men and 17 per cent for women. This is the visible measure of underemployment or under-utilisation of labour time of agricultural labourers. The daily status rate reflects the underemployment during the week and the intermittency of employment and uncertainty in availability of employment.

8.15 The underemployment of usual status agricultural labourers by CDS rates increased during the decade 1993/94 - 2004/05. In fact the CDS unemployment rate was exceptionally high at 16 per cent in 2004-05 (Table 8.6). In 2004-05 the female unemployment rates were higher in both the statuses compared to the males'.

Table 8.6: Percentage of Unemployed by CWS and CDS for Usual Status Rural Agricultural Labourers

	Unemployed by CDS		
Gender	1993-1994	1999-2000	2004-2005
Male	9.7	12.9	15.6
Female	9.8	11.4	17.3
Total	9.7	12.4	16.2

Source: Same as in Table 8.1.

8.16 The report on the employment and unemployment survey for the 61st Round gives a measure of the invisible unemployment rate by asking the usually employed if they were more or less regularly employed throughout the year.

8.17 Among the various categories, proportion of those usual status workers who did not consider themselves more or less regularly employed was the highest for casual workers and particularly so in agriculture (Table 8.7). It is more than double of the self-employed and four times of the regular workers. To sum up agricultural labourers / casual workers in agriculture have high rates of unemployment and underemployment due to irregularity of and non-availability of employment. This makes the group even more vulnerable and creates insecurity in regular flow of income. Thus to meet their subsistence levels and supplement their incomes during lean periods they need to migrate to adjoining semi-urban and urban centers to work as casual labourers. They also borrow to survive which further worsens their situation and make them subject to forced or bonded labour.

Table 8.7: Percentage of Employed Persons (15 years and above) Who Did Not Work More or Less Regularly throughout the Year, Rural, 2004-05

Broad Usual Principal Status	Male	Female
Casual labour in :		
Agriculture	20.0	23.7
Non-agriculture	19.1	19.8
Self-employed in:		
Agriculture	7.9	8.8
Non-agriculture	5.1	6.1
Regular Wage Worker in:		
Agriculture	4.3	4.6
Non-agriculture	3.1	3.1
All	**11.0**	**13.9**

Source: NSSO 2006a

8.18 This scenario has to be kept in mind while designing and implementing public employment programmes. The recent enactment of a national legislation to guarantee manual work to all those rural workers who seek it - called National Rural Employment Guarantee or NREG for short - is essentially a form of social protection to cover the employment gap for the working poor and enable them to realise at least minimum wages relevant for the area. Proper implementation of the NREG can go a long way in not only assuring a minimum income for the rural working poor but also contribute to enhancing the reserve price of such labour which is currently so low that it is nothing but starvation

Employment for agricultural labourers is irregular and unassured. This reflects the intermittency of employment and uncertainty in availability of employment

wages (i.e. one that will not help cross the poverty threshold).

Health and Occupational Hazards

8.19 Besides the normal health problems, agricultural workers, in general, suffer from certain specific health hazards due to extensive use of fertilizers, insecticides and pesticides and mechanization. The increasing use of chemicals and biological agents with hazard potential unknown to people; the indiscriminate use of agro-chemicals including pesticides, agricultural machineries and equipment, and their impact on health and safety of exposed population; pose serious safety and health risks for agricultural workers. Since the occupational safety and health services are out of the reach of this group their vulnerability is further accentuated. Pesticides are usually sprayed and it has been observed (Nag and Nag 2004) that the sprayer operators experience fatigue mainly due to carrying the sprayer load. The vibration arising out of powered sprayers also causes discomfort to the operator. The pesticide applicators, mixers and loaders are at the risk of exposure to toxic chemicals. It is not uncommon that the farmers broadcast pesticides or prepare pesticide solutions with bare hands. Improper handling of pesticides, spraying without wearing personal protective devises, oral poisoning of pesticides, etc. led to many sprayer related accidents. Also due to low education and awareness levels among the group they are subject to greater health and occupational hazards.

8.20 Since the farming sector is unorganized in character, there is an absence of statistics on farm related accidents and injuries. A study observed (Nag and Nag, 2004), that the tractor incidents (overturning, falling from the tractor, etc.) were the highest (27.7 per cent), followed by thresher (14.6 per cent), sprayer/duster (12.2 per cent), sugarcane crusher (8.1 per cent), and chaff cutter accidents (7.8 per cent) (Fig. 8.2). Most of the fatal accidents resulted from the powered machinery, with the annual fatality rate estimated at 22 per 100,000 farmers. The hand tools related injuries (8 per cent of the total accidents) were non-fatal in nature. In spite of the enactment of legislation, the shortcomings in production and monitoring of the machinery in field use may be responsible for the high rate of accidents (e.g., 42 thresher accidents/1,000 mechanical threshers/year in Southern India).

8.21 A field study surveyed power thresher accidents in Punjab (Northern India) and reported that about 73 per cent of the accidents were due to human factors, 13 per cent due to machine factors, and the remaining 14 per cent were due to crop and other factors. The All India Coordinated Research Projects (AICRP) on human engineering and safety in agriculture reported accident and injury data (1995-1999) from forty-four sample villages of Eastern, Southern, Central and Northern regions points out that while farm mechanization is more in the Northern India, accidents were more in the villages in Southern India. Tractor and tractor implements, thresher, sprayer, sugar cane crusher and chaff cutters accidents accounted for 70 per cent of the total farm accidents (Fig. 8.2).

Fig. 8.2 Distribution of Traumatic Accidents with Different Farm Machinery and Activities

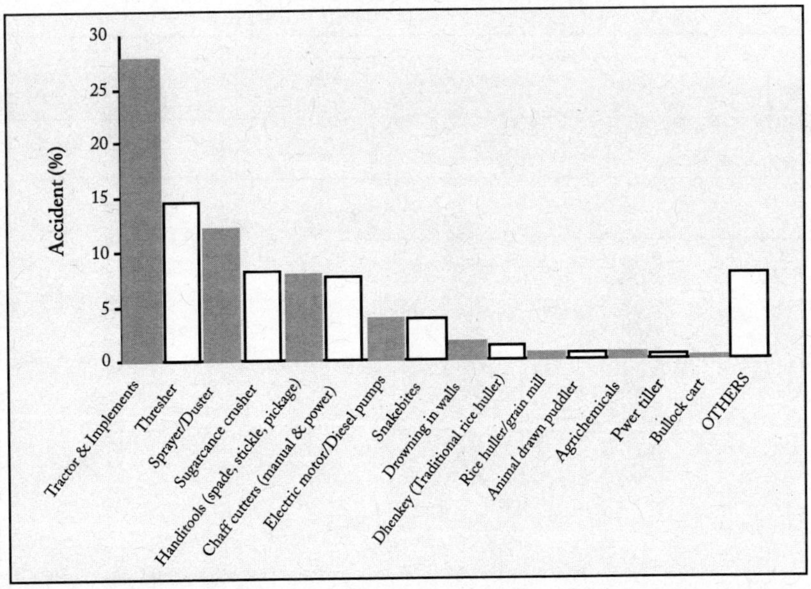

Source: Nag and Nag 2004

Agricultural labourers have high rates of unemployment and underemployment due to irregularity of and non-availability of employment. This makes the group even more vulnerable and creates insecurity in regular flow of income.

8.22 The risks to life of agricultural workers are greatly increased due to low levels of health security. Low income levels and consequent low nutritional intake and constant physical labour increases health problems. Poor health status further affects their productivity and forces them to spend their limited earnings on expensive health care. In most cases, the workers in the informal sector do not obtain any support for meeting the medical cost. Lack of resources to pay for the health care often forces the poor workers either to forego it or become indebted or improvised while trying to pay for it.

Seasonal Migration

8.23 The NCRL report suggests that labourers and land-poor farmers have a high propensity to migrate as seasonal labourers. These migrants are highly disadvantaged as they are poverty ridden with very little bargaining power. They are employed in the unorganized sector, where the lack of regulation compounds their vulnerability. They are largely ignored by the government and NGO programmes and labour laws dealing with them are weakly implemented (Srivastava and Sasikumar 2005).

Fig. 8.3: Distribution of Total Migrants by Industry Groups: All India 1991 (all Duration)

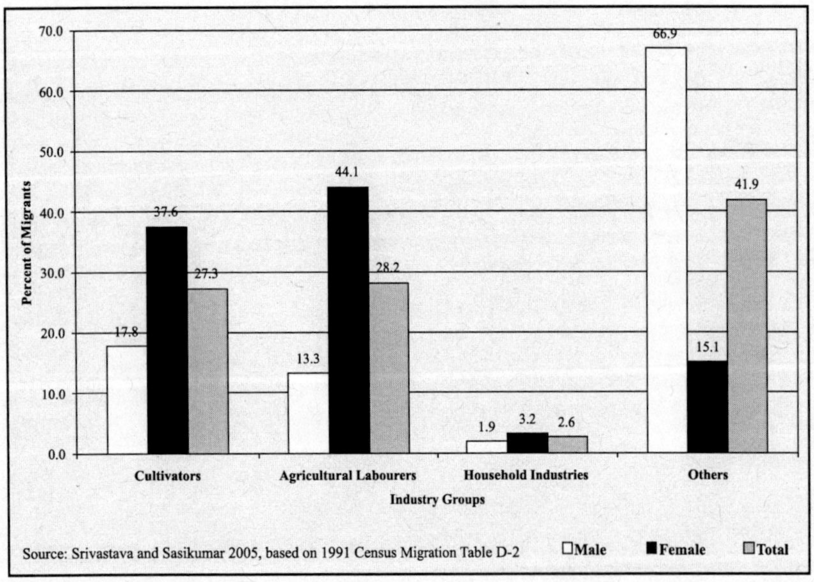

8.24 Women migration for employment was most prominent among agricultural labourers, while male migrants were mainly the non-agricultural workers (Fig. 8.3). Seasonality of agricultural operations is one of the factors that lead to migration of agricultural labourers in search of employment during lean periods. The NCRL (1991) indicates that uneven development of agriculture across different states/regions of the country has led to the migration of labourers from low wage regions/states to states and regions where both the demand and wages are higher. This is particularly so after the Green Revolution when higher agricultural development led to migration of labour from states such as Bihar to Punjab, Haryana and Uttar Pradesh. Further, low rate of public investment in agricultural infrastructure in the less-developed regions has resulted in highly uneven development of agriculture between different regions of the country. The NCRL report recommends that the potential of the backward regions from where out-migration takes place, should be tapped by investment in the development of the regions in areas such as irrigation facilities, dry land farming with emphasis on horticulture and allied activities which would create employment opportunities and raise wages in such regions. This inter-regional migration of labour however is not altogether undesirable as it helps bring down inter-regional wage disparities.

8.25 As per the NCRL there were more than 10 million seasonal/circular rural migrant labourers in the country. Growth of input intensive agriculture and commercialisation of agriculture since the late 1960s has led to peak periods of labour demand, often also coinciding with a decline in local labour deployment (Srivastava and Sasikumar 2005). As observed, migration also takes place when workers in source areas lack suitable options for employment/ livelihood. This may be particularly true when there has been stagnancy in employment generation in agriculture during the nineties along with a slow pace of diversification to non-farm employment in rural areas.

8.26 However the migrant labour is highly disadvantaged as they are subject to exploitation by middlemen and employers, often leading to forced labour. It also entails hazards of travel, deplorable living conditions, lower wages, irregular payments and unfamiliar working conditions and odd and long hours of work. Women migrants fare the worst; they are generally paid less than male migrants and are even more vulnerable. Labourers working in harsh circumstances and living in unhygienic conditions suffer from serious occupational health problems and are vulnerable to disease. Migrant labourers are exposed to serious uncertainties in the potential job market. Their recruitment is often through middlemen. In the agricultural sector, labourers are, sometimes, directly recruited by the employer (Srivastava and Sasikumar 2005), which can be at railway stations or bus stands. At times contractors, who often belong to the same caste and community, are the medium for recruitment in the agricultural and rural sectors. In parts of Punjab, agents or traders are also active in recruitment. The vulnerability of migrant labourers is accentuated due to lack of and ineffective laws and regulations concerning working conditions of the migrants.

8.27 A number of field studies over the 1990s provide rough estimates of the magnitude of seasonal migration in different parts of India. A study in the rice belt of West Bengal indicated that the number of migrants moving into the area during peak seasons, belonging to Muslim tribes, exceeds half a million and it has been increasing over time. Several such instances of mass migration by socially and economically relegated groups such as SCs/STs who have poor physical and human asset base in states like Gujarat, Madhya Pradesh, Rajasthan, Andhra Pradesh, Karnataka and Maharashtra are noted (quoted in Srivastava and Sasikumar 2005).

Forced/Bonded Labour

8.28 Bonded or forced labour whereby one is compelled to work and accept employment at wages or remuneration less than statutory minimum wage or at times even without it, in lieu of payment of debt, has been in existence even after the enactment of the Bonded Labour System (Abolition) Act, 1976. As per the NCRL (1991) 89 per cent of the employers of bonded labourers were agriculturists who mainly belonged to upper castes and engaged the lower caste labourers belonging to STs and SCs for cultivation activities. Wages/ remuneration paid is very meagre and in most cases the labourer is not permitted to undertake additional work elsewhere to supplement incomes. Often the creditors of these labourers engage them as bonded labour and pay much lower wages by deducting the debt. As a result the labourers are caught in a vicious circle and have no means to get out of the bondage and often the other family members were also compelled to offer their services. Abject poverty leads to perpetuation of the bondage.

8.29 The main causes of bonded labour in agriculture as highlighted by NCRL (1991) are the social and caste disabilities aggravated by the seasonal nature of employment in agriculture. "The abject poverty compels them to take resort to loans for subsistence and social customs, usually from the landlord, who also desires captive labour. The kernel of bondedness lies in unrepayable debt and loss of freedom to seek alternate employment through the market process". Thus, economic backwardness, poor infrastructure and low employment, high migrant labour, acute poverty and high incidence of inequality generally characterise areas where bonded labour is high.

8.30 Coexistence of poor agrarian regions with regions of capitalist development through labour migration often also enables agrarian capitalists to impose poor working conditions and high restrictions on the freedom on migrant labourers, even though local farm servants may enjoy superior working conditions (Srivastava 2005). Such instances are found in Punjab, western Uttar Pradesh, and in the cottonseed farms in Andhra Pradesh. While bonded labour was considered as a thing of the past, prevalent in a colonial era, it has been found that new forms of attachment have been rising in developed agriculture, the phenomenon of a 'U' shaped relationship between labour attachment and agricultural development i.e. after an initial decline as agriculture develops, it starts to increase again at later stages.

While bonded labour was considered as a thing of the past, prevalent in a colonial era, it has been found that new forms of attachment have been rising in developed agriculture, the phenomenon of a 'U' shaped relationship between labour attachment and agricultural development i.e. after an initial decline as agriculture develops, it starts to increase again at later stages.

8.31 Recent evidences also corroborate the findings of the NCRL (1991). The NHRC (2001) notes that there is still a sizeable incidence of bonded labour in agriculture which reflects the changing labour requirements of employers under the impact of capitalist development. Debt bondage is the most prominent form of attached labour especially in Punjab, Haryana and Uttar Pradesh. Labour in lieu of debt payment is used as a pretext to perpetuate bondage of not only the victim but also his/her family. With the development of capitalist agriculture, employers have been resorting to contractual forms and labour control strategies, which minimize labour costs and ensure availability of labour. These interlinked contracts place constraints to freedom and mobility of labour (Srivastava 2000).

8.32 There has been some change in the nature and incidence of bonded labour in India as a result of various factors, including the impact of social change and social movements, economic modernisation and state intervention. While these processes have impacted positively on the unfree status of labour in traditional agriculture and in some other sectors, the incidence of bonded labour still remains high in some segments of unorganised industry, the informal sector and in the relatively modern segments of agriculture in some areas (Srivastava 2005). Despite the law abolishing bonded labour, release and rehabilitation of bonded labourers has been a slow process, primarily because of the difficulty in identifying cases of forced labour.

Child Labour

8.33 As noted in Chapter 6, roughly 67 per cent of India's estimated 8.6 million child labourers worked in agriculture in 2004-05 (Chapter 3), 63 per cent of the girls and 71 per cent of the boys. But the bigger problem, as we emphasised in Chapter 3, was that 45.2 million children belonged to out-of-school category, including the child workers. The positive part was, however, that the number and proportion of the out-of-school children and child workers declined substantially over the past decade, 1993/1994-2004/2005, from about 32 per cent to about 18 per cent in the case of former and from 6.2 per cent to 3.4 per cent in the case of the latter. This is at least partly due to the various forms of governmental and non-governmental interventions in the area of child schooling.

8.34 Through the years there has also been a decline in the proportion of child labourers among the rural agricultural labourers, from 3.2 per cent in 1993-94 to 1.9 per cent in 2004-05. Contrary to popular perception, majority of these children are principal workers (71 per cent), working for most of the time during the year, and assist their families on the household farms (68 per cent). About one-third (31 per cent) also works as paid casual labourers (Table 8.8).

8.35 There still are a number of worrying trends as far as the child workers are concerned. With liberalisation

Table 8..8: Percentage of Child Workers in Agriculture across Different Employment Statuses by Sex 2004-2005

Sex	Self Employed			Wage Workers			All Workers		
	Principal	Subsidiary	Principal+ Subsidiary	Principal	Subsidiary	Principal+ Subsidiary	Principal	Subsidiary	Principal+ Subsidiary
Child Labour (5 - 14 years)									
Male	49.6	20.2	69.9	27.2	2.9	30.1	76.8	23.2	100.0
Female	37.1	28.7	65.7	28.5	5.8	34.3	65.6	34.4	100.0
Total	43.4	24.4	67.8	27.9	4.3	32.2	71.3	28.7	100.0
All Workers (5 & Above)									
Male	61.7	2.3	64.0	35.7	0.3	36.0	97.4	2.6	100.0
Female	40.6	23.8	64.4	31.3	4.3	35.6	71.9	28.1	100.0
Total	52.9	11.2	64.2	33.9	2.0	35.8	86.8	13.2	100.0

Note: Subsidiary status is considered only for non-workers by the principal status.
Source: NSS 61st Round 2004 - 2005, Employment-Unemployment Survey. Computed .

and opening up of the economy there is a growing new demand for child workers in agriculture, e.g. in cotton hybrid seeds. Further, there are instances of forced or bonded labour among children. Often children of indebted labourers are offered to work in return of debt to the creditor. Such child labourers are subject to long working hours and even to hazards like exposure to pesticides and accidents from agricultural implements. These children are even more vulnerable to physical abuse and exploitation.

8.36 The Commission is unequivocal in its position that there should be no child labour in the country and in addition, all children between the ages of 11 and 14 years should be in schools. The Child Labour (Prohibition and Regulation) Act, 1986 does not take such a clear position. The Act bans child labour in a few industries in Part A of the Schedule and this includes industries such as transport, within the limits of any port, in foundries and in handling toxic or inflammable substances. Child labour is not explicitly banned in agricultural activities. However, child labour is banned in certain processes and that includes some activities in agriculture such as handling of pesticides and insecticides, processes where tractors, threshing and harvesting machines are used, chaff-cutting and sericulture processing.

8.37 Though the range of hazardous occupations in which child workers are banned has now been expanded under the Child Labour Act, most child labourers including those working in agriculture continue to be 'regulated' to an official maximum of 6 hours a day. Children are also not permitted to work at night from 7 p.m. to 8 a.m. As noted above, working in agriculture is not officially recognized as hazardous work and to that extent there is no ban on child labour in agriculture. Working days in agriculture are normally long and there is frequent exposure to pesticides. The children working in agricultural fields are exposed to the hazards of farming, such as machinery, pesticides, fuels, noxious gases, airborne irritants, noise and vibration.

8.38 A policy framework for child labour needs to clearly place emphasis on education of all children in the school-going age and, if required, increase the supply of schools to facilitate this process. If it is perceived that there is no demand for education among such farm labour households, then more vocational oriented courses or other ways to make schooling attractive needs to be devised.

8.39 While the majority of child workers in agriculture are working on family farms, about a third of them do work as wage workers. Some form of regulation needs to be considered for children in paid work. There should be a ban on child labour in agriculture during the school sessions and paid work could be entertained only during the vacation period. This would prompt parents to keep children in school. Further, children, in the age group 11-14 years, working during vacations, should be allowed to do so only part-time, for less than 4 hours/day, instead

Fig. 8.4: Mandays of Rural Agricultural Labourers by Type of Operation and Gender, 2004-2005

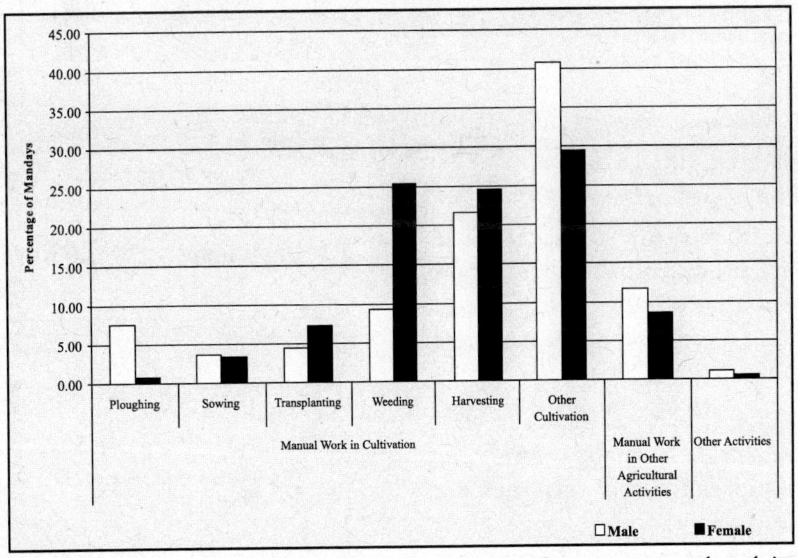

Note: Other activities include manual work in non-agriculture, non-manual work in cultivation and other than cultivation.

Source: NSS 61st Round 2004 - 2005, Employment-Unemployment Survey. Computed .

While operations predominantly done by women, like transplanting is a very skilled activity and weeding is a back-breaking work, the minimum wages appear to take into account the use of technology to categorise an activity as semi-skilled or skilled. Such a categorization works against the interest of women.

of the six hours limit prescribed in the Child Labour Act.

Gender Dimension of Agricultural Work

8.40 Earlier in the chapter, we have highlighted the gender differences in work in agriculture. Women workers in agriculture obtained fewer days of work throughout the year (Table 8.4). The average daily wage earnings were lower for women than for men (Table 8.1). While there was a catch-up of the women wages, with higher growth rates in the nineties (Table 8.1), the disparities by gender have grown since 2000 (Table 8.2) with male wages growing at a faster rate than women's.

Fig. 8.5: Average Earnings per Manday (Rs.) of Rural Agricultural Labourers in Manual Work in Cultivation Operations by Gender 2004-2005

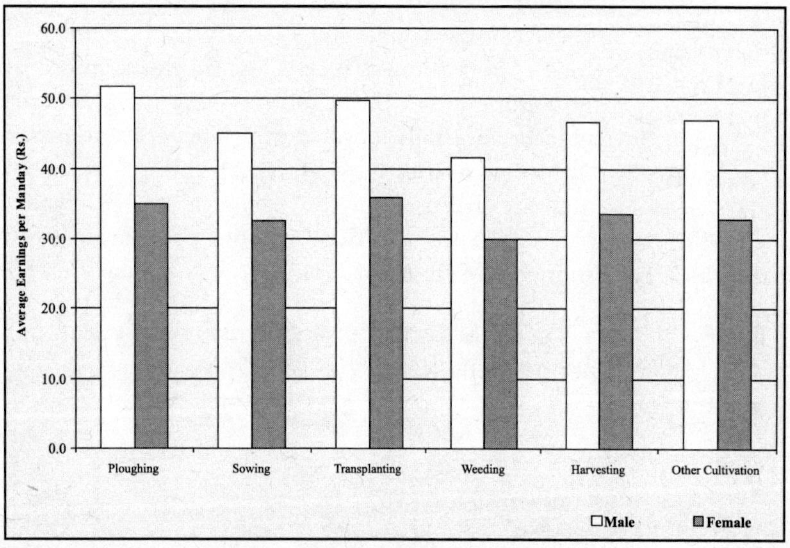

Source : ibid.

8.41 Besides the fact that women got fewer days of work, we found that their activities are concentrated in a few operations within agriculture such as weeding, transplanting and harvesting (Fig. 8.4). Further, even in agricultural operations where the work was primarily done by women, they received lower wages than men (Fig. 8.5). Another form of discrimination referred to in Chapter 5 relates to the fixing of minimum wages. According to the Notification issued by the Ministry of Labour, Government of India on November 11, 1999, all the agricultural operations where women predominate such as sowing, transplanting, weeding and harvesting have minimum wages fixed in the unskilled category. Ploughing, which is predominantly a male operation has a minimum wage fixed in the semi-skilled category and use of a tractor or operation of a tube well is categorized as a skilled activity and accordingly the minimum wages fixed are higher. This has implications for the actual wages received by the workers since the minimum wages gave the signal that the operations identified as women's work are unskilled and could be paid at lower rates. While transplanting is a very skilled activity and weeding is a back-breaking work, the minimum wages appear to take into account the use of technology to categorise an activity as semi-skilled or skilled. Such a categorization works against the interest of women.

8.42 In the earlier chapter, we had observed that there was no feminisation of agriculture till 2000, however, the share of women workers in agriculture in 2004-05 showed an increase. The obverse is observed for the process of casualisation of female workforce in agriculture, i.e., proportion of agricultural labourers among

Fig. 8.6: Casualisation of the Rural Agricultural Workforce by Gender, 2004-2005

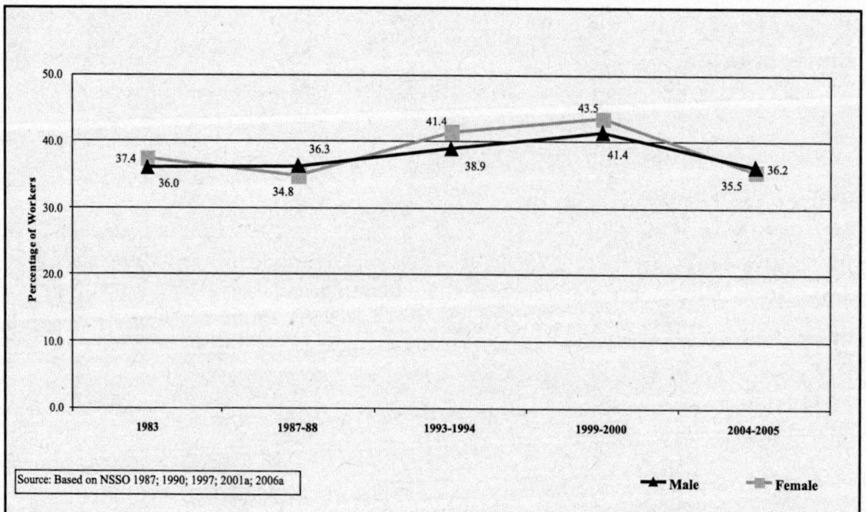

female workers in agriculture. Casualisation of the workforce in agriculture occurred from 1983 to 2000 for men and women and in 2004-05 when the feminisation of the workforce seemed to have occurred, there was no further casualisation of the workforce (Fig. 8.6). Therefore, the recent increase in self-employed workers in 2004-05 in agriculture was true for women workers as well, with the proportion of women cultivators showing a rise.

Social Security

8.43 Overall agricultural labourers suffer under highly insecure and vulnerable working conditions. There are no social security measures to provide risk coverage and ensure maintenance of basic living standards in times of crises such as unemployment or health issues. There are no laws to ensure they work under suitable working conditions and are not subject to any health hazards. There is no fixity of working hours, no compliance to minimum wages and in most cases these are governed by local factors. The insecurity, lack of safety, occupational hazards and incidence of exploitation is even more in the case of migrant labourers and forced labour. This is because of lack of organization and unionization among the group, which is mainly on account of poor literacy and awareness levels and high levels of poverty prevalent among the group. Also there is very little legal protection available and whatever laws or provisions are in place suffered from poor implementation and enforcement.

8.44 The only law that applies to agricultural labourers is the Minimum Wages Act, which is supposed to address their working conditions. However, we have shown here that even this existing legislative provision is more often observed in the breach, and therefore failed to provide much relief to the agricultural labourers except in some states where the unions of such workers are strong or where there is low landlessness leading to a somewhat tight labour market.

Conclusion

8.45 Agricultural labourers are unable to secure even the minimally acceptable standard of living for himself and his family. This is mainly due to the seasonal nature of agricultural work where they do not receive full days of employment during the year. Further, the wage rates for agricultural operations are very low so that the income needs of the labourers are not met adequately. The consequence is the high levels of poverty among the agricultural labourers. Further in the absence of any provisions for social security for the informal sector in general and particularly for agricultural workers, their condition is still worse.

9 Working Conditions of Farmers

Introduction

9.1 Farming still continues to remain the primary source of employment for a large majority of workers in rural areas. Of the total of 166 million farmers, 86 per cent belong to the marginal and small categories and the produce from such activities helps them merely maintain subsistence levels of living. Income from cultivation for these categories of farmers is very low and they often have to resort to wage employment to meet their expenditure. On the other hand, the medium and large farmers, relatively well off with better economic assets and social status, are usually net employers of labour. The small and marginal farmers constitute a highly impoverished group, particularly those who belong to the backward classes like Scheduled Castes and Scheduled Tribes. Hardly having any form of organisation they lack a common forum to articulate their problems and often issues of concern to them are not addressed adequately. These categories of farmers have limited access to credit facilities and often depend on large and medium farmers for purchase of inputs and at times even for wage employment as the latter group is a net employer of wage labour. It is, thus, clear that within the unorganised sector, issues pertaining to marginal and small farmers call for a special focus.

9.2 The problems of farmers, particularly of the small and marginal land holders, have been further compounded by the slow down in the agriculture sector during the nineties. Several studies (e.g. Bhalla 2000; Thamarajakshi 1999; Balakrishnan 2000) highlight that the high growth rate observed in the agriculture sector in the eighties could not be sustained through the nineties. The Mid-Term Appraisal of the Tenth Five-Year Plan (Planning Commission 2005) and the Steering Group on Agriculture of the 11th Plan (Planning Commission 2007) have further confirmed the deceleration in agriculture, particularly in the crop sector after 1996-97. This is in contrast to the gains visualized through improved terms of trade, with the removal of bias against the sector after the process of liberalization was initiated. Studies carried out in the nineties (Bhalla 1995 & 1997) show that the price gains have not been actually realized. Besides, the declining institutional support, particularly of investment in irrigation, research and extension has had adverse impacts on agricultural growth. Private investment in the sector, though increased, has not been able to substitute for the declining public investment. The sector has also not seen a major breakthrough in agriculture technology after the Green Revolution. Productivity deceleration was identified as an underlying factor responsible for the decline in agricultural output. This concurred with the downturn in world prices, which impacted domestic farm prices more than in the earlier decades because of greater openness. The consequence has been that farm incomes became more volatile and decelerated more than the output in many cases (Planning Commission 2007).

9.3 This Commission views the current situation as an agrarian crisis, the magnitude of which can be assessed from the spate of farmers' suicides in the recent past, especially in the states of Maharashtra and Andhra Pradesh. The National Agricultural Policy of 2000 observed "Agriculture has become a relatively unrewarding profession due to generally unfavourable price regime and low value addition, causing abandoning of farming and increasing migration from rural areas....". Several factors contribute to this situation. These include shift in cropping pattern towards cash crops, lack of level playing field for farmers in the global market, increased dependence on high-cost inputs which increases the cost of cultivation and indebtedness, enhanced risks, falling profitability and declining public support. While all sections of farmers in the focal areas of the crisis have been vulnerable, studies show that marginal and small farmers undertaking commercial agriculture have been especially affected.

9.4 It is in this background that the Commission would like to draw the attention of all stakeholders on the conditions of work and livelihood of the marginal and small farmers in this chapter, with relevant comparisons with medium and big farmers wherever necessary.

Credit and Indebtedness

9.5 Small and marginal farmers' households need credit to meet both consumption needs to maintain subsistence levels as well as for production purposes to meet the increasing costs of cultivation. Increased indebtedness is noted as a major reason for the spurt in farmer suicides during recent times across a number of states. Many states including Punjab, Andhra Pradesh, Karnataka, Maharashtra and Kerala have recorded a spurt in distress driven suicides among farmers. In most, if not all, such cases, the economic status of the suicide victim was very poor, being small and marginal farmers. Among the reasons for suicides, indebtedness featured as the prime reason (Gill & Singh 2006). Although a direct link between distress and indebtedness has not always been established, the spate of suicides has been associated with it (Deshpande & Prabhu 2005). After the Green Revolution agricultural activities have become cash based individual enterprises requiring high investment in modern inputs and wage labour (Suri 2006). This is evident from the list of states with high incidence of farmer suicides, which are not necessarily backward or predominantly agrarian or with low income. A common feature that we discern is the high level of commercialization of agriculture and the trend towards cash crops in these states. Increased liberalisation and globalisation have in fact lead to a shift in cropping pattern from staple crops to cash crops like oilseeds and cotton, requiring high investment in modern inputs and wage labour, and increasing credit needs but when the prices declined farmers had no means to supplement their incomes (Bandopadhyay 2004). As in the case of Andhra Pradesh and Karnataka, when the global prices of cotton went up, many farmers, particularly, small and even some marginal ones switched over to cotton production abandoning their traditional staple crop (minor cereals) based agriculture. Traditional agriculture with multi-cropping provided some degree of economic and food security. Cotton is a highly input intensive crop. Small and marginal farmers had hardly any access to institutional finance and had to depend heavily on private moneylenders who charged very high rates of interest. When crops failed and or prices went down they had no means to repay the loans, which drove them to the wall, as the saying goes. Desperate as they were and further burdened by a sense of social shame, ending one's own life might have provided an easy exit. Further, unlike the industrialists, farmers do not have access to debt relief under any law. Being indebted to the private moneylenders they cannot go to public authorities to declare themselves insolvent or to get any kind of debt relief. In most cases the suicide victims were small and marginal farmers who could not sustain frequent price shocks. With mounting debt burden along with the rising risks in production and price fluctuations leading to low remuneration, it is no wonder that a lot of distress is generated among the farmers.

9.6 Loans outstanding against a particular household have both positive (as an indicator of financial access)

Box 9.1 Farmers' Suicides

The main feature that emerged from a number of studies has been that, among the socio-economic factors which led to spurt in farmer suicides in various states, indebtedness was the most prominent. In most cases, the deceased had greater dependence on informal sources of credit and the loans were taken to meet more of consumption needs than for productive purposes. Also a majority of these farmers were illiterate and belong to small and marginal farmers category who had poor access to formal sources of credit. Thus, it appears that, given their poor economic conditions, the small and marginal farmers fail to overcome the seasonal variations in agriculture performance and price shocks and are caught in a vicious circle of indebtedness as they have to resort to loans to meet their consumption needs, leading to immense distress among them.

and negative ramifications (as an indicator of debt burden). About 48 per cent of farmer households had loans outstanding in 2002-03 (Based on Situation Assessment Survey of Farmers 2003). Incidence of indebtedness among farmer households was the highest in Andhra Pradesh (82 per cent), followed by Tamil Nadu (75 per cent) and Punjab (65 per cent).

Table 9.1: Prevalence Rate of Indebtedness by Farm Size, All India (Percentage) 2003

Land size (Hectares)	Formal	Informal	Both	Total
Sub-marginal	12.7	30.3	3.5	46.5
Marginal	18.8	21.7	4.6	45.0
Small	25.9	17.9	7.0	50.8
Medium-Large	34.7	14.4	8.6	57.8
Total	20.4	23.0	5.3	48.6

Note: Sub-Marginal (<= 0.40), Marginal (0.41 - 1.00), Small (1.01 - 2.00), Medium-Large (> 2.00) Hectares.
Source: NSS 59th Round 2003, Situation Assessment Survey of Farmers. Computed.

9.7 The prevalence of outstanding loans was the highest among medium and large categories of farmers (58 per cent) (Table 9.1). Prevalence rate for formal sources among marginal and small farmers was much lower than for large farmers, while in the case of informal sources the reverse was true. The medium and large farmers have better access to institutional sources as they are better endowed in terms of assets to offer as collaterals for loans than marginal and small farmers[1].

9.8 Among the social groups the prevalence rate was the lowest among Scheduled Tribes. While no more than 20.4 per cent of the farmer households had loans outstanding from formal sources, their percentage was the highest among higher caste groups (25.1 per cent) and lowest among STs (16.6 per cent) and SCs (17.1 per cent). Among the Scheduled Castes and Other Backward Classes the prevalence rate was high for informal sources (Table 9.2). It is thus evident that the economically and socially backward groups including small and marginal farmers and Scheduled Castes and Other Backward Classes are more dependent on informal sources compared to the higher castes and medium and large farmers.

Table 9.2: Prevalence Rate of Indebtedness by Social Groups: All India (Percentages) (2003)

Social group	Formal	Informal	Both	Total
ST	16.6	16.8	2.9	36.3
SC	17.1	28.3	4.7	50.2
OBC	19.8	25.6	6.0	51.4
Others	25.1	18.6	5.7	49.4
Total	20.4	23.0	5.3	48.7

Source: Same as in Table 9.1

Quantum of Loans by Source

9.9 The average outstanding loans among indebted farmer households stands at Rs.25895 per household, increasing from Rs. 14866 among sub-marginal households to Rs. 51726 among large farmer households[2]. The picture obtained earlier with regard to the dependence on formal and informal loans, changes slightly when we see the quantum of loans by source (as the loan size from institutional sources is larger on average). It is observed (Table 9.3) that institutional sources account for more than half the outstanding loans in the case of all categories of farmers, other than sub-marginal ones. Among the formal sources, banks and co-operatives are the most important. The importance of institutional sources increases with farm size. But moneylenders continue to be a very important source of loan among all categories, and account for a third of the total quantum of loans to sub-marginal farmers.

9.10 Given their economic conditions, the poorer farmers, with no collateral to offer in lieu of loans and with incapacity and difficulty in following the required procedural formalities to access formal sources, these farmers prefer to approach the easily reachable informal sources such as private moneylenders and traders. This increases their vulnerability and also checks their entrepreneurial initiatives to invest in agriculture to

[1] Andhra Pradesh, Tamil Nadu, Punjab and Kerala have the highest indebtedness among farmer households across all land sizes (Appendix Table A9.1). While Kerala has higher incidence of indebtedness among the sub-marginal and marginal farmers, it is higher among the larger farmer households in Gujarat, Maharashtra and Madhya Pradesh. In the poorer states of Assam, Bihar and Jharkhand the overall indebtedness was low and tends to be concentrated among the marginal farmers.

[2] The average outstanding loan per farmer household was the highest, above or close to Rs.50000 in Kerala, Punjab and Haryana across all land sizes (Appendix Table A9.2). Gujarat, Rajasthan and Tamil Nadu reported average outstanding loans close to Rs.30000. In most states the medium and large farmers had high average outstanding loans per household perhaps implying higher credit-worthiness and repaying capacity.

Table 9.3: Percentage Distribution of Outstanding Loans by Farm Size and Sources, 2003

Source of loan	Size Class of Land Possessed (hectares)			
	Less than and equal to 0.40	0.41-1.00	1.01-2.00	Above 2.00
Government	3.9	3.8	1.7	1.4
Co-operative society	14.1	17.0	20.5	22.8
Bank	24.4	32.0	35.4	42.6
Total: Institutional	**42.4**	**52.8**	**57.6**	**66.8**
Agricultural/ professional moneylender	32.4	30.8	25.9	20.0
Trader	4.9	4.6	4.2	6.0
Relatives & friends	15.2	9.1	8.8	5.2
Doctor, lawyer & other professionals	1.4	0.7	0.8	0.8
Others	3.6	2.0	2.6	1.2
Total: Non-Institutional	**57.6**	**47.2**	**42.4**	**33.2**

Source: NSS 2005b

increase productivity and income levels. The SC and OBC farmers are also more likely to rely on informal sources of credit (Fig. 9.1).

9.11 Our direct estimates shows that of the total loans outstanding from formal sources in 2002-03 (Rs. 50125 crores), the group of farmers who cultivated less than 0.4 hectares of land (35.9 per cent of the total) had only 13.6 per cent of formal sector loans, while those who cultivated between 0.4 and 1 hectares of land (31.1 per cent of the total) availed 21.8 per cent of the loan. Small farmers (16.8 per cent) availed 19.4 per cent of the formal loans, while medium and large farmers (10 per cent and 6.2 per cent of the total respectively) availed 21.7 per cent and 23.4 per cent of formal loans respectively. The major credit constraint, therefore, appears to lie with the two-thirds of the farmers who are marginal landholders, possessing less than 1 hectares of land (NSSO 2005b).

Fig. 9.1: Percentage of Outstanding Loans by Source & Social Groups 2003

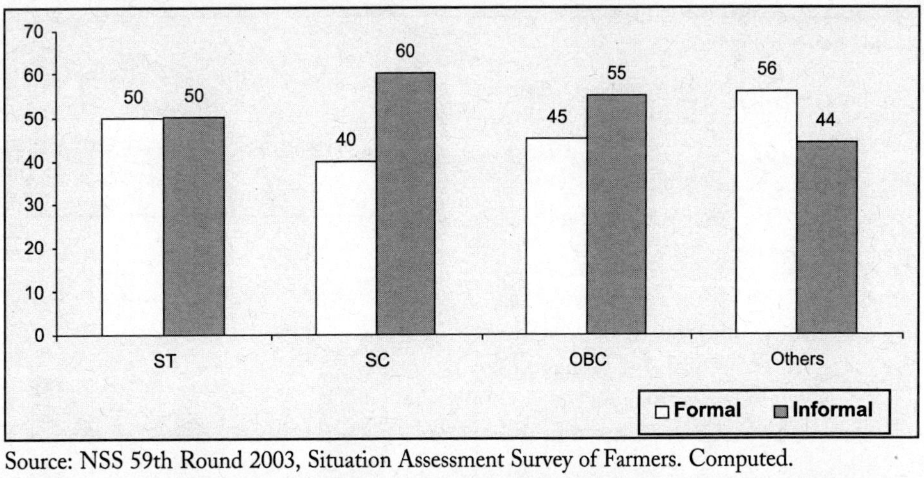

Source: NSS 59th Round 2003, Situation Assessment Survey of Farmers. Computed.

Purpose of Loan

9.12 As already mentioned, rising costs of cultivation and poor returns due to low profitability and viability of small farmers' operations have increased the indebtedness of farmers who require loans to meet both production and consumption needs. The average outstanding loan per farmer household was Rs.12585 in 2002-03. Expenditure in farm business (capital + current) accounted for 58 per cent of the total loan (Fig. 9.2). This was followed by marriages accounting for 11 per cent of the total loan and consumption expenditure at 9 per cent. The main purpose of debt in the case of farmer households is thus to meet the operational costs.

9.13 Loans for productive capital and current expenditure as percentage of total loans outstanding increase with farm size. The significance of loans for consumption and unproductive purposes such as marriages and consumption expenditure is higher among the marginal and small farmers (Fig. 9.3). SCs have the highest share of consumption and unproductive loans,

The economically and socially backward groups, particularly the marginal farmers and the SCs, are most vulnerable to indebtedness. This is so because they are more dependent on informal sources and for consumption purposes. Given their poor economic situation, they face the credit constraint and the possibility of being wedged in a perpetual debt trap.

Fig. 9.2 Percentage of Outstanding Loans by Purpose of Loan 2003

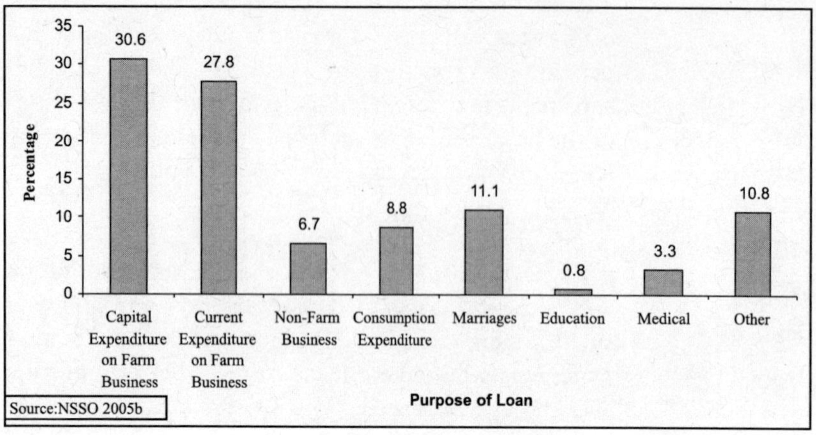

Fig. 9.3: Percentage of Outstanding Loans by Purpose & Land Size Classes 2003

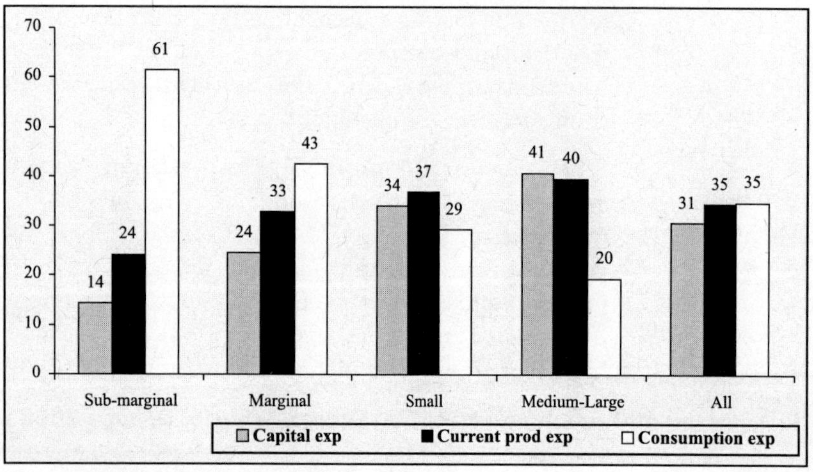

Source: Same as Fig. 9.1

followed by the OBCs and the STs (Fig. 9.4). Among the higher castes, unproductive loans account for less than 30 per cent of the total outstanding loans.

9.14 The indebtedness situation clearly shows that the economically and socially backward groups, particularly the marginal farmers and the scheduled castes, are far more vulnerable than the medium and large farmers and the higher castes. This is so because the former group is more dependent on informal sources and for consumption purposes. Given their poor economic situation, they face the credit constraint on the one hand, and on the other, the possibility of being wedged in a perpetual debt trap.

Irrigation and Input Use

9.15 Cultivation is dependent on timely input use and irrigation. Planning Commission's Steering Group on Agriculture (Planning Commission 2007) identified declining public investment in irrigation as one of the main reasons for declining agricultural productivity during the nineties.

9.16 The proportion of area irrigated was as low as 35 per cent in 1992 (NSSO 1992). Nearly half of the cropped area is still without irrigation facilities (NSSO 2005c). Gross irrigated area accounted for 42 per cent of the cropped area during kharif and 66 per cent during rabi seasons. Punjab, Haryana, and Bihar have the highest gross irrigated area while Assam and Orissa had the lowest. The area irrigated was low across all sizes of farms with no particular disadvantage accruing to small and marginal farmers. However, large farmers capitalized on cheaper sources (e.g. higher percentage of irrigation from canals which is a cheaper irrigation option while smaller farmers have to rent water). While about 40 per cent of the irrigated area in the case of farmers above 10 hectares was from

Fig. 9.4: Percentage of Outstanding Loans by Purpose and Social Groups 2003

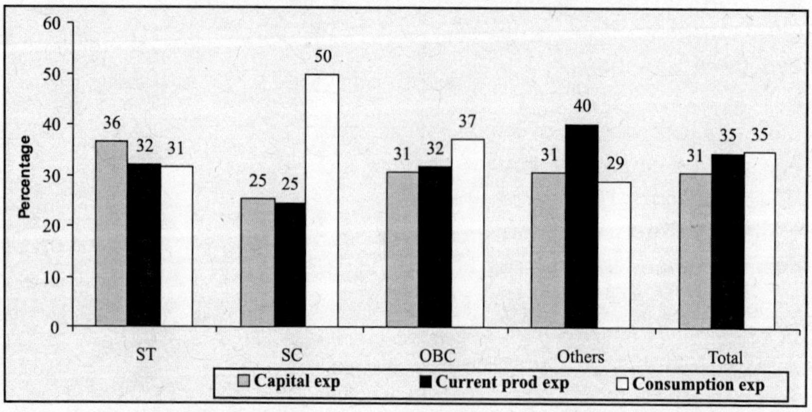

Source: ibid.

canals, it was less than 25 per cent in the case of marginal and small farmers.

9.17 The number of productive assets particularly mechanical equipment/ implements and tractors are very low among smaller sized holdings. The small and marginal farmers thus have to rent such equipment, which adds to their cost of cultivation.

9.18 Input use to enhance productivity has greatly increased since the Green Revolution, which is also one of the reasons for increased cost of cultivation. At the same time these inputs have greatly increased productivity, particularly through the eighties. Timely availability of HYV seeds and usage of fertilizers and pesticides are thus very important to ensure a good crop. Farmers in general, and marginal and small farmers in particular, often face problems regarding easy and timely availability and quality of these inputs as also the costs and knowledge of use of these inputs in the right quantities. Among the various inputs such as pesticides, fertilizers, HYV seeds, organic manure and veterinary services, only organic manure is most readily available within the village. In most cases the inputs are available in the nearest large village which is more than 2-5 kms away. Farmer households have to travel more than 10 kms for seeds and pesticides. Equipment is in most cases rented from medium and large farmers who charge exorbitant rates.

9.19 While usage, quantity and quality of fertilizers and organic manure are considered as optimum, timely and adequate use of improved seeds and pesticides has been low. While about 80 per cent of the farmers of all size classes used fertilisers, the use of organic manure, improved seeds and pesticides has been higher among the medium and large land size farmers. About 48 per cent of the farmer households made use of purchased seeds and 47 per cent used farm saved seeds. Seed replacement rates were found to be low. About 30 per cent farmers replaced seed variety every year and 17 per cent changed it after 4 years. Replacement rates were the lowest among marginal farmers. Only 24 per cent of the sub-marginal farmers and 29 per cent of the marginal farmers replaced seeds every year, compared to 40 per cent of the large farmers (NSSO 2005d).

9.20 Testing facilities for fertilizers and pesticides are hardly available to the farmer households. Only states like Punjab and Tamil Nadu reported some usage of such facilities. With rampant adulteration seeds are often of poor quality. Similar has been the case with fertilisers and pesticides. Often farmers are also not aware of the correct proportions of fertilisers to be used. They depend on sellers or on the demonstration effect of large farmers. Incorrect usage of inputs and environmental hazards are the fallouts from such instances.

9.21 Despite the low capacity to invest in productive assets, the small and marginal farmers have been undertaking more intensive cultivation than their large counterparts. As mentioned above, apart from irrigation, the usage of fertilizer per hectare of both fertilized area and per hectare of gross cropped area is much higher in their case than the large farmers.

9.22 Based on the Cost of Cultivation Studies' data for the 80s and the 90s, some scholars (e.g. Sen and Bhatia 2004) have observed that the negative relationship between farm size and productivity, noted for earlier periods, is less evident now. However, recent data shows that the inverse relationship between gross value of crop output per hectare and farm size continues to hold in a majority of states (Based on Situation Assessment Survey of Farmers 2003). It is also observed that as long as small farmers have access to similar infrastructure and irrigation as the large farmers, they neither suffer from scale disadvantages nor are they disadvantaged by the higher prices they pay for the inputs. Cropping intensity as well as a more intensive use of family labour is also noticeable on smaller farms. However, small farmers are still faced with higher unit costs on indivisible fixed inputs. Their access to cheaper inputs is limited and they have to rent equipments at higher rates which add to the costs. In addition, they face several other constraints, which lower their productivity and income.

The Tenancy Issue

9.23 A large percentage of farmers lease-in land in order to augment their holdings. Under the tenancy laws, which followed the Abolition of Intermediary Acts promulgated after Independence, most states abolished

Tenancy reform had the perverse impact of driving tenancy underground, and making it more difficult for tenants to lease land on secure and reasonable conditions. Landless and poor tenants continued to lease-in land, but remained unrecorded tenants, without security of tenure and without the benefit of rent regulation.

leasing, except for a very small category of households which were legally permitted to lease-in or lease-out. Since the objective of land reform was to provide proprietorship to erstwhile tenants no further leasing was needed to be permitted, except in a small category of cases. In these cases, the states also laid down procedures for regulating rents and providing security of tenure through recorded tenancies.

9.24 In reality, tenancy reform was not able to cover the unrecorded tenancies, which prevailed at the time of reform. Further, because of the pressure on land, landless and poor tenants continued to lease-in land, but remained unrecorded tenants, without security of tenure and without the benefit of rent regulation. Tenancy reform had the perverse impact of driving tenancy underground, and making it more difficult for tenants to lease land on secure and reasonable conditions.

9.25 From the very beginning, tenancy conditions in India differed between the usually arid and semi-arid regions where the land-man ratio was favourable and extensive cultivation was practised, and the other regions, where there was more intensive cultivation. In the former areas, often very small landowners preferred to lease-out land to bigger cultivators. With the spread of capital intensive agriculture, this trend also spread into the areas of developed capitalist farming, notably in the northern states of Punjab and Haryana. As regards terms of tenancy, during the British period, there was already a differentiation, with the upper stratum of secure tenants usually paying cash rents, while the tenants-at-will usually remaining sharecroppers. After the former category became proprietors, sharecropping became the predominant form of rent, but with the spread of capitalist and commercial farming, once again fixed and cash rents have become more important.

9.26 For policy purposes, therefore, one has to recognise that the tenants are differentiated because they face different conditions and levels of insecurity. At the same time, tenants as a class also face some common issues mainly due to the difference between their de jure and de facto statuses. Besides the usual risks and problems faced by other cultivators, tenant cultivators have the additional burden of high rents. Due to the lack of documented proof, as it is merely a verbal agreement, the tenants are deprived of any tenancy rights. This increases the hardships of tenant cultivators as lack of documented proof keeps them outside the ambit of formal credit. Thus, rising costs of inputs and enhanced rents along with the high costs of informal leasing increases the vulnerability of the group. Studies of agrarian distress in the recent past indicate that marginal and small tenants are an especially vulnerable class, as rents in the areas of commercial agriculture go up to reflect high profitability in good years, but constitute a heavy burden in the years of distress.

9.27 Since tenancy is largely concealed, land holding surveys cannot be expected to throw up very reliable figures. Nevertheless, these surveys, carried out since 1953-54 are still the best source of data on land tenancy. About 10 per cent holdings are tenanted holdings and recent surveys (NSSO 1992; 2006b) indicate that the percentage of such holdings has seen an overall decline between 1991-1992 and 2002-2003, albeit a very small one (Fig. 9.5).

9.28 The total area leased-in has remained roughly stable since 1981-82, after a decline in the initial three decades. The area leased as a proportion of the operated area was 20.55 per cent in 1953-54, which went down to below 11 per cent in 1961-62 and 1971-72. It further declined to 7.2 per cent in 1981-82 but increased slightly to 8.3 per cent in 1991-92. The total area leased-in shows a decline to 6.5 per cent in 2002-03.

9.29 The share of marginal and small holdings in the total leased area rose from 35.6 per cent to 52.3 per cent with a corresponding decline in the share of leased area in the medium holdings (Fig.9.6). It is interesting to note,

Fig. 9.5: Tenant Holdings by Categories of Operational Holdings (Percentages) 1991-92 and 2002-03 (Kharif only)

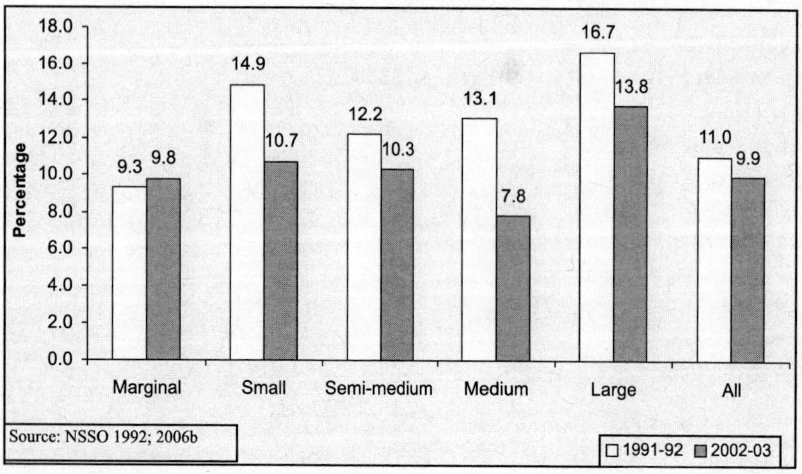

Source: NSSO 1992; 2006b

Fig. 9.6: Percentage Shares in Leased-in Area 1992 - 2003

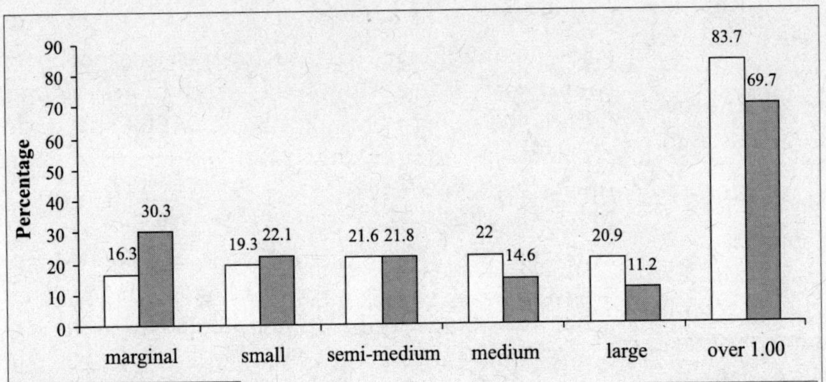

Source: NSSO 1992; 2006b

however, that the overwhelming proportion of land (55.1 per cent) is leased-in by the households owning less than 1 hectare of land (Srivastava, Saxena and Thorat, 2003).[3] Since the first landholding survey was carried out in 1953-54, sharecropping has been the predominant form of leasing in India. Comparison across the years is not straightforward as the lease type is not stated for a large percentage of leased area (which varies from survey to survey). Leaving aside this, in 1991-92, 34.4 per cent of the leased area was under sharecropping, while 33.5 per cent was under fixed cash or kind rents. In 2002-03, the respective percentages were 40.3 and 49.8 (Table 9.4). The advantages and disadvantages of each type of tenancy are well discussed in the literature. Sharecropping reduces efficiency but allows risk sharing. Fixed rents provide for greater incentives to the tenant but put the entire burden of risk on her. This is notable, especially because, as we stated earlier, in areas of commercial agriculture, where vulnerability to price and output fluctuations is high, small tenants are subject to high risks.

Table 9.4: Percentage of Leased-In Area by Terms of Lease and Broad Size Class 1991-92 and 2003

Broad Size Class (In hectares)	Fixed Money	Fixed Produce	Share of Produce	From Relatives: No Terms	Others
			1991-92		
0.002 - 0.20	24.4	7.5	19.2	18.0	30.9
0.21- 0.50	18.5	13.6	38.7	9.8	19.4
0.51- 1.00	11.6	16.0	41.6	5.2	25.6
1.01-2.00	15.1	19.1	40.9	4.3	20.6
2.01-4.00	24.2	14.8	30.1	4.6	26.3
4.01-10.00	26.4	12.3	27.2	3.4	30.7
Over 10.00	35.5	11.1	19.0	5.3	29.1
All Sizes	19.0	14.5	34.4	7.4	24.7
			2003		
Equal to 0.04	26.6	7.0	0.9	21.5	44.0
0.04-0.5	17.2	24.6	49.0	3.5	5.6
0.5-1.0	19.7	17.8	53.1	1.9	7.4
1.0-2.0	22.9	22.4	47.1	2.1	5.6
2.0-4.0	37.1	16.9	31.2	7.2	7.5
4.0-10.0	50.8	9.4	31.9	3.2	4.7
Over10.0	28.5	36.0	26.7	7.0	1.8
All Sizes	29.5	20.3	40.3	4.0	5.9

Sources: NSSO 1992 ; 2005b

9.30 We have already pointed out that most tenancies are unrecorded. The share of recorded tenancy is almost negligible, 0.74 per cent in 2003, which has declined from 1.31 per cent in 1991-92. This goes to show that the tenant cultivators are highly vulnerable.

9.31 It is clear that a new round of tenancy reform should be high on the policy agenda. The Tenth Plan and the Eleventh Plan have already suggested that tenancy should be legalised subject to the ceiling limit already specified in law, security of tenure should be encouraged and the new law should protect the rights of both landowners and tenants. At the same time, banks should not insist on copies of land records for credit purposes.

Other Constraints

9.32 Being a nature-based activity, cultivation is a highly risky. Further, in the liberalised scenario price risks have also increased (Suri 2006; Jodhka 2006). Heightened dependence on market has exposed the farmers to fluctuating price regimes, more so in the areas of commercial farming. This is of particular concern for the small and marginal farmers who do not have the means to cope with such shocks, either through market support or through insurance.

9.33 The entire crop of the small holders comes to the market at one time. The small

[3] Appendix Table A9.3 gives the state-wise trends in tenant holdings. Tenant holdings/area leased is the lowest in Gujarat and Rajasthan and the highest in Haryana. All the states except Gujarat, Bihar and Orissa register a decline in area and holdings under lease between 1992 and 2003.

cultivator, who is often heavily indebted, has poor bargaining strength to get a favourable deal from the more resourceful traders. In such a situation the state support price system is of prime importance in protecting the interest of the farmer. However, the government's attempts to mitigate these risks through such measures as the Minimum Support Price (MSP) have also not been very successful as the coverage of the scheme in terms of crops and area is small. The small farmer is thus not assured of a minimum return on his labour and investment. As Jodka (2006) noted, public marketing services have also declined in spread and scope, again increasing the role of private traders. The now dilapidated public extension support system has increased the dependence of the farmer on private dealers, often resulting in inappropriate choice of crops and inputs. In several states, the Agricultural Produce Marketing Corporation Acts have either been amended or repealed, providing freer entry to private organised trade. Contract farming is also now being considered as a way of integrating farmers to markets. With such integration, crop diversification is likely to receive a fillip. But this may not automatically translate into higher returns to small farmers due to high transaction costs for the firms and the weak bargaining strength of the farmers, who will remain so unless the small and marginal farmers can be federated into groups.

9.34 In case of crop failures, insurance is important. However, crop insurance has made little headway except where it is built into other transactions such as co-operative credit. Insurance is an uncommon practice with only 4 per cent farmers having ever insured their crop. Nearly 57 per cent of the farmers who had never insured their crops were unaware of the crop insurance schemes. Inability to pay the premium was reported as a reason by only 3 per cent. Marginal and small farmers were less likely to have crop insurance. Compared to 14 per cent of the large farmers, only around 2 per cent of the sub-marginal farmers, 2 per cent of the marginal farmers and 5 per cent of the small farmers had crop insurance. Even among farmers with insured crops, follow up and payment by insurance companies in case of crop failure is still a weak area (Based on Situation Assessment Survey of Farmers 2003).

9.35 Low literacy, lack of organisation and poor connectivity lead to low levels of awareness among farmers, regarding technology usage, institutional credit schemes and sources and the government's support initiatives. Awareness levels about bio-fertilisers, Minimum Support Price (MSP), WTO etc. are associated with the educational levels. States of Kerala, Tamil Nadu and Punjab reported high awareness levels about these issues. At the all India level, only 18 per cent of the farmers were aware of bio-fertilisers, 29 per cent are aware about the MSP and only 8 per cent of the farmers have heard of WTO (Appendix Table A9.4)[4]. Variations are prominent across farmer households, the level of awareness of bio-fertilizers, MSP and WTO increases with increase in land size.

9.36 The Eleventh Plan Steering Group on Agriculture (Planning commission 2007) has noted that technology has become a crucial constraint on growth of agriculture. It points to the two aspects of this constraint - development of new technologies and the gaps in the application of existing technologies. Extension services can serve as a critical tool in closing this gap. The Steering Group has noted that public extension services have become extremely weak. This conclusion has been echoed in a number of other reports including those by the National Farmers' Commission.

9.37 Nearly 60 per cent of the farmer households have not accessed any source of information on modern technology (NSSO 2005d). Among those who had accessed such information, the three main sources were other progressive farmers (16.7 per cent), input dealers (13.1 per cent) and the radio (13 per cent). Government agencies such as the Krishi Vigyan Kendra, extension workers, farmer visits, or even demonstrations and fairs have come to play a negligible role in disseminating information on modern technology. For instance, extension workers were a source of information in only 5.7 per cent of the cases (Appendix Table A9.5). Both government and other sources of information were least

The majority of the farmer households have not accessed any source of information on modern technology. Government agencies such as the Krishi Vigyan Kendra, extension workers, farmer visits, or even demonstrations and fairs have come to play a negligible role in disseminating information on modern technology.

4 The state level picture regarding awareness of bio-fertilizers, MSP and WTO by farm size is reported in Appendix Table A9.4. Awareness regarding these was highest across states among the medium and large farmer households.

accessed by the marginal and small farmers. Given that the government extension services are needed precisely to overcome market failures, which is more acute in the case of marginal and small farmers, this disparity is of considerable concern. As against 10 per cent of the medium and large farmers, only around 4 per cent of the sub-marginal and marginal farmers and 8 per cent of the small farmers accessed information regarding improved practices and technology from extension workers. Similarly, participation in training programmes, exposure to Krishi Vigyan Kendras, study tours etc. constituted the least source for the smallest groups. Moreover, the quality and reliability of extension services appeared to be a major concern of the cultivators.[5]

9.38 Farmers' groups and co-operatives help the farmers overcome diseconomies of small size and access credit, inputs and markets. Only about 30 per cent of the farmer households are members of cooperative societies (Appendix Table A9.7). Among the sub-marginal farmer households only 18 per cent are members of the cooperatives, while among the larger households, with land size above 4 hectares nearly 50 per cent are members of cooperative societies.[6] About 10 per cent of them, though were members of the co-operatives, did not make use of the services. Thus, only 20 per cent of the farmer households availed the cooperatives' services, and 9 per cent of them availed credit and seed procurement services. Compared to the 37 per cent large farmers, only 11 per cent sub-marginal farmers and 19 per cent marginal farmers availed services of the co-operatives.

9.39 At all India level, only 2 per cent of the farmer households were associated with organizations while 5 per cent of them had at least one as a member of the Self-Help Groups (SHGs). Across land sizes, percentage of farmer households with membership of registered farmers' agencies increase from 1.7 among sub-marginal and marginal farmers to 3.7 among medium-large farmers. The share of farmer households with membership of SHGs was higher than for any registered farmers' association. It ranged from 4.4 per cent among sub-marginal and marginal farmer households to 5.4 per cent among medium-large households. It was slightly higher among the small farmer households, 5.7 per cent (Appendix Table A9.8). Membership of farmers' organizations and SHGs is higher in the southern states of Kerala, Tamil Nadu, Karnataka and Andhra Pradesh[7]. Thus, presently, economic organisation of farmers, particularly the marginal and small farmers, which could have helped them overcome the size constraint, is extremely insignificant.

9.40 Rising costs of cultivation, low remunerations, high risks with frequent crop failures, declining agricultural growth, and mounting debts have all led the farmer to a distress like situation. Nearly 40 per cent of the farmer households disliked their occupation (Appendix Table A9.9). The disinclination to farming is higher among smaller farmers. While nearly 44 per cent of the sub-marginal and marginal farmers reported they disliked farming, only 28 per cent of the medium and large farmers said so[8]. The main reasons for this disinclination were the lack of viability of farming, followed by its perceived risks.

Conclusion

9.41 Indian agriculture sustains a large cultivating population on the meagre land resource. Land ownership distribution remains highly skewed and the average size of landholding has been steadily declining. An overwhelming majority of farmers are marginal and small

5 Percentage of farmer households accessing extension service worker or any government agency as a source of information on modern technology increases with increase in farmer households' land size in most states (Appendix Table A9.5 and Appendix Table A9.6).

6 Appendix Table A9.7 presents the share of farmer households that are members of the cooperatives by land size. Overall the cooperative movement is not very strong in Uttaranchal, Jharkhand and Bihar. The share of farmers who are cooperatives' members is exceptionally high in Kerala, Maharashtra, Chhattisgarh, Himachal Pradesh and Gujarat. While in Himachal Pradesh and Kerala the medium farm size holders are more likely to be members of the cooperatives, in the other three states large farmers dominate. The percentage difference between sub-marginal and large farmer households that are members of the cooperatives is very large across the states, especially in Punjab, Madhya Pradesh, Gujarat, Maharashtra and Uttar Pradesh.

7 Across the states negligible share of farmer households have membership in registered farmers' associations among the land size classes (Appendix Table A9.8). The only exceptions in this regard are the states of Kerala in all land size classes, Gujarat, Tamil Nadu and Karnataka among medium-large farmer households and Assam among sub-marginal and marginal farmers. Similar to the national pattern, the share of farmer household members in SHGs is higher among the small farmers than among the medium-large farmers in most states. Medium-large farmer households from the continuous belt from eastern India, Bihar, Jharkhand, Chhatisgarh, Madhya Pradesh, Rajasthan up to Gujarat and Punjab in the West have higher share of membership in SHGs. In the southern states the small farmers are more likely to be members of SHGs. Bihar, Jammu & Kashmir and Rajasthan have negligible share of farmer households with membership of SHG.

8 Across the states it was mainly the sub-marginal and marginal farmers who reported that they disliked their occupation (Appendix Table A9.9), the highest being in the eastern states of Bihar, Jharkhand, Orissa Chhattisgarh and Uttaranchal. Lowest share of the medium-large farmers who reported that they disliked farming were from Uttaranchal, Andhra Pradesh and Gujarat.

cultivators. These farmers use available inputs intensively and, except in some regions, show higher efficiency.

9.42 The sector as a whole showed poor performance in the last decade. Agricultural growth rate had declined and food grains production had virtually stagnated. Signs of agrarian distress were visible in some years. The spate of farmers' suicides in many areas is the most disconcerting manifestation of this distress. Marginal and small farmers have borne the brunt of the adverse circumstances in agriculture.

9.43 While there were efforts such as those to promote institutional credit to rural areas, improved access to inputs, subsidies on fertilisers and electricity, minimum support price etc. these have not been fully successful in protecting the interest of the farmers in general, and marginal/small farmers in particular. The analysis of results from the Farmers' Survey clearly establishes that these farmers have inadequate access to information, to agencies promoting technological change, to co-operative networks and related organisations and are less able to benefit from the plethora of governmental interventions. This is significant since; in any case, these farmers are less well placed to take advantage of the markets.

9.44 A focused initiative is clearly required to facilitate the growth of small farm agriculture. It is imperative that the government takes initiatives to expand the network of institutional credit facilities in the rural areas and that the credit needs of the small and marginal farmers are met through earmarking credit for the group. Extension and marketing initiatives need to focus on this segment. At the same time, group initiatives need to be encouraged and awareness among the group has to be increased. The procedural formalities also have to be made less stringent to make the system more user-friendly for the largely illiterate group. Further it is of prime importance that the educational levels and skill development among the farmers are enhanced so that there is increased occupational diversification among them, as more than forty per cent of the marginal and small farmer households dislike their occupation and would rather give it up. Improved education levels among them will increase their awareness levels and may also lead to greater cooperation among them. This will make them better organized for collective action and better equipped to anticipate the market trends. This also will increase their exposure to the new techniques of production and other initiatives taken by the government to protect their interest. In view of the poor conditions of the farmers the revised National Policy for Farmers emphasizes the need to improve their well-being rather than concentrating solely on enhancing the production. It needs to be realised that the gains of several initiatives in this context have not been reaching the majority of small and marginal farmers. This issue needs to be appropriately addressed.

9.45 A thrust area of this Commission (which has been endorsed by the National Policy for Farmers) is on the need to introduce a universal social security system as a support for farmers. It is important to ensure the protective social security of the landless and marginal and small farmers. Given the high risk and low profitability of the farmer's activities such a social security measure that provides for health expenses, life and unemployment insurance and old age pensions is important. Presently, there have hardly been any welfare provisions for farmers. This is of concern as it discourages entrepreneurship among the farmers as also to undertake and adopt new ventures. Given the distress among the farmers, it is important that a safety-net programme is introduced to ensure a minimum income for the farmers. Also the risk factor has to be mitigated through adequate insurance and credit facilities. At the same time, the outreach and efficiency of the institutional credit sources have to be improved. This is important to protect the small and marginal farmers who still heavily rely on private moneylenders who charge high interest rates and follow unscrupulous means to perpetuate indebtedness. Land reforms particularly related to tenancy laws, land leasing, distribution of ceiling surplus land and providing adequate access to common property is also urgently needed.

10 International Experience of Regulation of Minimum Conditions of Work

Introduction

10.1 The international community has long been engaged on a discussion of the rights of workers, whether wage employed or self-employed. A distinction is usually made between the 'core' rights of workers, which are usually 'negative' rights, and other rights of workers, which may be subject to the specific country/industry context and which may be subject to what has been termed as progressive realisation in the human rights literature. The rights of different categories of workers are dealt with in the declarations, treaties and conventions of the United Nations, and the deliberations and conventions of the International Labour Organisation, which is the pivotal multi-lateral organisation dealing with issues pertaining to workers.

United Nations Framework of Rights

10.2 Human rights were first articulated in 1948 with the Universal Declaration of Human Rights. While this declaration proclaimed both political and economic rights two separate protocols were drafted subsequently, dividing rights into civil and political rights and economic, social and cultural rights, The International Covenant on Civil and Political Rights, and The International Covenant on Economic, Social and Cultural Rights were adopted in 1966 and entered into force in 1976. Civil and political rights were thought of as "negative rights". In other words, governments should refrain from impinging on these rights but the realization of these rights required little direct government intervention. In contrast, economic, social and civic rights are "positive rights" since the government must do more than provide individual entitlements. These were seen as exorbitantly costly requiring massive state-provided welfare. Further, while civil and political rights were seen as precise and possible to implement immediately, economic rights were subject to progressive realisation.

10.3 The United Nations has also given effect to a number of Declarations and Conventions (ratified by states), which have a bearing on the treatment of workers. For example, the Convention on the Elimination of all forms of Discrimination against Women (CEDAW) is the most comprehensive treaty on women's rights and is often described as the international bill of rights of women. It was adopted by the United Nations General Assembly in 1979 and came into force in 1981. As of April 2000, the Convention had been ratified and acceded to by 165 States, making it the second most ratified international human rights treaty (United Nations 2000).

The ILO Framework

10.4 The International Labour Organisation has adopted a number of Declarations and Conventions for the treatment of workers. The ILO, in its International Labour Conference, June

1998 adopted the Declaration on Fundamental Principles and Rights at Work. The worker's rights, referred to as the "core labour standards" of the ILO, included eight ILO Conventions. These Conventions focus on issues of the right of freedom of association and effective recognition of the right to collective bargaining (Conventions No. 87, 1948 and 98, 1949); elimination of all forms of forced or compulsory labour (No. 29, 1930 and 105); effective abolition of child labour and minimum age (No 138, 1973 and No. 182, 1999), elimination of discrimination in respect of employment and occupation, equal remuneration (No. 100, 1951 and 111, 1958).

10.5 Of the eight Conventions included in the ILO core labour standard, only three have been ratified by India relating to forced labour, equal remuneration and discrimination. The insecurities faced by informal workers require a whole matrix of rights and the core labour standards, as formulated above, do not address these. India has ratified a series of other Conventions pertaining to the conditions of workers, mainly of the organised sector workers.

10.6 Since 1999, the ILO set itself the challenge to achieve decent work for all by promoting 'opportunities for women and men to obtain decent and productive work, in conditions of freedom, equity, security and human dignity' (ILO 1999). Interest in achieving this outcome for all implicitly extended the ILO's reach from its traditional base of formal sector wage workers to include the self-employed and other workers outside traditional employee-employer relations (ILO 1999, 2001; Sen 2000). It extended its outreach to the informal economy. In 2002 it made this expansion explicit through the International Labour Conference's focus on 'decent work and the informal economy' (ILO 2002b).

10.7 The embrace of 'decent work for all' illustrates the ILO's interest in incorporating a greater development focus which places the needs of the working poor, particularly the informal workers, more central to its aims (ILO 1999). Decent work integrates the ILO's four strategic objectives, and can be linked to poverty reduction since increased opportunities for work, increased rights at work, social protection and greater voice in the workplace are associated with improvements in capabilities and well being (Chen, Vanek and Carr 2004; Saith 2004). The key point is that it is not just the number of jobs created but the quality of those opportunities that makes the work decent and which links decent work to poverty reduction (ILO 1999, 2002b; Chen, Vanek and Carr 2004).

International experience in adhering to Minimum Conditions of Work

10.8 A large number of countries across the world, both developed and developing, large and small, have converted the international community's commitment to minimum conditions of work for all workers, into enforceable legislation, and in some cases (such as the European Union) have committed themselves to providing a social floor (in which the rights-based framework evolved by the international community can apply) for all workers, irrespective of their social and geographical origin.

OECD Countries

10.9 A review of the conditions of work of the workers in the OECD countries (Australia, Canada, Italy, Japan, Netherlands, United Kingdom, United States) and European Union by the Commission shows that all countries prescribe certain minimum conditions of work for their workers.

10.10 Minimum wages are followed by all OECD countries. In Canada the minimum wage varies across jurisdictions. Canadian law requires different rates for regional and occupational categories. Though minimum wages are set by the Fair Labour Standards Act, some states in the US follow their own minimum wages.

10.11 The hours of work are limited to 38-40 hours per week in the OECD countries except in the UK and the US which do not limit the hours of work. The hours of work in the US and UK are based on the agreement between the employer and the employee.

10.12 The workers are entitled to rest days, holidays and paid leave as per the law in all the OECD countries except in the UK where there is no general legislation specifying the number of rest days and holidays. UK has relatively high proportions of employees working shifts, at night and weekends. Netherlands, Canada, Italy and Australia have provisions for maternity and child care leave.

ILO's "core labour standards" refer to eight ILO Conventions focussing on the right to freedom of association and collective bargaining, elimination of forced labour, child labour and discrimination in employment and occupation, and equal remuneration.

10.13 The minimum age of work is 15-16 years. There are also provisions for occupational safety of workers and prevention of discrimination of workers against sex, nationality, race, colour, etc.

10.14 Labour laws of OECD countries give protection to formation of trade unions and right to bargain collectively. Netherlands has fairly rigid standards. Dutch employers are required to operate within a fairly rigid system of statutory rights and obligations. In Australia, to register in the federal system, the trade unions must have at least 50 members who are employees along with other conditions. There must be no other trade union to which the members of the association could more conveniently belong.

10.15 The Social Charter of the European Union has made it imperative for the countries to have minimum conditions of work for the workers. Among the countries of the European Union, legislations involving most of the minimum standards exist. United Kingdom is the only country with relatively freer labour market conditions. In general we could say that the minimum conditions of work are met for workers in all the OECD countries.

US Fair Labour Standards

10.16 The US Fair Labour Standards ensures minimum standards at work for workers in the United States. The US has the most flexible labour laws among the OECD countries. Although labour market regulation in the US is the most idiosyncratic and cannot be applied mechanically to other situations where labour markets have their own institutional and historical specificity, it is instructive to note that the US sets certain universal minimum standards of work for its workers, leaving other conditions to be worked out through employment contracts.

10.17 The Fair Labour Standards Act (FLSA) is a United States Federal law that was enacted in 1938. Amendments have been made to this law since it was passed. The Act (FLSA) is the federal law that establishes a federal minimum wage, overtime compensation requirements, payday rules, child labour and record keeping requirements affecting full-time and part-time workers in the private sector and in Federal, State, and local governments. The FLSA was passed to protect unskilled labourers, minors, and others who work in low paying jobs. The FLSA does not cover certain categories of employees, specifically professional, administrative, and executive employees.

10.18 The FLSA legislates a federal minimum wage but some states have set their own minimum wages, in which case, a worker must be paid whichever minimum wage is higher. Certain categories of employees such as apprentices, those under training, or workers with disabilities may be paid less than the minimum wage under special certificates issued by the Department of Labour. Overtime pay at a rate of not less than one-and-a-half times their regular rates of pay is required after 40 hours of work in a workweek. An employee must be at least 16 years old to work in most non-farm jobs and at least 18 years to work in non-farm jobs declared hazardous by the Secretary of Labour. Youths, 14-15 years old, may work outside school hours in various non-manufacturing, non-mining, non-hazardous jobs for specified hours of work. The FLSA does not limit the number of hours in a day or days in a week an employee may be required or scheduled to work if the employee is at least 16 years old. These matters are for agreement between the employer and the employees or their authorized representatives.

Social Charter of the European Union

10.19 The countries which are part of the European Union have adopted a social charter to give effect to the social and economic rights of their citizens and working people. The Charter consists of a number of protective as well as promotional measures, which lead up to the ILO's definition of 'decent work', discussed earlier.

10.20 The European Social Charter is a document signed by the members of the Council of Europe in 1961 in which they agreed to secure to their populations the social rights specified there in order to improve their standard of living and their social well-being. It was intended to fill a gap left by the Convention for the Protection of Human Rights and Fundamental Freedoms, which essentially covers only civil and political rights. Member-states that have ratified the charter must submit reports every two years concerning the implementation of the articles of the Charter in their legal systems. The implementation is supervised by the Committee of Social Rights, composed of the representatives of the Ministers Committee and by the Intergovernmental Committee, which prepares the Ministers Committee decisions.

At the international level most countries have legislated for minimum conditions of work for all workers. Minimum wage policy is practiced in most countries.

Finally the Ministers Committee makes recommendations to member countries that are not in compliance with the Charter's requirements. The Charter was revised in Strasbourg, on 3 May 1996. The Charter, thus, sets out rights and freedoms and establishes a supervisory mechanism guaranteeing their respect by the state parties.

10.21 The Charter protects rights such as to work, to just conditions of work, fair working conditions as regards pay and working hours, safe and healthy working conditions, freedom of association, social security, benefit from social welfare services and social protection for the elderly as well as other groups needing special treatment. It gives the workers a right to a fair remuneration sufficient for a decent standard of living for themselves and their families.

10.22 Under the Charter, children and young persons have the right to a special protection against the physical and moral hazards to which they are exposed. Employed women, in case of maternity, have the right to a special protection. Workers have protection against sexual and psychological harassment. The Charter prohibits employment of children under the age of 15 and asks for special working conditions for young persons between 15 and 18 years of age. It also prohibits forced labour.

10.23 The Charter emphasises non-discrimination, and special policies to protect the interests of migrant workers. It protects the workers against arbitrary dismissals and calls for their participation in decision-making. It also guarantees the workers' right of association as well as their right to strike.

10.24 The states are enjoined to make economic and social policy designed to ensure full employment. They are also enjoined to prevent social exclusion to provide health, housing and education facilities to all citizens. In addition, the Charter lays down that the states must undertake promotional measures to provide training and skills and to create productive employment for all workers.

10.25 In order to ensure that the state parties follow the guidelines of the Charter, the European Committee of Social Rights ascertains whether countries have honoured the undertakings set out in the Charter. It has thirteen members for a period of six years, and determines whether or not the national laws and practices in the States Parties are in conformity with the Charter. Every year the States Parties submit a report indicating how they implement the Charter in law and in practice. Each report concerns some of the accepted provisions of the Charter. Under a protocol opened for signature in 1995, which came into force in 1998, complaints of violations of the Charter, may be lodged with the European Committee of Social Rights. As a result of the monitoring system, states make changes to their legislation and/or practice in order to bring the situation into line with the Charter.

Low and Middle Income Countries

10.26 A review of labour market regulation in some low and middle income Asian and Latin American countries shows that several of them have also attempted to legislate for minimum working conditions for workers. China has ratified 23 ILO Conventions and formulated a Labour Act in 1994. Two Asian countries, Vietnam and Indonesia have developed a 'Labour Code' ensuring minimum conditions of work for workers. Most of these legislations include issues of minimum wages, working hours and holidays (Sugiyarto et.al. 2006; Herlina 1997).

10.27 Minimum wage policy is practiced in all of these countries. In Brazil, employees have the right to an additional salary bonus every year. Employees working in hazardous activities are paid additional monthly allowance. In Mexico, China and Indonesia, the minimum wage varies across provinces and is set by the local governments (Ghellab 1998). In China wages are determined by a mixture of market forces and government intervention. Lowest living expenses, number of family members supported, average wage levels, productivity, the local labour market and regional differences in employment are also considered while fixing minimum wage. In Vietnam, Foreign invested enterprises are required to pay their employees minimum wages that are more than twice that of their domestic counterparts (Brassard 2006; Li Qi et. al., 2003). In China, Mexico and Brazil the overtime payment rate is one and half times, double or triple the normal hourly wage depending on the day worked (normal, rest, holiday respectively).

10.28 The maximum hours of work vary between 7 and 8 hours a day and 40 and 48 hours a week. Overtime is limited to 1-4 hours per day. Mexico has a system of 3 work shifts consisting of day shift, night shift and the mixed shift (part day shift and part night shift). South Korea has a provision for flexible working hours wherein either through an employment rule or a written agreement with workers' representatives, working hours can be extended. In Vietnam workers employed in hard, harmful or dangerous work are entitled to work 1-2 hours less daily, female workers employed in unsafe conditions are entitled to work 2 hours less daily and elderly workers are allowed to work 4 hours less daily. The Vietnam law also prohibits women from working at night shifts (Nguyen et. al. 2006).

10.29 All workers are entitled to one day of remunerated rest in a week. All the countries have provisions for annual leave. In Brazil 30 days vacation is permitted to employees working with the same company who are not absent from work for more than five days. Indonesia and South Korea have special provisions for menstrual and maternity and child care leave for women (Hanartani 2005).

10.30 The minimum working age in these countries is 15-16 years. In Indonesia children aged between 13 and 15 years are allowed to do light work. While in Brazil apprenticeship can be started at the age of 14.

10.31 Special provisions are made for occupational safety and health (OSH) in the law of China, Mexico and Vietnam (Lum 2003). The legal framework of Brazil for occupational health regulation is complex. No specific piece of legislation defines a standard-setting process.

10.32 Discrimination against sex, nationality, social background, religion, race, language, etc., is prohibited by law in all these countries.

10.33 Trade union is a part of labour law in all the countries studied. Brazil has a "unicidade" system, which stipulates that there can only be one trade union per economic or occupational category in each territorial area. Collective bargaining is allowed only on a small number of issues. South Korea has Workplace Associations of public officials (grade 6 and above) other than in important defence industries. But these Workplace Associations do not have the right to collectively bargain. Other workers are free to establish trade unions, and require at least two employees to file a report with relevant government office. Public employees do not have the right to bargain collectively. In Indonesia, minimum 10 workers are required to form a union.

Globalisation and 'New' Regulatory Environment

10.34 The extent of autonomy with which a country can pursue national economic policies has been changing continuously during the process of globalisation. Globalisation is not only bringing with it new social concerns but also influences policy choices and the framework of governance and regulation. Economic globalisation, besides offering opportunities for economic growth, has also given rise to a number of interrelated concerns in the social and environmental realms. These include the impacts on employment and distribution of income, emergence of new forms of vulnerability and the provision of welfare and social safety nets through collective or planned systems. These concerns with social and environmental issues have also influenced regulatory frameworks and compel countries to evaluate the scope and potential of government regulations and consider its relation with the new regulatory environment, often called as civil regulation.

10.35 The emerging framework of international regulation, embodied, for example, in the World Trade Organization (WTO) and that proposed under the Multilateral Agreement on Investment, is advancing corporate rights over those of nation-states. Along with this, globally, competitive forces are encouraging companies to externalize negative social and environmental costs on to the wider community and future generations. All these are weakening the existing state led regulatory provisions and also encouraging social and environmental standards to be pressured downward in national economies.

10.36 A growing body of thought and practice has been attempting to increase the pressure on companies to behave in a socially responsible manner through corporate self-regulation and voluntary initiatives. The 1990s saw a proliferation of corporate codes of conduct and an increased emphasis on corporate responsibility, which is in consonance with the change in the paradigm of how the global capital should be governed. Voluntary approaches, such as the OECD Guidelines on Multinational Corporations, were a direct response to UN initiatives in the 1970s to regulate the activities of Trans-National Corporations (TNC). Several changes in the global economy have contributed to the growing interest in corporate responsibility and codes of conduct. The deregulation and 'free market' environment of the 1980s gave greater legitimacy to the self-regulation model. The growth of "global value chains", through which Northern buyers control web of suppliers in the South, has led to calls for the former to take responsibility not only for aspects such as quality and delivery dates, but also for working conditions and environmental impacts. At the same time, the increased significance of brands and corporate reputation makes leading companies particularly vulnerable to bad publicity. Changing public attitudes are also an important part of the context in which corporate codes of conduct have been adopted. Companies in the north can no longer ignore with impunity the impact of their activities on the environment. Developments in global communications, which have enabled corporations to control production activities on an ever-widening scale, have also facilitated the international transmission of information about working-conditions in their overseas suppliers, increasing public awareness and facilitating campaigning activities.

10.37 Globalisation has meant that people located anywhere in the world can engage with each other in one world - physically, legally, culturally, and psychologically. While there is reconfiguration of space, territory continues to matter. We do not live in a borderless world. Territorial production, governance mechanisms, ecology, and identities remain significant. States are involved in trans-world laws and regional arrangements as well as national regulations and relations with provincial and local authorities; what is internal and domestic cannot be separated from the external and foreign. Even the global rules on trade enforced by the international institutions (e.g., WTO) are not independent of nation-states. Nation-states provide the legal framework within which all markets operate. The notion of a 'free market' is a myth because all markets are governed by regulations, though the nature and degree of regulation may vary from market to market. Even the self-regulation model would lack legitimacy if it was not backed by a government decree.

10.38 States are accountable to their citizens, and it is only through national regulatory measures that implementation of international frameworks is facilitated. International rules do not reduce the importance of national regulation. On the contrary, international law looks first to states to enforce its rules. If international law says that companies must respect human rights, it is primarily up to states to make sure that this happens through the domestic laws. Though international rules are not a substitute for national law or regulation, they can help harmonize rules at a time of weak national regulation. They can act as a common reference point for national law, setting benchmarks, drawing attention to core minimum requirements and clearly establishing what is permissible.

10.39 In some contexts, voluntary initiatives can constitute stepping stones for enforceable international rules. If we look carefully, we find that the companies that currently respond to civil society pressure are actually not taking "voluntary action" nor complying with public regulation. They are in fact responding to an organic "civil regulatory environment." Civil regulation of Northern TNCs, has, in the main, been driven by civil society organizations based in the North. Over the last decade, the cumulative effects of civil action have been to create a civil regulatory environment that increasingly covers codes of conduct, commitments to transparency, and corporate governance. Civil society can leverage companies by influencing the thinking of the time, in terms of better environmental and labour standards, which the business community follows in exploiting markets for financial gains. Companies that are at the cutting edge of technology, who provide global leadership to their industries, will use the civil society synergy to their best advantage. This obviously excludes vast numbers of companies in developing countries, thereby limiting the scope and significance of voluntary initiatives in these countries.

10.40 In a dual context where neo-liberalism was weakening certain state institutions and discrediting the idea of "command and control" regulation and where certain state-based and international regulatory initiatives had failed, voluntary approaches were seen as the way forward (Utting 2001). The early 1990s, therefore, saw the emergence of a wave of corporate codes. These codes were mainly focused on the impact of corporate activity on labour and the environment. They differed from the earlier generation of codes in at least two ways. First, these codes were voluntary initiatives, adopted by the business sector itself, rather than a means of regulation of Multinational Corporations by international bodies (Jenkins 2001). Second, codes in the 1990s emerged largely as a result of activist and consumer pressure from developed countries. This was in keeping with the north-driven argument of linking trade to labour and environmental standards and incorporating a social clause in the WTO.

10.41 Codes of conduct refer to standards or principles that are adopted by a corporate entity, an association of businesses or a group of multiple stakeholders. Codes could be related to improving working conditions for labour, preserving and protecting the environment or fulfilling some other social responsibilities. An increasing number of companies are voluntarily adopting codes of conduct to fulfil their environmental and social obligations. These voluntary initiatives may be unilaterally developed by industry, designed and run by government, jointly developed by government and industry, or developed and run by non-governmental organizations (Utting 2000). A majority of voluntary codes developed in the 1990s tend to be multiple stakeholder initiatives (MSI), which address the needs and concerns of some or all stakeholders of a corporation (Freeman 1984). Broadly speaking, voluntary initiatives can be divided into five main types: specific company codes (e.g., those adopted by Tata Corporate Governance Code, Nike, H&M, Next etc); business association codes (e.g., KPMG-CII 10/10 Stakeholder Charter for Indian entertainment industry, CII-ITC Centre for Excellence for Sustainable Development); multi-stakeholder codes (e.g., the collaboration of the Centre of Education and Communication in India with the Fair Wear Foundation, Netherlands; Ethical Trading Initiative); inter-governmental codes (e.g., the UNCTAD multilaterally agreed equitable principle and rules for the control of restrictive business practices, 1980; ILO declaration on multinational enterprises and social policy and OECD Guidelines on international investment and multinational enterprises), and international framework agreements (such as UNI global unions' five agreements with: Telefonica, Spain - telecom sector; H&M, Sweden - commerce sector; Carrefour, France - commerce sector; OTE, Greece - telecom sector; ISS, Denmark - property services sector). Global Union Federations have signed agreements with companies such as: IFBWW - IKEA (furniture), Sweden and Faber-Castell (pencils), Germany; IUF - Danone (food), France and Accor (hotels), France; IMF - Volkswagen (cars), Germany and Daimler Chrysler, (cars) Germany; ICEM, Statoil (energy), Norway and Endesa (electricity), Spain.

Scope and Limitations of Voluntary Labour Codes: Global Lessons

10.42 Initially corporate codes were designed as unilateral instruments of self-regulation, an approach that provoked widespread criticism. Implementation of the codes was weak and marked by a complete absence of independent monitoring and verification (Ascoly, N. and I. Zeldenrust 2001). The responsibility of achieving standards adopted by Multinational Corporations was sometimes thrust upon their suppliers and sub-contractors, who were not, provided financial assistance for raising their standards (Utting 2001). Worse, company claims were often inflated and closer inspection revealed that codes were not being adopted meaningfully. Some criticism has also been directed towards the bewildering multiplicity of codes. An OECD study identified 246 codes of conduct, of which 83 per cent were company or industry/trade association codes. These codes did not focus on a consistent and well-researched set of issues, preferring instead to adopt the ad-hoc approach of addressing only those social issues that were relevant at that point in time. The numbers and variety of concerns addressed by corporate codes weakened their impact considerably. In fact, many of them ignored key issues such as labour rights, bribery, and taxation (Gordon, K. and M. Miyake 2000, quoted in Utting 2001).

10.43 Adoption of codes of conduct is usually motivated by external pressure. As a result, two broad categories of companies are most likely to initiate codes of conduct in the developing countries - those that export to northern countries and those that form part of the supply chain of a north-based corporate or MNC that has adopted a code. Companies that manufacture entirely for domestic consumption usually avoid implementing labour codes.

10.44 Often, initiatives to impose codes of conduct may be highly protectionist in nature. UNCTAD suggests that such initiatives could "function like non-tariff barriers or significantly raise the cost of competitive entry into global markets" (UNCTAD 1999). The protectionist impact has its own financial implications - some suppliers and perhaps countries may be priced out of the export market completely if strict adherence to international labour standards is expected. On the other hand, non-adoption of voluntary labour codes appears to be associated with adverse financial effects, particularly for retailers and companies with high-profile brands. The adoption of voluntary codes is a soft option that is preferred over the harder option of government legislation. Moreover, voluntary labour codes are often adopted simply as a defensive strategy to guard against civil society pressure and resultant government legislative intervention.

10.45 The adoption of voluntary codes of conduct for labour militates, however, against short-term positive financial benefits both for developed and developing countries. For large firms in developed countries, cross-border sub-contracting of production activity is financially attractive because of low labour costs. The absence of labour standards in special economic zones or among informal sector workers ensures precisely this objective.

Codes of conduct refer to standards or principles that are adopted by a corporate utility, business associates or multiple stakeholders. They are voluntary and not meant to replace existing labour legislation.

For developing countries, cheap and abundant labour is a comparative advantage that they are reluctant to relinquish. Fitzgerald (2001) also points out that small firms, which provide the bulk of employment in developing countries would find international standards too expensive and be forced to close down. Given the highly competitive export market and the tight margins under which most small and medium sized suppliers operate, it is usually not viable for them to undertake to improve labour conditions without external financial support. A possible consequence of promoting labour standards throughout the supply chain is that smaller suppliers may be dropped due to their inability to bear the costs of compliance and production contracts may switch to larger, national chains.

10.46 Despite their diversity, the majority of codes of conduct are concerned with working conditions and environmental issues. They tend to be concentrated in a few business sectors. Codes related to labour issues, for instance, are generally found in sectors where consumer brand image is paramount, such as footwear, apparel, sports goods, toys, and retail. Environmental codes are usually found in the chemicals, forestry, oil, and mining sectors.

10.47 Codes vary considerably in both their scope and application. Very few codes accept the core labour standards prescribed by the ILO. Corporate codes often set standards that are lower than existing national regulations. For instance, labour codes recognize the right to freedom of association but do not provide the right to strike. In many countries, such as India, the right to strike is a legally recognized instrument.

10.48 Although codes increasingly cover the company's main suppliers, they tend not to include every link in the supply chain. Codes rarely encompass workers in the informal sector even though they could form a critical link in the company's supply chain. In terms of ensuring compliance, only a small proportion of codes include provisions for independent monitoring. Multi-stakeholder initiatives involve only a small fraction of the world's largest companies, including the TNCs, and the informal sector accounts for the majority of the labour force in developing countries.

10.49 Labour, women's and non-governmental organizations in the North and South continue to be divided on whether such initiatives will actually benefit workers on the ground, and whether or how to engage with various competing initiatives. Not surprisingly, the emergence of these new players in the labour rights field is exacerbating already existing divisions among these organizations over questions, such as: Will these voluntary systems usurp the regulatory role of national governments and privatize labour standards regulation, or prompt governments to more actively monitor compliance with national labour laws? Can commercial auditing firms carry out quality social audits that accurately assess worker rights violations, and if not, who can and should play this role? Will local NGOs and/or labour organizations have a significant role in code monitoring and verification, or will this field continue to be dominated by commercial auditing firms and NGOs/commercial hybrids? Will the presence of local NGO monitoring groups in factories facilitate or discourage workers' organisations? Will workers themselves have an active role in workplace monitoring, or will they remain objects to be studied by outside organisations hired by companies or northern multi-stakeholder institutions?

10.50 Codes do not necessarily accord with the social priorities of public policy. A country's social services may be better assisted by companies simply complying with their fiscal obligations. In the particular case of India, very few civil society organisations and almost no trade unions are involved in the shaping of the codes agenda. Most companies operating in India prefer self-regulation, when it comes to partnerships with civil society organisations their participation is limited to the implementation of community development projects.

10.51 All these imply that corporate codes of conduct are not meant to replace existing labour legislation; at best, they can be viewed as self-regulatory mechanisms that complement existing labour laws and ensure at least minimum labour standards to workers. Voluntary codes are most likely to be adopted by a registered corporation or firm - any corporate structure that exists as a distinct legal entity. The applicability of codes is, thus, limited to the formal sector. Organizations where production activities are carried out in the informal sector or through homeworkers are effectively excluded from adopting labour initiatives. The exclusion of informal sector activity from voluntary codes has serious implications for developing countries.

10.52 Both legal and voluntary approaches are needed, and they can be complementary. Voluntary codes will make binding regulation more likely to succeed because they have started to build consensus, or at least understanding, around some core rights. Willing consent to such norms will be helpful when binding regulations are introduced in the future. As companies introduce new management practices to implement codes they develop business expertise that will also be essential to the successful implementation of binding regulations.

Conclusion

10.53 In this chapter, we have focused on an analysis of international experience of ensuring minimum conditions of work to all wage workers. It is clear that the international rights framework provides the basic linchpin around which minimum rights of workers are guaranteed in different countries. A large number of countries - both developed and developing - have evolved minimum yardsticks of conditions of work covering issues and principles such as minimum wages, regulation of hours of work, child/adolescent work, overtime, non-discrimination, forced labour, and association, and legislating safeguards for ensuring that these are available for all workers. This is consistent with the approach that the Commission has adopted.

10.54 With globalisation, there is now a shift to voluntary codes of conduct and their enforcement through third party inspection. Such codes of conduct may be useful in preventing a 'race to the bottom' as countries and firms may compete to lower labour costs. But their success would depend upon: the extent to which the states can themselves regulate the conditions of work of the unorganised workers, if the codes can themselves encompass core labour standards and if the presence of codes can facilitate workers organise and ensure that they themselves can have an active role in workplace monitoring of codes.

10.55 Voluntary codes of conduct can never substitute for state regulations. Nor can they substitute for labour and community rights. At best, voluntary codes can complement state regulations and provide an opportunity to raise environmental, health, labour, and other public interest issues.

11 Regulations of Conditions of Unorganised Workers in India

Introduction

11.1 In this Report the unorganised sector workers are categorised as wage labourers, home-workers and the self-employed. We have reiterated that the conditions of work of wage labourers (and to some extent of home-workers) are contingent upon the employers making these available to the workers. Although the bulk of the employers of such labourers are very small, there is a very strong case that the working conditions subscribe to a basic minimum.

11.2 Vast majority of the unorganised sector workers (60 per cent) are, however, independent (self-employed) or dependent (homeworker) operators (including those who may employ some labour, and with or without contributory family labour). The conditions of such workers are inextricably linked with the conditions of their enterprises (in the case of the wage workers, the conditions of work depend upon both the willingness as well as the ability of employers to subscribe to a set of conditions). The improvement in the conditions of livelihood of the unorganised workers depends not only on their own agency, but also on a policy and a regulatory framework, as well as programmes, which create the conditions, which allow them to expand their livelihoods. The main responsibility for creating such conditions rests with the State, although other stakeholders may also play important roles.

11.3 In this Chapter, we review the existing context of the regulation of conditions of work of the unorganised wage workers in India.

The Constitutional Framework

11.4 Indian Constitution provides an overarching framework for regulation of conditions of work as well as protection and promotion of livelihoods. The Fundamental Rights guaranteed by the Constitution prohibit the exploitation of labour through the use of forced labour and child labour in factories and mines or in hazardous occupations (Articles 13 and 14). It also guarantees non-discrimination by the State and equality of opportunity in matters of public employment (Articles 15 and 16). The Right to form associations and unions is also a Fundamental Right under Article 19.

11.5 The Directive Principles of the Constitution (in Part IV) lay down goal posts and the direction of State Policy. While the right to work is not a fundamental right for the citizens of India, it is included in the Directive Principles of State Policy. It states "The state shall within the limits of its economic capacity and development, make effective provision for securing the right to work". The Directive Principles also include provision for just and human conditions of work and maternity relief. Further, "The state shall endeavour to secure by suitable legislation, or economic organisation or any other way, to all workers, agricultural, industrial or otherwise, work, a living wage, and conditions of work ensuring a decent standard of life"

Ratification of International Conventions

11.6 India has been a signatory to a number of international conventions and human rights instruments. Within the ILO framework the Conventions ratified by India, those that relate to the unorganised sector are a limited few. Of about 41 Conventions ratified (Table 11.1) it is mainly the Minimum Wages legislations that cover the informal workers. The recent ILO Home Work Convention, 1996 (No. 177) is not included in the core labour standards of the ILO and is also not ratified by India. As these workers form a large segment of the unorganised workers India should review the Convention and proceed for its ratification.

Legal Regulation of Conditions of Work

11.7 Labour is on the concurrent list in the Indian Constitution, and regulatory provisions of the conditions of work (entries 22, 23 and 24 of List III in the 7th Schedule) are, therefore, in the domain of both the state and the Central governments. Labour laws can be legislated both by the Central and state governments. The Centre has passed a number of laws, but here too, the coverage of these laws as well as the rules regarding their implementation can be framed by the state governments. There are two types of state laws. In the first case, the Central laws are enacted by the Central Government but amendments can be made by the state governments in conformity with the Central laws with the approval of the Central Government. In the second case, the states may, on their own, pass laws relating to the working conditions of some sections of the workers in the states sphere.

11.8 Almost all labour laws are circumscribed by the scope of their coverage, which could be defined in terms of the type of employment, type of employment relationship, nature and size of the 'establishment', including the number of workers, and area. There are very few laws that apply universally to all workers, whether in the organised or in the unorganised sectors. Other laws apply unequivocally to the organised sector. A third set of laws is applicable to some segments of the workers in the unorganised sector (in a few cases, they may also cover some segments of the organised sector). Overall, the unorganised sector workers are covered in a piece meal fashion in various legislations and lack comprehensive protection of the minimum conditions of work.

Central Laws for Unorganised Sector Workers

11.9 Central laws, which regulate conditions of work in the unorganised sector fall into three groups. The first group applies generally to the unorganised sector. The second group of laws applies to certain groups of workers in the unorganised sector and the scope of application is restricted by the nature of employment, or size of employment. The third group of laws apply mainly to the organised sector workers (viz. factories, establishments, or enterprises employing 10 or more workers), but in certain cases, or by relaxing the employment criterion these laws can (be made to) apply to some sections of workers in the unorganised sector.

First set (Laws which apply to all sections of the unorganised sector labour)

1. The Equal Remuneration Act, 1976
2. The Bonded Labour System (Abolition) Act, 1976

Second set (Laws which apply to some sections of the unorganised sector labour)

3. Minimum Wages Act, 1948
4. Child Labour (Prohibition and Regulation) Act, 1986
5. Dangerous Machines (Regulation) Act, 1983
6. The Employment of Manual Scavengers and Construction of Dry Latrines (Prohibition) Act, 1993
7. Inter-State Migrant Workmen (Regulation of Employment and Conditions of Service) Act, 1979
8. Motor Transport Workers Act, 1961
9. Sales Promotion Employees (Conditions of Services) Act, 1976
10. Trade Unions Act, 1926

Third set (Laws which can be extended to the Unorganised Sector)

11. The Beedi and Cigar Workers (Conditions of Employment) Act, 1966.

Central labour laws can be categorised into three broad types: Laws that apply to all workers in the unorganised sector, laws that apply to some segments of workers in the unorganised sector and laws that can be extended to the unorganised sector.

Table 11.1: List of International Labour Organisation Conventions Ratified by India

Sl. No.	No. and Title of Convention	Date of Ratification
1.	No.1 Hours of Work (Industry) Convention, 1919	14.07.1921
2.[1]	No.2 Unemployment Convention, 1919	14.07.1921
3.	No.4 Night Work (Women) Convention, 1919	14.07.1921
4.	No.5 Minimum Age (Industry) Convention, 1919	09.09.1955
5.	No.6 Night Work of Young Persons (Industry) Convention, 1919	14.07.1921
6.	No.11 Right of Association (Agriculture) Convention, 1921	11.05.1923
7.	No.14 Weekly Rest (Industry) Convention, 1921	11.05.1923
8.	No.15 Minimum Age (Trimmers and Stokers) Convention, 1921	20.11.1922
9.	No.16 Medical Examination of Young Persons (Sea) Convention, 1921	20.11.1922
10.	No.18 Workmen's Compensation (Occupational Diseases) Convention, 1925	30.09.1927
11.	No.19 Equality of Treatment (Accident Compensation) Convention, 1925	30.09.1927
12.	No.21 Inspection of Emigrants Convention, 1926	14.01.1928
13.	No.22 Seamen's Articles of Agreement Convention, 1926	31.10.1932
14.	No.26 Minimum Wage-Fixing Machinery, Convention, 1928	10.01.1955
15.	No.27 Marking of Weight (Packages Transported by Vessels) Convention, 1929	07.09.1931
16.	No.29 Forced Labour Convention, 1930	30.11.1954
17.	No.32 Protection Against Accidents (Dockers) Convention (Revised), 1932	10.02.1947
18.[2]	No.41 Night Work (Women) Convention (Revised), 1934	22.11.1935
19.	No.42 Workmen's Compensation (Occupational Diseases) Convention (Revised), 1934	13.01.1964
20.	No.45 Underground Work (Women) Convention, 1935	25.03.1938
21.	No.80 Final Articles Revision Convention, 1946	17.11.1947
22.[3]	No.81 Labour Inspection Convention, 1947	07.04.1949
23.	No.88 Employment Services Convention, 1948	24.06.1959
24.	No.89 Night Work (Women) Convention (Revised), 1948	27.02.1950
25.	No.90 Night Work of Young Persons (Industry) conventions (Revised), 1948	27.02.1950
26.	No.100 Equal Remuneration Convention, 1951	25.09.1958
27.	No.107 Indigenous and Tribal Population Convention, 1957	29.09.1958
28.	No.111 Discrimination (Employment & Occupation) Convention, 1958	03.06.1960
29.	No.116 Final Articles Revision Convention, 1961	21.06.1962
30.[4]	No.118 Equality of Treatment (Social Security) Convention, 1962	19.08.1964
31.[5]	No.123 Minimum Age (Underground Work) Convention, 1965	20.03.1975
32.	No.115 Radiation Protection Convention, 1960	17.11.1975
33.	No.141 Rural Workers' Organisation Convention, 1975	18.08.1977
34.	No.144 Tripartite Consultation (International Labour Standards) Convention, 1976	27.02.1978
35.	No.136 Benzene Convention, 1971	11.06.1991
36	No.160 Labour Statistics Convention, 1985 (Article 8 of Part - II)	01.04.1992
37.[6]	No.147 Merchant Shipping (Minimum Standards), 1976	26.09.1996
38.	No.122 Employment Policy Convention 1964	17.11.1998
39.	No.105 Abolition of Forced Labour, 1957	18.05.2000
40.	P89 Protocol of 1990 to the Night Work (Women) Convention (Revised), 1948	21.11.2003
41.	No.108 Seafarers' Identity Documents Convention, 1958	17.01.2005

1 Later denounced. The Convention requires, internal furnishing of statistics concerning unemployment every three months which is considered not practicable

2 Convention denounced (ON 27.02.1950) as a result of ratification of Convention No.89.

3 Excluding Part II.

4 Branches (c) and (g) and Branches (a) to (c) and (i).

5 Minimum Age initially specified was 16 years but was raised to 18 years in 1989.

6 Article 8 of Part II

Source: Website, Ministry of Labour & Employment, Government of India

12. Payment of Wages Act, 1936
13. The Building and Other Construction Workers (Regulations of Employment and Conditions of Service) Act, 1996.
14. The Contract Labour (Regulation & Abolition) Act, 1970
15. The Maternity Benefit Act, 1961
16. Workmen's Compensation Act, 1923
17. Weekly Holidays Act, 1942

11.10 The applicability criteria, coverage and restrictions existing in the important legislations applicable to the unorganised sector workers are presented later.

11.11 Based on the five sets of issues on the conditions of work we had defined in Chapter 1, we present in Table 11.2 the laws identified above that have provisions for these conditions. We exclude the laws relating to social security as they are discussed in the Report on Social Security (NCEUS 2006).

Table 11.2: Central Labour and Industry Laws that Deal with Conditions of Work

Sl. No.	Broad Categories of Conditions of Work	Description/Details	Laws that Have Provisions to Regulate the Conditions of Work
1a	Physical conditions of work	Space, ventilation, illumination, temperature, humidity, hygiene, occupational health and safety.	The Dangerous Machines (Regulation) Act, (1983), Inter-State Migrant Workmen Act (1979), The Building and Other Construction Workers Act, (1996), The Beedi and Cigar Workers (Conditions of Employment) Act, (1966).
1b	Duration and timing of work	Hours of work, spread over, hours of rest, overtime work, hours of work per week, night work, paid holidays during the week	The Minimum Wages Act, (1948), Inter-State Migrant Workmen Act (1979), The Building and Other Construction Workers Act, (1996), Child Labour (Prohibition and Regulation) Act, (1986), The Beedi and Cigar Workers (Conditions of Employment) Act, (1966).
2	Remuneration at work	Wages, wage forms, pay period, advances, bonus, gratuity, pension, provident fund.	The Minimum Wages Act, (1948), Inter-State Migrant Workmen Act (1979), The Building and Other Construction Workers Act, (1996), The Equal Remuneration Act, (1976), The Payment of Wages Act, (1936), The Bonded Labour System (Abolition) Act, (1976), The Beedi and Cigar Workers (Conditions of Employment) Act, (1966).
3	Industrial and labour relations	Recognition of trade unions, redressal of grievances and dispute resolution.	The Trade Union Act (1926), The Bonded Labour System (Abolition) Act, (1976), The Payment of Wages Act, (1936), The Minimum Wages Act, (1948), Child Labour (Prohibition and Regulation) Act, (1986), The Equal Remuneration Act, (1976), Inter-State Migrant Workmen Act (1979), The Beedi and Cigar Workers (Conditions of Employment) Act, 1966, The Building and Other Construction Workers Act, (1996)
4	Conditions of work of disadvantaged workers	Disabled workers, women workers, migrant workers, minority workers, bonded labour, other forms of forced labour, child labour	The Dangerous Machines (Regulation) Act, (1983), Inter-State Migrant Workmen Act (1979), The Building and Other Construction Workers Act, (1996), The Equal Remuneration Act, (1976), Child Labour (Prohibition and Regulation) Act, (1986) and The Bonded Labour System (Abolition) Act, (1976)

Note: The set of issues related to social security are not considered for purposes of the condition of work.

11.12 The provisions, in brief, of some important laws relating to conditions of work in the unorganised sector are as under:

Laws Which Apply to All Sections of Unorganised Sector

11.13 The provisions of some of the important laws in this respect are briefly described below. It will be noticed that all these laws have a minimum size of employment restriction and apply to particular employments only.

1. Equal Remuneration Act, 1976

11.14 The Act is applicable to the women workers and provides for the payment of equal remuneration to men and women workers and for the prevention of discrimination, on the ground of sex, against women in matters of employment.

11.15 Under the Act, the employer has to pay equal remuneration to men and women workers for same work or work of a similar nature. By same work or work of a similar nature is meant work in respect of which the skill, effort and responsibility required are the same, when performed under similar working conditions. The Act also provides against discrimination made while recruiting men and women workers.

2. The Bonded Labour System (Abolition) Act, (1976)

11.16 Forced labour violates the fundamental rights guaranteed to all citizens by the Indian Constitution. Article 23(1) in Part III relating to Fundamental Rights, states "Traffic in human beings and begar and other forms of forced labour are prohibited and any contravention of the provision shall be an offence, punishable by law".

11.17 The Bonded Labour System (Abolition) Act, (1976) dealing with bonded and forced labour was legislated by Indian Parliament in 1976 in view of the above provision. The Act is applicable to bonded labour and provides for the abolition of bonded labour system with a view to preventing the economic and physical exploitation of the weaker sections of the people. The Act defines 'bonded labour' as a service rendered under the 'bonded labour system'. This is a system of forced, or partly forced, labour under which the debtor enters into an agreement, oral or written, with the creditor. According to this agreement, in consideration of an 'advance' obtained by the debtor or by any of his lineal ascendants and in consideration of interest on such an advance or in pursuance of any customary obligation or by reason of his birth in any particular caste or community, the debtor agrees to render, by himself or through any member of his family, labour for the creditor for a specified or unspecified period of time either without wages or for nominal wages, or forfeits the freedom of employment or other means of livelihood, or forfeits the right to move freely throughout India, or forfeits the right to appropriate or sell at market value any of his property or the product of his own or any of his family members'. It may be noted that the Supreme Court in the case of 'Bandhua Mukti Morcha, 1983 has held that the burden of proof that a worker is not a bonded labour is on the employer and that the court would presume the existence of bonded labour unless it is rebutted by satisfactory evidence.

Laws Which Apply to Some Sections of the Unorganised Sector Labour

3. The Minimum Wages Act, 1948

11.18 The Act is applicable to the workers engaged in the scheduled employments and provides for fixing minimum rates of wages in certain employments. It is applicable both to agricultural, non-agricultural and to rural as well as urban workers. The Government may, however, increase the scope of this Act by adding schedules. Units employing even one worker are covered by the Act. Thus, the Act covers wage worker, homeworker but not the self-employed. Supreme Court in the case of Bandhua Mukti Morcha (1984) SCC 389 held that even a piece rated worker is entitled for minimum wages. Under the Act, the appropriate government shall fix the minimum rates of wages payable to employees in a specified employment and review the rates at such intervals as it may think fit, such intervals not exceeding five years. The Government also fixes a minimum rate of wages for time rated work, a minimum rate of wages for piece work, a minimum rate of remuneration to apply in the case of employees on piece work for the purpose of securing to such employees a minimum rate of wages on a time work basis, a minimum rate (whether a time rate or a piece rate) to apply in substitution for the minimum rate which would otherwise be applicable, in respect of overtime work done by employees. Different minimum rates of wages may be fixed for different scheduled employments; different classes of work in the same scheduled employment; adults, adolescents, children and apprentices; or different localities. Similarly, minimum rates of wages may be fixed by the hour, day, month, or by such other larger wage-period as may be prescribed. Any minimum rate of wages fixed or revised by the government in respect of the scheduled employments may consist of a basic rate of wages and cost of living allowance; or a basic rate of wages with or without the cost of living allowance, and the cash value of the concessions in respect of supplies of essential commodities at concessional rates, or, an all-inclusive rate allowing for the basic rate, the cost of living allowance and the cash value of the concessions. Minimum wages are generally payable in cash unless authorised by the Government considering the prevailing custom or practice. Further, the Government may fix the number of hours of work which shall constitute a normal working day, inclusive of one or more specified intervals; provide for a day of rest in every period of seven days which shall be allowed to all employees or to any specified class of employees and for the payment of remuneration in respect of such days of rest; and provide for payment for work on a day of rest at a rate not less than the overtime rate. Under the Rules, ordinarily Sunday is the weekly day of rest. For an adult nine hours and for a child 4 ½ hours constitute a normal working day. Overtime is payable at 1½ times the wage in agriculture and double the rate in other cases of scheduled employment.

4. Child Labour (Regulation and Prohibition) Act, 1986

11.19 The Act is applicable to child labour (person who has not completed fourteen years of age) and prohibits the engagement of children in certain occupations as specified in Part A of the Schedule or processes as specified in Part B of the Schedule. The Central Government may, if considered appropriate, add any occupation or process to the Schedule. Besides in Part III, the Act contains provisions for regulation of conditions of work of children in establishments or a class of establishments in which none of the occupations or processes referred to above is carried on. The Act provides for prohibition of work by children beyond certain number of hours, period of work and interval of breaks, prohibits work between 7 p.m. and 8 a.m, prohibits overtime and weekly holidays. The Government is empowered to frame rules for the health and safety of the children employed or permitted to work in any establishment or class of establishments.

11.20 Thus, this Act is applicable both to agricultural and non- agricultural workers, covers wage worker, homeworker and is applicable to rural as well as urban workers.

5. Dangerous Machines (Regulation) Act, 1983

11.21 The Act is applicable to the operators engaged on the dangerous machines and provides for the regulation of trade and commerce in and production supply, distribution and use of, the product of any industry producing dangerous machines with a view to securing the welfare of labour operating any such machine and for payment of compensation for the death or bodily injury suffered by any labourers while operating any such machine. It is only applicable to machines intended to be used in rural or agricultural sector.

11.22 The manufacturer has to ensure that every part of a dangerous machine conforms to prescribed standards. The manufacturer has to supply operator's manual with each dangerous machine. The manufacturers and dealer has to give a certificate and guarantee for the dangerous machine that it is as per prescribed standard. Liability of the manufacturer for reimbursement arises whenever any person operating a dangerous machine suffers death or dismemberment of any limb or any other bodily injury by reason of any manufacturing defect in the machine whereby such death, dismemberment or injury was caused, or by reason of the omission of the manufacturer to comply with the provisions of this Act such manufacturer shall be liable to reimburse the person by whom compensation had to be paid under this Act to the members of the family of the person whose death was caused by such machine or, to the person by whom such dismemberment or bodily injury was suffered. Employer's liability for compensation under the Act arises if, during the employment as an operator of a dangerous machine, death or dismemberment of any limb or any other bodily injury is caused to such operator with certain specified exceptions.

6. The Employment of Manual Scavengers and Construction of Dry Latrines (Prohibition) Act, 1993

11.23 The Act is applicable to the manual scavengers and provides for the prohibition of employment of manual scavengers as well as construction or continuance of dry latrine and provides for the regulation of construction and maintenance of water-seal latrines. Under the Act, no person shall engage in or employ for or permit to be engaged in or employed for any other person for manually carrying human excreta; or to construct or maintain a dry latrine.

7. Inter-State Migrant Workmen (Regulation of Employment and Conditions of Service) Act, 1979

11.24 The Act is applicable to every establishment in which five or more inter-state migrant workmen are employed and to every contractor who employs five or more inter-state migrant workmen. The establishments engaging less than five interstate migrant workmen are not covered under this act. For the purposes of this Act, "workman" means any person employed in or in connection with the work of any establishment to do any skilled, semi - skilled or unskilled, manual, supervisory, technical or clerical work for hire or reward, but does not include any person who is employed mainly in a managerial or administration capacity; or who, being employed in a supervisory capacity, draws wages exceeding five hundred rupees per month.

11.25 The Act provides that the wage rates, holidays, hours of work and other conditions of service of an inter - state migrant workman shall be the same as those applicable to such other workman performing the same or similar kind of work and cannot be less that the wages fixed under the Minimum Wages Act, 1948 (41 of 1948) and are payable in cash. It also provides for payment of displacement allowance and journey allowance. The contractor has the liability for regular payment of wages; ensuring equal pay for equal work irrespective of sex; ensuring suitable conditions of work; to provide and maintain suitable residential accommodation to such workmen during the period of their employment; to provide the prescribed medical facilities to the workmen, free of charge; to provide protective clothing to the workmen; and in case of fatal accident or serious bodily injury to any such workman to report to the specified authorities of both the states and also the next-of-kin of the workman. The primary responsibility for payment of wages is on the contractor and on his failure on the principal employer.

8. Motor Transport Workers Act, 1961

11.26 The Act applies to every motor transport undertaking employing five or more motor transport workers. The state government may however extend the applicability of this Act to undertaking employing less than five motor transport workers.

11.27 The Act provides for provision of canteens, rest rooms, uniforms, raincoats or other like amenities for protection from rain or cold, washing allowance, medical and first-aid facilities. The Act also specifies the hours of work for adult workers and adolescents. Adolescents are prohibited to work from 10 P.M. to 6 A.M. It also contains provisions regarding daily intervals for rest (at least half-an-hour), spread-over, split duty, etc. The Act provides for a day of weekly rest, compensatory day of rest, extra wages for overtime at a rate twice his ordinary rate of wages in respect of the overtime work or the work done on the day of rest, annual leave with wages, wages during leave period rate etc. The Act prohibits employment of children.

9. Sales Promotion Employees (Conditions of Services) Act, 1976

11.28 The Act is applicable to the sales promotion employees engaged in pharmaceutical industry and regulates certain conditions of service in certain establishments. The Central Government may apply the provision of this Act to any other establishment engaged in any notified industry.

11.29 The Act provides for leave in addition to holidays, casual leave or other kinds of leave, namely, earned leave on full wages for not less than one-eleventh of the period spent on duty; and leave on medical certificate etc. It also provides for cash compensation when the sales promotion employee voluntarily relinquishes his post or retires from service, or when his services are terminated for any reason whatsoever (not being termination as punishment).

10. The Trade Unions Act, 1926

11.30 The Act is applicable to the trade unions and provides for the registration of trade unions and in certain respect defines the law relating to register trade unions. Any seven or more members of a trade union may by subscribing their names to the rules of the trade union and by otherwise complying with the provisions of this Act with respect to registration, apply for registration of the trade union. However, vide the Trade Unions (Amendment) Act, 2001, it is provided that at least 10 per cent of the members or 100 workmen (which ever is less) engaged or employed in the industry with which the trade union is connected should be the members of the trade union. The Act provides for the objects, on which general funds of the trade union may be spent, constitution of a separate fund for political purposes, immunity to office bearers from criminal conspiracy in trade disputes if it is for furthering the objects of the trade union and provides for immunity from civil suit to certain cases.

Laws, Extendable to the Unorganised Sector

11. Beedi and Cigar Workers (Conditions of Employment) Act, 1966

11.31 The Act is applicable to the workers engaged in Beedi and Cigar establishments. It provides for the welfare and regulates the conditions of their work. It applies to wage workers and homeworkers but not the self-employed workers/persons in private dwelling houses.

11.32 The Act provides for cleanliness of industrial premises free from effluvia arising from any drain, privy or other nuisance. It seeks to maintain cleanliness including white washing, colour washing, varnishing, or painting. In order to prevent injury to the health of the persons, the industrial premise has to maintain proper lighting, ventilation and temperature. To prevent overcrowding, the Act prescribes at least four and a quarter cubic metres of space for every person in the work-room. It also provides for sufficient supply of wholesome drinking water, sufficient latrine and urinal accommodation, adequate washing facilities, crèches, adequate first aid facilities and canteens. It also provides for working hours in any one day and in any week, overtime, interval for rest, spread over in any day, weekly holidays, substituted holiday etc. There is prohibition of employment of children altogether and prohibition of employment of women or young persons during hours except between 6 a.m. and 7 p.m. It also contains provisions regarding annual leave with wages and wages during the leave period.

12. Payment of Wages Act, 1936

11.33 The Act is applicable to the workers engaged in factories and industries or other establishments as specified in the Act and regulates the payment of wages to certain class of employed persons. The class of persons or the list of such industries or establishments may be extended by the Government. This Act applies to wages payable to an employed person in respect of a wage period if such wages for that wage period do not exceed Rs.6500 per month or such other higher sum notified by the Central Government. Thus, this Act covers certain specified classes of both agricultural and non-agricultural workers (including contract labour) who are wage earners with wage a limit of less than Rs.6500/- per month only.

11.34 The Act fixes the responsibility on the employer for the payment of all wages wages to persons employed by him. It also provides for fixation of wage-periods which shall not exceed one month. Time of payment of wages also needs to be fixed and wages are to be paid in current coin or currency notes only. The deductions authorised under the Act, for example for absence from duty, for damage or loss caused by the worker, for services rendered and accepted by the worker, for recovery of advances or loans received by the worker, or for payments to co-operative societies and insurance schemes, only may be made from the wages. There are strict provisions regarding imposition of fines on the worker.

13. Building and Other Construction Workers' (Regulation of Employment and Conditions of Service) Act, 1996

11.35 The Act is applicable to the establishments engaging ten or more building and other constructions workers. It seeks to regulate the employment and conditions of service of building and other construction workers and provides for their safety health and other welfare measures. The establishments engaging less than ten workers are not covered under this Act.

11.36 The Act provides for fixing hours for normal working day inclusive of one or more specified intervals; provides for a day to rest in every period of seven days, payment of work on a day of rest at a rate not less than the overtime rate, wages at the rate twice his ordinary rate of wages for overtime work. The Act prohibits a person who is deaf or has defective vision to undertake such work. It also provides for adequate drinking water, latrines and urinals and accommodation for workers, crèches, first-aid and canteens. The appropriate government is empowered to make rules for the safety and health of building workers.

14. Contract Labour (Regulation and Abolition) Act, 1970

11.37 This Act is applicable to every establishment in which twenty or more workmen are employed or were employed on any day of the preceding twelve months as contract labour and to every contractor who employs or who employed twenty or more workmen on any day preceding twelve months. However, the appropriate government may, after giving not less than two months' notice and by notification in the Official Gazette, apply the provisions of this Act to any establishment or contractor employing less than twenty workmen. This Act does not apply to establishments in which work of only an intermittent or casual nature is performed. Workman means any person employed in or in connection with the work of any establishment to do any skilled, semi-skilled or unskilled manual, supervisory, technical or clerical work for hire or reward, whether the terms of employment be express or implied. It does not include any person employed mainly in a managerial or administrative capacity; or a person employed in a supervisory capacity drawing wages exceeding five hundred rupees per month or an out-worker (homeworker).

11.38 Under the Act, the appropriate government may prohibit employment of contract labour in any process, operation or other work in any establishment, having regard to the conditions of work and benefits provided for the contract labour in that establishment and other relevant factors, such as whether nature of work is incidental or necessary to the main operation, whether it is of perennial nature, that is to say, it has sufficient duration, whether it is done ordinarily through regular workmen in that/other establishment(s), and whether it is sufficient to employ considerable number of whole-time workmen. The Act also provides for licence to be taken subject to such conditions including, in particular, as to hours of work, fixation of wages and other essential amenities in respect of contract labour. The Act also contains provisions regarding welfare and health of contract labour, e.g. canteens, rest rooms, other facilities such as drinking water, urinals and, first aid facilities. For security of payment of wages the Act provides for its payment by the contractor, and in case of failure by the principal employer.

15. Maternity Benefits Act, 1961

11.39 The Act is applicable to the women workers and seeks to regulate employment of women in certain establishments for certain periods before and after childbirth and provides for maternity and certain other benefits. It applies to every establishment, being a factory, mine or plantation including any such establishment belonging to Government. This Act is not applicable to the establishments engaging less than 10 persons. The Government may however extend its applicability to any other establishment or class of establishments. This Act does not apply to any factory or other establishments to which the provisions of the Employees' State Insurance Act, 1948, (34 of 1948) apply.

11.40 The Act prohibits employment of, or work by, women during the six weeks immediately following the day of her delivery or miscarriage. Women worker are entitled to maternity benefit at specified rates for specified periods. It also provides for payment of maternity benefit to the nominee in case of death, payment of medical bonus, leave for miscarriage for a period of six weeks immediately following the day of her miscarriage, leave for illness arising out of pregnancy, delivery, premature childbirth, or miscarriage, nursing breaks etc.

16. Workmen's Compensation Act, 1923

11.41 The Act is applicable to workmen and provides for the payment by certain classes of employers to their workmen of compensation for injury by accident. This Act is applicable to both agricultural and non agricultural workers. "Workman" means any person (other than a person whose employment is of a casual nature and who is employed for purposes other than of the employer's trade or business) as specified in the Act and its Schedule. However, the Central Government or the state government may add to the Schedule any class of persons employed in any occupation which, it is satisfied, is a hazardous occupation.

11.42 The Act provides for Employer's liability for compensation, if personal injury is caused to a workman by accident arising out of and in the course of his employment with certain exceptions. The Act also specifies a list of diseases, which, if contracted by the worker, would be deemed to be occupational disease peculiar to that employment which shall be deemed to be an injury by accident liable for compensation under the Act.

17. Weekly Holidays Act, 1942

11.43 The Act provides for the grant of weekly holiday to persons employed in shops, restaurants and theatres. Every shop shall remain entirely closed on one day of the week, which shall not be altered by the shop-keeper more often than once in three months. Every person (employed other than in a confidential capacity or in a position of management) in any shop, restaurant or theatre shall be allowed in each week a holiday of one whole day for which there shall be no deductions from wages, with certain specified exceptions. The state government may also provide for additional half-day holiday in specified establishments.

Laws Relating to Agricultural Workers

11.44 Agricultural workers constitute, by far, the largest segment in the unorganised sector. They are extremely vulnerable to exploitation on account of low level of literacy, lack of awareness, persistent social backwardness and absence of unionisation and other forms of viable organisation. Further, the high rates of migration because of the seasonality of operations and lack of stability of employment subject them to all sorts of hazards and exploitation.

11.45 Among the measures adopted to protect the interest of the agricultural workers has been the Minimum Wages Act, 1948. Subsequently, the Plantation Labour Act, 1951 was enacted to provide certain basic facilities to plantation workers (organised sector). This Act is applicable to plantations measuring 5 hectares or more and in which fifteen or more persons are employed. The state government may however extend the provisions of this Act to plantations even to cases with less than 5 hectares, or less than 15 persons are employed.

11.46 The Act provides for safe drinking water, sufficient number of latrines and urinals in a clean and sanitary condition, proper medical facilities, canteens, crèches, recreational facilities, educational facilities, housing facilities, umbrellas, blankets, rain coats or other like amenities for the protection of workers from rain or cold. There are regulations of weekly hours of work, overtime for work done on any closed holiday, weekly holidays, daily intervals for rest, and spread-over. Night work for women and children is prohibited. The Act provides for annual leave with wages during the leave period, sickness and maternity benefits.

11.47 Other legislation which, though are applicable to plantation workers also have enabling provisions to be extended to agricultural labour. These include Payment of Wages Act, 1936, Maternity Benefit Act, 1961, Payment of Gratuity Act, 1972, and the Workmen Compensation Act, 1943. The Equal Remuneration Act, 1976, and the Inter-state Migrant Workmen (RECS) Act, 1979 etc. also apply to agricultural workers. Similarly, there are other Acts applicable to the agricultural workers viz., Minimum Wages Act, 1948, Bonded Labour System (Abolition) Act, 1976, Child Labour (Prohibition and Regulation) Act, 1986, and Trade Union's Act, 1926. There is only one specific law applicable only to agricultural workers viz. Dangerous Machines (Regulation) Act, 1983.

11.48 However, the physical working conditions of unorganised agricultural workers are not protected by law, except where state level laws exist. This highlights the need for a comprehensive legislation to safeguard the interests of agricultural workers and to protect their working conditions.

State Laws

11.49 There have been some attempts at the state level to regulate conditions of work in the unorganised sector and of conditions of work of agricultural workers. Important examples are the Kerala Agricultural Workers Act (1974) and the Maharashtra Mathadi, Hamal and Other Manual Workers (Regulation of Employment and Welfare) Act, 1969. A list of such Acts is given in Appendix A11.1. We have excluded the Welfare Acts, which the Commission has dealt in detail in its Report on Social Security.

11.50 Among the laws enacted by the states, the Shops and Establishments Act is the most wide-ranging. The coverage of this Act varies from state to state and is given in Appendix A11.2. The working of the legislation governing conditions of employment in shops, commercial establishments, theatres, hotels and restaurants has been analysed by the Ministry of Labour for the year 2003. The states' Shops and Establishment Acts regulate inter alia, the daily and weekly hours of establishments, payment of wages, overtime, holidays with pay, annual leave, etc. The Acts prohibit the employment of children below 14 years of age and women at night. These Acts apply in the first instance to shops and commercial establishments, restaurants, hotels and places of amusement in certain notified urban areas. The state governments are, however, empowered to extend the application of the Acts to such other areas or to such categories of undertakings, as they may consider necessary. However, certain types of employees, such as those employed in a confidential capacity or where the work is of intermittent nature, are excluded from the provisions of the Acts.

11.51 In recent years, a number of states (Karnataka, Andhra Pradesh, Kerala, to name a few) have extended the coverage of the legislation to the entire state. Even so, a small part of the workers in various types of establishments are only covered. For example, in Andhra Pradesh, only about 3.4 lakh workers in 3.5 lakh establishments are covered by the Act. Examination of the number of shops and commercial establishments covered under the Acts, number of persons employed therein, number of shops being run independently by the owners and those being run with the help of employees in states and union territories during 2004 (excluding Maharashtra), reveals that out of the 36.5 lakh shops, as many as 26.3 lakhs (72 per cent) were run independently by the owners while the rest were being run with the help of employees with or without family members (Appendix A11.3). In 2003 the highest number of establishments registered under this Act (10.3 lakhs) was in the state of Mahrashtra, the corresponding workers employed by them being 5.9 lakhs. The average number of persons employed per shop for all the reporting states / union territories works out to less than one. On the whole, however, these Acts cover only 29.2 lakh hired workers which is a small percentage of non-agricultural workers in the unorganised sector.

Organisational Structure for Implementation Labour Laws

11.52 The state-wise organisational structure is given in Appendix A11.4. The Labour Departments in the states are mainly responsible for the implementation of the Central and state labour laws. The organisational structure of the departments consists of the Labour Inspector/ Assistant Labour Officer at the base and the Labour Commissioner at the apex. The Labour Inspectors/Assistant Labour Officers are the enforcement officers, but their jurisdiction varies among the states (ranging from a group of Mandals in AP, a Block in Bihar, Jharkhand and UP and to a group of Blocks in a district in some states. The posting of Assistant Labour Commissioners also depends upon the quantum of work generated in a district or group of districts. Usually, officers in the rank of a Labour Officer and above are responsible for conciliation under the Industrial Dispute Act. Inspections under the Factories Act come within the purview of the Chief Factories Inspector and his staff. The office of the Chief Inspector (Boilers) also functions under the Labour Commissioner in some states.

11.53 There are some states where the organisational structure for implementation of laws relating to agriculture or rural areas is distinct or even separate. In Tamil Nadu, the enforcement of the Minimum Wages Act in agriculture and the Agricultural Welfare Act is the responsibility of the Revenue Department. In Gujarat, the Department of the Rural Labour Commissioner is responsible for the implementation of unorganised sector laws in the rural areas. In Bihar, there is a Director (Agriculture Labour) under the Labour Commissioner, who is responsible for the implementation of the Minimum Wages Act in agriculture. In UP, the state has designated the revenue officials, the Block officials and the panchayat officials as inspectors under the Minimum Wages Act.

11.54 For the administration of the Shops and Establishment Acts the states of Andhra Pradesh, Jammu & Kashmir, Orissa, Punjab, West Bengal and the Union Territory of Chandigarh have appointed Chief Inspectors of Shops and Commercial Establishments. In other states, it is the responsibility either of the Labour Commissioner or the Factory Inspectors or of the officials of the Health or Revenue Department. In Maharashtra, it is administered by the local authorities.

Experience of Implementation of Laws for the Unorganised Sector

11.55 As has been pointed out in the preceding chapters, the implementation of the existing laws is abysmally poor.

Minimum Wages

11.56 For Minimum Wages, which is the most widely applicable law for the unorganised sector workers, the analysis carried out by the Commission and presented in Chapters 3 and 8 shows that the non-observance of these laws is widespread. Generally, states have relied upon the labour department machinery, but in the case of some states, the revenue machinery, and even the panchayat officers have been empowered to enforce the Act.

11.57 During 2004-05, the Ministry of Labour, Government of India reported that 587397 inspections took place under the Minimum Wages Act by the Central, states and the UTs except in Mizoram, Sikkim and Lakshadweep (Appendix A11.5). Irregularities were detected in the respect of 622673 workers and rectified in respect of 399921. While claims were filed for Rs.90 million, settlements were made worth only Rs.50599. During the year, 9572 prosecutions were launched while there were 56,099 pending cases, but only 5925 cases were resolved. The compensation awarded was Rs.70.5 million. Fines of Rs.10.9 million were imposed and the recovery was Rs1.7 million.

11.58 The data on inspections made, prosecutions launched, cases disposed of by the courts and the amount of fines realized under the Shops and Establishments Act during 2003 (Appendix A11.6) do not give the provisions under which the prosecutions were launched. The highest numbers of inspections reported were 511187 in Maharashtra, while the prosecutions launched numbering 21378 were the highest in the Union Territory

Considering the large proportion of workers, e.g more than 70 per cent of agricultural labourers not receiving minimum wages (Chapter 8), the number of inspections, irregularities detected and prosecutions launched were negligible.

Chandigarh. The highest number of cases (25690) disposed off was in Gujarat and the maximum total amount of fine realized was Rs.6.7 million in Maharashtra.

11.59 Administrative authorities generally followed a policy of persuasion for ensuring compliance with the provisions of the Acts and instituted prosecutions only as a last resort in extreme cases of continuing defaults. The irregularities detected during the period under report were attributed to non-payment of wages, arrears, bonus, overtime, leave with wages; non-maintenance of prescribed records and registers; non-display of notices and non-observance of working hours, weekly holidays, etc. However, in the course of the Commission's discussions with labour departments, it has been pointed out that through the implementation of the Acts the authorities monitored mainly aspects such as the registration of the establishments, their opening and closing hours and their observance of holidays. In some cases, some of the safety conditions may also be monitored. The working conditions of the workers are monitored generally indirectly.

Migrant Workers

11.60 Migrant wage workers are rendered vulnerable to economic exploitation because of the lack of or ineffective implementation of the labour laws that would protect their specific interests. Among the existing laws some laws that are for all workers are also extended to the migrant labourers. These include Minimum Wages Act 1948, Contract Labour (Regulation and Abolition) Act 1970, the Equal Remuneration Act 1976, the Building and Other Construction Workers (Regulation of Employment and Conditions of Service) Act 1996, the Workmen's Compensation Act 1923, the Payment of Wages Act 1936, the Child Labour (Prohibition and Regulation) Act 1986 and the Bonded Labour Act 1976.

11.61 In addition to the above, a separate Act for migrant workers, the Inter State Migrant Workmen (Regulation and Condition of Service) Act, 1979 has been to address the specific problems of migrant workers such as malpractices in recruitment and employment of workers who migrate across state-boundaries. The Act has limited coverage as it is only extended to inter-state migrants recruited through middlemen and contractors and those establishments that employ five or more such workers. The main provisions of the Act include the following: a) Contractors and establishments are required to be licensed and registered by a notified registering authority; b) The contractor is required to issue a passbook to every worker, giving details about the worker, including payments and advances, and pay each worker a displacement allowance and a journey allowance; c) Contractors must pay timely wages equal to or higher than the Minimum Wage; provide suitable residential accommodation, prescribed medical facilities and protective clothing; and notify accidents and casualties to specified authorities and kin. The Act lays down the machinery to resolve industrial disputes and provides for migrant workers to approach the authorities in the destination states or in their home states if they have already returned home. The Act sets penalties including imprisonment for non-compliance, but provides an escape route to principal employers if they can show that the transgressions were committed without their knowledge.

11.62 The Inter-State Migrant Workers Act (1979) has been ineffective because of the lack of implementation as also the lack of awareness among the workers regarding existence of the laws and their rights. Very small number of contractors has taken licenses and very few enterprises employing interstate migrant workers have registered under the Act. The record of prosecutions and dispute settlement has been very weak. Migrant workers do not possess pass books, prescribed by law, and which form the basic record of their identity and their transactions with the contractor and employers. Several studies have revealed violation of all these acts. Further migrant workers are harassed by the police, postal department, owners of the establishments, owners of workers' dwellings, shopkeepers, labour contractors and the railway police during their journey. Migrants contribute to growth by providing cheap and flexible labour, yet they remain without an identity and are unable to get access to government programmes and schemes related to health and education meant for the poor.

Child Labour

11.63 Studies on child labour in recent years, especially after the enactment of the Child Labour Act (1986), have argued that success of state action has been limited. These studies have attributed a part of the invisibility of child labour in the late 1980s and the 1990s to the successful elimination of child labour from formal industry. This has led to a substantial increase, by some estimates even in absolute terms, in child labour in unorganised workshops and home-based units that are relatively hidden and isolated from the authorities (Burra 1995). Part of the problem is identified by scholars as the loopholes in the child labour regulations which bans child labour in certain processes and industries, while excluding any process or occupation that is carried out by the family within the household (Burra 1989).

Bonded Labour System

11.64 The Bonded Labour System (Abolition) Act created a legislative framework for the elimination of bonded labour in 1976. But, as both the Supreme Court and the NHRC have shown, its implementation by the states has remained generally weak. The Expert Group constituted by the NHRC in 2000 and the institution of the Special Rapporteurs has breathed some life into the legislative system and has given support to the grass-root NGOs that have been involved in taking up issues of bonded labour. Several attempts at releasing bonded labourers have been made but it has been found that rehabilitation of such labour is a difficult task.

11.65 Ministry of Labour, Government of India had initiated a Centrally Sponsored Scheme under which Rs.4,000 was initially provided for the rehabilitation of each bonded labourer, to be equally contributed by the Central and the state governments. The amount has since been gradually raised, reaching Rs.20,000 in May 2000. The Central government also provides assistance for surveys, awareness campaigns and evaluations. Released bonded labourers are given priority in a number of government programmes, such as the distribution of government land, and some states have initiated specific programmes for their rehabilitation. But, by and large, the process of rehabilitation is frequently delayed, particularly in the case of inter-state bonded migrant labourers, and the degree of concerted convergent action required on the part of the administration is rarely forthcoming. Prosecution of the employers is also weak. Since the bonded labourers are very poor and assetless, some can relapse into bondage, while others may experience only a very marginal increase in income. Since bondage results from severe deprivation arising from the lack of assets and adequate livelihood opportunities, a key focus of rehabilitation has to be on providing assets and means of livelihood to the bonded labourers. Efforts to do this are more likely to succeed if the poor are empowered and collectively organised, and if they have the capacity to undertake new activities.

Constraints on Effective Implementation

11.66 The Commission has examined the constraints on the implementation of the existing laws. The main reasons for this appear to be the following: small size of the enforcement machinery in relation to the large and dispersed workforce and inadequate infrastructure; almost exclusive focus on the organised sector; lack of voice for the unorganised workers and no participation of their representatives in ensuring effective implementation; and lack of or inadequate sensitivity among those responsible for implementation.

11.67 The issue of inadequate number of personnel and infrastructure emerged clearly during the course of the Commission's visits to the states. The Commission was struck by the fact that the labour inspectors, who had to cover dispersed and far flung areas, did not have the requisite transport and other infrastructure made available to them. As discussed in the section on implementation structure, the inspectors who are the enforcement officers have to cover a huge population segment (sometimes the major part of a district, but never less than a development Block, which could include a population of up to 100,000). They are responsible for the implementation of more than 30 Central and state laws and have poor facilities to help them do so.

11.68 The Institute for Studies for Industrial Development (ISID) undertook a research project on "Labour Regulation in Indian Industry: A Study of Its Impact on Growth, Investment and Employment" in four states i.e. Maharashtra, Uttar Pradesh, Andhra Pradesh and West Bengal to assess the impact of labour regulation on Indian industry. The study covers laws for the organised sector and the unorganised sector. The ISID study pointed out that the labour machinery was inadequate in relation to the needs of enforcement. The Labour Department of UP is responsible for the enforcement and administration of 33 labour laws and related rules. For effective enforcement, the Department has some officers from Revenue Departments, Co-operatives and Panchayats as inspectors under the Minimum Wages Act. However, despite this, there has been no significant improvement in the enforcement of prescribed Minimum Wages and the study concluded that the enforcement machinery should be further extended to the block levels. In Andhra Pradesh, the number of inspectors was insufficient to carry out the mandatory number of inspections (although the number of required inspections had itself declined). This was also the case in West Bengal, where the studies noted that although the cases of infringement detected by the Labour Department had increased, it was not able to keep pace with the growing informalisation of labour and the denial of labour rights to informal labour.The Second National Commission on Labour (SNCL 2002) concluded that among the major constraints in implementation were inadequate logistic support, lack of proper training and proper status to the officials of the concerned departments, and shortage of manpower and infrastructure. The SNCL (2002) had clearly observed that officers of the Labour

Department should be provided with offices, infrastructure and facilities commensurate with the functions they have, and the dignity they should have. The Commission has also noted the lack of adequately trained professional staff in some states. One of its important recommendations to the Central Government was to determine some norms for the inspector ratio and the infrastructure of the Labour Departments. Such norms should, no doubt, be determined after due deliberation and taking into account the International Labour Standards concerning Labour Administration formulated by the International Labour Organisation in 1978.

11.69 The SNCL (2002) had noted that there was not much scope for increasing the staff. It had stressed that the concern should, therefore, be on improving the efficiency of the existing staff and infrastructure, without depending on increasing the size of the machinery. While we agree with this recommendation, we are of the view that the implementation machinery should be commensurate to with the tasks assigned to it. We will return to this issue in Chapter 13.

11.70 Another basic issue that has emerged from this Commission's discussion is that the major focus of the Labour Department is on the implementation of labour laws for the organised sector. For example, the Conciliation Machinery is focused on the Industrial Disputes Act.

11.71 The pronounced emphasis on creating a facilitating business environment and increased informalisation of labour had reduced the emphasis on the pro-active enforcement of labour laws, apart from making this more difficult. In almost all the states, the ISID study, referred to earlier, noted that there was a trend towards hiring of contract labour who did not receive statutory benefits. The state governments did not want to encourage pro-active enforcement through inspections, which was seen to discourage an industrial climate. The net result was that there was a declining trend in enforcement of labour laws. In Maharashtra, the study noted that inspections, prosecutions and convictions (under Shops and Establishments Act, Factories Act, Minimum Wages Act and all Labour Laws) showed a declining trend.

Scope for Self-Certification

11.72 Multiplicity of inspections and burden of compliance are often cited as among the main day to day problems faced by the small enterprises. Within the liberalisation framework being followed in India, both the Central as well as the state governments have been conscious of the difficulties faced by enterprises in the era of Inspector Raj and have taken a number of steps to make the entrepreneur- government interface less cumbersome. As most of these inspections are prescribed under the applicable statutes and are implemented through administrative practices, these initiatives include both legislative as well as administrative measures.

11.73 The Commission has reviewed the process of simplification of laws and procedures with regard to inspections in about seven states, viz. Uttar Pradesh, Andhra Pradesh, Punjab, Gujarat, Karnataka, Orissa and Rajasthan. Most of these states reported that there is multiplicity of Acts, 17 or more, that lend to inspection of the small enterprises by various government departments. All these states have since 1994 tried to reduce the number of inspections required either in terms of percentage of enterprises to be inspected, or number of visits by inspectors allowed in a year, or restricting visits to one in year or even in five years.

11.74 The states of Gujarat, Punjab and Rajasthan have also introduced a Self-certification Scheme for compliance with the existing laws. The main features of this scheme is the reduction in the number of visits by inspectors, filing a single return on compliance and once opted the Scheme remains valid for five years. However, all these states noted that the Scheme has not been very successful and that very few enterprises have actually registered or opted for the Scheme. One of the reasons cited for the lack of enthusiasm among the enterprises to come forward for self-certification was the requirement to give a blanket certificate of compliance with all the laws and regulations. The difficulty also lies with the concerned government official to certify for such a blanket compliance of all regulations. In case the enterprise comes up for inspection and is found not to have complied with any one regulation the consequences could be quite

In the liberalisation framework being followed in India, the central and the state governments have started a process of simplification of laws and procedures to reduce the burden of compliance. Three states introduced a self-certification scheme, but it has not been successful so far. It also has limited impact on the unorganised sector.

damaging for it. The result of all these efforts at simplifying the existing laws and reducing inspection is that the enterprises have less incentive to comply with the regulations. The conditions of the workers can only deteriorate under such circumstances.

11.75 The self-certification scheme while having limited impact so far, really lend itself only to compliance with the labour and other regulations that exist for the large and registered companies. The small enterprises, that are not registered, and the micro enterprises where the majority of workers are engaged, are not under any obligation to follow the self-certification scheme. Self-certification, therefore would have limited impact on the enterprises in the unorganised sector.

Voluntary Codes of Conduct for Minimum Conditions of Work

11.76 With globalisation and the increasing export intensity of Indian manufactures, the application of voluntary codes of conduct (labour standards) has become an important issue in the country. Many of the items in which buyer-driven commodity chains operate are produced in the small-scale sector and/or are outsourced to homeworkers.

11.77 One area where social labels are prominent in India concerns child labour related issues. According to the Global Report on Child Labour by the ILO in 2002, there were more than 200 million child labourers worldwide, and the incidence of child labour was the highest in the Asia-Pacific region, with South Asia being the worst (ILO 2002c). Greater public awareness about the much-publicized issue of child labour resulted in some organizations coming up with social labels in India also. Currently, child labour-related social labelling in India is limited to the carpet industry, for which there is a multiplicity of labels. There are four labelling programmes in the carpet industry in India (Rugmark, Kaleen, STEP and Care and Fair), and these programmes differ both in their mechanisms as well as the approaches adopted and their stated objectives (Sharma et al. 2000). Rugmark and Kaleen labels are affixed to individual carpets, while STEP and Care and Fair programme certifies specific companies. With the exception of Care and Fair, the labelling initiatives operate with inspection and monitoring mechanisms of different types (Sharma et al. 2000).

11.78 The Rugmark Foundation, established in India in 1994, is an independent body that offers a voluntary certification programme for carpet exporters in India to ensure that carpets are not made by children. The Rugmark stamp of approval is a "smiling carpet" label. The cost of the inspections is borne by the exporters who pay 0.25 per cent of the value of their rugs toward monitoring the system, and by importers, who contribute 1 per cent of the carpets' value. Since 1995, according to the facts provided by the Rugmark Foundation, 1334 children have been liberated from carpet looms by Rugmark India.[7] Approximately 15 per cent of all registered carpet looms (some 230 Indian exporters) are licensed under Rugmark. However, the limitations of the programme's reach can be gleaned from the fact that according to Rugmark's own estimate, there were 300,000 children working on the looms in India in 1993.

11.79 Christian Aid and South Asian Coalition on Child Servitude (SACCS) has also been working on child labour initiatives. It has been instrumental in increasing the visibility of the abysmal work conditions, especially of child labourers, and called for Indian Government's adherence to the UN Convention on the Rights of the Child (Article 32).[8] Recently, these organizations have looked at India's sporting goods manufacturers who employ approximately 300,000 workers in 1500 factories and smaller manufacturing units, and in subcontracted arrangements (ibid). Indian companies supply sporting goods to many international brands including Adidas, Mitre (Pentland Group), Umbro, Gunn and Moore, Dunlop Slazenger, Kookaburra Sports and Cosco. The report describes that, either with their families or in small stitching centres, these children work to produce some of the 200 different products manufactured by the Indian sports goods industry. Christian Aid and SACCS have found that Indian children as young as 7 years stitch footballs in their homes, while boys as young as ten are employed as stitchers or trimmers producing boxing and cricket gloves. Tanneries that supply leather to the industry's main exporters also employ children, exposing them to hazardous chemicals. These include tanneries located in Jalandhar in Punjab and Meerut in Uttar Pradesh, which supply leather for cricket balls and gloves. Kashmiri sawmills that supply willow clefts for crafting into cricket bats also operate under extremely poor conditions. Children and teenage apprentices who work in factories or small workshops are routinely paid a

7 See www.rugmark.org, accessed 22 June 2005.

8 See www.christianaid.org.uk/world/where/asia/indiap.htm, accessed on 22 June 2005.

fraction of the adult minimum wage. Meanwhile, some adult workers are not only poorly paid but also denied sick pay, union rights and company contributions to benefits such as employee provident fund and insurance schemes. The Sports Goods Export Promotion Council of India has downplayed these findings and challenged the World Federation of Sporting Goods Industries to inspect factories and provide evidence of any use of child labour (ibid).

11.80 Christian Aid has developed a code of practice based on internationally agreed standards, including ILO conventions and the United Nations Convention on the Rights of the Child. This code addresses not only the employment of child labourers in the sports goods and other industries, but also the adult working conditions in factories manufacturing footballs, boxing and cricket gloves, volleyballs, cricket pads and shuttlecocks. The code also covers the manufacturer of cut synthetic jewels, the weaving of silk saris and carpets and the production of glass bangles (ibid).

11.81 One of the more recent certificates is the social accountability standard, SA 8000. Initiated by Social Accountability International, SA 8000 is an auditable standard for third party verification based on 11 ILO conventions, the Universal Declaration of Human Rights and the United Nations Convention on the Rights of the Child. The standard covers eight workplace conditions: child labour, forced labour, health and safety, freedom of association and the right to collective bargaining, discrimination, disciplinary practices, working hours, and compensation. A ninth area covers management systems, which stipulates the necessary systems for ensuring the ongoing conformity with the requirements of the standard. The standard covers not only the company that adopts these standards, but also the suppliers[9] and subcontractor.[10] The code is expected to maximize benefits in the areas of preserving and enhancing company and brand reputation; improving employee recruitment, retention and performance; better supply chain management; and opportunities to develop partnerships with other organizations.

11.82 According to Mishra (2005), Indian manufacturers are now more aware about social compliance and are increasingly interested in social accountability. However, manufacturers do not have much choice as the buyers insist upon it. Mishra (2005) claims that "post-MFA [Multi-Fibre Arrangement], social accountability has to be an integral part of business because importers, buyers and retailers from the United States and Europe will choose suppliers from other countries based on stringent social accountability norms." Exporters and suppliers in India have become aware of this fact over the past couple of years as they prepared for the end of the MFA in January 2005. There has therefore been a significant increase in the number of companies in India that have gone for social audits, especially in the leather and textile sectors.

11.83 As in March 2004, 30 Indian companies were SA 8000 certified from a total of over 200 companies worldwide (Mishra 2005). In India, social accountability audits are done only at the behest of buyers. Companies will not do it for domestic consumers because it is expensive (Mishra 2005).

11.84 Some Indian companies have adopted the Global Sullivan Principles of Social Responsibility, a code of conduct to which socially responsible companies and organizations can be aligned.[11] The objectives of the Global Sullivan Principles are to support economic, social and political justice by companies where they do business; to support human rights and to encourage equal opportunity at all levels of employment, including racial and gender diversity on decision making committees and boards; to train and advance disadvantaged workers for technical, supervisory and management opportunities; and to assist with greater tolerance and understanding among peoples; thereby, helping to improve the quality of life for communities, workers and children with dignity and equality. At present, the Global Sullivan Principles appear more to be a statement of intent as there is no inherent system of monitoring or auditing built into it.

Voluntary Codes of Conduct and standards as it exists now covers a very small fraction of the Indian market, especially the Indian labour market. However, there has been a significant increase in the number of companies in India that have gone for social audits, especially in the leather and textile sectors.

9 "Supplier" is defined as a business entity that provides the company with goods and/or services integral to, and utilized in/for the production of the company's goods or services.

10 "Subcontractor" is defined as a business entity in the supply chain, which, directly or indirectly, provides the supplier with goods and/or services integral to, and utilized in/for the production of company's goods and/or services.

11 See www.thesullivanfoundation.org/gsp/default.asp, accessed on 22 June 2005.

11.85 Another global programme, the Global Reporting Initiative (GRI), is a multi-stakeholder process and an independent institution with a mission to develop and disseminate the globally applicable Sustainability Reporting Guidelines.[12] The GRI Guidelines are for voluntary use by organizations reporting on the economic, environmental and social dimensions of their activities, products and services. The GRI incorporates the active participation of representatives from business, accountancy and investment as well as environmental, human rights, research and labour organizations from around the world. It was started in 1997 by the Coalition for Environmentally Responsible Economies (CERES) in partnership with the United Nations Environment Programme (UNEP). The GRI became independent in 2002, and is now an official collaborating centre of UNEP and works in cooperation with the UN Global Compact. The GRI Sustainability Reporting Guidelines are applicable to national and multinational organizations in both industrial and developing countries. The ultimate objective of the GRI is the global harmonization of corporate reporting information covering the environment and social performance.

11.86 There is limited association between the GRI and Indian business. Only four companies in India had submitted a report to GRI by the end of 2004, with TISCO being the first Indian company to do so, in 2002. However, several Indians are involved in the GRI. By 2005, Dr. Jamshed J. Irani, Director of Tata Sons Limited, was on the Board of the GRI; there are four other Indians who are GRI Stakeholder Council Members; and CII is an organizational stakeholder.

11.87 Indian companies are more strongly associated with the UN Global Compact. At the end of 2004, over 90 companies had committed themselves to its principles. The Global Compact was created after the United Nations Secretary-General Kofi Annan challenged business leaders, in an address to the World Economic Forum on 31 January 1999, to join an international initiative that was meant to bring companies together with UN agencies, labour and civil society to support nine (now ten) principles in the areas of human rights, labour, environment and anti-corruption (the last principle was adopted during the first Global Compact Leaders Summit in June 2004).[13] The Global Compact is a learning network, and its operational phase was launched at the UN headquarters in New York on 26 July 2000.

11.88 India was one of the first countries in which the Global Compact was launched, and its New Delhi and Mumbai Networks were established in 2001. Realizing the need for a nationwide network, a third network-the India Partnership Forum, a joint UNDP/CII initiative-was added. This was followed by the formation of a UN Global Compact Society India in 2003. A number of industry associations, employer organizations and professional bodies in India have joined the Global Compact, and these bodies play an important role in promoting it to their members.

11.89 Civil society and multi-stakeholder initiatives such as the Clean Clothes Campaign (CCC), though active in India since the 1990s (Ascoly and Zeldenrust 2001), have yet to develop a critical mass. The CCC Task Force for Tamil Nadu that focuses on the textile mills in southern India reported violations of workers' rights, including low wages and long working hours, intimidation and unjust dismissals, and the use of child labour. The CCC Task Force for Tamil Nadu is made up of 30 NGOs and seven trade unions working on labour rights issues in the region.

11.90 In order to facilitate the compliance of labour standards in the supply chains of companies, the Ethical Trading Initiative (ETI)-a tripartite alliance of NGOs, trade union organizations and global companies, funded by the UK Department of International Development and membership contributions[14]-formulated a model code of conduct called the ETI Base Code[15]. Several ETI member companies have included elements of the code in their company codes of conduct, and their suppliers are required to comply with the agreed standards. In this manner, ETI incorporates models of ethical business practices into the supply chain management and consequently, impact the lives of the workers in the supply chain.

11.91 ETI has been in operation in India since the mid-2000s. However, it still has some weaknesses. Like the other stakeholder initiative operatives in India discussed above, it has not yet developed a critical mass and remains focused on the export-driven market. The

12 See www.globalreporting.org, accessed on 22 June 2005.
13 See www.unglobalcompact.org, accessed on 22 June 2005.
14 www.eti2.org.uk/Z/lib/2006/media/CSRAsiaWkly-Vol2Week2.pdf.
15 ETI base code includes nine elements: Employment freely chosen; Freedom of Association; Working conditions safe and hygienic; Child labour shall not be used; Living wages are paid; Working hours are not excessive; No discrimination practised; Regular employment provided; No harsh or inhumane treatment

ETI code has not been able to successfully incorporate home-based workers into its monitoring model and has been able to build only limited trust with workers, thereby restricting their active participation in better implementing the base code. The code does not necessarily ensure subsistence wage for workers either, in spite of the provision that member countries should pay the existing legal wage. A recent study on the impact assessment of ETI base code in the Garment Sector of Delhi reports that the most significant impact has been on health and safety and not on wages, unionisation or terms of employment (Barrientos, Sood and Mathur 2006).

11.92 Despite considerable publicity surrounding codes of conduct related with labour, adoption of the codes is limited. Consumer goods industries that have an export market, for instance, garments, carpets, textiles, leather and related accessories, where brand name and corporate image matter and firms that are part of the global supply chain of large TNCs are the ones that voluntarily adopt "standardized" labour practices either in order to compete with their rivals from South and Southeast Asia, or in response to pressures from international buying houses and retail chains. There are hardly any examples of companies manufacturing for the domestic markets adopting voluntary codes of conduct dealing with labour issues (Sood 2003). The weak domestic pressure for adoption of better labour and environmental practices creates a hiatus between firms that supply to the domestic market and those that supply to the global market. This implies that the reality of codes and standards in India as it exists now covers a very small fraction of the Indian market, especially the Indian labour market. Further, within the export sector itself, the new standards regime is mainly followed by large registered firms because such firms are more institutionalised. The implementation of the standards in small and medium-sized firms is more difficult and costly in relative terms compared to a big firm. Home-based workers and those outside the institutionalised organized sector can be covered by codes only in cases where the codes' implementation is related to the supply chain and where there are provisions for auditing and monitoring by third parties, or exclusive groups within the company overseeing it. Declarations without constant monitoring and auditing do not serve much purpose, like many domestic laws where the constitutional provisions are never fulfilled. Companies could always find ways to circumvent the laws.

11.93 Codes may have limited success because (a) as the experience of ILO conventions (codes accepted by governments) suggests, countries bypass them; (b) as the experience of impact of trade on employment in developing countries suggests, a race to the bottom; (c) the applicability of codes is mostly limited to the formal sector; and (d) there is a sectoral limitation to the application of codes, covering mostly consumer goods sector. However, codes serve a useful purpose in so far as they keep the labour conditions on the global agenda and help labour rights campaign to be effective by raising awareness. Consumer conscientisation does have a positive linkage with political support for workers rights.

11.94 For voluntary codes of conduct to positively influence the conditions of labour in developing countries, the enactment and enforcement of legislation by national governments, consistent with ILO Conventions and other standards (right to collective bargaining and freedom of association, along with reasonable levels of social insurance provision) is necessary. Indeed, corporate codes of conduct are not meant to replace existing labour legislation; at best, they can be viewed as self-regulatory mechanisms that complement existing labour laws to ensure at least minimum labour standards to workers.

Conclusion

11.95 The examination of the regulatory framework for ensuring minimum conditions of work for unorganised wage workers in the preceding sections has shown that: (a) there are lack of comprehensive and appropriate regulation in India; and (b) even where regulations exist, there is inadequate and ineffective implementation mechanisms. The Commission has also noted that self-regulation will not, by itself, lead to an improvement in the working conditions.

11.96 It appears that there is a need for a comprehensive legislation, which can provide a regulatory framework for minimum conditions of work in the country. Such a legislative framework would need to distinguish between the different segments of workers, especially agricultural and non-agricultural workers. It would also need to consider the regulatory framework for homeworkers as well as other vulnerable segments of the labour force. It would also need to take into account the main factors, which lead to poor implementation of the existing laws. The Commission has reviewed and analysed the various perspectives on a comprehensive legislative framework for unorganised wage workers, and has made appropriate recommendations in Chapter 13 of this Report.

12 Towards Protection and Promotion of Livelihoods of Unorganised Workers

Introduction

12.1 The Constitution of India clearly recognized the link between decent conditions of work and the promotion of enterprises in the unorganised sector. Articles 39 and 42 of the Directive Principles emphasised the goals of just and humane conditions of work, while Article 43 required the State to work towards not only the provision of a minimum wage but also the "conditions of work ensuring a decent life" and for this, "promote cottage industries on an individual or co-operative basis." Article 49 emphasised the need to develop agriculture and livestock towards this end.

12.2 It is well known that the expected transformation of developing economies from the unorganised to the organised has not yet occurred. Not only has the unorganised sector continued to be predominant, its relative size (in employment terms) has grown in most countries. The growth of the informal sector and of the informal work is part of a world-wide phenomenon, in which the informal sector and informal labour have registered an increase in all categories of countries, but most of all in developing countries (ILO 2002d). Growth of the informal sector and of the informal workers is due to a number of reasons including structural adjustment, privatisation, liberalisation and globalisation, and the growth of the new knowledge economy. In many countries, this is also a result of the global commodity and value chains seeking more decentralised production venues and 'flexibilisation' of labour relations. However, while the informal sector continues to be pervasive in countries like India, the context of its survival and the growth of the informal sector enterprises have changed significantly in recent years, with the emergence of many new challenges.

12.3 The International Labour Conference of 2002 has explicitly considered issues relating to the protection and promotion of informal workers. These are the application of core labour standards and extension of labour regulation (discussed in Chapters 10 and 11 of this Report), extension of social security (discussed in the NCEUS Report on Social Security and in Chapter 13 of this Report), creation of proper institutional and legal safeguards and instruments, including the creation of property rights; provision of equitable resources and a level playing field to this sector, and providing specialised services needed for the development of this sector and its graduation into the (formal)

The growth of the informal sector and of the informal work is part of a world-wide phenomenon, in which the informal sector and informal labour have registered an increase in all categories of countries, but most of all in developing countries.

Box 12.1: The Case for a Multifaceted Approach

Because the root causes of the informal economy are multifaceted, legalization alone is not enough to promote decent work. Strong and effective judicial, political, economic and other market and non-market institutions and equitable access to these institutions are essential. Informal workers and enterprises also need access to resources, information, markets, technology, public infrastructure and social services; they need a "level playing field" (similar rights, facilities and access) vis-à-vis those in the formal economy. Those who are particularly disadvantaged or discriminated against may need special measures. For the poor without property rights, measures to ensure that the legal system records property and titles assets of the poor in standardized, simple and cost-effective ways would enable them to transform their assets into productive capital and investments. Most importantly, those in the informal economy need representation and voice as a fundamental right and an enabling right to enhance their access to a range of other rights at work. It is also important to promote good governance and to reduce the costs to governments of informality and informalization. Often, informal workers and entrepreneurs are subject to harassment, bribery and extortion practiced by corrupt officials and face prohibitive costs and complexity of bureaucratic procedures for setting up and operating enterprises. (ILO 2002b)

organised sector. In short, the ILO stresses that a multifaceted approach is needed so that the informal workers can progress towards the objective of "decent work" (Box 12.1).

Creating the Foundations of Decent Work

12.4 The challenge of transforming the informal economy is essentially a challenge of development for a poor and unequal society like India. While the focus of this report is on the informal economy, the Commission has already noted from the very beginning (see Chapter 1) the high congruence between poverty and vulnerability of an overwhelming proportion of the population and the informal work status. The subsequent analytical chapters in this Report have demonstrated strongly that the unorganised workers position in the world of work is strongly influenced by their social status and their capabilities. The latter are dependent on her or his access to education, good health, decent housing, sanitation, and other basic amenities. Education, in particular, has emerged as an important signifier of the individual's work status, wages and poverty. While this Report has focused on the worker's employment and livelihood, we consider issues that determine the worker's capability as being foundational. These foundational issues are related to public interventions in the fields of education, health and sanitation and, housing, to name three most important ones. The biggest beneficiaries of effective public policies and systems in these fields will no doubt be the poor and vulnerable and, by implication, those who work in the informal economy. While there are several public schemes, their outreach is still far below what is warranted by the magnitude of the problem. More importantly for a political democracy, the approach to such public intervention has to graduate from 'ad hoc' schemes and projects to constitutional entitlements of citizens.

12.5 Within this overarching foundational framework, there is also the recognition that target-oriented public intervention is also necessary given the size of those who live in abject poverty. This has given rise to a number of public interventions by way of schemes and programmes. The Public Distribution System though limited in coverage, the Mid-Day Meal for school children, pension for the destitutes and a host of other schemes especially for those belonging to SCs and STs can be cited as good examples. Here again, the question of outreach as well as effective delivery are quite critical.

12.6 However, during the last few years, the perception of the role of the State in creating these foundational conditions has been variable, to say the least. At one level, there is a perception that the state has withdrawn from the provision of these foundational capabilities. At another level, the state has assumed greater and specific

While this Report has focused on the worker's employment and livelihood, we consider issues that determine the worker's capability as being foundational. These foundational issues are related to public interventions in the fields of education, health and sanitation and, housing, to name three most important ones.

responsibilities in certain spheres (such as elementary education, which is now a fundamental right). There is no doubt, in our view, that the state has displayed a degree of positive commitment in recent years and has launched several large programmes - notably in the field of elementary education (Sarva Shiksha Abhiyan) and basic health (Rural Health Mission), and a right-based manual employment guarantee for rural households (National Rural Guarantee Programme). We see these as positive developments. The view of this Commission is that the state needs to give the highest priority to the above mentioned issues, and that these by themselves will have the potential of transforming the workers' status both in, and outside the work place. The Commission recognises that the government has set itself clear goals in these areas and we believe that the government should formulate clear and unequivocal strategies to pursue these goals.

12.7 The mandate of this Commission has been to examine the problems and suggest measures for transforming the informal economy. As such we have concentrated on measures that are to be initiated from the point of informal work status. This is in no way interpreted to be a substitute for the foundational as well as target-oriented public initiatives mentioned above. What it underlies is the need for an approach that is firmly rooted in the sphere of work recognising the contribution of the people in the informal economy not only to the growth of national income but of employment as well. In fact, as we have shown in this Report (see Table 1.1), much of the incremental employment in the economy in recent years has been the contribution of the informal economy i.e. those working as informal workers in the unorganised sector as well as in the organised sector. This certainly calls for a quid pro quo by way of, and at the least, minimum conditions of work, social security and a measure of promotional policies and programmes for protecting and enhancing livelihood opportunities.

Dealing with the Negatives: Impact of Certain Laws and Regulation on Livelihoods

12.8 This Report is about ensuring minimum conditions at work and the expansion of employment and livelihoods. But as we have shown in chapters 4 and 5, policies, laws and regulations, if not well conceived, also have the potential of impacting negatively on both. The Constitution of India provides its citizens with the right to life (Article 21) and the right to carry out trade and business (Article 19 (g)). These rights are subject to reasonable restrictions, particularly on grounds of infringing upon the fundamental rights of other citizens. Public policy has the task of maintaining the balance between the rights of groups of citizens in the context of growth and development (which implies the increase of the public good over time). This requires it to address issues of current as well as inter-temporal priorities. It is only reasonable that when faced with choices, governments should place the highest priority on the poor and the weak, and ensure that these groups are adequately compensated whenever their livelihoods are threatened by specific policies, laws and regulations. Further, any successful policy requires that those who are likely to be affected are involved in the decision-making. However, government policies and programmes, regulations and laws, sometimes, fail this test, and have adverse effects on the livelihood of the poor and especially those in the unorganized sector. Moreover, the interpretation of laws by the courts may exacerbate the livelihood crisis faced by the poor if governments do not step in to help meet the compliance costs, which may be well beyond what the poor workers can afford, or to otherwise compensate them. We consider below the examples of such policies and laws/regulations that have had negative impacts on the livelihoods of the poor.

Land Acquisition for Public Projects

12.9 The acquisition of land under the Land Acquisition Act and the displacement of people for the sake of public works such as dams and roads has been a cause of concern for some time. While these initiatives are important for development, and they also generate alternative employment, the principal constraint is the principles underlying compensation for land and assets, resettlement of the displaced persons and access to alternative employment opportunities.

12.10 The construction of dams leads to displacement of the local inhabitants for what is considered to be the larger public interest. The displacement occurs with the loss of property and livelihoods. There is usually lack of consultation and adequate information about even the precise contours of submergence [Roy 1999; Desai 1993]. Typically, the displaced are rarely consulted or even

It is only reasonable that when faced with choices, governments should place the highest priority on the poor and the weak, and ensure that these groups are adequately compensated whenever their livelihoods are threatened by specific policies, laws and regulations.

Box 12.2: NCEUS on Special Economic Zones (SEZs)

- Proposes Growth Poles as an alternative form of SEZs:
  - Based on Cluster Approach, Agglomeration Economies and Infrastructural Development
  - Relies on linkages - forward & backward, complimentarity of goods produced by units in SEZs, access to common infrastructural facilities.
  - Once developed multiplier effect would make them viable, reduce unit costs, specialization, result in infrastructural development
- NCEUS argues for initial treatment of SEZs as 'infant industry' and its function as 'extended EPZs', coupled with a 'big push' for the SMEs in the SEZs, primarily in unorganised sector.
- Benefits to SEZs include:
  - Production Subsidy, Export Subsidy, Tax Concessions, Fiscal Benefits, Trade Arrangements, Risk Sharing, Provision of Public Goods and infrastructural services at subsidized prices, Support for Agglomeration
- NCEUS stand on provisions of current SEZ Act 2006:
  - Public Support/ subsidies should be restricted to SMEs not viable on their own and needing infant industry treatment - else it would result in profits not being related to efficiency and perpetuate a form of dependent industrialization
  - Single Window Clearance for central and state approvals applicable not only to SEZs but extended all activities all over the country
  - Notification of SEZs based on infant industry
  - SMEs and units in a cluster/ GP/ SEZs must have linkages and complimentarity so that they spurn off multiplier effects and enable economies to be realized
  - Restriction of export subsidy only to times when Rupee is overvalued and for non-traditional items export where markets, product designs are yet to be developed
  - Infrastructure development for SEZs should not be based on land acquisition and sale of vast tracks of land and from its rental income (resulting in limiting land acquisition)
  - Infrastructural development should be based on:
    - Public support (limited though necessarily to some) especially in risk sharing
    - Largely from schemes of PPP - existing and new ones of government to promote infrastructure like PURA
    - Capitalizing on future returns and borrowings from the capital market
  - Not relating development of township with SEZs (resulting in no land acquisition)
- In addition, if SEZs are evolved as Growth Poles as proposed by NCEUS -
  - existing clusters - especially ones with potential can be further developed as SEZs
  - making them reap benefit (economies, externalities common services and social overhead capital, export & fiscal incentives available to SEZs) from initial infant industry treatment
  - become viable on their own and continue to expand, extend
  - and thereafter spurn off development of adjoining regions (incorporating in their fold social and economic benefits as well)
- Growth Pole can be developed and promoted by independent authorities and through PPP
- Funded by a combination of Central, State Governments, Banks and User/ Private Agencies.

(See Box 12.5 on NCEUS on Growth Poles for details)

informed about the phasing and content of their rehabilitation package, their entitlements and their choices. The practice is to pay compensation for fixed assets like agricultural land at the prevailing market rate, calculated as an average of the registered sales prices of land of similar quality and location in the preceding three or five years. However, it is well known that most land transactions in India are grossly undervalued. Hence, the displaced are not compensated for their land or houses at rates, which would enable them to buy land or construct houses elsewhere similar to those that are lost. The compensation that is fixed is paid as a rule in cash rather than in kind. Tribal people, and to a lesser degree most rural people, have little experience in handling cash. Moreover, tenants, sharecroppers, wage-labourers, artisans and encroachers are usually not considered eligible for compensation because they do not have legal title to agricultural land, whereas they are paradoxically the most vulnerable and in need of support. Community assets like grazing grounds and forests, which again may be critical for the livelihood of the poorest, are not compensated for under the Land Acquisition Act.

12.11 The Special Economic Zones (SEZ) Act was passed in 2005 to build infrastructure, promote exports and generate employment through development of technology parks and industrial zones (Box 12.2). This measure requires the acquisition of vast stretches of land, which raises issues similar to the ones discussed earlier, but with the difference that the land is acquired for private entrepreneurs. This has highlighted the fact that the Land Acquisition Act needs to be modified to clearly define 'public purpose'.

12.12 The basic issue is that while, at present, the Land Acquisition Act 'compensates' loss of assets it should more basically compensate the loss of livelihood. The relative loss may be much higher for a landless labourer or sharecropper on the fields of an absentee landlord, but it is only the latter who is eligible for compensation. The Narmada Award is perhaps the first that recognizes the right of landless labourers, artisans and adult co-landholders to land compensation, but this should be prescribed in law. Rehabilitation should not be discretionary, but should be clearly defined as a legal duty of the State, with the provision that acquisition proceedings would stand annulled in the event of the failure of the State to perform its duty. Along with the notice under section 4 (1), the details of the compensation package should also be published and widely publicized. In particular, in cases of land acquisition for an irrigation project, the first right on the land of the command area must be of the displaced oustee. Acquisition and allotment of land in the command area for rehabilitation must precede acquisition of land for submergence. A significant share from the profits/ registration fees of future transactions in the sale and purchase of that land should go to the original farmer.

Regulation of Environmental Standards

12.13 There are three principal Acts, viz. the Environmental Protection Act, the Water Pollution Act and the Air Pollution Act that are in effect for environment protection. There are several loopholes in these Acts, which can be exploited by the powerful to circumvent these Acts. However, workers employed in such industries also face uncertainty of employment and undergo the fear of punishment. Ban on tiny and small scale industries in cities like Delhi and Calcutta in order to prevent pollution of the Yamuna and Ganga rivers has also led to loss of livelihood for a number of workers in these industries. The Supreme Court had passed orders in 1996 to close down all industries that led to pollution of these rivers. Thousands of tiny units identified by these directives were sealed in Delhi, which affected a large number of casual, contract and informal workers engaged in these industries. A large number of them were migrant labourers from the states of U.P and Bihar. Majority of them had to return to their native lands as they could not afford the cost of living in the city without any employment. Although the affected were small entrepreneurs and migrant workers, no systematic study was ever carried out to assess the environment costs of these units and the cost of their possible relocation nor was any scheme evolved to assist in the relocation of the tiny entrepreneurs and the workers.

Street Vendors

12.14 The status of street vendors and the impact of laws and regulations on them has been examined in depth by this Commission, both in a separate Report (Box 12.3) and in chapter 4 of this Report. There are

The basic issue is that while, at present, the Land Acquisition Act 'compensates' loss of assets it should more basically compensate the loss of livelihood. The relative loss may be much higher for a landless labourer or sharecropper on the fields of an absentee landlord, but it is only the latter who is eligible for compensation.

Box 12.3: NCEUS Recommendations on Urban Street Vendors

- Provide, promote supportive environment for earning livelihood to urban street vendors
- Restriction of street vending in urban areas to only on the consent of owners
- 3 level monitoring mechanism: Town Vending Committee (TVC) ward level; CEO Municipal Level; Official at state level
  - Constitution of TVC in each ward of all towns by municipal authorities
  - TVC to have greater participation of vendors ; RWAs, Market and Traders Associations to have no role
  - TVC to identify 3 zones - no restriction for hawking, with certain restrictions, no vending
  - Hawking zones to be city specific
  - Regulate space based on space available, previous occupancy, lottery if applicants exceed space to be undertaken by TVC
  - Allocation against payment of fee as recommended by TVC
  - TVC to collect revenue to ensure prefixed rate only charged
  - Registration and issue of identity card to street vendors by TVC
  - Registered street vendors given preference for new shops when licences for new ones issued
  - TVC to monitor, provide facilities.
  - Dissemination of information on credit, linking of street vendors with micro credit agencies by TVCs
  - Maintenance of hygiene and cleanliness by vendors themselves
  - Appropriate redressal mechanism to be maintained by TVC
  - Municipal authority to implement decisions by hawkers
- Amendment of Section 283 IPC and Section 34 Police Act to exempt street vendors from their purview with reasonable restrictions
- Mechanism for eviction
- Issue of notice prior to eviction - giving due date and time
- Imposition of fine if space not cleared within due date
- Confiscated goods may be obtained by payment of fine and within fixed durations
- Incentives to state governments and municipalities to tackle issue of street vendors
- Formulation of action plan for various levels
- Application of legislation regarding Social Security and Conditions of Work to address the issues pertaining to the livelihood needs of urban street vendors.

several laws and regulations that directly affect the employment opportunities of roadside vendors selling food items. A recent directive by the Supreme Court has put several constraints on the street food shops selling food items in Delhi. Laws such as Food Adulteration Act called the Prevention of Food Adulteration Act (PFA) 1955, is the principal instrument of law, to ensure that clean and wholesome articles of human consumption are sold to the public. While the PFA Act by itself is not a very complicated piece of legislation, the accompanying rules are. Also there are a number of procedural problems in the implementation of this law. The food inspectors can act arbitrarily and the license raj breeds corruption. Further the law lacks transparency. The really poor often have neither the capital or credit nor the enterprise to set up shops, and eke out a hand to mouth existence as street vendors, especially in urban areas. They live in constant fear of being forcibly moved or "pay" someone in order to remain undisturbed. With street vendors there is also the anomalous situation that they cannot vend without a license and yet there is almost a blanket ban on the issue of licenses. Even if a license is issued there is always the additional whim of the traffic police to deal with. Although in recent times, judicial intervention has played a significant role in asking municipal authorities to demarcate hawking and no hawking zones, executive response has been slow. In a few cases authorities have demarcated the no-hawking areas, but the areas, which are to be reserved for hawking have not been delineated. Not only does the entire process need to be expedited in those areas, which come under the jurisdiction of these pronouncements but a similar exercise needs to be systematically undertaken in all the urban areas in line with the revised Street Vendors Policy (Box 12.3).

12.15 Unless accompanied by suitable executive action, there is a high risk that judicial pronouncements restricting street vending will penalise the poor without affecting the systems that already restrict their livelihood operations while extracting 'rents' from them. The judicial pronouncements affect the livelihood of hundreds of thousands of hawkers in metropolitan cities and also have ramifications for small-scale industries and the farm sector. There is need to build upon successful experiments in many parts of India where civic authorities are working constructively with street vendors (Bahuguna 2007). It should be noted that with retail business being undertaken by big business houses, and with the introduction of FDI in the sector under the liberalized economy, the conditions faced by the small time grocery shop owners have become more adverse since they are unlikely to be able to compete with the giants and their price cutting policies.

Urban Planning

12.16 The meagre incomes of the workers in the unorganised sector force them to live in make-shift shanties and slums. Besides the miseries of living in terrible living conditions with lack of entitlement to basic amenities such as water or electricity, they also have to live in constant fear of being dislodged from their homes in the name of slum clearance. Since most of them are forced to be encroachers, they get caught in a vicious cycle of degraded living conditions without minimal facilities. This kind of dislocation not only deprives them of their homes but also affects their livelihood as unorganised workers. The slum dwellers are usually urban migrants who come to the city because of abject rural poverty and unemployment in their areas of origin. Clearly, a large programme of urban low cost housing and shared residential facility should be part of any master plan, which enables workers including seasonal migrants to access housing at reasonable cost and relocation costs (if any) to the workers should be shared by the employers.

12.17 The sealing drive in Delhi under the Master Plan, which has again exposed the weakness of urban planning, has led to loss of employment of a large number of petty shop owners and small time self-employed who had their shops in residential areas. Along with the shop owners those employed in these shops as helpers also lost their jobs and had to look for alternative employment with government providing no rehabilitation for them. It was the petty shop owners who were most adversely affected by this sealing as the bigger shop owners were able to resettle in other legal shops or able to get a stay order on the sealing. Such alternatives were beyond the capacity of the small shop owners.

12.18 Non-mechanical transport is an important, inexpensive and environment friendly means of transport in India. Lately, there have been regulations and court directives that directly affect the livelihood of those driving such transport as rickshaw pullers. These include the banning of such means of transport in certain areas in big cities in the name of reducing congestion such as the banning of rickshaws in the Chandni Chowk area of Delhi. Certain elite areas are also out of bound for the rickshaw pullers and other non-mechanical means of carriage and transport in the name of beautification of the city. These measures adversely affect the rickshaw pullers as their very means of livelihood is taken away without provision of any other alternative means of earning or employment.

12.19 These examples show that policies and programmes, laws and regulations can have a negative impact on the livelihoods of poor unorganised workers. In the recent past, the propensity of such decisions being taken has been very high. Given that the negative impact falls upon the poor whose livelihoods are affected they must be involved in any decisions. The Commission is of the view that it is not enough for government to demonstrate that there are public benefits of its actions. Alternative livelihoods must be provided to the affected poor without inordinately increasing the large existing burden on them. One of the existing problems is that when policy changes occur, their impact on the poor and

The Commission is of the view that it is not enough for government to demonstrate that there are public benefits of its actions. Alternative livelihoods must be provided to the affected poor without inordinately increasing the large existing burden on them.

on their livelihoods is not taken into account either by those departments/ ministries initiating the change or by any other coordinating institution within the government. We believe that a thorough review of policies from this perspective at their inception stage is absolutely essential and we also recommend that there should be a systematic review and monitoring of all policies and programmes which impact on unorganised sector workers.

Promotional Policies for Non-agricultural Unorganised Sector

12.20 Since independence, policies in India emphasised accelerated industrial growth and other important goals such as achieving self-reliance, reduction in disparities across regions in the country and prevention of concentration of economic power in private hands. These goals implied that other objectives such as creation of employment opportunities, assisting the development of small-scale and village and household industries, and protecting the consumer from the private sector monopolies were also to be addressed.

12.21 Rural industrialization and growth were seen to have major potential for production of goods and services and for the generation of employment of skilled, semi-skilled and unskilled labour. The Industrial Policy Resolution of 1948 assigned this important role to the cottage and small scale industries. In the Second Plan, the Mahalonobis strategy called for the rapid development of small scale and cottage industries to meet the demand for consumer goods. Industrial Policy Resolution, 1956, also assigned a key role to the cottage, village and small scale industries, for their distinct advantage in generating large scale employment and effective mobilization of resources, capital and skills (Kurien 1978). India was probably unique in the world for widespread policies to protect the small scale industries and the village and household industries (Mohan 2001). Policies for protection and development of small village and household industries were devised to help fulfil the role of this sector in the creation of employment and supply of consumer goods. Khadi and Village Industries Commission (KVIC) was set up in 1955 by an Act of Parliament. In 1978 the Districts Industries Centres were set up to provide services and support required by the small and village entrepreneurs under a single roof. These services were to extend the provision of raw material, supply of machinery and equipment, arrangement of credit facilities and helping to set up marketing linkages.

12.22 The nomenclature used to address the smallest segments of industries in India has been varied - village and small industries, khadi and village industries, tiny enterprises, micro-enterprises etc. At the base are the rural manufacturing household enterprises - usually subsumed in the KVI segment. The other units are distinguishable in terms of their size of investment. It is to be noted that the Factories Act employs the use of power and the size of employment as defining criteria. But India is again perhaps unique in defining its small scale industries (SSI) using investment ceilings which have changed with time. The Micro, Small and Medium Enterprises Act, 2006 has classified the enterprises in the manufacturing and service sectors into three categories. The micro enterprises in manufacturing are those having investment in plant and machinery of less than Rs.2.5 million and in services less than Rs.1 million. Small scale industries are those with investments between Rs.2.5 million and Rs. 50 million in manufacturing and Rs.1.0 million and Rs.20 million in services. The positive feature of this Act is that it recognizes a micro enterprise sector, but by clubbing it with the small as well as the medium enterprises the chances of the benefits flowing into the micro sector may be greatly reduced. The difference between cottage and village industries and SSI is in terms of their absolute size and technological characteristics. However, a major difference between the two is their links with the rest of the economy. The SSI industries are generally connected with the large scale industries in terms of technical and input-output linkages.

12.23 The broad approaches that have been followed to support the unorganised and the SSI sector have included support to various traditional industries, enterprise development, micro-credit, technology development and skill training. A massive administrative structure is in place to support these efforts (Appendix Table A12.1). These include institutions specifically designed to cater to the needs of the small sector, specialised credit institutions and a series of Boards under various ministries.

12.24 The policy framework that was developed in India to support the unorganised sector was based on several assumptions. These included imperfections in the input, output and credit markets, information asymmetries and economies of scale for large-scale production. The main advantages in favour of the unorganised manufacturing enterprises were considered to be their labour intensive character, decentralised location and the ability to provide varied products/services on a dispersed basis. Under these assumptions, the promotional policy was based on active state intervention directed at protecting the sector, providing it cheap and canalised inputs, fiscal incentives, assisting it in credit and marketing either through encouraging co-operative associations or through other means. The onset of liberalisation has now shifted the emphasis to a policy regime in which it is no longer considered expedient to interfere with the advantages conferred by the market and the role of promotional policy is restricted to assisting unorganised enterprises to take advantage of market conditions.

12.25 One of the main instruments for the development of this sector was through the reservation of certain items of production. Reservation of certain products for the small-scale sector was introduced in the Industrial Policy notification of 1973. The number of products reserved rose from 47 in 1967 to 504 in 1978 and in the second phase to 807. The latter increase was partly because the reserved list followed the codes adopted in the NIC classification. The number of reserved products went up to 872 in 1984. The choice of products reserved was not always made on clear criteria (Mohan 2001). The Abid Hussain Committee Report (1997) averred that the reservation of products for the small sector has not actually helped the growth of the sector and thatunits, which were exposed to competition actually grew faster than units in the reserved category. The Report argued that reservation may have militated against the growth of enterprises in sectors (such as textiles and leather) which were labour intensive and may have created a bias against employment growth in sectors which may also have been export oriented (Mohan 2001). The Government has gradually de-reserved a number of products with the current number of reserved products standing only at 239 (Economic Survey 2006-07). However, there is, as yet, no systematic study to show the impact of de-reservation on employment and productivity growth of specific sectors.

Availability of Institutional Credit

12.26 One of the key policy instruments to provide access to credit to the small industries was the RBI directions on 'priority sector' lending. The commercial banks were asked to advance 40 per cent of their net bank credit to the priority sector. This included the small and tiny enterprises for which , however, no separate targets were specified. In the case of co-operative banks the priority sector lending was to be 60 per cent. A large institutional structure was also created to facilitate the flow of credit to this sector.

12.27 However, there has been a change in the banking policy since the economic reforms of 1991. The concept of priority sector lending itself has come under attack, with the suggestion by the Narsimhan Committee Report (1993) that the 40 per cent direct credit to the priority sector should be phased out. While this recommendation has not been implemented, there has been a dilution of the priority sector lending policy. The operational relevance of the priority sector lending has been weakened by the inclusion of a vast number of items, including agricultural machinery, direct finance to the housing sector etc. Following the financial sector reform, and the imperative to restructure the existing credit institutions, the nature of credit support to the sector has undergone a change and the direct outreach of the institutional structure, especially in rural areas, has declined. Currently, credit support to the small enterprises follows a multi agency approach through the following: direct lending, indirect lending in the form of micro credit through intermediaries, credit and enterprise development support through schemes, and schemes such as Credit Guarantee to commercial banks to encourage lending to the small enterprises (NCEUS 2007).

12.28 There has clearly been a decline in the credit flow from public sector banks and commercial banks to the SSI sector and to the tiny enterprises, particularly since the mid-1990s. The NCEUS has examined the credit related issues of the non-agricultural unorganised sector in detail. It set up a Task Force under the Chairpersonship of Prof. V. S. Vyas, which has submitted its findings. These show a very limited outreach of institutional finance and sharp contraction of formal credit to the unorganised sector since 1991 (NCEUS 2007; see also Box 12.4). Alternative ways of financing the sector's requirements including through micro-credit have had limited success. Based on the recommendations of the Task Force, this Commission has made a number of far-reaching recommendations towards increasing the flow of credit to the unorganised sector (ibid.). In this Report, we have recommended that change in guidelines be taken up on an immediate basis in order to ensure that priority sector credit may become available to this sector and to

In this Report, we have recommended that change in guidelines be taken up on an immediate basis in order to ensure that priority sector credit may become available to this sector and to other needy sectors.

Box 12.4 NCEUS Tack Force on Credit

- This Report addresses itself mainly to that segment of non - farm unorganized enterprises whose investment in plant and machinery is less than Rs.0.5 million
- **Key Findings:**
  - 93.8% of the SSIs' investment in plant and machinery is less than Rs.0.5 million (3rd Census of SSI);
  - 97.4% of the non - farm enterprises employed not more than 5 persons (55th NSS Round)
  - 14.3% of the SSI units in registered sector availed bank finance, while only 3.1% of the unregistered units had access to bank finance (3rd Census of SSI, 2001-02)
  - Almost equal number of enterprises (4.1%) had access to institutional credit and to non - institutional credit including those from relatives and money lenders (55th Round)
  - The number of SSI accounts declined from 3.0 per cent of the total to 1.2 per cent and the credit from 11.5 per cent of the net bank credit to 4.1 per cent.
  - Decline in SSI credit as per cent of net bank credit from 15.4% in 1997-98 to 6.4% in 2005-06
  - Agriculture sector received only 11.9% of bank credit against the stipulation of 18%
  - Insistence on collaterals even on loan upto Rs.0.5 million, in spite of the RBI guidelines to this effect
  - The share of small loans (below Rs. 25000) in the total outstanding of scheduled commercial banks declined from 21% in June 1985 to 3.7% in March 2005
  - Disinterest of banks in advancing loans under Credit Guarantee Scheme which is available for loans up to Rs 2.5 million
  - Higher cost of credit for unorganized enterprises
  - Inadequate institutional infrastructure at field level
- **Recommendations**
  - Treating units with investment in plant and machinery up to Rs. 0.5 million as Special Sub-Group of Micro Enterprise (SSME) for lending under Priority Sector Lending Policy
  - 8% of the net bank credit be fixed for SSMEs- this growth in credit to be achieved in a phased manner in 5 years
  - Proper monitoring of credit to small & medium enterprises and micro enterprises with investment in P&M up to Rs.0.5 million and those between Rs0.5 million to Rs. 2.5 million separately
  - Extending credit plus services like credit plus insurance, guidance and counselling of entrepreneurs, training of personnel, linking skill with project development
  - Rationalising and reducing cost of credit by controlling the rate of interest which need to be governed by the overall cost and not specific high cost of lending of small loans alone
  - The rate of interest on loan up to Rs.0.5 million to farm and non - farm unorganized enterprises should be same as in the case of agriculture; employment intensive farm and non - farm unorganized enterprises deserve the same treatment as agriculture (cultivation)
  - Loans under Credit Guarantee Scheme up to Rs.0.5 million be made mandatory and guarantee cover be enhanced to 90% on loans up to Rs.0.5 million; 1.5% of guarantee fee on loan up to Rs.0.5 million should be met by the government, out of the available corpus of proposed National Fund.
  - Rate of margin money be uniform at 25% in respect of all credit linked Government Schemes.
  - Strengthening delivery points by making it mandatory for each bank branch in the country to open fresh loan accounts of non-farm unorganised sector enterprises every year.
  - Issue multipurpose Swarojgar Credit Cards for the self-employed persons in non- farm unorganised sector
  - National Fund for refinancing, financing and development of unorganised sector enterprises and workers should be created and named as "National Fund for Unorganized Sector" (NAFUS), to carry out development, financial, legal & administrative functions in the form of a registered society. The Fund will have an initial corpus of Rs.50 million out of which Rs.20 million would be Govt of India's contribution. The corpus may be raised to Rs.100 million in the next 5 years i.e. by 2012.

other needy sectors. Some other immediate measures, which aim at enhancing the flow of credit to the unorganised non-agricultural sector have also been included in the Action Programme spelt out in Chapter 14.

Micro Credit and SHGs

12.29 The potential of SHGs to develop as local financial intermediaries to reach the poor has gained recognition in India due to their community based participatory approach and sustainability. Recovery rates in micro-credit programmes have been significantly higher than those achieved by commercial banks in spite of loans going to poor, unorganised individuals without security or collateral. At the all India level, the number of SHGs has increased from about 110 thousand in 1999-00 to over 2.2 million by the end of March, 2006 and the volume of micro credit has increased from Rs.1.9 billion to over Rs.114 billion during the same period. By March, 2006, about 1.6 million SHGs were formed under the SHG-Bank Linkage Programme. SHGs, however, have shown uneven regional growth. Till March, 2001, over 70 per cent of SHGs were concentrated in the Southern states. Though things have improved since then, over 44 per cent of SHGs are located in the Southern states even now. The present number of NGO-MFIs is estimated to be 1,000, cooperative MFIs about 30,000. In addition, there are 20 MFIs working as companies, which provide about 70 per cent of credit advanced through MFIs in the country.

12.30 The Government of India has four major public micro-credit programmes: Swayamsidha, Swashakti, Rashtriya Mahila Kosh and SGSY. The NGO sector also has a number of large and successful micro-finance models such as Basix, SEWA, WWF, and MYRADA. The National Bank for Agriculture and Rural Development [NABARD] launched a scheme, linking the SHGs with banks, to augment the resources of micro finance institutions. All the major categories of the banks, viz. commercial banks, cooperative banks and regional rural banks are participating in delivery of micro finance services. Three distinct linkage models are being followed. Under Model I, banks provide micro finance to non-governmental organisations for on-lending to the SHGs and ultimately to the micro entrepreneurs. Under Model II, banks provide direct financing directly to SHGs for on-lending to the micro entrepreneurs. Under Model III banks finance directly to SHGs for on-lending to micro entrepreneurs, with the intervention of NGOs as social mobilisers and facilitators. During the year 2004, 14.1 per cent of the credit flowed to SHGs directly from banks, 81.1 per cent from banks to SHGs formed by NGOs, and 4.9 per cent to SHGs through the NGOs which had also helped in their formation.

12.31 Despite the success of the micro credit models, many reports reveal inadequacy of loan size, which does lead to asset creation and is unable to lift households above poverty line on a sustainable basis. Another area of attention is the addition to the number of products as also the extension of the products from thrift and credit to insurance, and money transfer, etc. Thus, a major aspect for a viable micro financing system is capacity building of the players like members of SHGs, MFIs, and NGOs so that micro finance graduates to micro enterprise, financing with adequate facilities for forward and backward linkages. Given that most SHGs are today concentrated in a few regions of the country, their growth in other parts needs to be pro-actively fostered.

12.32 The Commission has recommended a number of measures to encourage the growth of SHGs and micro-finance, especially in backward regions. These measures, which are described in Chapter 14, include the creation of an incentive fund to facilitate the growth of SHGs, incentivising the MFIs to expand the scope of their activities, pooling the individual subsidy component of SGSY into the funds made available under the programme for capacity building and establishing infrastructure and backward-forward linkages; and examining and removing the variety of restrictions imposed on MFIs due to which they are not in a position to expand their operations and grow beyond a certain size.

Raw Material

12.33 One of the major problems faced by the unorganised sector enterprises is procurement of raw materials. The problem arises mainly because the requirement of raw materials is of small quantities, partly due to small scale of operation and partly due to financial constraints. The capacity to withstand the market fluctuation of prices of raw material is also limited. Consequently they are not able to derive the benefits of bulk purchase. For small manufacturing enterprises the National and Small Industries Development Corporations (and similar agencies) were set up especially for the procurement and distribution of raw materials to the small scale industries. For the Handloom sector, National Handloom Development Corporation (NHDC) has been entrusted with the task of implementing 'Mill Gate Price Scheme', introduced in 1992-93 to provide yarn to the handloom weavers at the Mill Gate prices. However, this is not adequate and the micro enterprises require special measures to protect them from these contingencies (Sinha 2006). The Commission has examined in detail the difficulties faced by the enterprises in various industries, such as handlooms and textiles, in procuring raw materials. The Commission underlines the need for special measures to mitigate these difficulties and provide raw material at reasonable prices to small enterprises. It will be finalising its recommendations on these issues in a separate report.

Marketing

12.34 A major constraint faced by the unorganised enterprises is marketing of their products. The lack of marketing facilities was identified as a major problem by a large proportion of unorganised enterprises, particularly so in rural areas (Chapter 4). Marketing constraints arise from a number of interrelated factors like lack of information about markets for products, capacity to exploit the existing markets or to reach new markets, the scale of operation or volume of production, and cost of undertaking these operations. In the liberalised era, competition from larger units is a major constraint and this was noted particularly by the larger establishments in the urban areas. The Government has a number of schemes to support marketing linkages for the small enterprises. A Report prepared for the Commission on the Constraints Faced by Small Enterprises (Sinha 2006) has noted that schemes supporting management, technology, design interventions and the availability of credit can be drawn upon by unorganised enterprises to boost the marketing potential of their products but most of them are not able to avail of these facilities either for want of knowledge or inability to cross hurdles in accessing these facilities. It suggested a diametrically opposite kind of assistance, which would propel larger, more powerful units to take the initiative, link their growth prospects with the growth of unorganised enterprises and so to say, bring marketing to the doorstep of the small enterprises. The Commission is presently examining this issue in greater depth and will be making recommendations in a separate Report.

Cluster Development and Growth Poles

12.35 The experience of cluster approach has been found to be encouraging and successful in many countries. The clusters are defined as a sectoral and geographical concentration of enterprises, institutions, service providers and related regulatory bodies, engaged in the production of homogeneous or inter-related products and faced with common opportunities and threats. The existing literature brings out several major characteristics of clusters, especially the industrial ones - geographical proximity, sectoral specialization, close inter-firm collaboration (linkages substituting for vertical integration of activities within the firm), inter-firm competition (based on innovation rather than lowering of wages), social embeddedness and State support. However, the literature survey also shows that most clusters have an autonomous origin and are rarely induced, emerging around local skill or natural resource bases. But there are instances of product specific industrial estates subsequently emerging as clusters following the setting up of some kind of lead industry. UNIDO (United Nations Industrial Development Organization) and other UN agencies, OECD (Organization of Economic Cooperation and Development), the World Bank and assorted other organizations have all taken interest in promoting clusters in developing countries in Asia, Africa and Latin America.

12.36 At a conceptual level, there are three kinds of clusters that one can visualize - relatively modern, small-firm dominated industrial clusters that often tend to be located in urban areas; artisan and rural industry based clusters; and clusters that are based on the agro-economy. The last two, particularly the last, tend to be natural resource-based. Most policy interventions have focused on the first of the three, rather than the last two.

12.37 There have been many attempts to identify industrial and service clusters following different approaches. UNIDO has compiled a list of 388 clusters of modern small industries. The Development Commissioner, Small Scale Industries, has a figure of 2042 clusters of small-scale industries. The Entrepreneurship Development Institute (EDI), Ahmedabad, estimates 3511 clusters, 1422 urban and 1820 rural. Besides these SME (small and medium enterprise) clusters, there are 3332 artisan clusters and 372 handloom clusters. The Department of Industrial Policy and Promotion has a list of 100 clusters identified for development. Several other ministries / departments including Small Scale Industries, Agro & Rural Industries, Rural Development, Panchayati Raj, Commerce, Food Processing Industries, Textiles, Information Technology, as well as Science and Technology have their own cluster development programmes. Cluster development is also supported by a number of other agencies including the Small Industries Development Bank of India (SIDBI), Commissioner of Handlooms, Coir Board, Department

Box 12.5: NCEUS on Unorganised Sector Growth Poles (GP)

- **Growth Pole envisaged by NCEUS - based on Cluster Approach.**
  - GP is a continuous geographical location with a number of clusters.
  - GP approach relies on economies of scale, interdependencies and inter-linkages within & between SMEs in a cluster and between clusters in a geographical region.
  - Extension of SEZs benefits to GP clusters initially - citing their 'infant' nature in terms of access to capital, level of technology and competitiveness
  - Based on assumption that clusters once developed would leash out multiplier effect - expand production and employment - help tap positive (production linkages, common social overhead capital, different service delivery networks) and tackle negative externalities - resulting in spread effect and engulfing larger areas.
- **Key Features:**
  - land acquisition not involved as existing clusters to be developed further
  - providing fiscal incentives to export of goods from the area - gaining in terms of both economic (foreign exchange) and social value (multiplier effect), even after expansion
  - units in the cluster being treated as "deemed exports treatment" for their products
- **Implementation involves:**
  - Identification of clusters with potential to evolve to growth poles (by state governments)
  - Selection of cluster for Pilot Project from those identified above (by state governments)
  - Promoted thereafter and developed by independent authorities like corporations, PPP, with conditions and responsibility to focus on SMEs and provide support services themselves by involving other stakeholders.
  - Evolve a prototype of growth pole - leading to development of a model to be replicated
  - Wherever possible combining PURA scheme with Growth Pole Strategy to develop townships around GP
- **Six Projects identified till date:**
  - Sikandra and adjoining areas of Dausa district in Rajasthan.
  - Panchala and adjoining area of Domjur blocks of Howrah district in West Bengal.
  - Perinad (Kadavoor) Perumon, Eravipuram & Sasthamcotta of Kollam district, Kerala.
  - Janjgir in Champa district in Chhattisgarh.
  - Dasholi, Karnaprayag, Ghat, Naryanbagar, Tharali and Dewal of Chamoli district in Uttarakand.
  - Rampur, Chayani - Bardur; Chhaygaon; Bangaon; Boko-Bangaon; Goroimari and Hajo South-Western Kamrup district in Assam.
- **Funding for Growth Pole Strategy**
  - Fiscal Incentives - no loss of revenue as SMEs pay only small proportion of taxes
  - Government of India - 49 per cent - for basic infrastructure - equipment and machinery and technology upgradation with training and skill development
  - User/ private agencies - 25 per cent
  - Banks and state governments - 26 per cent - for credit expansion, technology upgradation, facility centres, social infrastructure development
- **In formulation of Growth Pole Strategy - focus on maintaining**
  - Diversity of products
  - Diversity and complementary in nature of SMEs or activities undertaken by SMEs
  - Dispersed geographical location of clusters.

of Science and Technology, State Bank of India, as well as numerous state governments.

12.38 Earlier attempts at cluster formation have not always been successful, as they often tended to be ad hoc, piecemeal and tried to induce the industrial units to set up operations in green field areas. The current approach is based upon strengthening natural clustering of units due to economies in skill acquisition, technology development, marketing, etc. However, the existing efforts are still scattered, small-scale and lack co-ordination. Up-scaling these efforts is possible through the provision of common infrastructure, service centres etc. The Commission has piloted the "Growth Poles" for the unorganized sector, based on a concept of developing a cluster of clusters in project mode with public-private partnership (Box 12.5). This is designed to take the existing cluster development approach to the next level. In Chapter 14, we have recommended that the Government set up 25 Growth Poles - one in each State- during the 11th Five Year Plan.

National Fund for the Unorganised Sector

12.39 As discussed above, the unorganised sector faces various types of constraints in terms of inadequacy of credit, low level of technology; difficulty in arranging critical raw materials; marketing of products; lack of skills etc. At present, there is no exclusive agency to address these requirements. The Commission's Report on credit has brought out that institutions such as SIDBI and NABARD which were created to cater to segments of the unorganised sector are not able to render these promotional services adequately. The Commission is of the view that there is need for an exclusive agency to take care of the integrated needs of the entire unorganised sector covering both financial and promotional requirement.

12.40 The Commission has proposed the creation of the National Fund for the Unorganised Sector (NAFUS). Some details of the Fund have been discussed in Chapter 14 and are being submitted separately to the Government as part of the Commissions' report on credit. The aims and functions of the Fund would not merely be to enable better access to credit of farm and non-farm enterprises alone but to enable the unorganised sector to benefit in the areas of marketing, technology, skill and entrepreneurship, guidance and counselling and capacity building. The target group of the Fund on the other hand, would be the micro enterprises, with focus on those below an investment of Rs. 0.5 million which constitute 94 per cent of the small enterprises.

Policy Initiatives, Programmes and Schemes for Agricultural Workers

12.41 Agricultural labourers, and marginal and small farmers are a highly vulnerable section of the rural population. There is clear evidence that in recent years, agricultural growth particularly in food grains has declined. This has had an adverse effect on the growth of agricultural wages that have shown signs of deceleration in the nineties making the situation even more unfavourable for the agricultural labourers. On the other hand the farmers particularly the marginal and small farmers are also facing a crisis due to high input costs and uncertain output markets. In these conditions government support in the form of policy initiatives and schemes to protect the interest of agricultural workers becomes even more pertinent. However, in the post-nineties period, there has been a decline in government support in the form of declining investment in agriculture and subsidies to the sector are also being rationalized. The withdrawal of the State has led to a much greater dependence on private sources for inputs, extension, markets and credit. Farmer suicides have been widespread in the last several years and the victims have largely been marginal and small farmers. Increasing costs of cultivation leading to higher indebtedness, crop failures and incapacity to face price shocks with greater liberalization of the agricultural sector has driven farmers to the extreme. This has prompted the Central and state governments to set up several Commissions including the National Commission on Farmers and the Committee on Agricultural Indebtedness to suggest remedial steps.

12.42 Agricultural policy followed during the last five decades can be broadly distinguished in three phases.

The Commission has proposed the creation of the National Fund for the Unorganised Sector (NAFUS). The aims and functions of the Fund would not merely be to enable better access to credit of farm and non-farm enterprises alone but to enable the unorganised sector to benefit in the areas of marketing, technology, skill and entrepreneurship, guidance and counselling and capacity building.

Phase one, immediately after independence, witnessed several institutional changes through land reforms and initiation of major irrigation projects. The second phase since the mid-sixties was aimed at increasing agricultural productivity to attain self-sufficiency in food grains through technological revolution and public support to credit, marketing, extension etc. This was followed by the current phase since the late eighties, aimed at making the agricultural sector more market oriented.

12.43 Several studies in the 1960s and 1970s indicated that the Green Revolution had a scale, size and capital bias and small and marginal farmers could not make the most of it. Despite this view, productivity gains were gradually realized even among the small and marginal farmers as indicated by the high, sustained agricultural growth through the eighties which also spread to several agriculturally stagnant areas. The main reasons for this spread appear to be that the new agricultural technologies were divisible, and the government pro-actively fostered the spread of credit, marketing and extension institutions and also facilitated their adoption by small and marginal farmers. An important role in the consolidation and spread of agricultural growth was also played by the special programmes, which were initiated by the government from time to time. The Small Farmers Development Agencies (SFDA) programme was instituted in 1971 with the objective of assisting marginal and small farmers in raising their income level. This was to be achieved by helping them to adopt improved agricultural technology and acquire means of increasing agricultural production like minor irrigation sources on the one hand, and to diversify their farm economy through subsidiary activities like animal husbandry, dairying, horticulture etc on the other. Two area based programmes, namely the Drought Prone Area Programme and the Desert Development Programme were started with a view to encouraging sustainable resource management and agricultural development in specific agro-ecological settings. The Million Wells scheme was introduced with the prime objective of catering to the irrigation needs of the small and marginal farmers to increase the productivity of their holdings. Although the scheme faced various impediments, it has contributed to increasing the irrigation potential of the small/marginal farms. A review of agricultural policy over the last decade or so however shows that no notable efforts have been made to overcome the handicaps faced by the marginal and small farmers.

12.44 Since the nineties it has been noticed that the productivity gains from the Green Revolution have started receding. The agriculture sector in general is going through a slow down. Among other factors, it has been indicated that the change in priorities and stance on state support has had an adverse effect on the development of rural areas in general and agricultural sector in particular. The gains to the sector visualized through improved terms of trade, with the removal of the bias against the sector after the process of liberalization was initiated, have not emerged while increasing price volatility has added to the vulnerability of the farmers. High level of distress has been witnessed among the farmers across a number of states, and the case of rising indebtedness was discussed in Chapter 9. The small and marginal farmers, given their poor economic conditions, fail to overcome the seasonal and price shocks and are caught in a vicious circle of indebtedness as they have to take loans to meet their consumption needs, given low income level, which is causing immense distress among them.

12.45 In the liberalised scenario and with increased integration with the global markets it has become even more imperative to protect the interests of the marginal and small farmers through measures that help promote and stabilize incomes, reduce risks and increase profitability and at the same time improve availability and access to inputs, markets and credit. However we have observed in Chapter 9 that the dependence on private sources for inputs, irrigation and most importantly for credit among the small and marginal farmers has increased in recent years reversing the earlier trend towards expansion in access.

12.46 The Government constituted the National Commission on Farmers (NCF) under the chairmanship of Dr. M.S. Swaminathan to specifically look into all aspects concerning the protection of interest of farmers. The key recommendations of the NCF are incorporated in its proposed National Policy for Farmers. The policy document recognizes the misery of the poor farmers and observes "agriculture has become a relatively unrewarding profession due to generally unfavourable price regime and low value addition, causing abandoning of farming and increasing migration from rural areas....". Several factors contributed to this situation. These include shift in cropping pattern towards cash crops, lack of level playing field for farmers in the global market, increased dependence on high-cost inputs which is increasing costs of cultivation and indebtedness, increasing risks, declining profitability and declining public support. In this context, the NCF has noted that the Government had initiated a number of measures such as Bharat Nirman, NREGA, expansion of credit at lower rates of interest, promotion of horticulture, fisheries, changes in the Agriculture Produce Marketing Committee Act (APMC) etc. But most of these measures are still in the initial stages. The NCF has also recognised the need for a social security system and has endorsed the recommendations of the NCEUS in this regard. The Eleventh Plan Steering Group on Agriculture (Planning Commission 2007) and the Planning Commission's note to the National Development Council also amply recognise the adverse conditions faced by agriculture and have advocated strategies to reverse the downturn.

12.47 In the Commission's view, marginal and small farms are the backbone of Indian agriculture. The analysis in Chapter 9 clearly brings out that 84 per cent of the households with land up to 2 hectares own 43 per cent of the area and operate 46 per cent of the land. These farmers face various disadvantages in dealing with the markets and at the same time, the Commission's analysis clearly brings out that government interventions also tend to be less effective with respect to them. The Commission feels that there is need for a focused strategy with respect to marginal and small farmers. Organisationally, such a strategy must focus on group approaches so that the appropriate transaction costs can be reduced and farmers can benefit from economies of scale. The Commission has therefore advocated the setting up of a special programme for marginal and small farmers (Chapter 14). The programme may be used to incentivise the formation of farmers' groups and apex organisations, and facilitate in finding solutions to problems of irrigation, inputs, markets, procurement and risk. Also the risk factor has to be mitigated through appropriate farming strategies as well as adequate insurance. There is a need for insurance instruments that cover for production and also for market risks for all crops to reduce the financial risks and increase viability.

12.48 This Report has clearly brought out the role of the credit situation in the distress of the farmers and agricultural workers. It needs to be noted that the growth in agriculture in the early periods was facilitated by the spread of rural credit institutions and improved access to credit. A step in this direction was the nationalisation of banks in 1969 and making imperative that the banks expand their rural coverage. The RBI also introduced measures for the vulnerable groups such as Scheduled Castes and Scheduled Tribes, as also the small and marginal farmers. The interest rate was regulated. Cooperative banks were also initiated in the area along with the Regional Rural Banks (RRBs) and the Land Development Banks (LDBs). The National Bank for Agriculture and Rural Development (NABARD) was constituted in the early eighties as the apex Development Bank with a mandate for facilitating credit flow for promotion and development of agriculture, small-scale industries, cottage and village industries, handicrafts and other rural crafts. It also has the mandate to support all other allied economic activities in rural areas, promote integrated and sustainable rural development and secure prosperity of rural areas.

12.49 The Commission is concerned that the position of institutional credit with respect to agriculture, and more so, with respect to marginal and small farmers continues to be extremely unsatisfactory. The share of agricultural credit in the Net Bank Credit (NBC) declined from 17 per cent in 1994 to 9 per cent in 2004. The Government is currently seized with the issue of extending affordable credit to the agricultural sector. Banks have been asked to increase credit by 25 per cent each year, and the rate of interest has been pegged at 7 per cent. In areas of high agrarian distress, debt waivers and moratorium on debt waivers have s been declared. A committee under Prof. R. Radhakrishna has been appointed to look into all aspects related to agricultural indebtedness in the areas of high agrarian distress.

12.50 The announcement of Government Policy in 2004 requiring the doubling of agricultural credit in three years, has undoubtedly led to an increase in the volume of credit, but as a percentage of NBC it still stands at a low 11.9 per cent in 2006. As far as marginal and small farmers are concerned, the RBI does not maintain a separate record of their credit off-take but surveys such as the Farmers Survey bring out a dismal picture. The Commission is of the view, that in addition to the steps already taken by the Government and the banking system, a number of other measures need to be initiated on an urgent basis, focusing particularly on the issue of credit availability to marginal and small farmers.

12.51 The Commission has recommended the following four sets of measures as an immediate Action Plan: (1) Separate monitoring of the credit flow to this

The Commission is of the view, that in addition to the steps already taken by the Government and the banking system, a number of other measures need to be initiated on an urgent basis, focusing particularly on the issue of credit availability to marginal and small farmers.

segment of farmers i.e. marginal and small farmers. (2) Change in the priority sector guidelines with a target of 10 per cent needs to be fixed for marginal and small farmers. (3) Measures to increase the outreach of the banking sector in rural areas and in areas of financial exclusion. (4) Measures to extend credit to the 20 - 40 per cent of the marginal and small farmers who are excluded from the formal financial sector due to lack of patta and title deeds. These measures are spelt out in Chapter 14. Apart from them, steps to strengthen and revive the rural banking sector and co-operatives are needed. The efforts of SHGs also need to be encouraged.

12.52 The NCF and the Steering Group on Agriculture have stressed the need to focus on rain-fed and dry-land farming. These and various other committees have also emphasised the role of efficient land and water management. In the Commission's view land and water management is the key to equitable and sustained growth in rural livelihoods. The problems of land and water management as well as solutions to these problems vary from region to region -well irrigated tracts, high rain-fall rain-fed areas, flood prone areas, low rainfall rain-fed areas, etc. These problems affect marginal and small farmers more than the bigger farmers. The Commission is of the view that programmes of land and water management must be significantly upscaled and an accelerated programme of watershed management should be implemented during the 11th Plan. We note that a number of studies have pointed out that the benefit-cost ratio of such a programme is high.

12.53 The Commission also views convergence of watershed development activities with other programmes as an issue of high importance. A number of activities undertaken in the Watershed Development Programme (WDP) pertains to wage employment. These activities can be converged with NREGP and SGRY. Shelves of projects related to water conservation, plantation and afforestation, renovation of the existing water structures, soil conservation and structures dealing with drought should be appropriately linked to the Watershed Development Work Plans at Block level. The Watershed Development Teams should work for convergence of WDPs with NREG activities. Panchayats should be trained to ensure convergence in implementation. The Eleventh Plan has recommended preparation of district plans with activity planning for different levels of the PRIs. Integration of land and water improvement programmes should be ensured in activity mapping and in the district plans.

12.54 The Commission has analysed the acute distress faced by the farmers in some parts of the country. It has also examined the reasons and impact of the crisis on farmers. While these reasons are broadly linked to a number of diverse reasons, their impact has been felt mostly by the marginal and small farmers. The access of these farmers to institutional credit being limited, they are compelled to take recourse to non-institutional sources of credit. Failure to repay these loans on time due to one of the several causes of the crisis leads to tremendous vulnerability of this group of farmers.

12.55 The Government has already initiated a number of measures to alleviate the distress faced by the farmers. With respect to 31 districts, in the four states of Andhra Pradesh, Maharashtra, Karnataka and Kerala, where the incidence of farmers' suicides has been very high, the Government has decided to launch a special rehabilitation package to mitigate the distress of farmers. The package will be implemented over a period of 3 years and includes both immediate and medium term measures. The rehabilitation package aims at establishing a sustainable and viable farming and livelihood support system, crop centric approach to agriculture, assured irrigation facilities, watershed management, better extension and farming support services, improved marketing facilities and subsidiary income opportunities through horticulture, livestock, dairying, fisheries etc. A special package has also been announced for the districts in Vidarbha, which face an agrarian distress. On the credit front, this package consisted of a debt relief package to restructure/reschedule overdue loans, so that the farmers become eligible for fresh loans; waiver of overdue interest on agricultural loans amounting to about Rs. 7 billion, and steps to increase the flow of institutional credit to farmers in these districts. The package will be implemented through a State Level Committee for coordination and supervision, including representatives of the Government of India and the state government, district level committees and PRIs.

12.56 In view of the special problems faced by the marginal and small farmers in the 31 districts, the Commission is of the view that the government should separately monitor the conditions of these farmers, including the implementation of the existing packages and take additional measures for strengthening agriculture and provision of price and income support.

12.57 A major problem in these areas is that since the marginal and small farmers in these areas do not have access to institutional credit, they have to approach informal lenders to meet their credit requirement. They, therefore, have a high burden of debt to these lenders. In order to address this problem, the Kerala Government has set up the Kerala State Farmers' Debt Relief Commission (2007) and the Commission has declared Idukki and Wyanad districts as distress prone districts. This approach is aimed to tackle the debt burden on farmers due to private moneylenders. The Commission recommends that the Central government could support the setting up of State Farmers' Commission's along these lines where required. The Debt Relief Commissions, as part of their award, could also examine and institute measures, which ensure the entitlement of the marginal/ small farmers to institutional credit. These recommendations are spelt out in Chapter 14.

12.58 It is now increasingly clear that the capacity of the agricultural sector to absorb the increasing labour force is limited and there is a need to diversify to other non-farm and off farm employment in rural areas. There is, thus, a clear need to generate more employment opportunities through rural diversification and development of off-farm and non-farm activities. An expanding non-farm sector impacts agricultural wages positively by tightening the rural wage worker market. Poor and socially backward workers also have access to it as it is not a land -based activity. Thus, even when the non-farm activity is low productive and of residual nature, it is still beneficial to the poor, for it acts as a safety-net and prevents further accentuation of poverty (Kundu et. al. 2005). From a gender point of view, it has been observed that non-farm activities which are based on traditional skills and take the form of small-scale cottage industries can be taken up by female labourers within or closer to their homes without disrupting their household chores, and also thus can lessen the gender inequalities as well (Unni and Rani 2005b). Overall the expansion of the non-farm activities helps reduce poverty levels by providing employment outside agriculture at a higher remuneration. A shift of the labour force out of agriculture into the non-agricultural sector can only happen if our growth strategy generates high growth in labour intensive manufacturing and in productive services sectors. Given the limited scope for employment generation in agriculture and the increasing vulnerability of the small and marginal farmers as also of the agricultural labourers in the liberalized scenario, it is imperative that the Government takes initiatives that promote both the expansion of non-farm employment opportunities in the rural areas. It must also take steps to improve the access of these vulnerable groups to these jobs through skill development and improving their capital and human asset base.

Promotional Measures for Expansion of Employment

12.59 The main promotional measures for wage workers fall into three main categories: (1) Measures to provide them with assets either through credit based programmes or through land distribution. (2) Measures to improve their marketable skills. (3) Measures to provide them with employment opportunities through direct employment creation or expansion of employment in the economy.

Land Reform

12.60 There is strong evidence that relatively successful implementation of even a modest package of land reforms dramatically improves the prospect of the poor. Poverty in rural areas is associated with landlessness and comparatively successful, although modest, land reforms, are able to unleash the productive potential of the rural economy and reduce poverty. There is, thus, in our view, a strong continuing case for redistributive land reforms viz. one which improves the access of the rural poor to land through expropriation and distribution of ceiling surplus lands and cultivable wastelands, tenurial reform and better operation of the land-lease market and the land sales market. However, these reforms will succeed in their intent only if supportive policies and institutions are in place, which allows the rural poor to access new technologies and economies of scale in marketing, wherever necessary. Large gains for poor farmers could still ensue if the tenancy market is liberalised, subject to the existing land ceiling and effective regulation to promote long-term tenancies and reasonable rents. The land sales market is very sluggish in poor regions and could be used to promote transfers to the land poor through long-term loans. The updating and computerisation of land records is bound to lower transaction costs in effecting land mutations, but the

There is strong evidence that relatively successful implementation of even a modest package of land reforms dramatically improves the prospect of the poor. Poverty in rural areas is associated with landlessness and comparatively successful, although modest, land reforms, are able to unleash the productive potential of the rural economy and reduce poverty.

specific impact on the poor needs to be investigated in greater detail.

12.61 Gender concerns in land reform have only been highlighted in the last few years. In land distribution programmes, deeds (pattas) are being given in the name of women only or in the joint names of wife and the husband. Priority is also being given to distributing land to widows. Land legislations have been amended in several states to remove the gender bias, but a number of issues remain. Moreover, improving women's access to land and assets is also linked to other cultural norms and practices, which need to be simultaneously addressed. Self-help groups have provided other mechanisms to improve women's access to land (through individual or joint leasing and cultivation of land), which needs to be carefully nurtured.

Self-employment Programmes

12.62 As we have shown in the earlier chapters, more than three-fifths of the unorganised workers in India are self-employed and asset ownership and operation lowers poverty in most cases. Thus, strategies, which promote self-employment and income growth of the self-employed are important components of a pro-poor development strategy in India. Four major schemes launched by the Central Government to facilitate self-employed enterprise development through easing credit flow and other assistance are the Prime Minister's Rojgar Yojana (PMRY) started in 1993, Rural Employment Guarantee Generation Programme (REGP) of the KVIC started in 1995, Swaranjaynati Gram Swarozgar Yojana (SGSY) of the Ministry of Rural Development started in 1999 and the Swaranjaynati Shahari Swarozgar Yojana (SSSY) of the Ministry of Urban employment and Poverty Alleviation since 1997, the latter two being integrated to the previously existing self-employment schemes. These programmes are mainly in the nature of poverty alleviation schemes, with the highest average investment of Rs.50000-65000 per enterprise being available in the PMRY. Some of them follow a group enterprise or the Self-Help Group formation approach to enterprise development. These programmes have made a significant contribution in not only enhancing income levels of the poor but have been helpful in stemming the rural and urban migration of the poor also. During the 10th Plan approximately 1.2 million projects were set up under PMRY and REGP programmes resulting in an additional employment of approximately 41 lakh person years at present. For greater impact of the programmes, it is essential that some rationalization of the various programmes be undertaken urgently. The Ministry of Small of Small and Medium Enterprises (MSME) has recently recommended the merger of the PMRY and the REGP, in order to have a better focus and concentration of efforts for generating employment in the non-farm sector. Further rationalisation that could be considered is to have integrated self-employment programmes for the rural and urban sector respectively, which draw upon the lessons of the existing programmes.

Wage Employment Programmes and NREGA

12.63 Programmes to create direct employment opportunities for wage workers are presently confined to rural wage workers, although they may be extended to urban workers in due course. The problem of employment in rural areas is mainly of seasonal unemployment and underemployment. Thus, the focus of these measures has been generation of supplementary employment opportunities especially during lean periods. Wage employment programmes, have been an important component of the anti-poverty strategy. These provide employment opportunities not only during lean agricultural seasons but also in times of floods, droughts and other natural calamities. These programmes also contribute directly to the creation of durable assets for the community. The rural infrastructure so created is expected to enhance further economic activity. Wage employment programmes also put an upward pressure on the market wage rates by attracting people to public works programmes, thereby reducing labour supply and pushing up demand for labour.

12.64 The National Rural Employment Guarantee Act, 2005 (NREGA) is a major step in the direction of providing assurance and security of employment to rural workers by providing at least one hundred days of guaranteed wage employment in every year to every household whose adult members volunteer to do unskilled manual work. The Act marks a historic step towards

The National Rural Employment Guarantee Act, 2005 (NREGA) is a major step in the direction of providing assurance and security of employment to rural workers by providing at least one hundred days of guaranteed wage employment in every year to every household whose adult members volunteer to do unskilled manual work.

recognising and ensuring work as a right of the people. The programme was launched on February 2006 in 200 districts of India and has been extended to 330 districts a year later. It aims to provide employment through public works, which lead to development of infrastructure, land development, irrigation, and construction. The main aim is the empowerment of labourers by making employment a right and the guarantee of employment an assurance by which the rural workers can demand employment.

12.65 Though it is still too early to assess the success of the Scheme but concurrent studies indicate that there have been mixed but, on the whole, positive results. The Commission is of the view that sufficient experience has been gained in the implementation of the programme to extend it to the remaining districts in the third year itself. Further, in line with the demand driven character of the programme, the Commission recommends that the employment ceiling of 100 days per household should be removed. Admissible administrative charges being low in the programme, states are unduly constrained in administering the programme and in innovating systems of delivery. The Commission is of the view that the administrative charges should be raised to 5 per cent and some part of these charges should be treated as fixed. Some of the other major challenges in improving the performance include: low awareness among the rural population, absence of institutional arrangements though the Gram Panchayats for facilitating the registration of the applications and issuance of job cards, little involvement of the local bodies in the identification of public works, low levels of work application, non-payment of minimum wages and delays in wage payment, and undertaking of unproductive work. Finally, greater transparency, building capacity of the local Panchayats and better local planning are the key to improved performance towards ensuring a good performance and a lasting impact. In view of the significance of the NREG, the Commission has summarized some of its important recommendations with respect to the programme in Chapter 14.

Skill Training

12.66 Skill development programmes have been undertaken at various levels and by a number of organizations. At the level of the Central Government, at present, around 24 ministries/ departments are organizing or funding skill development programmes. The main ministries are the Ministry of Human Resource Development and the Ministry of Labour and Employment. Most of the initiatives by other ministries/ departments are sectoral in nature and target-group oriented. Moreover, many state governments are also running programmes for skill development. Numerous non-governmental organizations (NGOs)/industry organizations are also providing training to various segments of the workforce. A number of private institutions have also entered the training arena. The main programmes organized and/or funded by the Central ministries/ departments are presented in Appendix Table A12.2.

12.67 The two flagship schemes of DGE&T under Ministry of Labour and Employment are the Craftsmen Training Scheme (CTS) and the Apprenticeship Training Scheme (ATS). The CTS provides institutional training whereas ATS is a combination of institutional as well as on the job training in which trainees are exposed to real life industrial environment.

12.68 As in other spheres, a large number of NGOs are involved in the initiatives geared towards enhancing the skill base of the labour force to enable them to earn better wages. While some NGOs provide only basic or upgraded skills and then leave the trainees to seek wage employment or start their own enterprise, a large number of NGOs attempt to provide a package of skills , basic entrepreneurship training and assistance availing credit facilities etc. Some NGOs even `handhold' the trainees for certain period till they are able to stand independently. A study by Educational Consultants India Ltd. for the World Bank in 2003 covered more significant providers of such facilities in eight states. The study showed that the size of non-public training market is small. About 8 - 10 lakh individuals were likely to have been enrolled in these institutions nationally. Majority of the students enrolled are in non-engineering and IT related trades. Most of these institutions are financed by fees. About 20 per cent, mostly NGOs, were dependent on Govt. as the major source of revenue. Moreover, a large proportion of the private providers are not accredited.

12.69 As per the NSSO 61st Round of the persons of age 15-29 years, about 1 per cent was receiving formal vocational training in 2004-05, about 2 per cent have received formal vocational training and another 8 per cent have received non-formal vocational training. The

The Commission is of the view that sufficient experience has been gained in the implementation of the NREGP to extend it to the remaining districts in the third year itself.

proportion was lower in the case of females than the males in both the rural and urban areas. Moreover, as expected, the proportion was higher in the urban areas than in the rural areas.

12.70 The formal vocational training system is basically geared to catering to the needs of the organized sector. At present, there is no structured way in which skills are imparted to the workers in the informal sector. Typically, skills are handed down from one generation to the next. The formal training system is not suited to cater to the less educated persons because of, among others, its educational entry requirements and the long duration of the training courses. Many of the schemes for skill formation operated by the government agencies at different levels focus on the organized sector and are for 8th or 10th standard pass workers. Hence a major initiative is urgently required at the national level for upgrading the skills in a more structured manner, with particular emphasis on those who do not possess the entry level educational qualifications required for the existing schemes.

12.71 The DGE&T under Ministry of Labour and Employment has established the Modular Employable Skills (MES) system of training, testing and certification under the Skill Development Initiative (SDI) of the Govt. of India in a Public Private Partnership mode. The Initiative aims at skilling and certification of one million persons over a period of five years and thereafter one million every year. Under MES course, curricula are prepared in consultation with concerned industries and trade experts. Training could be provided by any training/ educational institute, industry etc. with flexible delivery mechanism (part time, weekends, full time, onsite/offsite) to suit the needs of various target groups. ITIs/ITCs can also run short-term courses by the optimal utilization of the infrastructure available with them. Testing for National Certification is done by professional bodies/ industry associations jointly with the respective state directorates. The cost of the SDI is estimated at Rs. 5000 per worker.

12.72 The initiatives to be planned under the public private partnership model must keep in mind the vast scale on which training facilities are required in the country. A number of training programmes are being undertaken with innovative features by the NGOs / industry organizations. However, these are generally confined to small areas and train in small numbers. The issue of scalability of many of these initiatives need to be addressed thoroughly. As emphasized by the Draft Approach Paper to the Eleventh Plan, vocational training needs to be expanded from the present capacity of a mere 2 -3 million to 15 million new entrants to the labour force. While India has 5000 ITIs and 7000 Vocational Schools, China has about 5, 00,000 Secondary Vocational Schools. Moreover, the number of skills for which training is provided also needs to be expanded to include new skills. ITIs in India typically cater to around 40 skills compared to 4000 in China. Another aspect, which has to be kept in mind while formulating strategy for training of informal workers through public private partnership model is the opportunity cost of training to them. A worker in the informal sector would be engaged in some activity or the other for sheer sustenance. Training programmes will either have to be organized during non-working hours or the workers to be trained will have to be compensated for their loss of earnings during the training period.

12.73 The Commission is currently preparing a report on skill development of unorganised workers, which would place emphasis on providing marketable skills to those workers who have not been able to successfully complete their middle or secondary education (or who have just completed but without any acquired skills) with a view to increasing their employability. The focus of the programmes recommended by the Commission would be on semi-urban / smaller towns which have relatively less training facilities. The initiative would take into account the best practices from many successful schemes in this field being already undertaken by NGOs / industry associations in various parts of the country. It would also draw upon the experiences of other countries, which have already passed through or are passing through a similar stage of development. It would be a public-private partnership aiming to make fullest possible use of the existing infrastructure so as to get the maximum leverage out of the available resources. The aim would be to cover the target group in five years' time. At present, the Commission

The Commission has proposed an on-the-job training-cum-employment assurance programme for workers who are trained or certified under the Ministry of Labour's SDI. The programme, which will be dovetailed with the SDI would provide for on-the-job training for workers for a year, with a wage/cost subsidy of Rs. 5000 being given to the employer at the end of the period.

has proposed an on-the-job training-cum-employment assurance programme for workers who are trained or certified under the Ministry of Labour's SDI. The programme, which will be dovetailed with the SDI would provide for on-the-job training for workers for a year, with a wage/cost subsidy of Rs. 5000 being given to the employer at the end of the period. The objective is to link the SDI with the strengthening of training and job induction, thereby making the training programme more relevant for the workers. The contours of the programme are spelt out in the Action Programme proposed in Chapter 14 of this Report.

Institutional Support for Protection and Promotion of Livelihoods

12.74 The Commission is of the view that at present there is no apex institution or focal point in the country or in the states, which can take a holistic view of developments related to the informal sector of the economy. The Commission's finding is also that there is a lack of coordination between different agencies responsible for interventions to promote livelihoods for the unorganised sector. This Commission therefore recommends that the Government create a focal point for the protection and promotion of livelihoods in the unorganised sector either within the Planning Commission or outside it in the form of a National Livelihood Council chaired by the Prime Minister or her/his nominee. Similar focal points may also be created at the state level. These focal points will have the following main functions:

(a) Review of the existing policies and programmes that have an impact on the sector with a view to ensure that such policies factor in the livelihood concerns of the workers in the sector.

(b) Identification of programmes and measures for livelihood promotion and the growth of unorganized sector enterprises, including skill development, marketing support, organizational support, credit support etc.

(c) Ensuring better coordination between different ministries, departments and agencies involved in the growth of the unorganized sector.

12.75 The Commission has also recommended the creation of the National and State Boards for unorganized agricultural and non-agricultural workers in the two comprehensive Bills (see Chapter 13 and the proposed Bills). The primary purpose of these Boards will be to frame, and implement social security programmes. These Boards have also been given a wider role in reviewing the conditions of workers, taking steps to protect their working conditions and to improve their welfare and livelihoods.

12.76 Since the maximum synergy from the existing activities can be achieved at the district level where the local bodies (both the urban bodies and the three tier rural PRIs) are increasingly playing an important role, and the planning efforts are being synthesized through the District Planning Committees (DPCs), the Commission also recommends that the creation of the Standing Committees for Livelihood Promotion be mandated in all the local governments. The aim of these committees will be to prepare plans and schemes, with the co-operation of all the stakeholders, which will encourage group formation, promote livelihoods, and ensure convergence of all activities at the local level to create sustainable livelihood structure. The Committees will also review the impact of all such activities on the creation of livelihoods, with special focus on the poor, on SCs/STs and the socially marginal groups, and on women. At the district level, the CEO of the Zilla Parishad may be the convener of the Standing Committee.

12.77 The Department of Panchayati Raj has already prepared an ambitious plan for capacity building of the panchayats and augmentation of their local planning capacity. These are a large component of the activities planned under the Backward Region Grant Fund (BRGF). It is recommended that the creation and promotion of sustainable livelihoods be treated as a central objective in the activity planning envisaged for the creation of the local plans.

Conclusion

12.78 The current economic environment is one, which promotes informalisation -of enterprises and of workers- both in the national sphere and also internationally. Further, liberalisation and globalisation have accentuated the risks and vulnerability faced by the unorganised

The Commission is of the view that at present there is no apex institution or focal point in the country or in the states, which can take a holistic view of developments related to the informal sector of the economy.

enterprises and workers. The policy framework is often discriminatory in effect and the laws/regulations are biased in favour of large producers and the well-off, while impacting negatively on the livelihoods of the poorer unorganised workers.

12.79 There is undoubtedly in existence a broad framework of promotional policies within which the Government has attempted to improve the livelihoods of the unorganised workers. It has also set up very elaborate paraphernalia to implement these policies and programmes. However, in spite of all these efforts, the reach has been very limited and a large segment of the self-employed remains engaged with enterprises that have very low returns. In fact, with economic reforms there has been a hand-off policy towards regulation of the enterprises and the mainstream institutions such as the RBI have been following a policy, which further pushes the smaller among the unorganised enterprises into the market to fend for themselves.

12.80 While India has one the most elaborate institutional and policy frameworks for the growth of the enterprises in the unorganised sector, the sectoral initiatives are disparate and piecemeal. Moreover, many elements of this framework have been discarded in recent years. Economic reforms and globalisation have focused on the centrality of the market-based instruments. Due to the presence of economies of scale, these instruments favour the large organised sector in the pricing and allocation of resources, although the share of the unorganised sector, and even more particularly of the unorganised workers, in total employment continues to increase. Policy changes in the period of globalisation have in fact reduced the unorganised sector's access to assets and resources, reducing the returns and increasing their vulnerability.

12.81 That the unorganised sector has a central place in the Indian economy - certainly in terms of employment, but also in terms of output - is often lost sight of. However, the Eleventh Plan has now accepted that the entire burden of employment creation in the next few years will be on the unorganised sector. Moreover the Plan has accepted that labour productivity in this sector needs to increase at an annual rate of 4 per cent and this would require consistent support to this sector through capital deepening and many other measures.

12.82 Given these imperatives, and the scenario depicted in the earlier chapters, the institutional arrangements, which will oversee the development of this sector need to be strengthened. A number of other steps are also required to accelerate the growth of productivity of the unorganised non-agricultural sector and of marginal-small holdings in agriculture. The objective of these measures must be to increase employment and incomes of the unorganised workers. As outlined earlier and also in this Chapter, the Commission is preparing detailed reports on several aspects relating to the unorganised sector. At the same time, based on the examination of issues in this Report, the Commission is recommending (in chapter 14) an immediate Action Plan for the unorganised sector.

Policy changes in the period of globalisation have in fact reduced the unorganised sector's access to assets and resources, reducing the returns and increasing their vulnerability.

13 Recommendations on Legislative Protection for Minimum Conditions of Work and Comprehensive Legislation

Introduction

13.1 In the earlier chapters, we have analysed the workers' conditions in the unorganised sector in India. We had observed that, for those workers who are not the self-employed, there are some minimum standards of work being regulated in a large number of countries across the world. We have also examined the regulation of the workers' conditions in the unorganised sector in India and discussed the laws that apply to wage workers in the unorganised sector, fully or partially. The Commission has concluded that the existing laws cover the basic conditions of work of unorganised workers in a piece-meal and inadequate manner.

13.2 Further, focused attention is clearly required to enhance the earnings and livelihoods of these workers. We have considered the large number of initiatives that already exist to achieve this. However, the Commission does not find the present scope of policies and programmes adequate to protect and promote the livelihoods of these workers. Indeed, several of the recent changes made it more difficult for the unorganised workers in many sectors and locations to eke out a living and for the unorganised enterprises to survive and grow. This Commission views the protection and promotion of livelihoods as essential for ensuring decent conditions of work to the unorganised sector workers.

13.3 In this Chapter we have examined the findings of the earlier Commissions and made a number of recommendations relating to various dimensions of the conditions of work. We have also recommended two comprehensive legislations for unorganised agricultural and non-agricultural workers, combining all aspects of the conditions of work, including social security.

A Review of the Principal Recommendations of the Earlier Commissions

13.4 The First National Commission on Labour (FNCL 1969) under the Chairmanship of Justice P. B. Gajendragadkar submitted its Report in 1969. The FNCL (1969) devoted its attention to labour in the unorganised sector. The main recommendations of the Gajendragadkar Commission included:

a) First hand detailed surveys from time to time to understand the problems of different categories of unorganised labour.

b) Legislative protection by the state for unorganised/ unprotected labour.

c) Simplification of legislative and administrative procedures applicable to small establishments.

d) Expediting education and organization in the field of unorganised labour.

e) Reinforcement and strengthening of the inspection system as there is no alternative to the existing implementation machinery

f) Steps for the protection of workers against middlemen, and development of self-help through co-operatives. Co-operatives should pay adequate wages and bonus, and give employment opportunities to the underemployed and unemployed among them (pp.434-35).

13.5 The National Commission on Self-employed Women and Women Workers (NCSEW) in the Informal Sector (GOI 1988), under the Chairpersonship of Smt. Ela Bhatt submitted its Report in 1988. The NCSEW recommended enlargement of the definition of work done by women to include all paid and unpaid activities performed within the home or outside as an employee or on own account.

13.6 According to the NCSEW the single most important intervention towards improving the economic status of poor women working in the informal sector of the economy would be to devise strategies, which would enhance their ownership and control over productive assets.

13.7 The NCSEW noted the flagrant violation of statutory provisions regarding payment of wages, safety regulations, provision of housing and medical facilities, accident compensation and so on. It felt the need for more stringent observance of the existing labour laws and the introduction of deterrent penalty clauses. The NCSEW recommended simplification of judicial procedures, particularly to enable unorganised workers to obtain legal redress without undue harassment.

13.8 For domestic workers, the NCSEW recommended the introduction of a system of registration. It felt that, in view of the existing trends of exploitation, it was extremely important to fix a minimum wage, and to legislate on to regulate conditions of employment, social security and security of employment.

13.9 The NCSEW observed that the rates of minimum wages are low and have to be increased keeping in view the requirements of the woman worker and her family. Piece-rates must be so fixed as to enable women workers to earn for 8 hours of work a wage equal to the time-rated Minimum Wage. Where the work is carried out at home due to which the employer saves on installation cost and equipment, an additional amount at 25 per cent of the Minimum Wage should be paid. There should also be a national or regional Minimum Wage. Despite the Equal Remuneration Act 1976, wage discrimination is widely prevalent. This must be corrected through better enforcement and wider dissemination of the law. The NCSEW concluded that there was a tendency to classify the tasks generally done by women as those of a slightly inferior nature. It recommended that this should be corrected, and one way of doing this was to broad base into a single category the activities requiring work of a similar nature.

13.10 The NCSEW recommended the setting up of an Equal Opportunities Commission under a Central law, and also that such a Commission should have wide powers of investigation, direction, advice and monitoring.

13.11 It further recommended the establishment of Tripartite Boards, as no law, however well conceived, would benefit women workers unless they had a major hand in the implementation of the laws. The Tripartite Boards have to be constituted in such a manner that workers have as many representatives as the government and the employers. The Tripartite Boards will regulate implementation of the legislation and also contribute to making women workers visible, and empower them to be equal partners and participants in the production process.

13.12 Another recommendation of the NCSEW was that a separate wing should be set up in the Labour Department for unorganised workers with adequate number of women employees at various places.

13.13 The NCSEW also felt that no solution to the problems of women at work would be complete without taking into account their reproductive functions, which can be effectively facilitated through maternity benefit and childcare. Maternity benefits, on the scale provided under the Maternity Benefit Act, should be universally available to all women. The responsibility for this should be borne by all employers, irrespective of whether or not they employed women, through a levy calculated as a percentage of the wage bill, and placed in a separate fund from which maternity benefit could be provided. In the case of a large number of women like homeworkers and others, where the employer is not identifiable, the responsibility for providing maternity benefits must lie with the state governments.

13.14 The NCSEW noted that though childcare facilities were provided in various labour laws, these were not being implemented, and had in fact led to the retrenchment of women workers since the employers wanted to avoid the statutory responsibilities the law imposed. Hence, it was necessary to introduce an extended system of childcare throughout the country to reduce the burden on women and to facilitate the all round development of the child.

13.15 The NCSEW emphasized the need for regulating working hours in the informal sector where there is considerable exploitation of the poor. It recommended that piece-rates be converted into daily wages based on the normal quantum of work completed at a healthy pace, and that health insurance including compensation for accidents should be available to women workers. Every workplace had to assure safety to the workers. It recommended that a comprehensive law on health and safety be formulated and enacted.

13.16 The National Commission on Rural Labour (NCRL) was appointed in 1987 "to look into the working conditions of this vulnerable section of our society and the implementation of social legislation for their protection". The NCRL submitted its Report in 1991. The NCRL (1991) recommended a multi-dimensional strategy to lift rural labourers out of poverty. This included creation of an infrastructure to improve productivity and employment; enforcement of minimum wages and social security; introduction of central legislation for agricultural labour to provide security of employment, prescribed hours of work, payment of prescribed wages and a machinery for dispute settlement; introduction of a system of registration and to provide identity cards to these workers; and the creation of a welfare fund to be set up with employers' contributions in the form of a cess on land, and a nominal contribution from agricultural labour.

13.17 The NCRL (1991) made specific recommendations for various categories of workers, including from handlooms beedi making, construction, brick-kilns, toddy tapping, fisheries, leather and also the sweepers, boned labourers and migrant labourers. It recommended a change in the Beedi Cigar Workers Act 1966, in order to establish unambiguously the employer-employee relationship in the case of homeworkers. It also suggested some changes in the existing Inter State Migrant Workmen (Regulation of Employment and Conditions of Service) Act, 1979 (ISMW). It recommended that the definition of migrant workmen should be expanded to cover all migrants, whether they came on their own or through the contractors, or changed the contractors after entering a recipient state. Amendments should be made to allow third parties to file complaints. The liability of the principal employer should be defined more clearly to prevent him from escaping the liability. The contractor should be made liable for the breach of the Act either by him or by the subcontractor.

13.18 The NCRL (1991) also recommended a minimum wage of Rs. 20 per day at 1990 prices as the subsistence wage, below which no employment should be allowed anywhere in the country.

13.19 The Second National Commission of Labour (SNCL), which submitted its Report in 2002, made a number of significant recommendations on reform and simplification of labour laws in the country. It recommended the grouping of laws into five broad categories and new legislation to cover workers in industries employing twenty or more workers.

13.20 The SNCL (2002) was specifically asked to make recommendations on an umbrella legislation for the unorganised sector workers and it made a specific proposal in this regard, the details of which we discuss below.

13.21 Thus, the earlier Commissions have tended to view the regulation of conditions of work and the protection and promotion of livelihoods in an integrated framework. This is also the approach of this Commission.

Comprehensive Legislation: Earlier Views

13.22 In the preceding chapters, the Commission has brought out the lack of comprehensive legal protection to the minimum conditions of work for unorganised sector workers. It is also clear that voluntary efforts to ensure minimum conditions of work can, at best, supplement the primary efforts by the state to ensure these conditions.

13.23 The approach towards ensuring minimum conditions of work through legislation can follow one of the three possible approaches viz. (i) extension of the coverage of existing laws to the unorganised sector; (ii) provision of a comprehensive legislation, replacing the existing laws, to cover the unorganised sector; and (iii) provision of a comprehensive legislation which extends protection to the unprotected/unorganised worker, and which provides a universal minimum working conditions, but which allows them to secure better working conditions through the existing laws. In the discussion that follows, we note that all the three approaches were under consideration from time to time.

13.24 In the 37th session of the Labour Ministers Conference in 1987, the general view was that the problem was not of the lack of Central legislation, but of the implementation of the existing laws such as the Minimum Wages Act, the Equal Remunerations Act and such other laws as are applicable to the unorganised sector workers including those in agriculture. However, since then, the issue of a new and separate regulation for workers in the unorganised sector has been discussed and consistently recommended by successive sessions of the Labour Ministers' Conference, and the Indian Labour Conference, and also by various commissions and committees.

13.25 We have earlier noted that whereas the NCSEW favoured simplification of the existing laws and strengthening of the tri-partite structure of implementation, the NCRL (1991) had recommended a Central legislation for agricultural workers.

13.26 Following the recommendations of the NCRL (1991), the Ministry of Labour and Employment (MOLE) proposed a comprehensive legislation for regulation of employment, conditions of service and for the provision of welfare measures for agricultural workers in 1997. The Bill contained provisions for regulation of conditions of work, welfare, and social security. The definition of agricultural workers covered wage workers only. For carrying out the welfare provisions, the Bill provided for registration of labourers and issue of identity cards and the constitution of Agricultural Welfare Boards. The provisions with respect to regulation of the conditions of work included those of hours of work, overtime rates, payment of prescribed wages, continuity of employment, childcare facilities, safety measures as prescribed. It also prohibited unfair labour practices which interfered with the rights of agricultural workers to enrol or continue as union members, discriminating against, restraining, or coercing any agricultural worker because of trade union activity, and victimizing any agricultural worker. For dispute resolution, the Bill provided for a three-tier structure with conciliation officers for mediating in and promoting the settlement of agricultural disputes, appointment of arbitrators at second level and appellate authorities at the third level.

13.27 The SNCL (2002) was specifically asked to examine the issue of comprehensive legislation for unorganised sector workers. The SNCL (2002) proposed an Act to consolidate and amend the laws relating to the regulation of employment and workers' welfare in the unorganised sector in India and to provide for protection and social security to these workers. The comprehensive legislation proposed by the SNCL (2002) was, thus, intended to cover social security and welfare, regulation of employment and conditions of work, as well as promotion of livelihoods. The legislation was intended to cover employments, both in the agricultural and non-agricultural sectors, which were to be listed in the Schedule appended to the proposed Act.

13.28 The essence of the proposed umbrella legislation was the removal of poverty among India's working population through improving their productivity, quality of work, enhancing income earning abilities and increasing their bargaining power. Its aim was to improve the quality of employment, provide a decent life to the workers and integrate them with the growing opportunities in the country. The basic approach of the legislation is the recognition and protection for all types of unorganised sector workers regardless of industry, occupation, work status, and personal characteristics.

13.29 The provisions covered by the umbrella legislation included social security, health and safety, working hours, holidays, prohibition of child labour, workers' right to access the common natural resources to develop and increase the productivity through work, traditional rights related to work and space, protection from unfair labour practices, retrenchment without a reasonable cause, education, and training and skill development. The proposed legislation also recommended record maintenance such as a register of workers employed, muster roll-cum-wage-payment register and wage slips to be issued to the workers with the seal of the employer. The SNCL (2002) recommended that the umbrella legislation should be integrated into the existing laws, policies and schemes that basically control the economies of these sectors to be more effective.

13.30 The SNCL (2002) proposed a Central Board at the Centre and State Boards at the state levels for the administration of the Act. It recommended employment based Boards at the state levels. It has also recommended the district level Boards and Worker Facilitation Centres (WFCs) at lower levels. The State Boards (SB) were vested with the responsibility of arbitration in disputes between the employers and workers' organisations, if agreed by the parties and conciliate and arbitrate in disputes pertaining to the use of common property resources by the workers in the event of the matter being brought before it by one or more District Boards. The SB also had the responsibility to ensure payment of minimum wages to workers as prescribed under the law by the Central or the state governments and also ensure timely payment of dues of such workers. In relation to the self- employed workers, the SB was to take suitable measures to ensure that they earn fair incomes, receive benefits of social security, training, and other development services, facilitate a support system that provide access to financial services, market infrastructure, and infrastructure like power, roads, warehousing, workplace, information and skill development interlinked in a holistic way. The District Boards had the responsibility to ensure implementation of the Act and other relevant labour legislations; conciliate or arbitrate in disputes pertaining to common property resources in the event of such matter being brought before it by one or more WFCs. The WFC had the responsibility to resolve any dispute arising out of the employment relating to wages and working conditions through tripartite or multipartite conciliation. In the case of failure of conciliation, WFCs should undertake arbitration to facilitate speedy resolution of disputes. They may also take the help of Lok Adalats or Labour Courts.

13.31 No separate grievance redressal mechanism was suggested in the draft Bill by the SNCL (2002). However, the Board was to encourage the parties to settle their issues and disputes relating to wages and conditions of work peacefully by bi-partite or multi-partite negotiations. The Labour Court or Lok Adalat having jurisdiction over that area shall be empowered to hear disputes and try offences under this Act. The State Government shall constitute the concerned Appellate Authority for the above matters.

13.32 As a follow up to the SNCL (2002) recommendations, the MOLE also proposed a comprehensive legislation for regulation of employment and conditions of service of unorganised sector workers and to provide for their safety, social security, health and welfare (The Unorganised Sector Workers Bill, 2004, was subsequently also revised by the Ministry in 2005). This Draft Bill drew upon the recommendations of the SNCL (2002) and covered both wage workers as well as self-employed workers, in all the sectors. However, only workers in scheduled employments were proposed for coverage. The Bill provided for schemes of social welfare to be funded through contributions by governments and workers and their implementation through Workers Facilitation Centres (WFCs) and State/Central Welfare Boards. The Bill also has provisions for minimum conditions of work, including an eight hours work-day with half an hour break, overtime at the rate of twice his ordinary rate of wages; and payment of wages at prescribed rates not less than the Statutory Minimum Wages. No separate dispute resolution mechanism was provided in the Draft Bill.

13.33 Another comprehensive legislation for regulation of employment, conditions of service, and provision of welfare measures of agricultural workers has been made in a private member's Bill (Hannan Mollah 2001). The definition, coverage and the main provisions of the Bill are broadly similar to the MOLE Bill (1997). It, however, proposes a system of enforcement by inspectors and a two- tier dispute resolution structure consisting of the conciliation machinery and an agricultural tribunal.

13.34 Two Bills proposing comprehensive legislation for regulation of employment and conditions of service, social security and welfare of unorganised sector workers have also been proposed by the National Centre for Labour and the National Campaign Committee for Unorganised Sector Workers in 2005. The Bills cover wage workers, home-based and out-workers duly registered under the Act but do not include those in agriculture, plantations, sericulture, horticulture, poultry farming, animal husbandry and also allied workers and the persons employed in factories and mines. The Bill provide for the right to livelihood including the right over common properties and natural resources. They also include provisions for regulation of working conditions, provide for continuity of employment, bonus and social security, non-discrimination, and provisions against harassment of women workers. They also provide for the right to have a uniform social security card; occupational and other safety measures; vocational training and guidance, and ensuring special protection for migrant workers. The tri-partite Boards formed under the proposed Act will be responsible for its administration. Enforcement will be through a system of inspections and trade unions will be vested with powers of inspectors. For dispute resolution, the Bill provides for Dispute Resolution Councils and appellate authorities.

13.35 The comprehensive Bill formulated by the Ministry of Labour and Employment, was forwarded to this Commission for review and comments. The National Advisory Council of the Government formulated a stand alone Bill on social security for unorganised sector workers which was also forwarded to this Commission for review.

The Commission deliberated on the issues of social security, conditions of work and livelihoods, and prepared two separate Draft Bills on social security and conditions of work, which were circulated for feedback.

13.36 These Bills, along with the Bills prepared earlier by the Ministry of Labour and the National Advisory Council were considered in the 40th Indian Labour Conference, which is the main tri-partite consultative forum, in its meeting held in December 2005. The Conference suggested that the NCEUS Draft Bill be used as a basis for further discussions. It, however, suggested that social security and conditions of work be integrated in the same Bill and that separate Bills be formulated for agricultural and non-agricultural workers.

13.37 The Commission considered the views of the ILC, along with the views and feedbacks from the other stakeholders and the states. In May 2006, the Commission finalised its report on social security and its recommendations on a Bill and a National Social Security Scheme to which all unorganised workers would be eligible within a period of five years. It may be noted that the Commission submitted a standalone proposal on social security at this stage because it considered that such a proposal would be institutionally feasible and implementation could begin within a short period of time.

13.38 The Commission's proposal on social security has been considered by the Ministry of Labour and Employment and by the Cabinet. The views of the Ministry and the Government have been summarised in the Ministry's report to the 41st ILC held in April 2007.

Comprehensive Legislations for Agricultural and Non-agricultural Workers

13.39 The preceding discussion shows that there has been a growing consensus on the need for a comprehensive legislation. There is some agreement among the stakeholders that the new law needs to have a different implementation mechanism involving tripartite regulatory bodies and having inbuilt systems of self-regulation. There is also some consensus that the needs of the agricultural and non-agricultural workers with regard to their working conditions are very different and that the proposed Bill should address the needs of agricultural and non-agricultural workers separately either within the same Bill or in two distinct Bills, one each for agriculture and non-agricultural sectors.

13.40 The Commission has examined these proposals in the light of its own findings on the conditions of unorganised sector workers, and its analysis of the existing state of regulation of conditions of work, as well as protection and promotion of livelihood of the workers in the sector as a whole. It is noted that the existing proposals differ in scope, coverage and institutional mechanisms. The general scope of these proposals extends to working conditions, social security and welfare, and protection and promotion of livelihoods. The coverage of these proposals varies in as much as some of them are confined only to agricultural wage workers. While some cover both wage workers and the self-employed in the non-agricultural unorganised sector only, others encompass all workers in both the agricultural and non-agricultural sectors. Further, the coverage may also be confined to listed Schedules of employment.

13.41 The Commission concurs with the need for a comprehensive legislation for the unorganised sector. With regard to social security, the Commission has already recommended a National Minimum Social Security Scheme for all unorganised sector workers, which can be added upon by the states, and has suggested Draft legislation. Issues contained therein are already under consideration by the Government. The Commission therefore proposed a legislative framework to ensure minimum conditions of work for all the unorganised workers, with special attention being given to the special needs of vulnerable sections of the unorganised workers (women, migrants, and homeworkers). However, given the differences between agricultural and non-agricultural workers, the Commission recommended two separate Bills (for the agricultural and non-agricultural workers). Part 1 of these Bills related to the conditions of work. The Commission also made recommendations with respect to livelihood promotion in Part 2 of the Bills. These two Draft Bills were publicised by the Commission in February 2007, and a series of state, regional and national level consultations were held with all the stakeholders on the contents of these Bills. In particular, two national consultations were held with Central Trade Unions and other national organisations representing unorganised sector workers. A number of views emerged in these consultations, which have been helpful in finalising these Bills. Views received by the Commission have also been appended to this Report.

13.42 Two main views emerged, however, which had a bearing on the structure of the Draft Bills as prepared by the Commission in February 2007. First, it was argued by the trade unions and national organisations that, although they welcomed the Commission's proposals, the Indian Labour Conference (40th Session) had resolved for composite Bills incorporating both social security and conditions or work proposals. Second, a number of responses stated that the Commission's proposals on livelihood promotion could be dealt more appropriately through the recommendation of policies or programmes, rather than through legislation.

13.43 The Commission deliberated at length on these two issues. With respect to the first, while the Commission could have left it to the Government to synthesise the two proposals if it so desired, the Commission felt that it could itself combine the earlier proposal on social security with those on the conditions of work in to two separate Bills for agricultural and non-agricultural workers. As far as the Government was concerned, nothing would be altered as far as the social security proposals of the NCEUS were concerned. But the synthesised Bills would be in line with the tri-partite conclusions and would, therefore, have greater acceptability among the stake-holders. Further, it was felt that the new synthesised Draft Bill for agricultural workers would be more in line with the commitment of the UPA government to a comprehensive protective legislation for agricultural workers in its Common Minimum Programme. For these reasons, the legislative content of the social security proposals have been incorporated in the two final Bills.

13.44 As regard the second issue, the Commission has given some responsibility for welfare and livelihood promotion to the Social Security and Welfare Boards proposed in the final draft of the Bills. However, the principal recommendations of the Commission with respect to livelihood promotion are now being suggested outside of the proposed legislative framework and are summarised in the form of an Action Plan in Chapter 14.

Need for Separate Bills

13.45 The Commission has proposed two draft Bills regarding the conditions of work and social security. These are the Agricultural Workers' Conditions of Work and Social Security Bill, 2007 (hereafter referred to as AWB), and the Unorganised Non-agricultural Workers Conditions of Work and Social Security Bill, 2007 (hereafter referred to as NAWB). The first Bill (AWB) is applicable to the unorganised agricultural workers (all agricultural wage workers excluding those eligible for protection under the Plantation Workers Act, and all marginal and small farmers). The second Bill (NAWB) is applicable to the unorganised non-agricultural workers in the unorganised sector as well as unorganised workers in the organised sector who are not protected by existing laws applicable to that sector, subject to an income ceiling. Although most of the conditions of work specified under the Agricultural Workers Bill and the Unorganised Non-agricultural Workers Bill are similar, the two separate Bills have been provided to take care of the specific issues being faced by the two different sets of workers. The working conditions differ and separate sets of measures have been proposed wherever considered necessary. Further, in some states like Tamil Nadu, the present machinery for enforcement of labour laws for agricultural and non-agricultural workers is different. The laws relating to non-agricultural workers are enforced by the Labour Department whereas for non-agricultural workers enforcement is carried out by the Revenue Department or by another separate machinery. For this reason, the two Bills prescribe different provisions for the dispute resolution machinery in the agricultural and non-agricultural sectors.

13.46 As discussed above, each of the Bills incorporate provisions for regulation of conditions of work and social security. Chapter II of the Bills deals with conditions of work of the unorganised non-agricultural and agricultural workers respectively. Chapters III - VIII of the Bills relate

Two Draft Bills proposed for
- *Agricultural Workers*
- *Non-agricultural Workers in the Unorganised Sector*

Each Draft Bill comprises nine chapters. Apart from the preliminary matters, these chapters deal with: (1) Regulation of Conditions of Work; (2) Social Security Benefits; (3) the National Social Security Fund; (4) the National Social Security and Welfare Board; (5) the State Social Security and Welfare Boards; (6) Registration of Workers; (7) Delivery of Benefits; and (8) Enforcement and Dispute Resolution.

to Social Security, Constitution of the Social Security Funds, Constitution, Powers and Functions of the National and State Social Security and Welfare Boards, and provisions for registration and implementation of the Scheme. The provisions with respect to the National Social Security Scheme, the National Social Security Fund and the National Social Security and Welfare Boards are identical in the two Bills and are based on the earlier proposals of the Commission to the Government. The Dispute Resolution Mechanism for settlement of disputes arising due to non- observance of the provisions relating to conditions of work is specified in Chapter IX of the respective Acts.

Main Recommendations Relating to Conditions of Work

13.47 Some of the main recommendations (covered by the Bills) are discussed below. We also discuss those recommendations, which are not part of the proposed Bills.

13.48 The Commission is well aware that there are a number of laws, which are partly applicable to the unorganised workers. However, their domain is restricted either in terms of coverage of the unorganised workers or in terms of the benefits provided by those laws. Hence, the Commission has offered a framework that provides for minimum conditions of work to all unorganised workers. The proposed law will, however, not affect the application of any other State or Central Acts which apply to the unorganised worker, and if under any existing law, the unorganised agricultural/ non-agricultural worker is eligible for superior or better benefits, he shall continue to be entitled for such superior benefits provided under those Acts. Further, as the entitlements as provided for in the Act are bare minimum, a wage worker can enter into an agreement with his/her employer for granting him/her rights or privileges in respect of any matter which are more favourable to him/ her than those to which he/she would be entitled to under this Act.[1]

13.49 The conditions of work which are prescribed for both the agricultural and non-agricultural unorganised wage workers include an eight-hour working day with at least half-hour break, one paid day of rest per week, a national minimum wage for employments not notified under the state's Minimum Wages Act, piece-rate wages to equal time-rated wages, employments specifically done by women to be brought on par with employment certified as equivalent, due payment of wages in time the failure of which would attract penal interest, no deduction of wages in the form of fines, right to organise, non-discrimination on the basis of gender, social origin, incidence of HIV AIDS and place or origin; provision of adequate safety equipment, compensation for accident, protection from sexual harassment, provision of child care; provision of basic amenities at the workplace etc.[2]

National Minimum Wage

13.50 The Constitution of India envisages a just and humane society and accordingly gives place to the concept of living wage in the Chapter on Directive Principles of State Policy Wages in the organized sector

Salient Features of Conditions of Work Proposals

- *Eight-hour working day with half-hour break*
- *One paid day of rest per week*
- *National Minimum Wage for all employments not in the Minimum Wages Act.*
- *Piece-rate wage to equal time rate wage*
- *Women's work to be remunerated on par*
- *Deferred payment of wages attract penal interest*
- *Deductions in wages attract fines*
- *Right to organise*
- *Non-discrimination*
- *Safety equipment and compensation for accident*
- *Protection from sexual harassment*
- *Provision of child-care and basic amenities at workplace*

1 See Section 35(2) and 36(2) of the Bills.
2 See Chapter 5 of the Bills

are determined through negotiations and settlements between the employer and the employees. In the unorganised sector, where labour is vulnerable to exploitation due to illiteracy and having no effective bargaining power, the wages can not be left to be determined entirely by the interplay of market forces and, therefore, intervention of the government becomes necessary both from the perspective of social justice, and also for increasing the efficiency and productivity in the economy.

13.51 On the recommendation of the Eighth Standing Labour Committee, the Minimum Wages Bill was introduced in the Central Legislative Assembly in April 1946 and the Act came into force in 1948. Under the Act both the state and Central governments are "Appropriate Governments" for fixation and revision of Minimum Rates of Wages for employments covered by the Schedule to the Act. The Schedule is in two parts, part II of which is applicable to employment in agriculture. The appropriate governments have notified the list of scheduled employments in part I and part II. At present some employments are not included in the Schedule and the benefits under the Minimum Wages Act are not applicable to the workers in such employments.

13.52 The appropriate governments fix the minimum rates of wages payable to employees in an employment either specified in part I and Part II of the Schedule or added to either part by notification under section 27, and review these wages at intervals not exceeding five years. In fixing or revising the Minimum Rates of Wages, the appropriate government can appoint as many committees and sub-committees as it considered necessary.

13.53 In the absence of any attempt to define the concept of Minimum Wages the principles and components decided in cases of Minimum Wage fixation differ at both Central and state levels and the concerned Advisory Boards use discretion and their judgment in the absence of a standard set of criteria. This absence of a uniform set of criteria has been sought to be filled later on by various attempts, which did not prove very useful because of several shortcomings and constraints.

Principles of Fixation

13.54 Minimum Wages depend upon the set of minimum needs of the worker and her family that should be met out of wage earnings and the capacity to pay of a particular industry. In general, there must be an irreducible 'minimum', which must correspond to a basic subsistence, which Minimum Wages must meet. The Judgment of the Supreme Court of India in the Case - Crown Aluminium vs. Workmen, mentions a bare subsistence or Minimum Wage and stresses that any employer who pays wages below this minimum would have no right to conduct his enterprise on such terms.

13.55 Since the factors that could go into the determination of Minimum Wage could vary depending upon the economic circumstances of the industry/country, a clearer elucidation is needed of these factors. In December, 1947 the Government of India appointed a Central Advisory Council for advising on the issues of fair wage to labour and fair return on capital. This Council appointed a high-powered tripartite committee called the Committee on Fair Wages, which was asked "to determine the principles on which fair wages should be based and to suggest the line on which these principles should be applied". The Committee, in its report submitted in 1948, drew a distinction between 'minimum wage', 'fair wage' and 'living wage'. 'Minimum Wage' according to the Committee should provide for the maintenance of the efficiency of the worker as well as his other (current) basic needs. The three concepts were elucidated by the Committee as follows:

- Living Wage should enable the wage earner to provide for himself and his family not merely the bare essentials of food, clothing and shelter but also a measure of frugal comfort including education of children, protection against ill health, requirements of social needs and a measure of insurance against the more important contingencies like old age.
- Minimum Wage must provide not merely for the bare sustenance of life but for preservation of the efficiency of the worker. For this purpose the Minimum Wage must also provide for some measure of education, medical requirements and amenities.
- Fair Wage: while the lower limit of the fair wage must obviously be the Minimum wage, the upper limit is equally set by what may broadly be called the capacity of the industry to pay.

13.56 In 1957 the 15th Session of Indian Labour Conference (ILC) emphasized that the Minimum Wage should be need-based in order to ensure the minimum human needs of the industrial workers. The following 5 norms were recommended by ILC which till date are generally taken as the basis for fixation of the minimum rates of wages: -

(i) Three consumption units for one earner;

(ii) Minimum food requirement for 2700/ day calories per average adult;

(iii) 18 yards of per capita cloth consumption for 4 members i.e. 72 yards per annum per family;

(iv) Rent corresponding to the minimum area provided for under Government's Industrial Housing Scheme, and

(v) Fuel, lighting and other 'miscellaneous' items of expenditure to constitute 20 per cent of the total Minimum Wages.

13.57 These norms were to be followed by all the wage-fixing authorities in India. In cases where the Minimum Wage fixed fell short of the above level recommended by the ILC, it was incumbent on the concerned authorities to justify the circumstances, which prevented them from pursuing the above norms.

13.58 The Supreme Court of India delivered a Judgement in 1992 in the case of Reptakos Brett and Co. vs. its workmen that "Children's education, medical requirement, minimum recreation including festival/ ceremonies and provision for old age, marriage, etc., should further constitute 25 per cent of the total Minimum Wage and used as a guideline in the determination of Minimum Wage".

13.59 The First National Commission on Labour (1969) stated clearly that while determining the need-based Minimum Wages the employer's capacity to pay should be considered. The FNCL (1969) did not make any attempt to define the Minimum Wage. The FNCL (1969) remarked that though the national minimum in the sense of a uniform monetary recommendation for the country as a whole was neither feasible nor desirable, it was possible and necessary to fix regional minima for different homogeneous regions in each state.

13.60 The Third Central Pay Commission (1970-73) broadly accepted the ILC norms for Minimum Wage fixation but reviewed the minimum necessary nutritional standard in order to prepare its diet schedule as the basis for expenditure estimates at January 1973 prices. Thus, the Third Central Pay Commission (1970-73) recommended a Minimum Wage of Rs.196 per month for the lowest category of Central Government employees.

13.61 The question of a National Minimum Wage engaged the attention of the Committee on Wage Policy (1973) appointed by Planning Commission. This Committee headed by Prof. S. Chakraborty, the then Member, Planning Commission, recommended the National Minimum Wage as also the General Minimum Wage, Centre-wise and region-wise. The Committee observed, "Rs. 40 at the October, 1972 prices as the National Minimum". The Study Group on Wages, Incomes and Prices (1978), chaired by S. Bhootalingam, after carrying out an elaborate exercise, recommended a monthly wage of Rs. 100/- per month (at 1978 prices) as the National Minimum, to be gradually raised to Rs. 150/- per month (at 1978 prices).

13.62 The 31st session of the Labour Ministers' Conference held in July, 1980 stressed that Minimum Wages should not be prescribed below the poverty line worked out by the Planning Commission and wherever the existing wages are below this line they should be brought at par with it.

13.63 The Committee of Secretaries, in its meeting held in July, 1981 noted that in view of the numerous spatial and characteristic diversities of various employments and their locations in our large country, the fixation and implementation of Minimum Wages have to overcome a lot of conceptual problems and operational constraints. The Committee suggested a duality of Minimum Wages: an absolute minimum called the 'National Floor Level' should be applicable to those employments which have not been included in the Schedule of the Act, while the other, pegged at a higher level (i.e. higher than the National Floor Level). The idea of a National Floor Level was conceived as a statutory rock-bottom below which the Minimum Wages cannot be legally allowed to fall in any employment anywhere in India. But there should be no bar to the fixation of Minimum Mages above this floor level wherever it would be possible to peg it up.

13.64 A similar concept was mooted by another Committee of Secretaries of six States (viz. Bihar, Kerala, Manipur, Uttar Pradesh, West Bengal and Pondicherry) constituted in 1981 on the recommendations of the Sub-committee of the Labour Ministers' Standing Committee. This Committee introduced another new concept of 'General Minimum Wage', which was defined as the lowest wage essential to meet the bare minimum needs of workers and their families. The General Minimum Wage envisaged the statutory bottom level below which wage rate in any Schedule employment is not legally permitted to fall; but according to the Committee there should be no bar on fixing of Minimum Wage above this General Minimum in cases where concerned employment with a better financial health might be capable of paying higher wages.

13.65 The Indian Labour Conference in its meeting held in November 1985, expressed the view that till such time a National Wage was not feasible, it would be desirable to have Regional Minimum Wages in regard to which Central Government may lay down the guidelines. The Minimum Wages should be revised at regular periodicity and should be linked with rise in the cost of living. Accordingly, the Government issued guidelines in July, 1987 for setting up of Regional Minimum Wages Advisory Committees. These Committees, renamed subsequently as Regional Labour Ministers' Conference, made a number of recommendations which include reduction in disparities in Minimum Wages of different states of a region, setting up of Inter-State Co-ordination Council, consultation with neighbouring states while fixing / revising the Minimum Wages, etc.

13.66 The National Commission on Rural Labour (1991) defined the Minimum Wage as a minimum subsistence wage, which must be paid to workers by all employers on socio-economic considerations. If the worker was paid below the minimum wage his efficiency would suffer and as a result productivity would decline. Minimum Wage, being the subsistence wage, cannot differ much in physical terms from employment to employment and from employer to employer. Taking into account the poverty line as determined by the Planning Commission, the average number of earners in an agricultural labour household, the average number of employment days, and three consumption units per earner, the NCRL determined Rs. 20 as being the Minimum Wage in rural India in 1990-91. Following the principles enunciated by the NCRL (1991), the Central Government raised the national floor level Minimum Wage to Rs.40 per day in 1998 and further to Rs.45 from December 1, 1999 and Rs.50 per day from September 1, 2002 keeping in view the rise in Consumer Price Index.

13.67 The Second National Commission on Labour (2002) also considered the issue of Minimum age and recommended a National Minimum Wage based on the principles recommended by the 15th ILC. The SNCL (2002) recommended that the wage be revised from time to time and have a component of dearness allowance linked to the cost of living so that it could be adjusted every six months. The wage itself could be revised every five years and the states could notify the Minimum Wage, which could vary from region to region, but could not be less than the National Minimum Wage. The SNCL (2002) recommended that wages should not be fixed separately for each Scheduled employment as is presently the case.

13.68 Expressing concern at the wide disparity in the Minimum Wages that existed and the lack of clarity on the concept, norms and parameters of wage fixation, the Central Advisory Board, constituted a Working Group in 2003 to go into these issues. The Working Group submitted its report in 2003.

13.69 The Working Group decided to adopt the principles laid down by the ILC of 1957 and elaborated by the Supreme Court judgment of 1992. Accordingly, it considered a daily minimum calorie norm of 2700 per consumption unit, 3 consumption units per earner and the estimated wage employment days for agricultural labourers. The Group then used the NSS 50th Round survey data on consumption expenditure to fix the average consumption expenditure which would yield a consumption of 2700 calories per consumption unit. It found that this expenditure level covered adequate non-food expenditure (as per norm). Working backward, it determined Rs. 66 to be the National Minimum Wage as in 2002-03. The Committee recommended that this wage could replace the different state level Minimum Wages for different Schedules of employment. With effect from February 2004, all the state/UT governments have been requested by the Labour Minister to ensure fixation/ revision of Minimum Rates of Wages in all the Scheduled employments at not below Rs.66 per day. However, there is no legal backup to the national floor level Minimum Wage fixed by the Government of India.

13.70 From the review of the existing analysis and recommendations on the subject of Minimum Wage, it is clear that it has been felt throughout that a Minimum Wage linked to the core subsistence needs of the workers should be available to all the workers. It is further clear that the existing wide variation in the Minimum Wages have been a matter of concern to most committees/ commissions. With regard to the issue of whether a single Minimum Wage should be available to all the workers, or should form the floor only, there are differences of opinion.

13.71 This Commission has taken the view that there should be a statutory National Minimum Wage, which shall represent the lowest level of wage for any employment in the country. This wage shall be applicable to all employments presently not covered under the Minimum Wages Act of the state concerned, and would be applicable to both wage workers and homeworkers. Even with respect to the employments covered under the Minimum Wages Act, the state government has to ensure that the Minimum Wage fixed under the

Minimum Wages Act, is not lower than the National Minimum Wage. In case the prescribed Minimum Wage under the Minimum Wages Act is lower than the National Minimum Wage, the state government shall immediately amend the prescribed Minimum Wage, to bring it in conformity with the National Minimum Wage. Even during the intervening period, till the time the state government has not amended the prescribed wage under the Minimum Wages Act, the worker shall not suffer and shall be eligible to receive the higher National Minimum Wage.[3]

13.72 The National Minimum Wage shall be fixed by the Central Government, which shall follow a tri-partite consultative process, and will be announced within one year. The general principles in the fixation of the National Minimum Wage will be the minimum basic needs of the wage worker and the homeworker and his/her family. It is seen that the cost of living among different states, districts or even between the rural and urban areas within one district vary considerably. The government shall consider all such factors or any other relevant parameters for fixation of the National Minimum Wage.[4] However, the Commission has also examined and elaborated on the relevant principles in 13.75 below.

13.73 The Commission finds that several committees have adopted a normative approach to define subsistence needs and Minimum Wage. The Indian Labour Conference had, in 1957, decided five norms, to which the Supreme Court judgment of 1992 added a sixth. The 30th Session of the Labour Ministers Conference in 1980 and NCRL (1991), however, adopted an approach, which was grounded more on the notion of a 'poverty line' as determined by the Planning Commission. It needs to be mentioned that the ILC norms, were set half a century ago, when the debate on minimum nutritional norms was in its infancy. Further, even if these norms were fully valid 50 years ago, they need to be redefined in the present context. In any case, the challenge has been to convert the basic norms into monetary value since this can be done in a number of alternative ways.

13.74 Since 1993, the Government of India has adopted a definition of 'poverty line', which is benchmarked to the consumption of a minimum amount of calories (2400 K. calorie in rural areas, and 2100 K. calorie in urban areas) on a per capita basis in 1973-74, and non-food expenditure by the expenditure class consuming these calories. The poverty line has provided an inter-state and inter-temporal basis for interpreting minimum subsistence. It has also provided a fulcrum for policy decisions. The poverty line is adjusted according to the cost of living in rural and urban areas and in different states. These parameters were not available before 1993. But, despite a considerable degree of debate, they have acquired wide acceptability as a notion of subsistence since then. It will be recalled that the poverty line includes expenditure on food and non-food items, including clothing, fuel, education, healthcare, housing etc. In other words, the poverty line is set at a level where it can cover the very basic requirements of a family, and except for old age security, includes some expenditure on the items mentioned by the ILC as well as the Supreme Court judgment. However, given the level of capability deprivation faced by the poor in India, it may be argued that the poverty line does not allow the minimum level of expenditure on some of the basic items such as education, health, and housing. A perusal of National Sample Survey data shows that, even as a proportion of their own consumption expenditure, the poor spend about eight per cent less than the average on the three items mentioned above. Similarly, there may be other items in the poor's consumption which reflect the deprivation, which the poor continue to face, which are not included in the poverty line. It is for similar reasons that the Supreme Court had suggested a 25 per cent increase over the basic expenditure level on the norms suggested by ILC. The Commission is of the view that the poverty line reflects the subsistence in the current context, which the ILC and other bodies have attempted to define through norms. However, this subsistence needs to be adjusted upwards to take care of the deprivation, particularly the capability deprivation that the poor continue to face. Since the items mentioned in the Supreme Court judgment are already included in the consumption basket, which constitutes the poverty line, a smaller mark-up over this level may be necessary to represent the expenditure to be met through minimum wage income. On this basis, the Commission recommends that that the following parameters could be taken into account in determining the National Minimum Wage:

a) The Monthly Per Capita Consumption Expenditure (MPCE) corresponding to the poverty line as determined by the Planning Commission;

[3] See Chapter 2, Section 6 of the Bills.

[4] Ibid., Section 6(2) ©

b) A mark-up over this expenditure to take account of the capability deprivation of poor households.

c) The average size of labour households, as shown in surveys

d) The average dependent-earner ratio in labour households

e) The average number of total days of employment for labourers as brought out by the National Sample Survey

f) The National Minimum Wage could be fixed for the country as a whole, on the basis of the above parameters, and the same could be adjusted for rural and urban areas and different states, as is done for estimating the poverty lines at present.

13.75 These parameters can be objectively determined on the basis of the National Sample Surveys on Consumption, and on Employment-Unemployment. Such a methodology could be considered by the Government in fixing the National Minimum Wage.

13.76 The fixation of National Minimum Wage by the government shall be done within one year of the implementation of the Act. Thereafter, the National Minimum Wage shall be periodically reviewed by the Central Government through a modality prescribed by the National Board for Social Security and Welfare for Unorganised Workers[5]. Till such time as the government fixes and announces the new National Minimum Wage, the National Minimum Wage fixed by the Labour Ministry shall, after adjustment for cost of living changes, be deemed to be the National Minimum Wage under this Act.

13.77 It would be noted that the Commission has not advocated the abolition of the different Schedules of the state level minimum wages. This is because the variation in circumstances between employments and/or states or locations may warrant a higher wage. However, there may be cases where the states may like to merge some employments and simplify existing Schedules. At the same time, the Commission is concerned that there are no clear guidelines regarding the fixation of Minimum Wages under the Minimum Wages Act, and this leads to considerable arbitrariness. It has therefore been proposed that the State Boards being constituted can go into these questions and can formulate appropriate guidelines for fixation of wages under the Minimum Wages Act.[6]

Other Issues relating to Wages

13.78 The Commission has analysed other aspects of payment of wages to unorganised sector workers. There are cases of delayed payments both for wage workers and homeworkers. We have, therefore, provided that the wages of workers shall be paid for the periods agreed upon by the employer and the worker, which can in no case exceed one month. If there is any delay in the payment of wages beyond one month, then the employer shall be liable to pay penal interest to the worker.[7] The Commission is aware of the lack of voice of workers in this sector and therefore the limitations in applicability of this suggestion. However a beginning needs to be made in this direction.

13.79 Due to non-availability of regular jobs the workers in the unorganised sector do not have enough bargaining power vis a vis the employers. The employers use all possible means and forms to squeeze the quantum of wages paid to a worker under one pretext or the other. There are no rules to control or monitor the deductions from wages. The deductions may be on account of advance to the worker, in the form of interest, payments to contractors or agents, overvaluation of goods supplied or basic amenities including accommodation in the case of seasonal migrant workers, fines, inadequate or poor quality output. These kinds of deductions are most rampant in the case of seasonal migrant workers who take advances from their employers/contractors, and also in the case of homeworkers. The Commission recommends that no deductions on these accounts be made, except in accordance with the rules made in this behalf by the state government. This provision is incorporated in the two Bills proposed by the Commission.[8]

13.80 The Minimum Wage Act provides for equivalence of wages between the time-rated Minimum Wages and the piece-rated wages. Where the wages of a wage worker or homeworker are determined by a piece-rate system, the earnings of a worker working for 8 hours under normal work intensity, should be at least equal to the time-rated Minimum Wages fixed for that category of work in the state concerned.[9] This would bring parity between the time-rated wage worker and a piece-rated wage worker. There may be certain employments where Minimum Wages have not been fixed under the Minimum Wages Act. In such cases the comparison and

[5] Chapter V, Section 13(m) of the Bills.
[6] Chapter VI, Section 18(t) of the Bills.
[7] Chapter II, Section 6(5)
[8] Chapter II, Section 6(6)

parity of piece- rated work should be with the National Minimum Wage.

Women Workers

13.81 We have shown that women workers in the unorganised sector suffer from a number of handicaps. The Equal Remuneration Act applies to the unorganised sector and has the object of ensuring that men and women receive equal remuneration for equal work. However, one of the reasons that this does not happen is that men and women are often segmented in different activities and activities in which women predominate are valued poorly, even in cases where work may be arduous or may require higher skills. This Commission recommends that an Employment Certification Committee be formed which will periodically evaluate employments in the state and bring on par with the wages in employments performed predominantly by women with employments certified as equivalent in value. This is in order to bring the wages of women on par with equivalent employment elsewhere. The National Commission for Self-employed Women Workers had also made a similar recommendation.[10]

13.82 Further, to facilitate the working of the women workers the Commission is of the view that there should be adequate childcare facilities made available at the local level for which the State Board for Promotion of Livelihood of the Unorganised Sector Workers shall make rules.

13.83 One of the issues with respect to women workers is that they are vulnerable to sexual harassment. It is fundamentally the responsibility of employers to ensure that this does not happen and that the women workers are treated with dignity.[11] The Commission also recommends, in this context, the creation of a Complaints Committee at the district and sub-district levels, within the structure of the Dispute Resolution Council and the Conciliation Committees to deal with complaints concerning sexual harassment of women at the workplace. This is in line with the Supreme Court Judgement in the Vishaka and Others vs. State of Rajasthan and others case.[12]

Homeworkers

13.84 We have shown that homeworkers constitute an important segment of self-employed workers, especially among the women workers. The conditions of work of such workers are less amenable to regulation because the relationship to their employers is indirect. Employers sometimes choose to outsource work to homeworkers precisely for this reason. It is, thus, extremely vital that the homeworkers' conditions of work is brought under the ambit of regulation, even after recognising the difficulties inherent in this task.

13.85 We have already discussed the issues relating to delayed payments, deductions in payments, non-equivalence of piece-rates and time-rates, and the valuation of work, which affects the homeworkers.

13.86 The homeworkers generally provide for their tools/ equipment or use part of their own dwellings for work purposes for which they get no separate compensation. In effect, the wages paid to the homeworker is less as compared to his counterparts who do the same work at the employers' premises with the aid of tools/ equipment and place of work provided by the employer. Thus, for the sake of equity, the Commission feels that they should be separately compensated at such percentages as may be decided by the state government.[13]

13.87 It should be noted that the conditions of work of the homeworkers are inseparable from their conditions of living. This calls for a promotional policy, which can assist such workers both by providing them with work sheds and common facilities, but also in making provision for better housing and basic facilities.

Migrant Workers

13.88 Migrant workers, especially seasonal migrants, suffer from a number of handicaps, including very poor working and living conditions. In mines, quarries, brick-kilns etc. where the system of contractor based recruitments is predominant, these workers are recruited against advances, and adjustments are made against their wages, which often include the contractor's commission, overcharging for provisions and interest rate. The Commission recommends that these adjustments be declared as illegal and be made subject to the dispute resolution mechanism proposed in the Bills.[14]

13.89 The migrant workers contribute significantly to the rural and urban economies and still their vulnerabilities and deprivations are not factored in the planning process.

[9] Chapter II, Section 6(3)
[10] Chapter II, Section 6(4) of the Bills.
[11] Chapter II, Section 4(4) of the Bills.
[12] Chapter IX, Section 29(3) of the Bills.
[13] Chapter II, Section 6(7) of the NAWB.

The Commission has proposed that the promotional policies of the State ensure that migrant workers receive their due entitlement and that their basic needs are factored in the regional planning processes.

Disadvantaged Workers

13.90 Workers belonging to the socially deprived groups and women usually form the core of disadvantaged workers employed as bonded labour, child labour, seasonal migrants, or suffering from various forms of social exclusion and discrimination. The National Commission for Self-employed Women and Women Workers in the Informal Sector and, more recently, the Prime Minister's High Level Committee on Muslim Minorities have recommended the constitution of an Equal Opportunities Commission to deal with broader aspects of discrimination and social exclusion (GOI 2006).

13.91 In the sphere of work, the Equal Remuneration Act protects workers against discrimination in wage payments. The proposal made by this Commission on the Certification Committee is aimed at protecting women workers against subtler forms of wage discrimination linked to segmentation of labour markets. The Commission has put discrimination on the basis of sex, caste, religion, incidence of HIV-AIDS, migration status, and place of origin in employment, wage rates and conditions of work within the purview of the proposed legislations.[15]

13.92 The Commission has examined the child labourers' position in the Report. Although the percentage of child workers in the workforce appears to be declining, a large number of children are still engaged in full time work as wage labourers. The sectors in which children can be found to be working are both those where child labour is now prohibited as the work is deemed to be hazardous as well as others where child work is presently not prohibited. In this Report, we have pointed out that as a result of increasing awareness and also the impact of promotional policies, mainly the expansion of elementary education, child labour has declined in both the prohibited and non-prohibited sectors. However, new sources of the demand for child wage labour are also rising which causes children from vulnerable households to be pushed into the labour force. The Commission is of the view that there is considerable urgency to regulate and check this trend. Further, we are of the view that instead of only relying on Part II of the Child Labour (Prohibition and Regulation) Act, 1986, suitable amendments should be made to Part III of the Act (Regulation of Conditions of Work of Children), so that: (i) it would be punishable to employ any child under the age of 11 years; (ii) no child between the age of 11 and up to 14 years can be employed in any occupation during school sessions; and otherwise for more than 4 hours a day.

Availability of Records

13.93 The Commission has considered the issue of record keeping as a method of verifying the terms and conditions of employment of the workers. A proportion of the small employers in the unorganised non-agricultural sector and a sizeable proportion in the agricultural sector are illiterate. Besides, the process of record keeping can be quite cumbersome for such employers. At the same time, the Minimum Wage Acts and the Shops and Establishments Act already prescribe some record keeping. In agriculture, however, many states provide exemptions to certain categories of employers. The Commission is in favour of according some degree of formality to the informal labour markets within pragmatic limits. We therefore recommend that the employers of regular workers in the non-agricultural sector be required to provide, in writing, the terms and conditions of employment to the workers.[16] In all cases of non-agricultural employment, including in the case of casual workers, wage slips may be provided.[17] This is, however, not feasible in the agricultural sector, where we recommend that regular workers be provided a record of their terms and conditions of employment. The Bills that the Commission has proposed put the onus of proof on the employers, and they might, therefore, keep such records as might be necessary to verify their claims of payment.[18]

Compensation in the Case of Injury

13.94 The wide variety of employments and the various categories of work in the unorganised sector entail varying hazards and risks. The employer should provide the unorganised wage worker or the homeworker with adequate safety equipment while handling hazardous substances and equipments.[19]

[14] Chapter II, Section 6(6)
[15] Chapter II, Section 6(9) of the AWB, and Section 6(10) of the NAWB.
[16] Chapter 2, Section 6, Clause 7(b) in the AWB and Clause 8(b) in the NAWB.
[17] Chapter 2, Section 6, Clause 8(a) in the NAWB. A general provision is also included in Clause 8(a) of the AWB.

13.95 Further if there is any accident or occupational hazard arising out of or in the course of employment that results in any temporary, permanent, partial or total disablement of the wage worker the employer shall compensate the wage or homeworker for it, which shall not be lower than the benefits provided under the National Social Security Scheme, being recommended by the Commission.[20] The Commission further suggests that where the wage worker is covered under the National Social Security Scheme, the employer shall not pay such compensation. This shall act as an incentive for the employers to get their employees registered under the Scheme.

Implementation of Regulations and Dispute Resolution

13.96 Although the Commission has recommended comprehensive legislation for regulation of conditions of work in the unorganised agricultural and non-agricultural sectors, the factors which will constrain the effectiveness with which the proposed legislations are likely to be implemented will be similar to those which affect the functioning of the existing laws.

13.97 The large scale violation of the existing laws such as the Minimum Wage Acts is indicative of the lack of awareness on the part of the workers and the employers and also the employers' unwillingness to enforce the existing regulations. It is important that the government carries out a large scale education programme for the workers, employers and other stakeholders aimed at inculcating the importance of assuring the workers the basic dignity and minimum conditions of work. The National and State Boards proposed by the Commission should also play a part in this campaign.

13.98 Another set of constraints on the implementation of laws for the unorganised sector springs from the large and dispersed nature of such employments, the limited outreach of the existing labour departments, the focus of the conciliation machinery on the organised sector, and the lack of infrastructure with the implementation departments. We propose that steps be taken to improve the infrastructure of the departments, focus on increasing its efficiency and education and sensitisation programmes of its officials.

13.99 Perhaps the biggest constraint arises from the lack of voice of the unorganised workers and their weak bargaining power. These problems can only be corrected through concerted efforts at strengthening the bargaining capacity of these workers. One of the ways in which this can be done is by giving them due representation in the dispute resolution mechanisms and the authority to raise issues as disputes.[21]

13.100 The Commission has noted that the Trade Unions (Amendment) Act, 2001 (Act No. 31 of 2001) has made amendments to Section 4 of the Trade Union Act, 1926, which makes it more difficult for the trade unions to work among unorganised sector workers, and to register themselves wherever there is no fixed employer-employee relationship. This amendment requires that "no trade union shall be registered unless at least ten per cent or one hundred of the workmen, which ever is less, engaged or employed in the establishment or industry with which it is connected are the members of such Trade Union. We, therefore recommend that a specific provision be made in the Act, which allows such unions to register whenever a union has seven or more members. The Commission notes that the SNCL (2002) has also made this recommendation.

13.101 The Commission has recommended the constitution of Conciliation Committees and Dispute Resolution Councils for both agricultural and non-agricultural workers respectively, which are tri-partite in character. In each of the Bills, the Commission has proposed that the state government will constitute Dispute Resolution Councils (DRC) at district level and Conciliation Committees (CC) at an appropriate level below the districts, i.e. Block/Tehsil/Mandal, level, for resolution of disputes relating to the non-observance of the provisions of the Acts arising among the unorganised wage workers/ homeworkers and the employers. The

Dispute Resolution Structure
- *Conciliation Committees*
- *Dispute Resolution Councils*
- *Adjudication*

[18] Chapter 2, Section 6, Clause 7(c) of the AWB and Clause 8(c) of the NAWB.
[19] Chapter 2, Section 4(2) of the Bills.
[20] Chapter 2, Section 4(3) of the Bills.
[21] Chapter 5, Section 14 (1) and Chapter 6, Section 16(1) of the Bills.

Composition of the DRCs and CCs will be tri-partite in character and will consist of representatives of employers, workers and an officer designated by the state government to be the member secretary.[22]

13.102 The primary focus of the proposed dispute resolution machinery will be on conciliation. The Conciliation Committee shall, for the purpose of bringing about a settlement of the dispute, without delay, investigate the dispute and all matters connected therewith or require the matters to be investigated by the Labour Inspectors under this Act, and may do all such things as they think fit for the purpose of inducing the parties to come to a fair and amicable settlement of the dispute.[23] In case of failure of conciliation, the DRC shall record its finding and refer the matter directly to an Adjudicator, within 4 weeks of the reference of the dispute.[24] The proposal provides that the state government shall also issue such notifications and directions as are necessary to ensure that the adjudication proceedings are concluded expeditiously with minimum loss of time and costs to the parties involved.

13.103 Where the dispute pertains to any matter covered by any law mentioned in Section 4(1), the DRC shall forward the complaint to the appropriate authority created under the relevant Act for adjudication.

Provisions for Social Security

13.104 The Commission has examined the issue of social security for unorganised workers in detail in its Report on Social Security for Unorganised Workers, submitted to the Government in May 2006. The Commission had made a specific recommendation for an Act and a National Social Security Scheme for which all unorganised workers could register and be eligible to receive benefits. The Commission has recommended that the Scheme cover all eligible unorganised workers within a period of five years. These provisions are included in the present Bills in Chapter III of the Comprehensive Bills (Section 7, Clauses 1 and 3). The eligibility of the workers under the scheme was to be determined subject to a ceiling on land held (two hectares) in the case of agricultural workers, or income (Rs. 6500 per month, as on 1.1. 2006, as discussed in the 40th Indian Labour Conference), in the case of non-agricultural workers (as per Section 20 of the Bills). The Commission's approach has been to ensure that a minimum level of social protection is seen by the workers as a statutory right and an entitlement and not simply as an ad hoc largesse bestowed by the government.

13.105 The statutory National Social Security Scheme which the Commission has proposed consists of a package of the following minimum benefits[25]:

a) Hospitalisation benefit for the worker and his family to the tune of Rs 15,000 per year, maternity benefit to the extent of Rs 1000 to the worker/ spouse, and sickness allowance for 15 days beyond three days of hospitalisation.

b) Life and disability insurance to the tune of Rs 30,000 in the event of untimely natural death of the worker; Rs. 75,000 in the event of accidental death or total disability; and Rs. 17,500 in the event of partial disability.

c) Old age cover in the form of a pension of Rs. 200 p.m. to all BPL workers above the age of 60 years, and Provident Fund for all other registered workers.

13.106 It may be mentioned that the Commission has estimated the total financial cost of the Scheme, at 2006-07 prices, on complete implementation, to be about Rs. 33350 crores (Rs. 19400 crores for agricultural workers and Rs 12950 crores for non-agricultural workers), as laid down in the Schedule to the Bills. The Commission has recommended a contributory scheme, in which the poor workers are exempt from making any contribution, and the other workers do not contribute more than one-third. However, in the proposed Bills, the actual pattern of financing has been left to the Central Government, which can meet the financial expenditure on the Scheme through grants and loans, contributions from employers and workers, cess or tax (see Section 8 of the Bills).

Institutional Framework

13.107 The Commission had, in its Report on Social Security for Unorganised Workers, proposed a federal structure for implementation of the Scheme. The present Comprehensive Bills incorporate this structure with few changes. The proposed structure is described in Chapters 4 - 8 of the comprehensive Bills as well as in the Schedule to the Bills. It is proposed that the National Board for

22 Chapter 9, Section 29 of the Bills.
23 Chapter 9, Section 30 (4-8) of the Bills.
24 Chapter 9, Section 30 (14) of the Bills.
25 Chapter 3, Section 7 (2) of the Bills lays down the type of benefits. The quantum of minimum benefits in the package is laid down in the Schedule to the Bills.

Social Security and Welfare will implement the scheme at the Central level, while State Boards for Social Security and Welfare will do the same at the state and district levels[26]. Worker Facilitation Centres (WFCs), which may be NGOs, trade unions, or PRIs will facilitate the scheme including the registration of workers[27]. The actual registration of the workers as well as issue of identity cards will be the responsibility of the State Boards. Further, in the Commission's proposal, there is possibility of incorporation of the existing structures and schemes at the state level as well as add-ons.

13.108 While the functions of the WFCs remain the same in this Report, we have proposed a broadening of the functions of the National and State Boards in relation to functions that we had proposed to these organisations in the 2006 Report. The functions of the National Social Security and Welfare Board for Unorganised Workers will include Social Security and Welfare functions, along with provisions for the oversight of the regulation of the conditions of work. The Board, which is an apex institution, will be common to both the agricultural and non-agricultural workers. The Commission has proposed that the National Board be constituted by the Central Government and consists of stakeholders among trade unions, employers, government bodies and public agencies, experts and other non-governmental institutions dealing with the unorganised sector[28]. The exact constitution of the Boards is set out in the Bills proposed by the Commission.

13.109 The Chairperson shall be a person of eminence appointed by the government, and an officer in the rank of the Secretary to the Government of India, shall be the full-time Member-Secretary, who shall be its Chief executive Officer[29]. The National Board shall have a secretariat with adequate professional and other staff. The staff of the National Board for promotion of livelihood of Unorganised Workers (agricultural/non-agricultural) shall be governed by the Central Government rules and regulations existing from time to time.

13.110 A National Social Security and Welfare Fund (NSSF) would be created and operated by the National Board (see Section 8 of the Bills). The contribution of the Central Government will be credited to the NSSF at the beginning of each year[30]. Similarly, State Funds would be created under the State Boards (whose functions are discussed below), to which state level sources of finances for the National Social Security Scheme as well as finances for other schemes would accrue.

13.111 The National Board will perform the following pivotal functions for the protection and promotion of the unorganised agricultural and non-agricultural sector workers[31]:

a) Administration of this Act and formulation of policies at the national level, and shall have such powers as may be laid down to direct, co-ordinate, supervise, and monitor the functioning of State Boards and the Central Welfare Boards;

Main Functions of the National Board

- Administration of this Act and monitoring its functioning at the state level.
- Formulation of social security policies and programmes, including gradual strengthening of such policies with respect to unorganised sector workers and extension of organised sector schemes to sections of these workers.
- Monitoring and review of the impact of existing schemes, policies and programmes for the unorganised sector workers.
- Advise the government regarding the promotion of gainful employment opportunities and promotion of livelihood options;
- Identification of skill and training requirements;
- Advise the government on special protection measures for migrant workers;
- Periodic review of the national minimum wage.

26 Chapters 5 and 6 of the Bills.
27 Chapter 8, Section 27 of the Bills.
28 Chapter 5, Section 14 (1) of the Bills.
29 Chapter 5, Section 14 (4) of the Bills.
30 Chapter 4, Section 8 of the Bills.

b) Review the working including auditing of the State Boards and the Central Welfare Boards every four years and make suitable recommendations to the government(s) concerned for further improvement;

c) Manage and maintain the National Social Security and Welfare Fund, provide financial assistance to State Boards; recommend new schemes and programmes and projects for implementation through the Fund;

d) Advise the Central Government on policy matters relating to social security, and extension of schemes of social security such as Employees State Insurance (ESI) and Employees Provident Fund (EPF) to the unorganised sector workers; and their health, safety and welfare. ;

e) Assist in capacity building of the State Boards.

f) Collect, compile and publish statistics relating to the unorganised sector and undertake such promotional activities as may be decided from time to time.

g) Monitor and review the impact of the existing schemes, policies and programmes of various ministries and departments of Government of India on the unorganised sector workers and make appropriate recommendations;

h) Advise the Government regarding the promotion of gainful employment opportunities and promotion of livelihood options and matters relating to welfare of unorganised sector workers;

i) Identify skill and training requirements for unorganised workers and to advise the government accordingly;

j) Carry out periodic surveys on the conditions of work in the unorganised sector and make suitable recommendations to the government;

k) Hold public hearings to entertain petitions submitted by the unorganised sector workers and make appropriate recommendations;

l) Advise the Government on special protection measures for the migrant workers and their families in providing the ration cards, housing and education to their children;

m) Provide for guidelines of periodic review of the National Minimum Wages fixed by the Central Government after taking into account the minimum basic needs of the wage workers and their families.

13.112 In consonance with the federal character, we have proposed that State Boards for Social Security and Welfare for Agricultural Workers and Non-agricultural Workers be set up under the provisions of the two Bills respectively. The organisational structure of the State Boards is similar to the National Boards. The State Boards have, however, more direct responsibilities with respect to the implementation of the National Social Security Scheme. They can also frame their own schemes and undertake other welfare and livelihood promotion activities. Besides, the State Boards will also undertake specific oversight functions with respect to regulation of conditions of work. For instance, they will make guidelines for fixation of Minimum Wages; determine the safety and health standards required to be maintained in various occupations; carry out periodic surveys of occupational health hazards; and constitute an Employment Certification Committee to bring the wages in employments performed mainly by women on par with other employments certified as equivalent in value.

13.113 Thus, it is envisaged that the National and State Boards will play a pivotal role with respect to the National Social Security Scheme, in progressively enhancing the scope of social security and welfare measures for unorganised sector workers, in monitoring the conditions of work in the sector and regulating these conditions; and in undertaking promotional measures to enhance employability and employment of the unorganised sector workers.

Conclusion

13.114 The purpose of this Report has been to present a rationale as well as a proposal for comprehensive protective legislations for agricultural workers and the unorganised non-agricultural workers respectively. These legislations include provisions for regulating minimum conditions of work, social security, welfare, and livelihood promotion and are appended to this report. The recommendation of the Commission with respect to conditions of work is discussed in this Report while its recommendations on Social Security have been submitted earlier to the Government. The Commission's recommendations on livelihood promotion are presented in Chapter 14 of this Report.

13.115 We have noted that although there are existing laws which provide some provisions for conditions of

[31] Chapter 3, Section 13 of the Bills.

work to certain sections of wage workers, and there are also some initiatives by the corporate sector to provide for minimum conditions of work through voluntary codes, there is no comprehensive framework which provides for basic and minimum conditions of work for wage workers and homeworkers. The laws that exist are also poorly implemented because of the inadequacies of the implementation machinery and lack of voice among unorganised workers.

13.116 The Commission has therefore suggested a comprehensive regulatory framework to prescribe minimum conditions of work for all unorganised workers. Given some differences between the agricultural and the non-agricultural workers in their conditions of work, two separate Bills have been proposed. Instead of relying on bureaucratic implementation and costly and time consuming legal redressal procedures, the Commission has accorded priority to conciliation and has proposed the participation of workers' representatives and elected representatives of the local bodies in the conciliation and dispute resolution committees. Further, if adjudication is required, the Commission has emphasised expeditiousness and the Bill requires that the state government prescribes modalities by which this might be ensured.

13.117 The Commission had earlier proposed a standalone social security legislation along with its comprehensive Report on Social Security for Unorganised Workers. During its consultations on working conditions and livelihood promotion, the Commission has been apprised that tri-partite consultations held under the auspices of the Ministry of Labour have advocated two comprehensive legislations in which the provisions for social security are incorporated along with the provisions for regulation of conditions of work and livelihood promotion. The Commission has considered these views carefully. It has also considered the fact that its recommendations on social security are already under consideration of the Government. While it is still of the opinion that its social security proposals are fully viable on a standalone basis, it has taken the view that incorporation of its existing recommendations on social security along with its current recommendations on the regulation of minimum conditions of work and livelihood promotion in the two comprehensive Bills (separately for agricultural and non-agricultural workers) may be helpful in building a broader consensus around these important issues. It has accordingly recommended two comprehensive Bills, separately for agricultural and unorganised non-agricultural workers, covering working conditions, welfare and livelihood promotion, and (its earlier recommendations on) social security.

13.118 As a consequence of the fact, that a primary problem relating to the poor living and working conditions of both the self-employed and the wage employed lies in the low productivity of the unorganised enterprises, the Commission's view is that protection and promotion of livelihoods is also an integral part of any strategy which aims at improving the conditions of unorganised sector workers. Further, although a number of promotion initiatives for the unorganised sector are available, no single agency provides an overview of the problems and constraints faced by this sector or are able to mobilise the necessary resources to help the sector overcome such constraints and facilitate its growth. The Commission, is therefore of the view that the appropriate governments take a number of necessary steps to protect and promote these livelihoods through suitable policies and programmes. It separately recommended the creation of a National Fund, which can play a catalytic role in the promotion of livelihoods of the unorganised sector workers. The next and final Chapter of this Report spells out an Action Programme proposed by the Commission which includes the two dimensions viz. social protection and regulation of conditions of work, and a number of measures which, in the Commission's view, are required to be undertaken on a priority basis to expand employment and improve livelihoods and incomes of unorganised sector workers.

14 An Action Programme for the Unorganised Sector

Introduction

14.1 The Commission's mandate requires it to examine, among other issues, (i) measures necessary for bringing about improvement in the productivity of enterprises and generation of large scale employment opportunities (ii) labour laws in the informal sector, consistent with labour rights; (iii) expansion in the social security system available for labour in the informal sector. The present report on conditions of work and livelihood opportunities addresses the above mentioned issues.

14.2 The Commission is aware that certain fundamental and foundational issues such as the provision of education, health, rural roads, sanitation, housing, provision of electricity and other basic infrastructure impact on the well being and livelihoods of the workers in the unorganised sector. The provision of these services and infrastructure is being addressed in various schemes of central and the state governments. While recognizing the importance of these issues, the Commission has chosen to focus on issues which are directly concerned with unorganised sector workers qua workers and the growth of enterprises in this sector.

14.3 In doing this, the Commission has followed a three-fold approach. It has advocated a minimum level of protective social security for the workers, which can be both progressively enhanced and supplemented, as elaborated in its first Report. It has recommended a set of measures, most of which are incorporated, along with the proposed social security measures, in two comprehensive Bills, for regulation of minimum conditions of work in the unorganised agricultural and non-agricultural sectors, presented to the Government in its second Report. This Report elaborates the basis of the recommendations made by the Commission in its second Report. It has further examined the scope of enhancement of employment, incomes, and livelihoods in the unorganised sector. The Commission is separately preparing several reports such as those on credit, marketing and technology; skill development; and growth poles, with detailed recommendations on these aspects. However, the main recommendations, which in its opinion should

The Commission has followed a three-fold approach. It has advocated a minimum level of protective social security for the workers, which can be both progressively enhanced and supplemented, as elaborated in its first Report. It has recommended a set of measures, most of which are incorporated, along with the proposed social security measures, in two comprehensive Bills, for regulation of minimum conditions of work. It has further examined the scope of enhancement of employment, incomes, and livelihoods in the unorganised sector.

get overriding and immediate priority, are listed below in the form of an Action Programme for the Unorganised Sector. While doing so we aim to address the issues relating to the Unorganised Sector in a holistic manner.

A. Protective Measures for Unorganised Workers

1. Ensuring Minimum Conditions of Work

14.4 The Commission has examined in detail in this Report the conditions of work in the unorganised sector and the rationale and experience of ensuring of minimum conditions of work both internationally and in India. It has noted that since the Second National Commission on Labour there has been a consensus on a comprehensive legislative approach for regulation of the conditions of work, welfare and social security of the unorganised sector workers. Given that the tri-partite consultations in this country have favoured two separate Bills for the agricultural and non-agricultural workers and that the Common Minimum Programme of the UPA government calls for a separate comprehensive protective legislation for agricultural workers, the Commission has recommended two comprehensive Bills for agricultural workers and unorganised non-agricultural workers respectively.

14.5 The minimum conditions of work which are prescribed in the comprehensive Bills, both for agricultural and non-agricultural unorganised wage workers, include an eight-hour working day with at least half-hour break, a weekly paid day of rest, a National Minimum Wage, piece-rate wages to equal time-rated wages, employments specifically done by women to be brought on par with employment certified as equivalent value, timely payment of wages the failure of which would attract penal interest, no deduction of wages in the form of fines, right to organise, non-discrimination on the basis of sex, caste and religion, incidence of HIV AIDS or place or origin; provision of adequate safety equipment, compensation for accident, protection from sexual harassment, provision of child care and basic amenities at the workplace etc.

14.6 The Commission has carefully considered and prescribed a tri-partite Dispute Resolution Machinery focused on conciliation, which will give the stakeholders a role in implementation of the proposed laws, and which, in its view is likely to be more effective than the implementation machinery for a few of the laws that are in force for workers in the unorganised sector.

2. Minimum Level of Social Security

14.7 The Commission has already proposed in May 2006, on a stand alone basis, a universal national minimum social security scheme covering life, health and disability, maternity and old age protection which should be provided to workers in the unorganised sector both in the agriculture and non-agriculture sectors. The scheme and the accompanying Bill mandated specific obligations on the Government through creation of a clear entitlement (Right) for the unorganised workers. Since the Commission has now decided to recommend two comprehensive Bills separately for the agricultural and non-agricultural workers, which also cover the social security aspect, the template of the Bill proposed earlier has now been incorporated in the two comprehensive Bills.

14.8 The scheme recommended by the NCEUS envisages the following benefits:--

i) **Life Insurance:** Rs. 30,000 for natural death or Rs. 75,000 in the event of accidental death or total disability.

ii) **Health Insurance:** Hospitalization for each worker and his family members, costing Rs. 15,000 a year with Rs. 10,000 per ailment in designated hospitals. The scheme covers transportation as well.

iii) **Old Age Security:** All BPL workers will get a monthly pension of Rs. 200 at the age of 60 plus; all workers other than BPL will be entitled to a Provident Fund. The PF scheme envisages unemployment insurance also wherein the workers would be entitled to draw up to 50 per cent of the accumulated sum as unemployment benefits for six months, after a specified lock in period.

14.9 The National Social Security Scheme will be phased over five years. It envisages an organizational model which is federal where the implementation will be done by the grass roots organizations at the sate level, supervised and monitored by a central agency.

14.10 Further, the proposed scheme is based on a financial cost of Rs. 1095 per worker per year which implies a total cost for both the agricultural and non-agricultural workers, when all 30 crore unorganised workers will be registered, to be about Rs. 33,950 crores at 2006-07 prices. On the assumption that GDP will grow at the rate of 8 per cent in the next 5 years, we note that the cost of the scheme will be 0.20 per cent of GDP in the year of inception of the scheme. This will rise to 0.48 per cent of GDP 2010-11, when the entire unorganised sector workers are expected to be covered.

14.11 The scheme would be financed through the National Social Security and Welfare Fund (NSSWF). The Commission has suggested various options for financing the scheme including: a) Grants and loans from the Central Government; b) Contributions from workers, employers and state governments; c) Any tax or cess that the Central Government may impose for the purpose of providing social security for unorganised workers; and d) Any tax or cess that the Central Government may impose on commodities and/or services in lieu of the employers' contributions. However, the share of contribution of the BPL workers, if any, would be borne by the Central Government. The government's cost may be entirely borne by the Central Government or it may be shared between the Centre and States.

B. A Package of Measures for the Marginal and Small farmers

14.12 The Commission has reviewed the condition of marginal and small farmers, along with agricultural labourers in this Report. These farmers, with less than 2 hectares of land, constitute about 84 per cent of all farmer households, owned 43 per cent of the area and operated about 46 per cent of the land. The Situation Assessment Survey of Farmers (2003) shows that in most parts of the country, small farms are as productive, if not more than the medium-large farms. However, household income of these farmers from cultivation are low. The main issue of concern, which the Survey highlights, is that the marginal and small farmers suffer from a comparative disadvantage in the markets for credit, input, and output, and also to secure in obtaining access to new technological practices.

14.13 Many of the general issues relating to the farmers have been highlighted by the National Farmers Commission and the Planning Commission (2007) Steering Group Report on Agriculture for the 11th Plan and have also been reviewed by the Commission. This Commission recommends that focused attention should be given to the issues confronting the marginal and small farmers so that they may be able to achieve higher incomes from agriculture, with lower risks. Since, due to their small size, these farmers suffer more from the prevailing market failures in agriculture in matters relating to credit, input supplies and marketing of output, access to new technologies etc., the Commission has recommended the following package of measures for this segment of farmers:

3. *Special Programme for Marginal and Small Farmers*

14.14 The Commission's analysis has shown that till the 1980s, the Government had specific focus on the problems of marginal and small farmers. Besides large public investments in agriculture, and initiatives to extend institutional outreach, there were specific programmes to facilitate access to credit, inputs, modern technology and provide extension services to the small and marginal farmers, such as the Marginal Farmers and Agricultural Labourers Scheme, (MFAL), the Small Farmers Development Agency (SFDA), and the Million Wells Scheme. Such a focus on the weaker sections within the agricultural sector was able to raise the productivity and incomes of these farmers. The programmes were later withdrawn or integrated with other sector-specific programmes loosing the focus on the small and marginal farmers as their primary concern.

14.15 In this context, the Commission recommends that during the Eleventh Plan period, the government should revive a targeted programme focusing on small and marginal farmers, with an initial thrust on areas where the existing yield gap is also considered to be high. For this purpose a special agency or coordinating mechanism may be set up if required. The objective of the Government's intervention would be to promote state and area specific interventions which could improve the condition of marginal and small farmers. The Government could take as its priority tasks the development of area specific irrigation schemes; crop procurement, measures for reduction of risk; formation of producer groups among such farmers (e.g., SHG or cooperative approaches) with respect to sharing of irrigation resources, inputs and marketing arrangements; tenancy reform and group farming; strengthening of extension services and development of technological platforms which could be accessed by such farmers etc. A mechanism should be

The Commission recommends that during the Eleventh Plan period, the government should revive a targeted programme focusing on small and marginal farmers, with an initial thrust on areas where the existing yield gap is also considered to be high.

set up under the programme to oversee the arrangements in the districts for purchase of inputs and marketing of output, the area where market failures severely affect small and marginal farmers.

4. Emphasis on Accelerated Land and Water Management.

14.16 Land and Water management is the key to equitable and sustained growth in rural livelihoods. The problems of land and water management as well as solutions to these problems vary from region to region. But these problems affect marginal and small farmers more than bigger farmers. The Commission is of the view that the programmes of land and water management must be significantly upscaled.

14.17 Further, in the rainfed areas, the watershed development programmes are of crucial significance and have a high benefit cost ratio. About 45 million hectares have been covered in some way under watershed programmes till date, while about 75 million hectares remain to be covered. Therefore, the Commission recommends the accelerated expansion of the watershed development programmes and Rainfed Area Programmes in the country to revive agriculture in the rainfed agricultural land, on which a large number of the rural poor are dependent, as an immediate priority.

14.18 The Commission also views convergence of watershed development activities with other programmes as an issue of high importance. A number of activities undertaken in the Watershed Development Programme pertain to wage employment. These activities can be converged with NREGP and SGRY. Shelves of projects related to water conservation, plantation and afforestation, renovation of existing water structures, soil conservation and structures dealing with drought should be appropriately linked to the Watershed Development Work Plans at Block level. The Watershed Development Teams should work for convergence of WDPs with NREG activities. Panchayats should be trained to ensure convergence in implementation. The Eleventh Plan has recommended preparation of district plans with activity planning for different levels of the PRIs. Integration of land and water improvement programmes should be ensured in activity mapping and in the district plans with specific focus on benefits to the small and marginal farmers.

5. Credit for Marginal-Small Farmers

14.19 The position of institutional credit with respect to agriculture, and more so, with respect to marginal and small farmers has been reviewed by the Commission and is found to be extremely unsatisfactory. As far as marginal and small farmers are concerned, the RBI does not maintain separate record of their credit off-take, which is a great drawback to any Government committed to the improvement of the poor and vulnerable in our country. But surveys such as the Situation Assessment Survey of Farmers (2003) bring out their dismal state. The Commission is of the view, that in addition to the steps already taken by Government and the banking system, the following measures need to be initiated:

14.20 First, the priority sector guidelines need to be revised and a target of 10 per cent needs to be fixed for marginal and small farmers. At present, the revised priority sector lending guidelines announced by the RBI on 30th April, 2007 fix a quota of 18 per cent for agriculture, 10 per cent for weaker sections, including marginal and small farmers, and 12 per cent for other designated purposes. However, the agricultural quota includes direct agricultural loans to corporate entities up to Rs. 10 million and for even higher amounts for indirect agricultural activities. The limit of loan for activities eligible for direct agriculture has been raised to Rs. 2 million. The Commission recommends that the priority sector guidelines of the RBI be amended and a 10 per cent quota, out of the 18 per cent presently assigned for agriculture, be fixed for farmers with land holdings below 2 hectares. The weaker section quota for small and marginal farmers may then be released for other socio-economically weaker segments.

14.21 Second, the Reserve Bank should separately monitor the credit flow to this segment of farmers i.e. marginal and small farmers.

14.22 Third, the Commission, in its detailed report on credit has recommended measures to increase the outreach of the banking sector in rural areas and in areas of financial exclusion. These recommendations should be considered and implemented by government on an urgent basis.

The Commission recommends the accelerated expansion of the watershed development programmes and Rainfed Area Programmes in the country to revive agriculture in the rainfed agricultural land, on which a large number of the rural poor are dependent, as an immediate priority.

The Commission is of the view that the Central Government could provide guidelines and assistance to other states experiencing agrarian distress, both natural and market related, for setting up Farmers Debt Relief Commissions. It is recommended that the Government, as part of the relief package, could extend assistance to the State Commissions on a 75:25 basis.

14.23 Fourth, 20 - 40 per cent of marginal and small farmers are excluded from the formal financial sector due to lack of patta and title deeds. The majority of these farmers are informal tenants. The RBI has issued guidelines, following the Swarnakar Committee recommendations that such farmers be extended credit on the basis of certificates issued by the panchayats. These guidelines should be complied with by the banks and the procedures simplified to the extent necessary. However, in order to reduce the perceived risk of default of this excluded segment, as well as the larger segment of marginal and small farmers, due to which the banks do not approach these farmers actively, the Commission is of the view that the Government may set up a Credit Guarantee Fund in NABARD, on the lines of the CGF set up by the Ministry of Micro, Small and Medium Enterprises which provides guarantee cover on loans to small units.

6. Farmers' Debt Relief Commission

14.24 The Commission has analysed the overall condition of farmers as well as the acute distress faced by them in some parts of the country. The impact of the agrarian distress has been felt most by marginal and small farmers. The access of these farmers to institutional credit being limited, they are compelled to take recourse to non-institutional sources of credit. Failure to repay these loans on time is one of the several causes of the crisis leading to tremendous vulnerability of this group of farmers.

14.25 The government has already initiated a number of measures to alleviate the distress faced by farmers specially with respect to 31 districts, in the four states of Andhra Pradesh, Maharashtra, Karnataka, and Kerala, for which a special package has been launched. The measures aim at removing the causes of distress, restoring and increasing the flow of institutional credit, and reducing the debt burden to institutional agencies. But the affected farmers, particularly the marginal and small farmers are indebted to non-institutional sources, and due to absence of title deeds etc (more so in the case of tenants), they are not able to approach the institutional agencies. In order to address the problem of debt burden due to private moneylenders, the Kerala Government has set up the Kerala State Farmers' Debt Relief Commission (in 2007), to look at these problems on a case by case basis.

14.26 The Commission is of the view that the Central Government could provide guidelines and assistance to other states experiencing agrarian distress, both natural and market related, for setting up Farmers Debt Relief Commissions. It is recommended that the Government, as part of the relief package, could extend assistance to the State Commissions on a 75:25 basis. The Debt Relief Commissions, as part of their award, should also examine and institute measures which ensure the entitlement of the marginal/small farmers to institutional credit. These measures would complement the measures already announced by the Government.

C. Measures to Improve Growth of the Non-agricultural Sector

7. Improve Credit Flow to the Non-agricultural Sector.

14.27 The Commission has analysed the credit situation for the unorganised non-agricultural sector in detail in a separate Report. This shows the extremely poor as also declining access of this sector to institutional credit. The Commission's Report on Credit contains a set of detailed recommendations for improving the access of the sector to bank credit, which address both the demand and the supply side of credit for the unorganised sector. This proposed Action Plan, however, highlights some of the key recommendations of this report which, in our view should be taken up on an immediate basis.

The Commission's Report on Credit contains a set of detailed recommendations for improving the access of the sector to bank credit, which address both the demand and the supply side of credit for the unorganised sector. This proposed Action Plan, however, highlights some of the key recommendations of this report which, in our view should be taken up on an immediate basis.

(a) Priority Sector Lending Policy was introduced in early seventies to improve credit flow to the relatively low bankable sectors. However, over the years, particularly after the mid-nineties, relatively high credit worthy activities like housing, education, transportation, and loans to professionals have been included in the priority sector. This has affected unfavourably the credit flow to the needy sectors. At present the priority sector targets are as follows: agriculture - 18 per cent; weaker sections - 10 per cent; others including small and micro enterprises - 12 per cent. There is no separate designated target for small and micro enterprises. The Commission recommends that an explicit target of 10 per cent be set for lending to small and micro enterprises. Within this, a 4 per cent target be set with respect to micro enterprises with capital investment (other than land and building) up to Rs.0.5 million. Since the priority sector quota for agriculture is 18 per cent (of which 10 per cent should be reserved for the small and marginal farmers), and another 10 per cent as suggested above for small and micro enterprises, this would leave a quota of 12 per cent from the total priority sector allocation of 40 per cent, which, in the Commission's view, should be allocated for socio-economically weaker sections, for purposes of housing, education, professions etc. with a loan ceiling of Rs. 0.5 million.

(b) The Commission has made a number of recommendations in its Report on credit to overcome the problem of shrinking outreach in rural areas. This includes clubbing of branches for assessment of profit and incentives for opening branches in unserved areas. It is recommended that the RBI issue necessary guidelines in this respect. Further, the RBI, based on the recommendations of the Khan Committee, has permitted the banks to adopt the agency model consisting of business correspondents and business facilitators, by utilizing civil society organizations, and existing infrastructure. However, banks are not inclined to adopt this model because of cost considerations, Hence, the Commission is of the view that some incentives may be provided to the banks, in the form of tax or other benefits, to adopt this model.

(c) As we have suggested in the case of credit to marginal and small farmers, the RBI should issue guidelines for monitoring of credit flow to the micro-enterprise sector, with capital investment up to Rs.0.5million and between Rs.0.5 to 2.5 million.

(d) The cost of credit to the unorganised non-agricultural sector should be affordable and should be kept on par with the agricultural sector.

8. *Encouraging SHGs and MFIs for Livelihood Promotion*

14.28 The Commission's review of micro-credit in its Report on Credit, as well as earlier in this Report has shown that micro credit has grown over the years as a major instrument in reducing financial exclusion. Micro-credit in India is generally extended through the self-help group approach.

14.29 Despite the success of the different micro credit models, the main problems/constraints being experienced in the expansion of micro-credit, are: (i) regional imbalance, (ii) distortion arising out of subsidy under SGSY programme and (iii) difficulty in graduating to micro enterprise financing; (iv) the difficulty of the sector in offering a range of suitable products due to regulatory and other issues. To overcome these, the Commission suggests the following measures:

(a) Keeping in view the need and success achieved under the micro credit programme there is need to encourage the growth of SHGs and microfinance in financially excluded regions. As the sector covers the weaker sections of society, the government should consider setting up as an incentive fund desirably located in the National Fund proposed by the Commission, which could be utilized for promoting SHGs through NGOs and capacity building of the agencies involved.

(b) Apart from this, it is also necessary to encourage the micro finance institutions (MFIs) by way of permitting them to expand the scope of their activities to insurance, acting as bank correspondents, as also give them performance based tax rebates etc.

(c) The availability of subsidy for the members of the SHGs under SGSY programme tends to shorten the life of SHGs as they are formed for garnering the subsidy, which also may encourage migration of members from one programme to the other. It is therefore suggested that subsidy component of SGSY be pooled into the funds made available under the programme for capacity building and establishing infrastructure and backward-forward linkages.

(d) There is an urgent need to examine issues relating to a variety of restrictions and regulations by multiple authorities, areas of operation, tax regime, entry level capital requirement, integrated provision of credit, thrift, social security, marketing and other support services; as a result of which MFIs are not in a position to expand their operations and grow beyond a certain size.

9. Creation of a National Fund (NAFUS)

14.30 Apart from the inadequacy of credit, a low level of technology, difficulty in arranging critical raw materials, marketing of products, lack of skills etc. are among the significant issues which need to be addressed in the case of the unorganised sector. The Commission's work on credit has brought out that the institutions such as SIDBI and NABARD are not rendering these promotional services effectively. In view of the above, there is need for an agency to specifically take care of the integrated requirements of the entire unorganised sector covering both financial and promotional requirement.

14.31 The Commission recommends an agency be created for the development of the unorganised sector which shall be called **National Fund for the Unorganised Sector (NAFUS).** The NAFUS will be a statutory body with an initial corpus of Rs. 50 billion which will be funded by Central government, public sector banks, financial sector institutions and other government agencies. Details of the Fund are being submitted separately to Government as part of the Commissions' Report on credit.

14.32 The aims and functions of the Fund would not merely be to enable better access of credit to farm and non-farm enterprises alone but to enable the unorganised sector to benefit in the areas of marketing, technology, skill and entrepreneurship, guidance and counseling and capacity building. Though some of these areas are mentioned as objectives of NABARD and SIDBI, but they get subsumed primarily in their credit related activities. It may be noted that SIDBI's mandate now also covers medium enterprises up to investment limit of Rs. 100 million. Micro units are generally out of its purview.

14.33 The target group of the Fund on the other hand, would be the micro enterprises, with focus on those below an investment of Rs. 0.5 million. These constitute 94 per cent of the small enterprises in the country but they receive approximately two per cent of the Net Bank Credit despite providing employment to 70 million people and contributing 30 per cent of industrial production (NCEUS 2007). As the fund would have the flexibility of entering into an arrangement with financing and developmental agencies in the public and private sector, it is expected to ensure convergence among the various institutions and programmes and supplement their efforts through refinancing and confidence building schemes for the banks.

14.34 In effect, the NAFUS, recommended by the Commission, would cater to the requirements of the unorganised sector, much the same way as NABARD and SIDBI cater to the needs of the rural sector and the small enterprises respectively, but with a broader developmental perspective.

10. Upscaling Cluster Development through Growth Poles

14.35 The Commission has piloted "Growth Poles" for the unorganised sector, based on a concept of developing a cluster of clusters in project mode with public-private partnership. The outcomes of the pilot approach, reflected in the Detailed Project Reports prepared for the states of Rajasthan, West Bengal, Kerala, Chhattisgarh, Uttarakhand and Assam has now led the Commission to recommend the adoption of 'Growth Pole' model for cluster development.

14.36 The Commission's recommendation of 'Growth Poles' involves an upscaling of cluster development efforts through provision of common infrastructure, service centres etc. designed to take the existing cluster development approach to the next level. It is based upon strengthening natural clustering of industrial units to achieve economies of scale in skill acquisition, technology development, marketing etc. This recommendation of the Commission is based on the assumption that clusters once developed would lead to a multiplier effect on production and employment as also a spread effect in rural areas.

In effect, the NAFUS, recommended by the Commission, would cater to the requirements of the unorganised sector, much the same way as NABARD and SIDBI cater to the needs of the rural sector and the small enterprises respectively, but with a broader developmental perspective.

As part of this Action Plan, the Commission recommends that twenty-five growth poles (one in each state) be supported during the 11th Plan. The Commission also recommends that 'Growth Poles' should be given the same incentives currently being offered to Special Economic Zones. This will facilitate the unorganised sector infant enterprises and thus have a stimulating multiplier effect on the economy.

The NCEUS proposes that an SPV may be formed for the Growth Pole consisting of stakeholders from within and outside the area to enable focused development in the region. This is proposed to be initiated under a strong public private partnership approach where the stakeholders are participants from the inception of the programme.

14.37 As part of this Action Plan, the Commission recommends that twenty-five growth poles (one in each state) be supported during the 11th Plan.

14.38 The Commission also recommends that 'Growth Poles' should be given the same incentives currently being offered to Special Economic Zones. This will facilitate the unorganised sector infant enterprises and thus have a stimulating multiplier effect on the economy.

D. Measures to Expand Employment and Improve Employability

11. Expand Employment through Strengthening Self-employment Programmes

14.39 As shown earlier in this Report, more than 60 per cent of the unorganised workers are engaged in self-employment. The Commission has reviewed the four major self-employment generation programmes namely, Prime Minister's Rozgar Yojana (PMRY), Rural employment Generation Programme (REGP), Swarnjayanti Gram Swarozgar Yojana (SGSY) and Swarnjayanti Shahari Rozgar Yojana (SJSRY) with a component of Urban Self-Employment Programme (USEP), which are available for rural and urban persons seeking opportunities for self-employment. Nearly 9.4 million persons were assisted during the 10th Plan period under these self-employment programmes.

14.40 The Ministry of MSME has recently examined two programmes/schemes, namely, PMRY and REGP, being handled by it, and has proposed their merger to have a better focus and concentration of efforts for generating employment and balanced and sustainable industrialization in the non-farm sector. The new merged scheme proposed by the Ministry of MSME, to be called Prime Minister Employment Generation Programme (PMEGP), targets generation of 10 million additional employment opportunities in the 11th Plan.

14.41 The Commission is of the view that the move to merge these two programmes is a positive step. Further, the Commission is also of the view that there is a good case for consideration of a single self-employment programme for the rural areas, and a separate one for the urban areas. Also as a broad objective, there is a case for rationalization of various programmes as the grass roots administration is being overburdened with enhanced financial allocations and enhanced pressures of implementing increasing number of missions and schemes.

14.42 The Commission's report on credit has revealed that the bank credit to the micro segment has largely piggy backed on the above schemes. Therefore, keeping in view (a) the impact of the programmes; (b) that banks are more comfortable lending to the unorganised sector under the government's self-employment programmes; (c) large number of jobs have to inevitably come from the non-farm unorganised sector, it is essential that the self-employment programmes be strengthened considerably. For these reasons, the Commission recommends that the target of employment under the self-employment schemes should be raised to at least 5 million per year as against about 2 million per year proposed at present by the 11th Plan.

12. Universalise and Strengthen NREGA

14.43 The Commission strongly endorses the approach of providing a minimum guarantee of employment through the National Rural Employment Guarantee

the Commission recommends that the target of employment under the self-employment schemes should be raised to at least 5 million per year as against about 2 million per year proposed at present by the 11th Plan.

Programme. Apart from providing a guarantee of minimum employment, the Programme has created a precedence by integrating labour standards and an insurance safety net in the programme, and building in greater transparency and accountability. The Commission suggests the following measures to strengthen the ongoing programme:

i. The programme can be universalized ahead of schedule, in the third year itself. Since the Government has already succeeded in scaling up the programme to 330 poorest districts in two years, and the uncovered districts are not high-need districts, the financial implications of doing this will not be high.

ii. A number of measures need to be taken to ensure good performance of the programme. For this, the following issues should be addressed on a priority basis: (i) Constraints on administrative capacity and training need to be removed and the permissible administrative cost needs to be increased to 5 per cent; (ii) On the employment front, the cap on employment of 100 days a year to be provided per household should be removed and the programme should be purely demand based, on the lines of the Maharashtra Employment Guarantee Scheme. Other important issues relate to issuance of job cards, measurement of work, gender disparity in wages and delay in wage payments. (iii) Clearer provision needs to be made with respect to work site facilities such as crèche, drinking water and first aid; (iv) the list of works in Schedule 1 of the Act should be enlarged. In particular, the unskilled work required to improve the quality of social sector programmes can be brought under this list.

iii. A number of states have introduced innovations in the maintenance of accounts and records, wage payments and improving transparency. These developments need to be encouraged. The Centre may allocate some part of the administrative charge to such innovations. It may be noted that these developments are in line with the Commission's recommendations on the use of universal ID cards for social security registration and transactions through a book-keeper (the post office), with shadow accounts being maintained by the National Social Security Board.

iv. Along with providing an employment safety net, the NREG's objective is also to increase the productive capacity of rural areas and create sustainable rural livelihoods. This requires increased local capacity, good local planning, creation of a shelf of projects, and a dovetailing with other major programmes, especially around improved land and water management.

13. Increasing the Employability through Skill Development

14.44 The Commission has reviewed the skill development initiatives presently been undertaken in the country and is preparing a detailed Report on the subject. The Report brings out the inadequacy of skill development programmes for unorganised sector workers who have low levels of education. The Commission has noted that a Centrally Sponsored Scheme with 100 per cent Central Assistance, "Skill Development Initiative" (SDI), has been approved recently by the Cabinet Committee on Economic Affairs for implementation at a total cost of Rs. 5.5 billion. The objective of the Scheme is to provide training to school leavers, existing workers, ITI graduates, etc. to improve their employability by optimally utilizing the infrastructure available in government and private institutions and industry. The Scheme aims to train or test and certify one million persons or their existing skills tested and certified over a period of five years. About 200 modules for employable skills as per industry and labour market demands would be identified and course curriculum developed. On an average, an expenditure of Rs. 5000/- per person is expected to be incurred on imparting training and certification of work force under the SDI scheme.

14.45 The Commission is of the view that even as the DGET proposal is in the right direction. The Commission further recommends that the DGET scheme as approved could be expanded through a supplementary on-job-training cum employment-assurance programme for an additional sum of Rs. 5000 per person to be provided as one time payment as incentive to any employer

The NREGA can be universalized ahead of schedule, in the third year itself. Since the Government has already succeeded in scaling up the programme to 330 poorest districts in two years, and the uncovered districts are not high-need districts, the financial implications of doing this will not be high.

who is willing to provide on job training for skill enhancement for at least one year to the trained worker. This incentive will be released to the employer after verification at the end of the year. It may be mentioned here that the NREG also provides for a sum of Rs. 10,000 per rural household requiring employment. The employer for this purpose need not be covered by the Apprenticeship Act. As in the case of the DGET Skill Development programme, the regional directorates of apprenticeship training would monitor both skill development and the on-the-job training.

14.46 The Commission is also of the view that since the SDI and the programme proposed by it, are crucial programmes for increasing the employability of the unorganised sector workers, the target of the programme should be at least doubled from the present with more pro-active collaboration of the State Governments.

References

Abraham, V. and Sharma, R.K. 2005. "New Technology and the Emerging Labour Market: A Study of Indian IT Industry", *Indian Journal of Labour Economics*, 48 (4).

Acharya, S. and Jose. A.V. 1991. *"Employment and Mobility: A Study among Workers of Low-Income Households in Bombay City"*, I1O-ARTEP Working Papers, New Delhi.

Advani, R. 1998. "Legal Status of Street Vendors", *Labour File*, A4 (11) November-December.

Anand, V. 1991. "*Small Enterprises and Urban Economy*", Chugh Publications, Allahabad.

Anant, T. C. A. and Sundaram, K. 1998. "Wage Policy in India: A Review", *The Indian Journal of Labour Economics*, 41(4): 815-34.

Anker, R. 1998. "*Gender and Jobs: Sex Segregation of Occupations in the Worlds*", International Labor Organisation, Geneva.

Ascoly, N. and Zeldenrust, I. 2001. "*Discussing Key Elements of Monitoring and Verification, Amsterdam*", Centre for Research on Multinational Corporations.

Babu, R. P. 2004. "Cyber Coolies in BPO: Insecurities and Vulnerabilities of Non-Standard Work", *Economic and Political Weekly,* Jan 31

Bahuguna, N.J. 2007. "Smart streets, shattered lives", *Women's Feature Service*, March 26th, www.wfsnews.org.

Balakrishnan, P. 2000. "Agriculture and Economic Reforms – Growth and Welfare" *Economic and Political Weekly,* 35(14): 1143

Bandohpadhyay D. 2004. "Preventable Deaths" Commentary *Economic and Political Weekly,* July 24

Banerjee, N. and Nihila, M. 1999. "Business Organisation in Leather Industries of Calcutta and Chennai", in Bagchi A. K. (ed.). *Economy and Organisation: Indian Industries under the Neo-liberal Regime*, Sage Publications. New Delhi.

Barat, T. 2004. "*The Dark side of Indian Homes*", http://www.indiatogether.org/2004/nov/hrt-domhelp.htm accessed on 18-02-2007

Baririentos, S., Sood, A and Mathur, K. 2006. *"Findings and Recommendations from a Case Study in India"*, IDS, Sussex, 2006

Bhagat, B. R. 2005. *"Conceptual Issues in Measurement of Internal Migration in India"*, paper presented at the XXVth IUSSP International Conference held in Tours, France.

Bhagat, M. 1997. "Poverty and Minimum Wages", *The Indian Journal of Labour Economics*, 40(4): 721-30.

Bhalla, G.S. 1995. "Introduction," in Bhalla, G.S. (ed.), *Economic Liberalisation and Indian Agriculture*, Institute of Studies in Industrial Development, New Delhi.

Bhalla, G.S. 1997. "Structural Adjustment and the Agricultural Sector in India," in Chadha, G.K. and Alakh N. Sharma (eds), *Growth, Employment and Poverty: Change and Continuity in Rural India*, Vikas Publishing House, New Delhi.

Bhalla, G.S. 2000. "Political Economy of Indian Development in the 20th Century: India's Road to Freedom and Growth," Presidential Address, 83rd Conference Indian Economic Association, *Indian Economic Journal*, 48(3).

Bhat, Ela R. 1994. "The Unprotected Labour", *The Indian Journal of Labour Economics*, 37(3).

Bhattacharya, B. B. and Sakthivel., S. 2004. *"Economic Reforms and Jobless Growth in India"*. Working Paper Series No. E/245/2004. Institute of Economic Growth.

Bhowmik, S.K. undated. "*Hawkers and the Urban Informal Sector: A Study of Street Vending in Seven Cities*", National Alliance of Street Vendors of India. http://www.streetnet.org.za/English/ page10.htm

Brassard, C. 2006. "Impact of Wage and Labour Regulation in Vietnam", in Brassard, C. and Acharya, S. (eds.), *Labour Market Regulation and Deregulation in Asia*: 81-110, Acedemic Foundation, New Delhi.

Breman, J. 1996. "*Footloose Labour: Working in India's Informal Economy*", Cambridge University Press, Cambridge.

Burra, N. 1989. *"Child Labour in the Brass-Ware Industry of Moradabad, Uttar Pradesh"*, International Labor

Organization/Asian Regional Team for Employment Promotion, New Delhi.

Burra, N. 1995. "*Born to Work*", Oxford University Press, New Delhi.

Carr, M. and Chen, M.A. 2001. *"Globalization and the Informal Economy: How Global Trade and Investment Impact on the Working Poor"*, Working Paper, Women in Informal Employment Globalizing and Organizing (WIEGO).

Census of India 2001. *"Migration Tables – India"*, Office of Registrar General, India.

Chadha, G. K. and Sahu, P.P. 2002. "Post-Reform Setbacks in Rural Employment: Issues that Need Further Scrutiny". *Economic and Political Weekly*, May 25: 1998-2026.

Chandra, N. (1999. "Legal Regulation of Labour Market", *The Indian Journal of Labour Economics*, 42 (4).

Chandrasekhar, C. P. 1997. "The Economics Consequences of Abolition of Child Labour: An Indian Case Study", *The Journal of Peasant Studies*, 24(3):137-179.

Chen, M., Vanek, J. and Carr, M., 2004. *"Mainstreaming Informal Employment and Gender in Poverty Reduction: A Handbook for Policy Makers and Other Stakeholders"'* Commonwealth Secretariat, London.

CSO 2000. "*Report of the Time Use Survey*", Central Statistical Organisation Ministry of Statsitics and Programme Implementation, New Delhi.

Das, B. 1994. "Slums, Migrations and the Urban Informal Sector in Surat City", *The Indian Journal of Labour Economics*, 37(3).

Das, K. 2003. "Income and Employment in Informal Manufacturing: A case Study", in Renana Jhabvala, Rathan Sudarshan and Jeemol Unni (eds) *Informal Economy Centrestage: New Structures of Employment*, Sage Publications, New Delhi.

Desai, K. and Raj, D. 2001. *"Child Labour in Diamond Industry of Surat"*, NLI Research Studies Series No 19/ 2001, V.V. Giri National Labour Institute, Noida Uttar Pradesh.

Desai, M. 1993. "The People's Tribunal on Bargi", *Lokayan Bulletin.*

Deshpande R.S and Prabhu, N. 2005. "Farmers Distress Proof Beyond Question" *Economic and Political Weekly*, October 29.

Dev, M.S., Galab, S., Reddy, P.P., Vinayan, S., Rani, G.S., and Raju,D.S.R 2005. "*Handloom Sector in Andhra Pradesh: Problems, Prospects and Policy Options*", Centre for Economic and Social Studies, Begumpet, Hyderabad.

Dewan, R. 2001. "*Ethics of Employment and Exports: Societal Dialogue and Fish Processing Export Units in India*", in Oberai, A.S., Sivananthiran, A. and Venkata Ratnam, C.S. (eds) *'Labour Issues in Export Processing Zones: Role of Social Dialogue'*, I.L.O: 221 – 273.

Dewan, R. 2005. "*Gender Budget Perspectives on Macro and Micro Policies in Small Urban Manufacturies in Greater Mumbai*", Discussion Paper Series-12, Human Development Resource Centre, UNDP, New Delhi.

Dharmalingam, A. 1995. "Conditions of Work in a South Indian Village", *Economic and Political Weekly*, November 25

Dhavse, R. 2004. "Organising Inside the_Home", http:// www.indiatogether.org/2004/apr/eco-domestic.htm, accessed on 18-02-2007

Economic Survey 2006 – 2007. "Economic Survey", *Government of India. Ministry of Finance. New Delhi.*

Engelshoven, M. 1999. "Diamonds and Patels: A Report on the Diamond Industry in Surat", in J. P. Parry, J. Breman, and K. Kapadia (eds.) The World's of Indian Industrial Labour, *Sage, New Delhi: 353-377.*

FitzGerald, E.V.K. 2001. "*Regulating Large International Firms*", Technology, Business and Society Paper No. 5, United Nations Research Institute for Social Development.

Freeman, R. 1984. "*Strategic Management: A Stakeholder Approach*", Pitman, Boston

Ghellab, Y. 1998. "*Minimum Wages and Youth Employment*", Employment and Training Papers 26, ILO Geneva.

Ghosh, R. 2004. *"Brick Kiln Workers: A Study of Migration, Labour process and Employment"*, NLI Research Studies Series No 57/2004, V.V. Giri National Labour Institute, Noida Uttar Pradesh.

Ghosh, R. and Sharma, R. 2003. *"Child Labour in the Glass Bangle Industry of Firozabad"*, NLI Research Studies Series No 40/2003, V.V. Giri National Labour Institute, Noida Uttar Pradesh.

Gill Anita and Singh, L. 2006. "Farmer's Suicides and Response of Public Policy, Evidences, Diagnosis and Alternatives Form Punjab", *Economic and Political Weekly*, June 30: 2762-2768

GOI 1988. *"Shramshakti: Report of the National Commission on Self-employed Women and Women in the Informal Sector"*, Department of Women and Child Development, Ministry of Human Resource Development, Government of India, New Delhi.

GOI 2004-2005. *"Annual Report – 2004-2005"*, Ministry of Labour, Government of India.

GOI 2006. "Social, Economic and Educational Status of the Muslim Community of India: A Report", *Prime Minister's High Level Committee, Cabinet Secretariat, New Delhi.*

GOM 2001. *"The Minimum Wages Act, 1948: Act No.11 of 1948 and The Maharashtra Minimum Wages Rules 1963, with Notifications"*, Labour Law Agency, Mumbai.

Gordon, K. and Miyake, M. 2001. *"Deciphering Codes of Corporate Conduct: A Review of* Comments", Paris, OECD in Utting, 92001. *Regulating Business vis 'Multistakeholder Initiatives': A Preliminary* Assessment", United Nations Research Institute for Social Development.

Gothoskar, S. et al 1998. *"Neither Bread nor Roses, a Comparative Study of Women and Men Workers in the Galas of Industrial Estates in Mumbai"*, Worker's Solidarity Centre, Mumbai.

GOTN 1998. *"Report of the Committee Constituted to Study the Problems and Issues of Unorganised Labour in Tamil Nadu"*, Office of the Commissioner of Labour, government of Tamil Nadu, Chennai,

Goyal P. K. 2005. *"Street Children and the Child Labour"*, Vista International Publications, Delhi.

Gupta, J. 2003. "Informal Labour in Brick Kilns: Need for Regulation", *Economic and Political Weekly*, August 2.

Haberfeld, Y., Menaria, R.K., Sahoo, B.B. and Vyas, R.N. 1999. "Seasonal migration of rural labor in India", *Population Research and Policy Review*, 18 (5), Netherlands.

Hanartani, M.M. 2005. *"Decent Work Programme In Indonesia"*, Report submit to 2nd Sub Regional Tripartite Forum on Decent Work in South East Asia and the Pacific, Melbourne, Australia, 5-8 April 2005, http://www.ilo.org/public/english/region/asro/manila/downloads/dwind.pdf , accessed on 21-12-2006

Hannan, M. 2001. *"The Agricultural Workers Welfare Bill, 2001"*.

Herlina, A. 1997. *"Workers' Conditions in Indonesia (5) - Hearing On The Social ... Public Hearing On The Social Clause: Human Rights Promotion Or Protectionism?"*, Committee On Foreign Affairs, Security And Defence Policy, Subcommittee On Human Rights, Brussels, 17 and 18 June 1997, http://www.europarl.europa.eu/hearings/19970617/droi/doc5_en.htm , accessed on 21-12-2006.

Homenet South Asia and ISST. 2006. "S*ocial Protection for Home-based Women Workers in South Asia: Learning from Action and Research"*, Unpublished, Institute of Social Studies Trust, New Delhi, June.

IDS 2006. *"The Informal Economy Workers, Especially Women, in the State of Rajasthan"*, Study commissioned by the International Labour Organisation, New Delhi, Draft Report, Institute of Development Studies, Jaipur.

ILO 1999. *"Decent Work for All"*, International Labour Organisation, Geneva.

ILO 2001. *"Reducing the Decent Work Deficit: A Global Challenge"*, 89th Session, Report 1(A), International Labour Conference, Geneva.

ILO 2002a. "Report of Seventeenth International Conference of Labour Statisticians", *International Labour Organisation, Geneva.*

ILO 2002b. *"Decent Work and the Informal Economy,"* Report VI, International Labour Conference, 90th Session 2002

ILO 2002c. *"A Future without Child Labour"*. ILO Global Report of the Director-General., International Labour Organization, Geneva.

ILO 2002d. "Women and Men in the Informal Economy: A Statistical Picture", *Employment Sector, International Labour Organization, Geneva.*

ILO 2003. "Making End Meet: Bidi Workers in India today: A Study of Four States", Sectoral Activities Programme, *Working Paper, International Labour Organization, Geneva.*

Jenkins, R. 2001. "*Corporate Codes of Conduct: Self Regulation in a Global Economy*", Technology, Business and Society Paper No. 2, United Nations Research Institute for Social Development.

Jeyarajan, J. 2002. *"Child Labour in Chrompet Leather Manufacturing Units of Tamil Nadu*", NLI Research Studies Series No 35/2002, V.V. Giri National Labour Institute, Noida Uttar Pradesh.

Jhabvala, R. 1998. "Minimum Wages Based on Worker's Needs", *Economic and Political Weekly*, 33(10): 500-502.

Jhabvala, R. 2000. "Roles and Perceptions", *Seminar*, 491 (July).

Jodhka, S. S. (2006. "Beyond 'Crisis' Rethinking Contemporary Punjab Agriculture", *Economic and Political Weekly*, April 22: 1530- 1537

John, J. 2000. "The Saga of Rickshaw Pullers", *Labour File*, A6(8).

John, J. and Ghosh, R. 2002. *"Study of Child Labour in the Zardosi and Hathari Units of Varansi*", NLI Research Studies Series No 38/2002, V.V. Giri National Labour Institute, Noida Uttar Pradesh.

Joshi, H, and V. Joshi 1976. "*Surplus Labour and the City: A Case Study of Bombay"* Oxford University Press, Delhi.

Kaur, R., Ghosh, P.K. and Ratna, M. S. 2007. "Trade Liberalization and Informality in the Rice Processing Industry", *in Barbara Harris-White and Anushree Sinha, edited, Trade Liberalization and India's Informal Economy", Oxford University Press, Delhi.*

Kundu, A., Sarangi, N. and Paritosh, B. 2005. "Non-Farm Employment and Rural-Urban Inter-Linkages" in Nayyar, R. and Sharma, A.N. (ed.) *Rural Transformation in India: The Role of Non-farm Sector*, Institute for Human Development, New Delhi.

Kurien, C.T. 1978. "Small Sector in New Industrial Policy", *Economic and Political Weekly*, March 4.

Labour Bureau 1979. 'Report on the Working and Living Conditions of Workers in Building Construction Industry in Delhi", *Labour Bureau, Ministry of Labour, Government of India, Chandigarh/Shimla*

Labour Bureau 1981. 'Report on the Working and Living Conditions of Workers in Metalware Industry at Jagadhari (Haryana)", *Labour Bureau, Ministry of Labour, Government of India, Chandigarh/Shimla*

Labour Bureau 1982. 'Report on the Working and Living Conditions of Workers in Brick kiln Industry in Chandigarh Union Territory", *Labour Bureau, Ministry of Labour, Government of India, Chandigarh/Shimla*

Labour Bureau 1992a. 'Report on the Working and Living Conditions of Workers in Handloom Industry in India", *Labour Bureau, Ministry of Labour, Government of India, Chandigarh/Shimla.*

Labour Bureau 1992b. 'Report on the Working and Living Conditions of Workers in Powerloom Industry in India", *Labour Bureau, Ministry of Labour, Government of India, Chandigarh/Shimla*

Labour Bureau 1992c. "*Report on the Working and Living Conditions of Workers in the Unorganised Sector, Toys and Dolls Industry in India"*, Ministry of Labour, Shimla/ Chandigarh.

Labour Bureau 1995a. "*Report on the Working and Living Conditions of Workers in the Unorganised Sector, Beedi Industry in India"*, Ministry of Labour, Shimla/ Chandigarh.

Labour Bureau 1995b. 'Report on the Working and Living Conditions of Workers in Readymade Garment Industry in India", *Labour Bureau, Ministry of Labour, Government of India, Chandigarh/Shimla*

Labour Bureau 1996. 'Report on the Working and Living Conditions of Workers in Beedi Industry in India", *Labour Bureau, Ministry of Labour, Government of India, Chandigarh/Shimla*

Labour Bureau 1998. 'Report on the Working and Living Conditions of Workers in Man Made Fibre Textile Industry in India", *Labour Bureau, Ministry of Labour, Government of India, Chandigarh/Shimla*

Labour Bureau 2000. 'Report on the Working and Living Conditions of Workers in Artistic Metalware Industry in India", *Labour Bureau, Ministry of Labour, Government of India, Chandigarh/Shimla*

Labour Bureau 2007. Indian Labour Journal, *Ministry of Labour and Employment, Government of India, 48 (1. 7.*

Labour File. 1998a. "Do Tokri Ki Jagah", *Labour File*, A4 (11) November-December.

Labour File. 1998b. "The Bellagio International Declaration of Street Vendors", *Labour File*, A4 (11) November-December.

Lahiri, S. 1998. "A Matter of Policy", *Labour File*, A4 (11) November-December.

Laskar, B. I. 2000. "Conditions of Child Labour in Aligarh Lock Industry", *Economic and Political Weekly*, Feb 12-18

Li Qi, Taylor, B. and Frost, S. 2003. "*Labour Relations and Regulation in Vietnam: Theory and Practice*", University of Hong Kong Working Paper Series No. 53.

Lum, T. 2003. *"Workplace Codes of Conduct in China and Related Labor Conditions*", Report for Congress, Order Code RL 31862. Congressional Research Service, The library of Congress.

Lustig, N.C and McLeod, D. 1997. "Minimum Wages and Poverty in Developing Countries: Some Empirical Evidence", *Labor Markets in Latin America*, Brookings Institution Press, Washington DC.

Majumdar, B. 2006. *"Influx of Forced Labour: Nature and Causes", The Indian Journal of Labor Economics, 49 (1): 133 - 141.*

Mamgain, R. P. 1996. "Employment Conditions in the Indian Food Processing Industy: Retrospect and Prospects", *Indian Journal of Labour Economics, 39 (2): 299-315.*

McCormick, D. and Hubert, S. 2002. "*Manual for Value Chain Research on Homeworkers in the Garment Industry*", Institute of Development Studies, University of Sussex.

Mehrotra and Biggeri (edited). 2007. "Asian Informal Workers: Global Risks, Local Protection", *Routledge New York.*

Menon, S. 1998. "A Voice from Janpath", *Labour File*, A4 (11) November-December.

Menon, S. 2000. 'Delhi: The Relentless Struggle of Rickshaw Pullers', *Labour File*, A6(8).

Mishra, N. K., and Srivastava, R. S. 2002. "Labour and Employment in the Informal Textile Industry in Kanpur", *Labour and Development*, 8 (1-2): 27-61.

Mishra, S.S. 2005. "2005 onwards SA certifications will surely pick up" *Express Textile*, 6 January.

Mitra, S. 2002. "Lessons in Regulating the Informal Sector: The Case of Rickshaw Pullers' Sector in Delhi', *Indian Journal of Labour Economics*, 45(2): 387-394.

Mitra, S. undated. "*Licences and Livelihood: Rickshaw Pullers in Nashik*", Centre for Civil Society, Working Paper No. 0064.

Mohan, R. 2001. *"Small Scale Industry Policy in India: A Critical Evaluation"*, NCAER, New Delhi.

MOLE 2003. *"Report of the Working Group 'To Go Into Codification of The Concept of Minimum Wages, Listing Out Guidelines Based on Critical Evaluation of Various Parameters and Also to Study the Problems in Implementation of Minimum Wages"*, Ministry of Labour, Government of India.

MOLE 2007. *"Annual Report 2006-2007"*, Ministry of Labour & Employment, Government of India.

Mukherjee, M and Mukherjee, P. 2000. "Calcutta: Unhappy Elements in the City of Joy", *Labour File*, A6(8).

Nag, P. K. and Nag, A. 2004. *"Drudgery, Accidents and Injuries in Indian Agriculture"*, *Industrial Health*, 42, 149–162, National Institute of Occupational health, Indian Council of Medical Research, Meghani Nagar, Ahmedabad

Nangia, P. 1981. *"Child work in India: A Preliminary Analysis"*, M Phil Dissertation, Jawaharlal Nehru University, Delhi.

NCAER. 2007. *"Examining Employment Figures on the Handloom Sector"*, Project Leader Sinha, A., commissioned by the All India Artisans and Craftworkers Welfare Association (AIACA).

NCEUS (forthcoming). *"Definitional and Statistical Issues, (Task Force Report)"*, National Commission for Enterprises in the Unorganised Sector, Govt. of India.

NCEUS 2006. *"Report on Social Security for Unorganised Workers"*, National Commission for Enterprises in the Unorganised Sector, Govt. of India.

NCEUS 2007. "Financing of Enterprises in Unorganised Sector", Report of the Task Force on Access to Finance, Raw Material and Marketing to Unorganised Sector, *National Commission for Enterprises in the Unorganised Sector, Draft Report, January* (www.nceus.gov.in).

NCRL 1969. "*Report of the National Commission on Labour*", Ministry of Labour, Government of India, New Delhi

NCRL 1991. "*Report of the National Commission on Rural Labour*", Ministry of Labour, Government of India, New Delhi

Neetha, N. 2002. "Flexible Production, Feminisation and Disorganization: Evidence from Tiruppur Knitwear Industry", *Economic and Political Weekly,* May 25.

Nguyen, N.T., Loi, C.C. and Nguyen, C.T. 2006. "A Stock Taking of Vietnam's Labor Market Policies", in Felipe, J. and Hasan, R. (eds.), *Labour Markets in Asia: Issues and Perspectives*: 301-366, Palgrave Macmillan, New York.

NHRC 2001. "*Report on the Expert Group on Bonded Labour*", National Human Rights Commission, New Delhi (unpublished).

Nihila, Millie 2002. "Growing Industries, Sick Workers: A Study of Leather Tanning Industry of Dindigul from an Occupational Health Perspective", *Review of Development and Change,* 7(1): 134-166.

NSSO 1987. *"Report on Third Quinquennial Survey on Employment-Unemployment Survey Results (All India)"*, 1983, Round 38th, Report No. 341, Ministry of Statistics and Program Implementation. Government of India. New Delhi.

NSSO 1990. *"Report on Employment-Unemployment Situation in India"*, 1987-1988, Round 43rd, Report No. 371, Ministry of Statistics and Program Implementation. Government of India. New Delhi.

NSSO 1992. "*Land and Livestock Holding Survey, Report on Operational Land Holdings in India: Salient Features*", 1992, Round 48th, Report No. 407, Ministry of Statistics and Program Implementation. Government of India. New Delhi

NSSO 1997. *"Employment-Unemployment Situation in India 1993 – 1994"*, Round, Round 50th, Report No. 409, Ministry of Statistics and Program Implementation. Government of India. New Delhi.

NSSO 2001a. *"Employment-Unemployment Situation in India 1999-2000"*, Round 55th, Report No. 458 – I and II (55/10/2), Ministry of Statistics and Program Implementation. Government of India. New Delhi.

NSSO 2001b. "*Migration in India*", 1999-2000, Round 55th, Report No. 470, Ministry of Statistics and Program Implementation. Government of India. New Delhi

NSSO 2005a. "*Situation Assessment Survey of Farmer Households 2003*", Round 59th, Report No. 497a (59/33/5), Ministry of Statistics and Programme Implementation. Government of India. New Delhi.

NSSO 2005b. "*Situation Assessment Survey of Farmer Households 2003*", Round 59th, Report No. 498b (59/33/1), Ministry of Statistics and Programme Implementation. Government of India. New Delhi.

NSSO 2005c. "*Situation Assessment Survey of Farmer Households 2003*", Round 59th, Report No. 496c (59/33/3), Ministry of Statistics and Programme Implementation. Government of India. New Delhi.

NSSO 2005d. "*Situation Assessment Survey of Farmer Households 2003*", Round 59th, Report No. 499d (59/33/2), Ministry of Statistics and Programme Implementation. Government of India. New Delhi.

NSSO 2006a. *"Employment-Unemployment Situation in India 2004 – 2005"*, Round 61st, Report No. 515 – I and II (61/10/1&2), Ministry of Statistics and Program Implementation. Government of India. New Delhi.

NSSO 2006b. "*Some Aspects of Operational Land Holdings in India*", 2003, Round 59th, Report No. 492, Ministry of Statistics and Program Implementation. Government of India. New Delhi

Pais, J. 2002. *"Industrial Structure and Industrial Employment in India in the era of Liberalisation and Globalisation: A Study of Workers in the Leather Accessories Manufacture in Dharavi, Mumbai"*, Presentation June 12, OXFAM GB, New Delhi.

Pais, J. 2003. "*Production Units and the Workforce in Urban Informal Sector: A Case Study from Mumbai*", PhD thesis, Indira Gandhi Institute of Development Research, Mumbai.

Patrick, M. 2001. "Unorganised Women in a Urban Setting: Opportunities and Challenges", In A. Kundu and A.N.Sharma, *Informal Sector in India: Perspectives and Policies*, Institute of Human Development, New Delhi.

Planning Commission 2005. *"Mid-Term Appraisal of the Tenth Five Year Plan"*, http://planningcommission.nic.in/midterm/midtermapp.html, accessed on 26th March 2007.

Planning Commission 2007. "Report of the Steering Committee on Agriculture and Allied Sectors for the Formulation of the Eleventh Five Year Plan", Government of India, http://planningcommission.nic.in/aboutus/committee/strgrp11/str11_agriall.pdf accessed on 25th may 2007.

Raj, N. and Srivastava, R. 2000. *"Children of Carpet Looms: A Study of Home-based Productions of Carpet in Uttar Pradesh"*, NLI Research Studies Series No 11/2000, V.V. Giri National Labour Institute, Noida Uttar Pradesh.

Rajasekhar D. and G. Sreedhar, 2001. "Changing Face of Beedi Industry: A Study of Karnatka", *Economic and Political Weekly*, September 28.

Ramirez-Machado, J. M. 2003. "Domestic Work, conditions of Work and Employment: A Legal Perspective", *Conditions of Work and Employment Series* No. 7, International Labour Office, Geneva.

Rao, R. V. and Hussain, S. 1997. "Women Workers and Struggles in the Garment Export Industry-A Case Study of Delhi", in Sujatha Gothaskar, edited, *Struggles of Women at Work*, Vikas Publishing House, Delhi.

Rawal, V. 2006. "The Labour Process in Rural Haryana (India): A Field-Report from Two Villages", *Journal of Agrarian Change*, 6(4): 538–583.

Roy, A. 1999. "The Greater Common Good, The Human Costs Of Big Dams", Cover Essay, *Frontline*, 16 (11) May. 22 - June 04.

Roy, A. 2000. "Breaking the Shackles: Kol Trial Labourer", *Economic and Political Weekly*, Feb: 5-11.

Rural Labour Enquiry 1993-1994. "Report on Wages & Earnings of Rural Labour Households (50th Round of N.S.S.) 1993-1994", *Government of India.*

Rural Labour Enquiry 1999-2000. *"Report on Wages & Earnings of Rural Labour Households (55th Round of N.S.S.) 1999-2000"*, Government of India, (http://labourbureau.nic.inRLE992k%20WageEarn%20St%203p1a.html) , accessed on 28-06-2007.

Rustagi, P. undated. *"Women in the Context of Migration: Addressing Vulnerabilities and Policy Issues"*, http://www.migrationindia.org/articles WOMEN%20AND%20MIGRATION-%202007.pdf, accessed on 14-01-2007

Saith, Ashwani, 2004. *"Social Protection, Decent Work and Development"*, Discussion Paper, DP/152/2004, International institute for Labour Studies, Geneva.

Sankaran, S. R. 1997. "Minimum Wage Legislation", *The Indian Journal of Labour Economics*, 40(4): 705-13.

Sarmah, S. 2001. "Agricultural Wages in India: A Study of States and Regions", *The Indian Journal Of Labour Economics*, 45(1): 89-116.

Sarvanan and Velayutham, 2002. "Women's Employment and Reduction in Child Workers: Beedi Workers in Rural Tamil Nadu", *Economic and Political Weekly*, December 28.

Sekar R. H. and Mohammad, N. 2001. *"Child Labour in Home Based Lock Industries of Aligarh"*, NLI Research Studies Series No 18/2001, V.V. Giri National Labour Institute, Noida Uttar Pradesh.

Sekar, R. H. 2003. *"Child Labour in Hazardous Industries: A Case of Slaughter House and Allied Occupations"*, NLI Research Studies Series No 47/2003, V.V. Giri National Labour Institute, Noida Uttar Pradesh.

Seminar 2000. "Genesis of Municipal Laws Regarding Vendors", *Seminar*, 491 (July).

Sen 2000. *"A Decade of Human Development"*, Journal of Human Development, 1(1).

Sen, A. and Bhatia, M.S. 2004. "State of the Indian Farmer A millennium Study", Volume 14 *Cost of Cultivation and Farm Income*, Department of Agriculture and Cooperation, Ministry of Agriculture G.O.I, Academic Foundation New Delhi

Sharma, A.N., Sharma, R. and Raj, N. 2000. *"The Impact of Social Labelling on Child Labour in India's Carpet Industry"*, ILO/IPEC (International Labour Organization/ International Programme on the Elimination of Child Labour) Working Paper. Institute for Human Development, New Delhi.

Sharma, K. 2003. "In the Name of Servitude", http://www.indiatogether.org/2003/sep/ksh-domestic.htm, accessed on 18-02-2007

Shukla, V. 2000a. "Kanpur: Rickshaw, A Convenient Convenient", *Labour File*, A6(8).

Shukla, V. 2000b. "Patna: Rickshaw, A Convenient Conveyance", *Labour File*, A6(8).

Shyam, G. 2000. "The New Millennium Cycle Rickshaw", *Labour File*, A6(8).

Singh, A. 2000. "Organizing street vendors", *Seminar*, 491 (July).

Singh, A.K., Joshi, A. and Singh, Y.P. 2006. *"Diagnostic Study of Handloom Clusters in Uttar Pradesh"*, Giri Institute of Development Studies, Lucknow.

Singh, G. 2004. "Retail Trade and Urban Policy" *Economic and Political Weekly*, June 05.

Singh, N. and Sapre, M 2007. "Liberalization in Trade and Finance: India's Garment Sector", in Barbara Harris-White and Anushree Sinha, edited, *Trade Liberalization and India's Informal Economy*", Oxford University Press, Delhi.

Sinha, A. 2006. *"Study Report on Constraints Faced by Small Enterprises – Freedom of Carrying out the Enterprises, Access to Raw Materials, Finance, Skills, Entrepreneurship Development, Infrastructure, Technology and Markets"*, Report Prepared for NCEUS, New Delhi.

SNCL 2002. *"Second National Commission on Labour Report"*, Ministry of Labour, GOI, http://labour.nic.in/lcomm2/nlc_report.html accessed on 09-10-2006

Sood, A. 2003. *"Voluntary Self-Regulation versus Mandatory Legislative Schemes for Implementing Labour Standards: An Issues Paper on the New Regulatory Regime"*, CUTS Centre for International Trade, Economics and Environment, Jaipur.

Srivastava, R. 2000. "Changes in Contractual Relations in Land and Labour in India", *Indian Journal of Agricultural Economics*, 45(3): 253-282

Srivastava, R. 2005. *"Bonded Labor in India: Its Incidence and Pattern"* In Focus Programme on Promoting the Declaration on Fundamental, International Labour Office Cornell University Year 2005

Srivastava, R. 2006. *"Trends In Rural Employment In India With Special Reference To Agricultural Employment"*, Paper presented at Conference on Labour and Employment Issues in India, July 27-29, 2006, New Delhi, organized by Institute for Human Development (IHD) and World Bank.

Srivastava, R. and Sasikumar, S.K. 2005. "An overview of migration in India, its impacts and key issues", *Paper presented at the Regional Conference on Migration, Development and Pro-Poor Policy Choices in Asia, Dhaka, Bangladesh 2003.*

Srivastava, R. and Singh, R. 2005. "Economic Reforms and Agricultural Wages in India", *The Indian Journal Of Labour Economics*, 48(2): 407-424

Srivastava, R. and Singh, R. 2006. "Rural Wages during the 1990s: A Re-estimation," *Economic and Political Weekly*, September 23: 4054-4062

Srivastava, R. S. 1999. "Rural Labour in U.P: Emerging Features of Subsistence Contradiction and Resistance", *Journal of Peasant Studies*, 26 (2-3), January and April, London, Frank Cass & Co.

Srivastava, R.S., Saxena, N.C. and Thorat, S.K. 2003. "*Land Institutions, Policy and Reform in India*" in the International JNU-IFPRI International Conference on 'The Dragon and the Elephant: A Comparative Study of Economic and Agricultural Reforms in China and India", March, New Delhi.

Standing, G. 1983. *"A labour status approach to labour statistics"*, Working Paper of the Population and Labour Policies Programme, WEP 2-21/WP.139, International Labour Office, Geneva.

Sugirtharaj, Felix and Sait 1995. *"Report of the Commission on Bonded Labour in Tamil Nadu"*. Report submitted to the Supreme Court of India in Civil Writ Petition No. 3922 of 1985.

Sugiyarto, G., Oey-Gardiner, M. and Triaswati, N. 2006. "Labor Markets in Indonesia: Key Challenges and Policy Issues", in Felipe, J. and Hasan, R. (eds.), *Labour Markets in Asia: Issues and Perspectives*: 301-366, Palgrave Macmillan, New York.

Suri, K.C. 2006. "Political Economy of Agrarian Distress", *Economic and Political Weekly*, April 22: 1523 1529

Suryanarayanan, S.S. 2004. *"Labour Laws, Contractual Parameters and Conditions of Construction Workers: A Study in Chennai"*, NLI Research Studies Series No 50/2004, V.V. Giri National Labour Institute, Noida Uttar Pradesh.

Suryanarayanan, S.S. and Rao, B.V.L.N. 2000. "Employment in Food Processing Industries" *NLI Research Studies Series No. 008/2000, V.V. Giri National Labour Institute, Noida.*

Swaminathan, M. 1998. "Economic Growth and the Persistence of Child Labour: Evidence from an Indian City", *World Development*, 26(8): 1513-28.

Swaminathan, P. 2005. "*Trapped in to Living: Women's Work Environment and their Perceptions of Health*", Cehat, Mumbai.

Thamarajakshi, R 1999. "Agriculture and Economic Reforms," *Economic and Political Weekly*, 34 (33).

Tiwari, G. 2000a. "Encroachers or service providers?", *Seminar*, 491 (July).

Tiwari, G. 2000b. "Cycle Rickshaws and Non Motorized Vehicles in Delhi", *Labour File*, A6(8).

UNCTAD 1999. "*World Investment Report 1999: Foreign Direct Investment and the Challenge of Development*", Geneva.

United Nations 2000. *"The World Women 2000: Trends and Statistics"*, UN Press, NY

Unni, J. 1997. "Employment and Wages among Rural Labourers: Some Recent Trends." *Indian Journal of Agricultural Economics*, 52 (1): 59-72.

Unni, J. 1998. "Employment and Wages in the Unorganised Sector: Issues in Wage Policy", *The Indian Journal of Labour Economics*, 41(4), October–December.

Unni, J. and Bali, N. 2002. "Subcontracted Women Workers in the Garment Industry in India", in Radhika Balakrishnan, edited, *The Hidden Assembly Line: Gender Dynamics of Subcontracted Work in a Global Economy,* Kumarian Press, Connecticut.

Unni, J. and Rani, U. 2005a. "Impact of Recent Policies on Home-based Work in India", HDRC, Discussion Paper Series-10, UNDP, New Delhi.

Unni, J. and Rani, U. 2005b. "Gender and Non-farm Employment" in *Rural Transformation in India: The Role of Non-farm Sector* Edited by Rohini Nayyar and Alakh N. Sharma, Institute for Human Development, New Delhi.

Unni, J. and Raveendran, R.G. 2007. "Growth of Employment (1993-94 to 2004-2005): Illusion of Inclusiveness", *Economic and Political Weekly*, 42(3):196-202.

Usha, P. 1984. "*Leather Industry of Tamil Nadu- Study of Structural Change During 1960-1980 (with Special Reference to the Export Trade Control Policy)*", unpublished PhD. Dissertation, University of Madras.

Utting, P. 2000. "*Business Responsibility for Sustainable Development*", Occasional Paper 2, United Nations Research Institute for Social Development.

Utting, P. 2001. "*Regulating Business vis 'Multistakeholder Initiatives': A Preliminary* Assessment", United Nations Research Institute for Social Development.

Vaid, 1997. "*Contract Labour in the Construction Industry in India*", NICMAR Publication Bureau, National Institute of Construction Management and Research, Mumbai.

Varma, S. and Kumar, M. 2006. "*From Leather Artisans to Brick-Kiln Workers: Narratives of Weary Travelers*", NLI Research Studies Series No. 71/2006, V.V. Giri National Labour Institute, Noida.

Vidyasagar and Kumarababu, G. 2001. "*Child Labour in the Home Based Match Industries of Sivakasi*", NLI Research Studies Series No 28/2001, V.V. Giri National Labour Institute, Noida Uttar Pradesh

Vijayabhaskar, M. 2002. "Garment Industry in India", in Gopal Joshi, edited, *Garment Industry in South Asia: Rags to Riches: Competitiveness, Productivity and Job Quality in Post MFA Environment*, International Labour Organisation, SAAT, New Delhi.

Watanabe, S. (ed.) 1983. *"Technology Marketing and Industrialisation: Linkages between Large and Small Enterprises"*, Macmillian India Limited, Delhi.

Weiner, M. 1991. "*The Child and The State in India: Child Labor and Education Policy Comparative Perspective*". Princeton University Press, Princeton,

WEBSITES

http://lawmin.nic.in/coi.htm : Ministry of Law and Justice, Government of India

http://www.christianaid.org.uk/world/where/asia/indiap.htm, accessed on 22 June 2005: Christian Aid

http://www.eti2.org.uk/Z/lib/2006/media/CSRAsiaWkly-Vol2Week2.pdf. : Ethical Trading Initiative http://www.globalreporting.org, accessed on 22 June 2005 : Global Reporting Initiative

http://www.mhupa.gov.in/policies/natpol.htm accessed on 16th May 2007 : Ministry of Housing and Urban Poverty Alleviation: Policies, National Policy for Urban Street Vendors

http://www.nasvinet.org : National Alliance of Street Vendors

http://www.nceus.gov.in : National Commission for Enterprises in Unorganised Sector

http://www.rugmark.org, accessed 22 June 2005: Rugmark Foundation

http://www.thesullivanfoundation.org/gsp/default.asp, accessed on 22 June 2005 : Global Suvillan Principles of Social Responsibility

http://www.unglobalcompact.org, accessed on 22 June 2005 : United Nations Global Impact

OSHA: U.S. Department of Labor, Occupational Safety & Health Administration: www.osha.gov

Abbreviations & Acronyms

AICRP	All India Coordinated Research and Planning
AIDS	Acquired Immuno-Deficiency Syndrome
APMC	Agriculture Produce Marketing Committee Act
ATS	Apprenticeship Training Scheme
AWB	Agricultural Workers' Conditions of Work and Social Security Bill, 2007
BPL	Below Poverty Line
BPO	Bussiness Process Outsourcing
BRGF	Backward Region Grant Fund
CBSP	Scheme of Capacity Building for Service Providers
CC	Conciliation Committees
CCC	Clean Clothes Campaign
CDS	Current Daily Status
CEDAW	Convention on the Elimination of all forms of Discrimination against Women
CERES	Coalition for Environmentally Responsible Economies
CFNEU	Community Food and Nutrition Extension Units
CGF	Credit Guarantee Fund
CIDC	Training by Construction Industry Development Council
CII	Confederation of Indian Industries
CIPET	Central Institute of Plastics Engineering and Technology
CITS	Crafts Instructor Training Scheme
CMP	Common Minimum Program
CPSE	Central Public Sector Enterprises
CSO	Central Statistical Organisation
CTS	Craftsmen Training Scheme
CW	Casual Worker
DGET	Directorate General of Employment & Training
DOEACC	Department of Electronics Accreditation for Computer Courses
DPC	District Planning Committee
DRC	Dispute Resolution Councils
DTP	Modified Decentralised Training Programme for Handloom weavers
EDI	Entrepreneurship Development Institute
EDP	Entrepreneurial Development Programme
EPF	Employees Provident Fund
EPZ	Economic Processing Zones
ESIS	Employees State Insurance Scheme

ETI	Ethical Trading Initiative
FDI	Foreign Direct Investment
FLSA	Fair Labour Standards Act
FNCL	First National Commission on Labour
FPTC	Food Processing & Training Centres
FWP	Food for Work
GDP	Gross Domestic Product
GOI	Government of India
GOM	Government of Maharashtra
GOTN	Government of Tamil Nadu
GP	Growth Pole
GRI	Global Reporting Initiative
GVA	Gross Value Added
HIV	Human Immunodeficiency Virus
HRLN	Human Rights Law Network
HS	Higher Secondary
HUDCO	Housing and Development Corporation of India
HYV	High Yielding Varieties
ICLS	International Conference of Labor Statisticians
ICSE	International Classification of Status in Employment
IDS	Institute of Development Studies
IHTP	Integrated Handloom Training Project
ILC	Indian Labour Conference
ILO	International Labour Organisation
ISID	Institute for Studies in Industrial Development
ISMW	Inter State Migrant Workmen
ISST	Institute of Social Studies Trust
ITI/C	Industrial Training Institutes/ Centres
KVIC	Khadi and Village Industries Commission
LDB	Land Development Banks
LPR	Labour force Participation Rate
MES	Modular Employable Skills
MFA	Multi-Fibre Arrangement
MFAL	Marginal Farmers and Agricultural Labourers Scheme
Mfg./M	Manufacturing
MFI	Micro Finance Institutions
MNC	Multinational Corporation
MOLE	Ministry of Labour and Employment

MPCE	Monthly Per Capita Consumption Expenditure
MSI	Multiple Stakeholder Initiatives
MSME	Ministry of Small of Small and Medium Enterprises
MSP	Minimum Support Price
MYRADA	Mysore Resettlement and Development Agency
NABARD	National Bank for Agriculture and Rural Development
NAFUS	National Fund for the Unorganised Sector
NASVI	National Alliance for Street Vendors
NAWB	Unorganised Non-agricultural Workers Conditions of Work and Social Security Bill, 2007
NBC	Net Bank Credit
NCAER	National Council for Applied Economic Research
NCEUS	National Commission for Enterprises in the Unorganised Sector
NCF	National Commission on Farmers
NCL	National Commission of Labour
NCRL	National Commission on Rural Labour
NCSEW	National Commission on Self-employed Women and Women Workers
NDMC	New Delhi Municipal Corporation
NGO	Non-Governmental Organisation
NHDC	National Handloom Development Corporation
NHRC	National Human Rights Commission
NIC	National Industrial Classification
NID	National Institute of Design
NIRD	National Institute of Rural Development
NREGA/ NREG	National Rural Employment Guarantee Act, 2005
NSDP	National State Domestic Product
NSS/ NSSO	National Sample Survey (Organisation)
NSSF	National Social Security and Welfare Fund
NSSF	National Social Security and Welfare Fund
NYK	Nehru Yuva Kendra
OAE	Own Account Enterprises (without hired labour)
OAW	Own Account Worker
OBC	Other Backward Classes
OECD	Organization of Economic Cooperation and Development
OS	Organised Sector
OSHA	Occupational Safety and Health Administration, USA
p.a.	Per Annum
p.c.p.d.	Per Capita Per Day
p.d.	Per Day

PFA	Prevention of Food Adulteration Act, 1955
PMEGP	Prime Minister Employment Generation Programme
PMRY	Prime Minister's Rojgar Yojana
PPP	Purchasing Power Parity
PRI	Panchayati Raj Institutions
RBI	Reserve Bank of India
RD&TCs	Regional Design and Technical Development Centres
RECS	Regulation of Employment and Conditions of Service
REGP	Rural Employment Guarantee Generation Programme
RRB	Regional Rural Banks
RW	Regular Worker
RWA	Resident Welfare Association
SACCS	Christian Aid and South Asian Coalition on Child Servitude
SC	Schedule Castes
SDI	Skill Development Initiative
SDP	Skill Development Program
SE	Self Employment
SEWA	Self Employment Women's Association
SEZ	Special Economic Zones
SFDA	Small Farmers Development Agencies
SFURTI	Scheme of Fund for Regeneration of Traditional Industries
SGSY	Swaranjaynati Gram Swarozgar Yojana
SHG	Self Help Group
SIDBI	Small Industries Development Bank of India
SJSRY	Urban Self Employment Programme under Swarna Jayanti Shahari Rozgar Yojana
SME	Small and Micro Enterprises
SNA	System of National Accounts
SNCL	Second National Commission of Labour
SSI	Small Scale Industry
SSME	Special Sub-group of Micro Enterprises
SSSY	Swaranjaynati Shahari Swarozgar Yojana
ST	Scheduled Tribes
STEP	Support to Training and Employment Programme for Women
TISCO	Tata Iron and Steel Co Ltd
TNC	Trans-National Corporations
TVC	Town Vending Committee
UFW	Unpaid Family Worker
UN	United Nations

UNCTAD	United Nations Conference on Trade and Development
UNDP	United Nations Development Program
UNEP	United Nations Environment Programme
UNICEF	United Nations
UNIDO	United Nations Industrial Development Organization
UPA	United Progressive Alliance
UPSS	Usual Principal and Subsidiary Status (Subsidiary only for non-workers in principal status)
US	Unorganised Sector
USEP	Urban Self-Employment Programme
UW	Unorganised Worker
UW in OS	Unorganised Worker in the Organised Sector
VoTEG	Vocational Training for Employment Generation
VTC	Vocational Training Centres
WDP	Watershed Development Program
WFC	Workers Facilitation Centres
WTO	World Trade Organisation
WWF	Working Women's Forum

Appendix Tables

Appendix A1.1: Size & Distribution of the Organised and Unorganised Sector Workers by Industry and Status 2004 - 05

	Agriculture			Non-agriculture			All		
	Organised	Unorganised	Total	Organised	Unorganised	Total	Organised	Unorganised	Total
	Number of Workers (Million)								
SE	2.3	163.9	166.2	2.9	89.2	92.1	5.2	253.1	258.2
RW	1.2	1.6	2.8	41.9	24.8	66.7	43.2	26.4	69.5
CW	2.5	87.4	89.9	11.7	28.1	39.8	14.2	115.5	129.7
Total	6.1	252.8	258.9	56.5	142.1	198.5	62.6	394.9	457.5
	Percentage Distribution of Workers								
SE	38.1	64.8	64.2	5.1	62.8	46.4	8.3	64.1	56.5
RW	20.1	0.6	1.1	74.3	17.4	33.6	69.0	6.7	15.2
CW	41.8	34.6	34.7	20.7	19.8	20.0	22.7	29.2	28.3
Total	100.0	100.0	100.0	100.0	100.0	100.0	100.0	100.0	100.0
Percentage to total	2.4	97.6	100.0	28.4	71.6	100.0	13.7	86.3	100.0

Note: SE = Self -employed; RW= Regular Worker; CW=Casual Worker.
Source: NSS 61st Round 2004 - 2005, Employment-Unemployment Survey. Computed.

Appendix A1.2: Estimates of Organised and Unorganised Workers/Employment by Industry (Million)

Category	Combined		
	Male	Female	Total
Total Workers	**309.4**	**148.0**	**457.5**
Agriculture	151.2	107.7	258.9
Non-agriculture	158.2	40.3	198.5
Organised Worker	**28.8**	**6.0**	**34.9**
Agriculture	2.0	0.8	2.9
Non-agriculture	26.8	5.2	32.0
Unorganised Worker	**280.6**	**142.0**	**422.6**
Agriculture	149.2	106.9	256.1
Non-agriculture	131.4	35.1	166.5

Source: ibid.

Appendix A1.3: Percentage of Workers in Unorganised Sector and Unorganised Workers by Gender across the States 2004-2005

State	Unorganised Sector			Unorganised Worker		
	Male	Female	Total	Male	Female	Total
Andhra Pradesh	85.3	92.7	88.3	92.5	96.1	94.0
Arunachal Pradesh	79.3	93.4	84.9	83.9	96.4	88.9
Assam	85.6	80.6	84.4	89.8	91.4	90.2
Bihar	95.6	98.4	96.2	97.1	99.2	97.5
Goa	60.2	67.3	62.2	71.9	75.1	72.8
Gujarat	78.1	92.3	82.8	88.6	97.6	91.6
Haryana	79.0	93.5	83.5	87.4	96.6	90.2
Himachal Pradesh	76.5	92.2	83.7	85.5	95.8	90.2
Jammu & Kashmir	77.8	92.2	81.7	85.7	96.3	88.5
Karnataka	84.6	90.1	86.6	90.0	95.3	91.9
Kerala	63.9	62.4	63.4	82.0	79.6	81.3
Madhya Pradesh	87.3	92.5	89.1	93.1	98.2	94.8
Maharashtra	77.3	90.4	82.0	86.6	95.0	89.6
Manipur	82.1	92.5	86.0	84.8	95.5	88.8
Meghalaya	83.1	86.4	84.5	88.4	91.1	89.6
Mizoram	79.3	91.1	83.8	81.0	92.9	85.5
Nagaland	75.1	92.8	82.6	76.0	94.7	83.9
Orissa	88.2	93.9	90.1	92.9	97.7	94.5
Punjab	83.1	90.4	85.2	89.5	94.3	90.9
Rajasthan	88.3	95.5	91.2	93.0	98.5	95.2
Sikkim	72.5	83.6	76.1	82.2	90.5	84.8
Tamil Nadu	77.5	86.1	80.8	87.2	94.3	89.9
Tripura	83.9	74.8	82.7	89.5	88.5	89.4
Uttar Pradesh	90.7	97.1	92.5	94.6	98.8	95.8
West Bengal	84.6	88.3	85.4	90.5	93.8	91.2
Delhi	62.6	51.6	61.4	77.0	64.5	75.6
Jharkhand	84.4	94.0	87.6	91.8	98.3	94.0
Chhattisgarh	85.5	95.6	89.7	92.7	98.6	95.2
Uttaranchal	81.7	96.0	87.4	87.0	97.1	91.0
All India	84.0	91.3	86.3	90.7	95.9	92.4

Source: ibid.

Appendix A1.4: Number (Millions) of Workers in Unorganised Non-agricultural Sector by Status of Employment 1999-2000

Status of Employment	Rural			Urban			Total		
	Male	Female	Total	Male	Female	Total	Male	Female	Total
Self- employed:									
Independent	23.1	6.3	29.4	26.4	4.9	31.3	49.5	11.2	60.7
Homeworkers	2.0	3.0	5.0	1.5	1.8	3.2	3.4	4.8	8.2
All Self- employed	25.1	9.3	34.4	27.9	6.7	34.5	52.9	16.0	68.9
All Unorganised Non-agriculture	41.2	11.9	53.1	46.7	10.6	57.3	87.9	22.5	110.4

Source : NSS 55th Round 1999-2000, Employment and Unemployment. Computed.

Appendix A2.1: Distribution of Rural Non-agricultural Workers by Land Size Class and Socio-Religious Groups 2004 - 2005

Employment Status	Landless	Sub-Marginal	Marginal	Small	Medium-Large	Total
			Hindu ST			
US: Casual Workers	13.2	45.6	31.9	7.0	2.3	100.0
US: Regular Workers	9.9	53.8	10.8	20.2	5.3	100.0
US: Self Employed Workers	16.1	48.4	20.9	7.6	6.9	100.0
Unorganised Sector Workers	14.3	47.4	25.8	8.1	4.5	100.0
Organised Sector Workers	14.6	35.7	24.0	12.0	6.8	100.0
Non-Agricultural Workers	14.7	44.4	25.8	9.7	5.4	100.0
			Hindu SC			
US: Casual Workers	18.5	67.5	8.8	3.0	2.2	100.0
US: Regular Workers	21.8	60.3	11.4	3.9	2.6	100.0
US: Self Employed Workers	17.6	64.4	11.0	5.0	2.0	100.0
Unorganised Sector Workers	18.4	65.1	10.3	4.2	2.1	100.0
Organised Sector Workers	21.3	54.8	11.8	5.0	3.5	100.0
Non-Agricultural Workers	19.2	63.1	10.8	4.4	2.5	100.0
			Hindu OBC			
US: Casual Workers	15.8	62.4	14.6	4.9	2.3	100.0
US: Regular Workers	18.8	51.5	13.8	8.2	7.6	100.0
US: Self Employed Workers	13.8	60.5	14.5	6.3	5.0	100.0
Unorganised Sector Workers	14.8	59.8	14.4	6.2	4.7	100.0
Organised Sector Workers	17.9	46.2	13.3	7.3	7.6	100.0
Non-Agricultural Workers	15.8	57.7	14.4	6.6	5.5	100.0
			Hindu Upper Castes			
US: Casual Workers	12.6	62.1	13.8	7.3	4.2	100.0
US: Regular Workers	14.0	53.7	14.6	8.5	9.2	100.0
US: Self Employed Workers	10.9	57.7	14.5	8.2	8.7	100.0
Unorganised Sector Workers	11.6	57.8	14.4	8.1	8.1	100.0
Organised Sector Workers	12.4	43.1	12.8	8.0	11.8	100.0
Non-Agricultural Workers	12.3	55.0	14.5	8.4	9.7	100.0
			Muslims OBC			
US: Casual Workers	13.9	75.0	8.8	1.8	0.6	100.0
US: Regular Workers	14.8	71.0	10.1	2.6	1.5	100.0
US: Self Employed Workers	15.3	73.2	7.2	3.1	1.2	100.0
Unorganised Sector Workers	15.0	73.3	7.7	2.8	1.1	100.0
Organised Sector Workers	14.3	68.0	12.8	2.6	2.2	100.0
Non-Agricultural Workers	14.9	72.8	8.3	2.8	1.3	100.0
			Muslims Others			
US: Casual Workers	16.3	68.4	9.6	3.5	2.2	100.0
US: Regular Workers	19.4	61.7	11.8	5.5	1.6	100.0
US: Self Employed Workers	13.1	67.2	11.8	5.3	2.6	100.0
Unorganised Sector Workers	14.2	67.1	11.4	4.9	2.5	100.0
Organised Sector Workers	10.0	63.2	13.8	8.1	4.8	100.0
Non-Agricultural Workers	13.5	66.5	11.7	5.4	2.8	100.0

Employment Status	Landless	Sub-Marginal	Marginal	Small	Medium-Large	Total
			Muslims OBC			
US: Casual Workers	16.3	73.9	6.4	2.1	1.2	100.0
US: Regular Workers	13.2	67.5	8.3	4.9	6.2	100.0
US: Self Employed Workers	9.4	66.3	12.2	6.1	6.0	100.0
Unorganised Sector Workers	12.0	68.6	10.0	4.8	4.7	100.0
Organised Sector Workers	11.1	56.0	9.4	8.2	7.6	100.0
Non-Agricultural Workers	12.0	66.2	10.0	6.0	5.8	100.0
			All Socio-Religious Groups (includes unspecified)			
US: Casual Workers	16.0	63.7	13.6	4.4	2.3	100.0
US: Regular Workers	17.5	56.6	12.7	7.1	6.1	100.0
US: Self Employed Workers	13.8	62.2	13.2	6.1	4.7	100.0
Unorganised Sector Workers	14.8	61.9	13.2	5.8	4.3	100.0
Organised Sector Workers	16.0	48.2	13.5	7.4	7.5	100.0
Non-Agricultural Workers	15.4	59.6	13.6	6.3	5.2	100.0

Note:

1. Agriculture includes only unorganised sector.
2. Land Possessed in hectares: Landless (< 0.01), Sub-Marginal (0.01 - 0.40), Marginal (0.41 - 1.00), Small (1.01 - 2.00), Medium-Large (> 2.00).

Source: NSS 61st Round 2004-2005, Employment Unemployment Survey. Computed.

Appendix A 2.2: Mean Years of Schooling of Non-agricultural Workers by Employment Status, Sector, Sex and Sector of Occupation 2004-2005

Employment Status	Rural			Urban			Total		
	Male	Female	Total	Male	Female	Total	Male	Female	Total
Unorganised Sector: Casual	3.6	1.5	3.3	4.3	2.1	3.9	3.8	1.7	3.5
Unorganised Sector: Regular Workers (RW)	7.0	5.6	6.8	7.1	4.8	6.7	7.1	5.0	6.7
Unorganised Sector: Self Employed	5.3	2.9	4.7	7.7	5.1	7.2	6.5	3.8	5.9
Unorganised Sector (Total)	**5.1**	**2.9**	**4.6**	**7.0**	**4.7**	**6.6**	**6.1**	**3.7**	**5.6**
Unorganised Worker in OS: RW	**7.9**	**7.2**	**7.7**	**8.8**	**9.6**	**9.0**	**8.5**	**8.5**	**8.5**
Unorganised Worker in OS	**5.3**	**4.0**	**5.0**	**7.4**	**7.3**	**7.4**	**6.4**	**5.5**	**6.2**
Organised Sector (OS) (Total)	**7.6**	**5.7**	**7.2**	**10.1**	**10.1**	**10.1**	**9.1**	**8.1**	**9.0**
All Workers	**5.7**	**3.6**	**5.2**	**8.1**	**6.3**	**7.7**	**6.9**	**4.9**	**6.5**

Note:

1. To compute the mean years of schooling the following years of schooling have been considered: Illiterate-0, literate below primary-1, primary-4, middle-8, secondary-10, higher secondary-12, diploma/ certificate course - 14, graduate - 15, postgraduate and above -17.
2. Regular unorganised workers in the organised sector consisted of 13.6 million workers.
3. Unorganised workers in the organised sector in non-agriculture were 25.9 million workers.

Source: ibid.

Appendix A2.3: Non-agricultural Workers' Mean Years of Schooling across Major States by Sector and Sex 2004 - 2005

State	Rural				Urban			
	Unorganised Sector		Organised Sector		Unorganised Sector		Organised Sector	
	Male	Female	Male	Female	Male	Female	Male	Female
Andhra Pradesh	4.6	2.6	6.7	3.7	6.1	3.0	9.7	8.3
Assam	4.6	2.9	9.2	7.9	7.2	4.7	11.0	11.5
Bihar	4.3	1.4	7.2	6.6	7.1	2.2	11.8	12.8
Gujarat	6.2	3.0	7.5	5.7	7.9	6.0	9.6	7.2
Haryana	5.5	3.2	8.1	5.4	7.6	6.9	9.2	10.9
Himachal Pradesh	6.3	5.5	8.1	10.1	7.4	5.8	8.2	7.4
Jammu & Kashmir	5.1	2.9	7.9	6.9	5.7	2.2	9.0	12.5
Karnataka	5.4	3.6	8.9	7.2	7.3	4.5	10.9	10.0
Kerala	7.4	6.9	9.5	9.1	8.2	6.4	10.8	12.1
Madhya Pradesh	4.6	1.4	7.3	2.3	7.4	4.7	10.2	8.9
Maharashtra	7.1	5.2	9.4	6.4	7.8	6.3	10.0	10.3
Orissa	4.7	2.1	6.7	3.7	6.7	3.5	10.0	10.1
Punjab	5.7	5.7	7.2	10.5	7.1	7.2	9.7	13.3
Rajasthan	4.1	1.1	6.4	2.6	5.9	3.0	10.5	11.0
Tamil Nadu	5.3	3.5	7.8	6.4	7.2	4.6	10.3	8.8
Uttar Pradesh	4.4	1.6	7.5	7.1	5.9	3.3	10.0	10.7
West Bengal	4.6	2.3	6.6	6.0	7.0	5.0	9.5	12.0
Jharkhand	3.9	1.4	5.0	3.3	8.8	3.1	10.3	9.2
Chhattisgarh	6.0	1.7	6.7	3.5	7.2	3.8	10.2	7.6
Uttaranchal	5.6	4.7	9.0	11.3	8.3	7.6	9.4	11.4
All India	**5.1**	**2.9**	**7.6**	**5.7**	**7.0**	**4.7**	**10.1**	**10.1**

Source: ibid.

Appendix A2.4: Percentage of Non-agricultural Workers according to Educational Attainment Levels, Sex and Sector 2004 - 2005

Educational Level	Illiterate & Below Primary	Primary	Middle	Secondary	HS & Above	Total
			Total Male			
Unorganised Sector: Casual	48.1	19.3	22.0	7.1	3.4	100.0
Unorganised Sector: Regular Workers (RW)	20.7	18.4	25.5	17.0	18.4	100.0
Unorganised Sector: Self Employed	30.2	15.6	20.0	14.3	19.9	100.0
Unorganised Sector	32.3	16.9	21.4	13.2	16.1	100.0
Unorganised Worker in OS: RW	16.8	14.1	21.3	14.9	32.9	100.0
Unorganised Worker in OS	31.3	16.8	20.6	11.3	20.1	100.0
Organised Sector (OS)	17.9	10.9	15.9	13.9	41.4	100.0
All Workers	28.1	15.2	19.8	13.4	23.4	100.0
			Total Female			
Unorganised Sector: Casual	75.0	12.6	8.5	1.8	2.0	100.0
Unorganised Sector: Regular Workers (RW)	49.6	11.3	12.0	8.3	18.8	100.0
Unorganised Sector: Self Employed	54.7	15.0	14.6	6.4	9.4	100.0
Unorganised Sector	56.8	14.0	13.3	6.0	9.9	100.0
Unorganised Worker in OS: RW	24.9	10.5	12.3	13.8	38.5	100.0
Unorganised Worker in OS	46.9	11.2	11.3	8.8	21.8	100.0
Organised Sector (OS)	31.7	8.5	8.7	10.2	40.9	100.0
All Workers	50.0	12.5	12.1	7.2	18.2	100.0
			Total			
Unorganised Sector: Casual	52.1	18.3	20.0	6.4	3.2	100.0
Unorganised Sector: Regular Workers (RW)	26.2	17.1	22.9	15.3	18.5	100.0
Unorganised Sector: Self Employed	35.9	15.5	18.7	12.4	17.5	100.0
Unorganised Sector	37.4	16.3	19.7	11.7	14.8	100.0
Unorganised Worker in OS: RW	18.7	13.2	19.2	14.6	34.2	100.0
Unorganised Worker in OS	34.9	15.5	18.4	10.7	20.5	100.0
Organised Sector (OS)	20.5	10.4	14.5	13.2	41.3	100.0
All Workers	32.6	14.6	18.3	12.2	22.4	100.0
			Rural Male			
Unorganised Sector: Casual	51.1	18.7	21.1	6.3	2.8	100.0
Unorganised Sector: Regular Workers (RW)	20.4	19.8	25.8	16.1	17.9	100.0
Unorganised Sector: Self Employed	38.2	16.9	20.7	11.7	12.5	100.0
Unorganised Sector	39.6	17.8	21.4	10.8	10.5	100.0

Educational Level	Illiterate & Below Primary	Primary	Middle	Secondary	HS & Above	Total
Unorganised Worker in OS: RW	21.7	12.2	20.0	17.7	28.3	100.0
Unorganised Worker in OS	39.8	16.8	18.8	11.0	13.6	100.0
Organised Sector (OS)	26.6	12.1	16.8	14.3	30.2	100.0
All Workers	36.5	16.4	20.3	11.6	15.2	100.0
			Rural Female			
Unorganised Sector: Casual	78.9	10.6	7.7	1.8	1.1	100.0
Unorganised Sector: Regular Workers (RW)	44.8	8.2	13.5	13.7	19.8	100.0
Unorganised Sector: Self Employed	61.9	15.0	13.4	5.0	4.7	100.0
Unorganised Sector	63.3	13.8	12.5	5.2	5.3	100.0
Unorganised Worker in OS: RW	31.8	10.3	15.7	14.7	27.5	100.0
Unorganised Worker in OS	57.0	10.8	11.8	7.9	12.6	100.0
Organised Sector (OS)	45.5	9.8	10.4	10.3	24.0	100.0
All Workers	59.1	12.8	12.0	6.4	9.8	100.0
			Rural Total			
Unorganised Sector: Casual	55.0	17.6	19.2	5.7	2.5	100.0
Unorganised Sector: Regular Workers (RW)	24.1	18.0	24.0	15.8	18.2	100.0
Unorganised Sector: Self Employed	44.4	16.4	18.8	9.9	10.5	100.0
Unorganised Sector	44.8	16.9	19.5	9.5	9.3	100.0
Unorganised Worker in OS: RW	24.6	11.7	18.8	16.9	28.1	100.0
Unorganised Worker in OS	44.2	15.3	17.0	10.2	13.3	100.0
Organised Sector (OS)	30.7	11.6	15.4	13.5	28.8	100.0
All Workers	41.4	15.6	18.5	10.5	14.0	100.0
			Urban Male			
Unorganised Sector: Casual	42.7	20.5	23.7	8.7	4.5	100.0
Unorganised Sector: Regular Workers (RW)	20.9	17.7	25.3	17.4	18.7	100.0
Unorganised Sector: Self Employed	22.6	14.3	19.3	16.7	27.1	100.0
Unorganised Sector	25.2	16.0	21.4	15.7	21.7	100.0
Unorganised Worker in OS: RW	14.0	15.1	22.0	13.4	35.5	100.0
Unorganised Worker in OS	23.2	16.8	22.2	11.5	26.2	100.0
Organised Sector (OS)	12.4	10.2	15.3	13.7	48.4	100.0
All Workers	21.0	14.1	19.4	15.0	30.5	100.0
			Urban Female			
Unorganised Sector: Casual	69.4	15.5	9.7	2.0	3.4	100.0
Unorganised Sector: Regular Workers (RW)	51.3	12.4	11.5	6.4	18.4	100.0
Unorganised Sector: Self Employed	44.4	14.9	16.3	8.3	16.1	100.0

Educational Level	Illiterate & Below Primary	Primary	Middle	Secondary	HS & Above	Total
Unorganised Sector	49.3	14.3	14.2	7.0	15.1	100.0
Unorganised Worker in OS: RW	19.1	10.7	9.4	13.0	47.8	100.0
Unorganised Worker in OS	34.0	11.6	10.7	10.0	33.6	100.0
Organised Sector (OS)	20.2	7.4	7.3	10.2	54.9	100.0
All Workers	40.5	12.2	12.1	8.0	27.1	100.0
			Urban Total			
Unorganised Sector: Casual	47.1	19.6	21.4	7.5	4.3	100.0
Unorganised Sector: Regular Workers (RW)	27.2	16.6	22.4	15.1	18.6	100.0
Unorganised Sector: Self Employed	26.8	14.4	18.7	15.1	24.9	100.0
Unorganised Sector	29.9	15.7	20.0	14.0	20.4	100.0
Unorganised Worker in OS: RW	15.1	14.2	19.5	13.3	38.0	100.0
Unorganised Worker in OS	25.4	15.8	19.9	11.2	27.7	100.0
Organised Sector (OS)	13.7	9.7	13.9	13.1	49.6	100.0
All Workers	24.6	13.8	18.0	13.7	29.9	100.0

Source: ibid.

Appendix A2.5: Non-agricultural workers' Educational Attainment Levels across Major States by Sector and Sex 2004 - 2005: Rural (Percentages)

State	Unorganised Sector				Organised Sector			
	Male		Female		Male		Female	
	Primary & Below	Middle & Above	Primary & Below	Middle & Above	Primary & Below	Middle & Above	Primary & Below	Middle & Above
Andhra Pradesh	61.2	38.8	78.7	21.3	47.0	53.0	69.9	30.1
Assam	62.0	38.0	77.7	22.3	25.8	74.2	33.8	66.2
Bihar	63.1	36.9	86.9	13.1	42.7	57.3	40.5	59.5
Gujarat	44.8	55.2	76.6	23.4	36.8	63.2	57.0	43.0
Haryana	57.5	42.5	78.3	21.7	40.0	60.0	59.	40.9
Himachal Pradesh	48.5	51.5	55.3	44.7	37.8	62.2	25.6	74.4
Jammu & Kashmir	52.6	47.4	79.1	20.9	29.2	70.8	41.3	58.7
Karnataka	52.5	47.5	68.8	31.2	27.7	72.3	37.4	62.6
Kerala	29.2	70.8	39.5	60.5	20.0	80.0	30.0	70.0
Madhya Pradesh	63.1	36.9	91.3	8.7	45.6	54.4	85.5	14.5
Maharashtra	35.6	64.4	54.7	45.3	25.2	74.8	52.8	47.2
Orissa	58.1	41.9	80.0	20.0	43.9	56.1	69.5	30.5
Punjab	52.2	47.8	55.3	44.7	40.8	59.2	21.5	78.5
Rajasthan	67.5	32.5	93.0	7.0	52.6	47.4	78.9	21.1
Tamil Nadu	57.8	42.2	72.6	27.4	34.5	65.5	51.7	48.3
Uttar Pradesh	62.6	37.4	88.1	11.9	40.1	59.9	46.6	53.4
West Bengal	65.8	34.2	87.6	12.4	49.2	50.8	49.5	50.5
Jharkhand	67.9	32.1	88.9	11.1	60.8	39.2	71.4	28.6
Chhattisgarh	51.4	48.6	88.8	11.2	47.1	52.9	73.0	27.0
Uttaranchal	52.9	47.1	66.3	33.7	29.3	70.7	21.3	78.7
All India	**57.3**	**42.7**	**77.0**	**23.0**	**38.7**	**61.3**	**55.3**	**44.7**

Source: ibid.

Appendix A2.6: Non-agricultural Workers' Educational Attainment Levels across Major States by Sector and Sex 2004 - 2005: Urban (percentages)

State	Unorganised Sector				Organised Sector			
	Male		Female		Male		Female	
	Primary & Below	Middle & Above	Primary & Below	Middle & Above	Primary & Below	Middle & Above	Primary & Below	Middle & Above
Andhra Pradesh	50.1	49.9	77.6	22.4	27.5	72.5	43.2	56.8
Assam	36.3	63.7	60.3	39.7	15.7	84.3	18.6	81.4
Bihar	43.4	56.6	87.9	12.1	11.3	88.7	8.5	91.5
Gujarat	32.9	67.1	48.5	51.5	22.0	78.0	42.7	57.3
Haryana	37.0	63.0	47.4	52.6	27.1	72.9	22.1	77.9
Himachal Pradesh	40.3	59.7	61.3	38.7	35.2	64.8	50.0	50.0
Jammu & Kashmir	47.8	52.2	82.6	17.4	26.6	73.4	9.6	90.4
Karnataka	36.2	63.8	60.8	39.2	15.5	84.5	22.7	77.3
Kerala	26.9	73.1	46.6	53.4	13.3	86.7	14.2	85.8
Madhya Pradesh	45.2	54.8	65.2	34.8	25.8	74.2	37.9	62.1
Maharashtra	30.9	69.1	50.7	49.3	19.2	80.8	24.9	75.1
Orissa	42.1	57.9	69.2	30.8	21.6	78.4	25.1	74.9
Punjab	41.5	58.5	49.2	50.8	26.2	73.8	10.1	89.9
Rajasthan	50.9	49.1	76.3	23.7	25.0	75.0	27.0	73.0
Tamil Nadu	40.8	59.2	65.0	35.0	23.2	76.8	37.3	62.7
Uttar Pradesh	52.1	47.9	76.4	23.6	28.6	71.4	29.9	70.1
West Bengal	43.5	56.5	62.3	37.7	26.8	73.2	13.5	86.5
Jharkhand	24.8	75.2	73.4	26.6	19.6	80.4	23.0	77.0
Chhattisgarh	47.8	52.2	72.0	28.0	23.6	76.4	47.3	52.7
Uttaranchal	33.3	66.7	42.7	57.3	27.5	72.5	16.2	83.8
All India	**41.2**	**58.8**	**63.7**	**36.3**	**22.5**	**77.5**	**27.6**	**72.4**

Source: ibid.

Appendix A2.7: Mean Years of Schooling of Non-agricultural Workers by Sector, Sex and Sector of Occupation among Social Groups 2004 - 2005: Total

Employment Status	Hindu				Muslims		Other Religious Groups	All Social Groups
	ST	SC	OBC	Upper	OBC	Others		
					Male			
Unorganised Sector: Casual	2.0	3.5	4.3	5.0	3.4	2.9	5.1	3.8
Unorganised Sector: Regular Workers (RW)	5.5	6.0	7.2	8.5	5.1	5.4	7.8	7.1
Unorganised Sector: Self Employed	4.2	4.4	6.1	9.4	4.0	4.8	8.9	6.5
Unorganised Sector	3.3	4.3	5.9	8.8	4.1	4.6	7.8	6.1
Unorganised Worker in OS: RW	6.9	6.2	8.2	10.1	6.3	7.7	9.6	8.5
Unorganised Worker in OS	3.6	4.8	6.3	8.8	4.6	5.3	7.1	6.4
Organised Sector (OS)	6.3	6.6	8.7	11.4	6.7	7.6	10.0	9.1
All Workers	4.4	5.0	6.7	9.8	4.4	5.1	8.5	6.9
					Female			
Unorganised Sector: Casual	0.5	1.4	2.1	2.6	1.4	1.0	3.2	1.7
Unorganised Sector: Regular Workers (RW)	2.8	2.9	4.8	7.2	5.5	3.4	6.3	5.0
Unorganised Sector: Self Employed	1.8	2.2	3.5	6.7	2.4	2.4	7.0	3.8
Unorganised Sector	1.4	2.2	3.5	6.5	2.5	2.4	6.3	3.7
Unorganised Worker in OS: RW	4.8	4.7	7.6	11.5	7.7	8.1	10.4	8.5
Unorganised Worker in OS	1.7	2.9	5.1	9.4	2.9	5.5	7.9	5.5
Organised Sector (OS)	3.2	4.3	6.9	11.9	5.8	7.8	10.6	8.1
All Workers	2.0	2.7	4.3	8.5	2.8	3.1	8.0	4.9
					Total			
Unorganised Sector: Casual	1.7	3.2	4.0	4.6	3.2	2.7	4.8	3.5
Unorganised Sector: Regular Workers (RW)	4.9	5.2	6.8	8.3	5.1	5.2	7.4	6.7
Unorganised Sector: Self Employed	3.3	3.8	5.5	8.9	3.7	4.3	8.5	5.9
Unorganised Sector	2.8	3.9	5.4	8.4	3.8	4.1	7.5	5.6
Unorganised Worker in OS: RW	6.4	5.8	8.1	10.4	6.5	7.8	9.8	8.5
Unorganised Worker in OS	3.0	4.4	6.0	8.9	4.3	5.3	7.4	6.2
Organised Sector (OS)	5.6	6.1	8.3	11.5	6.6	7.6	10.1	9.0
All Workers	3.8	4.5	6.2	9.5	4.1	4.7	8.4	6.5

Source: ibid.

Appendix A2.8: Mean Years of Schooling of Non-agricultural Workers by Sector, Sex and Sector of Occupation among Social Groups 2004 - 2005: Rural

Employment Status	Hindu				Muslims		Other Religious Groups	All Social Groups
	ST	SC	OBC	Upper	OBC	Others		
					Male			
Unorganised Sector: Casual	2.0	3.3	3.9	4.8	3.4	2.8	4.7	3.6
Unorganised Sector: Regular Workers (RW)	5.7	6.0	7.3	8.3	5.8	5.0	7.1	7.0
Unorganised Sector: Self Employed	3.6	4.1	5.4	7.8	3.5	3.7	7.2	5.3
Unorganised Sector	2.9	4.0	5.3	7.4	3.7	3.6	6.4	5.1
Unorganised Worker in OS: RW	7.0	6.2	7.9	9.8	6.5	7.0	7.9	7.9
Unorganised Worker in OS	3.3	4.5	5.6	7.7	4.3	3.6	5.5	5.3
Organised Sector (OS)	5.2	6.2	7.7	10.2	6.0	5.9	8.1	7.6
All Workers	3.6	4.5	5.8	8.2	4.0	4.0	6.9	5.7
					Female			
Unorganised Sector: Casual	0.4	1.4	1.9	2.0	1.1	0.5	3.3	1.5
Unorganised Sector: Regular Workers (RW)	4.9	3.8	5.3	7.6	8.6	4.6	7.2	5.6
Unorganised Sector: Self Employed	1.4	1.8	3.1	4.9	2.0	1.7	5.8	2.9
Unorganised Sector	1.2	1.9	3.1	4.9	2.2	1.6	5.7	2.9
Unorganised Worker in OS: RW	5.3	3.9	6.8	9.5	8.6	6.6	10.3	7.2
Unorganised Worker in OS	1.4	2.3	4.1	6.8	3.5	3.4	7.6	4.0
Organised Sector (OS)	2.5	3.5	5.3	8.9	5.6	4.8	9.1	5.7
All Workers	1.6	2.3	3.6	6.1	2.6	1.9	6.8	3.6
					Total			
Unorganised Sector: Casual	1.6	3.1	3.7	4.4	3.2	2.5	4.6	3.3
Unorganised Sector: Regular Workers (RW)	5.6	5.6	7.0	8.2	6.1	4.9	7.1	6.8
Unorganised Sector: Self Employed	2.8	3.5	4.8	7.1	3.2	3.1	6.8	4.7
Unorganised Sector	2.4	3.5	4.8	6.9	3.5	3.1	6.2	4.6
Unorganised Worker in OS: RW	6.5	5.6	7.6	9.7	6.9	6.9	8.7	7.7
Unorganised Worker in OS	2.8	4.0	5.2	7.5	4.1	3.5	6.1	5.0
Organised Sector (OS)	4.5	5.6	7.1	9.9	6.0	5.7	8.3	7.2
All Workers	3.1	4.0	5.3	7.8	3.7	3.5	6.9	5.2

Source: ibid.

Appendix A2.9: Mean Years of Schooling of Non-agricultural Workers by Sector, Sex and Sector of Occupation among Social Groups 2004 - 2005: Urban

Employment Status	Hindu				Muslims		Other Religious Groups	All Social Groups
	ST	SC	OBC	Upper	OBC	Others		
					Male			
Unorganised Sector: Casual	2.5	3.8	4.9	5.3	3.4	3.0	5.6	4.3
Unorganised Sector: Regular Workers (RW)	5.3	6.0	7.2	8.6	4.7	5.6	8.2	7.1
Unorganised Sector: Self Employed	5.5	4.9	7.0	10.2	4.5	5.8	10.1	7.7
Unorganised Sector	4.6	4.9	6.7	9.5	4.4	5.3	9.0	7.0
Unorganised Worker in OS: RW	6.9	6.2	8.5	10.3	6.2	7.9	10.6	8.8
Unorganised Worker in OS	4.8	5.3	7.1	9.3	5.0	6.4	8.7	7.4
Organised Sector (OS)	8.6	7.0	9.4	11.9	7.3	8.5	11.2	10.1
All Workers	6.2	5.6	7.5	10.5	4.7	5.9	9.8	8.1
					Female			
Unorganised Sector: Casual	0.6	1.4	2.4	3.1	1.6	1.9	3.2	2.1
Unorganised Sector: Regular Workers (RW)	2.1	2.5	4.6	7.1	3.9	3.2	5.9	4.8
Unorganised Sector: Self Employed	3.2	3.0	4.2	8.3	2.7	3.6	8.4	5.1
Unorganised Sector	2.1	2.5	4.1	7.5	2.7	3.4	6.9	4.7
Unorganised Worker in OS: RW	3.9	5.4	8.5	12.6	6.3	8.9	10.4	9.6
Unorganised Worker in OS	2.5	3.8	6.5	11.5	2.2	7.5	8.1	7.3
Organised Sector (OS)	4.8	5.0	8.7	13.1	5.9	10.0	11.4	10.1
All Workers	3.1	3.2	5.3	9.8	3.0	4.4	8.9	6.3
					Total			
Unorganised Sector: Casual	2.0	3.4	4.5	4.8	3.2	2.9	5.2	3.9
Unorganised Sector: Regular Workers (RW)	4.5	5.0	6.6	8.3	4.6	5.3	7.5	6.7
Unorganised Sector: Self Employed	4.9	4.5	6.4	9.9	4.1	5.4	9.8	7.2
Unorganised Sector	4.0	4.3	6.1	9.2	4.1	5.0	8.6	6.6
Unorganised Worker in OS: RW	6.0	6.0	8.5	10.7	6.2	8.0	10.6	9.0
Unorganised Worker in OS	3.9	4.9	7.0	9.7	4.5	6.6	8.5	7.4
Organised Sector (OS)	7.8	6.6	9.3	12.1	7.1	8.7	11.3	10.1
All Workers	5.5	5.1	7.1	10.4	4.4	5.7	9.6	7.7

Source: ibid.

Appendix A2.10: Percentage of Non-agricultural Workers by Employment Status, Sector and Gender among Socio-Religious Groups 2004-2005

Employment Status	Hindu				Muslims		Other Religious Groups	All Social Groups
	ST	SC	OBC	Upper	OBC	Others		
					Total: Male			
Unorganised Sector: Casual	30.4	25.0	15.5	6.0	15.7	15.1	15.3	15.1
Unorganised Sector: Regular Workers (RW)	8.7	11.4	13.1	13.2	12.3	13.7	12.7	12.7
Unorganised Sector: Self Employed	25.3	34.9	45.0	43.2	60.5	52.9	38.6	43.4
Unorganised Sector	64.4	71.4	73.7	62.4	88.5	81.7	66.7	71.2
Unorganised Worker in OS: RW	5.3	5.9	6.6	8.3	3.3	4.5	7.3	6.6
Unorganised Worker in OS	20.8	15.1	12.7	11.9	7.1	9.9	12.9	12.6
Organised Sector (OS)	35.6	28.6	26.3	37.6	11.5	18.3	33.3	28.8
All Workers	100.0	100.0	100.0	100.0	100.0	100.0	100.0	100.0
					Total: Female			
Unorganised Sector: Casual	25.3	15.3	9.8	5.6	8.5	8.5	7.9	10.4
Unorganised Sector: Regular Workers (RW)	6.6	14.6	11.0	13.2	7.3	7.3	16.5	11.7
Unorganised Sector: Self Employed	36.9	45.2	55.0	44.4	71.6	71.6	36.2	51.0
Unorganised Sector	68.7	75.1	75.8	63.2	87.4	87.4	60.5	73.1
Unorganised Worker in OS: RW	5.6	7.3	8.1	10.7	4.0	4.0	10.2	7.9
Unorganised Worker in OS	23.8	16.6	15.2	14.4	7.1	7.1	16.5	14.7
Organised Sector (OS)	31.3	24.9	24.2	36.8	12.6	12.6	39.5	26.9
All Workers	100.0	100.0	100.0	100.0	100.0	100.0	100.0	100.0
					Total: Total			
Unorganised Sector: Casual	29.0	22.9	14.3	5.9	14.4	13.9	13.6	14.1
Unorganised Sector: Regular Workers (RW)	8.1	12.1	12.7	13.2	11.0	12.5	13.6	12.5
Unorganised Sector: Self Employed	28.4	37.1	47.2	43.4	63.3	56.3	38.1	44.9
Unorganised Sector	65.6	72.2	74.1	62.5	88.8	82.7	65.3	71.6
Unorganised Worker in OS: RW	5.4	6.2	7.0	8.7	3.0	4.4	8.0	6.8
Unorganised Worker in OS	21.6	15.4	13.2	12.4	7.0	9.4	13.8	13.0
Organised Sector (OS)	34.4	27.8	25.9	37.5	11.2	17.3	34.7	28.4
All Workers	100.0	100.0	100.0	100.0	100.0	100.0	100.0	100.0
					Rural: Male			
Unorganised Sector: Casual	36.2	30.7	18.7	10.8	18.6	18.6	22.1	20.9
Unorganised Sector: Regular Workers (RW)	5.1	7.8	10.1	10.9	9.0	7.5	11.0	9.3
Unorganised Sector: Self Employed	25.0	37.2	49.1	47.7	61.8	57.4	36.8	45.8
Unorganised Sector	66.2	75.8	77.9	69.4	89.4	83.5	70.0	76.0
Unorganised Worker in OS: RW	5.1	4.5	5.1	7.0	2.7	2.2	6.4	5.0
Unorganised Worker in OS	24.0	15.4	12.5	12.2	7.3	9.6	14.0	13.2
Organised Sector (OS)	33.8	24.2	22.1	30.6	10.6	16.5	30.0	24.0
All Workers	100.0	100.0	100.0	100.0	100.0	100.0	100.0	100.0
					Rural: Female			
Unorganised Sector: Casual	27.3	16.4	10.3	6.5	7.5	9.9	9.7	12.0
Unorganised Sector: Regular Workers (RW)	2.4	7.7	5.8	6.1	3.8	2.0	12.0	5.9

Employment Status	Hindu				Muslims		Other Religious Groups	All Social Groups
	ST	SC	OBC	Upper	OBC	Others		
Unorganised Sector: Self Employed	40.3	53.0	60.7	55.9	77.8	78.6	46.2	58.4
Unorganised Sector	70.0	77.0	76.7	68.6	89.1	90.5	67.9	76.3
Unorganised Worker in OS: RW	4.8	6.4	7.7	10.6	2.3	2.4	9.4	7.0
Unorganised Worker in OS	24.2	17.9	16.2	17.5	7.5	6.3	17.1	16.1
Organised Sector (OS)	30.0	23.0	23.3	31.4	10.9	9.5	32.1	23.7
All Workers	100.0	100.0	100.0	100.0	100.0	100.0	100.0	100.0
					Rural: Total			
Unorganised Sector: Casual	33.7	27.7	16.8	9.9	16.4	16.6	19.2	19.0
Unorganised Sector: Regular Workers (RW)	4.3	7.8	9.1	10.0	8.0	6.2	11.2	8.5
Unorganised Sector: Self Employed	29.2	40.6	51.7	49.3	64.9	62.3	39.0	48.6
Unorganised Sector	67.3	76.1	77.6	69.2	89.3	85.1	69.5	76.0
Unorganised Worker in OS: RW	5.0	4.9	5.7	7.7	2.6	2.3	7.1	5.5
Unorganised Worker in OS	24.0	15.9	13.3	13.3	7.3	8.8	14.7	13.9
Organised Sector (OS)	32.7	23.9	22.4	30.8	10.7	14.9	30.5	24.0
All Workers	100.0	100.0	100.0	100.0	100.0	100.0	100.0	100.0
					Urban: Male			
Unorganised Sector: Casual	16.6	17.4	12.1	3.8	13.1	12.7	9.9	10.1
Unorganised Sector: Regular Workers (RW)	17.4	16.2	16.3	14.3	15.2	18.0	14.1	15.6
Unorganised Sector: Self Employed	25.9	31.8	40.7	41.1	59.4	49.7	40.1	41.3
Unorganised Sector	60.0	65.5	69.1	59.2	87.8	80.4	64.1	67.0
Unorganised Worker in OS: RW	5.9	7.8	8.2	8.9	3.8	6.1	8.0	7.9
Unorganised Worker in OS	13.2	14.7	12.9	11.8	7.0	10.1	12.1	12.1
Organised Sector (OS)	40.0	34.5	30.9	40.8	12.2	19.6	35.9	33.0
All Workers	100.0	100.0	100.0	100.0	100.0	100.0	100.0	100.0
					Urban: Female			
Unorganised Sector: Casual	19.6	13.9	9.2	5.1	10.4	6.7	6.5	8.7
Unorganised Sector: Regular Workers (RW)	18.4	23.7	17.7	17.1	7.0	13.8	20.0	17.8
Unorganised Sector: Self Employed	27.3	35.0	47.7	38.1	73.3	63.1	28.3	43.3
Unorganised Sector	65.3	72.5	74.7	60.2	90.8	83.6	54.8	69.8
Unorganised Worker in OS: RW	7.6	8.4	8.7	10.7	1.5	5.9	10.9	8.8
Unorganised Worker in OS	23.0	14.8	13.9	12.7	5.5	8.1	16.1	13.2
Organised Sector (OS)	34.7	27.5	25.3	39.8	9.2	16.4	45.2	30.2
All Workers	100.0	100.0	100.0	100.0	100.0	100.0	100.0	100.0
					Urban: Total			
Unorganised Sector: Casual	17.3	16.7	11.5	4.0	12.6	11.8	9.1	9.8
Unorganised Sector: Regular Workers (RW)	17.6	17.8	16.6	14.8	13.8	17.4	15.5	16.0
Unorganised Sector: Self Employed	26.3	32.5	42.1	40.6	61.9	51.6	37.3	41.7
Unorganised Sector	61.3	67.0	70.2	59.3	88.3	80.9	61.9	67.5
Unorganised Worker in OS: RW	6.3	8.0	8.3	9.2	3.4	6.1	8.7	8.0
Unorganised Worker in OS	15.6	14.7	13.1	11.9	6.7	9.8	13.0	12.3
Organised Sector (OS)	38.7	33.0	29.8	40.7	11.7	19.1	38.1	32.5
All Workers	100.0	100.0	100.0	100.0	100.0	100.0	100.0	100.0

Source: ibid.

Appendix A2.11: Percentage of Unorganised Workers among All Non-agricultural Workers in Industry Groups, across States 2004-2005

State	Mining, Electricity, Public Administration, Etc.	Manufacturing	Construction	Trade, Etc.	Hotels & Restaurant	Transport, Etc.	Finance, Real Estate, Business Services, Etc.	Education	Health, Social Work, Etc.	Other Services	Private Households	Total
Andhra Pradesh	10.8	74.6	70.8	94.6	93.7	77.5	56.6	24.5	48.6	93.2	98.2	73.6
Assam	3	82.4	72.3	98.5	96.2	82	43.5	15.5	32.4	93	95.6	74.1
Bihar	15.2	90.8	85.5	98.1	99.7	84.7	59.2	50.7	83	95.2	100	87
Gujarat	9.1	45.6	68.1	97	85.2	78.3	57.2	8.9	38.8	90.6	100	61.3
Haryana	5.3	53.6	71.6	95.2	86.3	83.5	61.9	31.5	45.7	85.1	99.1	67.5
Karnataka	8.4	77	85.3	94.1	79.1	81.9	37.7	12.8	40.2	87.7	98.9	72.8
Kerala	21	73.2	76.5	91.3	87.2	78.2	53.6	30.9	28.1	70.7	100	71.5
Madhya Pradesh	11.6	64.7	75.3	96.1	97.6	71.3	56.2	20.3	36.9	88.2	100	66.8
Maharashtra	4	55.1	65.6	93.3	71.1	64.4	45	18.6	46.1	81.6	99	62.4
Orissa	10.3	87.6	61.1	98.1	94.2	78.4	49.3	24.3	35.8	87.6	100	74
Punjab	2.1	74.4	85.8	95.2	87.9	78.7	53.9	19	52.5	77.2	95.5	72.8
Rajasthan	22.5	85.3	84.3	98.1	97.5	87.4	65.6	23	39.6	86.7	100	78.1
Tamil Nadu	3.2	67.2	72	93.2	91.3	65.8	54.5	19.7	32.6	86.7	99.9	68.2
Uttar Pradesh	11.3	83	87.5	97.7	94.6	78	67.7	33	63.7	97.5	99.3	81.4
West Bengal	3.9	78.6	75.4	96.5	87.4	81.8	56.1	57.9	51.6	85.3	99.1	77.6
Jharkhand	3.8	66.9	75.9	96.8	87.6	66.7	52.3	33.2	54.5	88.7	86.5	68.5
Chhattisgarh	6.3	61.1	39.5	89.8	60.7	62.7	70.5	16.7	39.5	87.2	100	57.2
Jammu & Kashmir, Himachal Pradesh, Uttaranchal	1.1	72.9	71.2	95.8	80.8	77.1	44.7	15.3	24.7	73.3	100	62
All India	**8.3**	**71.2**	**75.6**	**95.5**	**86.7**	**75.9**	**52.7**	**26.9**	**44.2**	**88.2**	**98.7**	**71.6**

Source: ibid.

Appendix A2.12: Percentage of Unorganised Workers among All Non-agricultural Workers in each Occupational Category across States 2004-2005

State	Professional, Technical, Etc.	Admini-strative, Managerial	Clerical, Etc.	Sales	Service	Farmers & Related	Production, Transport & Related	Total
Andhra Pradesh	40.8	81.0	29.1	95.0	80.8	65.4	73.7	73.6
Assam	21.8	85.6	15.1	97.8	59.4	11.6	83.6	73.4
Bihar	63.7	69.5	31.0	97.6	91.3	91.4	89.9	86.9
Gujarat	28.1	80.3	20.1	97.2	56.3	42.9	55.8	61.3
Haryana	39.7	51.2	27.0	96.1	58.9	9.0	72.3	67.5
Himachal Pradesh	16.6	83.5	7.2	95.1	53.2	38.3	63.0	56.3
Jammu & Kashmir	15.6	63.4	6.7	95.8	39.6	0.0	74.5	63.4
Karnataka	26.7	83.0	15.8	94.5	70.4	60.4	81.6	72.8
Kerala	37.0	77.7	25.5	92.7	74.6	26.9	76.4	71.5
Madhya Pradesh	32.9	70.0	9.9	95.4	65.2	47.7	69.8	66.8
Maharashtra	33.5	79.8	18.4	93.2	65.8	61.6	61.6	62.4
Orissa	37.1	82.7	18.6	95.3	79.1	73.1	77.6	74.0
Punjab	32.2	87.4	24.3	95.5	57.6	44.4	77.0	72.8
Rajasthan	41.4	87.5	14.9	95.3	78.6	47.8	83.6	78.1
Tamil Nadu	33.2	77.3	21.7	93.2	72.2	73.6	69.7	68.2
Uttar Pradesh	47.1	87.3	16.0	97.4	78.4	73.1	85.1	81.4
West Bengal	60.1	85.5	19.2	94.8	73.1	67.6	80.4	77.5
Jharkhand	38.5	82.0	15.5	95.5	72.3	79.9	66.2	68.0
Chhattisgarh	34.6	85.9	15.7	78.9	67.3	44.6	52.1	57.2
Uttaranchal	38.5	82.0	4.7	94.8	45.4	30.1	80.2	65.7
All India	**38.7**	**80.1**	**18.9**	**95.1**	**70.9**	**49.3**	**74.6**	**71.5**

Source: ibid.

Appendix A2.13: Percentage of Non-agricultural Workers across Occupational Categories by Status and Gender 2004-2005

Occupational Category	Casual Labour		Regular		Self Employed	
	US	OS	US	OS	US	OS
			Male			
Professional, Technical, Etc	0.5	0.4	6.7	21.0	5.3	8.3
Administrative, Managerial	0.0	0.0	1.1	5.1	15.0	46.2
Clerical, Etc	0.8	0.9	8.3	25.3	0.4	1.1
Sales	3.0	1.0	22.3	3.2	36.0	18.9
Service	3.7	2.9	10.9	11.6	6.9	2.2
Farmers & Related	0.4	0.4	0.4	0.7	0.2	0.1
Production, Transport & Related	91.6	94.3	50.3	33.1	36.2	23.1
Total	100.0	100.0	100.0	100.0	100.0	100.0
			Female			
Professional, Technical, Etc	0.4	1.1	17.4	46.1	5.3	5.8
Administrative, Managerial	0.3	0.1	0.4	2.6	10.3	22.2
Clerical, Etc	0.2	0.6	4.7	18.9	0.3	2.1
Sales	0.5	0.1	5.0	0.8	20.6	15.9
Service	22.0	5.7	59.5	14.2	9.9	3.8
Farmers & Related	0.3	0.8	0.1	0.2	0.1	0.0
Production, Transport & Related	76.3	91.6	12.8	17.2	53.4	50.1
Total	100.0	100.0	100.0	100.0	100.0	100.0
			Total			
Professional, Technical, Etc	0.4	0.6	8.7	25.7	5.3	7.9
Administrative, Managerial	0.1	0.0	1.0	4.6	14.0	42.5
Clerical, Etc	0.7	0.9	7.6	24.1	0.3	1.3
Sales	2.7	0.8	19.0	2.7	32.5	18.4
Service	6.4	3.5	20.2	12.1	7.6	2.5
Farmers & Related	0.4	0.5	0.3	0.6	0.2	0.1
Production, Transport & Related	89.4	93.7	43.2	30.1	40.2	27.3
Total	100.0	100.0	100.0	100.0	100.0	100.0

Source: ibid.

Appendix A2.14: Poverty Ratios among Unorganised Non-agriculture Workers by Social Groups

Socio-religious Group	Rural	Socio-religious Group	Urban
Hindu ST	34.3	Hindu ST	44.0
Hindu SC	24.4	Hindu SC	36.6
Muslims	20.7	Muslims	35.8
All India	17.2	Hindu OBC	26.1
Hindu OBC	13.9	All India	24.1
Other Religions	10.3	Other Religions	13.1
Hindu Others	8.3	Hindu Others	9.0

Source: ibid.

Appendix A2.15: Poverty Ratios among Unorganised Sector Workers by Sector & Industry 2004-2005

State	Agriculture		Non-agriculture			All	
	Total	Rural	Urban	Total	Rural	Urban	Total
Andhra Pradesh	7.9	3.7	24.7	13.5	6.3	25.0	9.9
Assam	12.1	18.7	2.4	14.9	13.6	2.8	12.9
Bihar	29.1	27.1	31.6	28.2	28.4	34.3	28.9
Gujarat	13.4	10.3	11.0	10.8	12.6	12.3	12.5
Haryana	5.2	12.2	11.3	11.8	7.1	10.5	7.8
Karnataka	12.4	7.7	31.1	22.1	10.5	33.1	15.6
Kerala	8.3	6.9	15.4	9.6	6.9	15.8	9.2
Madhya Pradesh	29.4	27.9	43.0	36.4	28.1	46.0	31.1
Maharashtra	23.3	15.6	31.6	27.1	20.8	34.3	24.6
Orissa	47.3	31.3	45.3	34.6	42.8	49.0	43.4
Punjab	5.1	3.9	3.5	3.7	4.8	3.5	4.4
Rajasthan	12.1	14.1	31.5	22.1	11.9	31.1	15.6
Tamil Nadu	17.4	9.6	20.7	16.1	14.1	22.9	16.7
Uttar Pradesh	21.9	24.0	28.4	25.9	22.3	28.1	23.3
West Bengal	23.0	19.4	12.7	16.3	21.7	13.3	19.7
Jharkhand	36.0	39.1	17.5	32.7	37.0	18.4	35.0
Chhattisgarh	31.9	29.1	43.5	36.4	30.9	48.6	32.6
Uttaranchal	27.5	38.7	31.3	35.1	29.1	32.1	29.6
All India	**20.5**	**17.2**	**24.1**	**20.6**	**19.3**	**25.5**	**20.5**

Source: ibid.

Appendix A2.16: Poverty Ratios among Unorganised Sector Workers by Employment Status and Industry 2004-2005

State	Unorganised Non-agriculture			
	Casual Labour	Regular	Self Employed	All
Andhra Pradesh	17.2	16.9	11.6	13.5
Bihar	43.7	33.0	25.6	28.2
Gujarat	23.5	8.7	8.5	10.8
Haryana	25.8	6.1	9.6	11.8
Karnataka	25.2	18.4	21.9	22.1
Kerala	12.6	9.2	7.3	9.6
Madhya Pradesh	57.0	36.6	29.6	36.4
Maharashtra	49.6	25.6	21.7	27.1
Orissa	51.6	29.0	30.7	34.6
Punjab	7.7	3.3	2.4	3.7
Rajasthan	26.2	24.3	19.5	22.1
Tamil Nadu	18.0	16.8	15.1	16.1
Uttar Pradesh	37.9	17.3	24.3	25.9
West Bengal	22.6	11.0	15.8	16.3
Jharkhand	43.2	16.4	28.3	32.7
Chhattisgarh	54.4	35.2	31.7	36.4
Uttaranchal	53.6	24.6	32.3	35.1
All India	29.8	17.4	18.6	20.6

Source: ibid.

Appendix A3.1: Average Daily Earnings of Casual Workers by Industry and Gender, Rural 2004-05

Industry Group	Average Daily Earnings (Rs.)			Per cent Below Minimum Wage		
	Male	Female	Total	Male	Female	Total
				National Minimum Wage Rs. 66		
Agriculture	47.88	33.15	42.48	86.56	96.71	90.46
Manufacturing	63.85	37.63	57.59	63.86	92.89	71.37
Construction	69.49	49.81	66.94	58.25	85.99	61.91
Trade & related, etc	59.46		58.79	64.26		65.05
Transport, storage & Communication	69.97		69.28	58.47		59.03
Education, health, other services, etc	59.68	41.07	52.66	62.46	82.95	70.51
Non-agriculture	67.53	44.05	63.79	60.14	87.97	64.70
All Casual Workers	54.62	34.72	48.49	77.98	95.56	83.72
				NCRL Min Wage Rs.49		
Agriculture				50.53	84.53	63.60
Non-agriculture				20.98	56.72	26.84
All Casual				40.93	80.88	53.98

Note: Average daily earnings are computed per manday.
Source: NSS 61st Round 2004 -2005, Employment-Unemployment Survey. Computed.

Appendix A3.2: Average Daily Earnings of Casual Workers by Industry and Gender, Urban 2004-05

Industry Group	Average Daily Earnings (Rs.)			Per cent Below Minimum Wage		
	Male	Female	Total	Male	Female	Total
				National Minimum Wage Rs. 66		
Agriculture	56.80	34.29	46.72	76.63	96.55	86.13
Manufacturing	68.85	41.04	63.95	52.68	92.77	60.68
Construction	84.85	57.19	81.64	36.45	72.21	40.94
Trade & related,	60.40	40.90	58.28	65.46		68.22
Transport, storage & communication	81.12	38.85	80.59	38.53		39.49
Education, health, other services, etc	66.98	45.94	53.63	56.35	82.84	73.10
Non-agriculture	76.12	47.62	71.29	45.48	82.98	51.94
All Casual Workers	74.30	43.58	68.10	48.68	87.51	57.20
				NCRL Min Wage Rs.49		
Agriculture				77.51	96.82	86.72
Non-agriculture				46.20	83.13	52.57
All Casual				49.42	87.70	57.82

Source: ibid.

Appendix A3.3: Average Daily Earnings of Casual Workers in Manufacturing by Industry and Sector 2004-05

Industry Group	Average Daily Earnings (Rs.)		Per cent Below Minimum Wage	
	Rural	Urban	Rural	Urban
Food products and beverages	55.20	60.16	75.19	57.94
Tobacco products	32.80	29.23	92.52	92.33
Textiles	49.84	56.14	79.33	67.45
Wearing apparel		63.07		65.75
Wood and of products	82.89	78.93	42.57	36.86
Other non-metallic mineral products	54.40	62.81	77.34	64.88
Fabricated metal products		62.11		57.70
Total Manufacturing	57.59	63.95	71.37	60.68
			NCRL Min Wage	
Total Manufacturing			**38.89**	**61.33**

Source: ibid.

Appendix A3.4: Average Daily Earnings of Casual Workers in Manufacturing by Industry and Gender 2004-05

Industry Group	Average Daily Earnings (Rs.)		Per cent Below National Minimum Wage		
	Male	Female	Total	Male	Female
Food products and beverages	60.61	46.09	56.41	64.96	84.72
Tobacco products	37.75	25.32	31.65	85.86	98.72
Textiles	58.78	33.96	52.31	65.17	96.59
Wearing apparel	60.86		56.16	61.81	
Wood and of products	84.83		81.44	36.92	
Other non-metallic mineral Products	59.35	43.59	55.64	70.13	91.81
Fabricated metal products	62.12		62.04	60.38	
Total Manufacturing.	65.68	38.62	59.69	59.82	92.85

Source: ibid.

Appendix A3.5: Average Daily Earnings of Regular Workers by Industry and Gender, Rural 2004-05

Industry Group	Average Daily Earnings (Rs.)			Per cent Below Minimum Wage		
	Male	Female	Total	Male	Female	Total
Unorganised Sector				**National Minimum Wage Rs.66**		
Manufacturing	69.32	36.21	64.98	53.86	86.80	58.21
Construction	-	-	-	-	-	-
Trade, hotels & restaurant	69.23	-	68.48	63.24	-	64.06
Transport, storage & communication	88.19	-	87.53	35.71	-	36.45
Financial intermediation, real estate & business	78.41	-	73.68	44.78	-	49.65
Public administration	76.69	-	73.09	68.08	-	70.28
Education, health, other services	98.49	59.37	85.28	53.93	74.51	60.88
Domestic services	61.55	29.59	38.55	76.62	92.74	88.21
All Non-agriculture	78.54	41.75	72.88	52.13	85.62	57.27
				NCRL Min Wage Rs.49		
All Non-agriculture				29.48	75.80	36.58
Regular Unorganised Workers in the Organised Sector				**National Minimum Wage Rs.66**		
Manufacturing	77.50	29.08	67.70	48.89	91.60	57.65
Construction	81.32	-	81.45	63.25	-	62.23
Trade, hotels & restaurant	85.15	-	78.09	41.63	-	46.76
Transport, storage & communication	102.49	-	99.27	21.49	-	24.94
Financial intermediation, real estate & business	-	-	-	-	-	-
Public administration	67.17	38.52	59.98	68.10	84.92	72.31
Education, health, other services	83.72	47.13	65.42	41.65	82.22	61.98
Domestic services	-	-	-	-	-	-
All Non-agriculture	83.36	44.30	72.27	46.40	82.95	56.80
				NCRL Min Wage Rs.49		
All Non-agriculture				24.80	71.44	38.07

Source: ibid.

Appendix A3.6: Average Daily Earnings of Regular Workers by Industry and Gender Urban 2004-05

Industry Group	Average Daily Earnings (Rs.)			Per cent Below Minimum Wage		
	Male	Female	Total	Male	Female	Total
Unorganised Sector				**National Minimum Wage Rs.66**		
Manufacturing	88.97	49.46	85.46	34.96	82.82	39.20
Construction	97.02	-	100.78	34.13	-	32.33
Trade, hotels & restaurant	83.12	61.89	81.99	44.95	63.47	45.93
Transport, storage & communication	106.32	-	105.98	28.34	-	28.79
Financial intermediation, real estate & business	133.98	-	133.59	38.09	-	41.35
Public administration	-	-	122.90	-	-	38.64
Education, health, other services	99.42	75.65	89.78	51.85	66.41	57.69
Domestic services	82.13	40.24	50.17	33.80	84.65	72.66
All Non-agriculture	92.36	52.80	83.93	38.81	78.36	47.20
				NCRL min wage Rs.67		
All Non-agriculture				40.76	78.92	48.86
Regular Unorganised Workers in the Organised Sector				**National Minimum Wage Rs.66**		
Manufacturing	107.43	52.60	99.80	29.92	73.71	36.08
Construction	156.79	-	155.66	26.19	-	24.42
Trade, hotels & restaurant	113.91	-	111.64	28.43	-	29.12
Transport, storage & communication	127.00	-	123.78	21.81	-	24.73
Financial intermediation, real estate & business	161.03	-	168.72	16.84	-	18.24
Public administration	140.93	-	129.94	37.61	-	38.34
Education, health, other services	130.59	77.08	104.26	26.02	59.37	42.35
Domestic services	-	-	-	-	-	-
All Non-agriculture	121.37	81.19	113.02	27.89	59.04	34.35
				NCRL Min Wage Rs.67		
All Non-agriculture				29.58	61.18	36.13

Source: ibid.

Appendix A4.1: Percentage of Self- employed Workers in Unorganised Non-agriculture across the States 2004-2005

State	OAW	UFW	Employer	Self-employed	All Workers (millions)
Andhra Pradesh	44.6	19.2	1.5	65.2	12.6
Assam	55.9	9.7	0.0	65.6	2.5
Bihar	63.8	16.9	0.0	80.8	5.8
Gujarat	45.2	16.3	1.6	63.1	6.8
Haryana	49.6	11.2	0.0	60.8	3.2
Himachal Pradesh	39.6	7.8	1.0	48.4	0.7
Jammu & Kashmir	51.6	21.9	0.2	73.7	0.9
Karnataka	41.2	15.8	1.6	58.6	7.6
Kerala	36.8	5.7	5.5	47.9	6.2
Madhya Pradesh	46.8	18.6	0.2	65.5	6.3
Maharashtra	42.4	11.5	5.9	59.7	14.3
Orissa	47.0	22.8	0.5	70.3	4.9
Punjab	41.5	10.3	2.6	54.4	4.2
Rajasthan	42.7	12.8	0.5	56.0	8.3
Tamil Nadu	38.6	15.7	3.2	57.5	11.7
Uttar Pradesh	49.3	18.4	0.4	68.1	21.7
West Bengal	55.8	11.7	0.7	68.2	14.3
Delhi	35.5	7.8	9.5	52.7	3.0
Jharkhand	43.8	10.3	0.0	54.1	2.8
Chhattisgarh	42.2	16.8	0.3	59.4	1.6
Uttaranchal	54.4	12.2	0.6	67.2	0.9
All India	**46.2**	**14.7**	**1.9**	**62.8**	**142.1**

Note: OAW: Own Account Worker, UFW: Unpaid Family Worker.
Source: NSS 61st Round 2004-2005, Employment-Unemployment Survey. Computed.

Appendix A4.2: Percentage of Enterprises by Size in Unorganised Non-agriculture across the States, 1999-2000

State	OAE	Establishments		All Enterprises
		2 - 5 Workers	6 - 9 Workers	
Andhra Pradesh	88.4	10.3	1.4	100.0
Assam	89.2	10.1	0.7	100.0
Bihar	95.0	4.5	0.5	100.0
Gujarat	81.9	15.1	3.0	100.0
Haryana	88.2	10.2	1.5	100.0
Himachal Pradesh	85.6	13.3	1.1	100.0
Jammu & Kashmir	88.3	9.9	1.7	100.0
Karnataka	82.4	14.8	2.8	100.0
Kerala	77.4	20.4	2.3	100.0
Madhya Pradesh	89.9	8.5	1.5	100.0
Maharashtra	80.8	16.0	3.2	100.0
Orissa	95.6	4.0	0.3	100.0
Punjab	82.0	16.5	1.6	100.0
Rajasthan	89.5	9.5	1.0	100.0
Tamil Nadu	83.4	14.1	2.5	100.0
Uttar Pradesh	91.9	7.2	0.9	100.0
West Bengal	91.0	8.0	1.0	100.0
All India	**87.4**	**10.9**	**1.7**	**100.0**

Note: OAE: Own Account Enterprises are enterprises without hired workers; Establishments are enterprises with hired workers.
Source: NSS 55th Round 1999-2000, Informal Enterprises Survey. Computed.

Appendix A4.3: Percentage of Total Workers by Size of the Enterprise in Unorganised Non-agriculture across the States 1999-2000

State	OAE	Establishments		All Enterprises
		2 - 5 Workers	6 - 9 Workers	
Andhra Pradesh	76.9	17.7	5.4	100.0
Assam	76.6	19.8	3.6	100.0
Bihar	88.8	8.9	2.4	100.0
Gujarat	65.1	24.0	11.0	100.0
Haryana	72.8	20.2	7.0	100.0
Himachal Pradesh	70.3	24.7	5.0	100.0
Jammu & Kashmir	74.7	17.4	7.9	100.0
Karnataka	65.8	23.9	10.3	100.0
Kerala	57.2	33.7	9.1	100.0
Madhya Pradesh	78.7	14.7	6.6	100.0
Maharashtra	61.8	25.8	12.3	100.0
Orissa	91.6	6.9	1.5	100.0
Punjab	62.7	30.3	7.0	100.0
Rajasthan	77.5	17.9	4.5	100.0
Tamil Nadu	67.7	22.8	9.6	100.0
Uttar Pradesh	82.3	13.5	4.2	100.0
West Bengal	79.7	15.9	4.3	100.0
All India	**73.4**	**19.4**	**7.2**	**100.0**

Source: ibid.

Appendix A4.4: Percentage of OAEs by Location and Broad Industry Group 1999-2000

Location of Enterprise	Broad Industry Group						
	M	C	T&RS	H&R	TSC	OS	Total
				Rural			
Within Household Premises	76.5	0.4	29.3	26.8	19.1	41.1	46.3
With Fixed Premises & Permanent Structure	14.3	0.0	37.5	55.9	3.5	24.6	23.4
With fixed premises & Temporary Structure	1.4	0.0	4.4	10.2	0.5	2.8	2.8
With fixed Premises but Without Structure	1.9	0.0	2.9	1.5	11.3	4.4	3.2
Mobile or without fixed premises	4.4	0.2	26.8	5.5	64.5	26.5	18.9
Construction Site	1.6	98.7	0.1	0.0	1.0	0.6	5.5
Total	**100.0**	**100.0**	**100.0**	**100.0**	**100.0**	**100.0**	**100.0**
				Urban			
Within Household Premises	62.8	0.7	16.7	17.6	12.9	37.1	28.2
With Fixed Premises & Permanent Structure	28.6	0.2	53.7	49.0	10.1	47.8	40.4
With fixed premises & Temporary Structure	1.6	0.0	5.2	14.5	0.8	3.1	3.8
With fixed Premises but Without Structure	1.4	0.1	3.4	5.8	11.2	1.7	3.6
Mobile or without fixed premises	4.3	0.2	21.0	13.1	58.6	9.9	19.8
Construction Site	1.3	98.8	0.1	0.0	0.2	0.5	4.2
Total	**100.0**	**100.0**	**100.0**	**100.0**	**100.0**	**100.0**	**100.0**

Note: M-Manufacturing, C-Construction, T&RS-Trade and retail services, H&R-Hotels and restaurants, TSC-Transport, storage, communication, OS-Other Services.

Source: ibid.

Appendix A4.5: Percentage of Enterprises without Any Registration by States 1999-2000

State	OAE	Establishments	All Enterprises
Andhra Pradesh	87.2	44.8	82.3
Assam	81.2	42.9	77.0
Bihar	95.3	65.7	93.8
Gujarat	69.8	22.5	61.2
Haryana	94.1	78.9	92.3
Himachal Pradesh	71.9	29.5	65.8
Jammu & Kashmir	66.6	30.4	62.3
Karnataka	74.2	32.8	67.0
Kerala	65.0	33.4	57.8
Madhya Pradesh	87.4	40.2	82.6
Maharashtra	65.8	31.3	59.2
Orissa	97.7	74.2	96.7
Punjab	84.4	55.4	79.2
Rajasthan	92.3	54.9	88.3
Tamil Nadu	85.0	53.3	79.7
Uttar Pradesh	89.3	64.1	87.2
West Bengal	89.5	48.7	85.9
All India	**84.9**	**46.9**	**80.1**

Source: ibid.

Appendix A4.6: Percentage of Homeworkers in Self- employed by States 1999-2000

State	Percentage of Homeworkers
Andhra Pradesh	9.4
Bihar	8.6
Gujarat	6.3
Jammu & Kashmir	13.0
Karnataka	13.4
Kerala	7.9
Madhya Pradesh	12.2
Maharashtra	6.5
Orissa	11.5
Rajasthan	7.0
Tamil Nadu	23.7
Uttar Pradesh	12.6
West Bengal	22.4
All India	**11.9**

NSS 55th Round 1999-2000, Employment-Unemployment Survey. Computed.

Appendix A5.1: Percentage of Unorganised Non-agricultural Women Wage Workers across Industrial Categories 2004-05

Industry Group	Casual Labour	Regular Workers	Wage Workers
Private Households	19.8	53.9	37.8
Manufacturing	28.6	13.1	20.4
Construction	38.9	0.7	18.7
Education	0.2	12.9	7.0
Trade & Repair, etc	2.6	6.0	4.4
Health & Social Work	0.4	4.7	2.7
Other Services, etc	2.7	2.4	2.5
Mining & Quarrying	3.7	0.1	1.8
Finance, Business Service	0.1	3.1	1.7
Hotels & Restaurants	1.7	1.5	1.6
Transport Storage, etc	1.2	1.5	1.4
Public Administration, etc	0.0	0.1	0.1
Electricity, Gas, etc	0.0	0.0	0.0
Total	100.0	100.0	100.0
Percentage Distribution	47.1	52.9	100.0

NSS 61st Round 2004-2005, Employment-Unemployment Survey. Computed.

Appendix A5.2: Percentage of Unorganised Non-agricultural Self-employed Female Workers across Industrial Categories 2004-2005

Industry Group	Own Account Worker	Employer	Unpaid Family Worker	Self-employed
Manufacturing	62.9	43.1	57.4	60.2
Trade & Repair, etc	18.5	15.1	23.5	20.8
Other Services, etc	6.7	13.4	8.7	7.7
Hotels & Restaurants	2.2	4.4	7.4	4.6
Education	6.6	4.3	0.8	3.9
Finance, Business Service	1.1	1.7	0.7	0.9
Transport Storage, etc	0.7	2.0	0.8	0.8
Health & Social Work	1.1	15.6	0.3	0.8
Construction	0.1	0.0	0.2	0.2
Mining & Quarrying	0.0	0.0	0.3	0.1
Electricity, Gas, etc	0.0	0.0	0.0	0.0
Public Administration, etc	0.0	0.2	0.0	0.0
Private Households	0.0	0.0	0.0	0.0
Total	100.0	100.0	100.0	100.0
Percentage Distribution	53.1	0.6	46.3	100.0

Source: ibid.

Appendix A5.3: Share of Male and Female Proprietary Enterprises by Most Serious Problem Faced (Percentage) 1999-2000

Most Serious Problem	Male Proprietary			Female Proprietary		
	OAEs	Establishments	Total	OAEs	Establishments	Total
No Specific Problem	29.0	35.2	29.8	37.9	41.0	38.1
Shortage of Capital	40.3	27.6	38.7	26.6	20.6	26.3
Power Related Problems	1.9	4.9	2.3	1.2	3.2	1.3
Lack of Marketing / Other Infrastructure Facilities	8.1	7.4	8.0	4.9	4.8	4.9
Local Problems	7.6	6.6	7.5	5.8	4.6	5.8
Competition from Larger Units	6.2	11.6	6.8	4.9	18.9	5.6
Labour Related Problems	0.5	1.6	0.6	0.2	1.8	0.3
Raw Materials/Fuel Not Available or Exorbitant Price	1.1	1.0	1.1	4.9	1.3	4.7
Non- recovery of Service Charges / Fees/ Credit	2.8	2.1	2.7	1.7	1.1	1.7
Others	2.4	1.8	2.3	11.7	2.6	11.2
Total	100.0	100.0	100.0	100.0	100.0	100.0

Note: OAE = Enterprises with no hired worker. Establishments are enterprises with one or more hired workers.
Source: NSS 55th Round 1999-2000, Informal Enterprises Survey. Computed.

Appendix A6.1: Incidence of Child Labour and Out -of-School Children (Labour Pool) (5 - 14 Years) across the States (Percentage) 2004 - 2005

State	Out of School Children	Child Labour	Out of School Children	Child Labour	Out of School Children	Child Labour
	Males		Females		Total	
Bihar	29.9	2.2	40.1	0.6	34.4	1.5
Jharkhand	20.0	2.4	27.4	2.7	23.4	2.5
Uttar Pradesh	20.3	4.7	25.7	3.4	22.8	4.1
Rajasthan	15.6	3.8	29.2	5.9	22.2	4.8
Madhya Pradesh	17.3	2.4	26.4	3.3	21.5	2.8
Orissa	17.3	5.3	23.7	4.6	20.4	5.0
Chhattisgarh	14.0	3.6	23.0	5.5	18.6	4.5
All India	15.4	3.5	20.8	3.3	17.9	3.4
West Bengal	16.7	4.3	18.1	3.2	17.4	3.7
Gujarat	12.0	2.7	18.1	2.3	14.8	2.5
Haryana	9.7	1.4	17.7	2.1	13.3	1.7
Assam	11.9	2.6	13.5	1.1	12.6	1.9
Andhra Pradesh	9.6	6.1	15.1	7.1	12.2	6.6
Uttaranchal	10.4	3.3	14.0	1.8	12.1	2.6
Jammu & Kashmir	7.6	1.6	16.8	4.1	12.1	2.8
Karnataka	10.4	4.3	13.7	4.8	12.0	4.6
Maharashtra	10.7	3.2	11.5	3.7	11.1	3.5
Punjab	9.4	2.8	11.3	1.3	10.2	2.1
Himachal Pradesh	5.2	2.0	8.2	3.5	6.6	2.7
Tamil Nadu	2.3	1.3	5.3	1.9	3.7	1.6
Kerala	2.9	0.4	2.0	0.1	2.5	0.3

Note: States arranged in descending order of total 'Out-of-School' children.
Source: NSS 61st Rounds 2004 - 2005, Employment-Unemployment Survey. Computed.

Appendix A7.1: State-wise Percentage Share of Agricultural Workers in Total Rural Workforce

State	Male			Female			Total		
	1983	1993-94	2004-05	1983	1993-94	2004-05	1983	1993-94	2004-05
Andhra Pradesh	77.1	75.6	66.4	83.7	83.7	78.5	80.0	79.3	71.8
Assam	78.7	77.5	69.6	80.8	82.4	88.3	79.1	78.5	74.3
Bihar	81.1	81.9	75.8	88.2	91.8	86.4	83.4	84.2	77.9
Gujarat	78.8	71.1	69.3	92.6	90.6	89.1	84.5	78.7	77.3
Haryana	71.6	60.8	49.4	90.3	93.2	90.6	77.4	71.9	64.1
Himachal Pradesh	77.0	65.8	49.4	97.6	95.5	91.0	87.1	80.2	69.6
Jammu & Kashmir	72.0	61.3	53.8	96.4	95.4	86.6	79.9	75.8	63.9
Karnataka	81.5	78.8	77.7	88.2	84.8	85.5	84.2	81.3	81.0
Kerala	57.8	52.8	37.1	70.8	62.8	51.7	63.1	56.1	42.0
Madhya Pradesh	87.1	87.2	79.1	93.9	93.8	88.1	90.0	89.8	82.5
Maharashtra	79.6	75.3	71.4	92.9	91.2	90.7	85.7	82.5	80.0
Orissa	78.1	78.8	65.9	81.0	85.1	74.6	79.1	81.0	69.0
Punjab	77.5	68.1	54.7	92.6	92.7	89.7	82.5	74.6	66.9
Rajasthan	81.0	69.5	60.2	93.9	93.0	89.5	86.7	79.8	72.9
Tamil Nadu	68.7	63.8	58.7	81.8	78.5	73.8	74.5	70.4	65.4
Uttar Pradesh	78.6	76.2	66.3	89.7	89.9	86.5	82.0	80.0	72.8
West Bengal	73.0	64.8	63.9	75.1	59.5	58.8	73.5	63.5	62.7
India	**77.6**	**74.0**	**66.5**	**87.7**	**86.2**	**83.3**	**81.4**	**78.4**	**72.7**

Note: Usual Principal and Subsidiary Status.
Source: Based on NSSO 1987; 1997; 2006a.

Appendix A7.2: State-wise Percentage of Rural Agricultural Workforce across Types of Employment

State	Farmers			Agricultural Labourers*		
	1993-94	1999-2000	2004-2005	1993-94	1999-2000	2004-2005
Himachal Pradesh	97.7	97.7	97.5	2.3	2.3	2.5
Jammu & Kashmir	96.7	95.3	95.2	3.4	4.7	4.8
Rajasthan	89.9	91.0	91.2	10.1	9.1	8.8
Uttar Pradesh	78.1	77.5	84.3	21.9	22.6	15.7
Haryana	76.6	79.7	82.6	23.3	20.3	17.4
Assam	61.0	65.6	77.2	39.0	34.4	22.8
Punjab	68.7	75.5	76.5	31.3	24.6	23.5
All India	60.1	57.8	64.1	39.9	42.2	35.9
Bihar	50.2	50.0	63.4	49.9	50.0	36.6
Madhya Pradesh	64.1	58.0	61.4	35.9	42.1	38.6
Kerala	52.0	55.6	59.9	48	44.5	40.1
Orissa	54.6	45.0	58.5	45.5	54.9	41.5
Gujarat	54.4	59.0	57.8	45.7	41.0	42.2
Maharashtra	49.6	45.5	53.1	50.3	54.6	46.9
West Bengal	53.8	43.7	50.6	46.1	56.2	49.4
Karnataka	55.1	50.0	49.2	44.9	50.0	50.8
Andhra Pradesh	44.1	43.2	44.8	55.9	56.8	55.2
Tamil Nadu	40.9	34.9	43.2	59.1	65.1	56.8

Source: NSS 50th, 55th and 61st Rounds, for 1993-94, 1999-2000 and 2004 - 2005, Employment and Unemployment Survey. Computed.

Appendix A7.3: State-wise Distribution of Households by Size of Land Possessed (Hectares): Rural (Percentage) 2004 - 2005

State	Landless	Marginal	Small	Semi-medium	Large	Total
Andhra Pradesh	17.1	61.2	10.8	7.0	3.9	100.0
Assam	2.2	62.8	21.6	12.1	1.3	100.0
Bihar	12.0	70.5	11.0	5.0	1.5	100.0
Chhattisgarh	9.5	51.6	17.3	16.7	4.9	100.0
Delhi	62.1	37.3	0.0	0.6	0.0	100.0
Gujarat	26.9	45.9	12.0	9.6	5.6	100.0
Haryana	20.0	54.8	10.1	9.8	5.3	100.0
Himachal Pradesh	8.3	75.9	10.5	4.1	1.2	100.0
Jammu & Kashmir	2.8	81.4	11.9	3.5	0.4	100.0
Jharkhand	5.0	77.5	14.0	2.8	0.7	100.0
Karnataka	22.9	48.3	13.7	10.0	5.1	100.0
Kerala	3.7	90.4	4.3	1.3	0.3	100.0
Madhya Pradesh	18.7	36.8	18.1	17.4	9.0	100.0
Maharashtra	23.9	44.7	13.4	11.3	6.7	100.0
Orissa	17.5	62.4	14.1	4.7	1.3	100.0
Punjab	14.6	63	7.5	9.1	5.8	100.0
Rajasthan	8.3	46.4	17.3	14.3	13.7	100.0
Tamil Nadu	22.6	66.6	7.3	2.5	1.0	100.0
Uttaranchal	11.5	78.9	5.5	2.6	1.5	100.0
Uttar Pradesh	10.1	69.6	12.7	5.8	1.8	100.0
West Bengal	8.0	84.3	6.0	1.5	0.2	100.0
All India	**14.4**	**62.5**	**12.0**	**7.5**	**3.6**	**100.0**

Source: ibid

Appendix A7.4: Percentage of Rural Agricultural Labour Households by Social Groups

State	STs		SCs		OBCs		Others	
	1999-2000	2004-2005	1999-2000	2004-2005	1999-2000	2004-2005	1999-2000	2004-2005
Andhra Pradesh	7.3	9.9	35.8	32.2	43.0	42.6	13.9	15.3
Assam	11.1	13.3	11.2	14.3	22.9	24.5	54.7	48.0
Bihar	5.7	1.2	39.8	44.3	45.1	47.9	9.4	6.6
Jharkhand		37.2		25.8		27.8		9.2
Gujarat	27.3	26.9	22.8	23.8	29.5	39.6	20.4	9.7
Haryana	3.9	0.0	54.1	72.8	30.6	21.7	11.4	5.5
Himachal Pradesh	4.8	2.9	40.5	56.8	14.3	0.0	40.5	40.2
Karnataka	11.1	12.1	34.4	29.3	35.7	37.9	18.8	20.6
Kerala	3.5	8.8	27.6	30.5	43.0	38.4	25.9	22.3
Madhya Pradesh	36.1	35.9	22.3	28.5	36.3	30.7	5.3	4.9
Chhattisgarh		29.8		22.8		46.0		1.5
Maharashtra	23.4	17.8	22.0	22.6	27.5	37.8	27.2	21.7
Orissa	36.4	37.0	24.9	26.3	26.3	29.7	12.4	7.1
Punjab	1.3	0.3	77.4	73.4	13.4	20.5	7.9	5.8
Rajasthan	20.1	15.1	41.0	46.9	23.1	29.7	15.7	8.3
Tamil Nadu	1.5	1.0	45.9	41.4	50.7	57.3	2.0	0.3
Uttar Pradesh	0.8	1.1	55.5	46.9	32.1	42.6	11.6	9.4
Uttaranchal		1.0		44.8		38.7		15.5
West Bengal	9.0	14.6	36.4	36.2	3.8	3.8	50.8	45.3
India	**13.6**	**14.1**	**35.3**	**34.1**	**33.5**	**36.4**	**17.7**	**15.4**

Source: Rural Labour Enquiry Report 1999-2000. NSS 61st Round, 2004 - 2005, Employment-Unemployment Survey.

Appendix A7.5: Average Monthly Income Per Farmer Household (Rs. / month) From Cultivation by Size Classes of Land Holdings (Hectares) 2003

STATE	Marginal	Small	Semi-medium	Medium	Large	All Sizes
A.P	243	1174	1999	4755	8553	743
Assam	1083	3102	6285	11643	***	1792
Bihar	474	1885	3494	7319	20891	846
Chhattisgarh	319	1024	2023	3288	9571	811
Gujarat	330	1408	2563	4616	4876	1164
Haryana	373	1987	3603	5018	14414	1494
J.K	1552	5479	7123	21618	***	2426
Jharkhand	555	1968	3624	4531	23433	852
Karnataka	400	1523	2549	4405	15142	1266
Kerala	734	3715	7199	8704	***	1120
Madhya Pradesh.	273	882	1725	3464	8171	996
Maharashtra	440	1440	2502	4431	12846	1263
Orissa	212	705	1198	2507	10599	336
Punjab	307	3027	5369	13088	26079	2822
Rajasthan	198	383	836	706	331	359
Tamil Nadu	281	978	2450	8821	14890	659
Uttar Pradesh	389	1746	2999	7282	8370	836
West Bengal	519	7225	4621	5263	***	737
All India	**435**	**1578**	**2685**	**4676**	**8321**	**969**

Note: Marginal (Less than 1.00), Small (1.01 - 2.00), Semi-Medium (2.00 - 4.00), Medium (4.00 - 10.00), Large (> 10.00) Hectares.
Source: NSSO 2005a

Appendix A8.1: Average Daily Earnings (Rs) of Men, Women and Children in Rural Labour Households in Agricultural Occupations, 1999-2000

States/ Union Territories	Wage Rate (Rs. per day)							Women's Wages as percentage to Men's	
	All Classes		Scheduled Castes (SC)		Scheduled Tribes (ST)				
	Men	Women	Men	Women	Men	Women	All Classes	SC	ST
Andhra Pradesh	39.80	26.49	40.58	27.24	39.14	29.77	67	67	76
Assam	43.13	39.02	38.91	34.26	45.49	35.68	90	88	78
Bihar	35.10	30.96	34.93	31.64	33.32	31.61	88	91	95
Gujarat	38.81	33.27	44.91	38.54	31.24	27.58	86	86	88
Haryana	60.04	53.28	65.31	55.54	62.87	-	89	85	-
Karnataka	40.32	27.21	38.72	26.74	36.21	25.22	67	69	70
Kerala	94.52	62.22	97.25	62.37	76.28	56.34	66	64	74
Madhya Pradesh	30.01	25.44	29.85	26.05	29.24	25.26	85	87	86
Maharashtra	37.67	24.34	37.32	23.59	35.84	24.87	65	63	69
Orissa	28.69	22.31	28.50	23.38	26.37	22.72	78	82	86
Punjab	63.57	73.98	62.90	72.70	-	-	116	116	-
Rajasthan	51.68	39.12	55.43	47.17	39.68	30.45	76	85	77
Tamil Nadu	52.36	30.48	50.40	30.19	53.67	24.83	58	60	46
Uttar Pradesh	38.29	29.05	36.53	28.11	25.74	17.92	76	77	70
West Bengal	43.45	37.03	43.85	36.38	40.97	36.93	85	83	90
Arunachal Pradesh	63.91	55.05	-	-	73.94	60.00	86		81
Chhattisgarh	26.31	22.92	25.56	21.83	27.16	23.21	87	85	85
Himachal Pradesh	63.52	56.79	57.19	40.00	81.02	62.56	89	70	77
Jammu & Kashmir	85.91	-	64.09	-	-	-	-	-	-
Jharkhand	34.45	28.71	35.23	26.21	32.73	30.01	83	74	92
Manipur	52.24	49.74	-	-	58.82	50.00	95	-	85
Meghalaya	50.58	35.44	-	-	50.16	35.48	70	-	71
Mizoram	87.57	114.50	-	-	87.57	114.50	131		131
Nagaland	111.86	-	-	-	135.91	-	-	-	-
Sikkim	50.67	39.08	51.40	32.12	52.09	30.00	77	62	58
Tripura	49.60	36.67	51.13	33.97	37.77	38.97	74	66	103
Uttaranchal	58.96	52.79	63.64	65.50	64.29	-	90	103	-
ALL-INDIA	**40.58**	**28.57**	**41.89**	**29.60**	**33.19**	**26.44**	70	71	80

Source: Rural Labour Enquiry Report 1999-2000.

Appendix A9.1: Incidence of Indebtedness among Farmer Households by Farm Size (Percentages) 2003

State	Farm Size in Hectares			
	Sub-Marginal & Marginal	Small	Medium-Large	Total
Andhra Pradesh	80.3	86.9	82.7	82.0
Assam	19.6	16.5	12.6	18.1
Bihar	35.7	20.8	21.4	33.0
Chhattisgarh	38.6	44.9	38.6	40.2
Gujarat	43.2	57.3	67.0	51.9
Haryana	47.8	59.4	64.0	53.1
Himachal Pradesh	32.7	35.2	39.1	33.4
Jammu &Kashmir	29.4	32.5	52.6	31.8
Jharkhand	21.1	20.5	18.5	20.9
Karnataka	58.8	65.8	64.2	61.6
Kerala	63.8	72.9	59.9	64.4
Madhya Pradesh	42.6	49.9	62.0	50.8
Maharashtra	44.9	56.9	66.7	54.8
Orissa	47.6	48.4	49.1	47.8
Punjab	58.6	75.3	77.6	65.4
Rajasthan	50.4	53.1	54.9	52.4
Tamil Nadu	74.5	75.5	73.5	74.5
Uttar Pradesh	39.3	42.1	46.0	40.3
Uttaranchal	6.1	25.6	2.0	7.2
West Bengal	51.1	44.7	41.5	50.1
All India	**45.8**	**50.8**	**57.8**	**48.6**

Note: Sub-Marginal & Marginal: <= 1 hectare; Small: 1 - 2 hectares; Medium-Large: >2 hectares.
Source: NSS 59th Round 2003, Situtation Assessment Survey of Farmers. Computed.

Appendix A9.2: Average Amount of Outstanding Loans per Indebted Farmer Household by Land Size (Rs.) 2003

State	Farm Size in Hectares				
	Sub-Marginal	Marginal	Small	Medium-Large	Total
Andhra Pradesh	17751	25704	37334	41813	29216
Assam	4369	3431	5707	7456	4486
Bihar	9498	16479	28436	38673	13552
Chhattisgarh	4579	5404	9228	25031	10256
Gujarat	16568	17280	22538	53934	29912
Haryana	24264	37516	52923	89557	48952
Himachal Pradesh	25925	21694	35157	58920	28759
Jammu & Kashmir	7157	4019	6692	9484	5977
Jharkhand	9564	10320	9370	25813	10564
Karnataka	14853	21131	24063	54200	29437
Kerala	43228	56570	89927	98777	52676
Madhya Pradesh	11019	18006	24529	40664	27987
Maharashtra	15844	18118	30292	43782	30948
Orissa	8996	14212	11387	19617	12275
Punjab	21090	51830	37801	156235	63529
Rajasthan	19199	21829	30388	56987	35044
Tamil Nadu	20596	29565	42951	60729	32178
Uttar Pradesh	11365	16444	22540	50138	18409
Uttaranchal	16726	9423	16441	75039	15429
West Bengal	7676	12194	21738	21556	10449
All India	**14866**	**20240**	**28428**	**51726**	**25895**

Note: Sub-Marginal: <= 0.40 hectares; Marginal: <= 1 hectare; Small: 1 - 2 hectares; Medium-Large: >2 hectares.
Source: ibid.

Appendix A9.3: Tenant Holdings & Operated Area Leased-In (Percentage) 1991-92 & 2002-03 (Kharif only)

State	Per cent of Tenant Holdings		Per cent Share of Leased-in Area	
	1991-92	2002-03	1991-92	2002-03
Andhra Pradesh	14.1	12.9	9.6	9
Assam	10.1	8.9	8.9	5.3
Bihar	5.6	12.7	3.9	8.9
Gujarat	3.7	5.3	3.3	5.1
Haryana	17.1	10.7	33.7	14.4
Karnataka	8	4.6	7.4	3.6
Kerala	5.2	5.1	2.9	4
Madhya Pradesh	9	7.3	6.3	3.6
Maharashtra	6.9	6.6	5.5	4.7
Orissa	16.9	19.4	9.5	13
Punjab	15.9	13.1	18.8	16.8
Rajasthan	6.5	2.9	5.2	2.8
Tamil Nadu	15.3	9.4	10.9	6
Uttar Pradesh	15.5	11.7	10.5	9.5
West Bengal	14.4	14.1	10.4	9.3
All-India	**11**	**9.9**	**8.3**	**6.5**

Source: NSS 1992; 2006b.

Appendix A9.4: Awareness of bio-fertilizer, MSP & WTO by Size of Holdings (Percentage of Farmer Households) 2003

State	Awareness of Bio fertilizers				Awareness of MSP Farm Size in Hectares				Awareness of WTO			
	Sub-Marginal & Marginal	Small	Medium-Large	Total	Sub-Marginal & Marginal	Small	Medium-Large	Total	Sub-Marginal & Marginal	Small	Medium-Large	Total
Andhra Pradesh	8.7	11.2	16.0	10.6	25.6	31.3	38.2	29.1	3.2	6.2	11.9	5.5
Assam	22.8	31.7	32.1	25.7	18.6	26.2	30.5	21.6	9.2	13.2	13.3	10.5
Bihar	11.4	19.8	20.5	13.0	15.9	28.3	36.6	18.7	6.3	16.7	19.1	8.3
Chhattisgarh	10.5	10.9	14.0	11.3	33.0	35.6	40.8	35.3	0.5	1.5	3.5	1.4
Gujarat	7.3	11.1	18.0	10.7	17.4	30.7	37.5	25.0	4.8	8.3	6.0	5.8
Haryana	4.9	10.1	18.8	8.7	49.7	72.5	78.5	59.6	7.4	9.1	24.7	11.4
Himachal Pradesh	10.7	14.7	14.5	11.6	19.1	32.7	32.5	22.0	7.1	14.6	5.8	8.2
Jammu &Kashmir	30.5	24.3	16.5	28.4	27.8	26.2	21.0	27.0	7.6	5.0	6.6	7.2
Jharkhand	22.2	25.9	30.7	23.2	11.2	15.6	22.1	12.5	9.5	14.3	17.9	10.7
Karnataka	15.7	29.4	30.2	22.2	22.8	32.7	40.0	29.2	3.9	8.5	12.4	7.0
Kerala	52.7	69.5	64.3	54.6	59.1	78.5	66.9	61.0	41.6	62.7	58.1	44.0
Madhya Pradesh	7.7	9.2	14.8	10.4	21.1	28.3	40.7	29.4	1.5	1.3	5.6	2.7
Maharashtra	19.1	27.5	28.5	24.2	17.1	30.9	39.4	27.6	3.5	3.7	10.7	5.8
Orissa	15.3	13.9	14.0	15.0	10.1	16.1	26.4	12.3	1.8	2.7	6.4	2.3
Punjab	1.3	10.3	18.0	6.4	45.8	81.0	89.4	61.0	13.1	39.6	39.6	23.1
Rajasthan	8.4	13.4	10.2	10.0	7.0	10.6	15.6	10.5	1.9	1.2	3.5	2.3
Tamil Nadu	44.5	50.0	57.5	47.0	43.7	51.0	60.1	46.9	8.9	17.7	23.9	12.1
Uttar Pradesh	13.0	19.8	21.3	14.7	27.5	44.8	57.0	32.6	2.9	8.7	12.1	4.5
Uttaranchal	26.6	19.6	26.4	26.2	20.2	46.9	39.4	23.0	11.0	29.8	26.4	13.0
West Bengal	20.6	30.8	30.2	21.9	28.7	39.3	42.9	30.2	10.6	20.9	17.7	11.8
All India	**16.6**	**20.2**	**21.5**	**18.0**	**24.8**	**33.8**	**41.0**	**28.9**	**6.5**	**9.0**	**11.4**	**7.7**

Note: Sub-Marginal & Marginal: <= 1 hectare; Small: 1 - 2 hectares; Medium-Large: >2 hectares.
Source: Same as in Appendix A9.1

Appendix A9.5: Access to Extension Service Workers as a Source of Information on Modern Technology for Farming by Size of Holdings (Percentage of Farmer Households) 2003

State	Farm Size in Hectares			
	Sub-Marginal & Marginal	Small	Medium-Large	Total
Andhra Pradesh	7.4	12.2	10.7	9.0
Assam	5.4	8.0	5.5	5.9
Bihar	0.4	0.6	0.3	0.4
Chhattisgarh	12.1	15.1	25.2	15.5
Gujarat	16.9	29.1	27.4	21.9
Haryana	0.6	7.0	4.8	2.5
Himachal Pradesh	1.5	4.2	4.0	2.1
Jammu & Kashmir	2.1	4.4	8.9	3.0
Jharkhand	0.1	0.0	0.0	0.0
Karnataka	8.0	12.9	18.1	11.5
Kerala	3.4	6.0	6.8	3.8
Madhya Pradesh	7.0	11.6	9.4	9.0
Maharashtra	5.4	8.0	10.2	7.6
Orissa	5.0	8.6	14.2	6.3
Punjab	0.4	1.4	3.9	1.4
Rajasthan	1.0	1.4	2.1	1.4
Tamil Nadu	12.2	15.1	17.8	13.3
Uttar Pradesh	0.8	1.2	3.1	1.1
Uttaranchal	0.4	0.0	16.3	1.2
West Bengal	3.6	5.7	11.7	4.1
All India	**4.1**	**8.1**	**10.1**	**5.7**

Note: Sub-Marginal & Marginal: <= 1 hectare; Small: 1 - 2 hectares; Medium-Large: >2 hectares.
Source: ibid.

Appendix A9.6: Access to Government Agencies as a Source of Information on Modern Technology by Size of Holdings (Percentage Farmer Households) 2003

State	Farm Size in Hectares			
	Sub-Marginal & Marginal	Small	Medium-Large	Total
Andhra Pradesh	10.7	10.9	14.0	11.4
Assam	4.3	6.0	9.6	5.3
Bihar	1.2	2.6	4.1	1.5
Chhattisgarh	4.9	8.1	9.7	6.7
Gujarat	12.3	15.8	17.1	14.2
Haryana	5.5	7.9	15.1	8.0
Himachal Pradesh	10.9	29.1	29.2	14.8
Jammu & Kashmir	2.5	0.9	1.6	2.2
Jharkhand	2.6	4.8	2.4	2.9
Karnataka	11.6	13.2	16.1	13.1
Kerala	16.6	32.7	27.2	18.3
Madhya Pradesh	7.6	10.1	16.3	11.1
Maharashtra	6.0	7.4	14.4	9.0
Orissa	3.9	3.1	6.2	4.0
Punjab	4.6	11.2	17.0	8.4
Rajasthan	2.4	5.6	4.5	3.7
Tamil Nadu	11.4	15.3	26.8	14.0
Uttar Pradesh	2.5	7.5	8.1	3.8
Uttaranchal	0.9	9.3	19.6	2.5
West Bengal	4.4	6.5	8.0	4.7
All India	**5.4**	**8.9**	**12.5**	**7.2**

Note: Sub-Marginal & Marginal: <= 1 hectare; Small: 1 - 2 hectares; Medium-Large: >2 hectares.
Source: ibid.

Appendix A9.7: Membership of Cooperative Society by Size of Holdings (Percentage Farmer Households) 2003

State	Farm Size in Hectares					
	Sub-Marginal	Marginal	Small	Medium	Large	Total
Andhra Pradesh	21.2	28.0	39.7	43.3	39.7	31.1
Assam	16.4	17.5	14.4	20.4	26.4	17.2
Bihar	6.1	7.9	6.9	11.3	10.3	7.0
Chhattisgarh	42.3	50.8	55.5	43.4	58.6	49.9
Gujarat	29.1	46.7	57.3	65.4	66.9	48.9
Haryana	19.7	45.9	50.7	53.4	40.0	37.3
Himachal Pradesh	51.9	58.3	60.7	83.1	66.9	57.1
Jammu &Kashmir	28.9	27.8	14.2	10.6	19.3	24.9
Jharkhand	2.5	1.6	3.9	2.1	7.3	2.4
Karnataka	25.5	28.0	41.2	50.1	48.7	35.8
Kerala	56.0	63.7	73.1	78.0	51.4	59.5
Madhya Pradesh	20.3	32.3	49.9	50.6	63.1	42.8
Maharashtra	30.4	50.0	59.5	62.6	67.6	54.0
Orissa	17.6	23.4	24.3	31.1	25.3	21.8
Punjab	19.5	40.7	56.8	72.0	65.6	38.9
Rajasthan	13.9	16.6	19.6	26.7	34.8	21.3
Tamil Nadu	29.5	43.8	51.6	70.5	58.4	42.4
Uttar Pradesh	10.5	22.1	34.4	37.1	48.2	20.1
Uttaranchal	3.6	4.1	10.4	5.9	-	4.2
West Bengal	18.2	22.4	30.9	34.7	6.1	20.8
All India	**18.1**	**27.9**	**38.8**	**45.6**	**49.5**	**29.3**

Note: Sub-Marginal: <= 0.40 hectares; Marginal: <= 1 hectare; Small: 1 - 2 hectares; Medium: 2 - 4 hectares; Large > 4 hectares.
Source: ibid.

Appendix A9.8: Membership of a Registered Farmers' Organization, Self-help Group by Size of Holdings (Percentage of Farmer Households) 2003

State	Registered Farmers' Organisation				Self-help Group			
	Farm Size in Hectares							
	Sub-Marginal & Marginal	Small	Medium-Large	Total	Sub-Marginal & Marginal	Small	Medium-Large	Total
Andhra Pradesh	2.2	2.0	3.4	2.4	17.1	18.8	18.4	17.7
Assam	6.5	10.5	4.4	7.0	7.7	9.9	8.0	8.2
Bihar	0.2	0.7	0.8	0.3	0.6	1.1	2.7	0.8
Chhattisgarh	0.8	5.7	3.0	2.4	5.5	6.4	9.2	6.5
Gujarat	2.0	6.1	14.3	5.9	2.2	3.3	5.2	3.2
Haryana	0.0	0.0	0.2	0.0	1.3	1.0	0.2	1.0
Himachal Pradesh	0.6	0.5	1.8	0.7	8.4	12.1	6.1	8.8
Jammu &Kashmir	0.2	0.2	4.8	0.6	0.3	0.0	0.2	0.2
Jharkhand	0.2	0.0	0.0	0.2	2.5	3.7	3.7	2.8
Karnataka	3.5	5.9	8.5	5.2	6.3	10.8	9.6	8.1
Kerala	8.9	23.5	17.5	10.5	19.5	22.3	23.4	19.9
Madhya Pradesh	0.6	0.9	1.0	0.8	2.3	2.2	3.5	2.7
Maharashtra	0.9	2.5	3.8	2.2	3.7	6.1	5.5	4.9
Orissa	0.3	0.1	0.0	0.2	2.7	3.5	2.1	2.8
Punjab	0.0	1.0	0.8	0.3	1.8	0.4	1.3	1.5
Rajasthan	0.2	0.8	0.5	0.4	0.8	0.2	0.5	0.6
Tamil Nadu	2.6	1.8	9.7	3.4	12.5	16.3	12.0	12.9
Uttar Pradesh	0.7	1.7	2.8	1.0	1.3	2.5	1.5	1.5
Uttaranchal	1.0	0.0	0.0	0.9	4.2	16.1	0.6	4.9
West Bengal	4.0	3.7	3.7	4.0	1.9	2.0	1.3	1.9
All India	**1.7**	**2.7**	**3.7**	**2.2**	**4.4**	**5.7**	**5.4**	**4.8**

Note: Sub-Marginal & Marginal: <= 1 hectares; Small: 1 - 2 hectares.

Source: ibid.

Appendix A9.9: Preference of Farming as Occupation by Size of Holdings (Percentage of Farmers) 2003

State	Farm Size in Hectares			
	Sub-Marginal & Marginal	Small	Medium-Large	Total
Andhra Pradesh	28.3	19.5	15.9	24.2
Assam	43.6	32.2	40.6	40.9
Bihar	51.7	43.9	47.4	50.5
Chhattisgarh	51.4	46.9	32.2	46.3
Gujarat	43.5	24.0	16.5	32.9
Haryana	40.6	41.2	29.2	38.3
Himachal Pradesh	38.6	23.3	20.5	35.1
Jammu &Kashmir	41.7	32.4	19.3	38.5
Jharkhand	49.4	40.4	30.3	47.0
Karnataka	48.3	42.5	33.0	43.3
Kerala	34.7	18.5	25.6	33.0
Madhya Pradesh	46.9	39.6	32.4	40.3
Maharashtra	47.1	38.9	29.0	39.3
Orissa	49.0	41.1	34.6	46.7
Punjab	47.0	24.4	17.2	36.9
Rajasthan	41.3	40.8	33.8	38.8
Tamil Nadu	33.2	29.1	20.8	31.0
Uttar Pradesh	44.1	33.2	21.7	40.5
Uttaranchal	55.8	48.1	15.0	53.2
West Bengal	47.4	32.6	32.0	45.5
All India	**44.2**	**35.3**	**28.1**	**40.1**

Note: Sub-Marginal & Marginal: <= 1 hectare; Small: 1 - 2 hectares.
Source: ibid.

Appendix A11.1: State Laws for Unorganised Sector Workers

Sl. No.	State	Various Labour laws enforced by the state Govt.
1.	Andhra Pradesh	• The Andhra Pradesh Factories and Establishment (National Festival and Other Holidays) Act, 1974 • Andhra Pradesh Muttah, Jattu, Hamal and Other Manual Workers (Regulation of Employment and Welfare) Act, 1976 • The Andhra Pradesh Welfare Fund Act, 1987 • The Andhra Pradesh Shops and Establishment Act, 1988 • Andhra Pradesh Unorganised Labour Welfare Fund, 2002
2	Arunachal Pradesh	• No state Act / Law has so far been enacted
3.	Assam	• Assam Plantation Employees Fund Act, 1959 • The Assam Shops and Establishments Act, 1971 • Employees Welfare Board Act, 1959 • The Assam Industrial Employment (Conferment of Permanent Status to workmen) Act, 1985
4.	Bihar	• Bihar Shops and Establishment Act, 1953
5.	Chhattisgarh	• Chhattisgarh Shops & Establishment Act, 1958 • Chhattisgarh Industrial Relations Act, 1960
6.	Delhi	• Delhi Shops and Establishment Act, 1958 • Bombay Labour Welfare Fund Act, 1953
7.	Goa	• The Goa Employment (Conditions of Service and Retirement) Benefit Act, 2001 • Goa, Daman and Diu Labour Welfare Fund Act, 1986 • Goa, Daman and Diu Shops and Establishments Act, 1973
8.	Gujarat	• The Bombay Relief Undertaking Act, 1958 • The Bombay Industrial Relations Act, 1946 • The Bombay Shops & Establishment Act, 1948 • The Gujarat Shops and Establishments (Employee's Life Insurance) Act, 1980 • The Gujarat Unprotected Manual Workers (Regulation of Employment and Welfare) Act, 1979 • The Bombay Labour Welfare Fund Act, 1953 • The Gujarat Payment of Unemployment Allowance to Workmen (In Factories) Act, 1981 • The Gujarat Physically Handicapped Persons (Employment in Factories) Act, 1982.
9.	Haryana	• Punjab Shops and Commercial Establishments Act, 1958 • Punjab Industrial Establishments (National & Festival Holiday and Casual and Sick Leave) Act, 1965 • The Punjab Industrial Housing Act, 1956 • The Punjab Labour Welfare Fund Act, 1965
10.	Himachal Pradesh	• Himachal Pradesh Shops and Commercial Establishment Act, 1969 • H.P. Industrial Establishments (National & Festival Holidays, Casual & Sick Leave) Act, 1969
11.	Jammu & Kashmir	• The Jammu and Kashmir Shops and Establishments Act, 1966 • J & K Industrial Establishments (National and Festival) Holidays Act, 1974 • J & K Employees Provident Funds Act/Scheme, 1961 • The Employees Deposit Linked Insurance Scheme, 2000.

Sl. No.	State	Various Labour laws enforced by the state Govt.
12	Jharkand	• The Jharkhand Shops and Establishments Act, 1953
13	Karnataka	• The Karnataka Shops And Commercial Establishments Act, 1961 • The Karnataka Industrial Establishments (National And Festival Holiday) Act, 1963 • The Karnataka Labour Welfare Fund Act, 1965 • Mysore Labour Welfare Act, 1965 • Karnataka Unorganised Workers Welfare Act, 2002
14	Kerala	• The Kerala Shops and Commercial Establishment Act, 1960 • The Kerala Loading and Unloading Act, 1979 • The Kerala Agricultural Workers Act, 1974 • The Kerala Casual, Temporary and Badli Workers Act, 1989 • Kerala Casual, Temporary and Badli Workers (Wages) Act, 1989
15	Nagaland	• Nagaland Shop & Establishment Act, 1986
16	Maharashtra	• Bombay Shops and Establishments Act, 1948 • Bombay Industrial Relations Act, 1946 • Maharashtra Recognization of Trade Unions & Prevention of Unfair Labour Practices Act, 1971 • Bombay Labour Welfare Fund Act, 1953 • The Maharashtra Mathadi, Hamal and Other Manual Workers' (Regulation of Employment and Welfare) Act, 1969 • Maharashtra Private Security Guards (Regulation of Employment and Welfare) Act, 1961 • Maharashtra Workmen's Minimum House Rent Allowance Act, 1983
17	Madhya Pradesh	• Madhya Pradesh Industrial Employment (Standing Orders) Act, 1961 • Madhya Pradesh Industrial Relations Act, 1960 • M.P. Shops & Establishments Act, 1958 • Madhya Pradesh Shram Kalyan Nidhi Adhiniyam, 1982 • The Madhya Pradesh Asangathit Karmkar Kalyan Adhiniyam, 2003
18	Manipur	• The Manipur Shops and Establishments Act, 1972
19	Meghalaya	• The Meghalaya Shops and Establishments Act, 2003
20	Mizoram	• No state Act / Law has so far been enacted
21	Orissa	• Orissa Shops & Commercial Establishments Act, 1956 • Orissa Industrial Establishment (National & Festival Holidays) Act, 1969.
22	Punjab	• The Punjab Industrial Establishments (National & festival Holiday and casual and sick leave) Act, 1965 • The Punjab Shops and Commercial Establishments Act, 1958 • The Punjab Industrial Housing Act, 1956 • The Punjab Labour Welfare Fund Act, 1965
23.	Rajasthan	• Rajasthan Shops and Commercial Establishment Act, 1958 • Rajasthan Shops and Commercial Establishment (Employees Life Insurance) Act, 1987
24	Sikkim	• The Sikkim Labour Protection Act, 2005 • The Sikkim Shops and Commercial Establishments Act, 1983

Sl. No.	State	Various Labour laws enforced by the state Govt.
25	Tamil Nadu	• Tamil Nadu Manual Workers' (Regulation of Employment and Conditions of Work) Act, 1982 • Tamil Nadu Catering Establishments Act, 1958 • Tamil Nadu Payment of Subsistence Allowance Act, 1981 • Tamil Nadu Industrial Establishment (Conferment of Permanent Status to Workmen) Act, 1981 • Tamil Nadu Shops and Establishments Act, 1947
26	Tripura	• Tripura Scheme for Unorganised Workers (Asangatith Shramik Shayika Prakalpa) • The Tripura Shops and Establishments Act, 1970 • The Tripura Agricultural Workers Act, 1986
27	Uttar Pradesh	• The U.P. Dookan Aur Vinijya Adhistan Adhiniyam Act, 1962 • The U.P. Employment of Substitute Workmen Act, 1978 • The U.P. Industrial Dispute Act, 1947 • The U.P. Industrial Establishment (National Holidays) Act, 1961 • The U.P. Industrial Peace (Timely Payment of Wages) Act, 1978 • The U.P. Industrial Undertaking Special Provision for Preventions (Unemployment) Act, 1966 • The U.P. Labour Welfare Fund Act, 1955 • The U.P. Premises (Eviction of Unauthorised Occupants) Act, 1972 • U.P. Industrial Housing Act, 1955.
28	Uttaranchal	• The U.P. Dookan Aur Vanijya Adhishthan Adhiniyam Act, 1962 • The U.P. Employment of Substitute Workmen Act, 1978 • The U.P. Industrial Dispute Act, 1947 • The U.P. Industrial Establishment (National Holidays) Act, 1961 • The U.P. Industrial Peace (Timely Payment of Wages) Act, 1978 • The U.P. Industrial Undertaking Special Provision for Preventions (Unemployment) Act, 1966 • The U.P. Labour Welfare Fund Act, 1955 • The U.P. Premises (Eviction of Unauthorised Occupants) Act, 1972 • U.P. Industrial Housing Act, 1955.
29	West Bengal	• The West Bengal Workmen's House Rent Allowance Act, 1974 • The West Bengal Provident Fund Scheme for Unorganised Workers, 2001 • West Bengal Payment of Subsistence Allowance Act, 1969 • The West Bengal Shops and Establishment Act, 1963
30	Andaman & Nicobar Islands	• A & N Islands Shops and Establishments Regulation, 2005
31	Chandigarh	• Punjab Shops and Commercial Establishments Act, 1958
32	Daman & Diu And Dadar Nagar Haveli	• Goa, Daman & Diu Shops & Establishment Act, 1973
33	Lakshadweep	• No state Act / Law has so far been enacted
34	Pondicherry	• The Pondicherry Shops & Establishment Act, 1964 • The Pondicherry Catering Establishment Act, 1964 • The Pondicherry Industrial Establishment (National & Festival Holidays) Act, 1964

Appendix A11.2: State-wise Coverage of Shops and Commercial Establishments under the State Acts during the year 2003

Sl. No.	State/Union Territory	Name of the Act	Areas Covered during 2003
1	Andhra Pradesh	The Andhra Pradesh Shops and Establishments Act, 1988	All the areas of the State
2	Assam	The Assam Shops and Establishments and Establishments Act, 1971	Guwahati Municipal Corporation, 127 Urban, Semi-urban and Rural Areas.
3	Goa	Goa Shop and Establishments (Amendment) Act, 2001	All Districts of Goa and Banks (Nationalised, Scheduled or Co-operative Banks)
4	Gujarat	The Bombay Shops and Establishments Act, 1948	134 Local Authorities
5	Haryana	The Punjab Shops and Establishments Act, 1958	91 Towns
6	Himachal Pradesh	The Himachal Pradesh Shops & Commercial Establishments Act, 1969	58 Places
7	Jammu & Kashmir	The J&K Shops and Commercial Establishments Act, 1966	55 Towns/Places
8	Karnataka	The Karnataka Shops and Commercial Establishments Act, 1961	29 Sub-Divisions
9	Kerala	The Kerala Shops and Commercial Establishments Act, 1960	283 places (which include Corporations, Municipalities and Panchayats)
10	Maharashtra	The Bombay Shops and Establishment Act, 1948	241 Local Areas
11	Manipur	The Maniipur Shops and Commercial Establishments Act, 1972	The whole State of Manipur, notified areas of Towns, Municipal Areas
12	Orissa	The Orissa Shops and Commercial Establishments	95 Municipal and Notified Area Councils
13	Punjab	The Punjab Shops and Commercial Establishments Act, 1958	130 Towns/ Cities
14	Rajasthan	The Rajasthan Shops and Commercial Establishment Act, 1958	35 Places
15	Tamil Nadu	The Tripura Shops and Establishment Act, 1970	City of Chennai, in all Municipalities, Towns, Panchyats and in certain areas specially no notified by the Government
16.	Tripura	The Tripura Shops and Establishments Act, 1970	Muncipal areas of Agartala town & sub-Divisional Towns of Dharamanagar, Kailashahar, Khowai, Radhakishorepure (Udaipur) & Belonia in Tripura
17.	West Bengal	The West Bengal Shops and Establishment Act, 1963	239 places covering all the districts in West Bengal
18.	Chandigarh	The Punjab Shops and Commercial Establishments Act, 1958	

Source: Labour Bureau (2007)

Appendix A11.3: Ownership of Shops and Employments Therein during the Year by States 2004

State / Union Territory	Independently Run by Owners	Number of Shops Run with the Help of Employees	Total	Number of Owners of Shops in Col. 4	Number of Persons Employed
Andhra Pradesh	231416	122123	353539	353539	335801
Assam	29175	26731	55906	26731	48990
Bihar	152375	N	152375	152375	152375
Goa	21285	7045	28330	28309	29027
Gujarat	498519	243276	741795	779242	624978
Haryana	117171	30494	147665	147665	99451
Himachal Pradesh	27009	9322	36331	36331	11123
Jammu & Kashmir	132832	12321	145153	140022	19738
Karnataka	114710	54006	168716	156366	197272
Kerala	159373	71673	231046	228403	205906
Meghalaya	1561	795	2356	2356	11999
Manipur	925	1120	2045	2056	1590
Orissa	N	13034	13034	13034	38675
Punjab	171098	39824	210922	211408	91278
Rajasthan	355432	84783	440215	474080	167420
Tamil Nadu	277914	79180	357094	357094	352428
Tripura	7887	8630	16517	5464	11991
Uttar Pradesh	NR	12662	12662	12662	118233
West Bengal	328143	190996	519139	642314	380495
A & N Islands	N	N	N	N	N
Chandigarh	5625	8722	14347	14046	16896
Total	**2632450**	**1016737**	**3649187**	**3783497**	**2915666**

Note:
1. N = Not reported.
2. The remaining States/Union Territories did not furnish the Annual Returns for the year, 2003.

Source: Same as in Appendix A11.2

Appendix A11.4: Organisational and Implementation Structure of Labour Laws in States & UTs

Sl. No.	State	Implementation Machinery
1	Andhra Pradesh	Labour Deptt. Machinery in the State comprises 1 Commissioner, 1 Addl. Commissioner, 3 Joint Labour Commissioners, 8 Dy. Commissioners, 35 Asstt. Labour Commissioners, 47 Labour Officers, 292 Asstt. Labour Officers. Assistant Labour Officers are responsible for enforcement of labour laws in a Group of Mandals. The implementation structure is common for agricultural and non-agricultural workers. Officers of the rank of labour officers and above are responsible for conciliation under the ID Act.
2	Arunachal Pradesh	Labour Department consisting of 1 Labour Commissioner, 1 Deputy Labour Commissioner, 1 Assistant Labour Commissioner, 1 Labour Officer (HQ) and 2 Labour Inspectors. At the District Level there are 13 Labour Officers
3	Assam	Labour Department consisting of 1 Labour Commissioner, 1 Additional Labour Commissioner, 3 Dy. Labour Commissioners, 11 Asstt. Labour Commissioners, 1 Labour Welfare Officer (HQ), 23 Labour Officers and 79 Labour Inspectors
4	Bihar	Labour Deptt. Machinery in the State comprises: 1 Labour Commissioner , 3 Joint Labour Commissioners, 13 Dy. Labour Commissioners, 19 Asstt. Labour Commissioners, 64 Labour Superintendents and 425 Labour Enforcement Officers.Dispute resolution machinery for agriculture comprises Director (Agriculture) at State level , Dy. Labour Commissioners (Agriculture), Asstt. Labour Commissioners (Agriculture) and Labour Superintendents (Agriculture) at Distt. Level and Labour Enforcement Officers at block level.The Labour Deptt. has an implementation structure up to block level where labour inspectors were stationed, labour superintendents were also conciliation officers at the district level. The enforcement at the block level is the responsibility of the labour inspector. Labour Enforcement Officers are posted at circle level of the state.
5	Chhattisgarh	Labour Deptt. Machinery in the State comprises:1 Labour Commissioner, 1 Add. Labour Commissioner, 2 Deputy Labour Commissioners, 5 Asst. Labour Commissioners, 6 Labour Officer, 5 Asst. Labour Officers, 63 Labour Inspectors, and 30 Labour Sub-Inspectors
6	Delhi	Labour Deptt. Machinery in the State comprises: 1 Labour Commissioner, 3 Joint Labour Commissioners, 9 Deputy Labour Commissioners, 11 Assistant Labour Commissioners, 11 Labour Officers, 20 Inspecting Officers and 72 Labour Inspectors.
7	Goa	Labour Deptt. Machinery in the State compris es: 1 Commissioner - Labour and Employment at State level and 2 Dy. Labour Commissioners, 3 Asstt. Labour Commissioners and 11 Labour Inspectors at district level.
8	Gujarat	Labour Deptt. Machinery in the State comprises: 1 Labour Commissioner, 1 Additional Labour Commissioner, 7 Deputy Labour Commissioners, 36 Additional Labour Commissioners and 90 Labour Officers. The State. has separate rural labour commissioner for implementation of labour laws in rural areas (Gram Panchayat) of the State. This department has a strength of 25 Labour Officers , 93 Assistant Labour Officers. The Shops and Establishment Act is implemented by the local authorities like municipal corporations, municipalities, nagar panchayats and gram panchayats under the supervision of labour and employment departments. The shops inspectors employed by local authorities are implementing provisions of the Act.

Sl. No.	State	Implementation Machinery
9	Haryana	Labour Deptt. Machinery in the State comprises: 1 Labour Commissioner, 2 Joint Labour Commissioners, 2 Deputy labour commissioners, 1 Addl. Chief Inspector (Industrial Safety and Health), 1 Deputy Chief Inspector (Industrial Safety and Health) and 2 Assistant Directors at 2 Headquarter level.?At Regional / District level there are 6 Deputy Labour Commissioners, 27 Labour cum-Conciliation Officers, 87 Labour Inspectors, 2 Certifying Surgeons 4 Medical Officers (Occupational Health), 22 Assistant Directors (Industrial Safety and Health) . The total number of sanctioned posts is 885 in the labour department including labour courts.
10	Himachal	Labour Deptt. Machinery in the State comprises 1 Labour Commissioner, 1 Joint Labour Commissioner, 1 Deputy Labour commissioner and 1 Additional Deputy Commissioner at the State LevelAt the Distt. Level there are 12 Labour Officers and 33 Labour Inspectors.
11	Jammu & Kashmir	Labour Deptt. Machinery in the State comprises 1 Labour Commissioner, 4 Deputy Labour Commissioners, 17 Assistant Labour Commissioners, 25 Labour Officers and 22 Labour Inspectors.
12	Jharkhand	Most of the Acts are implemented by the State Labour Deptt. The State has implementation structure up to block level where labour enforcement officers are stationed. There are separate directorate under the Labour Commissioner for implementation of Minimum Wages Act with respect to Agricultural Act. The Directorate has a Director (Minimum Wages) at State level, Deputy Labour Commissioner (Agricultural Labour) at zonal level, Assistant Labour Commissioner (Agricultural Labour) at divisional level, Labour Superintendent (Agricultural Labour) at district level and Labour Enforcement Officers at the block level. Labour Superintendents at the district level were also the conciliation officers under the I.D. Act.. There are about 250 officers at various levels in the Department. The Labour Enforcement Officers at the block level look after implementation of labour laws in agricultural and non-agricultural area.
13	Karnataka	Labour Deptt. Machinery in the State comprising 1 Commissioner of Labour, 2 Additional Labour Commissioners, 1 Joint Labour Commissioner,5 Deputy Labour Commissioners (at regional head quarters), 11 Assistant Labour Commissioners (at Divisional Level), 39 Labour Officers (at District and Sub- Divisional Levels), 55 Senior Labour Inspectors (who are entrusted with the work of Implementation in City Corporation and Plantation Areas.), and 217 Labour Inspectors (Implementing Offices at taluk level.)
14	Kerala	Labour Deptt. Machinery in the State comprising 1 Labour Commissioner, 2 Addl Labour Commissioners, 5 Joint Labour Commissioners, 9 Deputy Labour Commissioners, 25 District Labour Officers, 20 Deputy Labour Officers, 14 Additional Labour Officers (Gr. I), 10 Inspectors of Plantations and 102 Asstt. Labour Officers -(Gr. II)(at every Taluk)
15	Nagaland	Labour Deptt. Machinery in the State comprising 1 Labour Commissioner, 1 Asst. Labour Commissioner, 7 District Labour Officers, and Labour Inspectors. -
16	Maharashtra	Labour Deptt. Machinery in the State comprises 1 Commissioner of Labour, 1 Joint Labour Commissioner, (for mathadi & security), 3 Additional Labour Commissioners, 11 Deputy Labour Commissioners, 68 Asst. Labour Commissioners, 123 District Labour Officers, 232 Inspectors (Shops Act) and 180 Minimum Wages Inspectors for Agriculture.There is a separate wing for unorganised labour comprising 1 Development Commissioner (Unorganised Labour), 1 Asst. Labour Commissioner and 2 Labour Officers.

Sl. No.	State	Implementation Machinery
17	M.P	At the State level, there is 1 Labour Commissioner, 1 Director (IH&S), 2 Joint Directors, 8 Dy. Directors, 18 Asstt. Directors and 4 Dy. Labour Commissioners (Enforcement). At the District level there are 6 Asstt. Labour Commissioners, 27 Labour Officers, 2 Asstt. Labour Officers -and Medical Officers. There are 180 Labour Inspectors at Taluk and 12 Labour Inspectors at Block level.
18	Manipur	Labour Deptt. Machinery in the State comprises: 1 Labour Commissioner, 1 Deputy Labour Commissioner, 2 Labour Officers, 5 Labour Inspectors and 28 Rural Labour Inspectors.
19	Meghalaya	Labour Deptt. Machinery in the State comprises: 1 Labour Commissioner, 1 Joint Labour Commissioner, 1 Deputy Labour Commissioner and 1 Labour Inspector [HQ]At the District level there are 8 Labour Inspectors.
20	Mizoram	Labour Deptt. Machinery in the State comprises: ing 1 Labour Commissioner, 4 District Employment Officers, 23 Officers - at taluk and 26 officers at block level
21	Orissa	Labour Deptt. Machinery in the State comprises: 1 Labour Commissioner, 2 Joint Labour Commissioners, 4 Deputy Labour Commissioners, 11 Asst. Labour Commissioners, 38 District Labour Officers, 40 Asst. Labour Officers and 40 Labour Inspectors.
22	Punjab	Thirteen Central Acts are implemented by the Labour Department. Dangerous Machines Act is implemented by Agricultural Deptt. Employment of Manual Scavengers and Construction of Dry Latrines (Prohibition) Act is implemented by Social Welfare Deptt. through the local govts. Labour Department is the nodal department for implementation of bonded labour Act. However, at the field level this Act is implemented by District Magistrates and the SDMs. Labour Deptt. Machinery in the State comprises : 1 Labour Commissioner, 1 Additional Labour Commissioner, 1 Additional Director of Factories, and o0ther officers including about 80 IInspectors.
23.	Rajasthan	All Labour laws were being implemented by the Labour Department, which has offices in all the 32 districts. There are 60 divisions each headed by Labour Welfare Officers. In some of the larger districts Deputy Labour Commissioners or Assistant Labour Commissioners were also stationed. There are 80 Labour Inspectors who are stationed at the district level.
24	Sikkim	Labour Deptt. Machinery in the State comprises: 1 Labour Commissioner, 2 Deputy Labour Commissioners, 4 Assistant Labour Commissioners and 12 Labour Inspectors
25	Tamil Nadu	Labour Deptt. Machinery in the State comprises 1 Commissioner of Labour, 12 Joint Commissioners of Labour, 13 Deputy Commissioners of Labour, 23 Asst. Commissioners of Labour, 28 Inspectors of Labour, 23 Labour Officers, 3 Inspectors and 10 Plantation Inspectors
26	Tripura	Labour Deptt. Machinery in the State comprises: Labour Commissioner at State level, Chief Labour Officer at Distt. Level, Labour Officer at Distt. Level and Labour Inspector at Block level
27	Uttar Pradesh	Labour Deptt. Machinery in the State comprises: 1 Labour Commissioner, 5 Additional Labour Commissioners, 1 Joint Labour Commissioner, 1 Director of Factories, 7 Deputy Director of Factories, 1 Deputy Director of Factories (medical),38 Asst. Directors of Factories (Factory Inspectors), 1 Director of Boilers, 2 Deputy Directors of Boilers and 2 Asst. Directors of Boilers.At the Regional level there are 3 Additional Labour

Sl. No.	State	Implementation Machinery
		Commissioners, 14 Deputy Labour Commissioners and 36 Assistant Labour Commissioners. The Labour Commissioner's Office has 36 regional offices headed by Additional/Deputy/Assistant Labour Commissioners. All Tehsildars, Naib Tehsildars, Block Development Officers, Assistant Development Officers (Agricultural), Cooperative Members and Panchayat Members under the Minimum Wage Act are notified as 'Inspectors'.
28	Uttaranchal	Labour Deptt. Machinery in the State comprises: 1 Labour Commissioner, 1 Additional Labour Commissioner, 3 Deputy Labour Commissioners, 9 Asst. Labour Commissioners, 23 Labour Enforcement Officers and 2 Trade Union Inspectors
29	West Bengal	Labour Deptt. Machinery in the State comprises: 1 Labour Commissioner, 6 Additional Labour Commissioners, 7 Joint Labour Commissioners, 22 Deputy Labour Commissioners, 127 Asst. Labour Commissioners - and 500 Labour Inspectors
30	Andaman & Nicobar Islands	Labour Deptt. Machinery in the State comprises 1 Labour Commissioner, 4 Asst. Labour Commissioners, 3 Labour Inspectors and 1 Factory Inspector
31	Chandigarh	Labour Deptt. Machinery in the State comprises: 1 Labour Commissioner, 1 Asst. Labour Commissioner and 4 Inspectors.
32	Daman & Diu And Dadar Nagar Haveli	Labour Deptt. Machinery in the State comprises 1 Commissioner Labour, 1 Chief Inspector of Factories & Boilers , 1 Labour Inspector and Conciliation Officers
33	Lakshadweep	Labour Deptt. Machinery in the State comprises: 1 Labour Commissioner and 1 Labour Enforcement Officer .
34	Pondicherry	Labour Deptt. Machinery in the State comprises: 1 Labour Commissioner, 1 Deputy Labour Commissioner, 3 Employment Officers/Labour Officers and Labour Inspectors.

Appendix A11.5: Enforcement of Minimum Wages Act, 1948 during 2004-05 by Central and State Governments / UT's

S. No.	Name of the State/UTs	Inspections made	Irregularities		Claims		Prosecution cases			Compen-sation Awarded (Rs.'000)	Amount of Fine (Rs. '000)	
			Detected	Rectified	Filed	Settled	Pending	Filed	Decided		Imposed	Realized
1	2	3	4	5	6	7	8	9	10	11	12	13
CENTRAL SPHERE		17188	386124	212587	90443761	39241	6267	3235	NA	NA	NA	NA
STATE SPHERE												
1.	Arunachal Pradesh	120	35	32	NIL	NIL	NIL	3	NIL	NIL	NIL	NIL
2.	Bihar	199509	29132	29366	10380	7796	-	-	-	-	-	-
3.	Goa	1859	5748	3817	45	22	7	24	19	210	8	1
4.	Gujarat	13667	38048	18866	-	-	27057	2211	842	2392	-	1119
5.	Haryana	2715	19	19	1174	346	2764	83	137	709	8065	NA
6.	Himachal Pradesh	2353	1041	819	192	58	Nil	170	131	62	69	69
7	Karnataka	107896						2104	1172		1427	
8	Maharashtra	139038	125986	107924	5	6	5831	527	474	28	757	-
9	Meghalaya	569	Nil	Nil	Nil	Nil	Nil	Nil	Nil	Nil	Nil	Nil
10	Mizoram	Nil	Nil	Nil	Nil	Nil	Nil	Nil	Nil	Nil	Nil	Nil
11	Orissa	24437	20660	11494	96	10	0	317	104		21	-
12	Punjab	13794	-	-	331		-	-	442	-	-	158
13	Rajasthan	7168	387	124	299	334	809	326	217	2951	82	NA
14	Sikkim											-
15	Tripura	6611	193	193	-	302	-	-	-	-	-	
16	Uttar Pradesh	212	187	196	893	-	10944	29	2125	63649	259	259
17	Uttaranchal	4363	834	396	140	2310	42	298	229	393	110	110
18	West Bengal	29952	7465	7360	Nil	136	743	159	-	38	86	
19	A & N Islands	84	420	420	1	1	-	-	-	-	-	-
20	Chandigarh	207	257	171	53	Nil	417	86	33	145	18	18
21	Dadra & Nagar Haveli	78	24	24	-	37	-	-	-	-	-	-
22	Delhi	8045	6113	6113	-	-	1218	-	-	-	-	-
23	Lakshadweep	Nil	Nil	Nil	Nil	-	Nil	Nil	Nil	Nil	Nil	Nil
24	Pondicherry	7532	-	-	-	Nil	-	-	-	-	-	-

Note:
1. The information has not yet been received from the remaining States/Uts
2. NA- Not Available

Source: Same as in Appendix A11.2

Appendix A11.6: Number of Inspections, Prosecutions, Cases Disposed off by the Courts and Amount of Fine Realized Under the Shops and Commercial Establishments Acts during the Year 2003 (by States)

State / Union Territory	Inspections made	Prosecutions launched	Cases disposed off by the courts	Amount realized as fine (in Rs.)
Andhra Pradesh	210019	10796	7546	1014380
Assam	31138	1571	393	83560
Goa	3507	177	147	47740
Gujarat	195475	8200	25690+	1326615
Haryana	22390	1833	1470	1946245
Himachal Pradesh	5967	2490	1522	247015
Jammu & Kashmir	19413	3220	2452	707200
Karnataka	46255	2730	1421	1231665
Kerala	47830	723	725+	310680
Maharashtra	511187	2829	13104+	6720702
Manipur	900	-	-	-
Orissa	2482	91	54	5550
Punjab	76815	3926	5075+	1275200
Rajasthan	17224	2284	1937	312710
Tamil Nadu	368408	1272	1086	74420
Tripura	92661	873	432	69170
West Bengal	83334	3957	4141+	806075
A & N Islands	92	6	6	425
Chandigarh	44483	21378	20401	2978598
Total	**17,79,580**	**68,356**	**87,602**	**1,91,57,950**

Note:
1. + = Includes the cases brought forward from previous year.
2. - = Nil
3. The remaining States/Union Territories did not furnish the Annual Returns for the year 2003.

Source: Same as in Appendix A11.2

Appendix A12.1: Administrative Structure for Governance of Self-employed Workers and Enterprises

Industry	Agency	Administrative Department/Ministry
Small Scale Industry	Small IndustriesDevelopment Organisation	Dept. of SSI, Agro and Rural Industries
Power looms	Textile Commissioner	Ministry of Textiles
Traditional Industries		
Khadi and Village Industries (KVI)	Khadi and Villages Industries Commission	Dept. of Agro and Rural Industries
Handlooms	Development Commissioner (Handlooms)	Ministry of Textiles
Sericulture	Central Silk Board	Ministry of Textiles
Handicrafts	Development Commissioner (Handlooms)	Ministry of Textiles
Coir Fibre Coir Board	Dept. of SSI, Agro and Rural Industries	
Credit and Enterprise Development		
REGP	Khadi and Village Industries Commission	Dept. of Agro and Rural Industries
PMRY	Dept. of Agro and Rural Industries	
SGSY	Ministry of Rural Development	
SJSRY	Ministry of Urban Development	
Micro Credit		
SHG-Bank Linkage	NABARD	
Rashtriya Mahila Kosh		Ministry of Women and Child Welfare
Swashakti/Swayamsidha	Women's Development Corporations/Societies	Ministry of Women and Child Welfare
Skill Training		
ITI	DGET	Ministry of Human Resources
STEP	DGET	Ministry of Human Resources
Swalamban	Women's Development Corporations/Societies	Ministry of Women and Child Welfare

Source: Adapted from Mohan 2001, Statement 3.

Appendix A12.2: Government Ministries and Departments Engaged in Skill Training

Sl.No.	Ministry/ Department	Skill Development Programmes or Schemes Having Skill Development Component
1	M/o Human Resource Development	1. Vocationalisation of Secondary Education, 2. Community Polytechnic Scheme, 3. Jan Shikshan Sansthan, 4. National Institute of Open Schooling 5. Distance Vocational Education Programmes
2	M/o Labour & Employment (DGET)	1. Craftsmen Training Scheme (CTS), 2. Apprenticeship Training Scheme (ATS), 3. Short -term Courses based on Modular Employable Skills (MES), 4. Crafts Instructor Training Scheme (CITS), 5. Advanced Vocational Training Scheme, 6. Hi-tech Training Scheme, 7. Women Training Programme
3	M/o Rural Development	1. National Institute of Rural Development (NIRD), 2. Swarnjayanti Gram Swarozgar Yojana (SGSY)
4	M/o Small Scale Industries	1. Entrepreneurship Development Programme, 2. Skill Development Programme (SDP), 3. Management Development Programme
5	M/o Textiles	1. Modified Decentralised Training Programme for Handloom Weavers (DTP) 2. Integrated Handloom Training Project (IHTP) 3. Design Development & Training Programme 4. Design & Technology Dissemination Training Programmes 5. Training Programmes by the RD&TCs 6. Schemes for Supporting Skill Formation in Handicrafts and Handloom Artisans
6	M/o Urban Development	1. Urban Self- employment Programme under Swarna Jayanti Shahari Rozgar Yojana (SJSRY) 2. Building Centres of HUDCO 3. Training by Construction Industry Development Council (CIDC)
7	M/o Women & Child Development	1. Support to Training and Employment Programme for Women (STEP) 2. Swalamban 3. Training in Home Scale Preservation of Fruits and Vegetables (by Community Food and Nutrition Extension Units (CFNEUs) 4. Central Social Welfare Board 5. Kishori Shakti Yojana etc.
8	Ministry of Agro & Rural industries	1. PMRY 2. REGP 3. SFURTI
9	M/o Agriculture	1. Training in Agricultural Extension 1. Training in the Use of Agricultural Implements & Machinery 2. Soil Conservation Training Centre, 3. Cooperative Education and Training
10	M/o Food Processing Industries	1. Food Processing & Training Centres (FPTCs), 2. Central Food Technology Research Institute, 3. Paddy Processing Research Centre, 4. Entrepreneurial Development Programme (EDP).

Sl.No.	Ministry/ Department	Skill Development Programmes or Schemes Having Skill Development Component
11	M/o Health & Family Welfare	1. Basic Training of Multipurpose Health Worker (Female & Male), 2. Promotional Training of Female Health Assistant.
12	M/o Heavy Industries & Public Enterprises	1. Counselling, Retraining and Redeployment of Rationalized Workers of CPSEs
13	D/o Information Technology	1. DOEACC - 'O' level
14	M/o Social Justice & Empowerment	1. National Scheme of Liberation and Rehabilitation of Scavengers and their Dependents, 2. Vocational Training Programmes for Improving Livelihood Options
15	M/o Tourism	1. Scheme of Capacity Building for Service Providers (CBSP) 2. Training Programmes for the Training of Trainers 3. Guide Training Courses 4. Induction Training Programme for Regional Level Guides 5. Refresher Level Course for Regional Level Guides 6. Skill Up-gradation in General for Existing Service Providers 7. Language Courses for Guides and other Service Providers
16	M/o Tribal Affairs	1. Vocational Training Centres (VTC) in Tribal Areas.
17	D/o Science and Technology	1. Vocational Training for Employment Generation (VoTEG)
18	Ministry of Commerce & Industry	1. Vocational Courses for Gem Cutting, Testing etc. 2. Skill Formation Activities under Design Development activities by NID 3. Vocational Programmes for Coffee Growers, Cashew Growers, etc. on New Technology, Better Production/ Harvesting Techniques etc
19	Ministry of Youth Affairs & Sports	1. Scheme of Rural Information Technology Youth Development Centres 2. Vocational Training Programmes by NYKs 3. Local Need Based Programmes on various Activities by NYKs 4. Training in Self-employment Project
20.	Ministry of Environment & Forests	1. Employment Related Activities in Joint Forestry Management Programme 2. Need Based Training for New Technology Dissemination
21.	Ministry of New & Renewable Energy	1. Solar Power Programme 2. Biogas Development 3. National Programme on Improved Chulhas 4. Integrated Rural Energy Programme
22.	Ministry of Development of NE region	Vocational Training as a Part of various Poverty Alleviation and Local Economic Development Activities
23.	Ministry of Chemicals & Fertilizers	Trainings for Operation Practice on CNC EDM/Milling/Lathe; Design, Fabrication of Moulds for Plastics; Injection Moulding Practice, and EDPs by CIPET
24.	Ministry of Panchayati Raj	1. Rural Business Hubs 2. Panchayat Development & Training Scheme

Annexures

Annexure 1

AGRICULTURAL WORKERS' CONDITIONS OF WORK AND SOCIAL SECURITY BILL, 2007.

Statement of Objects and Reasons

Chapter I

PRELIMINARY

1. Short Title, Extent, Commencement and Application
2. Definitions
3. Rules of Evidence

Chapter II

CONDITIONS OF WORK TO BE ENSURED FOR THE WAGE WORKER

4. Physical Conditions of Work
5. Duration of Work
6. Conditions of Work and Payment of Wages

Chapter III

SOCIAL SECURITY BENEFITS

7. Framing of Schemes

Chapter IV

NATIONAL SOCIAL SECURITY AND WELFARE FUND FOR UNORGANISED WORKERS

8. Constitution of a National Fund
9. Existing Welfare Boards
10. Exemption from Income Tax
11. Utilisation of the National Fund

Chapter V

NATIONAL SOCIAL SECURITY AND WELFARE BOARD FOR UNORGANISED WORKERS

12. Establishment and Incorporation
13. Functions of the Board
14. Composition of the Board
15. Secretariat of the Board

Chapter VI

STATE SOCIAL SECURITY AND WELFARE BOARDS FOR AGRICULTURAL WORKERS

16. Establishment of State Boards
17. State Fund
18. Functions
19. Secretariat of the Board

Chapter VII

REGISTRATION OF AGRICULTURAL WORKERS

20. Eligibility for Registration and for Social Security Benefits
21. Unique Identification Social Security Number
22. Identity Card
23. Portability of Registration
24. Cessation of Registration
25. Membership of Existing Welfare Boards

Chapter VIII

DELIVERY OF SOCIAL SECURITY BENEFITS

26. Implementation Machinery
27. Workers' Facilitation Centres
28. Premium and compensation/benefits

Chapter IX

ENFORCEMENT AND DISPUTE RESOLUTION BODIES

29. Disputes Resolution Council and Conciliation Committees
30. Functions and Powers of the Conciliation Committee and Dispute Resolution Council
31. Adjudication and Constitution of Agricultural Tribunals
32. Contravention of Provisions Regarding Employment of Agricultural Workers

Chapter X

MISCELLANEOUS

33. Accounts and Audit
34. Power to Make Rules
35. Savings
36. Effect of Laws and Agreements Inconsistent with This Act

Statement of Objects and Reasons

The agricultural sector of the economy in India is the largest sector in terms of employment of the workforce. It consists of crop cultivation and other agricultural activities such as forestry, livestock and fishing. The workers in this sector may be broadly divided into wage workers, and farmers. Almost the entire agricultural sector (except the Plantation Sector) is unorganized i.e. it has neither any formal system of social security nor regulation of conditions of work. Hence, this Bill is intended to cover all unorganised agricultural workers, who are all agricultural wage workers not protected under the Plantations Workers Act, and marginal and small farmers. This Bill is intended to regulate the minimum conditions of work to agricultural wage workers and provide a measure of social security to agricultural wage workers and marginal and small farmers in the unorganised sector. The Bill mandates the Central and State governments to implement a package of National Minimum Social Security Scheme for which all agricultural workers would be entitled. This Bill is also intended to provide minimum conditions of work for agricultural wage workers whose minimum conditions of work are not regulated by any other legislation. It also provides a mechanism for dispute resolution for such workers.

AGRICULTURAL WORKERS' CONDITIONS OF WORK AND SOCIAL SECURITY BILL, 2007.

A
BILL

to provide for regulation of conditions of work, social security and welfare, and a dispute resolution mechanism for Agricultural workers and to provide for other matters connected therewith or incidental thereto.

BE it enacted by Parliament in the fifty-eighth year of the Republic of India as follows:-

Chapter I
PRELIMINARY

1. **Short Title, Extent, Commencement and Application**

   (1) This Act may be called Agricultural Workers' Conditions of Work and Social Security Act, 2007.

   (2) It extends to the whole of India.

   (3) It shall come into force on such date as the Government may, by notification in the Official Gazette, appoint, and different dates may be appointed for different States and different areas in a State and for different provisions of this Act, within six months from the date of the assent.

2. **Definitions**

   For the purposes of this Act, unless the context otherwise requires, -

   a) **"Adolescent"** means a person of the age of 14 years and above and who has not completed 18 years of age.

   b) **"Agricultural worker"** means either a farmer (as defined in clause g below) or a wage worker engaged in agriculture.

   Explanation: Workers eligible for protection under the Plantation Workers Act are excluded from the purview of this Act.

c) **"Agriculture" means** the following occupations:

   (i) Farming, including the cultivation and tillage of soil, etc;

   (ii) Dairy farming;

   (iii) Production, cultivation, growing and harvesting of any horticultural commodity;

   (iv) Raising of livestock, bee-keeping or poultry;

   (v) Fishing and/ or fish farming or sericulture;

   (vi) Any practice performed on a farm as incidental to, or in conjunction with, the farm operations (including any forestry or timbering operations and the preparation for market and delivery to storage or to market or to carriage for transportation of farm products);

   (vii) Growing fodder or thatching grass or for grazing cattle.

d) **"Casual worker"** means a **wage worker** engaged in agriculture in consideration of wages, whose employment is of casual nature.

e) **"Child"** means a person who has not completed 14 years of age.

f) **"Employer"** means a natural or juridical person, or an association of such persons, by whom any *agricultural* worker is engaged or employed either directly or otherwise, in consideration of wages.

g) **"Farmer"** means any person engaged in agricultural activities, either individually or with one or more persons, and not owning or operating a holding of more than two hectares or such limits as may be notified from time to time by the State government.

h) **"Government"** means either Central Government, or State Government, or Union Territory administration, or local government, or Cantonment Boards as the case may be.

i) **"Homeworker"** means an unorganised non-agricultural sector worker involved in the production of goods or services as specified by an employer, in his / her own home or other premises of his / her choice (other than the work place of the employer) for remuneration, irrespective of whether or not the employer provides the equipment, materials or other inputs.

j) **"Identity card"** means a card issued to an agricultural worker carrying a unique number issued by the authorised agency of the State Board.

k) **"Migrant worker"** includes inter state and intra state migrant workers.

l) **"National Board"** means the National Social Security and Welfare Board for unorganised workers.

m) **"Non-agriculture"** means all occupations other than those included in agriculture and includes occupations related to Mining and Quarrying, Manufacturing, Electricity, Gas and water supply and Construction sectors, and services (including trade; hotels; restaurants; transport, storage and communications; financing, insurance, real estate and business services; and community, social and personal services).

n) **"Registered *Agricultural* Worker"** means an *agricultural* worker registered for benefits under this Act.

o) **"Remuneration"** means as defined in the Equal Remuneration Act, 1976.

p) **"Sexual Harassment"** is such unwelcome sexually determined behavior such as physical contact, advances, sexually coloured remarks, showing pornography or making sexual demands, whether verbal, textual, graphic or electronic or by any other actions, which may -.

(i) contain implied or overt promise of preferential treatment in that wage worker's employment; or

(ii) contain an implied or overt threat of detrimental treatment in that wage worker's employment or an implied or overt threat about the present or future employment status of that wage worker and includes the creation of a hostile working environment; or

(iii) interfere with a wage worker's work or create an intimidating, hostile or offensive work environment; or

(iv) be humiliating and may constitute a health and safety problem.

Explanation1: Hostile Environment: A work environment is "hostile" when unwelcome verbal, non-verbal or physical behaviour focusing on sexuality is severe and pervasive enough to interfere with the victim's work performance or be intimidating or offensive to a reasonable person.

q) **"State Board"** means the (name of the State) State Social Security and Welfare Board for agricultural workers.

r) **"Self-employed non-agricultural worker"** means any person who operates a non-farm enterprise or engages in a non-agricultural profession, trade or business, either on own account individually or with one or more persons.

s) **'Unorganised non-agricultural sector**" consists of all unincorporated private non-agricultural enterprises owned by individuals or households engaged in the production and sale of non-agricultural goods and services and operated on a proprietary or a partnership basis and employing less than ten persons.

t) **Unorganised non-agricultural sector worker"** means a self-employed non-agricultural worker, a homeworker or a wage worker employed or engaged in the unorganised non-agricultural sector.

u) **""Unorganised non-agricultural worker"** means an unorganised non-agricultural sector worker and also includes workers in the organized non-agricultural sector not protected by the existing laws relating to conditions of work and/or social security.

v) **"Unorganised Worker**" means unorganised non-agricultural worker, and agricultural worker (except those eligible for protection under the Plantation Workers Act).

w) **"Wages"** means as defined in clause (vi) of section 2 of the Payment of Wages Act, 1936 (4 of 1936).

x) **"Wage worker"** means a person employed in agriculture for a remuneration directly by an employer or through any agency or contractor, whether exclusively for one employer or for one or more employers, whether simultaneously or otherwise, whether in cash and/or in kind whether as a temporary or casual worker, or as a migrant worker.

3. Rules of Evidence

In this Act, notwithstanding anything contained in the Indian Evidence Act, 1872, the burden of proof that compliance with the provisions of the Act and the Scheme has been effected shall be entirely on the employer and the units of the Board, wherever applicable.

[Explanatory Note: This section facilitates shifting the burden of proof from the workers to the employer. This is a departure from the normal practice and ordinary rules of evidence, which places the burden on the plaintiff.]

Chapter II

CONDITIONS OF WORK TO BE ENSURED FOR THE WAGE WORKER

4. **Physical Conditions of Work**

(1) Every employer shall provide in all the lands where agricultural work is carried on such basic amenities and first-aid facilities, and reasonable housing and provision of basic amenities for seasonal migrant workers, as may be prescribed.

(2) Every employer shall ensure that personal protective safety equipments are provided to such agricultural workers as are required to handle machinery and agro-chemicals as are hazardous to the life and limb of such workers. The State Board shall carry out periodic studies on occupational hazards arising in this sector and develop suitable outreach/extension programmes for this purpose.

(3) Every employer shall compensate a wage worker for any accident or occupational hazard arising out of or in the course of employment that results in any temporary, permanent, partial or total disablement of the wage worker, at rates to be specified in this behalf.

(4) The employer shall ensure that there is no sexual harassment of the agricultural wage worker at the place of work. The state government shall make appropriate rules concerning the disciplinary action that may be taken by an employer where a complaint of sexual harassment is established against a wage worker; and the compensation payable by an employer where a case of sexual harassment is established against the employer himself/herself.

(5) The State Board shall make rules with respect to child care facilities to be made available at local levels.

5. **Duration of Work**

(1) The normal hours of work of a agricultural wage worker shall be limited to eight hours a day beyond which a worker shall be paid overtime at one and a half the normal rate of wages per hour.

Provided that nothing contained in this section shall be deemed to prohibit an agreement between the employer and the wage workers engaged in agriculture for working for less than eight hours on any particular day or days or on all days of employment or to affect any custom or practice prevailing in the locality under which the wage worker engaged in agriculture is required to work for less than eight hours.

Explanation: Nothing contained in this section shall extend the normal hours of work beyond eight hours to give effect to any custom or practice prevailing in the locality.

(2) Every eight hour working day of the agricultural wage worker shall have at least an half hour break, so however that the spread over of work shall not exceed ten hours.

(3) Women and adolescents shall not be employed as agricultural wage workers between the hours of 9 p.m. and 5 a.m., except where permitted under rules made in this behalf.

(4) Every agricultural wage worker shall be entitled to one paid day of rest after completing six continuous days of employment by or under a single employer.

6. **Conditions of Work and Payment of Wages**

(1) No employer shall employ any agricultural wage worker, in contravention of the existing Acts which are applicable to the worker. In particular, the employer shall comply with the following Acts:

a) Bonded Labour System (Abolition) Act, 1976;

b) Child Labour (Prohibition and Regulation) Act, 1986;

c) Minimum Wages Act, 1948; and

d) Equal Remuneration Act, 1976

(2) (a) The Central government shall notify a National Minimum Wage.

(b) The National Minimum Wage shall apply to all agricultural wage workers in employments not notified under the Minimum Wages Act.

Provided that where the wage under the Minimum Wages Act is lower than the National Minimum Wage, the concerned State Government shall amend the prescribed Minimum Wage to bring it in conformity with the National Minimum Wage.

Provided further that till such time as this is done, the wage worker shall be entitled to receive the National Minimum Wage.

(c) The Central Government shall fix a National Minimum Wage for all employments, after taking into account the minimum basic needs of the wage and homeworkers and his/her family, variations in the cost of living in different areas and other parameters on the basis of consultation with a tripartite body consisting of workers, employers and the Government representatives.

(d) The National Minimum Wage shall be announced by the Central Government within one year of the implementation of this Act and shall be periodically reviewed through a modality prescribed by the National Board.

Provided that, till the announcement of the National Minimum Wage as above, the national floor level minimum wage recommended by the Ministry of Labour for 2004-05, shall, after adjusting for cost of living changes in different areas, be treated as the National Minimum Wage.

(3) Where the wages are determined by a piece rate system, the earnings of an agricultural worker working for 8 hours should be at least equal to the time rated minimum wages fixed for that category of work in the state concerned, and where the rates have not been fixed under the Minimum Wages Act, 1948 in the relevant state, the rates as fixed under clause (2) above.

(4) Wages in employments performed predominantly by women shall be brought on par with employments certified as equivalent in value by an Employment Certification Committee to be constituted by the State Board. The Employment Certification Committee shall periodically evaluate employments in the state for this purpose.

(5) Wages of agricultural workers shall be duly paid for the periods agreed upon. The wage period can on no account exceed one month; any delay in payment beyond this periods will require the employer to pay penal rates of interest, as specified in this behalf, for the period of the delay to the agricultural wage worker.

(6) There shall be no deduction from wages, including in such cases where such wages are paid as advance to the worker, in the form of interest, payments to contractors or agents, overvaluation of goods supplied or basic amenities provided including accommodation in the case of seasonal migrant workers, fines, inadequate or poor quality output, except in accordance with rules made in this behalf by the State Government.

(7) (a) Every employer shall provide an agricultural wage worker the details of remuneration received by him/her in such form as may be prescribed by the State Government.

(b) Every agricultural wage worker, except casual workers, shall receive a letter of employment from his/her employer, stating the terms of employment of his/her employment.

(c) Every employer shall maintain such registers and records as may be necessary to verify the employer's claim regarding the employment status of agricultural wage workers and details of payments made to them.

(8) All agricultural workers shall have the right to organise, by forming trade unions or other membership based organisations, for representation and collective bargaining in various fora. **(Note: This applies to both wage workers and farmers)**

(9) No employer shall discriminate against any agricultural wage worker on the grounds of sex, caste, religion, incidence of HIV-AIDS, migration status, place of origin, in employment, wage rates and conditions of work as laid down in this Act.

Chapter III

SOCIAL SECURITY BENEFITS

7. Framing of Schemes

(1) The Central Government shall formulate and notify in the Official Gazette a National Social Security Scheme containing such basic features as provided for in the Schedule to this Act.

(2) The National Social Security Scheme for the agricultural workers shall consist of a package of the following national minimum social security benefits:

(i) Health benefits for self, spouse and children below the age of 18 years, and maternity benefits for women workers or spouse of men workers;

(ii) Life and disability cover for natural or accidental death of the worker;

(iii) Old age security in the form of old age pension for workers above the age of 60 years or Provident Fund.

(3) The Scheme will be applicable to all eligible workers within a period of five years.

(4) In addition to the national minimum, the Central Government may frame on recommendations of the National Board such schemes as it may deem necessary or finance such schemes of the State governments/Welfare Boards as it may find appropriate, subject to availability of finance by such means as mentioned in Section 8 and may include those listed under (5) below.

(5) The State Government on recommendations of the State Board may formulate schemes for such unorganised workers as it may find appropriate to: (a) strengthen the national minimum social security by way of its own contribution, and/or (b) design and implement additional social security benefits through its own schemes. These may include:

a) Provident Fund schemes;

b) Employment injury benefit scheme;

c) Housing schemes;

d) Educational schemes for children of workers;

e) Skill up-gradation;

f) Funeral assistance;

g) Marriage of daughters; and

h) Any other schemes to enhance socio-economic security.

(6) The Central Government shall have the power to remove difficulties that arise in giving effect to the provisions of the Scheme by an order published in the Official Gazette, not inconsistent with the provisions of the Act, as appears to it necessary or expedient for the removal of the difficulty.

Chapter IV

NATIONAL SOCIAL SECURITY AND WELFARE FUND FOR UNORGANISED WORKERS

8. Constitution of a National Fund

The Central Government shall create a National Social Security and Welfare Fund to which contributions shall accrue from the following sources:

a) Grants and loans from the Central Government;

b) Contributions from workers, employers and Governments in the form and manner to be prescribed in the specified National Minimum Social Security Scheme, provided that the Central government may exempt any class of unorganised workers or employers from making their contribution under such conditions as may be specified;

c) Any tax or cess that the Central Government may impose for the purpose of providing social security for unorganized workers;

d) Any tax or cess that the Central Government may impose on commodities and/or services in lieu of employers' contributions (which are either difficult to collect or appropriate employers in the unorganised sector are not directly identifiable).

In addition to the above, contributions may also accrue from the following sources:

e) Contributions from the national financial/developmental institutions; and

f) Any voluntary contribution from individuals or institutions.

9. Existing Welfare Boards

Notwithstanding any other provision contained under any other law, the Appropriate Government may merge any existing Welfare Board/Boards and Welfare Fund/Funds constituted under any other law into the Board and Fund created under this Act.

10. Exemption from Income Tax

All financial contributions made by individuals and institutions to the National Social Security and Welfare Fund will be exempted from the payment of income tax under the Income Tax Act.

11. Utilisation of the National Fund

All contributions accruing to the National Board shall be credited to the Fund, which shall be applied for meeting the following:

a) Expenses on the National Social Security Scheme and any other social security schemes of the Central Government;

b) Grants to the State Boards, including for the purposes of the functioning of the Workers' Facilitation Centres;

c) Expenses on the administration of the scheme;

d) Investment in permitted schemes;

e) Any other item in connection with the administration of this Act.

Chapter V

NATIONAL SOCIAL SECURITY AND WELFARE BOARD FOR UNORGANISED WORKERS

12. Establishment and Incorporation

With effect from such date as the Central Government may, by notification appoint, there shall be established for the purposes of this Act, a Board to be called the National Social Security and Welfare Board for Unorganised Workers.

13. Functions of the Board

The National Board shall perform the following functions:

a) Administration of this Act and formulation of policies at the national level, and shall have such powers as may be laid down to direct, co-ordinate, supervise, and monitor the functioning of State Boards and the Central Welfare Boards;

b) Review the working including auditing of the State Boards and the Central Welfare Boards every four years and make suitable recommendations to the Government(s) concerned for further improvement;

c) Manage and maintain the National Social Security and Welfare Fund, provide financial assistance to State Boards; recommend new schemes and programmes and projects for implementation through the Fund;

d) Advise the Central Government on policy matters relating to social security, and extension of schemes of social security such as ESI and EPF to unorganised sector workers; and health, safety and welfare of workers;

e) Assist in capacity building of the State Boards;

f) Collect, compile and publish statistics relating to the unorganised sector and undertake such promotional activities as may be decided from time to time;

g) Monitor and review the impact of existing schemes, policies and programmes of various Ministries and Departments of Government of India on the unorganised sector workers and make appropriate recommendations;

h) Advise the Government regarding the promotion of gainful employment opportunities and promotion of livelihood options and matters relating to welfare of unorganised sector workers;

i) Identify skill and training requirements for unorganised workers and to advise the government accordingly;

j) Carry out periodic surveys on the condition of work in the unorganised sector and make suitable recommendations to the government;

k) Hold public hearings to entertain petitions submitted by the unorganized sector workers and make appropriate recommendations;

l) Advise government on special protection measures for migrant workers and their families in providing the ration cards, housing and education to their children; and

m) Provide for guidelines of periodic review of the national minimum wages fixed by the Central Government after taking into account the minimum basic needs of the wage workers and his/her family.

14. Composition of the Board

(1) The National Welfare Board for unorganised workers shall be constituted by the Central Government consisting of the following member organisations:

a) Central Trade Unions and Agricultural Worker Unions; National level organizations, including federation of such organizations, of unorganised sector workers including the self-employed;

b) National Level organisations of employers of unorganised sector workers;

c) Central Government Ministries, State Boards, Central Welfare Boards and Public Agencies; and

d) Experts in the area of management of insurance products and services; social security and related issues in the unorganized sector; management of finances, and other organizations and stakeholders working with the unorganized sector.

(2) The Central Government shall decide the criteria, number and names of such organisations to be represented on the National Board, with adequate representation of wage workers, self-employed workers and women representing the workers.

(3) The National Board shall work through a Secretariat.

(4) The Chairman of the National Board shall be nominated by the Central Government from amongst persons of eminence in the fields of labour welfare, management, finance, law and administration. The Member Secretary, who shall be the chief executive officer shall be designated by the Central Government being a person not below the rank of Secretary to the Government of India.

(5) The Board shall meet as often as possible but not less than twice a year.

15. Secretariat of the Board

The National Board shall have a secretariat with adequate professional and other staff. The staff of the National Board shall be governed by the Central Government rules and regulations existing from time to time. The annual budget of the National Board shall be prepared by the Secretariat and placed before the full Board for approval.

Chapter VI

STATE SOCIAL SECURITY AND WELFARE BOARDS FOR AGRICULTURAL WORKERS

16. Establishment of State Boards

(1) Each State shall have a State Board to implement the national minimum social security as well as design and implement State-level social security and welfare programmes for agricultural workers. Provided that wherever a similar Board is already in existence, the State government may merge or amalgamate the existing Board with the State Board. The State governments shall constitute the State Boards within one year of the date of commencement of this Act. The State Boards shall have the following as its members:

a) Trade Unions and Agricultural Worker Unions; State level organizations, including federation of such organizations of unorganised agricultural sector workers including the farmers;

b) State Level organisations of employers of unorganised agricultural sector workers;

c) State Government Ministries, Welfare Boards and Public Agencies; and

d) Experts in the area of management of insurance products and services; social security and related issues in the unorganized agricultural sector; management of finances, and other organizations and stakeholders working with the unorganized agricultural sector.

(2) The State Government shall decide the criteria, number and names of such organisations to be represented on the State Board, with adequate representation of wage workers, farmers and women representing the workers.

(3) The State Board shall work through a Secretariat.

(4) The Chairman of the State Board shall be nominated by the State Government from amongst persons of eminence in the fields of labour welfare, management, finance, law and administration. The Member Secretary, who shall be the chief executive officer shall be designated by the State Government being a person not below the rank of Secretary to the Government of the State.

(5) The Board shall meet as often as possible but not less than twice a year.

17. State Fund

(1) The State government shall create a State Social Security and welfare Fund to which contributions shall accrue from the following sources:

(i) Grants and loans from National Board and the State government;

(ii) Any tax or cess that the State government may impose on commodities and/or services in lieu of employers' contributions (which are either difficult to collect or appropriate employers in the unorganised Sector are not directly identifiable);

(iii) Contribution toward additional social security scheme (if any) formulated by the State Board;

(iv) Contributions from the national financial/developmental institutions; and

(v) Any voluntary contribution from individuals or institutions.

(2) All financial contributions made by individuals and institutions to the State Social Security and welfare Fund will be exempted from the payment of income tax under the Income Tax Act.

(3) All contributions accruing to the State Boards shall be credited to the State Social Security and Welfare Fund which shall be applied for meeting the following:

a) Expenses on the implementation of the national minimum social security and additional social security schemes of the State Government;

b) Grants to the Welfare Boards and the Workers' Facilitation Centres;

c) Expenses on the administration of the State Board as per the annual budget approved by the Executive Council;

d) Investment in permitted schemes; and

e) Any other item in connection with the administration of this Act.

18. Functions

The State Boards will perform the following functions:

a) Administer this Act at the State level including ensuring collection of contributions, maintenance of individual accounts of the registered agricultural workers and records of receipt of contribution from individual employers;

b) Implement the national minimum social security for agricultural workers through appropriate organisational arrangements, negotiate with the providers for the best possible offers, and stipulate norms for the evaluation of the work done by the Workers' Facilitation Centres;

c) Frame guidelines to ensure portability of benefits to workers;

d) Frame and implement social security schemes, in addition to the National Social Security Scheme, that the State Board may design in consultation with the State government;

e) Provide financial assistance to other member organisations implementing social security programmes;

f) Advise the State government on policy matters relating to social security, health and safety and welfare of agricultural workers;

g) Create awareness among the agricultural workers about the need for social security registration and the existence of various social security schemes;

h) Collect, compile and publish statistics, with the help of statistical organisations, regarding agricultural workers and their conditions of work, and employers who engage these workers at the *Panchayat*/Municipal, District, State levels with such details as gender and age, nature of occupation, level of earnings, etc.;

i) Review the working of the Welfare Boards and other implementing agencies on the basis of annual reports and statements of audited accounts or specially commissioned reports and make suitable recommendations to the government(s) concerned for further improvement;

j) Assist in capacity building of Workers Welfare Boards and Workers' Facilitation Centres;

k) Initiate innovative approaches, through interaction across sectors and constituencies, for the enhancement of welfare, working conditions and productivity of agricultural workers;

l) Submit annual report to the National Board within four months from the last day of the previous financial year along with an audited statement of accounts;

m) Monitor and review the impact of existing schemes, policies and programmes of various Ministries and Departments of the concerned State Government on agricultural workers and make appropriate recommendations;

n) Advise the Government regarding the promotion of gainful employment opportunities and promotion of livelihood options for agricultural workers;

o) Encourage the promotion of labour organizations and cooperatives to secure gainful employment and dignified conditions of work;

p) Identify skill and training requirements for agricultural workers and to advise the government accordingly;

q) Carry out periodic surveys on the condition of work in the agricultural sector and make suitable recommendations to the government;

r) Hold public hearings to entertain petitions submitted by agricultural workers and make appropriate recommendations;

s) Carry out surveys to determine the safety and health standards required in the agricultural sector, and publish manuals and outreach programmes for worker safety;

t) Review the Minimum Wages for the state after taking into account the cost of living and minimum basic needs of the agricultural wage workers and his/her family;

u) Constitute Employment Certification Committee to bring the wages in employments performed predominantly by women on par with employments certified as equivalent in value and periodically evaluate employments in the state for this purpose; and

v) Carry out periodic studies on occupational hazards arising in this sector and develop suitable outreach/extension programmes for this purpose;

19. Secretariat of the Board

The State Board shall have a secretariat with adequate professional and other staff. The staff of the State Board shall be governed by the State government rules and regulations existing from time to time.

Chapter VII

REGISTRATION OF AGRICULTURAL WORKERS

20. Eligibility for Registration and for Social Security Benefits

Every agricultural worker shall be eligible for registration subject to the following conditions:

a) He/she should have completed 18 years of age;

b) His monthly income does not exceed Rs.7000/- in 2007 (roughly equivalent to Rs. 6500/- per month recommended by the Indian Labour Conference held in December 2005); and

c) a self-declaration confirming that he/she is an agricultural worker not owning or operating a holding of more than two hectares or such limits as may be notified from time to time by the State government; .

21. Unique Identification Social Security Number

Each registered agricultural worker shall be eligible for receiving a Unique Identification Social Security Number in the form of an Identity Card issued in the name of the State Board.

22. Identity Card

The State Government shall decide the manner of registration of unorganized agricultural sector workers, issuance of identity cards and manner of record keeping at the district level.

23. Portability of Registration

The Identity Card issued to agricultural workers shall remain valid even in the case of migration to another district in the country and the new address can be changed on application to the authority concerned.

24. Cessation of Registration

The National Board shall draw up rules to decide on the period of validity of registration, renewals, cessation of registration and settlement of claims on the death of the card holder.

25. Membership of Existing Welfare Boards

In case, any agricultural worker is eligible for benefit under one or more existing Central or Welfare Boards, in addition to his eligibility for the National Minimum Social Security Scheme,

(1) The agricultural worker shall retain the option of membership of the Fund with the highest benefit.

(2) The National/State Board may decide the criteria on which the agricultural worker can be eligible for benefit under the National Minimum Social Security Scheme in addition to membership in other Boards/schemes.

Chapter VIII

DELIVERY OF SOCIAL SECURITY BENEFITS

26. Implementation Machinery

The State Boards shall be responsible for the delivery of mandatory minimum social security benefits and shall decide the manner in which social security benefits shall have to be delivered to the registered agricultural workers. This may include tie-ups with local organisations like banks, post offices and insurance companies.

27. Workers' Facilitation Centres

(1) In order to extend coverage and reach the agricultural workers in remote areas, the State Boards may designate any one or more of the following at the local level as Workers' Facilitation Centres (WFC):

a) Existing Worker Welfare Boards and their local offices;

b) Local Panchayati Raj Institutions (PRI);

c) Organisations of workers including trade unions, associations and co-operatives in the agricultural sector;

d) Self-help Groups (SHGs); and

e) Non-profit organisations working among the agricultural sector workers.

(2) Such designated Workers' Facilitation Centres shall perform the following functions:

a) Disseminate information on available social security schemes for the agricultural workers;

b) Facilitate the filling, processing and forwarding of application forms for registration of agricultural workers;

c) Obtain registration from the District Committee and deliver the Identity Cards to the registered agricultural workers;

d) Facilitate the enrolment of the registered agricultural workers in social security schemes; and

e) Facilitate the delivery of social security benefits through the institutions designated to deliver such social security (insurance companies, post offices, Departments of the State/ Central Government and other institutions concerned).

(3) The State Boards shall compensate the costs incurred by the Workers' Facilitation Centres for performance of its functions.

28. Premium and Compensation/Benefits:

(1) The National Board shall decide the amount and manner of payment of contribution/fee by the agricultural workers to the National Social Security Schemes.

(2) For schemes initiated by the State Boards, the State Board concerned shall decide the contributions of agricultural workers and employers.

(3) The claim of registered agricultural workers for social security benefits shall lie solely against the State Board and it shall be the responsibility of the State Board to settle the dues, if any.

Chapter IX

ENFORCEMENT AND DISPUTE RESOLUTION BODIES

29. Disputes Resolution Council and Conciliation Committees

(1) The State Government shall, by rules, constitute Dispute Resolution Council (DRC) at District level and Conciliation Committees (CC) at an appropriate level below the district level i.e Block/ Tehsil/Mandal level, for resolution of disputes relating to the non observance of provisions of this Act arising amongst the agricultural wage workers , employers, Workers' Facilitation Centres and State Boards.

(2) The Composition of the DRCs and CCs shall be tripartite and consist of an officer designated by the State Government to be the Member Secretary, one person nominated from the most representative of membership-based organisations of the agricultural workers in that State, having membership in the district, and a person nominated from the most representative organisation of employers' organisations in the agricultural sector in the state. The State government, may, if it thinks fit, appoint two persons as assessors to advice the conciliation Committee on the proceedings before it.

(3) When there is a complaint regarding sexual harassment, the CC/DRC shall co-opt two other members from the Panchayats/local bodies, who shall be women, at the time of dealing with such complaints. The CC/DRC, if satisfied that a case of sexual harassment is established, direct the employer to ensure that necessary action is taken against the person guilty of such conduct.

(4) The honorarium and/ or the allowances to be paid to the workers and employers representatives on the DRC shall be determined by the State Government.

(5) The persons to be appointed as members from each of the categories specified in sub-section (2), the term of office and other related conditions, the procedure to be followed in the discharge of their functions, conduct of meetings, periodicity of meetings and the manner of filling vacancies among the members of the CC/DRC, shall be such as may be prescribed by the State Government.

(Note: In order to determine the most representative organisation, membership figures including the verification of trade unions carried out by the CLC may be relied upon.)

30. Functions and Powers of the Conciliation Committee and Dispute Resolution Council

(1) Any agricultural wage worker or employer or an organisation representing such worker or Workers' Facilitation Centres or the State Board may raise a dispute relating to the non-observance of provisions of this Act by filing a complaint before the Conciliation Committee in the manner prescribed by the State Government. The DRC may also take *suo moto* cognizance of such disputes.

(2) Every complaint so filed shall be deemed to be a dispute under this Act notwithstanding that such a complaint had not been referred to the employer at the first instance, and been rejected.

(3) The status of employment of agricultural workers in the dispute raised before the CC or DRC shall not be affected merely for the reason that a complaint regarding non observance of provisions of this Act has been raised before the DRC or CC.

(4) (a) Upon reference of a dispute, the Conciliation Committee shall proceed to arrive at a conciliated settlement. The Conciliation Committee shall, for the purpose of bringing about a settlement of the dispute, without delay, investigate the dispute and all matters connected therewith, and may do all such things as they think fit for the purpose of inducing the parties to come to a fair and amicable settlement of the dispute.

(b) The inspectors appointed under the Minimum Wages Act, 1948, shall assist the CC/DRC in their duties and shall carry such investigation of complaints as required by the CC/DRC.

(c) Where the CC/DRC apprehends violation of the provisions of this Act the inspectors may be directed to investigate and report the matter expeditiously.

(5) The CC/DRC or the inspectors designated for this purpose under sub- section 4(b) above may for the purpose of investigating the dispute, after giving reasonable notice, enter the premises to which the dispute relates. The Conciliation Committee shall also have the powers under the Code of Civil Procedure 1908 to enforce the attendance of parties, compel the production of documents and material objects.

(6) The Conciliation Committee may if it thinks fit appoint one or more persons having special knowledge of the matter under consideration to advise it on the proceeding before it.

(7) The time limit for the conclusion of the proceedings of the CC shall not exceed four weeks. Where the parties to the dispute apply in the prescribed manner, whether jointly or separately, to the CC for the extension of such period and the member-secretary of the CC considers it necessary or expedient to extend such period, he/she may for reasons to be recorded in writing, extend such period by such further period as he/she may think fit;

Provided that no proceedings before a CC shall lapse merely on the ground that the period specified under this sub section has expired without such proceedings being completed.

(8) If the Conciliation Committee is able to arrive at a conciliated settlement, it shall record its finding to such effect and shall issue such directions as considered necessary.

(9) Upon failure of such conciliation proceedings, the Conciliation Committee shall record its findings and refer the dispute to the DRC, which shall within two weeks of receipt of reference, refer the matter to the adjudicator provided in this section.

(10) Where a dispute is raised directly before the DRC, the DRC shall ordinarily refer the dispute to the CC below it, under whose jurisdiction the dispute falls.

(11) In cases of disputes raised directly before it or referred to it by the CC under subsection (9) above, the DRC may itself seek to bring about a conciliated settlement.

(12) In such cases, the DRC shall have all the powers mentioned in section (4) and (5) specified above.

(13) If the DRC is able to arrive at a conciliated settlement, it shall record its finding to such effect and shall issue such directions as considered necessary.

(14) In case of failure of conciliation, the DRC shall record its finding and refer the matter directly to the Agricultural Tribunal referred to in section 31, within 4 weeks of the reference of the dispute. Where the parties to the dispute apply in the prescribed manner, whether jointly or separately, to the DRC for the extension of such period and the member-secretary of the DRC considers it necessary or expedient to extend such period, he/she may for reasons to be recorded in writing, extend such period by such further period as he/she may think fit.

Provided that no proceedings before a DRC shall lapse merely on the ground that the period specified under this sub section has expired without such proceedings being completed.

(15) The DRC shall also monitor the functioning of the CCs.

(16) Where the dispute pertains to any matter covered by any law mentioned in Section 6(1), the CC/DRC shall forward the complaint to the appropriate authority created under the relevant Act for adjudication.

31. Adjudication and Constitution of Agricultural Tribunals

(1) The State Government shall by notification in the Official Gazette constitute Agricultural Tribunals for each district for the purpose of adjudication of disputes relating to agricultural workers under this Act.

(2) The Agricultural Tribunal shall consist of a sole member who shall an officer of the Government not below the rank of a District Labour Officer or Deputy Collector for each district, or any officer with experience as Civil Judge or as Magistrate to be the Adjudicator under the section.

(3) The Agricultural Tribunal shall hold sessions in such Block/ Tehsil/Mandal towns and with such frequency, as may be specified in the rules made in this behalf by the State Government, in order to adjudicate upon the disputes referred to it by the DRCs at the Block/ Tehsil/Mandal level.

(Note: NO appeal has been provided for under this Act. Moving the High Courts under Art. 226 of the Constitution would of course be available).

(4) The State Government shall issue such notifications and directions as are necessary to ensure that the adjudication proceedings are concluded expeditiously with minimum loss of time and costs to the parties involved. The award of the Agricultural Tribunal shall be publicised in the manner as prescribed by the State Government.

(5) The designated department(s) of the State Government concerned shall be responsible for enforcement and implementation of the provisions of this Act.

32. Contravention of Provisions Regarding Employment of Agricultural Workers

(1) Whoever contravenes any provisions of this Act or the rules made there under, other than those made punishable under any other law, regarding the employment of agricultural workers shall be punishable with imprisonment for a term which may extend to one year, or with fine which may extend to five thousand rupees, or with both, and in case of continuing contravention, with additional fine which may extend up to one hundred rupees for every day during which such contravention continues.

(2) No court shall take cognizance of an offence punishable under this Act or the abetment of any such offence, save on a complaint made by, or the previous sanction in writing of or under the authority of the State Government. No court inferior to that of a Metropolitan Magistrate or a judicial magistrate of the first class shall try any offence punishable under this Act.

(3) No suit, prosecution or other legal proceeding shall lie against any person for anything done in good faith or intended to be done in pursuance of this Act or rules.

(4) No court shall take cognisance of an offence punishable under this Act unless the complaint is made within six months from the date on which the alleged commission of the offence came to the knowledge of the CC or the DRC concerned.

(5) Any person who commits a breach of any conciliated settlement arrived at in the CC or DRC or final award by the Tribunal, shall be punishable with imprisonment for a term which may extend to six months, or with fine, or with both, [and where the breach is a continuing one, with a further fine which may extend to two hundred rupees for every day during which the breach continues after the conviction for the first] and the Court trying the offence, if it fines the offender, may direct that the whole or any part of the fine realized from him shall be paid, by way of compensation, to any person who, in its opinion, has been injured by such breach.

(6) Where any money is due to an agricultural worker under a settlement or an award, the workman himself or any other person authorized by him in writing in this behalf, or, in the case of the death of the

workman, his assignee or heirs may, without prejudice to any other mode of recovery, make an application to the state government for the recovery of the money due to him, and if the state government is satisfied that any money is so due, it shall issue a certificate for that amount to the Collector who shall proceed to recover the same in the same manner as an arrear of land revenue.

Chapter X

MISCELLANEOUS

33. Accounts and Audit

(a) The National Board and the State Boards shall maintain proper accounts and other relevant records and prepare annual statements of accounts in such form as may be prescribed.

(b) The National Board shall furnish to the Central Government, before such date as may be prescribed, the audited copy of the consolidated account of itself and the Funds together with the auditor's report.

34. Power to Make Rules

The Central and State governments shall have the power to make rules for the purposes of carrying out the objects of the Act.

35. Savings

(1) This law will not affect the application of any other State or Central Acts which applies to the agricultural worker or to the employer under this Act. (Note: Even if the employer or establishment is covered, the agricultural worker who is not covered under the formal sector law would get benefit under this law for the matters covered here).

(2) Notwithstanding anything contained in this Act, wherever any agricultural worker is eligible for superior or better benefits under any existing law in force, the worker shall continue to be entitled for such benefits.

36. Effect of Laws and Agreements Inconsistent with This Act

(1) The provisions of this Act shall have effect notwithstanding anything inconsistent therewith contained in any other law or in the terms of any award, agreement or contract of service, whether made before or after the coming into force of this Act.

(2) Nothing contained in this Act shall be construed to preclude an agricultural worker from entering into an agreement with his/her employer for granting him/her rights or privileges in respect of any matter which are more favourable to him/ her than those to which he/she would be entitled under this Act.

Schedule of the Agricultural Workers Conditions of Work And Social Security Bill, 2007.

(See section 7 (1))

National Social Security Scheme for Agricultural Workers

Background

The agricultural workers in the Unorganised Sector face problems that arise out of deficiency or capability deprivation in terms of inadequate employment, low earnings, low health, etc., as well as of adversity in the absence of fall back mechanisms (safety net). These workers have limited or no formal social security cover which increases their vulnerability during times of illness, old age, unemployment and untimely death. The absence of social security mechanisms is a critical factor in downturns in the conditions of these households, many of whom are already very poor. It destroys the workers ability to contribute meaningfully, and to increasing production and productivity. It leads to disaffection increasing social costs, widespread crimes, and persistent ill health. Presently, less than 6% of the entire unorganised sector workforce has recourse to any social security cover.

Objectives

1. To provide for a right based entitlement for the agricultural workers, and
2. To provide for a universal national minimum social security scheme to cover all the workers in the unorganised agricultural sector in a phased manner within a period of 5 years.

Definitions

Words and expressions shall have the meaning respectively assigned to them under Section. 2 of the Act.

Coverage and Eligibility

This scheme may be called the National Social Security Scheme, 2007.

This scheme shall come into force on….

This scheme applies to all agricultural workers, hereafter referred to as 'worker' to whom the Act extends who

a) has completed 18 years of age;

b) whose monthly income does not exceed Rs.7000/- in 2007 (roughly equivalent to Rs. 6500/- per month recommended by the Indian Labour Conference held in December 2005);

c) has submitted a prescribed self-declaration form confirming that he/she is an agricultural worker not owning or operating a holding of more than two hectares or such limits as may be notified from time to time by the State government; and

d) has paid the contribution/ fee as prescribed.

Benefits

The national social security scheme shall provide for a package of the following minimum benefits:

(a) Health Insurance

(i) Each worker will be entitled to hospitalization for himself and his family members, costing Rs. 15000 a year in total with Rs. 10000 maximum per ailment in designated, hospitals or clinics, public or private, recognized by the State Board, with at least 15 beds. If there is no such clinic available within 10 kilometres from the worker's residence, he would be entitled to a transport cost to the nearest hospital on actuals upto a maximum of 5% of hospital cost. All payments will be made by the insurance company to the clinics/hospitals directly and except for the transportation cost, no cash payment will be made to the workers;

(ii) Maternity Benefits of Rs. 1000 maximum or actuals for the member or the spouse, per year;

(iii) Sickness cover of Rs 750/- for earning head of family (during hospitalisation) for 15 days (only in excess of 3 days) during the policy period @ Rs 50/- per day.

(b) Life and Disability Cover

In case of Natural Death:	Rs. 30,000/-
In case of Death or total disability due to accident:	Rs. 75,000/-
In case of Partial Permanent Disability due to accident:	Rs. 37,500/-

(c) Old Age Security

(i) All BPL agricultural workers will get a monthly pension of Rs. 200 at 60 plus. This would be irrespective of the year of his/her registration with the scheme.

(ii) All agricultural workers other than BPL and registered in the scheme will be entitled to a Provident Fund which will accumulate to his account from the year of his/her registration.

(iii) At the end of 60th year the APL agricultural workers will have 3 options. He can continue with the provident fund scheme by contributing the full premium i.e. both the government's and his contribution, or, withdraw the whole amount of the Provident Fund accumulated to that date, or alternatively, he could buy an Annuity with the accumulated amount and the returns would be like his pension.

(iv) The Provident Fund Scheme can also be used as unemployment insurance. After 10 years' contribution, the worker, if he becomes unemployed and is verified to be so by the Workers Facilitation Centre (WFC), he would be entitled to draw up to 50% of the accumulated sum as unemployment benefits for a period of 6 months. After six months or before that if he becomes employed again, the worker will be able to continue with the scheme by renewing his contribution.

Organization

The organization model is federal in character where the implementation will be the responsibility of the State Social Security and Welfare Board for agricultural workers (SSSWB) with the assistance of WFC at the grass root level, supervised and monitored by the National Social Security and Welfare Board.

The structure is as follows:

(i) There will be a National Social Security and Welfare Board (NSSWB) at the central level, representatively constituted, with the central government as the prime mover. This National Board will be supervising and monitoring the implementation of the scheme at different levels and will also be responsible for running for National Social Security and Welfare Fund.

At the state level there would be a State Social Security and Welfare Board for agricultural workers (SSSWB), representatively constituted, which will be the main implementing agency at the grassroots level through Workers Facilitation Centre (WFC).

(ii) The WFC would be appointed by the SSSWB, keeping in mind the need to make them as representative as possible with the participation of institutions/organisations listed under section 27(1) of the Bill. WFC would perform the various functions as listed in section 27(2) of the Bill.

(iii) SSSWBs will negotiate with the insurance agency and other service providers with the help of NSSWF, the best possible terms for providing the prescribed benefits and also the selection of health care institutions.

(iv) SSSWBs would also set up their State Social Security and Welfare Fund (SSSWF) from sources specified in section 17, which would accumulate till they are transferred to the accounts of the beneficiaries held by the designated institutions such as Post Offices/ banks. National Social Security and Welfare Fund (NSSWF) contribution should also be deposited with SSSWF for being transmitted to the workers account once the scheme starts implementation.

Financing

The scheme would be financed by the National Social Security and Welfare Fund (NSSWF) through any of the sources as specified in section 8 of the Act. However, the share of contribution of the BPL workers, if any, would be borne by the Central Government.

The total outlay of the scheme proposed for agricultural workers when all of them are covered is estimated at Rs 19400 crore, which may be entirely borne by the Central Government. If however, the total cost is shared between the Centre and States in the ratio of 75:25, then, the Centre's and the State Governments' share is estimated at Rs 14550 crore and Rs 4850 crore respectively. The share of both Centre and States could be further reduced, if contributions of employers and workers or tax/ cess as mentioned in section 8 are available.

Annexure 2

UNORGANISED NON-AGRICULTURAL WORKERS' CONDITIONS OF WORK AND SOCIAL SECURITY BILL, 2007.

Statement of Objects and Reasons

Chapter I

PRELIMINARY

1. Short Title, Extent, Commencement and Application
2. Definitions
3. Rules of Evidence

Chapter II

CONDITIONS OF WORK TO BE ENSURED FOR THE WAGE WORKER AND HOMEWORKER

4. Physical Conditions of Work
5. Duration of Work
6. Conditions of Work and Payment of Wages

Chapter III

SOCIAL SECURITY BENEFITS

7. Framing of Schemes.

Chapter IV

NATIONAL SOCIAL SECURITY AND WELFARE FUND FOR UNORGANISED WORKERS

8. Constitution of a National Fund
9. Existing Welfare Boards
10. Exemption from Income Tax
11. Utilisation of the National Fund

Chapter V

NATIONAL SOCIAL SECURITY AND WELFARE BOARD FOR UNORGANISED WORKERS

12. Establishment and Incorporation
13. Functions of the Board
14. Composition of the Board
15. Secretariat of the Board

Chapter VI

STATE SOCIAL SECURITY AND WELFARE BOARDS FOR UNORGANISED NON-AGRICULTURAL WORKERS

16. Establishment of State Boards
17. State Fund
18. Functions
19. Secretariat of the Board

Chapter VII

REGISTRATION OF UNORGANISED NON-AGRICULTURAL WORKERS

20. Eligibility for registration and for social security benefits
21. Unique Identification Social Security Number
22. Identity card
23. Portability of registration
24. Cessation of registration
25. Membership of Existing Welfare Boards

Chapter VIII

DELIVERY OF SOCIAL SECURITY BENEFITS

26. Implementation Machinery
27. Workers' Facilitation Centres
28. Premium and Compensation/ Benefits

Chapter IX

ENFORCEMENT AND DISPUTE RESOLUTION BODIES

29. Disputes Resolution Council and Conciliation Committees
30. Functions and Powers of the Conciliation Committee and Dispute Resolution Council
31. Adjudication
32. Contravention of Provisions Regarding Employment of Unorganised Non-agricultural Workers

Chapter X

MISCELLANEOUS

33. Accounts and Audit
34. Power to Make Rules
35. Savings
36. Effect of Laws and Agreements Inconsistent with This Act

Statement of Objects and Reasons

The unorganised non-agricultural sector of the economy in India employs about 30 per cent of the total workforce. The workers in this sector may be broadly divided into wage workers, and self-employed workers (comprising independent self-employed as well as homeworkers). This Bill is intended to provide minimum conditions of work for those unorganised workers who are wage and homeworkers in the unorganised sector, as well as other wage workers whose minimum conditions of work are not regulated by any other legislation. This Bill is also intended to provide a measure of social security to the workers in the unorganised sector as well as informal/ unorganized workers in the organized sector. It mandates the Central and State governments to implement a package of National Minimum Social Security Scheme to which all unorganized workers would be entitled. It also provides a mechanism for dispute resolution for the unorganised workers.

UNORGANISED NON-AGRICULTURAL WORKERS' CONDITIONS OF WORK AND SOCIAL SECURITY BILL, 2007.

A
BILL

to provide for regulation of conditions of work, social security and welfare, and a dispute resolution mechanism for unorganised Non-agricultural workers and to provide for other matters connected therewith or incidental thereto.

BE it enacted by Parliament in the fifty-eighth year of the Republic of India as follows:-

Chapter I

PRELIMINARY

1. Short Title, Extent, Commencement and Application

(1) This Act may be called Unorganised Non-agricultural Workers' Conditions of Work and Social Security Act, 2007.

(2) It extends to the whole of India.

(3) It shall come into force on such date as the Government may, by notification in the Official Gazette, appoint, and different dates may be appointed for different States and different areas in a State and for different provisions of this Act, within six months from the date of the assent.

2. Definitions

For the purposes of this Act, unless the context otherwise requires, -

a) **"Adolescent"** means a person of the age of 14 years and above and who has not completed 18 years of age.

b) **"Agricultural worker"** means either a farmer (as defined in clause g below) or a wage worker engaged in agriculture.

Explanation: Workers eligible for protection under the Plantation Workers Act are excluded from the purview of this Act.

c) **"Agriculture"** means the following occupations:

(i) Farming, including the cultivation and tillage of soil, etc;

(ii) Dairy farming;

(iii) Production, cultivation, growing and harvesting of any horticultural commodity;

(iv) Raising of livestock, bee-keeping or poultry;

(v) Fishing and/ or fish farming or sericulture;

(vi) Any practice performed on a farm as incidental to, or in conjunction with, the farm operations (including any forestry or timbering operations and the preparation for market and delivery to storage or to market or to carriage for transportation of farm products);

(vii) Growing fodder or thatching grass or for grazing cattle.

d) **"Casual worker"** means a **wage worker** engaged in agriculture in consideration of wages, whose employment is of casual nature.

e) **"Child"** means a person who has not completed 14 years of age.

f) **"Employer"** means a natural or juridical person, or an association of such persons, by whom any unorganised *non-agricultural* worker is engaged or employed either directly or otherwise, in consideration of wages.

g) **"Farmer"** means any person engaged in agricultural activities, either individually or with one or more persons, and not owning or operating a holding of more than two hectares or such limits as may be notified from time to time by the State government.

h) **"Government"** means either Central Government, or State Government, or Union Territory administration, or local government, or Cantonment Boards as the case may be.

i) **"Homeworker"** means an unorganised non-agricultural sector worker involved in the production of goods or services as specified by an employer, in his / her own home or other premises of his / her choice (other than the work place of the employer) for remuneration, irrespective of whether or not the employer provides the equipment, materials or other inputs.

j) **"Identity card"** means a card issued to a **non-agricultural** worker carrying a unique number issued by the authorised agency of the State Board.

k) **"Migrant worker"** includes inter state and intra state migrant workers.

l) **"National Board"** means the National Social Security and Welfare Board for unorganised workers.

m) **"Non-agriculture"** means all occupations other than those included in agriculture and includes occupations related to Mining and Quarrying, Manufacturing, Electricity, Gas and water supply and Construction sectors, and services (including trade; hotels; restaurants; transport, storage and communications; financing, insurance, real estate and business services; and community, social and personal services).

n) **"Registered Non-agricultural Worker"** means an unorganised *non-agricultural* worker registered for benefits under this Act.

o) **"Remuneration"** means as defined in the Equal Remuneration Act, 1976.

p) **"Sexual Harassment"** is such unwelcome sexually determined behavior such as physical contact, advances, sexually coloured remarks, showing pornography or making sexual demands, whether verbal, textual, graphic or electronic or by any other actions, which may -.

(i) contain implied or overt promise of preferential treatment in that wage worker's employment; or

(ii) contain an implied or overt threat of detrimental treatment in that wage worker's employment or an implied or overt threat about the present or future employment status of that wage worker and includes the creation of a hostile working environment; or

(iii) interfere with a wage worker's work or create an intimidating, hostile or offensive work environment; or

(iv) be humiliating and may constitute a health and safety problem

Explanation1: Hostile Environment: A work environment is "hostile" when unwelcome verbal, non-verbal or physical behaviour focusing on sexuality is severe and pervasive enough to interfere with the victim's work performance or be intimidating or offensive to a reasonable person.

q) **"State Board"** means the (name of the State) State Social Security and Welfare Board for unorganised *non-agricultural* workers.

r) **"Self-employed non-agricultural worker"** means any person who operates a non-farm enterprise or engages in a non-agricultural profession, trade or business, either on own account individually or with one or more persons.

s) **"Unorganised non-agricultural sector"** consists of all unincorporated private non-agricultural enterprises owned by individuals or households engaged in the production and sale of non-agricultural goods and services and operated on a proprietary or a partnership basis and employing less than ten persons.

t) **Unorganised non-agricultural sector worker"** means a self-employed non-agricultural worker, a homeworker or a wage worker employed or engaged in the unorganised non-agricultural sector.

u) **""Unorganised non-agricultural worker"** means an unorganised non-agricultural sector worker and also includes workers in the organized non-agricultural sector not protected by the existing laws relating to conditions of work and/or social security.

v) **"Unorganised Worker"** means unorganised non-agricultural worker, and agricultural worker (except those eligible for protection under the Plantation Workers Act).

w) **"Wages"** means as defined in clause (vi) of section 2 of the Payment of Wages Act, 1936 (4 of 1936).

x) **"Wage worker"** means a person employed for a remuneration as an unorganised non-agricultural worker, directly by an employer or through any agency or contractor, whether exclusively for one employer or for one or more employers, whether simultaneously or otherwise, whether in cash and/or in kind, whether as a temporary or casual worker, or as a migrant worker, or workers employed by households including domestic workers.

3. Rules of Evidence

In this Act, notwithstanding anything contained in the Indian Evidence Act, 1872, the burden of proof that compliance with the provisions of the Act and the Scheme has been effected shall be entirely on the employer and the units of the Board, wherever applicable.

[Explanatory Note: This section facilitates shifting the burden of proof from the workers to the employer. This is a departure from the normal practice and ordinary rules of evidence, which places the burden on the plaintiff.]

Chapter II

CONDITIONS OF WORK TO BE ENSURED FOR THE WAGE WORKER AND HOMEWORKER

4. Physical Conditions of Work

(1) Every unorganised non-agricultural wage worker shall be entitled to the provisions for lighting, ventilation, safe drinking water, washing facilities, first aid box available at a place of work maintained by the employer and reasonable housing and provision of basic amenities for seasonal migrant workers shall be as may be prescribed.

(2) Every employer shall provide the unorganised wage or homeworker with adequate safety equipment while handling hazardous substances and equipments. The State Board shall carry out periodic studies on occupational hazards arising in this sector and develop suitable outreach/extension programmes for this purpose.

(3) Every employer shall compensate a wage or homeworker for any accident or occupational hazard arising out of or in the course of employment that results in any temporary, permanent, partial or total disablement of the wage worker, at rates to be specified in this behalf.

(4) The employer shall ensure that there is no sexual harassment of the non-agricultural wage worker at the place of work. The state government shall make appropriate rules concerning the disciplinary action that may be taken by an employer where a complaint of sexual harassment is established against a wage worker; and the compensation payable by an employer where a case of sexual harassment is established against the employer himself/herself.

(5) The State Board shall make rules with respect to child care facilities to be made available at local levels.

5. Duration of Work

(1) The normal hours of work of a non-agricultural wage worker shall be limited to eight hours a day beyond which a worker shall be paid overtime at double the normal rate of wages per hour.

(2) Every eight hour working day of the non-agricultural wage worker shall have at least an half hour break, so however that the spread over of work shall not exceed ten hours.

(3) Women and adolescents shall not be employed as non-agricultural wage workers between the hours of 9 p.m. and 5 a.m., except where permitted under rules made in this behalf.

(4) Every non-agricultural wage worker shall be entitled to one paid day of rest after completing six continuous days of employment by or under a single employer.

6. Conditions of Work and Payment of Wages

(1) No employer shall employ any unorganised non-agricultural wage worker or homeworker, in contravention of the existing Acts which are applicable to the worker. In particular, the employer shall comply with the following Acts:

a) Bonded Labour System (Abolition) Act, 1976;

b) Child Labour (Prohibition and Regulation) Act, 1986;

c) The Employment of Manual scavengers and Construction of Dry Latrines (Prohibition) Act, 1993;

d) Minimum Wages Act, 1948; and

e) Equal Remuneration Act, 1976

(2) (a) The Central government shall notify a National Minimum Wage.

(b) The National Minimum Wage shall apply to all unorganised non-agricultural wage and homeworkers in employments not notified under the Minimum Wages Act.

Provided that where the wage under the Minimum Wages Act is lower than the National Minimum Wage, the concerned State Government shall amend the prescribed Minimum Wage to bring it in conformity with the National Minimum Wage.

Provided further that till such time as this is done, the wage worker shall be entitled to receive the National Minimum Wage.

(c) The Central Government shall fix a National Minimum Wage for all employments, after taking into account the minimum basic needs of the wage and homeworkers and his/her family, variations in the cost of living in different areas and other parameters on the basis of consultation with a tripartite body consisting of workers, employers and the Government representatives.

(d) The National Minimum Wage shall be announced by the Central Government within one year of the implementation of this Act and shall be periodically reviewed through a modality prescribed by the National Board.

Provided that, till the announcement of the National Minimum Wage as above, the national floor level minimum wage recommended by the Ministry of Labour for 2004-05, shall, after adjusting for cost of living changes in different areas, be treated as the National Minimum Wage.

(3) Where the wages of a wage worker or homeworker are determined by a piece rate system, the earnings of a non-agricultural worker working for 8 hours should be at least equal to the time rated minimum wages fixed for that category of work in the state concerned, and where the rates have not been fixed under the Minimum Wages Act, 1948 in the relevant state, the rates as fixed under clause (2) above.

(4) Wages in employments performed predominantly by women shall be brought on par with employments certified as equivalent in value by an Employment Certification Committee to be constituted by the State Board. The Employment Certification Committee shall periodically evaluate employments in the state for this purpose.

(5) Wages of non-agricultural workers shall be duly paid for the periods agreed upon. The wage period can on no account exceed one month; any delay in payment beyond this periods will require the employer to pay penal rates of interest, as specified in this behalf, for the period of the delay to the non-agricultural wage worker.

(6) There shall be no deduction from wages/remuneration due to a wage/homeworker, including in such cases where such wages are paid as advance to the worker, in the form of interest, payments to contractors or agents, overvaluation of goods supplied or basic amenities provided including accommodation in the case of seasonal migrant workers, fines, inadequate or poor quality output, except in accordance with rules made in this behalf by the State Government.

(7) Where a homeworker has supplied his/her own tools, equipment or used part of his/her own dwelling for any process, the value of such contribution shall be ascertained by the employer and be added to the wages payable to such worker; provided however that the amount imputed for this purpose shall not be less than such percentage or premium as specified by the State Government.

(8) (a) Every unorganised wage and homeworker shall receive a wage slip from his/her employer providing details of remuneration received by him/her.

(b) Every unorganised non-agricultural wage worker, except casual workers, shall receive a letter of employment from his/her employer, stating the terms of employment of his/her employment.

(c) Every employer shall maintain such registers and records as may be necessary to verify the employer's claim regarding the employment status of non-agricultural wage and homeworkers and details of payments made to them.

(9) All unorganised non-agricultural workers shall have the right to organise, by forming trade unions or other membership based organisations, for representation and collective bargaining in various fora. **(Note: This applies to both wage workers and self -mployed workers)**

(10) No employer shall discriminate against any unorganised non-agricultural wage worker on the grounds of sex, caste, religion, incidence of HIV-AIDS, migration status, place of origin, in employment, wage rates and conditions of work as laid down in this Act.

Chapter III

SOCIAL SECURITY BENEFITS

7. Framing of Schemes

(1) By this Act, the Central Government shall formulate and notify in the official Gazette a National Social Security Scheme containing such basic features as provided for in the Schedule to this Act.

(2) The National Social Security Scheme for the unorganised non-agricultural workers shall consist of a package of the following national minimum social security benefits:

(i) Health benefits for self, spouse and children below the age of 18 years, and maternity benefits for women workers or spouse of men workers;

(ii) Life and disability cover for natural or accidental death of the worker;

(iii) Old age security in the form of old age pension for workers above the age of 60 years or Provident Fund.

(3) The Scheme will be applicable to all eligible workers within a period of five years.

(4) In addition to the national minimum, the Central Government may frame on recommendations of the National Board such schemes as it may deem necessary or finance such schemes of the State governments/ Welfare Boards as it may find appropriate, subject to availability of finance by such means as mentioned in Section 8 and may include those listed under (5) below.

(5) The State Government on recommendations of the State Board may formulate such unorganised worker-based schemes as it may find appropriate to: (a) strengthen the national minimum social security by way of its own contribution, and/or (b) design and implement additional social security benefits through its own schemes. These may include:

a) Provident Fund schemes;
b) Employment injury benefit scheme;
c) Housing schemes;
d) Educational schemes for children of workers;
e) Skill up-gradation of workers;
f) Funeral assistance;
g) Marriage of daughters; and
h) Any other schemes to enhance the socio-economic security of the unorganised worker.

(6) The Central Government shall have the power to remove difficulties that arise in giving effect to the provisions of the Scheme by an order published in the Official Gazette, not inconsistent with the provisions of the Act, as appears to it necessary or expedient for the removal of the difficulty.

Chapter IV

NATIONAL SOCIAL SECURITY AND WELFARE FUND FOR UNORGANISED WORKERS

8. Constitution of a National Fund

The Central Government shall create a National Social Security and Welfare Fund to which contributions shall accrue from the following sources:

a) Grants and loans from the Central Government;

b) Contributions from workers, employers and Governments in the form and manner to be prescribed in the specified National Minimum Social Security Scheme, provided that the Central government may exempt any class of unorganised workers or employers from making their contribution under such conditions as may be specified;

c) Any tax or cess that the Central Government may impose for the purpose of providing social security for unorganised workers;

d) Any tax or cess that the Central Government may impose on commodities and/or services in lieu of employers' contributions (which are either difficult to collect or appropriate employers in the unorganised sector are not directly identifiable).

In addition to the above, contributions may also accrue from the following sources:

e) Contributions from the national financial/developmental institutions; and

f) Any voluntary contribution from individuals or institutions.

9. Existing Welfare Boards

Notwithstanding any other provision contained under any other law, the Appropriate Government may merge any existing Welfare Board/Boards and Welfare Fund/Funds constituted under any other law into the Board and Fund created under this Act.

10 Exemption from Income Tax

All financial contributions made by individuals and institutions to the National Social Security and Welfare Fund will be exempted from the payment of income tax under the Income Tax Act.

11. Utilisation of the National Fund

All contributions accruing to the National Board shall be credited to the Fund, which shall be applied for meeting the following:

a) Expenses on the National Social Security Scheme and any other social security schemes of the Central Government;

b) Grants to the State Boards, including for the purposes of the functioning of the Workers' Facilitation Centres;

c) Expenses on the administration of the schemes;

d) Investment in permitted schemes;

e) Any other item in connection with the administration of this Act.

Chapter V

NATIONAL SOCIAL SECURITY AND WELFARE BOARD FOR UNORGANISED WORKERS

12. Establishment and Incorporation

With effect from such date as the Central Government may, by notification appoint, there shall be established for the purposes of this Act, a Board to be called the National Social Security and Welfare Board for Unorganised Workers.

13. Functions of the Board

The National Board shall perform the following functions:

a) Administration of this Act and formulation of policies at the national level, and shall have such powers as may be laid down to direct, co-ordinate, supervise, and monitor the functioning of State Boards and the Central Welfare Boards;

b) Review the working including auditing of the State Boards and the Central Welfare Boards every four years and make suitable recommendations to the Government(s) concerned for further improvement;

c) Manage and maintain the National Social Security and Welfare Fund, provide financial assistance to State Boards; recommend new schemes and programmes and projects for implementation through the Fund;

d) Advise the Central Government on policy matters relating to social security, and extension of schemes of social security such as ESI and EPF to unorganised sector workers; and health, safety and welfare of workers;

e) Assist in capacity building of the State Boards;

f) Collect, compile and publish statistics relating to the unorganised sector and undertake such promotional activities as may be decided from time to time;

g) Monitor and review the impact of existing schemes, policies and programmes of various Ministries and Departments of Government of India on the unorganised sector workers and make appropriate recommendations;

h) Advise the Government regarding the promotion of gainful employment opportunities and promotion of livelihood options and matters relating to welfare of unorganised sector workers;

i) Identify skill and training requirements for unorganized workers and to advise the government accordingly;

j) Carry out periodic surveys on the condition of work in the unorganised sector and make suitable recommendations to the government;

k) Hold public hearings to entertain petitions submitted by the unorganised sector workers and make appropriate recommendations;

l) Advise government on special protection measures for migrant workers and their families in providing the ration cards, housing and education to their children; and

m) Provide for guidelines of periodic review of the national minimum wages fixed by the Central Government after taking into account the minimum basic needs of the wage workers and his/her family.

14. Composition of the Board

(1) The National Welfare Board for unorganised workers shall be constituted by the Central Government consisting of the following member organisations:

  a) Central Trade Unions and Agricultural Worker Unions; National level organizations, including federation of such organizations, of unorganised sector workers including the self-employed;

  b) National Level organisations of employers of unorganised sector workers such as associations of tiny and small scale industries;

  c) Central Government Ministries, State Boards, Central Welfare Boards and Public Agencies; and

  d) Experts in the area of management of insurance products and services; social security and related issues in the unorganized sector; management of finances, and other organizations and stakeholders working with the unorganized sector.

(2) The Central Government shall decide the criteria, number and names of such organisations to be represented on the National Board, with adequate representation of wage workers, self-employed workers and women representing the workers.

(3) The National Board shall work through a Secretariat.

(4) The Chairman of the National Board shall be nominated by the Central Government from amongst persons of eminence in the fields of labour welfare, management, finance, law and administration. The Member Secretary, who shall be the chief executive officer shall be designated by the Central Government being a person not below the rank of Secretary to the Government of India.

(5) The Board shall meet as often as possible but not less than twice a year.

15. Secretariat of the Board

The National Board shall have a secretariat with adequate professional and other staff. The staff of the National Board shall be governed by the Central Government rules and regulations existing from time to time.

The annual budget of the National Board shall be prepared by the Secretariat and placed before the full Board for approval.

Chapter VI

STATE SOCIAL SECURITY AND WELFARE BOARDS FOR UNORGANISED NON-AGRICULTURAL WORKERS

16. Establishment of State Boards

(1) Each State shall have a State Board to implement the national minimum social security as well as design and implement State-level social security and welfare programmes for unorganised non-agricultural workers. The State governments shall constitute the State Boards within one year of the date of commencement of this Act. The State Boards shall have the following as its members:

a) Trade Unions and non- agricultural Worker Unions; State level organizations, including federation of such organizations of unorganised non-agricultural sector workers including the self-employed;

b) State Level organisations of employers of unorganised non-agricultural sector workers;

c) State Government Ministries, Welfare Boards and Public Agencies; and

d) Experts in the area of management of insurance products and services; social security and related issues in the unorganized non-agricultural sector; management of finances, and other organizations and stakeholders working with the unorganized non-agricultural sector.

(2) The State Government shall decide the criteria, number and names of such organisations to be represented on the State Board, with adequate representation of wage workers, self-employed and women representing the workers.

(3) The State Board shall work through a Secretariat.

(4) The Chairman of the State Board shall be nominated by the State Government from amongst persons of eminence in the fields of labour welfare, management, finance, law and administration. The Member Secretary, who shall be the chief executive officer shall be designated by the State Government being a person not below the rank of Secretary to the Government of the State.

(5) The Board shall meet as often as possible but not less than twice a year.

17. State Fund

(1) The State government shall create a State Social Security and Welfare Fund to which contributions shall accrue from the following sources:

(i) Grants and loans from National Board and the State government;

(ii) Any tax or cess that the State government may impose on commodities and/or services in lieu of employers' contributions (which are either difficult to collect or appropriate employers in the unorganised Sector are not directly identifiable);

(iii) Contribution toward additional social security scheme (if any) formulated by the State Board;

(iv) Contributions from the national financial/developmental institutions; and

(v) Any voluntary contribution from individuals or institutions.

(2) All financial contributions made by individuals and institutions to the State Social Security and welfare Fund will be exempted from the payment of income tax under the Income Tax Act.

(3) All contributions accruing to the State Boards shall be credited to the State Social Security and Welfare Fund which shall be applied for meeting the following:

a) Expenses on the implementation of the national minimum social security and additional social security schemes of the State Government;

b) Grants to the Welfare Boards and the Workers' Facilitation Centres;

c) Expenses on the administration of the State Board as per the annual budget approved by the Executive Council;

d) Investment in permitted schemes; and

e) Any other item in connection with the administration of this Act.

18. Functions

The State Boards will perform the following functions:

a) Administer this Act at the State level including ensuring collection of contributions, maintenance of individual accounts of the registered non-agricultural workers and records of receipt of contribution from individual employers;

b) Implement the national minimum social security for unorganised non-agricultural workers through appropriate organisational arrangements, negotiate with the providers for the best possible offers, and stipulate norms for the evaluation of the work done by the Workers' Facilitation Centres;

c) Frame guidelines to ensure portability of benefits to workers;

d) Frame and implement social security schemes, in addition to the National Social Security Scheme, that the State Board may design in consultation with the State government;

e) Provide financial assistance to other member organisations implementing social security programmes;

f) Advise the State government on policy matters relating to social security, health and safety and welfare of non-agricultural workers;

g) Create awareness among the unorganised non-agricultural workers about the need for social security registration and the existence of various social security schemes;

h) Collect, compile and publish statistics, with the help of statistical organisations, regarding non-agricultural workers and their conditions of work, and employers who engage these workers at the *Panchayat*/ Municipal, District, State levels with such details as gender and age, nature of occupation, level of earnings, etc.;

i) Review the working of the Welfare Boards and other implementing agencies on the basis of annual reports and statements of audited accounts or specially commissioned reports and make suitable recommendations to the government(s) concerned for further improvement;

j) Assist in capacity building of Workers Welfare Boards and Workers' Facilitation Centres;

k) Initiate innovative approaches, through interaction across sectors and constituencies, for the enhancement of welfare, working conditions and productivity of unorganised non-agricultural workers;

l) Submit annual report to the National Board within four months from the last day of the previous financial year along with an audited statement of accounts;

m) Monitor and review the impact of existing schemes, policies and programmes of various Ministries and Departments of the concerned State Government on the unorganised non-agricultural sector workers and make appropriate recommendations;

n) Advise the Government regarding the promotion of gainful employment opportunities and promotion of livelihood options for unorganised non-agricultural sector workers;

o) Encourage the promotion of labour organizations and cooperatives to secure gainful employment and dignified conditions of work;

p) Identify skill and training requirements for both self-employed workers and wage workers in the unorganised non-agricultural sector and to advise the government accordingly;

q) Carry out periodic surveys on the condition of work in the unorganised non-agricultural sector and make suitable recommendations to the government;

r) Hold public hearings to entertain petitions submitted by the unorganised non-agricultural sector workers and make appropriate recommendations;

s) Carry out surveys to determine the safety and health standards required in different occupations and employments in the unorganised non-agricultural sector, and publish manuals and outreach programmes for worker safety;

t) Review the Minimum Wages for the state after taking into account the cost of living and minimum basic needs of the non-agricultural wage workers and his/her family;

u) Constitute Employment Certification Committee to bring the wages in employments performed predominantly by women on par with employments certified as equivalent in value and periodically evaluate employments in the state for this purpose;

v) Carry out periodic studies on occupational hazards arising in this sector and develop suitable outreach/ extension programmes for this purpose; and

w) Make provisions for improvement in housing, rational use of public spaces keeping in mind the needs of the self-employed non-agricultural workers working from their homes/rented premises/streets or public spaces to improve their working conditions .

19. Secretariat of the Board

The State Board shall have a secretariat with adequate professional and other staff. The staff of the State Board shall be governed by the State government rules and regulations existing from time to time.

Chapter VII

REGISTRATION OF UNORGANISED NON-AGRICULTURAL WORKERS

20. Eligibility for Registration and for Social Security Benefits

Every unorganised non-agricultural worker shall be eligible for registration subject to the following conditions:

a) He/she should have completed 18 years of age;

b) His monthly income does not exceed Rs.7000/- in 2007 (roughly equivalent to Rs. 6500/- per month recommended by the Indian Labour Conference held in December 2005); and

c) A self-declaration confirming that he/she is an unorganised non-agricultural worker.

21. Unique Identification Social Security Number

Each registered non-agricultural worker shall be eligible for receiving a Unique Identification Social Security Number in the form of an Identity Card issued in the name of the State Board.

22. Identity Card

The State Government shall decide the manner of registration of unorganized non-agricultural sector workers, issuance of identity cards and manner of record keeping at the district level.

23. Portability of Registration

The Identity Card issued to non-agricultural workers shall remain valid even in the case of migration to another district in the country and the new address can be changed on application to the authority concerned.

24. Cessation of Registration

The National Board shall draw up rules to decide on the period of validity of registration, renewals, cessation of registration and settlement of claims on the death of the card holder.

25. Membership of Existing Welfare Boards

In case, any unorganised non-agricultural worker is eligible for benefit under one or more existing Central or Welfare Boards, in addition to his eligibility for the National Minimum Social Security Scheme,

(1) The non-agricultural worker shall retain the option of membership of the Fund with the highest benefit.

(2) The National/State Board may decide the criteria on which the non-agricultural worker can be eligible for benefit under the National Minimum Social Security Scheme in addition to membership in other Boards/schemes.

Chapter VIII

DELIVERY OF SOCIAL SECURITY BENEFITS

26. Implementation Machinery

The State Boards shall be responsible for the delivery of mandatory minimum social security benefits and shall decide the manner in which social security benefits shall have to be delivered to the registered non-agricultural workers. This may include tie-ups with local organisations like banks, post offices and insurance companies.

27. Workers' Facilitation Centres

(1) In order to extend coverage and reach the unorganised non-agricultural workers in remote areas, the State Boards may designate any one or more of the following at the local level as Workers' Facilitation Centres (WFC):

a) Existing Worker Welfare Boards and their local offices;

b) Local Panchayati Raj Institutions (PRI) or urban local bodies;

c) Organisations of workers including trade unions, associations and co-operatives in the unorganised non-agricultural sector;

d) Self-help Groups (SHGs); and

e) Non-profit organisations working among the unorganised non-agricultural sector workers.

(2) Such designated Workers' Facilitation Centres shall perform the following functions:

a) Disseminate information on available social security schemes for the non-agricultural workers;

b) Facilitate the filling, processing and forwarding of application forms for registration of non-agricultural workers;

c) Obtain registration from the District Committee and deliver the Identity Cards to the registered non-agricultural workers;

d) Facilitate the enrollment of the registered non-agricultural workers in social security schemes; and

e) Facilitate the delivery of social security benefits through the institutions designated to deliver such social security (insurance companies, post offices, Departments of the State/ Central Government and other institutions concerned).

(3) The State Boards shall compensate the costs incurred by the Workers' Facilitation Centres for performance of its functions.

28. Premium and Compensation/Benefits

(1) The National Board shall decide the amount and manner of payment of contribution/fee by the non-agricultural workers to the National Social Security Schemes.

(2) For schemes initiated by the State Boards, the State Board concerned shall decide the contributions of non-agricultural workers and employers.

(3) The claim of registered non-agricultural workers for social security benefits shall lie solely against the State Board and it shall be the responsibility of the State Board to settle the dues, if any.

Chapter IX

ENFORCEMENT AND DISPUTE RESOLUTION BODIES

29. Disputes Resolution Council and Conciliation Committees

(1) The State Government shall, by rules, constitute Dispute Resolution Council (DRC) at District level and Conciliation Committees (CC) at an appropriate level below the district level i.e Block/Tehsil/ Mandal level, for resolution of disputes relating to the non observance of provisions of this Act arising amongst the Unorganised non-agricultural wage workers / homeworkers, employers, Workers' Facilitation Centres and State Boards.

(2) The Composition of the DRCs and CCs shall be tripartite and consist of an officer designated by the State Government to be the Member Secretary, one person nominated from the most representative of membership-based organisations of the unorganised non-agricultural workers in that State, having membership in the district, and a person nominated from the most representative organisation of employers' organisations in the unorganised non-agricultural sector in the state. The State government, may, if it thinks fit, appoint two persons as assessors to advice the conciliation Committee on the proceedings before it.

(3) When there is a complaint regarding sexual harassment, the CC/DRC shall co-opt two other members from the Panchayats/local bodies, who shall be women, at the time of dealing with such complaints. The CC/DRC, if satisfied that a case of sexual harassment is established, direct the employer to ensure that necessary action is taken against the person guilty of such conduct.

(4) The honorarium and/ or the allowances to be paid to the workers and employers representatives on the DRC shall be determined by the State Government.

(5) The persons to be appointed as members from each of the categories specified in sub-section (2), the term of office and other related conditions, the procedure to be followed in the discharge of their

functions, conduct of meetings, periodicity of meetings and the manner of filling vacancies among the members of the CC/DRC, shall be such as may be prescribed by the State Government.

(Note: In order to determine the most representative organisation, membership figures including the verification of trade unions carried out by the CLC may be relied upon.)

30. Functions and powers of the Conciliation Committee and Dispute Resolution Council

(1) Any unorganised non-agricultural wage worker or employer or an organisation representing such worker or Workers' Facilitation Centres or the State Board may raise a dispute relating to the non-observance of provisions of this Act by filing a complaint before the Conciliation Committee in the manner prescribed by the State Government. The DRC may also take *suo moto* cognizance of such disputes.

(2) Every complaint so filed shall be deemed to be a dispute under this Act notwithstanding that such a complaint had not been referred to the employer at the first instance, and been rejected.

(3) The status of employment of non-agricultural workers in the dispute raised before the CC or DRC shall not be affected merely for the reason that a complaint regarding non observance of provisions of this Act has been raised before the DRC or CC.

(4) (a) Upon reference of a dispute, the Conciliation Committee shall proceed to arrive at a conciliated settlement. The Conciliation Committee shall, for the purpose of bringing about a settlement of the dispute, without delay, investigate the dispute and all matters connected therewith, and may do all such things as they think fit for the purpose of inducing the parties to come to a fair and amicable settlement of the dispute.

(b) The Labour Enforcement Officers (LEOs) of the Labour Departments of the concerned state shall assist the CC/DRC in their duties and shall carry such investigation of complaints as required by the CC/DRC.

(c) Where the CC/DRC apprehends violation of the provisions of this Act the LEOs may be directed to investigate and report the matter expeditiously.

(5) The CC/DRC or the LEOs designated for this purpose under sub-section 4(b) above may for the purpose of investigating the dispute, after giving reasonable notice, enter the premises to which the dispute relates. The Conciliation Committee shall also have the powers under the Code of Civil Procedure 1908 to enforce the attendance of parties, compel the production of documents and material objects.

(6) The Conciliation Committee may if it thinks fit appoint one or more persons having special knowledge of the matter under consideration to advise it on the proceeding before it.

(7) The time limit for the conclusion of the proceedings of the CC shall not exceed four weeks. Where the parties to the dispute apply in the prescribed manner, whether jointly or separately, to the CC for the extension of such period and the member-secretary of the CC considers it necessary or expedient to extend such period, he/she may for reasons to be recorded in writing, extend such period by such further period as he/she may think fit;

Provided that no proceedings before a CC shall lapse merely on the ground that the period specified under this sub section has expired without such proceedings being completed.

(8) If the Conciliation Committee is able to arrive at a conciliated settlement, it shall record its finding to such effect and shall issue such directions as considered necessary.

(9) Upon failure of such conciliation proceedings, the Conciliation Committee shall record its findings and refer the dispute to the DRC, which shall within two weeks of receipt of reference, refer the matter to the adjudicator provided in this section.

(10) Where a dispute is raised directly before the DRC, the DRC shall ordinarily refer the dispute to the CC below it, under whose jurisdiction the dispute falls.

(11) In cases of disputes raised directly before it or referred to it by the CC under subsection (9) above, the DRC may itself seek to bring about a conciliated settlement.

(12) In such cases, the DRC shall have all the powers mentioned in section (4) and (5) specified above.

(13) If the DRC is able to arrive at a conciliated settlement, it shall record its finding to such effect and shall issue such directions as considered necessary.

(14) In case of failure of conciliation, the DRC shall record its finding and refer the matter directly to the Adjudicator referred to in section 31, within 4 weeks of the reference of the dispute. Where the parties to the dispute apply in the prescribed manner, whether jointly or separately, to the DRC for the extension of such period and the member-secretary of the DRC considers it necessary or expedient to extend such period, he/she may for reasons to be recorded in writing, extend such period by such further period as he/she may think fit.

Provided that no proceedings before a DRC shall lapse merely on the ground that the period specified under this sub section has expired without such proceedings being completed.

(15) The DRC shall also monitor the functioning of the CCs.

(16) Where the dispute pertains to any matter covered by any law mentioned in Section 6(1), the CC/DRC shall forward the complaint to the appropriate authority created under the relevant Act for adjudication.

31. Adjudication

(1) The State Government shall by notification in the Official Gazette appoint any officer of the Government not below the rank of a District Labour Officer for each district, or any officer with experience as Civil Judge or as Magistrate to be the Adjudicator under the section. The Adjudicator shall hold sessions in such Block/ Tehsil/Mandal towns and with such frequency, as may be specified in the rules made in this behalf by the State Government, in order to adjudicate upon the disputes referred to it by the DRCs at the Block/ Tehsil/Mandal level.

(Note: NO appeal has been provided for under this Act. Moving the High Courts under Art. 226 of the Constitution would of course be available).

(2) The State Government shall issue such notifications and directions as are necessary to ensure that the adjudication proceedings are concluded expeditiously with minimum loss of time and costs to the parties involved. The award of the Adjudicator shall be publicised in the manner as prescribed by the State Government.

(3) The designated department(s) of the State Government concerned shall be responsible for enforcement and implementation of the provisions of this Act.

32. Contravention of Provisions Regarding Employment of Unorganised Non-agricultural Workers

(1) Whoever contravenes any provisions of this Act or the rules made there under, other than those made punishable under any other law, regarding the employment of unorganised, **non-agricultural** workers shall be punishable with imprisonment for a term which may extend to one year, or with fine which may extend to five thousand rupees, or with both, and in case of continuing contravention, with additional fine which may extend up to one hundred rupees for every day during which such contravention continues.

(2). No court shall take cognizance of an offence punishable under this Act or the abetment of any such offence, save on a complaint made by, or the previous sanction in writing of or under the authority of the State Government. No court inferior to that of a Metropolitan Magistrate or a judicial magistrate of the first class shall try any offence punishable under this Act.

(3). No suit, prosecution or other legal proceeding shall lie against any person for anything done in good faith or intended to be done in pursuance of this Act or rules.

(4) No court shall take cognisance of an offence punishable under this Act unless the complaint is made within six months from the date on which the alleged commission of the offence came to the knowledge of the CC or the DRC concerned.

(5) Any person who commits a breach of any conciliated settlement arrived at in the CC or DRC or final award by the adjudicator, shall be punishable with imprisonment for a term which may extend to six months, or with fine, or with both, [and where the breach is a continuing one, with a further fine which may extend to two hundred rupees for every day during which the breach continues after the conviction for the first] and the Court trying the offence, if it fines the offender, may direct that the whole or any part of the fine realized from him shall be paid, by way of compensation, to any person who, in its opinion, has been injured by such breach.

(6) Where any money is due to a unorganised sector non-agricultural worker under a settlement or an award, the workman himself or any other person authorized by him in writing in this behalf, or, in the case of the death of the workman, his assignee or heirs may, without prejudice to any other mode of recovery, make an application to the state government for the recovery of the money due to him, and if the state government is satisfied that any money is so due, it shall issue a certificate for that amount to the Collector who shall proceed to recover the same in the same manner as an arrear of land revenue.

Chapter X

MISCELLANEOUS

33. Accounts and Audit

(a) The National Board and the State Boards shall maintain proper accounts and other relevant records and prepare annual statements of accounts in such form as may be prescribed.

(b) The National Board shall furnish to the Central Government, before such date as may be prescribed, the audited copy of the consolidated account of itself and the Funds together with the auditor's report.

34. Power to Make Rules

The Central and State governments shall have the power to make rules for the purposes of carrying out the objects of the Act.

35. Savings

(1) This law will not affect the application of any other State or Central Acts which applies to the unorganised non-agricultural worker or to the employer under this Act. (Note: Even if the employer or establishment is covered, the non-agricultural worker who is not covered under the formal sector law would get benefit under this law for the matter covered here).

(2) Notwithstanding anything contained in this Act, wherever any unorganised non-agricultural worker is eligible for superior or better benefits under any existing law in force the worker shall continue to be entitled for such benefits.

36. Effect of Laws and Agreements Inconsistent with This Act

(1) The provisions of this Act shall have effect notwithstanding anything inconsistent therewith contained in any other law or in the terms of any award, agreement or contract of service, whether made before or after the coming into force of this Act.

(2) Nothing contained in this Act shall be construed to preclude a unorganised non-agricultural worker from entering into an agreement with his/her employer for granting him/her rights or privileges in respect of any matter which are more favourable to him/ her than those to which he/she would be entitled under this Act.

******

Schedule of the Unorganised Non-agricultural Workers Conditions Of Work And Social Security Bill, 2007.

(See section 7 (1))

National Social Security Scheme for Unorganised Non-agricultural Workers

Back ground

The unorganised non-agricultural workers in the Unorganised Sector face problems that arise out of deficiency or capability deprivation in terms of inadequate employment, low earnings, low health, etc., as well as of adversity in the absence of fall back mechanisms (safety net). These workers have limited or no formal social security cover which increases their vulnerability during times of illness, old age, unemployment and untimely death. The absence of social security mechanisms is a critical factor in downturns in the conditions of these households, many of whom are already very poor. It destroys the workers ability to contribute meaningfully, and to increasing production and productivity. It leads to disaffection increasing social costs, widespread crimes, and persistent ill health. Presently, less than 6% of the entire unorganised sector workforce has recourse to any social security cover.

Objectives

1. To provide for a right based entitlement for the unorganised non-agricultural workers,_and
2. To provide for a universal national minimum social security scheme to cover all the workers in the unorganised non-agricultural sector in a phased manner within a period of 5 years.

Definitions

Words and expressions shall have the meaning respectively assigned to them under Section. 2 of the Act.

Coverage and eligibility

This scheme may be called the National Social Security Scheme, 2007.

This scheme shall come into force on....

This scheme applies to all unorganised non-agricultural workers, hereafter referred to as 'worker' to whom the Act extends who

a) has completed 18 years of age;

b) whose monthly income does not exceed Rs.7000/- in 2007 (roughly equivalent to Rs. 6500/- per month recommended by the Indian Labour Conference held in December 2005);

c) has submitted a prescribed self-declaration form confirming that he/she is an unorganised non-agricultural worker ; and

d) has paid the contribution/ fee as prescribed.

Benefits

The national social security scheme shall provide for a package of the following minimum benefits:

(a) Health Insurance

(i) Each worker will be entitled to hospitalization for himself and his family members, costing Rs. 15000 a year in total with Rs. 10000 maximum per ailment in designated, hospitals or clinics, public or private, recognized by the State Board, with at least 15 beds. If there is no such clinic available within

10 kilometers from the worker's residence, he would be entitled to a transport cost to the nearest hospital on actuals upto a maximum of 5% of hospital cost. All payments will be made by the insurance company to the clinics/hospitals directly and except for the transportation cost, no cash payment will be made to the workers;

(ii) Maternity Benefits of Rs. 1000 maximum or actuals for the member or the spouse, per year

(iii) Sickness cover of Rs 750/- for earning head of family (during hospitalisation) for 15 days (only in excess of 3 days) during the policy period @ Rs 50/- per day.

(b) Life and Disability Cover

In case of Natural Death:	Rs. 30,000/-
In case of Death or total disability due to accident:	Rs. 75,000/-
In case of Partial Permanent Disability due to accident:	Rs. 37,500/-

(c) Old Age Security

(v) All BPL unorganised non-agricultural workers will get a monthly pension of Rs. 200 at 60 plus. This would be irrespective of the year of his/her registration with the scheme.

(vi) All unorganised non-agricultural workers other than BPL and registered in the scheme will be entitled to a Provident Fund which will accumulate to his account from the year of his/her registration.

(vii) At the end of 60th year the APL unorganised non-agricultural worker will have 3 options. He can continue with the provident fund scheme by contributing the full premium i.e. both the government's and his contribution, or, withdraw the whole amount of the Provident Fund accumulated to that date, or alternatively, he could buy an Annuity with the accumulated amount and the returns would be like his pension.

(viii) The Provident Fund Scheme can also be used as unemployment insurance. After 10 years' contribution, the worker, if he becomes unemployed and is verified to be so by the Workers Facilitation Centre (WFC), he would be entitled to draw up to 50% of the accumulated sum as unemployment benefits for a period of 6 months. After six months or before that if he becomes employed again, the worker will be able to continue with the scheme by renewing his contribution.

Organization

The organization model is federal in character where the implementation will be the responsibility of the State Social Security and Welfare Board for unorganised non-agricultural workers (SSSWB) with the assistance of WFC at the grass root level, supervised and monitored by the National Social Security and Welfare Board.

The structure is as follows:

(i) There will be a National Social Security and Welfare Board (NSSWB) at the central level, representatively constituted, with the central government as the prime mover. This National Board will be supervising and monitoring the implementation of the scheme at different levels and will also be responsible for running for National Social Security and Welfare Fund (NSSWF).

At the state level there would be a State Social Security and Welfare Board for unorganised non-agricultural workers (SSSWB), representatively constituted, which will be the main implementing agency at the grassroots level through Workers Facilitation Centre (WFC).

(ii) The WFC would be appointed by the SSSWB, keeping in mind the need to make them as representative as possible with the participation of institutions/organisations listed under section 27(1) of the Bill. WFC would perform the various functions as listed in section 27(2) of the Bill.

(iii) SSSWBs will negotiate with the insurance agency and other service providers with the help of National Social Security and Welfare Fund (NSSWF), the best possible terms for providing the prescribed benefits and also the selection of health care institutions.

(iv) SSSWBs would also set up their State Social Security and Welfare Fund (SSSWF) from sources specified in section 17, which would accumulate till they are transferred to the accounts of the beneficiaries held by the designated institutions such as Post Offices/ banks. National Social Security and Welfare Fund (NSSWF) contribution should also be deposited with SSSWF for being transmitted to the workers account once the scheme starts implementation.

Financing

The scheme would be financed by the National Social Security and Welfare Fund (NSSWF) through any of the sources as specified in section 8 of the Act. However, the share of contribution of the BPL workers, if any, would be borne by the Central Government.

The total outlay of the scheme proposed for unorganised non-agricultural workers when all of them are covered is estimated at Rs 12950 crore, which may be entirely borne by the Central Government. If however, the total cost is shared between the Centre and States in the ratio of 75:25, then, the Centre's and the State Governments' share is estimated at Rs 9700 crore and Rs 3250 crore respectively. The share of both Centre and States could be further reduced, if contributions of employers and workers or tax/ cess as mentioned in section 8 are available.

Annexure 3

Terms of Reference of the Commission

The Government of India, constituted the National Commission for Enterprises in the Unorganised Sector (NCEUS) vide Ministry of Small Scale Industries Resolution No. 5(2)/2004-ICC dated 20th September, 2004, under the Chairmanship of Professor Arjun Sengupta. The Terms of Reference of the Commission are as follows:

i. Review the status of unorganized/informal sector in India including the nature of enterprises, their size, spread and scope, and magnitude of employment;

ii. Identify constraints faced by small enterprises with regard to freedom of carrying out the enterprise, access to raw materials, finance, skills, entrepreneurship development, infrastructure, technology and markets and suggest measures to provide institutional support and linkages to facilitate easy access to them;

iii. Suggest the legal and policy environment that should govern the informal/unorganized sector for growth, employment, exports and promotion;

iv. Examine the range of existing programmes that relate to employment generation in the informal/ unorganized sector and suggest improvement for their redesign;

v. Identify innovative legal and financing instruments to promote the growth of the informal sector;

vi. Review the existing arrangements for estimating employment and unemployment in the informal sector, and examine why the rate of growth in employment has stagnated in the 1990s;

vii. Suggest elements of an employment strategy focussing on the informal sector;

viii. Review Indian labour laws, consistent with labour rights, and with the requirements of expanding growth of industry and services, particularly in the informal sector, and improving productivity and competitiveness; and

ix. Review the social security system available for labour in the informal sector, and make recommendations for expanding their coverage

Annexure 4

Past and Present Composition of the Commission

The composition of the Commission is as follows:

Professor Arjun Sengupta Chairman, Centre for Development and Human Rights, New Delhi	**Chairman,** [From 20.09.2004 to 01.07.2005 and from 17.11.2005 till date]
Professor K. P. Kannan Fellow, Centre for Development Studies, Ulloor, Thiruvananthapuram 695011, Kerala	**Full-time Member** [From 01.11.2004 till date]
Professor Ravi S. Srivastava Professor, Centre for Studies in Regional Development, Jawaharlal Nehru University, New Delhi 110067	**Full-time Member** [From 01.05.2006 till date]
Shri V.K. Malhotra, IAS (Retd.)	**Member Secretary** [From 01. 03.2006 till date]
Shri B.N. Yugandhar Member, Planning Commission, New Delhi 110001	**Part-time Member** [From 05.11.2004 till date]
Professor T.S. Papola Director, Institute for Studies in Industrial Development, Vasant Kunj Institutional Area, New Delhi.110070	**Part-time Member** [From 06.04.2005 till date]
Professor K. Jayashankar Former Vice Chancellor, Kakatiya University, Warangal, Andhra Pradesh	**Full-time Member** [From 01.12.2004 to 9.03.2006]
Shri Bibek Debroy, Director, Rajiv Gandhi Institute for Contemporary Studies, New Delhi 110001.	**Part-time Member** [From 27.10.2004 to 20.12.2005]
Shri K.K. Jaswal, IAS (Retd.)	**Member Secretary** [From 01.11.2004 to 18.02.2006]

Annexure 5

Composition of the Advisory Board

1. **Professor Bhalchandra Mungekar,**
Member, Planning Commission,
Yojana Bhavan, New Delhi.

2. **Swami Agnivesh,**
President, Bonded Labour Liberation Front,
13, South Avenue, New Delhi.

3. **Professor Sheila Bhalla,**
(Formerly Professsor of Economics,
Jawaharlal Nehru University, New Delhi)
Institute of Human Development,
Old IAMI Building (3rd Floor).
I.P.Estate, Mahatma Gandhi Marg,
New Delhi-110002.

4. **Professor Mahendra Dev,**
Director, Centre for Economic and Social Studies,
Begumpet, Hyderabad.

5. **Ms. Madhu Kishwar,**
Editor, Manushi
C-1/3 Sangam Estate, 1, Underhill Road, Civil Lines,
Delhi-110054.

6. **Ms. Mirai Chatterjee,**
Self-Employed Women's Association (SEWA)
Opposite Victoria Garden, Bhadra, Ahmedabad-380001.

7. **Shri Joginder Kumar**
President,
Federation of Tiny & Small Scale Industries of India (FTSSI),
General Metal Industries, B-189, Industrial Estate,
Ludhiana, Punjab.

8. **Professor Jean Dreze,**
Delhi School of Economics, Department of Economics,
Delhi University, Delhi-110007.

9. **Professor Amit Bhaduri,**
Council for Social Development,
53, Lodhi Estate, New Delhi - 110003.

10. **Shri Nachiket Mor,**
Executive Director, ICICI Bank Limited
ICICI Tower, Bandra Kurla Complex,
Mumbai.

Annexure 6

Summary of Responses/Comments from the Ministries of Government of India to the Draft 2007 Bills.

Ministry	Response
Ministry of SSI & ARI	➢ The suggestion to impose strict enforcement of Minimum Wages for agricultural labour cannot be a total solution in itself as: ■ Wages have to be fixed as a factor based on the cost of production and the market price of the agricultural commodities, which varies from area to area, from season to season, from crop to crop, and cannot have a fixed element. ■ Huge government machinery would be required for enforcement of Minimum Wages at the level of each village and such enforcement may lead to law and order problems. ■ Such wages that are imposed from the top are hardly known or published at the ground level. ➢ Most important is the fact that remunerative crop prices are essential to ensure Minimum Wages and, therefore, all-out efforts have to be taken to raise agricultural prices, so that the farmer is in a position to pay proper Minimum Wages to the agricultural labour. ➢ At the same time, it is also a fact that agricultural workers are the poorest of the poor and depend upon the farmer for survival. Very often, there is also a caste element built in, as the farmers are from higher castes or from OBCs, while agricultural workers are from SCs / STs etc. ➢ Consensus is, therefore, the best way to arrive at wages, which can differ from village to village and from season to season. The opinion of the Village Panchayat is essential as it is only the Panchayat's enforcement that can actually succeed, not governmental or police intervention.
Department of Economic affairs, Insurance Division, MOF	➢ No Comments
Ministry of Food Processing Industries	➢ No Comments to offer and agrees with the proposed Bills.
Ministry of Women & Child Development	➢ The Dispute Resolution Committee and the Conciliation Committee that take up complaints regarding sexual harassment should be headed by women and at least 50% of the members comprising such committees should be women. ➢ Clause 4(1) in both the draft Bills mentions 3 Acts, which shall not be contravened in employing wage worker or home- based worker. Here Equal Remuneration Act, 1976 should be added.
Ministry of Health & family Welfare	➢ No comments to offer except that there is no provision for payment of expenses incurred towards treatment due to any accident or occupation hazard arising out of or in course of employment. As such there is need

for a provision to be made in part 1, Chapter II, Item No 4(7) in each of the Bill, which may be a liability on the employer.

Ministry of Panchayati Raj

- In the past there have been attempts to regulate the un-organised sector through the operation of Minimum Wages Act in the agriculture sector and through some other legislations. These have not been very successful in the past because of magnitude of the task and difficult logistics involved. Though the enactment is a sincere attempt, but the chances of the success appear to be remote because of the reason that it has not involved the grass root institutions available i.e. the Panchayats. The agriculture workers for instance and the workers in most related other rural areas are admittedly uncharted.
- The unorganised workers live in the villages where the Panchayats are expected to design functions. Hence, the Panchayats should have a dominant role, which is not reflected in the Bill. It is suggested that the term Panchayati Raj institutions should be included in the definition of appropriate level. It should read somewhat like this- "At an appropriate level of the district intermediate or Gram Panchayat".
- The meeting of DRC calls for an intimate knowledge of ground conditions, which are generally not available with the officials but are available with public representatives. The DRC should logically be headed by the President of Zila Panchayat or one of the prominent members of the Zila Panchayat and could function within the overall supervision and guidance of the Zila Parishad. Like wise the Conciliation Committee at the intermediate level or below should be headed by either the President of the Intermediate Panchayat or a Member of the Panchayat body at these levels and should contain larger representatives from the members of the Panchayat.
- At the Gram Panchayat level the body should be placed squarely under the Gram Panchayat and should function somewhat on the lines of the Standing Committee of the Gram Panchayat.
- As regards setting up of National Board for Promotion of Livelihood of Unorganised Sector is concerned, it has been noticed that representatives of the Panchayats have not been included. There should be five representatives of the Panchayats from the different tiers of Panchayats Raj structures.
- Likewise under Section 16, the representatives of two Zila Parishad and Gram Panchayats should be included in the State Board by rotation.
- The scheme would duly succeed with institutional support from the Panchayats.

Annexure 7

Summary of Responses/Comments from the State Governments to the Draft 2007 Bills'.

State	Response
Arunachal Pradesh	➢ No comments to offer on the proposed Bills. ➢ State Government would require financial assistance in the implementation of the proposed Act.
Assam	➢ Both the revised drafts are being examined. Comments shall be sent to you shortly.
Bihar	➢ We in principle agree to the proposed Bills. ➢ It is a nice attempt to bring special Bill/ Act for labour in the unorganised sector by which it has sought to take care of job guarantee as well as welfare avenues that were neglected so far. ➢ Proposal for the creation of two separate Boards for the welfare of Unorganised Agricultural and Non- agricultural Sectors are not required; rather one Board could function for both the sectors conveniently. This Board may be named as Unorganised Sector Labour Board. ➢ In the place of two different Acts, a consolidated Act for both the Agricultural as well as Non- agricultural workers will be more appropriate and convenient. Two Acts will create complication as well as duplication. So the Commission should consider to amalgamate both the Acts into one. ➢ Care should be taken to make the Acts less complicated and non-interfering by government officials. Presently both the Acts provide for official interference at many places. They may signal a return of Inspector Raj, which should be avoided. ➢ The Dispute Resolution Mechanism for the unorganised sector labour should be less complicated. The impression one gains from a cursory glimpse of the bills is that the provisions in the I.D. Act, 1948 have been taken as the basis. A fresh look is perhaps needed.
Delhi	➢ While drafting the bills the Government should be extremely cautions before introducing a new law. Recently, the Hon'ble High Court of Delhi, while disposing a Civil Writ Petition No. 3620 of 2003 in the Builders Association of India Vs. Union of India & Ors. quoted the judgment of the Hon'ble Supreme Court of India in Bandhua Mukti Morcha Vs. Union of India (1984) 3SCC 161 at 184. Gist of the judgment is that Court of law cannot compel the State Government through the judicial process to make provision by statutory enactment, but where legislation is already enacted by the State, the State can certainly be obligated to ensure observance of such legislation for inaction on the part of the State in securing implementation of such legislation would amount to denial of right to live with human dignity enshrined in Article 21.

- We are looking for simplification of labour laws; the same concept should be extended to the agricultural and unorganised sector also. While drafting the bill, it would also be appropriate to keep in mind the economic conditions of the farmers and employers engaged in non-agricultural sector who will be required to comply with these laws.
- The language in the Act should be simple, as these Acts are required to be implemented by farmers and petty employers, many of whom are illiterate.
- The Central Government may determine some norms for enforcement of the laws- inspector ratio and the infrastructure of the Labour Department.
- Whether Government's "Agricultural" activity would come within the ambit of this Act. The Government runs numerous institutions e.g. Agricultural Institute at Pusa, IVRI, Central Potato Research Farm etc.
- It will be difficult to enforce the provisions in the case of marginal farmers having small land holdings, buffaloes, livestock etc. Some of them may be at BPL level.
- Section 4 (1). No useful purpose is served by prohibiting something, which is already prohibited by another law.
- Section 4 (2). The capacity of the Government to enforce the hours of work has been challenged in the organised sector. The Government will be extremely vulnerable in the unorganised sector to enforce the provisions in this Section.
- Section 4 (3) No comments, except that it will be difficult for a large number of marginal farmers, who may themselves be illiterate, to maintain records, to issue letter of appointment etc. to their workers. We have not been able to ensure it in the organised sector.
- Section 4 (3) (i). The Section itself contains a contradiction in as much as if any worker is found without an appointment letter, the employer will say that he is a casual worker.
- Section 4 (8). The employer may not be in a position to exercise supervision in certain agricultural activities due to its spread. The prohibition should be imposed upon co-workers and the employer per se.
- Section 4 (9). The corresponding industrial law prescribes that crèche etc. facilities are to be prescribed in industries employing more than the specific number of women workers. This Bill does not have any such criterion.
- Section 4 (10). It may be difficult for the employer to provide these facilities, specially for the employers, who are at marginal level.
- Chapter III, "Enforcement And Dispute Resolution Bodies". Certain provisions have been lifted from the industrial law without taking into account the realities of the agricultural sector. The efficacy of the bodies created under this Bill seems to be doubtful, as a formal system is being created for an informal environment. It would be far better to allow the Local Panchayats to mediate in the matter.

- The contents of "Protection And Promotion of Livelihood Of Unorganised Agricultural Workers"(Chapter IV) should be specifically read in the light of the judgment of the Hon'ble Supreme Court in the Bandhua Mukti Morcha case.
- Constitution of a National Board and a State Board for promotion of livelihood of unorganised agricultural workers is a welcome step.
- Prima facie, the definition of Unorganised Non- Agricultural Sector (Section 2 (i)) seems to be coterminous with establishment as defined in the Delhi Shops and Establishments Act, 1954 and similar Acts in other states. Since a law is already in force in this regard, the need for a new law may be reconsidered.
- Combined reading of the definition of Unorganised Non- Agricultural sector and Wage Workers Brings out a conflict between the two. While the sector has 'enterprises' as a key word, the wage workers includes domestic workers.
- The existing Shops and Establishments Act prohibits employment of a person in more than one establishment, whereas this law supports employment by one or more employers. This can lead to a situation where a worker will work for 8 hours with one employer and for another 8 hours with another employer. It will have adverse impact on the worker.

Jammu & Kashmir

- Fully supports the proposals.

Meghalaya

- No views or comments to offer on the two draft bills. However, we are agreeable to whatever consensus that would be arrived at the national level.

Mizoram

- This would be a very important Bill for the relevant sector workers. The Bill envisaged providing minimum conditions of work for the wage workers. The Bill is recommended for implementation.

Rajasthan

- The decision of the Government of India to introduce the two Bills separately for the Agriculture/ Non- agriculture Unorganised Workers in the forthcoming session of the Parliament is welcome. The State Government agrees with the basic framework and most of the provisions of the Draft Bill. However, we would like to offer following comments for consideration.
- The Bills of 2007 have not proposed the provision of bipartite settlements while the bipartite settlement ought to be promoted by all corners because the bipartite settlements have their own merits and they are always preferable.
- There is a provision of Adjudicator under the proposed Bill, who delivers wards against any dispute but there is no provision in the bill of 2007 to get this award implemented. There is this shortcoming in the Industrial Disputes Act, 1947 also. This may be provided for.
- Under the Bill, 2007, it has been proposed that every employer shall compensate the worker for any accident or occupational hazard arising out of or in the course of employment that results in any temporary, permanent, partial or total disablement of the worker, at rates to be

specified in this behalf which shall not be lower than the benefits provided under the Unorganised Workers Social Security Act. Departments view is that the compensation should not be awarded in accordance with the unorganised workers social act but it should be in accordance with the Workmen Compensation Act, 1923 as it is a specific Act in the case of accidents.

- The Bill of 2007 has proposed the protection and promotion of livelihood of the unorganised workers. It ensures social security benefits covering health, disability, maternity, life and old age benefit but how the states would meet out these expenses and ensure provisions of social securities with appropriate funding. Although there is a provision under chapter V for National Board and National Fund for Unorganised Sector workers for Agriculture and Non-agriculture. But there is no provision how the fund will be operated.
- The Bill has envisaged a provision to constitute a State Board for promotion of livelihood of the unorganised workers but there is no provision for the State Fund to meet out the expenses to ensure the welfare and social securities of the workers.
- It is for the first time that the Central Government has proposed very comprehensive bills for the Unorgansied Workers and we welcome it.

Chandigarh

- The Drafts bills intend to safeguard the interest of the Unorganised Agricultural/ Non - Agricultural Workers and to promote the avenues of livelihood amongst such workers. Since a large percentage of the work force is engaged in these sectors the proposed legislations would provide a systematic and regulated growth of employment opportunities in these unorganised sectors and would also save such workers from exploitation on the one hand while securing Minimum Wages and working conditions for them on the other. Therefore, the proposed legislations are really the need of the hour and require to be supported in view of the objectives contained therein.

Pondicherry

- This Administration welcomes the Government of India's initiatives to bring the Unorganised Sector of Non-agricultural Workers and Agricultural Workers separately under the two Bills.
- To regulate service conditions and promote the livelihood of the unorgansied workers according to the above lines, this Administration suggests as follows:i) The definition given for the Agriculture and Non-agriculture Workers in both the Bills requires more clarity for easy understanding.ii) The members of the Unorganised Sector enrolled in the appropriate board have to avail remedies only under this Act and they should not seek any remedy under other labour laws. This provision should be specifically made in the Act designating the appropriate forum for remedy. For instance, a worker employed in a Shop or Establishment or Catering Establishment if registers his membership in the Unorganised Sector, has to seek the remedy only under the Unorganised Sector Workers Bill and not under the Shops and Establishment Act or Catering Establishment Act.iii) National Minimum Wages should be notified separately to the Non-agricultural an Agricultural Wage Workers, since the nature of the work differs.iv) Fixation of the National Minimum

Wage to the unorganised workers and its implementation should be with in the provisions of this Act so that the proposed Bill and the Minimum Wages Act shall not override with the provisions of each Act.v) Likewise Payment of wages, disputes redressal and service conditions and regulations made in this Bill should be implemented subject to the provisions of the Bill.vi) The Inspecting Authorities and their powers have not been specified in the two Bills to ensure the interest of the workers and promote their livelihood.vii) Both the bills provide for one paid day of rest after completing six continuous days of employment by or under a single employer. In the case of double employment it requires clarity regarding paid weekly holiday.viii) The Unorganised Non-agricultural Sector Workers Bill, 2007 provides for payment of double the rate of normal wages per hour for doing overtime work. Whereas Unorgansied Agricultural Sector Workers Bill, 2007 provides only one and a half of the normal d\rate of wages per hour for doing overtime. This disparity should be avoided considering the arduous nature of agricultural work.

- Further, it is stated that the provision made for the issue of letter of appointment and wage slip to the unorganised workers is a progressive step that can avoid unnecessary disputes regarding years of service, last pay drawn, nature of work, employer-employee relationship etc.Ø I t is a proposal that enables the unorganised workers to be brought under the conciliation machinery through the Dispute Resolution Council and Conciliation Committees. There was a prolonged demand from the workers who are not covered under the Industrial Disputes Act, 1947 to have such machinery to redress their grievances and settle their demands. The proposed conciliation machinery will definitely solve the problems of unorganised labour. However, for adjudication of disputes an officer not below the rank of the District Labour Officer should be nominated and banked with necessary delegation of powers for adjudication of disputes and related matters as enshrined in the Industrial Disputes Act 1947.
- Finally, it is also informed that for implementation of the above schemes, huge funds will be required but the Bills do not mention any source for the generation of the funds.

Annexure 8

Summary of Responses/Comments from the Trade Unions to the Draft 2007 Bills.

Trade Union	Response
Central Trade Unions (31-05-07)	We, the Central Trade Union Organisations (CTUOs), view with serious concern the reported decision by the Union Cabinet of May 24, 2007 that a Bill will be introduced in the Parliament as early as possible for social security of the Unorgansied Sector Workers and that the Bill would provide for setting up a National Advisory Board and enable the Central Government to notify welfare schemes from time to time. We strongly resent the arbitrary decision of the Government, which totally negates the declared commitment of the present Government and tripartite conclusions so far arrived at. **We wish to draw the attention of the Government of their long pending demand that there should be TWO separate but comprehensive legislations covering 1) the agricultural workers and 2) unorganised sector workers.** The National Common Minimum Programme adopted by the present Government had also specifically committed a comprehensive protective legislation for all agricultural workers and assured ensuring of the welfare and well being of all workers, particularly those in the unorganised sector who constitute 93 per cent of out workforce. We also reiterate that the Government should stick to this commitment. **Hence, we oppose the present move to bring an omnibus legislation, covering workers of both these sectors.** The issue of separate legislation for unorganised sector workers had been under tripartite dialogue ever since 2002. The Ministry of Labour and Employment had circulated several drafts on the unorganised sector workers Bill, the latest being the one published on the web site of the Ministry in 2007. The National Advisory Council had also presented a note and draft bill. The National Commission on Enterprises in the Unorgansied Sector had also come out with separate drafts- on social security and conditions of work relating to the workers in the agricultural and unorgansied sectors. Successive session of the Indian Labour Conference had deliberated on these issues and conclusions arrived there in are before the Government for implementation. In this backdrop, we are dismayed at the arbitrary move by the Union Cabinet to introduce a Bill, which has nothing in common with the long- drawn process of tripartite consultations. We reiterate that **the proposed legislation for the unorganised sector workers, as well as another one for the agricultural workers, should include conditions of work, regulation of employment, guarantee minimum wages, equal remuneration for women and social security, with an effective implementation machinery in place.** The attempts in the past to introduce social security schemes without statutory backing and guarantee resource allocation have ended up only as non- starters. In the light of this unsavoury experience, it is strange that the Union Cabinet has accorded approval for a legislation, which at best contains only vague enabling provisions, without any time frame to cover the 93 per cent of workforce in this country.

We strongly urge the Government to review its present decision and take immediate steps to reconvene tripartite consultations in order to finalise the drafts to TWO separate but comprehensive Bills for the agricultural workers and unorganised sector workers, keeping in line with the unanimous inputs provided by the CTUOs on more than one occasion in the past. We urge that such a process completed well in time, in order that the Bills, after appropriate revisions, may be introduced in the forthcoming session of the Parliament as envisaged.

Central Trade Unions (08.06.2007)

- The CTUOs also urge the Commission to recommend ***two separate but comprehensive Bills*** covering both the conditions of work as well as social security for (1) Agricultural Workers & (2) Unorganised Sector Workers. This alone will ensure that the issues in respect of these two segments of workers are correctly bifurcated and clearly demarcated. The present proposals contained in the draft Bill as well as the earlier Bill would result in putting in place multiple apex level boards, funds and other logistical arrangements, which are bound to have overlapping functions/ authority.
- The nomenclature used in the draft Bills viz. Unorganised Agricultural Sector Workers and Unorganised Non- agricultural Sector Workers need to be revised.
- The Commission may take into account and make appropriate recommendations in the draft report for relaxing the provision of 10% of membership and entitling any 7 workers to form and register a trade union.
- The Draft Report makes a detailed analysis about the norms to be applied for determination of the floor level Minimum Wages. Though the Government of India has arrived at a National Floor Level Minimum Wage of Rs. 66 per day, the same does not have any statutory basis and hence does not lend itself to mandatory implementation. The Commission has chosen to recommend, as a part of the proposed laws, the appointment of a Tripartite Committee to decide this issue. Instead of providing a scientific formula for periodical revision of this Floor Level Minimum Wage, on the basis of increase in cost of living, the Commission leaves it to the proposed National Board to prescribe a modality there for. This, in our view, will only serve to protract the issue without any decision being arrived at in the near future. Or worse still, it may even be misused to dilute the norms resulting in deflating the Minimum Wages. We, therefore, urge the Commission to straightway quantify the Floor Level Minimum Wages at current prices, on the basis of 15th ILC norms, further enlarged by the Raptakos Brett case judgment and make a specific recommendation there on. Similarly the Commission may also recommend an appropriate modality for periodical revision of the Floor Level Minimum Wages.
- The Draft Bills contain a provision for the establishment of a National Fund in each case. But they are silent on how the corpus of the fund will be created and where contributions will come from. We urge that the Commission may please make specific recommendations for

contributions from the Government of India as a percentage of GDP and from the employers by way of an appropriate levy.

- The Draft Report has annexed several suggestions emanating from different quarters. There may still be some, which had been left out. Te Commission may please make a compendium of all such suggestions and consider how best to incorporate them in the Draft Report/ Bills.
- The Commission may please make a comparative analysis of the different Draft Bills, including the one based on the NCRL report, and attempt a synthesis of the beneficial provisions of all such Bills.
- The Commission seeks to put in place Dispute Resolution Councils (DRC) at district level and Conciliation Committees (CC) at lower levels. There is also a provision for adjudication. These, perhaps correspond to the similar provisions attempted in the Industrial Relations Bill of 1977-78, which sought to impose a sort of compulsory arbitration. There is no reason why the labour departments of the Central/ state governments cannot serve as implementation machinery in respect of the proposed comprehensive legislation as well.

Bharatiya Mazdoor Sangh

- The draft Bills are silent on the three issues raised by the Secretary Labour, in the meeting of the Tripartite Working Group, which met at New Delhi on 23-06-2006 namely:
  - The sources of funds for the welfare schemes.
  - The machinery for implementation of the Legislation and resources for meeting the expenditure on the establishment.
  - Guarantee for the implementation of the legislation.
- Implementation Machinery:- The present set up of Labour Organization, both at the Centre and states, and their system of working has the contempt of the targeted workers, hence the implementation of the proposed legislation shall be entrusted to the existing set up. A separate establishment be created for the purpose of the proposed Legislation.
- The service conditions, wage, allowances and benefits, and social security measures shall not be less favourable than the provisions existing in the existing Legislations, and the norms decent work propounded by the ILO. These shall be specified and incorporated in the proposed Legislation.
- In sub. S. (3) of Sec. 8 of the Bills, the first word, 'No' be removed. The person or persons concerned shall be liable for actions in pursuance of the legislation.
- Section 13 and 16 concerning the composition of National and State Boards, the number or representatives or workers, employers shall be ten each, not five as proposed.
- In Sec. 2 definitions of the Unorganised Agricultural SectorWorkers (Conditions of Work and Livelihood Promotion Bill, 2007, add 'piggery, floriculture, growing of vegetables and fruits.

BMS (UP)

- The requirements of the self-employed workers are distinct from the requirements of wage workers.
- The workers in the enterprises in the unorganised and informal sectors are employed in the nature of temporary employment and due to this they change their jobs frequently in short spells. Hence, it is difficult to provide them social security benefits. Hence, if there is permanent stability of employment to the workers in these enterprises, the benefits of social security may be provided to them easily.
- At present the organizational structure in the Center and the states provides for implementation to cover only three crore workers in the organised sector; whereas no machinery exists for 36 crore workers in the unorganised sector. At the national level, Rural Labour Commissioner Organization should be set up separately for implementation in the unorganised sector.
- For generation of employment opportunities in the unorganised sector, labour oriented small and cottage industries should be promoted.
- The Minimum Rates of Wages notified by the state governments should not be less than the National Minimum Wage. After introducing National Minimum Wages the differentiation in the Minimum Rates of Wages in the States should be abolished and the uniform National Minimum Wages should be fixed for all workers in the country.
- A Tripartite Committee at national level should be set up comprising the representatives from employers, workers and subject matter specialists to determine National Minimum Wages after considering different standards and inflation and advise the Central Government on it.
- The piece-rated workers should get same wages as decided for the time-rated workers in the same category.
- The provision of overtime should be made after working of 8 hours.
- The provision for weekly off/rest should be made to the workers working continuously for 6 days with one employer.
- In case of dispute between the workers and their employers, for resolution of such disputes, proper and adequate machinery should be set up at Tehsil/Block/Mandal/District level, who shall try to settle the matters and produce a solution within a fixed time frame. In case of failure at this level, the matter should be referred to the Authority decided for this purpose.
- For better living standards of the Unorganised Sector Workers, the Central & state governments should make mechanisms for livelihood promotion.
- A national fund should be set up for the welfare of Unorganised Sector Workers.

NCC-USW (31.05.2007)

The Report is exhaustive in terms of giving details of the conditions of Unorganised Sector Workers. But the Recommendations and the 2 Bills do not address the basic issues namely:

- The contract and sub-contract systems and invisible and insecure employer-employee relationships leading to exploitation-economic and extra economic forms such as bonded labour, casteism, sexual exploitation etc. and the lack of implementation mechanisms in the existing laws such as the Minimum Wages Act etc.
- Globalisation policies leading to invisible retrenchments-job losses and deprivation of livelihoods in the agriculture, fisheries, handlooms, gem cutting, tea plantations, artisanal trades etc.
- The Bills lack the required steps of regulation of employment-conditions of service, social security as well as participatory policies and implementation to check globalization through Sectoral Tripartite Boards and they will serve continuance of the existing unjust system

Hence we put forward the following recommendations:

- ➢ Agricultural workers need a separate and integrated legislation on conditions of work and social security in the lines of Kerala Agricultural Workers Act.
- ➢ The Law for the Unorganised Sector Workers should be an integrated law in the lines of the model Bill submitted by NCC-USW.
- ➢ At least 3 per cent of the revenue of Central and state governments is set apart every year for the social security of 39 crore Unorganised Workers till a target of 3 per cent of the Gross Domestic Product is reached.
- ➢ ESI Act needs to be amended to enable the Act to be applicable to various categories of Unorganised Sector Workers through Tripartite Boards.
- ➢ The National Rural Employment Guarantee, which calls for amendments that would ensure time bound extension to the whole of India.

SEWA

- ➢ The definitions of different types of workers are cumbersome. There should be only one type of definition, may be something like the following: *"Unorganised Sector Workers" means a person who works for wages or income; directly or through any agency or contractor; or who works on his own or her own account or is self- employed; in any place of work including his or her home, field or any public place and who is earning below Rs. 5000 per month.*
- ➢ The four Acts cited are fine. But the Acts and their rules as they stand now need to be amended. We propose to add the following:
- Special model rules should be framed for the four basic Acts, which must be adopted by the state governments. These model rules should take into account characteristics of the unorganised sector.
- Special model rules for the Minimum Wages Act should include:

a. Inclusion and fixation of rates of Minimum Wages for all the trades of the unorganised sector.

b. Similar rates of Minimum Wages in all the states.

- There does not seem to be any enforcement mechanism for the Acts. The present enforcement mechanism is weak and hence these Acts are not implemented. We suggest addition of the following:

- Constitution of the Special Department in the Ministry of Labour and Employment for enforcement of this four Acts. In addition to Enforcement of these Acts the Department would also:

a. Register and recognize associations and trade unions of workers of the unorganised sector with itself (like the registration of SGSY groups with Department of Rural Development). These registered organizations would be included in the process of implementation of the Acts.

b. Registration of associations of employers in the unorganised sector.

c. The Bill should lay stress on the registration and providing identity cards to the workers.

d. The Bill should contain some mechanism to see that employers ensure all the conditions of work and benefits to the workers.

e. Constitution of Conciliation Committee should be changed to include representatives of the different unions.

- There is not a mechanism to either implement or monitor the benefits for the self-employed.

- Promotion of an unorganised sector worker members based organization should be included in the Bill.

Annexure 9

Summary of Responses/Comments from the NGOs, Academia and others to the Draft 2007 Bills.

NGOs/Academia	Response
Working Women's Forum	➢ As for the proposed Boards and the Fund it is nothing new as it was done by some of the state governments like Tamil Nadu and Kerala earlier. However, such funds have never reached quickly and in time to the affected persons. ➢ These Boards and Funds should not only be beneficial to the unorganised workers by making funds available to them in the most critical time the board should consist of more representatives of the unorganised sector also. ➢ The unions, organisations and NGOs have certainly assured an increase in their income, savings and provided cash capital to these workers and have made them entrepreneurs. In fact, these NGOs and unions of unorganised workers not only provided occupational safety, planned health services but also provided both social security and micro insurance to the most neglected workers at the grassroots.
Rajarshi Majumder	➢ It was clear from the Report and the draft Bills, that most of the issues have been quite well discussed, deliberated and analysed by the NCEUS. Congratulations for that - you have done a tremendous job. ➢ Record- keeping by employers may backfire in the presence of large scale illiteracy and unemployment. ➢ For agricultural workers, allowing one paid day of leave after every six days of continuous work is not practicable. ➢ Compensation for the Homeworkers for the infrastructure, tools that they provide is ethically right, but valuation of such compensation will be a complex issue.
Dipa Mukherji	➢ Implementing the NMW in units where the value added per worker is lower than the NMW will be impossible. Instead of the NMW norm, one can consider 'National Minimum Earnings' and aim for that. The difference between wages paid and NMW may be borne by the State as a subsidy. ➢ Resource mobilisation for unorganised sector can also be done through indirect methods like Sharing of Equipment, Infrastructure etc. The Cluster Approach may be followed. ➢ Such clusters should not be formed on the basis of the existing/traditional regional concentration of industries, but should be based on a comprehensive study of future linkages and sustainability. Regional comparative advantage can be a basis of selecting Growth Poles and the composition of industries under it.

- The NREGS will help the rural non-agricultural unorganised sector through demand creation, but such schemes should be able to create mandays of employment and not simply follow the Act by giving out Unemployment Allowance to the registered job-seekers. Sufficient Public Works must be undertaken and funds allocated for the associated capital expenditure. Success in NREGS is a part of Promotion of Livelihood.Ø Provision of Training, Credit and Marketing Support to unorganised entrepreneurs must take into consideration local resource and demand factors. In this connection substantial advancement has been made in rural areas of W Bengal through SHGs and Micro credit delivery system.

D.Narasimha Reddy

- The Commission deserves to be congratulated for the monumental effort in putting together a comprehensive report on such a complex subject that deals with the nature and diversity of work and livelihoods in the unorganised workers. The clarity and tenacity with which the concept of 'Unorganised Worker' is analysed in the first chapter is a definitive advance in the understanding of this critical but vexed concept. It sets the basis for designing an appropriate institutional framework for intervention in favour of the unprotected workers whose share is on the rise.
- Given the fact that still most of the unorganised workers belong to the caste based craft or artisanal activities like handlooms, footwear making, pottery, carpentry etc. where skill upgradation requires different institutional arrangements, there could have been a discussion on the caste-craft artisanal links.
- The concept and methodology advanced for the 'Notional Minimum Wage' is convincing. It also provides a detailed account of the 'enforcement deficit' of the present Minimum Wage Legislation.
- Poor organization of the unorganised workers is a major problem. There is need for provision of incentives for organizing the unorganised workers by all agencies including the unions of organised sector workers. There is a growing tendency all over the world towards 'social movement unionism' to counter the weak organization of labour in the context of growing informalisation of work. Such unionism needs to be encouraged by providing for certain functions and powers in the management of the resources provided for the benefit the unorganised workers.
- The discussion of international experience on regulation of Minimum Conditions of Work in the Ninth Chapter is useful to the extent as to how the present phase of economic globalisation that has brought pervasive flexibilisation of labour needs to be addressed by the experience of measures to face similar situations elsewhere. However, under the conditions prevailing in India, measures like voluntary code of conduct for employers of unorganised labour may actually worsen the situation. The Christian Aid experience in sports goods, cited in the Report, is due to pressure from consumer groups. Such initiatives are likely to be hardly of any significance in the Indian context. The experience relating to self-certification discussed in the Tenth Chapter also suggests executive orders like 'self-certification' can hardly serve as alternatives in the absence of vigilant workers' organizations.

- The Tenth Chapter could have reflected on the role of voice, agency or organization of the unorganised workers in ensuring compliance of even the voluntary codes.
- The Eleventh Chapter, which deals with 'Protection and Promotion of Livelihoods of Unorganised Workers', appears to extend too much into activities that are the domains of a plethora of ministries which deal with a number of policies and programmes which also impact unorganised workers.
- Operationally more important part of the Report is a set of "Recommendations" set out in Chapter 12.
- The proposal to have two separate Bills, one for workers in Agricultural and another for Unorganised Non-agricultural Workers goes well with certain basic differences between these domains of work.
- Part I of the proposed legislation to ensure minimum conditions of work for all unorganised workers is well thought out, and the institutional framework with an emphasis on negotiation and conciliation machinery at the district and lower levels is simple and less bureaucratic. However, there could be incentives built-in for organizational efforts of the unorganised workers.
- But Part II of the proposed Bill dealing with "Protection and Promotion of Livelihoods" turns out to be too much of an overarching effort that may prove to be counter-productive.

Ashok Khandelwal

- The Bill: (a) lacks provisions for employment security, registration, assured wages, and welfare measures, (b) there is a qualitative shift in the definition of ' Agricultural Worker' to the detriment of agricultural labour, and (c) there is wide unwieldy coverage of issues in Part 2. Ø Many provisions of Kerala Agricultural Workers Act are not included in the NCEUS Bill.
- Addition of Part 2 in the Bill dilutes the focus on provisions of the Part 1. By making the applicability of the Part 2 much wider and ambiguous the Report renders the provisions of the Part 1 further digressed. The two legislations are thus essentially different despite a set of work conditions included in the draft Bill.
- The Bill defines the 'Unorganised Agricultural Sector Worker' to include both the self-employed and wage workers [Sec 2(k)]. And the 'Self-employed Agricultural Worker' has been defined as "any person engaged in agricultural activities in own farm or holding, either individually or with one or more partners" [Sec 2(i)]. The former thus clubs together sellers of labour-power (capacity to work) and sellers of labour (sellers of goods produced by one's own labour) and the latter, without any qualification, is likely to include all the farmers.
- Clubbing of wage labourers and all-producers and the inclusion of a wide-range of issues concerning the broad category of agricultural workers ranging from education, training, credit, housing, water, social

security, labour rights and so on is only going to loose the focus on labour rights. The livelihood issues of small producers, is, no doubt, a serious concern to be addressed with a special legislation. They should be however sharply focussed on small and marginal farmers and other poor 'sellers of labour'. However the interests of the class of wage labour are different and must be addressed independently of any other needs and associated aspects.

- The Bill must categorically prohibit employment in agriculture of anyone who has not completed the age of 15 years.
- In Section 4(5) the Bill prohibits discrimination on various grounds but there is no reference to Age. It should therefore also clearly state that there will be no discrimination in the wages paid to workers on the basis of 'Age'.

Annexure 10

List of the Meetings, Discussions and Consultations on Conditions of work

Discussions at the NCEUS Office

Sl. No	With whom	Date
1	Discussions on Social Security Bill 2006 and Conditions of Work Bill with the Representatives of Central Trade Unions & Other Organizations	02-06-2006
2	Meeting with Representatives of SEWA and NCL	11-09-2006
3	Meeting with Ms. Jaya Arunachalam of Working Women's Forum, Chennai	20-12-2006
4	Discussions on the Draft Report on Conditions of Work and Promotion of Livelihood in the Unorganized Sector and the Revised Comprehensive Bills with the Advisory Board Members	22-12-2006
5	Discussions on the Draft Report on Conditions of Work and Promotion of Livelihood in the Unorganized Sector and Revised Comprehensive Bills with the Advisory Board Members	20-02-2007
6	Discussions on the Draft Report on Conditions of Work and Promotion of Livelihood in the Unorganized Sector and Revised Comprehensive Bills with the Advisory Board Members	13-03-2007
7	Discussions on the Draft Report on Conditions of Work and Promotion of Livelihood in the Unorganized Sector and Revised Comprehensive Bills with the Advisory Board Members	28-05-2007
8	Discussions on the Revised Comprehensive Bills and the Draft Report with Centre of Indian Trade Unions (CITU) and Other Organizations.	31-05-2007
9	Discussions on the Revised Comprehensive Bills with the Representatives of Centre of Indian Trade Unions (CITU)	13-06-2007
10	Discussions on the Revised Comprehensive Bills with the Representatives of Indian National Trade Union Congress (INTUC)	21-06-2007
11	Discussions on the Revised Comprehensive Bills with the Representatives of Central Trade Unions & other Organizations other Organizations	27-06-2007

State Visits

1	State Visit to Andhra Pradesh and Meeting of Dr. R.S.Srivastava, Member NCEUS at Hyderabad with Principal Secretary, Labour & Employment and other senior officers of the Labour Department.	31-12-2006
2	State Visit to Tamil Nadu and Meeting of Dr. R.S.Srivastava, Member, Dr.K.P.Kannan, Member, & Mr.Mahesh Kumar, Director, NCEUS at Tiruchirapalli, Tirupur and Chennai with Secretary, Labour, Labour Commissioner, and other senior officers of Labour Department.	07-01-2007 to 09-01-2007

Sl. No	With whom	Date
3	State Visit to Bihar and Meeting of Dr. R.S.Srivastava, Member, NCEUS at Patna with Secretary Labour & Employment, Labour Commissioner, and other senior officers of Labour Department.	19-01-2007
4	State Visit and Meeting of Mr. Mahesh Kumar, Director, NCEUS at Ranchi with Labour Commissioner, Government of Jharkhand and other senior officers of Labour Department.	22-01-2007
5	State Visit to Rajasthan and Meeting of Dr. R.S.Srivastava, Member, NCEUS at Jaipur with Secretary, Labour & Employment, Labour Commissioner, and other senior officers of Labour Department.	25-01-2007

Consultations

1	Regional consultation on the Draft Report on 'Conditions of Work and Promotion of Livelihood in the Unorganized Sector' and the two draft Bills for Agricultural and Non-agricultural Workers at Jaipur	2-05-2007
2	Regional consultation on the Draft Report on 'Conditions of Work and Promotion of Livelihood in the Unorganized Sector' and the two draft Bills for Agricultural and Non-agricultural Workers at Ranchi	11-05-1007
3	Regional consultation on the Draft Report on 'Conditions of work and Promotion of Livelihood in the Unorganized Sector' and the two draft Bills for Agricultural and Non-agricultural Workers at Banglore	22-05-2007
4	Regional consultation on the Draft Report on 'Conditions of work and Promotion of Livelihood in the Unorganized Sector' and the two draft Bills for Agricultural and Non-agricultural Workers at Kolkata	2-06-2007
5	National Consultation and Seminar on Social Security organized by NCEUS in association with Centre for Economics and Social Studies , Hyderabad	7-06-2006 8-06-2006

Field visits, seminars and other consultations

1	Visit to Handloom clusters at Mau Aima, Allahabad	25-05-2006
2	Visit to Handloom/ Weavers' clusters and NGOs at Bhubaneswar	30-05-2006 31-05-2006
3	National Consultation on 'Social Security for the Workers in the Unorganised Sector' organized by National Centre for Labour at New Delhi	10-07-2006
4	National Seminar on Urban Street Vendors- organized by Ministry of Urban Development & Poverty Alleviation, New Delhi	12-07-2006
5	Janasunvayi of Street Vendors - Public Meeting for Grievances and Experiences at Kamani Auditorium, New Delhi	26-07-2006
6	National Workshop on Unorganised Women Workers organized by National Campaign Committee at Gandhi Peace Foundation, New Delhi	04-08-2006
7	Symposium on Unorganised Workers Social Security Bill, 2006 (National Labour Institute) at India International Centre, New Delhi	10-08-2006

Sl. No	With whom	Date
8	IILS Conference on A Development Agenda for Employment and Decent Work in India at IGIDR, Mumbai	10-08-2006 11-08-2006
9	Meeting with National Executives of Hind Mazdoor Sabha at T.N. Bajpai Memorial Hall, 12, Chelmsford, N. Delhi	02-09.-006
10	Meeting of National Alliance of Agricultural Workers' Unions at Gandhi Peace Foundation, New Delhi	23-09-2006
11	Conference on Labor Regulation at ISID, Jaipur	21-11-2006 22-11-2006
12	Session at 48th Conference of Indian Society of labour Economics held at Tiruchurapalli on Conditions of Work in the Unorganized Sector	5-.01-2007 6-01-2007
13	Meeting with SSI and other public sector organizations and entrepreneurs on Unorganized Sector: field visits at Chennai and Kanchipuram	09-01-2007
14	National Seminar on 'Women Vendors in Urban Spaces' by Deptt. of Social Work, Delhi University	29-03-2007

Annexure 11

Summary of Responses/Comments from the Stakeholders at Regional Consultations

Jaipur May 2, 2007

- If strict laws are put in place the prospective employers might not employ workers altogether. As such a small number of participants did not favour the regulation of minimum wages.
- The draft of the Bill should also recognise bipartite resolution of the dispute wherein only the employer and the worker come together and settle their dispute. People from civil society organisations should be involved for arbitration. Dispute resolution mechanism should be speedy and time bound. The power of implementation authority needs to be clear and specific.
- 8 hours work day with at least an hour of break was not practical, especially in agriculture.
- Protection of livelihood is understandable, but how promotion can be a part of the bill is not clear. The promotion of livelihood diffuses the issue of rights of the workers.
- Registration should be made compulsory for anybody who gives work. This will bring transparency on the employers' side and make them accountable as well.
- There is no relation between employers' capacity to pay and minimum wage of the worker.
- All concerned parties should be properly sensitised for a better implementation of the provisions.
- Awareness generation among the labourers about their rights and entitlements is essential. This will create an environment for a rights-based approach.
- The draft Bill proposes creation of a National Fund for Unorganised Sector, but does not mention how this Fund would be generated.
- There should be proper management of common property resources
- Identification and registration of workers in unorganised sector is practically difficult..
- As 60% of unorganised workers are not getting Minimum Wages. They will be treated as bonded labour in view of the decision of the Supreme Court of India.
- What would be mechanism for implementation of Minimum Wages?
- There may be overlapping of the status of the workers as self-employed or wage worker.
- There should be specific provisions with a specified time frame for making rules by the state governments.
- Definition of 'regular worker' as mentioned in the Agricultural Bill is difficult to implement.
- Migrant labour conditions are not considered in the Bill and social security should also be part of this Bill. Whether the proposed Bill would cover migrant workers from other countries, i.e., the workers coming from Nepal and Bangladesh?. It was suggested that appropriate provisions should be made to apply the proposed Bill to the Indian citizens only.
- The Bill does not specify the benefits to be given to the identified workers in the unorganised sector.
- WC Act may be added in Clause 4(1) of the Bill.
- Status of implementation agencies in the states should be ascertained before giving role to the states.
- The Chairperson of the National Board should not be a minister and preferably he should be a social activist and the tenure of the Board should also be five years.

- For common property and common resources, the role of Panchayats and their powers should be specified in the Bill.

Ranchi May11, 2007

- The report and the draft Bills are based on a top down approach. It is a statist view that assumes that the state is committed to the welfare of the unorganised workers. Therefore, the state is well equipped to regulate the conditions of work as well as initiate policies and programmes for livelihood promotion. How realistic is this view? Will it work itself out in terms of policies, programmes and implementation structure? If not, what is the way out? Is it possible to take a perspective from below (as opposed to a perspective from the above) and articulate what unorganised workers can and should do to improve their conditions of work and livelihood promotion?
- How will the National Minimum Wage be determined? Will it be the same for all the states? Who will implement the National Minimum Wage? Do the state governments have the capacity to enforce the National Minimum Wage?
- The problems of tribal communities (and hence workers) belong to a class of its own. They are engaged in subsistence production, wage work and migration. Their sources of livelihood are either depleted (e.g. forest produce) or being alienated. They cannot compete with the other groups in the society. Therefore, a special treatment of their problems is warranted and it should be reflected in the Report as well as the draft Bills. Similar views were also expressed by some (including representatives of dalit organisations) with regard to the problems being faced by the Scheduled Castes.
- Destruction of livelihood in the name of economic reforms and growth was also highlighted by a number of participants.
- Some participants wanted the National Fund and Board to be placed in a decentralized framework, thereby projects can be initiated at the local level for protecting and promoting livelihood. They wanted the fund to be made available to the Panchayati Raj institutions. With regard to the National Board, they felt that the decisions should not be made at the national and state levels because the requirements of each regime might differ.
- Some participants suggested that the two draft Bills may be integrated into one Bill.
- Migrant workers should get identity cards and their working conditions and hours of work need proper regulation.
- Registration of unorganised workers should be done at National/State/District levels
- There should be one Board instead of two Boards.
- Women should get more hours of rest for feeding small kids.
- Provisions dealing with sexual harassment are very weak.
- Workers in agricultural sector do not get work continuously for six days, if so, provision of weekly rest is impractical.
- Enforcement of working hours in the unorganised sector is very difficult in practice. Especially in seasonal works at the time of festivals the painters and other workers are working day and night continuously to complete the work within time, so how can it be regulated and enforced practically?
- Implementation strategy should be specific and not left to the discretion of states.
- Community based organizations, village Panchayats and cooperative organizations should be involved in the implementation.
- Domestic workers and disabled workers should be covered in the proposed Law and their Minimum Wages should also be fixed.

- Sex workers are not covered under this Act and they should also get protection under this Act.
- There should be a list of occupations/ employments to be covered under the Act.
- National Fund and National Social Security Fund should be separate.

Bangalore May 22, 2007

- It was felt necessary to strengthen the Dispute Settlement Mechanism as provided in the Bill. There is need to specify penalty on responsible persons for non-compliance.
- Unionisation of unorganized workers and strengthening of the already existing organisation was emphasised.
- Discussion regarding Minimum Wages Act highlighted the administrative failures. A few participants also queried if the failures are inbuilt in the scheme or institutionalized by the mechanism itself. Some of the trade union leaders felt it necessary to address this issue at the earliest and also to make serious efforts to bring on ground the Minimum Wages Act in letter and spirit . They also emphasised that the fixation of Minimum Rates of Wages should be clear and specific on the basis of laid down policy and principles and not left to the discretion to the Board.
- Heterogeneity of workers and interest of the workers are at cross-roads in the context of liberalization and thus implementation of the Bills will be a tough task. The discussion pointed out that this heterogeneity should be taken into consideration and specifically the issues of cross interest have to be internalized.
- It was felt that the operation of the envisaged National Fund needs to be elaborated further and it was necessary to decide the participation of workers' representatives in the operation of the suggested institutional framework
- There is the need to give more details regarding functioning of the Boards. The representation of NGOs in the Boards and the method of selection is not clear. The source to the National Fund is not clear and the trade unions demanded 3% of GDP to this fund.
- Non-discrimination clause should include membership /non- membership of trade unions
- List of scheduled employments should be specifically provided.
- Elements of Social Security to be brought comprehensively in the two Bills.
- Combining the regulation on Condition of Work and Livelihood Promotion is not proper.
- Any bill without a scheme is of no use.
- There should be a binding provision in the Act for its implementation by the State.
- There is need to creating awareness and capacity building.
- Identity cards should be issued to all the unorganised workers.
- The Clause 4 (2) (a), (d) of the Bill regarding normal hours of working, hours of rest, weekly rest would be difficult to implement
- Panchayati Raj institutions should be involved in the implementation.

Kolkata June 2, 2007

- Dispute Resolution Council must be impartial. Legal persons should be the members of this Council. The process should have low cost, be less time consuming and ensure speedy disposal of disputes.
- There is need to examine inclusion and exclusion of workers in the unorganised sector like cooking of food to the farmers, transportation of farm produce services and cattle breeding etc. in the rural areas etc.
- There should be a comprehensive law combining Social Security and Conditions of Work etc. to the agriculture and the non-agriculture workers in the unorganised sector.

- There should be compulsory registration of employer and workers. They should be provided with unique identity cards to enable them to avail the facilities anywhere in the country. This unique identity card may be accessible for all purposes.
- There may be two level of agencies, one, at the block and above level to enforce provisions of these two draft Bills, and the other below the block level and in the villages which may be an elected body like Village Panchayat to register workers, supervise the payments of wages and create awareness about their rights among them etc.
- One day of paid weekly rest to the workers may be difficult to provide for by farmers especially by the marginal farmers. Further, to provide one day paid leave to the seasonal workers is not practical. Instead of this provision, double wages for working on the rest day may be considered.
- Small farmers cannot pay Minimum Wages since they themselves do not have proper and adequate earnings.
- There should be a single body for conciliation, enforcement and adjudication.
- The domestic workers should also be covered under this Act.
- As the workers are illiterate, the records can be misutilised by the employers against them.
- There is need to list out various welfare schemes and create awareness among the people.
- The method of functioning of the Board, components of the Funds, manner, mode mechanism of collection of Fund need to be more specific.
- The sources of funds are not clear in the Bills. As the workers cannot afford to pay, the government should pay their contribution.
- The provisions for appointment letters to the regular workers would be difficult to implement.
- The Commission should examine the feasibility and availability of self-help groups, which can be the better agencies for livelihood promotion schemes.
- The issues of physically and mentally challenged workers need to be addressed more in the Report under disadvantaged workers.

Annexure 12

List of Participants who attended the Regional Consultations on Conditions of Work & Promotion of Livelihoods in the Unorganised Sector

May 2, 2007 at Jaipur .

S.No.	Name	Address
1	Prof. Ravi Srivastava,	Member, NCEUS
2	Prof. Alakh N. Sharma,	Director, IHD
3	Prof. V.S. Vyas,	Chairman, IDS
4	Prof. Surjit Singh,	Acting Director, IDS
5	Dhan Raj Sharma	Labour Department, Rajasthan
6	Hari Dutt	National Society for HRD and Research, J&K
7	P.K. Parmar	Secy. Industries (Cottage), Government of Rajasthan
8	Satish K Batra	Bhartiya Vidhya Bhawan, Jaipur.
9	Anju Kohli	Department of Economics, MLSU, Udaipur
10	Arun Prabha Chandu	Department of Economics, MLSU, Udaipur
11	Rajendra Saiwal	Janwadi Lekhak Sangh
12	Mahitosh Bagoria	HEDCON
13	Arun D. Khaitan	GNK Memorial Trust
14	Manish Dubey	CUTS-CART, Jaipur
15	D.K Chengani	AITUC
16	Sanjeev	ARAVALI, Jaipur
17	Manu Sharma	Shuksma Vikas Sansthan
18	Satish Kumal	Centre for Dalit Rights
19	M.P. Choudhary	Centre for Dalit Rights
20	S.S. Dhillon	Guru Nanak Deve University, Amritsar
21	Prof. Pradeep Bhargav	Institute of Development Studies (IDS), Jaipur
22	Manju Balana	IDS, Jaipur
23	S.A. Tak	J&K SSIDS, Srinagar
24	Prof. M.S.Rathore	IDS, Jaipur
25	Anand Shukla,	Research Scholar, IIT Bombay
26	Sharique Mashhadi	Seva Mandir, Udaipur
27	Sunita Kumari	Seva Mandir, Udaipur
28	Gulzar Goria	BKMU
29	Tara Singh Siddhu	Rajasthan Kisan Sabha
30	Kailash Gehlot	Rajasthan Kisan Sabha
31	Prof. K.Gopal Iyer	Punjab University

S.No.	Name	Address
32	R.S. Bora	IEG, Delhi
33	Daman Ahuja	SOHAM, Himachal Pradesh
34	Ranveer Singh	Agro-economic Research Centre, HP Univ., Shimla
35	Dr. Sardip Sarkar	Institute for Human Development (IHD), Jaipur
36	M.M. Sheikh	ISDESR, Churu
37	Lalit K. Panwar	Government of Rajasthan
38	P.N.Pandey	Department of Industries, Government of Rajasthan
39	D.P.Singh	NCEUS
40	Harkesh Bugalia	Rajasthan Nirman Majdoor Sangathan
41	Meva Bharti	Mehnatkash Kalyan Avom Sandarbha Kendra
42	Nisha Siddhu	NFIW
43	Niranjan Sharma	Sauhard, Alwar
44	Prabhakar Goswami	Eye India, Jaipur
45	Shobhita Rajgopal	IDS, Jaipur
46	Narendra Singh	IDS Jaipur
47	Ladu Lal Sharma	IDS, Jaipur
48	Dr. Dev Nathan	IHD, New Delhi
49	S.M. Meena	Labour Commision
50	Srikishan Verma	CECOEDECON
51	Badrilal	CECOEDECON
52	Srilal	CECOEDECON
53	Bhajvan Singh	CECOEDECON
54	R.S. Sharma	IDS, Jaipur
55	Dr. Preet Rustagi	IHD, New Delhi
56	Sunil K. Mishra	IHD, New Delhi
57	Dalbir Singh	IHD, New Delhi
58	Vidya	IDS, Jaipur
59	Dr. Kanchan Mathur	IDS, Jaipur
60	Jais Rathore	IDS, Jaipur
61	Kalyan S. Kothari	IDS, Jaipur
62	Kavita Srivastava	PUCL
63	Prem	CECOEDECON
64	G.S. Rathore	IDS, Jaipur
65	R.P.Sharma	IDS, Jaipur
66	I.C. Srivastava	IAS (Retd.)
67	Mahesh Chandra Guha	Dy. Secy. Food and Health, Government of Rajasthan

May11, 2007 at Ranchi

S.No.	Name	Address
1..	Prof. R S Srivastava	Member, NCEUS, New Delhi
2.	Dr. K.P. Kannan	Member, NCEUS, New Delhi
3.	Prof. T.S. Papola	Pt. Member, NCEUS, New Delhi
4.	Sh. D.P.Singh	Under Secretary, NCEUS, New Delhi
5.	Dr. Alakh N. Sharma	Director,IHD, New Delhi
6.	Dr. Dalbir Singh	IHD, New Delhi
7.	Prof. N. K. Choudhary	Department of Economics, Patna University, Patna
8.	Dr. Prakash Ch. Deogharia	Department of Economics, Jharkhand
9.	Shri Mahipal Bhuriya	Centre for Tribal Culture and Art, M.P
10.	Shri Nalini Kant	MANAVI, Professors' Colony, Jharkhand
11.	Dr. Kailash Sarap	Sambalpur University, Sambalpur
12.	Dr. Premnand Panda	Department of Anthropology, Sambalpur University
13.	Sri Jijnyasu Panda	MASS(Manav Adhikar Seva Samiti, sambalpur
14.	Ms. Purbi Paul	Shramjivi Mahila Samiti, Jharkhand
15.	Sri Vijoy Kumar	Shramjivi Mahila Samiti, Jharkhand
16.	Sri Rajesh Ranjan	Agrarian Assistance Association, Jharkhand
17.	Sri Gaurav Kant Jha	Jharkhand Kala Kendra, Jharkhand
18.	Sri Swapna Kumar Mahto	Ghatshila, East Singhbhum, Jharkhand
19.	Sri Jamini Kant Mahto	Secretary, Singhbhum Legal Aid& Development Society
20.	Sri Madaneshwar	Pragati Luyadih, Palidih, East Singhbhum, Jharkhand
21.	Dr. Abdul Karim	West Singhbhum, Jharkhand
22.	Sri Pramod Kumar Singh Sansthan,Patna	Director Vidyasagar Samajik Surksha Evam Sodh
23.	Dr. Sri Raman	New Patliputra Colony, Patna
24.	Sri O. P. Gupta	Addl. Labour Commissioner, Varanasi, U. P
25.	Dr. Mokhtar-ul-Haque	Raviskalp, Station Road, nawada, Bihar
26.	Sri Ghanshyam Gupta	Kolar Road, Bhopal, M. P
27.	Prof. S. N. Chaudhary	Barkatullah University, Bhopal M.P
28.	Sri Utkalmani Satpathy	Unit 2 Bhubneshwar, Orissa
29.	Dr. Niraj Kumar	SATHEE, Chtragupta Colony, Godda, Jharkhand
30.	Prof. C. P. Sharma	Department of Political Science, Hazaribag, Jharkhand
31.	Sri Ashok Ram	Research Scholar, Hazaribag, Jharkhand
32.	Prof. D. V. Giri	Department of IRPM, Berhampur, Orissa
33.	Dr. G. C. Mahto	Ghatshila, East Singhbhum. Jharkhand
34.	Dr. G. B. Nath	Bidyut Niwas, Gopalmal, Sambalpur, Orissa

S.No.	Name	Address
35.	Sri Murari Shekhar	Maldah, Dist. Shekhpura, Bihar
36.	Ms. Rajni Kanti Devi	Salarpur, Patna, Bihar
37.	Sri K. B. Singh	Village-Govindpur, District Patna, Bihar
38.	Sri K. K. Pandit	TSRDS, Ghatotand, West Bokaro, Jharkhand
39.	Sri Javed Usmani	Bilaspur, Chattisgarh
40.	Prof. P. P. Ghosh	Director, ADRI, Patna, Bihar
41.	Prof. I. D. Sharma	A.N. Sinha Institute of Social Services Patna, Bihar
42.	Dr. A. K. Choudhary	A.N. Sinha Institute of Social Services, Patna, Bihar
43.	Dr, K. B. Singh	A.N. Sinha Institute of Social Services, Patna, Bihar
44.	Dr. Parmanand Singh	Department of Economics, Bhaghulpur University, Bihar
45.	Sri, B. K. Sinha	Department of Political Science, Ranchi
46.	Dr. M. Barla	Department of Economics, St. Xavier's College, Ranchi
47.	Dr. Anant	Purulia Road, Ranchi
48.	Dr. K. K. Bhagat	XISS, Purulia Road, Ranchi
49.	Dr. Ramesh Sharan	Department of Economics, Ranchi University Ranchi
50.	Dr. Binod Narayan	Department of Sociology, Ranchi University, Ranchi
51.	Sri Om Prakash Pathak	Manthan Yuva Sansthan, Hindpirhi, Ranchi
52.	Dr. Vijay Baraik	Jharkhand Space Research Centre, Ranchi
53.	Sri Ravi	Hidustan Times, Ranchi
54.	Sri Sanjay Yadav	Prabhat Khabar, Ranchi
55.	Sri Prafulla Linda	General Secretary, All India Kissan Sabha, Ranchi
56.	Sri Satendra Kumar	Secretary Jan Chetna Gramin Vikas Parishad, Ranchi
57.	Ms. Anupma Kumari	Samajik Gram Vikas Sansthan, Dhurwa, Ranchi.
58.	Nilima Upadhya	PRIA, Mandir Marg, Kadru Ranchi
59.	Dr. Harishwar Dayal,	Director, IHD, Eastern Regional Centre, Ranchi
60.	Sri Jyoti Prakash	Director, Kislay, Ratu, Ranchi
61.	Sri Satendra Kumar Singh	Project Coordinator, Bhartiye Kissan Sangh, Ranchi
62.	Dr. Madan C. Sarkar	Research Fellow, IHD, Eastern Regional Centre, Ranchi

May 22, 2007 at Banglore .

1	Dr. Ravi Srivastava,	Member, NCEUS, New Delhi
2	Dr. K.P. Kannan	Member, NCEUS, New Delhi
3	Dr. R.P. Mamgain	Fellow, Institute for Human Development, New Delhi.
4	Dr. D. Rajashekhar,	Institute for Social & Economic Change, Bangalore
5	Dr. S. Madheswaran	Institute for Social & Economic Change, Bangalore
6	Dr. Supriya Roychoudhary	Institute for Social & Economic Change, Bangalore

S.No.	Name	Address
7	Prof. S. Mahendra Dev	Director, Centre for Economic and Social Studies, Hyderabad
8	Prof. D.Narasimha Reddy	3-33-33, L. Venkat Reddy Colony, Ligampalli, Hyderabad
9	Prof Chandrashekar, B.K	Hon'ble Speaker, Legislative Council, Govt of Karnataka
10	Mr. Srinivas Murthy, M R,	Principal Secretary, Rural Development and Panchayat Raj Dept, Government of Karnataka
11	Shri Rao S.L	Chairman, ISEC, Nagarbhavi, Bangalore
12	.Prof.Jayaram N	Director,ISEC. Nagarabhavi ,Bangalore 5600072
13	Prof Deshpande, R S	Head, ADRTC, ISEC, Nagarabhavi Bangalore
14	Dr.Manjunath, K.S	Commissioner for Labour, Government of Karnataka
15	Ms. Poornima Chikarmane,	Activist. Kagad Kach Patra Kashtakari Panchayat, Pune
16	Mr. Rajkumar Ghayal	Jt.Secy, Maharashtra Rajya Hamal Mapadi, Maharashtra
17	Mr. Thangavelu.A	Jt.Commissioner for Labour, Chennai
18	Mr. Doss M.L	Gen. Secy, Tamil Nadu Trade Union Council, Chennai
19	Mr. Mani.T.R.S	Secy, AITUC, Chintadhilel, Chennai-2
20	Mr. M.M.Lawerence	Gen Secy, CITU- Thiruvananthapuram, Kerala
21	Mr. N.P.Samy	National Center for Labor, (NCL),Bangalore
22	Mr. Shreesha H R	
23	Ms. Prameela,.V	Project Co-ordinator, Sampark, Koramangala Bangalore
24	Mr. Ramachandra H	Gen Secy INTUC
25	Mr. Narasimhan M.C	President AITUC, Sheshadripuram, Bangalore
26	Dr. Baba Adhav	Activist 89, New Timber Market, Pune
27	Dr. M. Indira	University of Mysore, Mysore
28	Dr. D.P Singh	NCEUS, New Delhi
29	Mr. Upendranadh C.	IHD, New Delhi
30	Mr. Narayana Reddy A.	Rural Integrated Social Education Society, Anantapur
31	Prof. Narasimha Reddy D	Professor of Economics,University of Hyderabad, Hyderabad
32	Mr. Singaravelu . R.	Assistant General Secretary,CITU, Chennai 5
33	Mr. Ajaya Kumar P.	Secretary CITU, Hyderabad
34	Mr. Jithendran V. N.	Addl. Commissioner for Rural Development,Kerala
35	Dr. Rajashekaran.N	Ambedkar Center for Economic Studies, Madras University
36	Mr. Sundaresan	Commissioner for Labour, Pondichery
37	Dr. Shashi kumar	Reader in Economics, Bangalore University, Bangalore

S.No.	Name	Address
38	Mr.Premachandra Kurup K.S.	Labour Commissioner, Govt of Kerala, Thiruvananthapuram
39	Dr. Thangaraj	University of Madras,Chennai 5
40	Mr. Prasad M.S.N	
41	Mr. Rajan B.R	H.M.K.P. No 5, Rajajinagar, Bangalore 25
42	Ms. Rajyashree Reddy	# 1958, 14th cross HSR layout, Bangalore
43	Prof Rangaswami,	HoD, Dept of Economics, Bangalore University, Bangalore
44	Dr.Keshava S.R	Dept of Economics, Bangalore University, Bangalore
45	Dr Ramanjaneyulu M	Dept of Economics, Bangalore University, Bangalore
46	Mr. Madhu Sudhan	NCL No.17, 6th cross, Rangadasappa Layout,Bangalore
47	Mr. Sitamani C.M	CEO, Construction Workers and Labour Board. Bangalore
48	Mr. Sooryanarayana Rao .K.M	General Secretary, BMS, Karnataka, Bangalore
49	Mr. Jeevanand.S	Convener, South India National Centre for Labour, Bangalore
50	Mr. Shivshankar G.R.	President, TUCC, Bangalore-79
51	Mr Verma.V.G	President, Unorganised Worker Board Trade Union, Banglore
52	Mr. Dhanashekar D	Secy, KSCWC, Bangalore-560030
53	Mr. Palamkumar	General Secy, K.S.C.W.C Union, Bangalore-560030
54	Mr. Manjuntah .C	Correspondent, Kannada Prabha, Bangalore-1
55	Ms Sheela	Karnataka Gruha Karmikara Sangha, Bangalore-30
56	Mr. Nagaraj Gadekal	Chief Photographer, Chamrajpet Bangalore
57	Ms Shataj	Women's Voice, # 47, St.Maria Road, Bangalore
58	Dr. SridharKrishna	Consulting Editor,ICFAI Business School, Bangalore
59	Prof Nadakarni M.V.	ISEC, Nagarbhavi, Bangalore
60	Prof. Rao V.M	ISEC, Nagarbhavi, Bangalore
61	Prof. Aziz, Abdul	ISEC Nagarbhavi, Bangalore
62	Prof. M.R.Narayana	Faculty, ISEC, Bangalore
63	Prof Tharakan P K M	Faculty, ISEC, Bangalore
64	Dr. Usha Devi	Faculty, Education Unit, ISEC, Bangalore
65	Dr. Ramaswamy	Faculty, Sociology, ISEC, Bangalore
66	Dr. Nanjundaiah.C,	Faculty, ISEC, Bangalore
67	Dr. Ramaswamy	Faculty, Sociology, ISEC, Bangalore
68	Dr. Erappa	Faculty, ADRTC, ISEC, Bangalore
69	Dr. Maruthi	Faculty, ADRTC,ISEC Nagarabhavi Bangalore

June2, 2007 at Kolkatta .

S.No.	Name	Address
1.	Prof. Arjun Sengupta	Chairman, NCEUS, New Delhi
2.	V.K. Malhotra	Member Secretary, NCEUS, New Delhi
3.	Prof. R S Srivastava	Member, NCEUS, New Delhi
4.	Prof. Raj Kumar Sen	Rabindra Bharati University
5.	Dr.Dhiraj Kr.Bandopadhya	CVES, Deptt. of Economics, Calcutta University
6.	Prof. Krishna Mazumdar	Economic Research Unit, Indian Statistical Institute
7.	Ishita Mukhopadhyaya	Dept. of Economics, University of Calcutta
8.	Anghya Mukhopadhyaya	Door Darshan
9.	M.G. Raghunathan	Door Darshan
10.	Laishram Churchil	CADM, Imphal
11.	Dr. Walter Fernandese	NESRC, Guwahati
12.	Dr. Vandana Upadhyay	Deptt. of Economics, Rajiv Gandhi University, Itanagar,
13.	Dr. Debdas Banerjee	IDSK, Kolkata
14.	Indranil Sengupta	Addl. Labour Commissioner, Labour Deptt., WB
15.	P.K. Chakravarty	Resident Commissioner, Government of Tripura
16.	Dr. B.P. Syam Roy	Special Officer & Spl. Secy, Development - Planning Government of West Bengal
17.	B. Lyngdoh	Liaison Officer, Government of Meghalaya
18.	Dr. Panchanan Das	Lecturer, Economics, Taki Government College
19.	K.S. Singhwan	GM, SIDBI, Kolkota
20.	H..Ismorchandra Sharma	Manipur University
21.	Dr. S. Borbora	Deptt. Of Humanities & Social Science, IIT Guwahati
22.	Dr. Annapoorna. Shaw	IIM-Calcutta
23.	Dr. Arpita Ghosh	Jadavpur University
24.	Dr. Amit Kundu	Jadavpur University
25.	Dr. C.S. Prasad	Consultant, NCEUS, New Delhi
26.	A. Bhattacharya	Spl.Secy, FPIH, Govt of West Bengal
27.	U.Bhattacharya	IDSK
28.	Gautam Gupta	Jadavpur University
29.	Dr. Dalbir Singh	IHD
30.	P. Bhattacharyya	Joint Labour Commissioner, Government of West Bengal
31.	Dr. R.P. Mamgain	IHD
32.	B.K. Baksi	ICSI, 19/2, B.Narkar Road, Kolkata-63
33.	B.L. Baheti	Indian Federation of Tiny Enterprises, Howrah

S.No.	Name	Address
34	D.P. Singh	Under Secretary, NCEUS, New Delhi
35.	Swapan Sarkar	Jadhavpur University, Main Hostel
36.	Prof. A. Saha	Deptt. Of Economics, Tripura University, Tripura
37.	Dr. R. Srivastava	Member, NCEUS
38.	Dr. Shyamlendu Chatterjee	Fellow, CUES
39.	Dr. Rajarshi Majumdar	Reader & Head, University of Burdwan, Burdwan
40.	Dr. Dipa Mukherjee	Sr. Lecturer, Narasinha Dutt College, Howrah-711101
41.	Debanjan Chakrabarti	Secretary, CITU, W.B. State Committee
42.	Saleeree Gupta	Anand Bazar Patrika
43.	Prof. Biswajeet Chatterjee	Dean, Faculty of Social Sciences, Jadavpur University